NBEO Part II Study Guide

Dr. Kimberly Castillo, O.D.

ISBN: 9798880459421

ACKNOWLEDGMENTS

I want to thank my husband, Jason Castillo, for his everlasting support in all of my endeavors.
I also want to thank my mom, Sharon Kelley, for inspiring me to write this book.
Thank you for constructive feedback: DLV Vision including Drs Doughery and Vosoghi, and Ron Zepeda; and Drs. Carol Lafradez, Shasha Patel; and Roxanna Potter.
Thank you to Dr. Naids of National Vision for his permission to use retinal pictures from National Vision's patients.
Finally, thank you to Dr. Christopher Nguyen for his suggestions to improve Chapter 20.

The Companion Website for this NBEO PART II Study Guide is now available!

www.nbeopart2.com

Features Include:

1) This Study Guide as a video book.
2) Flashcards
3) Memorization Tables
4) Practice Questions

Dr. Castillo highly recommends pairing this book with this website. The website subscription is NOT included with the purchase of this book.

CONTENTS

CHAPTER 1
NBEO PART II OVERVIEW

This NBEO Part II Study Guide is designed to put all the information you need to know for the exam into one place. The first step I took in designing this book is I looked at the content matrix on the NBEO website as well as the score reports from three separate administrations to see how many questions were actually asked in each topic, and I re-ordered the topics from highest to lowest yield. This is the order in which I have presented the information in this textbook. Meaning, I cover the highest yield information first, and the lowest yield information last. That said, this study guide is designed for you to read from cover-to-cover to maximize your study time with the most important information first.

This table shows the topics covered in this text as well as the number of questions which the NBEO has historically asked from each topic. This said, this is also the order in which the topics are discussed in this book:

Topic	**Number of Questions**
Retina / Choroid / Vitreous	39.0 Questions
Conjunctiva / Cornea / Refractive Surgery	38.6 Questions
Optic Nerve / Neuro-Ophthalmic Pathways	30.6 Questions
Contact Lenses	23.6 Questions
Lens / Cataract / IOL / Pre- And Post-Operative Care	23.0 Questions
Glaucoma	21.3 Questions
Accommodative / Vergence / Oculomotor Conditions	20.6 Questions
Ametropia	18.6 Questions
Lids / Lashes / Lacrimal System / Ocular Adnexa / Orbit	18.6 Questions
Systemic Health	18.3 Questions
Emergencies / Trauma	18.3 Questions
Episclera / Sclera / Anterior / Uvea	16.3 Questions
Amblyopia / Strabismus	14.6 Questions
Public Health	13.3 Questions
Ophthalmic Optics	12.6 Questions
Perceptual Function / Color Vision	12.6 Questions
Low Vision	12.3 Questions
Visual And Human Development	5.0 Questions
Legal Issues / Ethics	5.6 Questions

In selecting which diseases to include in this study guide, I kept in mind that Part II is testing if you have the minimum knowledge necessary to be an optometrist, and if you are safe to the public. Also, the NBEO website states, "patient cases generally focus on either typical presentations of relatively high frequency conditions or conditions with low frequency but high criticality." This said, they are testing if you can recognize and treat the most common diseases and diseases with the most severe consequences. Therefore, I chose to include diseases in this text if they fit into one of these two categories. I have also placed an asterisk (*) next to diseases which, in my opinion, are likely to be the highest yield topics.

Be sure not to overlook the Appendix at the back of this book for it provides clinical associations which will be useful to know.

The NBEO Part II comprises of two sessions each containing 175 questions which you have to answer in 210 minutes. For pacing purposes, this means you have 1.2 minutes per question. I'd suggest that you use this as a fast way to keep track of your pacing. While you're taking the exam, you will have a counter indicating the time you have left, which question number you are on, and you will have access to a calculator on the computer. Do some simple division and you will know how much current time per question is left. If you have more than 1.2 minutes per question, then you can slow down and spend more time per question. If you have less than 1.2 minutes per question, you need to speed up your pace. Even if you are doing great with pacing while doing practice tests, be sure to keep track of your timing during the actual exam because you never know how the stress of the real exam will impact your speed.

Part II is comprised of cases that you have to read and a series of questions to answer about each case. For each case you will be asked about the proper treatment and management. In the end, you will receive two scores for Part II. One score will be for the overall test. The other will be for just the questions on Treatment and Management, also known as your TMOD score. This is similar to Part III where you get a score for your overall performance as well as a score for Injections. You need to pass Part II overall as well as TMOD in order to get your license in any state. TMOD makes up about 116 of the 350 questions on Part II, or approximately one-third of the test! So, be sure to pay special attention to Treatment and Management as you prepare for Part II.

Regarding pharmacology, the NBEO provides you with a list which you can use during the test that has both the generic and trade names for each drug. I would definitely recommend that you use this tool while you are taking the test. This way, while you are studying you can focus on learning the names of the drugs that are easiest for you to remember. On the actual test there will be a search function so that you can search either name of a drug instead of hunting through the list. You can find a copy of the drug list which is provided here: http://www.optometry.org/pdf/contents/PAM_Abbreviations.pdf

The last day or two prior to the test, I would HIGHLY SUGGEST that you download this tool to help you familiarize yourself with the test format: http://www.optometry.org/downloads/ABS_Tutorial.msi
It is designed to look EXACTLY LIKE the software you will be using during the test. Once you download it, you can peruse the program at your leisure and familiarize yourself with all the tools, how to look up drugs on the list, how to use the calculator, and most importantly (although I may be biased with this statement) familiarize yourself on how to use the highlighter tool! The highlighter tool will be your best friend, and it is not necessarily the most intuitive tool. You don't want to be stressing on how to get the software to behave as you are sitting down for the test, so be sure you know how to use it before the test day.

The highlighter tool is helpful because it will allow you to highlight the significant information in a case as you are reading it. This will allow you to quickly find relevant information as you are answering the questions. There is a lot of erroneous information given with the cases, so this tool will help you sift out what is most relevant.

The purpose of this study guide is to help you study for and pass the NBEO Part II. If you find any inaccuracies, or have constructive feedback to make this a better tool, please let me know. I can be reached at kcastillo@westernu.edu.

As a last comment, I do want to make a disclaimer that I do not know what questions will be asked on the NBEO Part II or TMOD, and I am not privy to what material will be covered.

CHAPTER 2
TREATMENT AND MANAGEMENT OF OCULAR DISEASE

Part II presents you with cases that you have to read and a series of questions to answer about each case. For each case you will be asked about the proper treatment and management. In the end, you will receive two scores for Part II. One score will be for the overall test. The other will be for just the questions on Treatment and Management of Ocular Disease, also known as your TMOD score. This is similar to Part III where you get a score for your overall performance as well as a score for Injections. You need to pass Part II overall as well as TMOD in order to get your license in any state. TMOD makes up about 116 of the 350 questions on Part II, or approximately one-third of the test! So, be sure to pay special attention to Treatment and Management as you prepare for Part II.

When it comes to Treatment and Management of Ocular Diseases, it is helpful to remember that there are only so many complications that can arise within the eye. While there are many diseases out there, they are simply the cause behind the finite complications we can treat. The first step in deciding how to treat a patient is to identify which of these ocular complications are present. The latter portion of this chapter discusses these complications.

After identifying the ocular complication you want to treat, next you need to consider the location of the problem. If the issue is located in the anterior segment, you will use a topical medication. If the issue is in the anterior chamber, you will need to use a medication which can penetrate the cornea. Complications of the vitreous will require an intravitreal injection or implant. If the issue is in the retina, you will need to use systemic medications (oral or IV) so that the blood will deliver the medication to the retina (although there are some topical medications which can penetrate back to the retina).

After identifying the nature and location of the problem, next you need to consider the severity. A severe anterior segment issue will require more frequent dosing than a mild issue. An acute vitreous complication can be treated with injections while a chronic issue of the vitreous may require an implant with a slow releasing medication. A mild retinal issue may possibly be addressed with just a topical medication, a moderate retinal issue will require oral medications, and a severe retinal problem will require IV treatment.

An example of how to approach treatment would be Neovascular Glaucoma. Just from the name you can determine what complications need to be treated: the neovascularization and the glaucoma.

- Neovascularization
    1. Neovascularization is treated with ANTI-VEGF medication or Pan Retinal Photocoagulation (PRP).
    2. Since the neovascularization will be present in the iris and retina, the ANTI-VEGF treatment needs to be delivered to both these sites, usually through intravitreal injections or laser to the retina.
    3. Given that Neovascular Glaucoma has a poor prognosis, treatment should be aggressive.
- Glaucoma / Increased IOP
    1. Glaucoma treatment is aimed at reducing IOP through reducing aqueous production or facilitating aqueous outflow (more common).
    2. Since aqueous is located in the anterior chamber, these structures can usually be reached via topical medications, laser procedures, and/or surgeries to the anterior chamber.
    3. Given that it is hard to control IOP with Neovascular Glaucoma, patients should be monitored closely. Treatment should be aggressive and will usually require surgery.

Treatment for every disease can be broken down into the three steps as shown above.

The NBEO is not going to expect you to know the exact concentration or frequency in which medications are prescribed. They are more interested that you know which drug class should be used in what case, and that you know when a drug is contraindicated because of a patient allergy or because of other medications the patient is taking. Part Two is not going to focus on the medication's mechanism of action because that was on Part One. With this being said, what you need to focus on is being able to identify which drug class a drug belongs to and when a drug is contraindicated.

ABBREVIATIONS

- QD = once a day
- QHS = once before bed
- BID = twice a day
- TID = three times a day
- QID = four times a day
- PRN = as needed
- q1h = every hour (q2h = every two hours, etc.)
- gtt = drop
- po = by mouth
- IM = intramuscularly
- IV = intravenous
- Ung = ointment

DOSING GUIDELINES

- For most cases, eye drops (including antibiotics and steroids) are dosed BID-QID depending on severity.
- In serious cases (like a central bacterial corneal ulcer), the eye drop would be used aggressively, Q1-2H.

Below is a glossary of the most common ocular complications with their treatments, and also all of the information I would recommend you know about Pharmacology for Part II.

GLOSSARY OF OCULAR COMPLICATIONS AND THEIR TREATMENTS

ACNE ROSACEA

Patients should be advised to avoid any triggering agent. Oral doxycycline, tetracycline, or erythromycin should be prescribed to treat the systemic pathology. Patients may also benefit from topical steroids to treat the inflammation. Ocular Rosacea can be treated with artificial tears and antibiotic ointments on the eyelid margins. The eyelids can also be treated with lid scrubs.

ALLERGY

Allergies are treated pharmacologically with antihistamines because histamine initiates the allergic response. Mast cells/basophils contain histamine. During an allergic reaction, calcium depolarizes the cell, allowing for histamine release. Once the histamine is released, it will bind to other cells causing itch and all the other signs of allergic reactions. This being said, there are three classes of antihistamines which are aimed at either inhibiting the binding of histamine to other cells (H_1 Blockers), stabilizing the mast cells to prevent calcium depolarization (Mast cell stabilizers), or a combination of both (combo).

All seven of the systemic/oral antihistamines are H_1 Blockers. The systemic antihistamines are broken down into first and second generations:

1. There are four first generation systemic antihistamines. Three of them have "phen" in the name (diphenhydramine, brompheniramine, chlorpheniramine), and the fourth is promethazine. Remember that the first generation antihistamines are able to cross the blood brain barrier, which can lead to CNS complications including drowsiness. Promethazine is also known to increase the amount of pigment found within the eye.
2. I remember the three second generation systemic antihistamines with the mnemonic "ZAC:" Zyrtec, Allegra, Claritin. The second generation antihistamines do not cross the blood brain barrier, and so they do not cause the CNS side effects seen with the first generation systemic antihistamines.

Topical antihistamines are found in all three of the drug classes:

1. H_1 Blocker: The only topical drug whose sole mechanism of action is to inhibit the binding of antihistamine is emedastine. Emedastine is good for relieving symptoms of allergy, but does not stop the reaction because it does not stabilize mast cells.
2. Mast cell stabilizers: There are four mast cell stabilizers, which I remember by "cro, alo, alo, ala." Their full names are crolom, alomide, alocril, and alamast. Remember these drugs are good at halting an allergic reaction from progressing, but they cannot relieve symptoms already present because they do not inhibit the binding of antihistamine once it has been released from the mast cell.
3. The six combination antihistamines which both prevent the binding of antihistamine as well as stabilize mast cells are bepreve, elestat, ketotifen, optivar, patady, and patanol. The combination topical antihistamines can both relieve symptoms of an already active allergic reaction while also preventing further progression of the allergic reaction.
   a. **Topical over the counter antihistamines** include Ketotifen (sold under the trade names of Zaditor and Alaway), Pataday, and Lastacaft.

In addition to antihistamines, steroids are used to treat allergic reactions due to their anti-inflammatory characteristics. Steroids are described below under "Inflammation."

AMBLYOPIA

Patients under the age of 12 with amblyopia should be treated with the following:

- Full cycloplegic refraction OR reduce the amount of hyperopia symmetrically in both eyes by ≥1.50D.
- Next the better seeing eye should be patched for 2-6 hours per day depending on the severity of the amblyopia for 1 week per year of age (10 year old should be patched for 10 weeks). Patients who see better than 20/100 should be patched for 2 hours per day, and patients who see worse than 20/100 should be patched for 6 hours per day. The patching does not need to be continuous, but can be cumulative throughout the day. The patient should be using their eyes during the patching (do not patch while sleeping, this is pointless), and it should include at least 1 hour of near activities. The reason for patching is to allow the amblyopic eye a chance to see without the better-seeing eye overriding it.
- An alternative to patching in noncompliant patients (e.g. children who insist upon removing the patch) is Atropine penalization: one drop of Atropine every day in the better seeing eye. This is effective in patients who have 20/100 or better in the amblyopic eye

AUTOIMMUNE DISEASES

Autoimmune diseases occur when the immune system becomes hyperactive and begins to attack the patient's body (non-foreign cells/structures). Therefore, the goal of treatment is to reduce the immune response. Patients should be treated with steroids (topical, oral, intravenous, sub-Tenon's) or immunosuppressive agents (cyclosporine) performed by a specialist. Treatment can be tapered very slowly upon signs of improvement.

BACTERIAL INFECTIONS

Any disease caused by bacteria will be treated with an antibiotic. Here is the information I would recommend you know regarding antibiotics:

- Fluoroquinolones have "flox" in their generic name. They are used to treat corneal ulcers, but should be avoided in children because they can cause damage to ligament formation.
    - Second generation (Only gram negative coverage)
        - Ciprofloxacin, Ofloxacin
    - Third generation (Only gram negative coverage)
        - Levofloxacin
    - Fourth generation (Both gram negative and positive coverage)
        - Besifloxacin, Gatifloxacin, Moxifloxacin
- Folic Acid Synthesis Inhibitors
    - "Sulfa" drugs should be avoided in patients who have sulfa allergies.
        - Sulfamethazine, Sulfadiazine
    - There are three drugs which should be avoided in children and pregnant women because they damage bone marrow.
        - Methotrexate
        - Pyrimethamine
        - Trimethoprim
    - Bactrim is a combination of Sulfamethazine and Trimethoprim. It is used to treat MRSA infections.
- Aminoglycosides: Gentamycin and Tobramycin
    - These drugs were historically used for corneal ulcers, but they are NO LONGER first line medications.
    - Aminoglycosides delay corneal healing and should be avoided in patients with reduced immune systems.

- Tetracyclines: "cycline" will be in the generic name. Do not use in pregnant women and children because these can cause issues with bone growth and teeth. The Tetracyclines are also associated with Pseudotumor Cerebri.
  - Tetracycline
  - Doxycycline is used to treat chlamydia and dry eye.
  - Minocycline is used to treat acne but causes blue sclera. I remember the blue sclera by thinking that "Minnows swim in blue water."
- Macrolides are used to treat chlamydia and gonorrhea. They all have "mycin" in their generic name.
  - Azithromycin is great for pregnant women because it is a very safe antibiotic.
  - Erythromycin is also very safe and is used on newborn infants prophylactically to prevent ocular gonorrhea infections.
  - Clarithromycin is used to treat respiratory infections.
  - Lincomycin is used to treat MRSA infections.
  - Clindamycin is also used to treat MRSA infections.
  - Three medications also have "mycin" in their names but ARE NOT macrolides. These exceptions include:
    - Gentamycin
    - Natamycin
    - Tobramycin
- Penicillins: "cillin" will be in the generic name. They should NOT be used with patients who are allergic to cephalosporins because they both have a beta-lactam ring in their molecular structure.
  - Penicillin
  - Dicloxacillin works against Gram Positive bacteria. It is not good for use against MRSA infections because they are penicillinase resistant.
  - Amoxicillin works against both Gram Positive and Negative bacteria.
- Cephalosporins: "ceph" will be in the generic name. They should NOT be used on patients who are allergic to penicillins because they both have a beta-lactam ring in their molecular structure. They also reduce Vitamin K absorption and so should not be used in combination with Warfarin because this can lead to excessive blood thinning.
  - Cephalexin is 1st generation and works against Gram Positive bacteria.
  - Ceftriaxone is 3rd generation and works against Gram Negative bacteria. It is also used to treat Gonorrhea.
- Cell Wall Inhibitors are ointments used to treat blepharitis.
  - Bacitracin: Good for gram-positive infections
  - Neomycin
  - Polymyxin-B: Good for gram-negative infections
  - Combination drugs include
    - Polysporin which is made of two drugs (Bacitracin and Polymyxin-B)
    - Neosporin which is made of three drugs (Bacitracin, Polymyxin-B, and Neomycin)

BLEPHARITIS

First line treatment for Blepharitis is lid hygiene and hot compress. Bacterial Blepharitis may also be treated with topical Erythromycin/Bacitracin to treat the bacterial infection. Demodex Blepharitis may also be treated with Xdemvy.

CARDIOVASCULAR DISEASE

Cardiovascular diseases are treated with blood thinners. Some blood thinners may cause excessive bleeding and bruising, including recurrent subconjunctival hemorrhages.

- Antiplatelets prevent platelets from adhering and causing clot formation. Examples of antiplatelets:

  - Clopidogrel (Plavix): Side effects include nosebleeds, fatigue, nausea, headaches, and dizziness.
  - NSAIDs: Aspirin is the only NSAID with a long duration of action (up to 10 days) because it binds **irreversibly** to platelets.
- Anticoagulants slow or prevent clot formation by competing with vitamin K or Factor XA. Anticoagulants provide a more aggressive treatment than Antiplatelets.
  - Coumadin (Warfarin): This should not be combined with Acetaminophen (Tylenol) or Cephalosporins because the combination may increase its blood thinning effect too much.
  - Heparin: This drug was developed in 1916, and it must be administered via injections.
  - Examples of anticoagulants which compete with Factor XA include Eliquis or Xarelto.

CATARACTS

Cataracts are treated with surgery which removes the natural lens and replaces it with an artificial lens. The most common lens implants used currently are Posterior Chamber Intraocular Lenses (PCIOLs), which are inserted into the capsular bag. Be aware that complications are more likely in patients with pseudoexfoliation syndrome (weakened zonules are most likely to allow the lens to dislocate). Patients who have a history of ever using Flomax or drugs ending in "ozin" (Terazosin) are at risk for developing intraoperative floppy iris syndrome during cataract surgery. There are several types of cataract surgeries.

- **Anterior Chamber Intraocular Lenses (ACIOLs)** may be used when PCIOLs are contraindicated.
- **Intracapsular Cataract Extraction (ICCE)** is an older procedure in which a large incision was made into the cornea in order to remove the entire lens and its capsule. No artificial lens was implanted, and so these patients would require high plus lenses to compensate. This procedure is not performed anymore.
- **Extracapsular Cataract Extraction (ECCE)** is another older procedure in which a large incision was made into the cornea in order to remove the entire lens. The capsule would remain, in which an IOL would replace the natural lens.
- **Phacoemulsification** is the newest procedure. Ultrasound is used to break up the lens. This allows for a small incision because the lens is sucked out. The eye's IOP will press against the small incision, effectively closing it without the need for sutures.

CHLAMYDIA

A single dose of oral Azithromycin should be used followed by daily use of oral doxycycline, erythromycin, or tetracycline TID-QID for 1-2 weeks. Topical antibiotics may be helpful as well.

CORNEAL EPITHELIAL DEFECTS

When the corneal epithelium is compromised, the cornea is at risk for bacterial infections and ulcers because it provides a pathway for bacteria to enter the stroma. Therefore, the goal of treating Corneal Epithelial Defects is to prevent a bacterial infection. This is accomplished by prescribing topical antibiotics (fluoroquinolones) QID.

CORNEAL SCARRING

All possible treatments are surgical.

- Phototherapeutic Keratectomy (PTK): A surgery which uses lasers to remove superficial corneal opacities and/or surface irregularities.
- Diffuse Lamellar Keratoplasty (DLK): A microkeratome is used to create a corneal flap, and then it is used to remove scarred stromal tissue.
- Superficial Keratectomy: surgical removal of corneal epithelium as well as anterior sub-epithelial fibrovascular or scarred tissue.

- Penetrating Keratoplasty: corneal transplant which replaces all the layers of the cornea but retains the peripheral cornea

CORNEAL ULCERS

Use topical antibiotic (fluoroquinolone) up to Q1H and a topical cycloplegic for comfort. Severe cases may require oral antibiotics and use of steroids to reduce inflammation after the infection has cleared and the cornea is intact. Patients should be followed daily for resolution and IOP check.

DRY EYE

Dry eye is typically sub-categorized as either evaporative (oil dysfunction) or aqueous deficiency. The correct course of treatment depends on the type of dry eye the patient is experiencing. They are listed below based on if the underlying etiology is evaporative or aqueous in nature:

- Artificial tears (AT's) can be recommended for any type of dry eye. If the patient is using the AT's more than QID, recommend use of preservative free AT's because excessive use of preservatives can have toxic effects to the cornea. If the patient needs sustained relief, recommend gel or ointment AT's because they evaporate less quickly. Both of these options will blur vision (the ointment more than the gel) and so depending on the patient's needs, they may use them only before going to bed.
- Evaporative (oil dysfunction)
    - Omega-3 artificial tears are most effective to supplement the oil deficiency.
    - Lid hygiene can be performed daily.
    - Hot compress can be performed for 10 minutes several times a day.
    - If bacteria are suspected to be behind MGD, consider prescribing topical Erythromycin for long-term management of bacterial growth.
    - Topical acetylcysteine can be used to treat filaments (mucous strands).
    - Supplement diet with omega-3 fatty acids.
    - Manual expression of the meibomian glands may also be performed in-office as well. It can be preceded by either hot compress, LipiFlow, or IPL (intense pulsed light therapy) to heat up the lids prior to the gland expression.
    - RF (Radio Frequency) therapy can also be used to not only clear the meibomian glands, but to also help rejuvenate the atrophied meibomian glands.
- Aqueous Deficiency
    - If inflammation is the cause of the dry eye, consider using a mild steroid for 1-2 weeks to get the inflammation under control. Afterwards, consider use of Xiidra or Restasis/Cequa for long-term management of inflammation.
    - Supplement the patient's diet with vitamin A if a deficiency is present.
    - Punctal plugs can be used to reduce tear drainage. First perform a trial run using collagen plugs which will dissolve after about 1-2 weeks. If the patient likes the collagen plugs, then proceed with either planned replacement plugs which will dissolve in either 3 or 6 months, or permanent silicone plugs. Silicone plugs run the highest risk of infection which may require surgical removal of the plug.
    - An amniotic membrane graft can be used for severe cases of Dry Eye.

EDEMA (CORNEAL)

Corneal edema should be treated with topical sodium chloride (Muro 128) and topical steroids.

EDEMA (RETINAL)

Prostaglandins are mediators for edema, and so pharmaceutical therapy is aimed at inhibiting prostaglandins in edematous eyes. The two drug classes which block prostaglandin activity are topical NSAIDs and topical steroids, which are discussed above under inflammation. In the case of retinal edema, a strong steroid should be selected because they are more likely to penetrate to the posterior anatomy of the eye.

Cellular release of VEGF can induce blood vessels to become hyper-permeable and thereby lead to retinal edema. Therefore, anti-VEGF injections (which are discussed under neovascularization) can be used as a treatment for retinal edema when it is suspected that VEGF is playing a hand in causing the edema.

Laser photocoagulation (cautery of retinal blood vessels with a laser) can be effective in treating macular edema; however, the mechanism behind how this works is not fully understood.

EXPOSURE KERATOPATHY

Exposure Keratopathy typically occurs secondary to an eyelid condition. Therefore, the eyelid abnormality should be addressed: taping eyelids closed at night, partial tarsorrhaphy (sewing together eyelids), eyelid reconstruction, and gold weight implant. Other treatments are aimed at the injured cornea: preservative free artificial tears up to Q1H, artificial tear ointment QHS, and amniotic membrane graft. If present, the corneal ulcer should be treated as such.

EYELID: INCOMPLETE CLOSURE

When the eyelids are not closing appropriately, the patient is at risk for developing dry eye and exposure keratopathy while they are sleeping. Treatment is aimed at aiding the eyelids to close and thereby avoiding these complications. Options include taping eyelids closed at night, wearing eye shields while sleeping, partial tarsorrhaphy (sewing together eyelids), eyelid reconstruction, and a gold weight implant. Prior to going to sleep patients can use an artificial tear ointment to form a barrier between the cornea and the environment as well as aid in prolonged maintenance of corneal lubrication. The dry eye should also be treated (see "Dry Eye" in this chapter).

FILAMENTS (CORNEA)

Filaments are strings of epithelial tissue combined with mucous. The goal of treatment is to remove them. This can be done with corneal debridement. Topical acetylcysteine QID can also be considered.

GONORRHEA

Gonorrhea should be treated aggressively with IV or IM Ceftriaxone. The macrolides (Azithromycin, Clarithromycin, Clindamycin, Erythromycin, Lincomycin) are also used to treat Gonorrhea. Topical antibiotics may also be used concurrently. Erythromycin is placed on newborn infants prophylactically to prevent ocular gonorrhea infections.

FUNGAL INFECTIONS

Cases of fungal infections should be treated with the following:

- Natamycin is the only FDA approved topical anti-Fungal, so be sure to know this. It can only be used topically because it is hard on the kidneys.
- Drugs that have "azole" in the name (ketoconazole, fluconazole, miconazole)
- Nystatin
- Amphotericin B
- Griseofulvin

HEMORRHAGE

Hemorrhages are usually initially observed because they typically will self-resolve/become absorbed. Non-resolving hemorrhages will require treatment. If the hemorrhage is in the retina, then a laser can be used to help "break it up" and aid the absorption of the blood into the surrounding tissue. Optic nerve hemorrhages indicate further workup for underlying causes such as glaucoma or optic neuritis/edema. A vitreous hemorrhage is initially treated with bedrest for a few days with an elevated head to allow the blood to settle inferiorly. If the vitreous hemorrhage is non-resolving after three months, it may require a vitrectomy.

HEREDITARY DISEASES

Usually there is no treatment available because the problem is diffuse throughout the patient's genes. The patient may benefit from referral to a genetic counselor.

HYPERCOAGULABLE BLOOD

The goal of treatment when a patient has hypercoagulable blood is to prevent the formation of unnecessary clots, especially because these can cause strokes and/or heart attacks. This is accomplished by thinning the blood with daily use of anti-platelets and anti-coagulants such as baby aspirin.

INCREASED INTRAOCULAR PRESSURE

Pharmacological treatment:

- These are the general dosing guidelines for the glaucoma meds. It is more important for the test that you know which meds are used to treat high IOP than to know the frequency of dosing, and so the dosing frequency information has been listed here as an FYI:
    - Prostaglandins: QHS
    - Beta blockers: BID
    - Alpha Agonists: TID
    - Carbonic Anhydrase Inhibitors (CAI): BID-TID
- Prostaglandins are the first choice drug for glaucoma because they reduce IOP more significantly than the other glaucoma drugs and require only once a day dosing. They can be identified because they have "prost" in their name (Travoprost, Bimatoprost, Latanoprost). Prostaglandins should be avoided in patients who have a history of ocular inflammation (iritis, uveitis, cystoid macular edema) and a history of ocular herpes simplex. Since prostaglandins can increase inflammation, patients should discontinue using them prior to ocular surgery. Other side effects of prostaglandins include increased pigmentation of the iris and surrounding skin, eyelash growth, and conjunctival hyperemia (redness). The onset of Prostaglandins is a minimum of two weeks, and since they do not give an immediate reduction of IOP, they are not typically used in emergent cases of increased IOP.
- Beta-Blockers can be identified because they have "olol" in their name (Atenolol, Betaxolol, Carteolol, Levobunolol, Metoprolol, Timolol). They all should be avoided in patients who have asthma, diabetes, and hyperthyroidism.
    - Beta-1 specific medications (Atenolol, Betaxolol, Metoprolol) work on the heart and have minimal IOP reduction. Meaning, these three beta-blockers are not first choice beta-blockers.

  - Beta-2 specific medications (Carteolol, Levobunolol, Timolol) work better on the eyes and lungs. Their impact on lungs is the reason why they should be avoided in patients with respiratory issues such as asthma. Of these three medications, Carteolol is best to use in patients who have heart disease.
- There is only one topical Alpha Agonist, Brimonidine (Alphagan). Remember that you should avoid using Brimonidine in combination with MAOIs.
- Carbonic anhydrase inhibitors (CAI) can be identified because they have "amide" in their name (Brinzolamide and Dorzolamide). They should be avoided in patients who have sulfa allergies.
- Initial treatment for Acute Angle Closure Glaucoma is aimed at breaking the attack (separate the iris from the lens) and urgently reducing IOP. The attack can be broken with indentation gonioscopy. The IOP can be reduced topically by following the ABC method: Alpha Agonist, Beta Blocker, and Carbonic Anhydrase Inhibitor (dorzolamide). The round of drops should be administered every fifteen minutes and each drop should be separated by five minutes. An IV osmotic or acetazolamide can also be employed. Side effects of acetazolamide include a myopic shift, depression, a metallic taste, aplastic anemia, and metabolic acidosis. Topical steroids can also be used to reduce inflammation. Prostaglandins usually take about two weeks to start showing significant reduction of IOP, and so are not the first line of treatment for an Acute Angle Closure Attack.

Surgical Treatment:

- Compression/Indentation gonioscopy is typically used as a first line against an angle closure attack. The doctor applies pressure to the cornea with a goniolens which opens the angle and may help to "break" the attack.
- Laser Peripheral Iridotomy (LPI): A laser is used to create a small hole, typically in the superior iris between 11:00-1:00. This facilitates movement of fluid between the anterior and posterior chambers, thus equalizing the pressure throughout the eye. Prior to the surgery, the patient may be given pilocarpine because it will make the pupil miotic, stretching the pupil taught for the procedure.
- Iridectomy can be performed instead of a Laser Peripheral Iridotomy (LPI). The difference between the two is the surgeon removes a triangular section of the iris with an iridectomy instead of creating just a small hole as is seen with an LPI.
- Iridoplasty: Argon laser is used to shrink spots of the peripheral iris, causing it to shrink and pull away from the angle. Iridoplasty is used when peripheral iridotomy is not effective, such as in Plateau Iris Syndrome.
- Argon Laser Trabeculoplasty (ALT): A laser is applied in a regular pattern 360 degrees around the trabecular meshwork to increase aqueous outflow. The benefit may decrease after 2-5 years, and this is not repeatable.
- Selective Laser Trabeculoplasty (SLT): Similar to ALT except that the laser is applied to selective areas of the trabecular meshwork to provide the maximum benefit. The benefit may also decrease after 2-5 years; however, SLT IS REPEATABLE.
- Trabeculectomy: A portion of the trabecular meshwork is surgically removed to help increase drainage.
- Shunt: A shunt can be surgically inserted in patients where a Trabeculectomy has failed. A plastic tube is inserted into the anterior chamber to facilitate drainage of aqueous humor into an attached silicone pouch located underneath the conjunctiva.
- Paracentesis: An ophthalmologist inserts a needle into the peripheral cornea, penetrating the cornea to allow aqueous humor to flow out of the globe from the anterior chamber, thereby reducing IOP. This is used in cases of acute increased IOP, or when IOP needs to be emergently reduced.

INFLAMMATION

The simplest treatment for inflammation of the anterior segment (typically secondary to trauma) is to use cold compress. If appropriate, consider discontinuing the use of prostaglandins due to their pro-inflammatory mechanism. Any time a case involves inflammation, either an NSAID or a steroid can be prescribed. NSAIDs should be used for mild cases and in children, while steroids should be used for serious cases.

Topical NSAIDs can be identified because they have "fenac" or "rolac" in their generic name. They can be used to treat Cystoid Macular Edema (CME). Be aware that topical NSAIDs can reduce corneal wound healing, and if used excessively can lead to corneal melt. The topical NSAIDs include the following:

1. Bromfenac
2. Diclofenac sodium (Voltaren)
3. Flurbiprofen
4. Ketorolac
5. Nepafenac

Systemic NSAIDs include the following:

1. Aspirin: irreversible binding causes medication to stay in the body for up to 30 days after use. Should be used with caution for children due to the risk of Reye's Syndrome.
2. Celecoxib: selective Cox-2 inhibitor. Good to use when patient has peptic ulcer issues.
3. Ibuprofen
4. Indomethacin: is used to treat gout but can cause pigmentary retinopathy and whorl keratopathy.
5. Misoprostol: selective Cox-2 inhibitor. Good to use when patient has peptic ulcer issues.
6. Naproxen
7. Naproxen sodium

The most important side effect of systemic NSAIDs to bear in mind is that they can lead to hemorrhaging because they reduce blood clotting. For this reason, patients should avoid NSAIDs prior to surgery. However, reduced clotting can be helpful in certain cases (like when patients have hypertension) which is why these patients take baby aspirin.

Steroids can be administered via several pathways depending on the severity and location of the inflammation: topical drops, oral, intravitreal implants, and posterior sub-Tenon's or intravitreal injections. All steroids (including topical and systemic steroids) can be identified because they have "lone," "pred," or "sone" in their name.

Side effects of topical steroids include increased IOP due to decreased corneoscleral outflow. This can lead to glaucoma!! Posterior subcapsular cataracts are also associated with topical steroids. It is important to remember that steroids retard the immune system, and so they should be avoided in any case where there is suspicion that the immune system is already compromised. Topical steroids can be broken down into strong vs. weak. Weak steroids should be used when the inflammation is on the anterior segment. Strong steroids should be used when the inflammation is posterior to the cornea.

- The two weak topical steroids are:
  - Fluorometholone (FML)
  - Loteprednol is the weakest steroid, best used in very mild cases of inflammation.
- The strong topical steroids are as follows:
  - Dexamethasone
  - Difluprednate (aka Durezol) is the strongest steroid!

- Pred Acetate needs to be shaken before use.
- Rimexolone

Side effects of systemic steroids include peptic ulcers, increased blood sugar due to insulin resistance which can lead to diabetes, decreased collagen synthesis, increased blood pressure, and psychiatric effects. There are three systemic steroids: Fluticasone, Hydrocortisone, and Triamcinolone.

MRSA (METHICILLIN RESISTANT STAPH AUREUS) INFECTIONS

The drugs which are used to treat MRSA include Bactrim, Clindamycin, Doxycycline, and Vancomycin.

MYDRIATICS

The Cholinergic Antagonists are the first choice class used to cause mydriasis. From longest to shortest duration of action, they include Atropine, Scopolamine, Homatropine, Cyclopentolate, Tropicamide. The first choice drug to cause cycloplegia is Cyclopentolate, followed by Homatropine. Atropine should be avoided in Children, Geriatric patients, and patients with Down's Syndrome.

Phenylephrine is another mydriatic. Remember that Phenylephrine also works on Mueller's Muscle, and so it lifts the superior eyelid, increasing the palpebral fissure. It comes in concentrations of 2.5% and 10%. The latter should be used with caution on patients who use MAOIs, tricyclic antidepressants, or who have Grave's Disease due to an additive effect of the sympathetic system leading to a hypertensive crisis.

Other drugs which can cause dilation include Visine, Naphazoline, motion sickness medications such as Scopolamine, and antiperspirants

NEOVASCULARIZATION/LEAKY BLOOD VESSELS

Neovascularization occurs when there is insufficient oxygen supply to the eye. The ischemic cells release VEGF as a signal to the body to grow more blood vessels and increase oxygen supply, leading to neovascularization. Therefore, treatment for neovascularization is aimed at either reducing the cell's demand for oxygen, or reducing the release of VEGF.

Panretinal photocoagulation (PRP) is used to reduce the cell's demand for oxygen. In this procedure, laser is systematically applied to the retinal tissue to kill the cells. Now that they are dead, the cells no longer demand oxygen. This is ideally done in a pattern to cause minimal reduction of vision while causing maximal reduction of oxygen demand.

The release of VEGF is reduced by using intravitreal anti-VEGF injections. Kenalog, Avastin, Lucentis, Eylea are all different anti-VEGF medications which can be injected into the vitreous. Typically these injections need to occur on a regular basis, typically once per month. Depending on the disease course, the injections may be tapered over time.

PAIN

Pain is treated symptomatically with cold compress, NSAIDs, and steroids, all of which are discussed above under inflammation. Oral acetaminophen (Tylenol) can also be used to treat pain. Remember that acetaminophen is NOT a NSAID because it does not have any anti-inflammatory behavior. Acetaminophen treats pain symptomatically by "tricking" the CNS into no longer appreciating the pain.

PENETRATING WOUND

If a penetrating wound is suspected, an optometrist is expected to shield the wound WITHOUT compression. Surgical treatment is aimed at closing the wound and preventing further decrease of IOP by using any combination of the following: bandage CL, suture, or cyanoacrylate glue.

RETINAL BREAKS/HOLES/TEARS

The goal of treatment for Retinal Breaks/Holes/Tears is to prevent further tearing of the retina and subsequent retinal detachments:

- Laser photocoagulation: cautery of retinal blood vessels with a laser.
- Cryotherapy: freezing of tissue.

RETINAL DETACHMENT

Retinal detachments which are caused by a systemic disease are usually resolved by treating the underlying issue. Rhegmatogenous Retinal Detachments may be treated with one of the following surgeries:

- Laser photocoagulation: cautery of retinal blood vessels with a laser.
- Cryotherapy: freezing of tissue.
- Pneumatic retinopexy: (gas bubble injection).
- Vitrectomy: removal of the vitreous.
- Scleral buckle: a piece of semi-hard plastic is placed around the eye, which causes it to flatten and the retinal break to close.

STRABISMUS

The first step in treating strabismus should be to correct any associated refractive error. If the strabismus is present in children, utilize patching (occlusion or Atropine) in order to reduce risk for amblyopia. Vision therapy can also be considered. Severe cases may require strabismus surgery.

- Esotropia: Base OUT prisms can be prescribed for esotropia. However, base IN prisms are used during vision therapy exercises. In severe cases, surgical treatment would include a medial rectus recession of the affected eye.
- Exotropia: Base IN prisms can be prescribed for exotropia. However, base OUT prisms are used during vision therapy exercises. In severe cases, surgical treatment would include a lateral rectus recession of the affected eye.

SYPHILIS

Order a VDRL and FTA-ABS to confirm the Syphilis diagnosis. Syphilis is treated with IV Penicillin G followed by IM Penicillin G. Tetracycline can be used instead if the patient is allergic to penicillin.

SYSTEMIC ETIOLOGY

Many complications within the eye are caused by an underlying systemic pathology. In these cases, the ocular signs and symptoms will improve or resolve if the underlying systemic pathology is treated.

TOXICITY

Discontinue use of the toxic substance. May require co-management with the prescribing doctor if applicable.

TUMORS

Treatment of tumors is aimed at reducing the size or removing the tumor. Options for treatment include:

- Argon Laser: a narrow beam of light is used to shrink or destroy the cancerous cells.
- Biopsy
- Chemotherapy: use of cytotoxic chemicals to destroy/inhibit growth of cancerous cells.
- Cryotherapy: freezing of tissue
- Enucleation: remove eyeball but leave the EOMs and other orbital content intact.
- Epitheliectomy: Removal of the epithelium of a tissue.
- Exteneration: Complete removal of the globe and all the contents of the eye socket. Usually performed for malignant tumors.
- Mitomycin C/Mitomycin/MMC: DNA synthesis inhibitor which stops the growth of cancer cells.
- Plaque Brachytherapy: concentrated dose of radiation to the tumor.
- Radiotherapy/Radiation: The use of radiation prior to surgery to reduce the size of the tumor and thus make it easier to excise.
- Surgical Excision: Cutting out the tumor.
- Topical Interferon: Interferons are part of our natural immune system. They are protein molecules which can inhibit viruses, regulate oncogenes, and activate immunocompetent cells.
- 5-fluorouracil is a DNA synthesis inhibitor, which specifically inhibits the synthesis of thymidine. This stops the growth of cancer cells.

UVEITIS

Uveitis is treated with topical steroids to reduce the inflammation and cycloplegic to immobilize the iris. You want to immobilize the iris to relieve the patient's photophobia and also to prevent the formation of synechiae. Patients should be followed every 1-14 days depending on severity and response to treatment. Be careful to watch for an increased IOP in steroid responders. After resolution, the patient will need to have a slow taper off the steroid to prevent rebound inflammation. A systemic workup to determine a systemic underlying cause of the uveitis is also indicated.

VIRAL INFECTIONS

As you know, conjunctivitis associated with the common cold does not have any treatment. The patient is educated about the infectious nature of their disease. They should avoid contact with other people, and be sure to clean their bedsheets and towels, etc. Patients should be advised to use artificial tears and cool compress to relieve symptoms. A Mild steroid may also be prescribed to help alleviate symptoms. Patients should be educated that the disease may get worse before it gets better.

The big way to identify all anti-viral medications is they have "vir" in either their trade or generic name.

- Oseltamivir (Tamiflu) is used to treat influenza.
- Ribavirin is used to treat Hepatitis C. It can cause a myriad of complications including conjunctivitis, cotton wool spots, optic neuritis, retinal detachments, retinal hemorrhages, and vessel occlusions.

The two big viral infections that have treatments are herpes and HIV.

This table lists the Herpes medications. The Route, Frequency, and Dosing information is all FYI. For the purpose of Part II, just be sure you can recognize the names of the Herpes medications.

Scheduling and Dosing of Herpes Medications				
Medication	**Route**	**Frequency**	**HSV Dose**	**HZO Dose**
Zirgan (Ganciclovir)	gtt	5x/day		
Trifluridine (Viroptic)	gtt	9x/day		
Famcyclovir	po	TID for 7 days	250 mg	500 mg
Acyclovir	po	5x/day for 7 days	400 mg	800 mg
Valacyclovir	po	TID for 7 days	500 mg	1000 mg

Patients who have HIV are generally treated with a cocktail of drugs, referred to antiretroviral therapy (HAART). If a HIV positive patients need treatment for an ocular viral disease, they will most benefit from topical, oral, IV, or intravitreal injections and implants.

- A specific AIDS medication is Zidovudine (Retrovir). It may cause amblyopia and macular edema.

VITREOUS OPACITY

Severe opacities of the vitreous which reduce BCVA are treated with a vitrectomy, or surgical removal of the vitreous.

VITREOUS PULLING ON RETINA

Vitreous tissue can contract and pull on the retina. If indicated, treatment in these cases includes surgery (membrane peel or vitrectomy) to remove the offending vitreous tissue.

CHAPTER 3
RETINA / CHOROID / VITREOUS
Edited By Dr. Christopher Wu, MD

The NBEO website states that 33-44 questions will be asked on Retina / Choroid / Vitreous. Historically they have asked about 39 questions, meaning this chapter covers approximately 11% of the material tested on the exam, or roughly 8 cases. This material IS included on TMOD.

~~~RETINA~~~

RETINAL VASCULAR DISEASES

VALSALVA RETINOPATHY

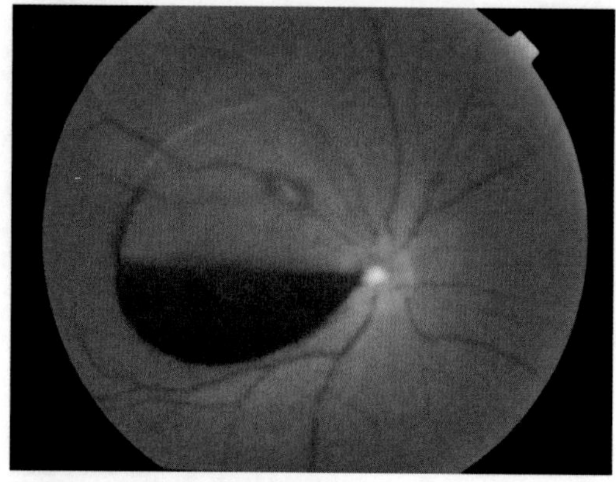
Retina Image Bank. File #26743

What to Know: Valsalva Retinopathy occurs after a patient performs a Valsalva maneuver, or forces an exhalation against a closed glottis. Examples of offending activities include blowing up a balloon, weight lifting, difficult bowel movements, vomiting, and coughing. A Valsalva maneuver will temporarily increase the intraocular venous pressure, and may rupture a macular capillary.

Symptoms: Patients may have no complaints (asymptomatic) or complain of reduced/blurry vision.

Signs: Patients present with one or more hemorrhages underneath the internal limiting membrane (ILM), typically located at the macula. Rarely, vitreous hemorrhage may occur. After a few days the blood may start to turn yellow (dehemoglobinized).

Treatment/Management: Usually Valsalva Retinopathy will resolve spontaneously. If it does not resolve after a few weeks, then a laser can be used to create an opening in the ILM/posterior hyaloid, allowing release of the enclosed hemorrhage.

DIABETIC RETINOPATHY*

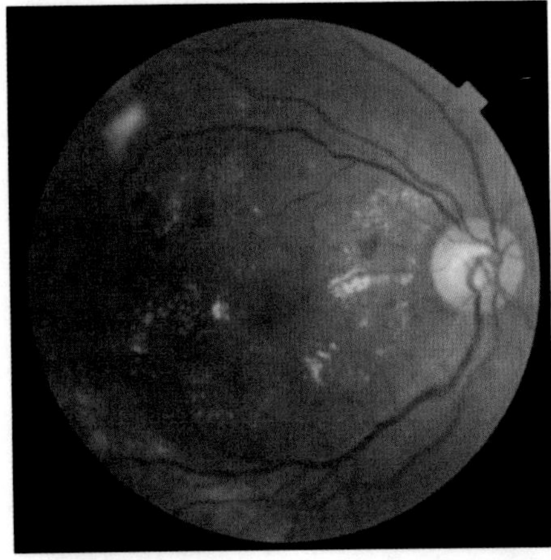

National Vision, Inc.

Kimberly Castillo, OD

What to Know:

Diabetic Retinopathy is the leading cause of blindness in the US among people aged 20-64. Diabetic retinopathy develops secondary to diabetes, especially those with long duration of disease and poor chronic glycemic control. Hypertension and pregnancy are other modifiable risk factors.

Symptoms

Patients will initially be asymptomatic. In later stages they may complain of blurry vision and floaters

Signs:

The two most common causes of vision loss in patients with Diabetic Retinopathy are Clinically Significant Macular Edema (CSME), and neovascularization. Diabetes is also associated with the formation of cataracts. Clinically Significant Macular Edema (CSME) is defined by any of the following criteria:

- Any retinal edema within 1/3DD (500 um) of the fovea
- Any hard exudates within 1/3DD (500 um) of the fovea with associated retinal edema
- Retinal edema with an area of at least 1DD (1500 um) within 1DD (1500 um) of the fovea

More recently, diabetic macular edema may be classified as center-involving if the center of the macula is involved on ophthalmoscopic examination, of if central subfield thickening is present on OCT, and non-center involving if the above criteria is not fulfilled (Baker et al. 2019).

Diabetic retinopathy is broken down into two categories: Nonproliferative (no neovascularization present) and proliferative (neovascularization present).

Nonproliferative diabetic retinopathy (NPDR) has **no neovascularization present**. It can present with **dot-blot** hemorrhages, microaneurysms, venous beading, intraretinal microvascular abnormalities (IRMA), cotton wool spots, and exudates. The 4-2-1 rule (below) is used to define Severe NPDR and Very Severe NPDR. Severe NPDR meets one of the criteria defined by the 4-2-1 rule, while Very Severe NPDR meets two of the criteria:

- 4 quadrants of hemorrhages
- 2 quadrants of venous beading
- 1 quadrant of IRMA

Proliferative Diabetic Retinopathy (PDR) **presents with neovascularization** as well as any of the findings described above. The neovascularization is described as NVI (neovascularization of the iris), NVD (neovascularization of the disc), and NVE (neovascularization elsewhere, aka anywhere else in the retina). For patients with PDR, we can predict who is most likely to lose their vision with the High Risk Characteristics:

- NVD greater than or equal to 1/4 to 1/3 DD in area
- Any NVD with an associated pre-retinal or vitreous hemorrhage.
- NVE greater than or equal to 1/2 DD in area with an associated pre-retinal or vitreous hemorrhage.

Treatment/Management

The Early Treatment Diabetic Retinopathy Study (ETDRS) drew three conclusions regarding treatment of Diabetic Retinopathy:

1. Focal photocoagulation for diabetic macular edema decreased risk of moderate vision loss, increased chance of moderate vision gain, and reduced retinal thickening.
2. Early scatter panretinal photocoagulation (PRP) resulted in small reduction in risk of severe vision loss (less than 5/200 for at least 4 months), but is not indicated for eyes with mild to moderate diabetic retinopathy. PRP helps to control neovascularization.
3. Aspirin use did not alter progression or complications of diabetic retinopathy nor affect vision.

The Adult Medication Study of the Restoring Insulin Secretion (RISE Study) showed that Anti-VEGF is an effective treatment for Diabetic Retinopathy. Anti-VEGF injections don't only prevent continued loss of vision, but can actually improve vision by controlling diabetic macular edema and controlling neovascularization/vitreous hemorrhage. This being said, anti-VEGF injections are the first line of treatment for patients with diabetic macular edema or neovascularization.

Vitrectomy can be considered for non-clearing vitreous hemorrhage and for patients with macula-involving tractional retinal detachments. Cataract surgery may also be necessary in many patients.

Patients should have a dilated eye exam within 5 years of diagnosis with diabetes and annually thereafter until NPDR is detected. NPDR should be monitored roughly every 6 months, and PDR should be monitored roughly every 3 months depending on the severity.

HYPERTENSIVE RETINOPATHY

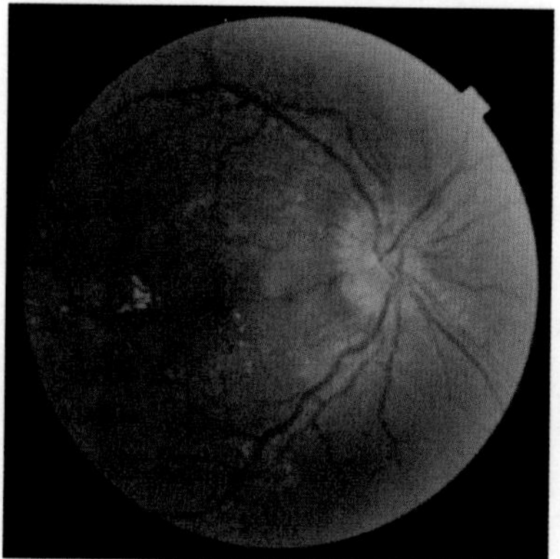

National Vision, Inc.

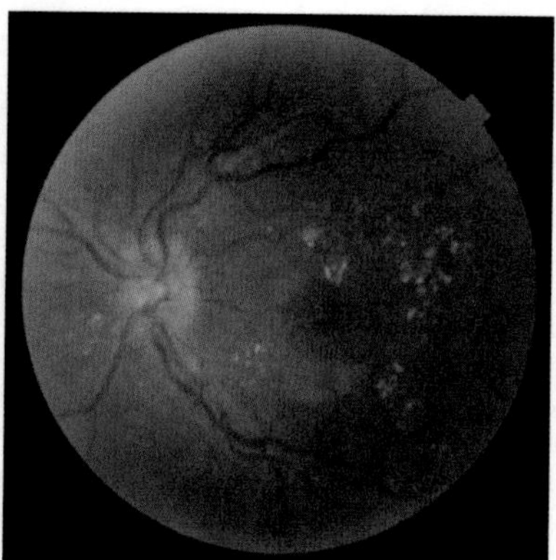

National Vision, Inc.

What to Know:

Hypertension is a common condition and may be divided into primary (aka essential) hypertension, and secondary hypertension. Primary hypertension is typically a chronic age-related condition without a clear cause. Atherosclerosis, or plaque buildup in arteries, is a risk factor for primary hypertension. Secondary hypertension occurs due to an underlying medical condition, such as kidney disease or adrenal gland tumors. Hypertension is associated with cardiovascular events, including myocardial infarctions, strokes, and retinal vascular occlusions. In particular, hypertension is a major risk factor for retinal vein occlusions presumably because it plays a role in causing the arteriosclerosis of retinal arterioles at arteriovenous crossings which can lead to compression, turbulence, and thrombus formation in the adjacent vein.

Hypertension is defined as chronic blood pressure above 130/80 mmHg, and Stage 2 if chronically greater than or equal to 140/90 mmHg. Chronic hypertension can damage the blood vessels within the retina, thereby causing them to become leaky, leading to hypertensive retinopathy.

Symptoms: Patients usually have no complaints (asymptomatic).

Signs: Hypertensive Retinopathy can be defined by the Keith-Wagner-Barker classification system:

- Group 1: Slight constriction of the retinal arterioles
- Group 2: Group 1 plus focal narrowing of retinal arterioles and AV nicking
- Group 3: Group 2 plus flame-shaped hemorrhages, cotton wool spots, and hard exudates
- Group 4: Group 3 plus optic disc swelling.

Other vascular changes seen with hypertensive retinopathy include narrowing, nicking, humping, and copper or silver wiring of the blood vessels, microaneurysms, and Elschnig spots (focal choroidal infarcts).

Malignant hypertensive retinopathy is defined as **blood pressure greater than 220/120** and will present with engorged blood vessels and a **swollen optic nerve head**.

IF a patient has hypertensive retinopathy in only one eye, then suspect a carotid artery obstruction ipsilateral to the NORMAL eye. The obstructed artery is shielding the ipsilateral eye from the effects of hypertension.

Treatment/Management Check the patient's blood pressure and manage the hypertension by referral to PCP. Patients with malignant hypertensive retinopathy need an emergent (same day) referral to the hospital due to risk of stroke or heart attack.

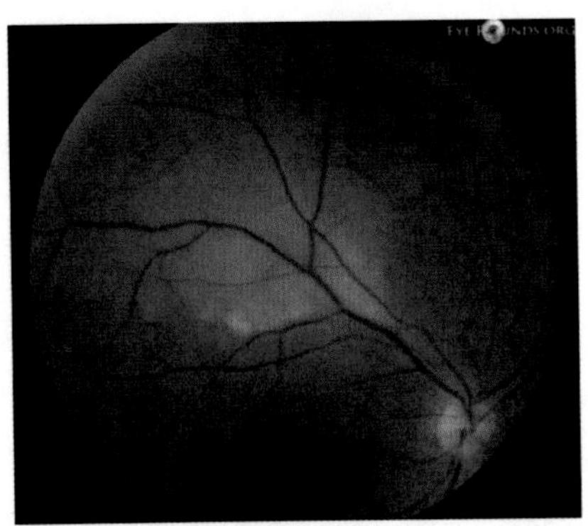
EyeRounds.org University of Iowa

RETINAL ARTERY OCCLUSIONS

What to Know: The first thing I remind myself when I come across artery occlusions is to remember that Arteries take blood Away from the heart. Meaning, arteries bring oxygenated blood to the eyes.

Retinal artery occlusions are usually caused by an embolus. The most commonly discussed types of emboli are Hollenhorst Plaques (cholesterol emboli originating from the carotid artery) and calcifications (originating from the heart valves). What happens is one of these emboli breaks loose from its point of origin, travels along the blood stream, and then gets wedged in a blood vessel, blocking the blood supply of everything downstream. Patients who experience a retinal artery occlusion are at an increased risk of stroke because they are prone to have emboli swimming around in their blood vessels.

Artery Occlusions are usually associated with systemic diseases with hypertension being the most common offender. Patients with hypertension have buildup of plaque inside their blood vessels which serves as the source for the emboli. Other associated systemic diseases include diabetes, cardiac valvular disease, and carotid occlusive disease.

Signs: As its blood supply is lost, the retina will take on a white appearance and will eventually atrophy/die. When this happens in the eye, it is a retinal artery occlusion. When this happens in the brain, it is a stroke. Therefore, a retinal artery occlusion is basically a “stroke” of the eye.

There are three types of artery occlusions which differ by where the embolus has become wedged within the eye’s arteries, described below in the order of severity:

1. Branch Retinal Artery Occlusion (BRAO): the embolus has traveled through the central retinal artery and has gotten itself wedged in one of the arterial branches within the retina. In this situation, only the section of the retina which is downstream of the emboli will be affected. Typically one quadrant or either the superior or inferior half of the retina will be involved. The embolus itself is likely to be small because these “branch arteries” are small. A small embolus will not get lodged in a large artery.
2. Central Retinal Artery Occlusion (CRAO): A CRAO occurs when an embolus gets wedged in the central retinal artery. The entire retina will be involved because it receives its blood from the central retinal artery and visual prognosis is poor. Usually this is caused by a larger, calcific embolus. The choroid will still have its blood supply because it receives its blood from the ophthalmic artery. The choroid will be visible through the whitened retina in the macular region because this is the area where the retina is the thinnest. This area of red choroid visible through the white retina is known as a “cherry-red spot.” In the case of a cilioretinal occlusion, there will be macular sparing and a better visual prognosis
3. Ophthalmic Artery Occlusion: When the Ophthalmic Artery is occluded, the entire retina and choroid of the affected eye will lose its blood supply. In these cases, no “cherry-red spots” will be present because the choroid has also lost its blood supply. Visual prognosis is dismal.

Since the eye is suffering from a lack of oxygen, a long-term complication of a Vein Occlusion may include neovascularization as the eye attempts to oxygenate the afflicted tissues.

Symptoms: Patients will complain of sudden, painless, unilateral loss of vision, with a visual field defect corresponding with the area which has been affected. Amaurosis fugax (or transient loss of vision) may occur as a precursor to the artery occlusion if an embolus gets wedged in a vessel momentarily, but then moves on with the blood stream.

Treatment/Management: Treatment needs to be initiated within 90 minutes of onset, otherwise the afflicted tissues will die from lack of oxygen. Since it is rare for a patient to be seen and treated within 90 minutes of onset, there have been few opportunities for research on the best treatment for these cases. At this time, treatment is aimed at reducing the pressure within the eye, hoping reduced pressure on the vessels will cause them to relax/dilate enough to allow the embolus to pass. Methods of reducing the pressure include: hyperventilation into a paper bag to induce respiratory acidosis and subsequent vasodilation, digital massage, systemic acetazolamide (Diamox IV or po), topical hypotensive drugs (Timolol drop every fifteen minutes), paracentesis (allowing outflow of aqueous from the globe by penetrating the cornea near the limbus with a needle).

Given the long-term risk of neovascularization, these patients should be monitored regularly and treated with Panretinal Photocoagulation (PRP) and/or anti-VEGF injections if neovascularization is found. The risk of neovascularization is lower with arterial occlusions when compared to venous occlusions.

Prognosis for artery occlusions is generally very poor; the visual field loss is usually permanent. BRAOs which do not involve the macula have the best prognosis. CRAOs and ophthalmic artery occlusions involve the entire retina (including the macula), and so they have the worst prognosis. Systemic prognosis is also concerning because any patient who has emboli swimming around the blood stream is at a higher risk of myocardial infarction (heart attack) and stroke.

In some ways, a patient who gets a retinal artery occlusion is lucky because the emboli decided to wedge itself in the retina instead of in the brain. This being said, other emboli could be moving around in the patient's blood stream, and the next one could very well travel up to the brain instead. Therefore, a patient who has had an artery occlusion should be urgently referred to determine and treat the underlying disease. In fact, the evaluation and treatment of amaurosis fugax and acute branch or central retinal artery occlusions are equivalent to that of transient ischemic attack and stroke.

Giant Cell Arteritis (GCA) needs to be ruled out in elderly patients who suffer from Central Retinal Artery Occlusions. Patients should be referred for immediate testing including an ESR, CRP, platelets, complete blood count, and possible temporal artery biopsy with possible initiation of systemic steroids if testing is positive.

RETINAL VEIN OCCLUSIONS

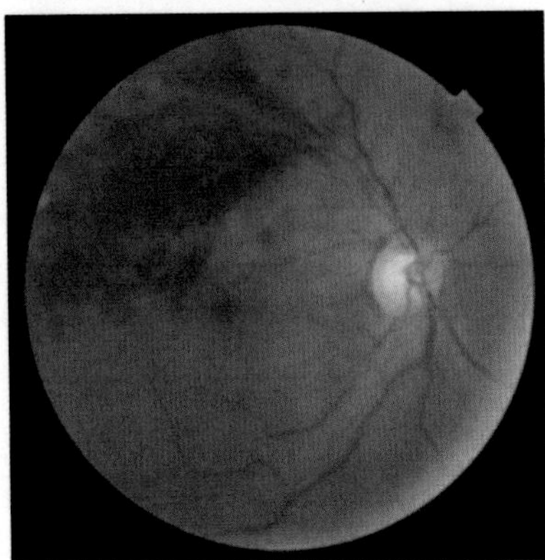

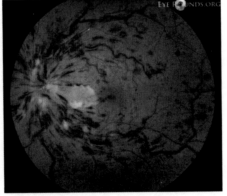

National Vision, Inc.

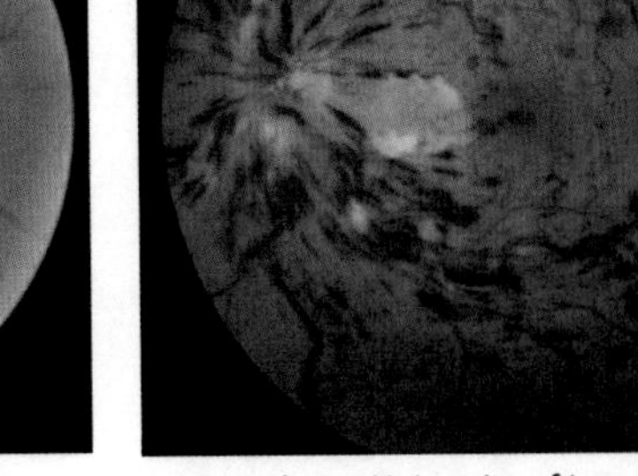

EyeRounds.org University of Iowa

What to Know: The first thing I remind myself when I come across vein occlusions is to remember that veins bring deoxygenated blood from the eye towards the heart.

Vein occlusions usually occur in patients who are at least 50 years old following a thrombotic event. Patients who are young and develop a Vein Occlusion may have hypercoagulable blood or take oral contraceptives. Finally, for unclear reasons, glaucoma appears to be a risk factor for both central and branch retinal vein occlusions.

Signs: Vein Occlusions present with retinal hemorrhages scattered throughout the afflicted area of the retina paired with engorged and tortuous retinal veins. Vein occlusions may also present with cotton-wool spots and edema of the macula and/or optic nerve. A RAPD may be present, and the severity of the RAPD corresponds with the severity of the ischemia.

Ischemia may be present with fluorescein angiography, and the more ischemia that is present, the more likely the patient will be to develop neovascular glaucoma (which is one of the most severe complications of vein occlusions). The reason why neovascularization occurs is the ischemic tissue secretes VEGF factors in an attempt to get oxygen. New abnormal blood vessels may begin to grow as a result, and that can lead to vitreous hemorrhage, tractional retinal detachments, and angle closure. The more ischemia that is present, the more VEGF is released, and the more likely neovascularization will occur.

There are three types of vein occlusions which differ by where the thrombus has become wedged within the retinal veins, described below:

1. Branch Retinal Vein Occlusion (BRVO): A BRVO occurs when a thrombus has formed in one of the small retinal veins prior to drainage into the central retinal vein. In these cases, diffuse retinal hemorrhages will usually be visible in just one quadrant of the retina (most commonly superotemporally). The closer the BRVO is located to the disc, the more area of the retina is involved, and so the more severe the case. There are two types of BRVOs which can be differentiated by fluorescein angiography (remember that when a tissue is ischemic, it is deprived of blood flow/oxygen):
    i. Nonischemic BRVOs show less than five disc diameters of capillary nonperfusion with FA. This is more common than ischemic BRVOs, presumably because they are smaller.
    ii. Ischemic BRVOs show greater than five disc diameters of capillary nonperfusion with FA. For obvious reasons, ischemic BRVOs have a poorer prognosis than nonischemic BRVOs.
2. Central Retinal Vein Occlusion (CRVO): A CRVO occurs when a thrombus forms within the central retinal vein. In these cases, diffuse retinal hemorrhages will be visible in all quadrants of the retina. Like BRVOs, there are also two types of CRVOs which can be differentiated by the area of ischemia as seen with fluorescein angiography:
    i. Nonischemic/Perfused is more common and is defined as less than 10 disc diameters of capillary nonperfusion on FA.
    ii. Ischemic/Nonperfused is less common and has greater than 10 disc diameters of capillary nonperfusion on FA.
3. Hemiretinal Vein Occlusion: Some individuals have two separate veins which drain the superior and inferior portions of the retina respectively, which do not merge into a central retinal vein. Therefore in lieu of a CRVO, these patients can develop a hemiretinal vein occlusion. These will present with diffuse retinal hemorrhages distinctively on either the superior or inferior half of the retina. Hemiretinal Vein Occlusions can also be defined as either Nonischemic or Ischemic by the same parameters as CRVOs.

"90-Day Glaucoma" is a term used for patients who develop glaucoma within 90 days after a Retinal Vein Occlusion attack. These are cases in which a patient gets neovascular glaucoma from a very ischemic eye secondary to a vein occlusion.

Symptoms: Patients will complain of sudden, painless, unilateral loss of vision, with a visual field defect corresponding to the area which has been affected. Patients with neovascularization may report associated ocular pain secondary to the acute severe intraocular pressure elevation or associated inflammation.

Treatment/Management: Ocular treatment is not necessary unless center-involving macular edema or neovascularization is present. Anti-VEGF agents and periocular steroids (as a second line) can be used to treat the macular edema, while anti-VEGF injections and panretinal photocoagulation can be used to treat neovascularization. These patients should be monitored monthly for the first six months for the development of edema or neovascularization. Treat the neovascular glaucoma should it develop.

The associated systemic disease should also be treated, and patients should be referred for a full cardiac evaluation. Patients with hypertension should have their blood pressure checked and also should consider taking aspirin prophylactically due to their high risk of cardiovascular disease. Oral contraceptive discontinuation may be discussed with younger patients.

Prognosis is good unless neovascularization develops. 33% of such cases develop neovascular glaucoma. The more ischemia that is present within the eye, the more likely the patient will develop neovascular glaucoma. This is a reason why it is good to know how much ischemia is present, it serves as a predictive factor.

OCULAR ISCHEMIC SYNDROME (OIS)

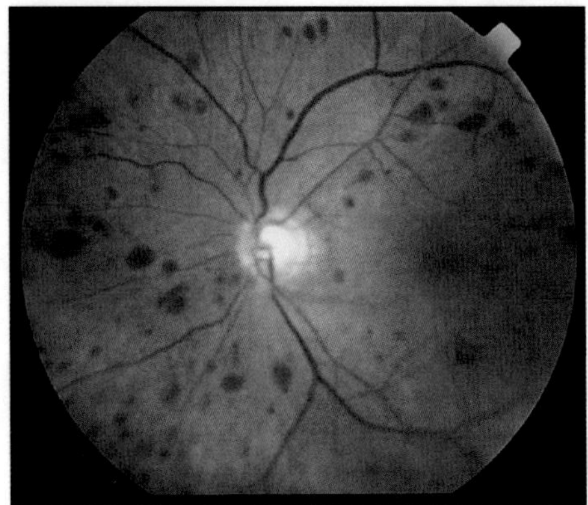

Retina Image Bank. File #3343

What to Know: OIS can present similarly to retinal vein occlusions, but typically lacks venous tortuosity and dilation. Both are associated with hypertension and cardiac disease. With OIS, the carotid artery is stenotic (narrowed) which can reduce blood flow to the entire eye. Both the anterior and posterior segments become ischemic. It is typically seen in men over the age of 50. After one year, vision will be reduced to count fingers or worse in 60% of patients. After five years, the mortality rate is 40%.

Symptoms: Patients may complain of amaurosis fugax (transient vision loss) and/or gradual vision loss (which can be as severe as NLP) as the eye is slowly choking. The patient may also have ocular angina (dull pain/headache).

Signs: OIS will present with **mid-peripheral** retinal hemorrhages. Since the eye's oxygen supply is being diminished, neovascularization may develop throughout the eye (anterior and posterior segments) in an attempt to oxygenate the ocular tissues. Neovascularization of the angle can increase IOP and lead to secondary neovascular glaucoma and associated rubeosis. There may be increased flare in the anterior chamber and corneal edema. This being said, it is important to note that OIS affects the front to the back of the eye.

Treatment/Management: Given the morbid prognosis, it is extremely important that patients with OIS are referred urgently for evaluation of neck and head vascular occlusive disease with special attention to the carotid arteries and for treatment of their hypertension or cardiovascular disease.

Ocular treatment will be aimed at halting the neovascularization and reducing any increased IOP. The neovascularization will be treated with panretinal photocoagulation (PRP) and anti-VEGF injections. Neovascular glaucoma is hard to stabilize, and may require incisional glaucoma surgery or cyclophotocoagulation (laser procedure that helps lower the eye pressure by targeting the ciliary processes).

RETINOPATHY OF PREMATURITY (ROP)

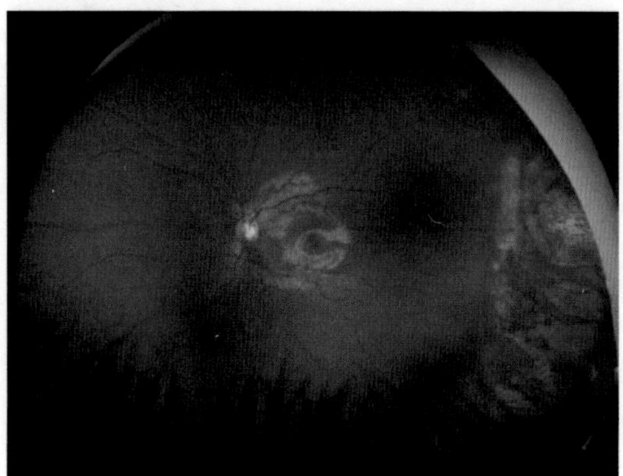

Kimberly Castillo, OD

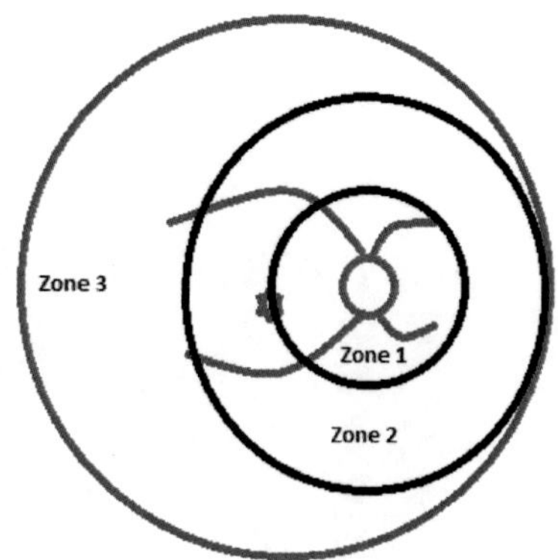

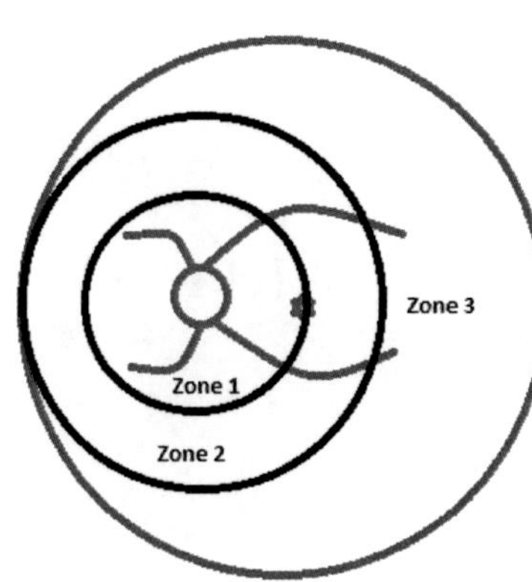

Kimberly Castillo, OD

Facts to Know: ROP occurs in certain premature and low birth weight infants, and early iatrogenic oxygen exposure (a high oxygen environment) is a major risk factor A major risk factor. When the retina is forming, it begins in the center and grows towards the periphery. When a baby is premature, the retina has not yet fully formed at birth. A high-oxygen environment disrupts the retinal development process, leading to an avascular peripheral retina. Babies who are at most risk have a **birth weight of less than 1500 grams or are born at less than 32 weeks (full term is 40 weeks**).

Symptoms: None, as the patients are premature infants and nonverbal.

Signs: ROP presents with a whitened, avascular peripheral retina, which may lead to leukocoria.

Stages:

1. Flat demarcation line separating the vascular from the avascular peripheral retina.
2. The demarcation line is ridged/elevated.
3. Fibrovascular proliferation or neovascularization along the demarcation line.
4. Partial retinal detachment, further defined by Stage 4A and Stage 4B:
    a. Macula on
    b. Macula off
5. Total retinal detachment.

- Plus Disease: Any ROP associated with abnormal dilated and tortuous blood vessels.

Zones:

1. A circle centered around the optic nerve head (ONH) in which the radius is the distance between the ONH and the fovea.
2. A circle centered around the optic nerve head (ONH) in which the radius is the distance between the ONH and nasal ora serrata and just outside Zone 1.
3. Includes the remaining temporal peripheral retina.

Treatment/Management Patients should be monitored every 1-2 weeks until the peripheral retina has become vascularized, monitoring to see if the blood vessels grow appropriately. Also be on the look-out for "rush disease" (aka Aggressive Posterior ROP) in which Plus Disease is seen in Zone 1 or Posterior Zone 2.

Since this is a disease of the retinal vasculature, it makes sense that treatment options are aimed at controlling neovascular complications. The avascular retina can be treated with laser photocoagulation (cautery of retinal blood vessels with a laser) and less commonly cryotherapy (freezing of tissue). If present, surgery may be indicated for any retinal detachments.

SILDENAFIL (VIAGRA) / TADALAFIL / VARDENAFIL

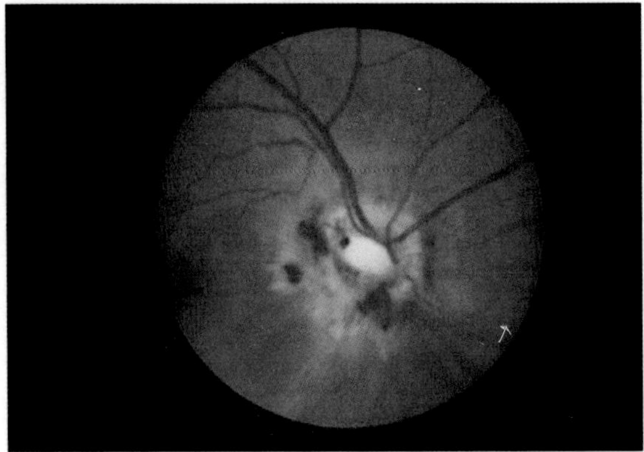

Retina Image Bank. File #13398

NBC 1

What to Know: Viagra is used to treat erectile dysfunction.

Symptoms: Patients may complain of a blue tint over their vision (cyanopsia). I imagine that the blue Viagra pills cause blue color vision changes.

Signs: Since Viagra changes how the blood behaves within the body, it will cause the patient to be more likely to have hemorrhages throughout the body, including retinal and subconjunctival hemorrhages. Other associated conditions include Non Arteritic Ischemic Optic Neuropathy (NAION), and retinal artery or vein occlusions.

Treatment/Management: Signs and symptoms will typically resolve when Viagra is discontinued. NAION and vascular occlusions have the worse prognosis.

RADIATION RETINOPATHY

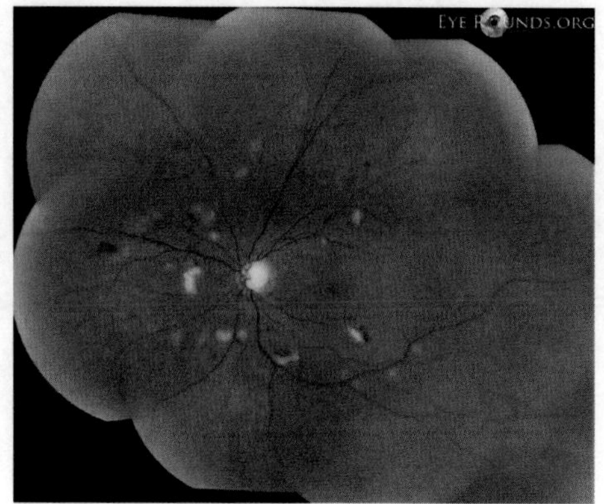

EyeRounds.org University of Iowa

What to Know: Radiation Retinopathy typically occurs within 6-24 months after a patient has been exposed to greater than 3000 rads of radiation. The threshold of necessary radiation is lower in patients who have diabetes or are undergoing chemotherapy. Prognosis is fair with two-thirds of patients maintaining between 20/20 to 20/200 vision.

Symptoms: Patients may have no complaints (asymptomatic). If the macula is involved they will complain of blurry vision.

Signs: Radiation Retinopathy presents similarly to Diabetic Retinopathy with hemorrhages, exudates, cotton wool spots, neovascularization, swollen optic nerve, macular edema, and cataracts.

Treatment/Management: Given its presentation is similar to Diabetic Retinopathy, Radiation Retinopathy is addressed with similar treatment. Macular edema is treated with anti-VEGF injections. Neovascularization is treated with anti-VEGF injections and panretinal photocoagulation (PRP).

COAT'S DISEASE

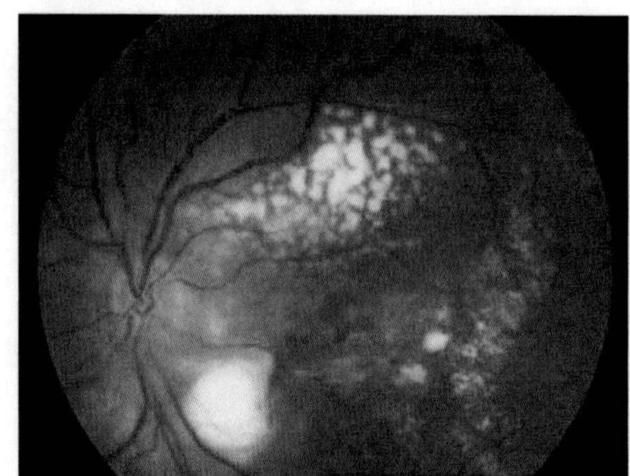
EyeRounds.org University of Iowa

What to Know: Coat's Disease is a progressive disease which usually starts in **young boys under the age of ten**, and is a vascular abnormality that causes a leakage of exudates. These exudates become thick and plentiful, and when severe enough will cause an exudative retinal detachment.

Symptoms Patients may complain of poor vision.

Signs: **Leukocoria** is a big sign that is always discussed with Coat's Disease. If onset is early enough, the patient may also have strabismus. Telangiectasia (abnormal dilated capillaries), multiple clumped lipid exudates, and exudative retinal detachments can be found. Advanced cases may present with glaucoma, and a blind painful eye.

Staging:

1. Telangiectasia only
2. Exudates
3. Retinal detachment
4. Glaucoma
5. End stage disease

Treatment/Management Treatment options are aimed at controlling leaking blood vessels with laser photocoagulation or cryotherapy (freezing of tissue). If present, treat the glaucoma. Retinoblastoma needs to be ruled out before treatment in all cases.

SICKLE CELL RETINOPATHY*

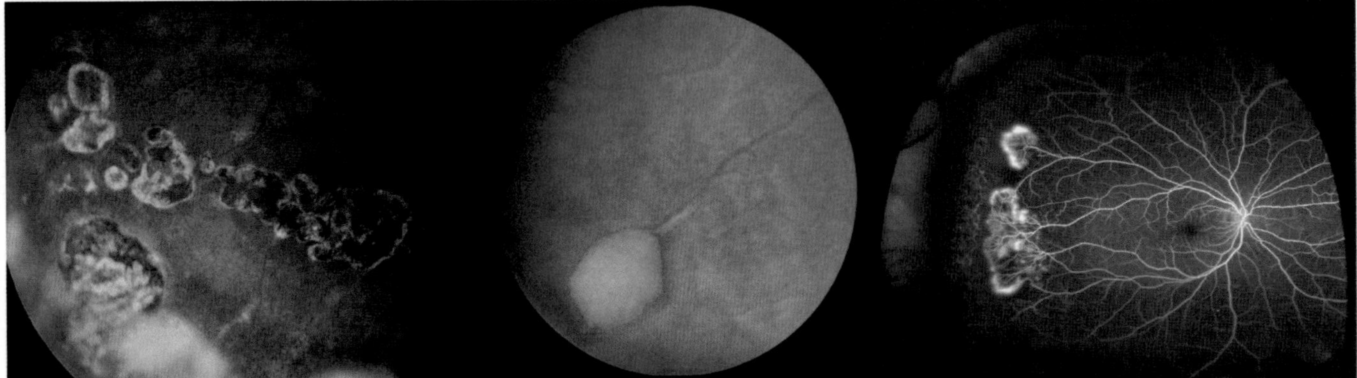

Retina Image Bank. File #26040 Retina Image Bank. File #1789 Retina Image Bank. File #721

What to Know: Sickle Cell is a genetic condition with a predilection for patients of African and Mediterranean descent. It causes their red blood cells to be shaped like a sickle instead of a healthy oval. Poor blood flow and ischemia arise because the sickled cells do not travel smoothly through the patient's vasculature like an oval-shaped red blood cell would.

Symptoms: Patients frequently have no complaints (asymptomatic).

Signs: Sickle Cell Retinopathy presents with five different stages. Stages One and Two are non-proliferative while stages 3-5 are proliferative:

1. Peripheral arterial occlusions.
2. Peripheral nonperfusion and arteriovenous anastomoses.
3. Sea Fan neovascularization, especially at the border of nonperfused retina.
4. Vitreous hemorrhage.
5. Tractional retinal detachment.

Findings may also include Salmon Patches (pink intraretinal hemorrhages) and Black Sunbursts (chorioretinal scars). This is a mnemonic I designed to help you remember the buzz words associated with Sickle Cell: Sickle Sell presents with Sunbursts, Salmon Patches, and Sea Fans.

Treatment/Management: The neovascularization should be as usual with anti-VEGF injections, laser photocoagulation (cautery of retinal blood vessels with a laser), and less commonly cryotherapy (freezing of tissue). These patients should also be referred for a hematology consult. They also require annual dilated exams.

RETINAL ARTERIAL MACROANEURYSM (RAM)

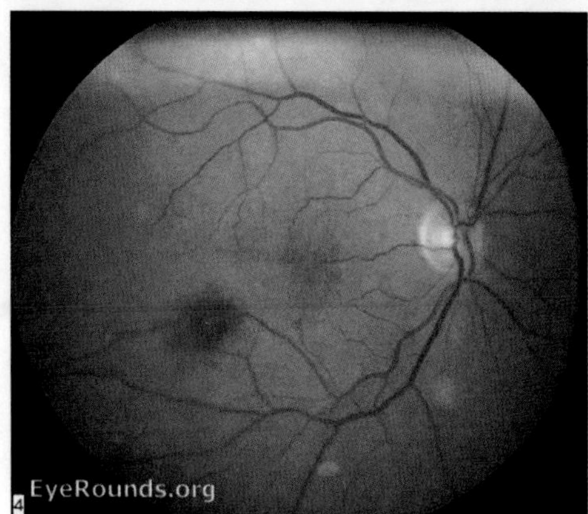

EyeRounds.org University of Iowa

What to Know: Retinal Arterial Macroaneurysms are most commonly found in elderly women who have hypertension and are taking multiple hypertensive medications. They are usually unilateral. The compromised artery will become dilated and could possibly rupture with associated hemorrhaging.

Symptoms: Patient may have no complaints (asymptomatic) prior to any rupture depending on location. If the macroaneurysm ruptures, then the patient may complain of sudden loss of vision secondary to the associated hemorrhage. Edema and exudates from aneurysmal leakage may lead to chronic vision loss.

Signs: Retinal Arterial Macroaneurysms present as a saccular dilated artery, which is unilateral and possibly associated with a pre-retinal or vitreal hemorrhage. The dilated artery may also leak without rupturing.

Treatment/Management Retinal Arterial Macroaneurysms often requires no treatment because the macroaneuryms usually resolve with spontaneous involution. If there is evidence that the vessel is leaking, it could be treated with laser photocoagulation (cautery of retinal blood vessels with a laser). Anti-VEGF and steroid injections may be used in some cases, though its efficacy is less well-studied when compared to diabetic macular edema or retinal vein occlusion. Non clearing vitreous hemorrhages can be treated with a vitrectomy, though this is rare.

All patients presenting with Retinal Arterial Macroaneurysms should be sent to their primary care physician (PCP) for management of their hypertension.

RACEMOSE HEMANGIOMATOSIS (WYBURN-MASON SYNDROME)

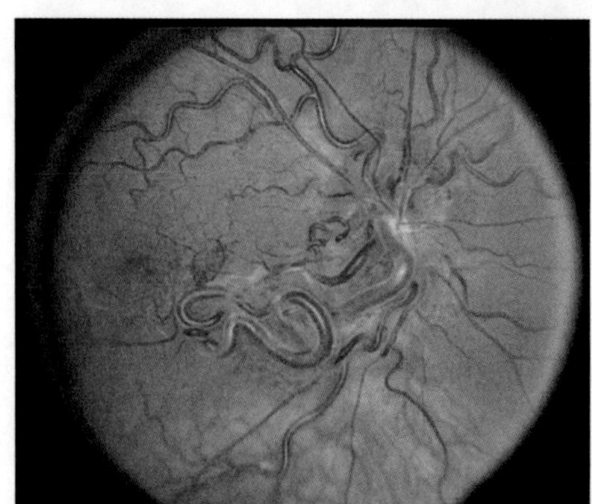
Retina Image Bank. File #4620

What to Know: Racemose Hemangiomatosis occurs when congenital arteriovenous malformations form in the retina and ipsilateral brain, face, orbit, and mandible.

Symptoms: Patients are usually visually asymptomatic, but may complain of headaches.

Signs: Racemose Hemangiomatosis presents with dilated vessels which may lead to any kind of hemorrhaging within the eye. It may have associated neovascular glaucoma and seizures. Intracranial vessel malformations and subsequent hemorrhages may lead to early mortality.

Treatment/Management: Treatment may not always be necessary, though laser photocoagulation (cautery of retinal blood vessels with a laser) may be used in exceptional symptomatic cases. Patients should be referred for a systemic evaluation.

TYPES OF DETACHMENTS / RETINAL LAYER DISRUPTIONS

<table>
<tr><th>LATTICE DEGENERATION</th><th>SNAIL TRACK DEGENERATION</th></tr>
<tr><td>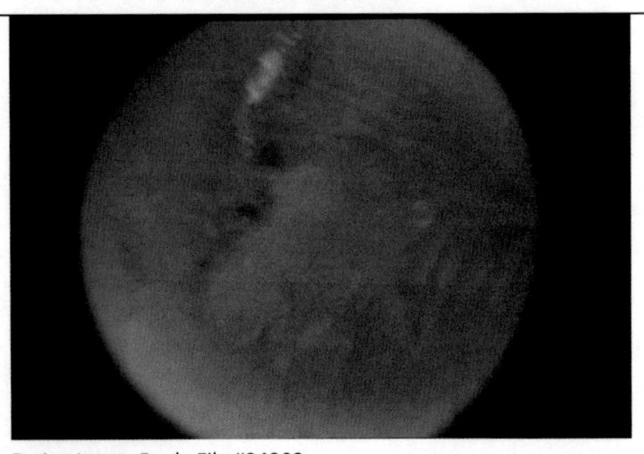
Retina Image Bank. File #24303</td><td>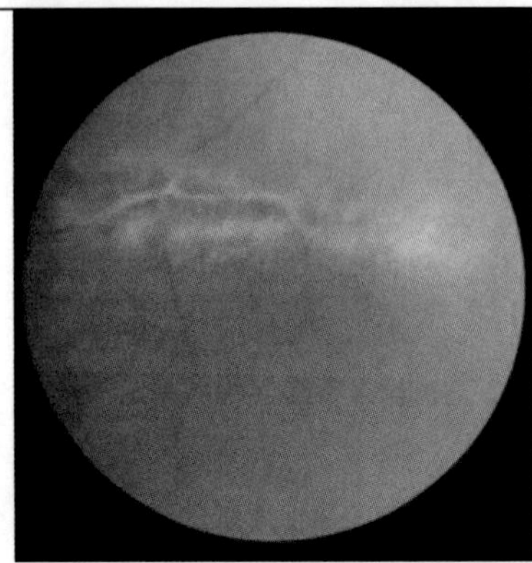
Retina Image Bank. File #2001</td></tr>
<tr><td colspan="2"><u>Similarities to Know:</u> Both are associated with high myopia and a higher risk of retinal holes and detachments.</td></tr>
<tr><td><u>Differences to Know:</u> Lattice Degeneration is comprised of areas of retinal thinning with overlying areas of liquefied vitreous. It is characterized by a strong adherence between the vitreous and the border of the lesion. This adherence leads to traction and the typical pigment seen in these lesions.</td><td><u>Differences to Know:</u> Snail Track Degeneration is comprised of areas of cystic lesions which lead to the separation of the neurosensory retina with corresponding scotomas. Snail Track Degeneration does NOT have a strong adherence between the vitreous and the border of the lesion.</td></tr>
<tr><td colspan="2"><u>Symptoms:</u> Patients may have no complaints (asymptomatic). Flashes and floaters may indicate the development of an associated retinal hole or detachment.</td></tr>
<tr><td><u>Signs:</u><ul><li>Long oval shape parallel to the ora serrata.</li><li>Located in the mid periphery. Usually superior temporal.</li><li>Dark crisscrossing areas.</li></ul></td><td><u>Signs:</u><ul><li>Long oval shape parallel to the ora serrata.</li><li>Located in the far periphery.</li><li>White crisscrossing areas with a glistening appearance like a snail's track.</li></ul></td></tr>
<tr><td colspan="2"><u>Treatment/Management:</u>
Patients who are asymptomatic should be educated on the symptoms of Retinal Detachment and instructed to return to clinic urgently if they observe these symptoms.

The goal with symptomatic patients is to prevent the development of any retinal tears or detachments. This is achieved with the prophylactic use of laser photocoagulation (cautery of retinal blood vessels with a laser), and less commonly cryotherapy (freezing of tissue). If a retinal tear or detachment develops, they should be treated as such.</td></tr>
</table>

RETINAL DETACHMENT

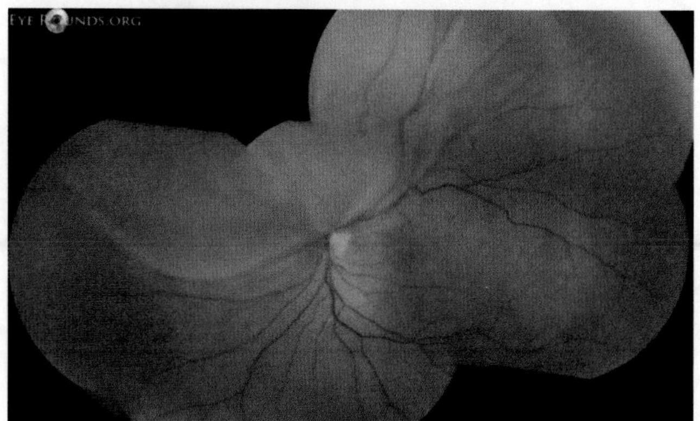

EyeRounds.org University of Iowa

Signs: Retinal detachments of any kind occur when fluid gets underneath the retina. There are three types of retinal detachments, differentiated by the mechanism by which the fluid gets underneath the retina. The three types include Rhegmatogenous, Exudative, and Tractional Detachments described below:

1. **Rhegmatogenous retinal detachments** occur when the retina is torn, causing a full thickness defect. Fluid from vitreous syneresis can now get underneath the retina. Because they are caused by a retinal break / tear / hole, these are the kinds of detachments where the patients will come in with symptoms of floaters, flashes of lights, a curtain / veil over their vision, or missing areas of vision. As with retinal breaks, a longstanding rhegmatogenous retinal detachment will show scarring presenting as a pigment demarcation line at the posterior border of the detachment. A patient with a rhegmatogenous detachment will have a ***relative*** visual defect, unlike retinoschisis which produces an ***absolute*** visual field defect.
2. **Exudative retinal detachments** occur when there is a breakdown in the blood-retinal barrier, and so fluid accumulates underneath the retina. The fluid is free to move around based on the position the person has assumed. While standing/sitting, the fluid will pool at the inferior portion of the retina. While lying down (in the supine position), the fluid will move to pool in the posterior pole. The detachment will appear convex and smooth, I think of this as being like a blister. The causes are all systemic diseases which obviously cause the breakdown between the blood-retinal barrier (non-exhaustive list: central serous retinopathy, VKH Syndrome, optic pit, morning-glory syndrome, coats disease)
3. **Tractional retinal detachments** occur when neovascularization from the retina grows into the vitreous, causing the two to be abnormally "connected" in locations where they normally would separate freely. The vitreous should not be abnormally tethered to the retina when a posterior vitreous detachment occurs. When the neovascularization connects the retina to the posterior hyaloid, it creates the possibility for the vitreous to tug on the retina when it moves and (aka traction) and when it contracts. Depending on the situation, the vitreous may break the neovascular blood vessels, which will present as pre-retinal or vitreous hemorrhages. Or, if the traction is strong enough, the retina may tear, leading to further accumulation of fluid under the retina, or a combined rhegmatogenous-tractional retinal detachment. The site of the traction may present with a vitreous membrane. Since neovascularization is necessary for a tractional retinal detachment to occur, the etiology behind these detachments are any diseases which can lead to neovascularization. The most common retinal diseases which can cause retinal neovascularization include diabetic retinopathy, retinopathy of prematurity, sickle cell retinopathy, and vessel occlusions.

Symptoms A **rhegmatogenous retinal detachment** is most likely to be symptomatic with the classic flashes, floaters, or "veils" over the patient's vision. The other two types of detachments may be asymptomatic or present with relative visual field defects.

Treatment/Management

Exudative retinal detachments are treated by addressing the underlying etiology.

The most important factor to consider prior to treating **rhegmatogenous and tractional retinal detachments** is whether or not the macula is involved. This can be determined based on the patient's BCVA and confirmed by using optical coherence tomography. If the BCVA is 20/50 or worse, then the macula is off. If the BCVA is 20/40 or better, then the macula is likely still on. If the macula is still on, then this needs to be referred for emergent same-day surgery because there is a possibility of saving the macula before it is detached as well. If the macula is already off, the surgery can be delayed; research shows the visual outcome does not change if the surgery is performed within 7 days. The surgeries which are used to treat rhegmatogenous and tractional detachments include pars plana vitrectomy with laser photocoagulation (cautery of retinal blood vessels with a laser), scleral buckle (a piece of semi-hard plastic is placed around the eye, which compresses and closes the retinal break from the outside), cryotherapy (freezing of tissue), and pneumatic retinopexy (gas bubble injection with appropriate positioning).

Patients treated for retinal detachments are followed up at 1 day; 1 and 2 weeks; 1, 2, 3, 6, and 12 months.

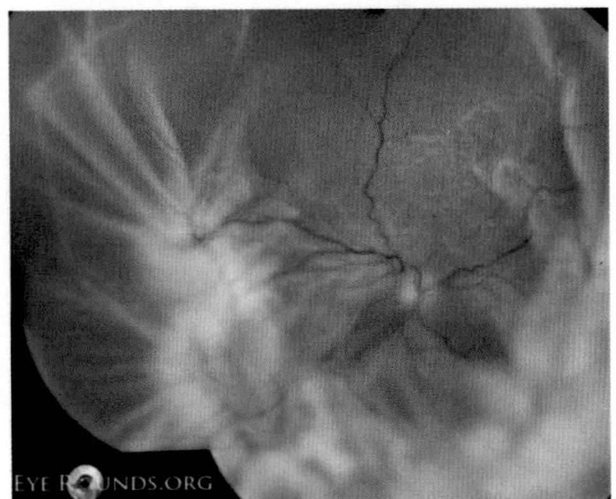

EyeRounds.org University of Iowa

The most common reason for failure of retinal detachment surgery is **Proliferative Vitretinopathy** (left image). It occurs 6-8 weeks after retinal detachment surgery. Proliferative fibrotic membranes contract and pull on the retina, causing re-detachment. Treatment includes surgery to remove the fibrotic tissue and reattach the retina. 70-90% of cases end with successful reattachment, but up to 40% end up with worse than 20/100 acuity.

RETINAL BREAK / HOLE / TEAR

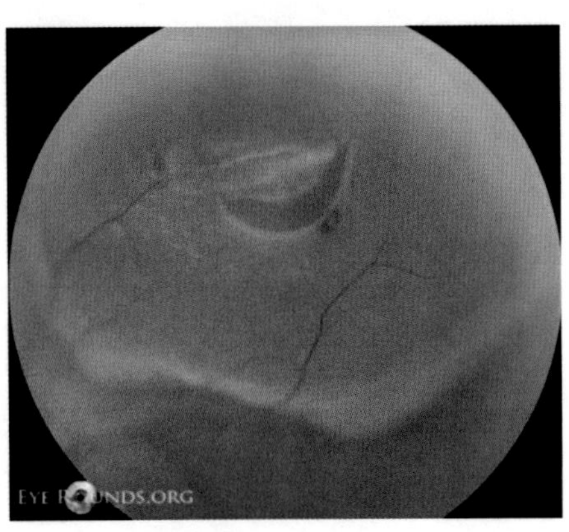

EyeRounds.org University of Iowa

What to Know: Risk Factors for a retinal break include high myopia, lattice degeneration, aphakia and pseudophakia (presumably secondary to surgery), and trauma (non-exhaustive list).

Symptoms: Patients may complain of flashes and floaters that move with the eye as it moves and blurry vision that fluctuates with eye movement. Symptoms may be indistinguishable from a PVD.

Signs: Retinal holes/breaks/tears have varying presentation depending on if the defect is new or long standing:

- New (aka acute) defects will display signs of recent damage to the eye. There may be subretinal or vitreal hemorrhaging or edema; Shafer's Sign will be present because of recently released pigment; torn retina in the form of a flap or operculum (a piece of retina floating in the vitreous) may be visible as well.

- Long standing (aka chronic) defects will have formed scars as pigment rings around the defects. This scar tissue is tough and binds the retina together, actually providing a protective measure against retinal detachment. In these cases, the eye has actually healed itself. A patient with a chronic defect will not complain of symptoms because at this point, everything has settled down. It looks far more interesting to the examiner than the patient.

Treatment/Management varies depending on if the break is acute or chronic:

- Treatment for acute breaks should be initiated within 24-72 hours after onset. It is aimed at stabilizing the tear so that the retina does not rip open further. Laser therapy or less commonly, cryotherapy (freezing of tissue) can be used to prevent progression to a retinal detachment.
- Chronic breaks are stable, and so they can be monitored. Photographs should be taken and the patient should be educated on the symptoms of a retinal detachment.

RETINOSCHISIS

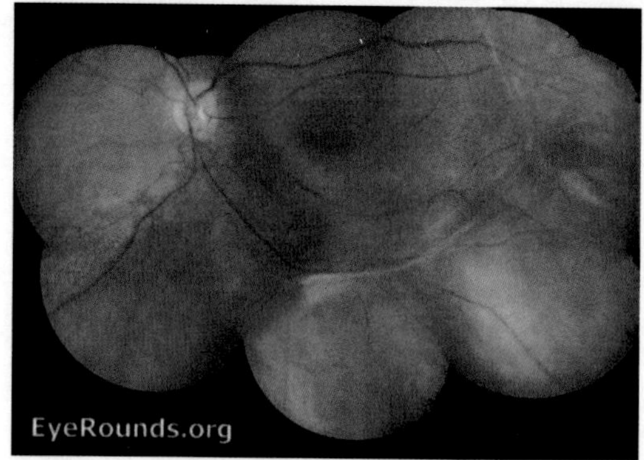

EyeRounds.org University of Iowa

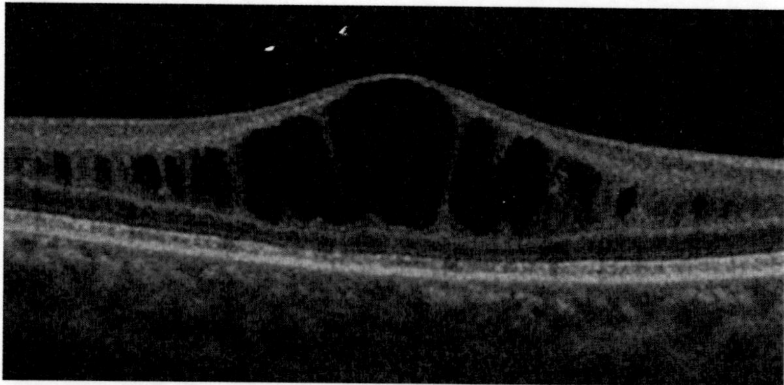

Retina Image Bank. File #28198

Signs: Retinoschisis is defined as splitting of the layers within the retina (as opposed to a retinal detachment which is when the retina is detached from the retinal pigment epithelium/choroid). It typically creates dome shaped lesions in the retinal periphery. Retinoschisis may look very similar to a retinal detachment. Since the intraretinal visual pathway is disrupted, retinoschisis leads to ***absolute*** visual field defects that have sharp borders (as opposed to retinal detachments which have ***relative*** visual field defects). Procedures which can help differentiate a Retinoschisis from a Retinal Detachment include visual field, scleral indentation, and OCT. Fluorescein Angiography cannot be used to differentiate them. Also note that Retinoschisis will present with no tobacco dust/Shafer's sign, which may be seen with a retinal detachment. Rarely retinoschisis can present with associated rhegmatogenous retinal detachments and vitreous hemorrhages. There are two types of Retinoschisis:

1. **Acquired Age Related:** more common, presents bilaterally and symmetrically. The location of the splitting is between the inner nuclear and outer plexiform layers (which can be remembered with OPL is the Old People's Layer). Etiology seems to be unclear.
2. **Juvenile (X-linked recessive):** less common and located in the nerve fiber layer (which can be remembered with young people play in the NFL). It presents with VA that progressively decreases from 20/25 to 20/80 due to macular involvement. Since this can be congenital, it may be amblyogenic with associated nystagmus and strabismus. It will often present as stellate maculopathy (spoke-like foveal cysts).

Symptoms: Patients may have no complaints (asymptomatic), or may complain of blurry vision if the macular is involved (ie. Juevenile cases).

Treatment/Management No treatment is needed for the retinoschisis itself. If it presents with an accompanying issue (hemorrhage, amblyopia, detachment, etc.) these should be treated as such. Children with juvenile retinoschisis should be educated to avoid physical activity (good luck) because minor "trauma" can lead to complications of hemorrhage or detachment. Genetic testing may be offered to confirm the diagnosis. Retinoschisis should be monitored every 6 months.

PATHOLOGICAL MYOPIA / MYOPIC DEGENERATION

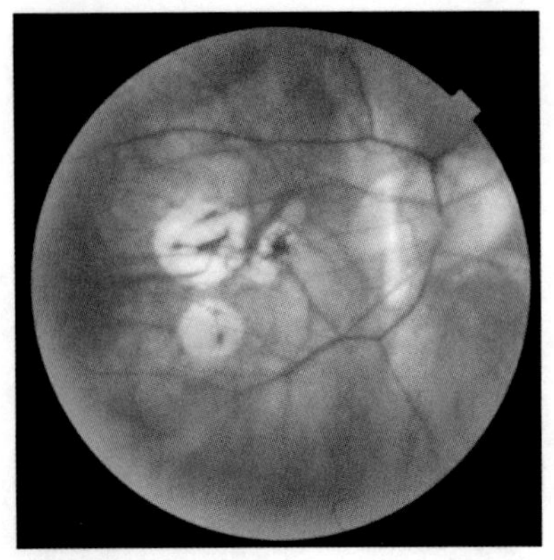

National Vision, Inc.

What to Know: Pathological Myopia occurs when patients have high grade and progressive myopia. All of the signs in these cases are due to the fact that the eyeball will not stop elongating. It occurs in patients who have greater than -6.00D of myopia or an axial length greater than 26mm. Not every patient who has high myopia has Pathological Myopia, just the ones where the myopia continues to progress and who present with the signs listed below. This disease has a hereditary component.

Symptoms: Patients may complain of decreased vision.

Signs: Pathological Myopia may present with a tilted disc, lacquer cracks, posterior staphyloma (outpouching of the posterior segment visible as white circles of visible choroid), peripapillary atrophy, Fuchs' spots (dark spots from RPE hyperplasia), retinal holes and detachments, posterior vitreous detachments, lattice degeneration, and choroidal neovascularization.

Treatment/Management: Contact lenses are often prescribed over glasses because they cause less image minification and prismatic effect. Recommend polycarbonate for patients who wear glasses. Choroidal neovascularization can be treated with anti-VEGF injections. Retinal holes and detachments should be treated as such. There are no treatments for the chorioretinal atrophy. These patients may benefit from low vision devices.

ANGIOID STREAKS

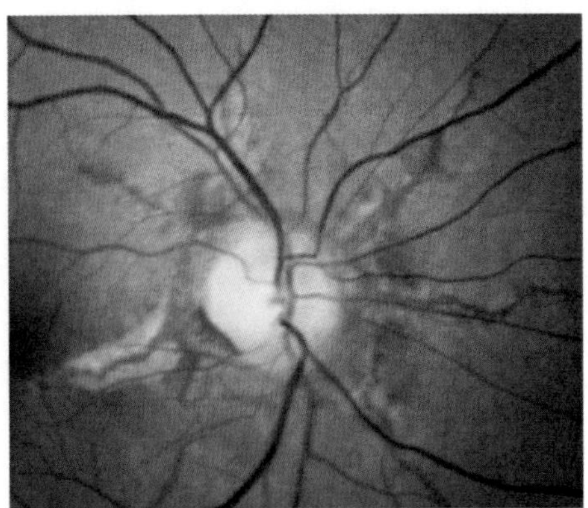

Eyerounds.org University of Iowa

What to Know: Angioid Streaks are most commonly idiopathic, but they can be associated with systemic diseases which can be remembered using PEPSI:

- Pseudoxanthoma Elasticum is a genetic disease characterized by mineralization of elastic tissues. It can lead to premature atherosclerosis (blockage of arteries).
- Ehlers Danlos Syndrome is a rare AD connective tissue disorder caused by a deficiency of hydroxylysine. It will cause connective tissues to become too flexible leading to joint dislocation, easy bruising, translucent skin, and dilation and rupture of blood vessels. Ocular complications may include angioid streaks, blue sclera, megalocornea, Ectopia Lentis, keratoconus, mitral valve prolapse, and aortic aneurysms.

- Paget's Disease is a chronic and progressive metabolic disease which causes malformation of bones.
- Sickle Cell Disease is a genetic condition which causes red blood cells to be shaped like a sickle instead of a healthy oval. Poor blood flow and ischemia arises because the sickled cells do not travel smoothly through the patient's vasculature like an oval-shaped red blood cell would.
- Idiopathic

Symptoms: Patients may have no complaints (asymptomatic), or complain of blur if a choroidal neovascular membrane (CNV) develops.

Signs: Angioid streaks present as pigmented full-thickness breaks in Bruch's Membrane that radiate out from the optic nerve head (ONH). Occasionally a choroidal neovascular membrane may arise from Angioid Streaks.

Treatment/Management: If a choroidal neovascular membrane is present, it should be treated using anti-VEGF injections. These patients should also be referred to rule out and treat any possible underlying systemic conditions.

HEREDITARY RETINOPATHIES
I remember that dystrophies are hereditary in nature with the rhyming in "you can get a dystrophy from your family."

RETINITIS PIGMENTOSA

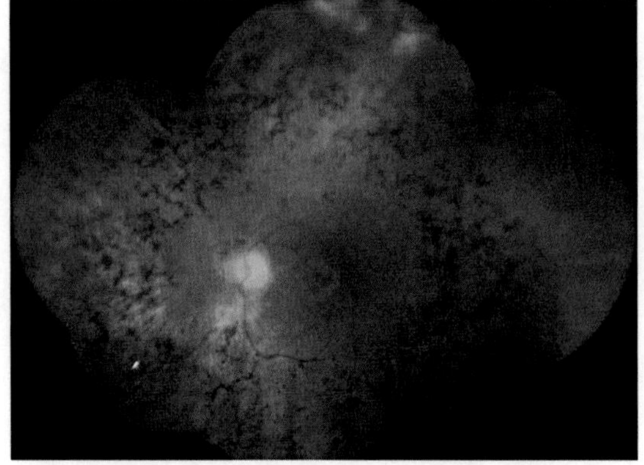

EyeRounds.org University of Iowa

What to Know: Retinitis Pigmentosa is the most common retinal dystrophy and has a variety of inheritance patterns ranging from autosomal recessive (AR) and autosomal dominant (AD) to X-linked Recessive. It is caused by abnormal photoreceptor protein production. Retinitis Pigmentosa is frequently found comorbid with other systemic diseases, the most classic being Bardet-Biedl Syndrome (polydactyly being a distinguishing characteristic) and Usher Syndrome (characterized by associated deafness. I remember this by thinking the singer Usher would be ruined if he became deaf).

Symptoms: Since rods are affected first, patients will complain of night blindness (nyctalopia) and a midperipheral ring scotoma which expands and leaves a central island of vision. Cones are affected second, with tritanopic color vision defects and progressive loss of central vision starting around the age of 20.

Signs: Retinitis Pigmentosa presents with a classic triad of waxy pallor of the optic nerve head, bone spicules (peripheral clumps of pigment), and vessel attenuation (narrowing). ERG will be drastically reduced. Cystoid macular edema, vitreous cells, and cataracts may develop as well.

Treatment/Management: Vitamin A supplementation is no longer recommended. Patients may benefit from sunglasses and a low vision consult. They are usually legally blind by the time they are in their 40s. Genetic testing is recommended to confirm the diagnosis and to determine candidacy for gene therapy treatments.

STARGARDT DISEASE

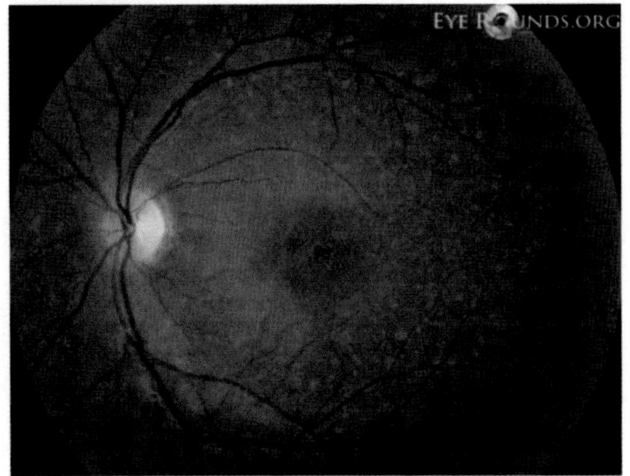

EyeRounds.org University of Iowa

What to Know: Stargardt Disease is the most common hereditary macular disease, and typically has an AR inheritance. Onset is before the patient is in their 20s, and prognosis is poor with vision decreasing to 20/200 while the patient is in their 30s.

Symptoms: Patients may have bilateral reduced vision before any fundus changes appear.

Signs: The classic findings in Stargardt Disease present bilaterally with yellow-white pisciform "fish tail" lipofuscin deposits at the level of the RPE, and RPE bullseye with a "beaten bronze" appearance. Patients may develop a central scotoma late in the disease. Fluorescein Angiography will show a silent choroid.

Treatment/Management: Patients should avoid vitamin A to slow down the accumulation of lipofuscin. Patients may benefit from UV blocking sunglasses, low vision aids, and genetic counseling as well. Genetic testing can be used to help confirm diagnosis and to determine patient's candidacy for gene therapy clinical trials.

BEST DISEASE / VITELLIFORM MACULAR DYSTROPHY

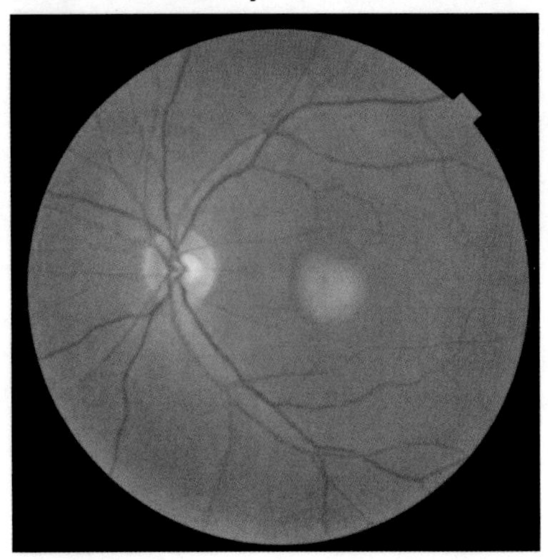
National Vision, Inc.

What to Know: Best Disease has an autosomal dominant (AD) inheritance.

Signs/Symptoms: Patients with Best Disease will have signs which are more severe than symptoms until they reach their 50s. The disease progresses as follows:

- The first indication the patient has Best Disease will be a **severely low EOG** before the patient is the age of 10 but with a normal appearing fundus. I remember that the EOG will be reduced by thinking of the "O" as looking like the classic yellow egg-yolk.
- The next sign will appear before the patient is 15 years old as an "egg yolk" lesion over the macula located at the level of the retinal pigmented epithelium (RPE), but with vision only mildly affected (20/40 being the worst).
- Vision will begin decreasing when the "egg yolk" turns into the "scrambled egg" appearance as the cyst begins to break apart.
- By the age of 50 the patient will have worse than 20/100 vision when the lesion has been completely reabsorbed leaving behind an area of atrophic RPE with scarring, choroidal neovascularization (CNV), or geographic atrophy).

Treatment/Management: No treatment is available unless CNV is present, then treat with anti-VEGF injections.

FAMILIAL EXUDATIVE VITREORETINOPATHY

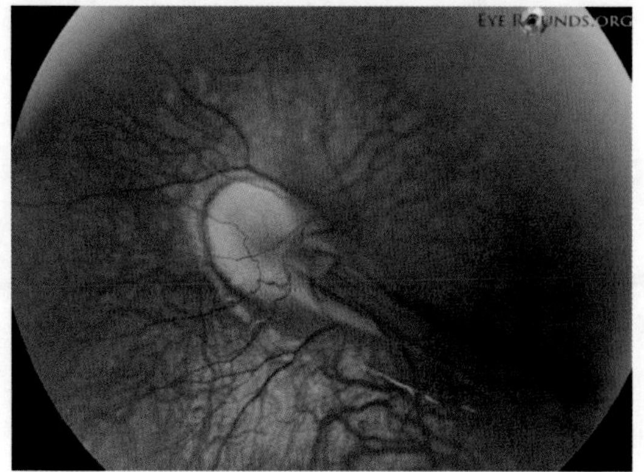

EyeRounds.org University of Iowa

What to Know: Familial Exudative Vitreoretinopathy most commonly has an autosomal dominant (AD) inheritance. It is an asymmetric bilateral degeneration which is present at birth and has a clinical appearance similar to Retinopathy of Prematurity but with no medical history of premature birth.

Symptoms: Most patients will have no complaints (asymptomatic). Patients may complain of blurry vision (as severe as 20/200), and it may be accompanied with amblyopia, strabismus, and nystagmus.

Signs: Familial Exudative Vitreoretinopathy may present with leukocoria in advanced cases with retina detachment. Characteristic vascular straightening in both eyes, avascular periphery, dragged macula, and exudative or tractional retinal detachments may be present.

Treatment/Management: Extraretinal vascularization is treated with laser photocoagulation, and retinal detachments are treated with surgery. Any amblyopia should be treated as well. Genetic testing may be offered to help confirm the diagnosis and to guide counseling. Family members should be evaluated as well as they may have asymptomatic disease.

LEBER'S CONGENITAL AMAUROSIS

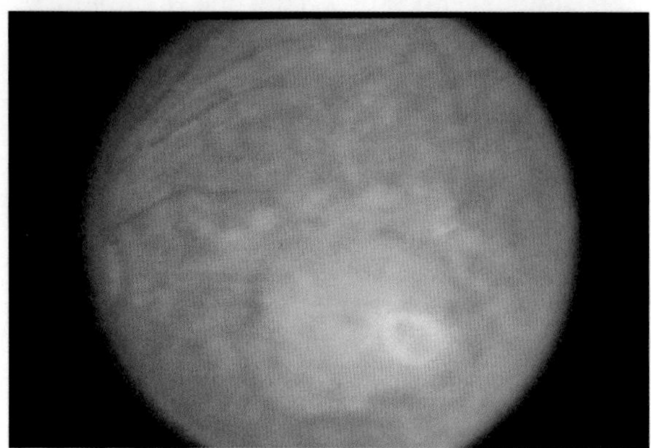

Retina Image Bank. File #24325

What to Know: Leber's Congenital Amaurosis is a progressive autosomal recessive (AR) rod-cone dystrophy which is the most common congenital cause of blindness in children. It is associated with the loss of retinal photoreceptors, outer segments, and outer nuclear layers.

Symptoms: Parents will notice a roving eye within the first few months of life. Patients will complain of reduced acuity and color perception, nyctalopia, and photophobia.

Signs: Leber's Congenital Amaurosis presents with an acuity which will be reduced from 20/40 to no light perception (NLP) with the average being 20/200. Early in life the fundus may appear normal, but it may progress to present with a myriad of findings including attenuated vessels, chorioretinal atrophy, significant macular pigmentation which may look like colobomas, pigmentary retinopathy, yellow flecks, and a tapetal/metallic sheen. Other ocular findings include sluggish pupils, nystagmus, significantly constricted visual fields, high hyperopia, keratoconus, keratoglobus, posterior subcapsular cataracts, oculo-digital sign (eye rubbing) which may cause atrophy of orbital fat and subsequent enophthalmos, and a severely reduced ERG. Systemic findings include deafness, skeletal and muscular conditions, renal/kidney abnormalities, endocrine dysfunction, mental handicap, and epilepsy.

Treatment/Management: Prognosis is poor. Refer to a low vision specialist. Genetic testing should be offered to help confirm the diagnosis and to help determine candidacy for gene therapy. One United States Food and Drug Administration-approved gene therapy exists in the form of Luxturna (voretigene neparvovec).

ENHANCED S-CONE SYNDROME / GOLDMANN-FAVRE SYNDROME

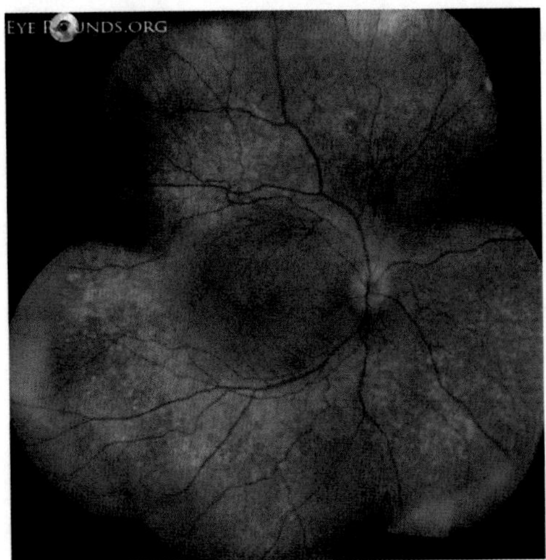

EyeRounds.org University of Iowa

What to Know: Goldmann-Favre Syndrome is an extremely rare, autosomal recessive (AR) degeneration which begins early in childhood. Goldmann-Favre Syndrome is a severe form of Enhanced S-Cone Syndrome.

Symptoms: Patients may complain of night blindness (nyctalopia), sensitivity to blue light, and blurry vision.

Signs: Goldmann-Favre Syndrome presents as a bilateral retinal pigmentary and vitreous degeneration with macular (and sometimes peripheral) retinoschisis.

Treatment/Management: Treatment, including topical carbonic anhydrase inhibitors, may be offered if cystoid macular edema is present. Prognosis is guarded because this is progressive.

ANGIOMATOSIS RETINAE (VON HIPPEL-LINDAU SYNDROME)

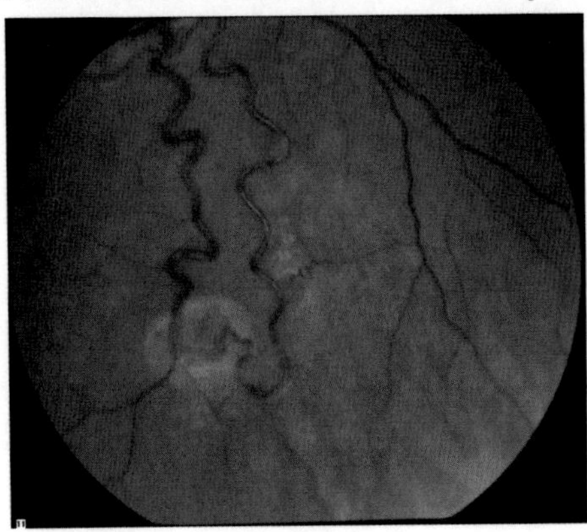
Retina Image Bank. File #2910

What to Know: Von Hippel-Lindau Syndrome occurs due to a tumor suppressor gene mutation which has autosomal dominant inheritance. As a result, hemangioblastomas may form in the retinal and central nervous system. Systemic tumors including renal cell carcinoma and pheochromocytoma among others may occur.

Symptoms: Patients may have no complaints (asymptomatic), or complain of blurry vision which may be worse than 20/100 in any affected eye.

Signs: Hemangioblastomas appears as an orange-red mass with feeder-vessels and drainage and is usually located in the superior temporal quadrant of the peripheral retina. There may be many hemangioblastomas and they may be bilateral. There may be an associated Epiretinal Membrane (ERM), tractional retina detachment, and exudative complications such as macular edema or exudative retinal detachment.

Treatment/Management: Asymptomatic cases may be observed. Treatment for symptomatic cases is aimed at destructive treatment of the tumors: cryotherapy (freezing of tissue), laser photocoagulation (cautery of retinal blood vessels with a laser), argon laser (a narrow beam of light is used to shrink or destroy the cancerous cells), diathermy, radiotherapy (use of radiation prior to surgery to reduce the size of the tumor), and surgical excision. Patients can be referred for genetic counseling.

PROGRESSIVE CONE DYSTROPHY

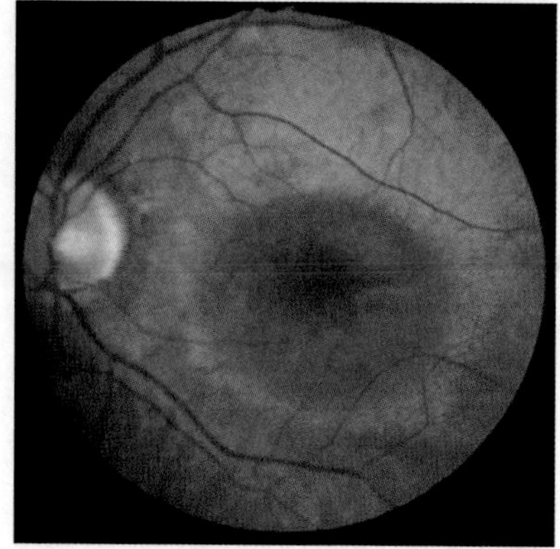

Retina Image Bank. File #3143

What to Know: Progressive Cone Dystrophy is also known as Progressive Cone-Rod Dystrophy, although it predominately affects the cones. It can be either autosomal dominant (AD) or autosomal recessive (AR). Onset is between the ages of 20-40 and progresses slowly with vision loss potentially ending at count fingers (CF).

Symptoms: Patients will complain of bilateral central blur with abnormal color vision and light sensitivity (photophobia). They will also experience Hemeralopia (difficulty seeing in bright light, the opposite of nyctalopia).

Signs: Progressive Cone Dystrophy will present with macular changes seen as a golden sheen which progress to a bulls-eye maculopathy, and eventually macular atrophy. Patients will have severe color vision abnormalities and central scotomas (which makes sense since cones are responsible for both color vision and central vision). Prognosis is poor with vision reaching 20/200 by the time the patient is in their 40s.

Treatment/Management: Treatment is focused on managing the symptoms of photophobia with sunglasses or tinted contact lenses. Patients can be referred for genetic counseling.

FAMILIAL DOMINANT DRUSEN

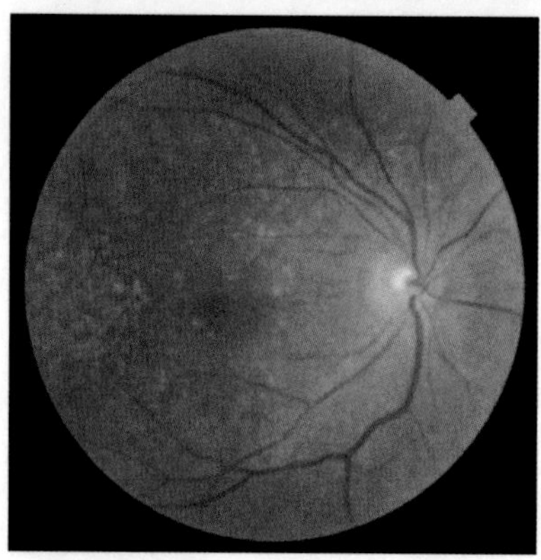

National Vision, Inc.

What to Know: Dominant Drusen have an AD inheritance and the onset is before the age of 20.

Signs: Familial Dominant Drusen will initially look similar to Age Related Macular Degeneration (ARMD). Fluorescein Angiography (FA) will display more drusen than is seen clinically. Once the patient reaches their 40s or 50s, the lesions may coalesce and form a honeycomb appearance, eventually turning into atrophy with possible choroidal neovascularization (CNV). The patient may also have a central scotoma.

Symptoms: Patients may have no complaints (asymptomatic) or complain of central vision loss if choroidal neovascularization (CNV) or atrophy is present in the macula. When the patient reaches their 40s or 50s they may complain of significant vision loss.

Treatment/Management: No treatment is available unless choroidal neovascularization (CNV) is present, then treat with anti-VEGF injections.

GYRATE ATROPHY

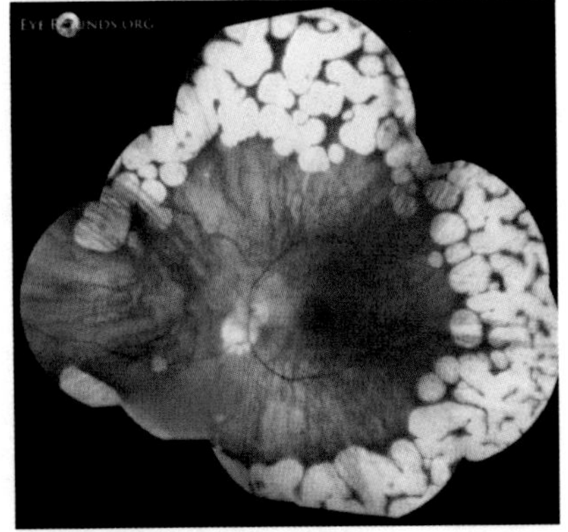

EyeRounds.org University of Iowa

What to Know: Gyrate Atrophy is autosomal recessive (AR). Onset is in the first decade of life, and will afflict the entire retina between the ages of 40-50 without treatment. Patients have a deficiency of ornithine aminotransferase, leading to urine and plasma ornithine levels increased by 10-20x greater than normal.

Symptoms: Patients may complain of night blindness (nyctalopia) and constricted visual field.

Signs: Gyrate Atrophy presents with peripheral areas of scalloped chorioretinal atrophy which enlarge and migrate posteriorly, affecting the macula last. It is associated with progressive myopia.

Treatment/Management: Arginine and protein are needed to create ornithine, and so restricting them in the patient's diet will help lower the ornithine levels. Patients should also supplement their diet with vitamin B6.

INFECTIOUS DISEASES

ACUTE RETINAL NECROSIS (ARN)

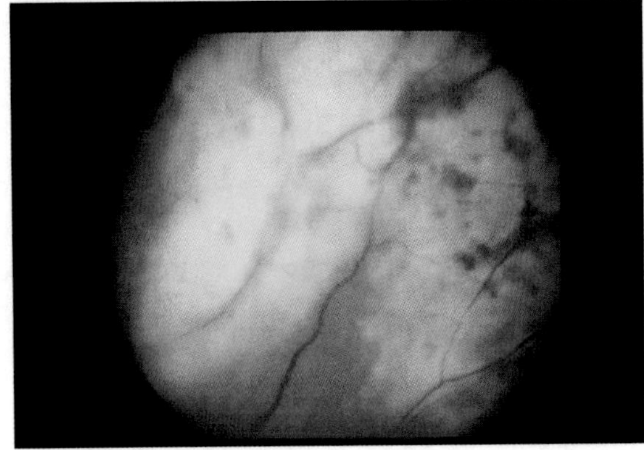

Retina Image Bank. File #8051

What to Know: Acute Retinal Necrosis (ARN) may occur in both immunocompetent or immunocompromised patients and is caused most commonly by varicella-zoster virus and herpes simplex virus type 1 and 2.

Symptoms: ARN may or may not be associated with recent herpetic disease or zoster. Patients typically complain of acute vision loss, pain, and photophobia.

Signs: Patients present with peripheral areas of well-demarcated white necrosis which will eventually spread circumferentially around the peripheral retina, sparing the posterior pole until late in the disease course. Anterior granulomatous uveitis and occlusive retinal vasculitis will be comorbid, and retinal detachments will occur in late stages. Acute Retinal Necrosis will begin unilaterally, but can spread to the second eye in 30% of cases if not treated appropriately.

Treatment/Management: Prognosis is poor with 70% of patients ending up with worse than 20/200 vision in the afflicted eye. Given this is a severe viral infection, treatment is aggressive with IV or oral antivirals followed by addition of oral steroids to control the inflammation. Adjunctive intravitreal antiviral injections should be strongly considered in severe cases. When anterior uveitis is comorbid, treat it with a topical steroid and cycloplegic as usual. If a retinal detachment occurs, it should be surgically repaired. Lifelong prophylactic antiviral after the acute episode is standard.

<table>
<tr><th>HISTOPLASMOSIS</th><th>TOXOPLASMOSIS</th></tr>
<tr><td colspan="2">Histoplasmosis and Toxoplasmosis are constantly compared, and a question on one will likely have the other listed as an option in the answer choices. Therefore, it is important to be able to differentiate these two diseases.</td></tr>
<tr><td>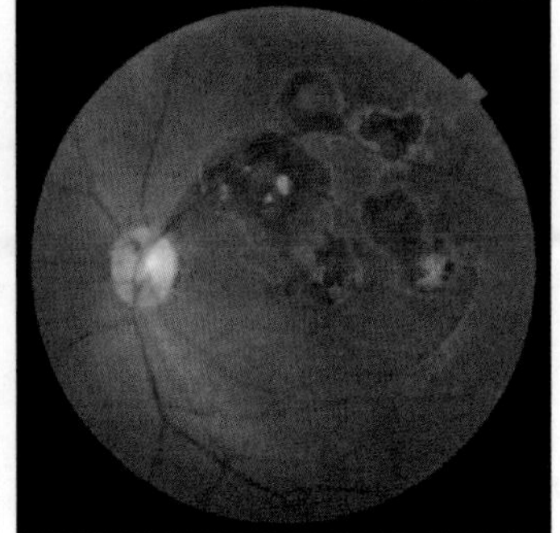</td><td>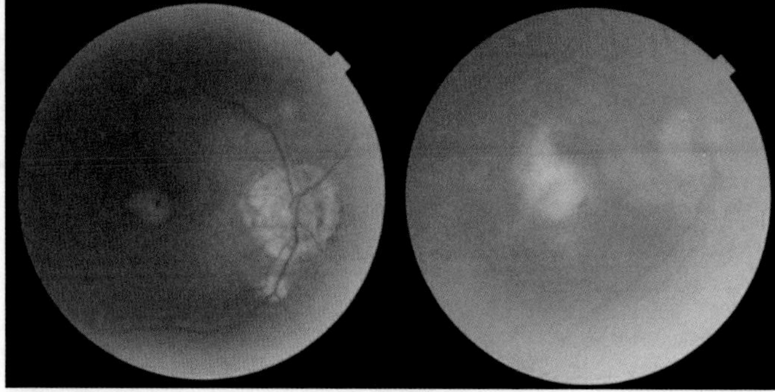</td></tr>
<tr><td>National Vision, Inc.</td><td>National Vision, Inc.</td></tr>
<tr><td>
<u>What to Know:</u>
Histoplasmosis is caused by the fungus Histoplasma capsulatum. The patient will typically become infected by inhaling the fungus from bat or bird (think of farmers) droppings. This is typically seen in the Ohio and Mississippi River valleys.

<u>Signs:</u>
Histoplasmosis presents with a classic triad, and two of the three findings need to be present for a diagnosis:
1. Multiple, small, yellow-white, punched-out lesions.
2. Peripapillary atrophy/scarring
3. Macular choroidal neovascular membrane (CNVM) appearing as a grey-green membrane.
NO vitritis is present!

<u>Symptoms:</u> Patients will complain of metamorphopsia if CNVM is present, otherwise they will be asymptomatic.

<u>Treatment/Management:</u>
Treatment for Histoplasmosis is aimed at controlling neovascularization (if present) with anti-VEGF injections. Antifungal treatment is not helpful!
</td><td>
<u>What to Know:</u> Toxoplasmosis is caused by the parasite Toxoplasma gondii. Patients will become infected through one of two courses:
• Acquired infections occur when the patient eats poorly cooked meat.
• Congenital infections account for the vast majority of cases, and occur when a pregnant mother comes in contact with contaminated cat feces, causing her baby to become infected.
Toxoplasmosis is the most common cause of posterior uveitis. It is a necrotizing (flesh eating!) disease when active.
<u>Signs:</u> An active case of Toxoplasmosis will present with fluffy yellow-white necrotic lesions and an overlying vitritis. When combined, these two look like the classic “headlights in a fog.” An anterior uveitis may be comorbid.
• Acquired cases will present as a typical active toxoplasmosis with an adjacent scar in most cases. Primary lesions may present less commonly with an associated chorioretinal scar because the scar has not had time to form yet.
• Congenital cases present classically with a deep macular chorioretinal scar and amblyopia. Other ocular findings may include cataracts and optic atrophy. Reactivation may occur adjacent to areas of scarring.
<u>Symptoms:</u> Patients will complain of blurry vision, floaters, and redness when they have an active infection. Otherwise they will be asymptomatic.

<u>Treatment/Management:</u> Trimethoprim, Sulfamethazole, Pyrimethamine, sulfadiazine, atovaquone, azithromycin, and clarithromycin are utilized to control protozoal proliferation. Prednisone is commonly added to control inflammation. Avoid periocular steroid injections.
</td></tr>
</table>

PROGRESSIVE OUTER RETINAL NECROSIS SYNDROME (PORN)

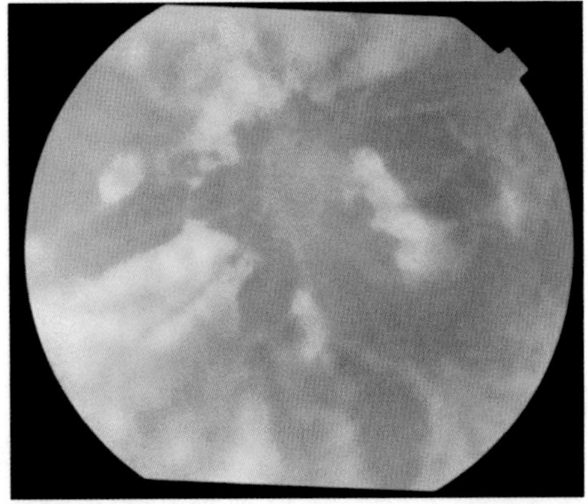

Retina Image Bank. File #1924

What to Know: It is only fitting that a disease which is called PORN is caused by an STD (Herpes Zoster Virus) and occurs in patients with HIV (as well as other immunocompromised patients). The compromised immune system allows the opportunistic HIV to behave aggressively, necrotizing (killing) the retinal flesh.

Symptoms: Patients will complain of blurry vision.

Signs: Characterized by rapidly progressive retinal necrosis with early posterior pole and contralateral eye involvement. There will be minimal retinal vasculitis and anterior or intermediate uveitis. Retinal detachments are common.

Treatment/Management: Given the viral origin, PORN should be treated with intravitreal anti-virals. If inflammation is present, then topical steroids should be considered. Any subsequent retinal detachments should be treated surgically. Treatment of the immunocompromise should be optimized.

TOXOCARIASIS

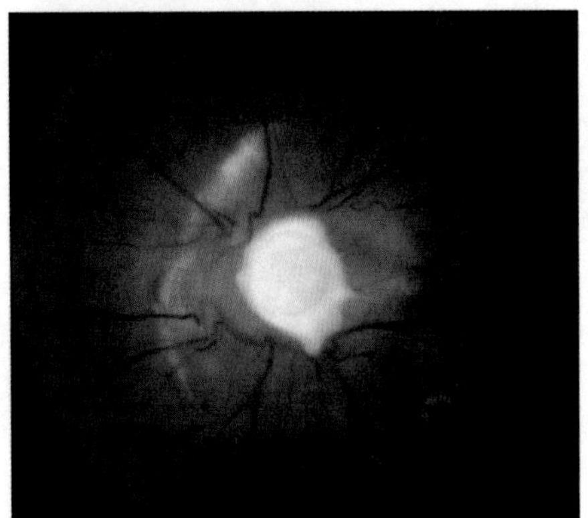

EyeRounds.org University of Iowa

Kira D. Foltz

What to Know: Toxocariasis typically occurs in children who ingest the nematode *Toxocara canis* from puppy feces by accident, via pica, or infant curiosity.

Symptoms: Patients will complain of blurry vision.

Signs: I like to think of white puppies with this disease because it is transmitted via puppies, and also has two significant ***white*** signs: endophthalmitis and leukocoria. The leukocoria is secondary to macular dragging due to a posterior pole granuloma (mass of vascular tissue produced in response to infection or ***inflammation***). Other related complications include chorioretinal scars and retinal detachment. Patients may also have papillitis and vitritis with associated vitreous infiltrates.

Treatment/Management: The inflammation should be treated with topical and/or oral steroids. If anterior uveitis is present, it should be treated with the usual steroid and cycloplegic. Retinal detachment should be repaired with surgery. Systemic antihelminthic medications can be given with assistance of infectious disease specialists.

CYSTICERCOSIS

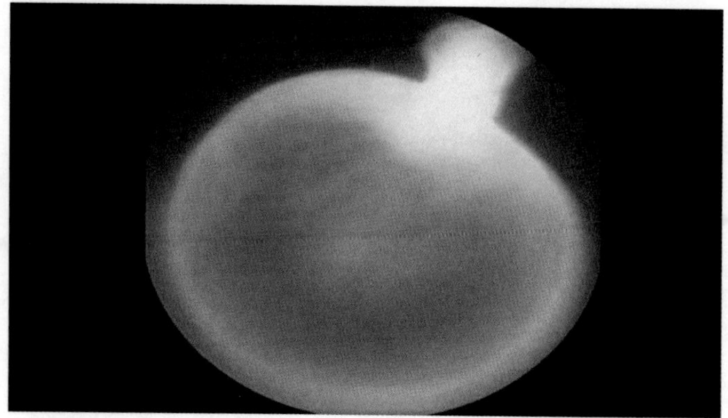

Retina Image Bank. File #26937

What to Know: Cysticercosis is a parasitic infection of *Cysticercus cellulosae*, which is the larval form of the tapeworm *Taenia solium*. Typically patients become infected by ingesting undercooked pork.

Symptoms: Patients will complain of progressive painless blurry vision with visual field defects.

Signs: Patients will present with inflammatory cysts caused by the larva which can be found in the vitreous, sub-retina- space, anterior chamber, and eyelids. The cysts can also be found in the brain, lungs, and muscles.

Treatment/Management: The inflammation is controlled with systemic (IV or oral) steroids. The larva should be surgically removed (vitrectomy) or addressed with laser photocoagulation. Systemic antihelminthic medications can be given with assistance of infectious disease specialists.

DIFFUSE UNILATERAL SUBACUTE NEURORETINITIS

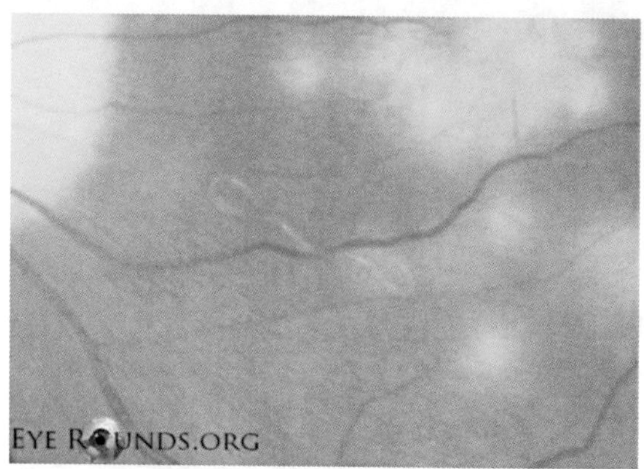

EyeRounds.org University of Iowa

What to Know: Diffuse Unilateral Subacute Neuroretinitis is most commonly caused by one of two worms: either the *Ancylostoma caninum* (dog hook worm) or the *Baylisascaris procyonis* (raccoon intestinal worm).

Symptoms: Patients will complain of unilateral blurry vision.

Signs: As the nematode wanders through the subretinal space, it can cause photoreceptor and RPE atrophy, leading pigmentary degeneration to visual field defects. When the worm dies, the retina will react with an inflammatory response with subsequent retinal scarring. Other findings include chorioretinal atrophy and optic nerve pallor.

Treatment/Management: Direct laser photocoagulation should be used against the worm if not macular involving. Systemic steroids should be used if inflammation arises. Systemic antihelminthic medications can be given with assistance of infectious disease specialists.

INFLAMMATORY DISEASE/UVEITIS

PARS PLANITIS

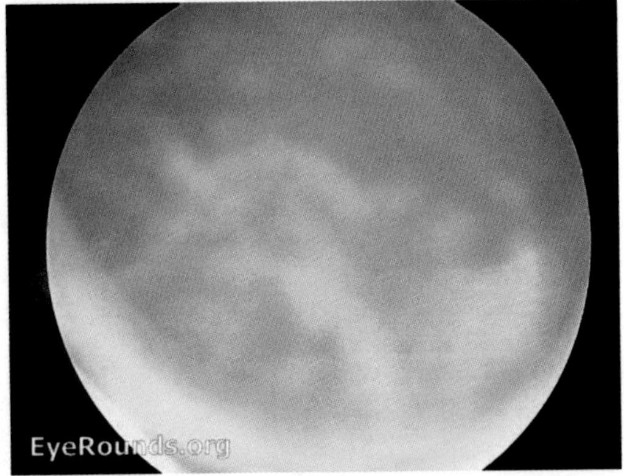

EyeRounds.org University of Iowa

Symptoms: Patients will complain of reduced vision and floaters with NO pain.

Signs: Pars Planitis is an idiopathic intermediate uveitis characterized by snowballs and/or snowbanks (fibrovascular exudates typically located in inferior pars plana). Other signs of inflammation may include vasculitis, cystoid macular edema, and papillitis. Exteriorly the eye will look white and quiet (it will not be red). Other causes of intermediate uveitis can include multiple sclerosis, sarcoidosis, and other granulomatous diseases.

Treatment/Management: Patients should be tested for systemic etiologies with a chest x-ray, TB testing (ie, QuantiFERON, PPD), ACE, and Syphilis testing (such as FTA-ABS). Given that this is an inflammatory disease, steroids should be used including topical, oral, IV, and sub-Tenon's injections depending on the severity of the case. Intravitreal steroid injections and implants can be considered in severe cases. Chronic vision-threatening cases will benefit from steroid-sparing immunomodulating medications. Vitrectomy with inferior peripheral laser photocoagulation may be useful in refractory pars planitis cases.

PRIMARY INTRAOCULAR LYMPHOMA (PRIMARY CNS LYMPHOMA)

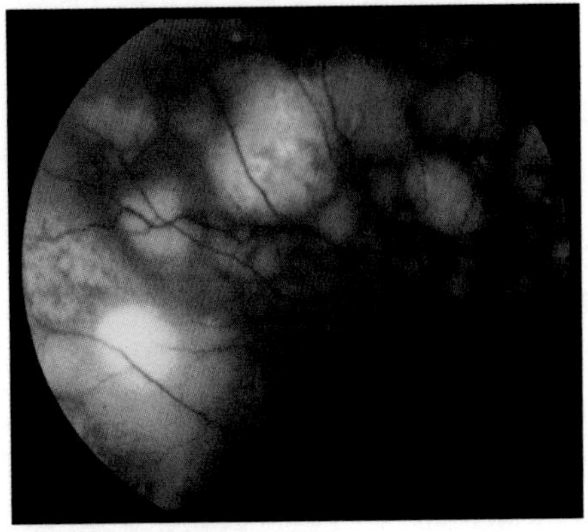

Retina Image Bank. File #135

What to Know: Primary Intraocular Lymphoma initially begins within the brain. Remember that the optic nerve is an extension of the brain, and so this tumor can manifest itself in the eye as well. Most patients will die within 2 years of diagnosis.

Symptoms: Patients will complain of blurry vision and floaters. There will not be inflammatory symptoms such as pain, redness, and photophobia.

Signs: Patients will present with most commonly with vitreous cells and subretinal and sub-RPE lesions.

Treatment/Management: A positive biopsy, most commonly of the vitreous, is necessary before initiation of systemic chemotherapy or radiation. A systemic workup with oncologist evaluation, including MRI brain, lumbar puncture, and bone marrow biopsy is necessary.

POSTERIOR SCLERITIS

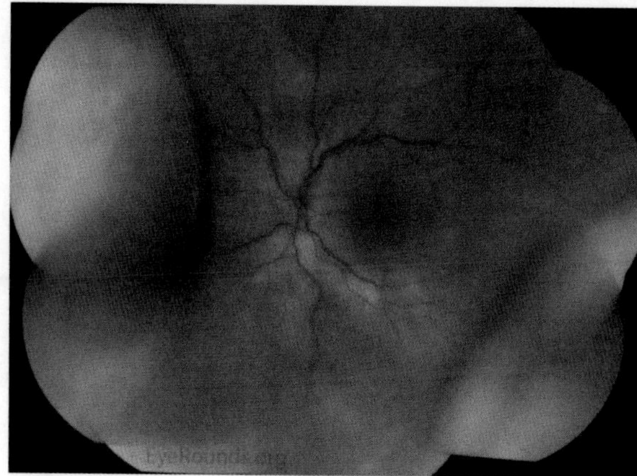

EyeRounds.org University of Iowa

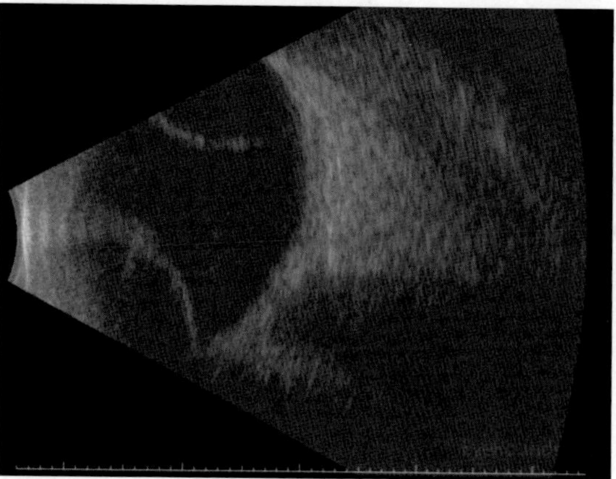
EyeRounds.org University of Iowa

What to Know: Posterior Scleritis is a very serious and potentially blinding condition associated with autoimmune diseases and typically occurs in 20-30 year old women.

Symptoms: Patients may complain of discomfort, pain with eye movement, and blurry vision.

Signs: Posterior Scleritis presents with inflammation of the sclera which causes an orange-red elevation in the posterior pole often associated with a retinal detachment or choroidal folds. T-Sign may be present on B-scan (see top right). The inflammation can cause limitation on EOM movement, and rapidly induced hyperopia (imagine the retina is being pushed forward, thereby shortening the distance between the retina and the cornea, leading to induced hyperopia).

Treatment/Management: Once other causes have been ruled out, the inflammation should be treated with systemic steroids (oral, or IV). Oral NSAIDs are also an option. The underlying autoimmune disease should be treated as well.

MISCELLANEOUS RETINOPATHIES

THIORIDAZINE RETINOPATHY

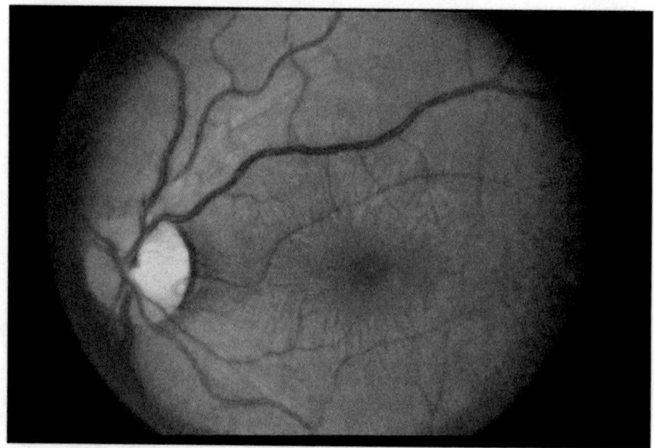
Retina Image Bank. File #15753

What to Know: Thioridazine is an anti-psychotic medication known to cause the accumulation of pigment within the eye.

Symptoms: Patients may complain of brown discoloration of their vision, nyctalopia (night blindness), blurry vision, and a ring/paracentral scotoma.

Signs: Thioridazine Retinopathy masquerades as other diseases. First it will have pigment clumping in the mid-periphery of the retina. Next, it can present with a salt and pepper fundus (like Syphilis). Finally, end stages can present with optic atrophy, attenuated vessels, and bone-spicules (like Retinitis Pigmentosa).

Treatment/Management: Patients taking Thioridazine should be monitored with regular dilated fundus examination. If early signs of toxicity develop, the medication should be discontinued.

RETINOBLASTOMA

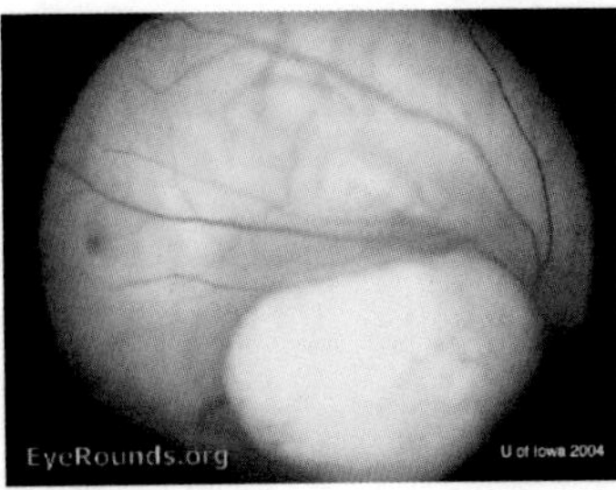

EyeRounds.org University of Iowa

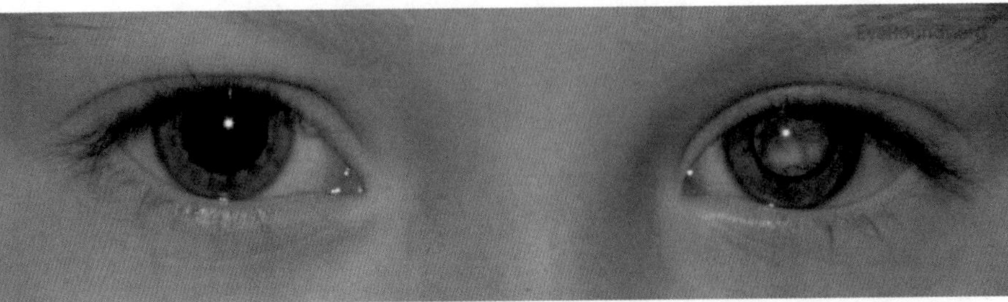

EyeRounds.org University of Iowa

What to Know: Retinoblastoma is the most common primary intraocular malignancy in children with diagnosis usually occurring before the child reaches the age of 5 years old. It is comprised of basophilic cells.

Symptoms: Parents will most commonly complain of leukocoria. They may also notice strabismus.

Signs: Retinoblastoma presents with a tumor which will usually be unilateral and appear as a dome shaped yellow-white globular mass which may have evidence of calcification. Patients may also have reduced acuity, recurrent uveitis from invasion of the uvea, pseudohypopyon, and secondary glaucoma with buphthalmos (globe enlargement). If left untreated, the tumor will spread to invade the orbit including the adjacent bony structures.

Treatment/Management: Diagnosis can be confirmed with examination under anesthesia. Testing includes B-scan, and MRI. Treatment includes the surgical options, most commonly including enucleation (remove eyeball but leave the EOMs and other orbital content intact) and chemotherapy. Prognosis is good, with survival rates 90%.

CONGENITAL HYPERTROPHY OF THE RETINAL PIGMENT EPITHELIUM (CHRPE)

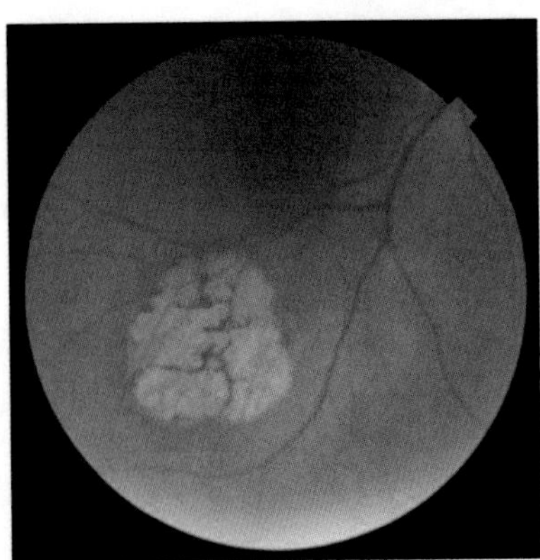

National Vision, Inc.

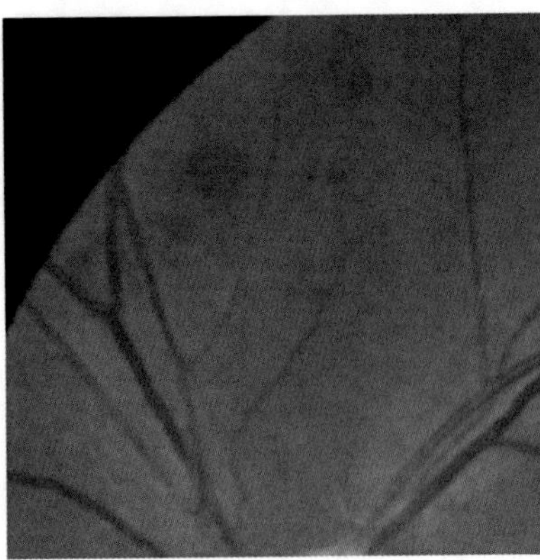

National Vision, Inc.

What to Know: Remember this is a CONGENITAL Hypertrophy, meaning a true CHRPE is present at birth. It will NOT disappear with the use of a red-free filter. I remember by thinking *if it's visible with the green then it's in the RPE*. In this case, the CHRPE WILL be visible with the green (red-free) filter, and so it is in the RPE.

Symptoms: Patients will have no complaints (asymptomatic).

Signs: A CHRPE is a singular flat brown "freckle" which will NOT disappear with the use of a red-free filter. Bilateral, multiple, small CHRPEs are known as "bear tracks" and are similarly benign. In contrast, lesions associated with familial adenomatous polyposis (FAP, also known as Gardner's syndrome) are more ovoid with a comet-shape and are multiple and bilateral.

Treatment/Management: A solitary CHRPE should be monitored and photographed for documentation purposes. Patients with characteristic lesions associated with FAP should be referred for a colonoscopy.

Gardener's Syndrome/FAP is typically diagnosed when the patient is in their 20s and will lead to colon cancer by the time the patient is in their 50s. Systemic findings may include polyps throughout the colon, soft tissue tumors (neurofibromas, cysts), and skeletal hamartomas.

MACULOPATHIES

MACULAR TELANGIECTASIA

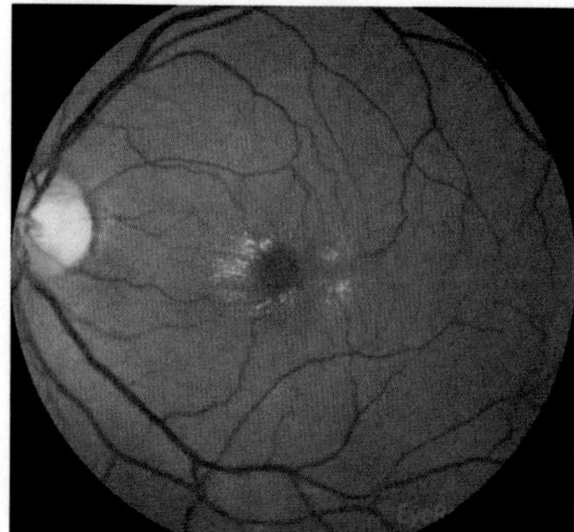

EyeRounds.org University of Iowa

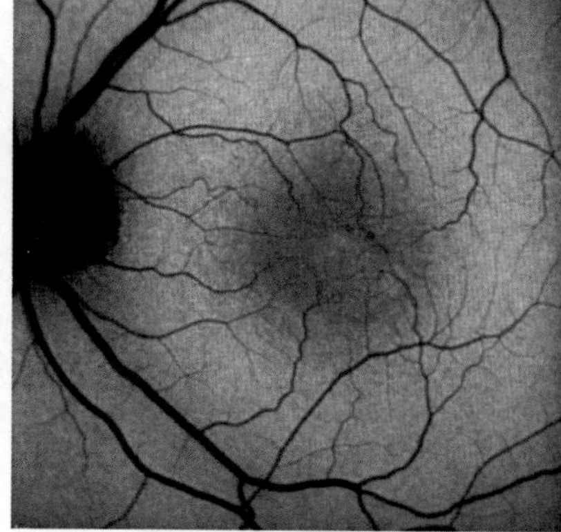

EyeRounds.org University of Iowa

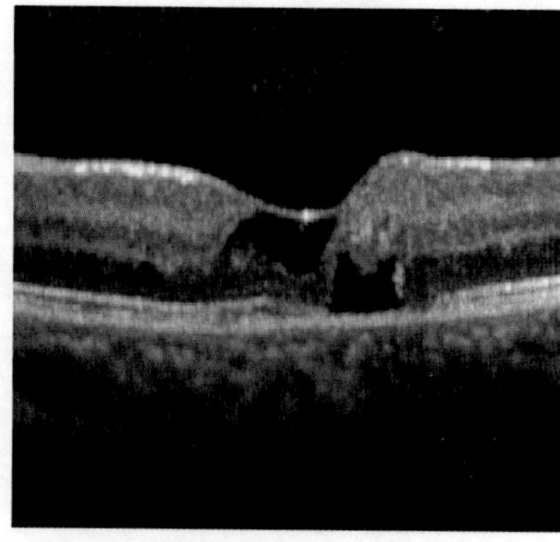

EyeRounds.org University of Iowa

What to Know: Telangiectasia (abnormal dilated capillaries) is usually caused by another retinal disease. Rarely the telangiectasia will be idiopathic, and in these cases it is called macular telangiectasia, of which there are three types. This is a progressive disease similar to Coat's Disease where the vascular abnormalities are leaky and lead to the deposition of hard exudates.

Symptoms: Patients may complain of progressive loss of central vision.

Signs: Macular findings including atrophy, exudates, pigmentary changes, and hemorrhage from choroidal neovascularization (CNV).

There are three types:

1. Exudates are found in the perifovea as well as the periphery. It is most commonly seen in middle aged men. Considered a form fruste of Coat's disease.
2. Neurodegenerative changes centered temporal to foveal center with characteristic ILM drape on OCT and exudates and hemorrhages from associated CNV. Atrophy and pigmentary changes in advanced cases. Type 2 is more common than Type 1 and has a worse visual prognosis.
3. Occlusive Telangiectasia: Extremely rare, occurs when the capillaries are occluded, very poor visual prognosis. It usually presents in the 6th decade of life.

Treatment/Management: Treat with anti-VEGF injections for the associated choroidal neovascularization (CNV)

MACULAR HOLE

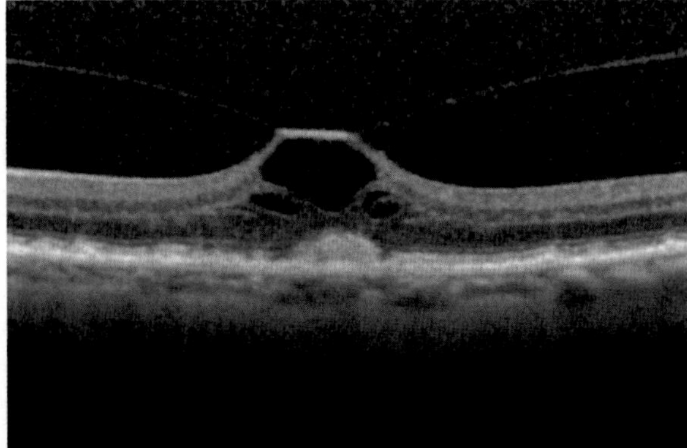

Retina Image Bank. File #173

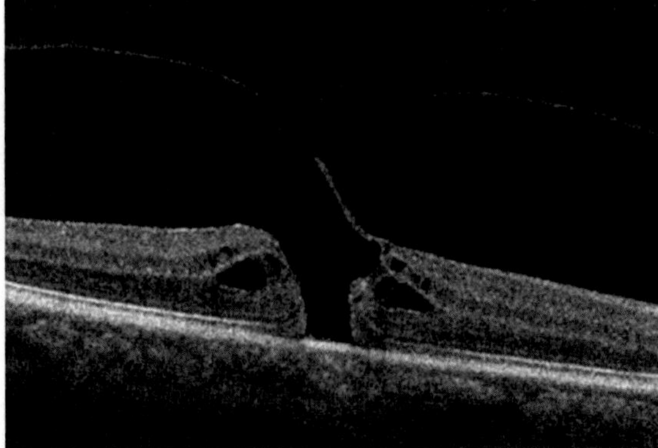

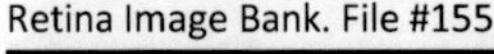

Retina Image Bank. File #155

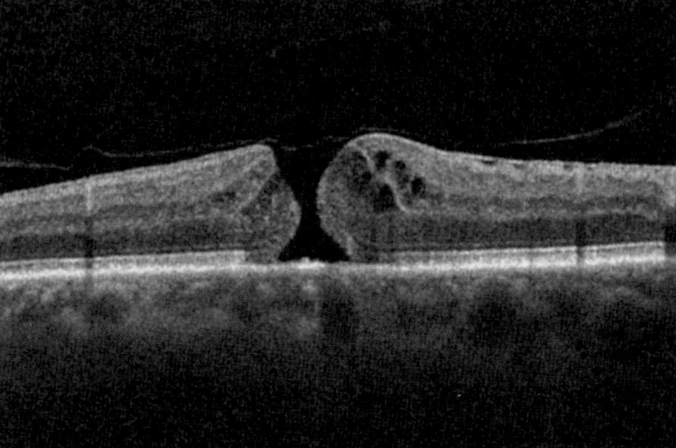

Retina Image Bank. File #156

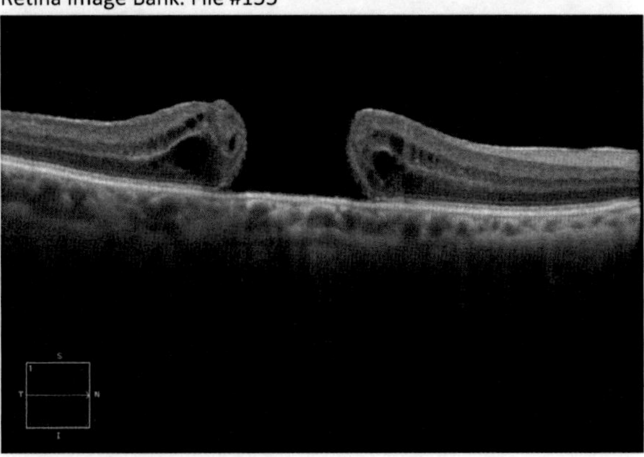

Retina Image Bank. File #7267

What to Know: Macular holes usually occur in women over the age of 60. Macular Holes can be idiopathic or caused by trauma, a tractional Epiretinal Membrane, or Cystoid Macular Edema. They are also caused by Vitreous Traction where the vitreous pulls on the macula, lifting/disrupting the underlying retinal layers, and eventually creating a hole.

Symptoms: Patients may complain of blurry vision ranging from 20/40 to counting fingers depending on the stage and central scotoma.

Signs: Macular holes are defined by four stages:

1. Impending hole (top left picture) designated as either stage 1a or stage 1b:
    a. Yellow foveal spot
    b. Yellow ring surrounding fovea
2. Small full thickness hole. Fovea has lost its depression on OCT as the vitreous is pulling up the fovea. This is vitreomacular traction. (top right picture)
3. Full thickness hole with the vitreous still attached, possibly creating an operculum/flap visible on OCT. Positive Watzke-Allen sign. (bottom left picture)
4. Full thickness hole with PVD. (bottom right picture)

Treatment/Management: No treatment is recommended for Stage 1 holes because 50% of them will spontaneously regress. Stage 2-4 holes can be treated with vitrectomy and membrane peel with the best results if performed within 6 months of onset.

CYSTOID MACULAR EDEMA (CME)

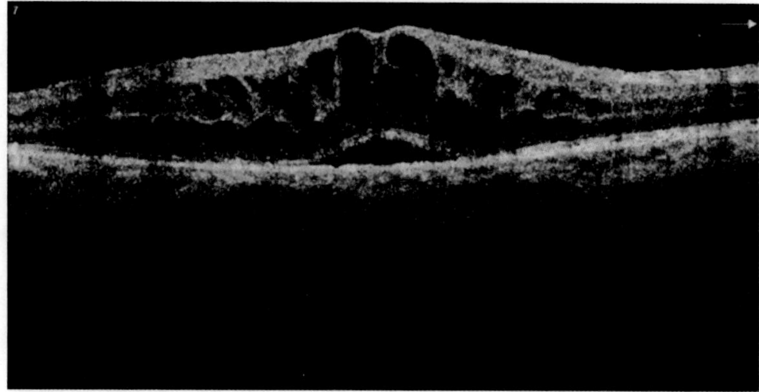
Retina Image Bank. File #24974

What to Know: CME is associated with a variety disorders which can be remembered with the DEPRIVENS mnemonic: Diabetes, Epinephrine, Pars Planitis, Retinitis Pigmentosa, Irvine-Gass, Vein Occlusion, E2-prostaglandin, Nicotinic acid and Niacin, and surgery. It can occur within three months of cataract surgery, in which case it is known as Irvine-Gass syndrome. If a patient is not correctable to better than 20/40 three months after cataract surgery, then CME should be suspected.

Symptoms: Patients may complain of blurry central vision.
Signs: CME presents with a loss of the foveal light reflex (FLR) and possible lipid exudates. OCT shows macular edema with enlarged holes of fluid "cysts."

Treatment/Management: Treat the underlying disorder if applicable.

Direct treatment is aimed at reducing inflammation. Discontinue use of prostaglandins due to their pro-inflammatory mechanism. Consider prescribing topical/oral NSAIDs and topical steroids. In cases that do not resolve after three months, consider steroid injections (posterior sub-Tenon's or intravitreal).

CENTRAL SEROUS CHORIORETINOPATHY (CSR)

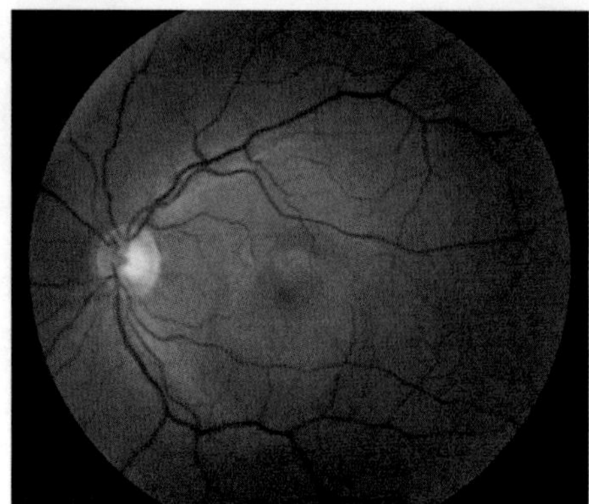
EyeRounds.org University of Iowa

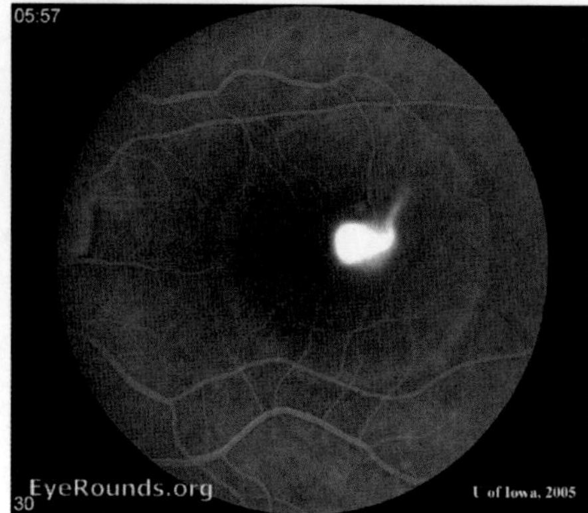

EyeRounds.org University of Iowa

What to Know: Patients who have CSR are experiencing idiopathic macular or peripheral subretinal fluid. CSR is most commonly found in **males with a Type A personality aged 20-50 years old**. It may also be associated with steroid use.

Symptoms: Patients will complain of sudden blurry vision and metamorphopsia (appreciated on Amsler Grid).
Signs: CSR may be hard to appreciate with DFE, although patients may have a loss of a foveal light reflex and there may be an appreciable swollen appearance underneath the macula. OCT will show sub-retinal fluid, and Fluorescein Angiogram (FA) may show an expansile dot or a classic **"smokestack"** which is pathognomonic.

Treatment/Management: Monitor as most cases of CSR will spontaneously resolve after three months. Photodynamic therapy, subthreshold laser, mineralocorticoid antagonists such as eplerenone may be used in refractory cases. Patients should be educated that recurrence is common, usually within a year.

AGE-RELATED MACULAR DEGENERATION (ARMD aka AMD)

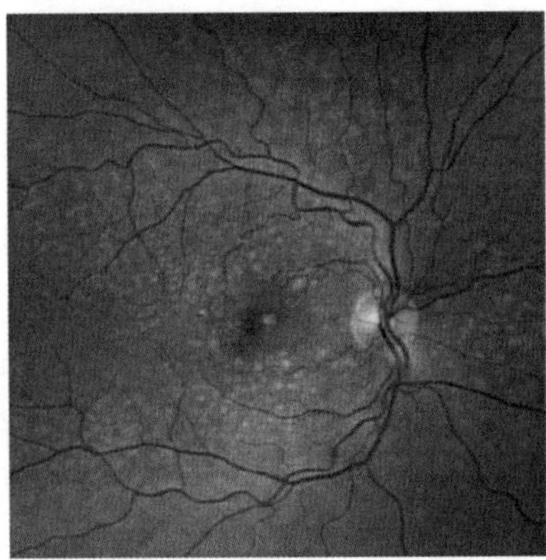
Kimberly Castillo, OD

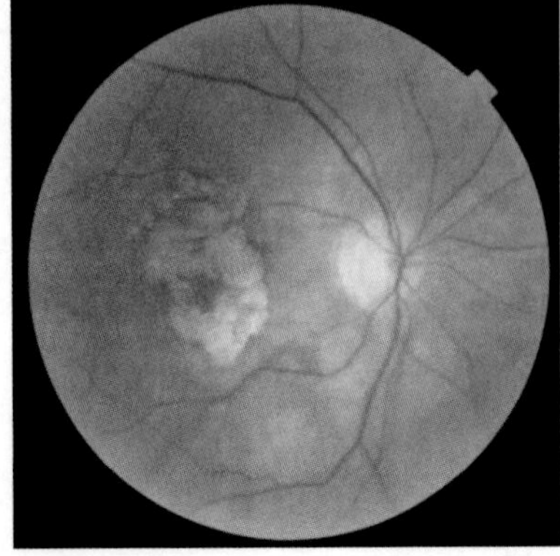
National Vision, Inc.

What to Know: ARMD is a progressive disease with early and intermediate stages defined by the presence of drusen in the macula secondary to a deteriorated retinal pigment epithelium, Bruch's membrane, and/or choriocapillaris. Risk factors include age, sun exposure, Caucasian ethnicity, high cholesterol, positive family history, and **smoking**. ARMD is the leading cause of blindness in people over the age of 50 in the US.

Symptoms: Patients may complain of blurry vision, loss of central vision, metamorphopsia, and central scotoma.

Signs: There are two types of ARMD:

1. Dry "nonexudative" ARMD: ***no*** choroidal neovascularization
    a. Small hard drusen are seen in the macula. Large, soft drusen are an indicator that the patient is at high risk of progressive to advanced disease. Dry ARMD may progress to geographic atrophy in advanced cases.
2. Wet "exudative" ARMD: choroidal neovascularization present
    a. Choroidal neovascularization with associated hemorrhaging, subretinal fluid, and pigment epithelial detachment.
    b. The neovascularization may be intraretinal, which is known as Retinal Angiomatous Proliferation.
    c. Choroidal Neovascularization (CNV) may progress to a subretinal disciform scar with macular atrophy and severe central vision loss.

Treatment/Management: Patients should be given an Amsler grid to take home for monitoring and they should be instructed to return to clinic if they notice any changes.

The AREDs vitamins slow the progression of moderate to severe AMD. Moderate AMD is defined as a minimum of 1 large drusen OR extensive intermediate sized drusen OR noncentral geographic atrophy. Patients who smoke should take the AREDS-2 vitamins to avoid the beta carotene found in AREDS-1 (which have been associated with increased risk of lung cancer in patients who smoke).

Treatment of Wet ARMD should be initiated promptly with anti-VEGF injections. Adjunctive photodynamic therapy may be utilized in refractory cases, especially those associated with polypoidal choroidal vasculopathy.

When advanced enough in both eyes, patients may benefit from low vision aids.

EPIRETINAL MEMBRANE (ERM)

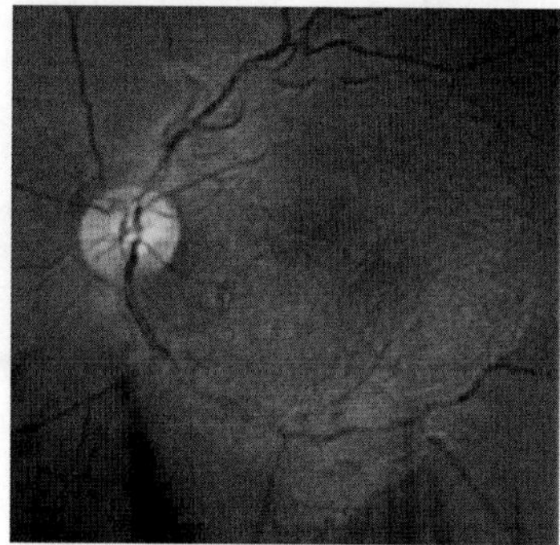

Kimberly Castillo, OD

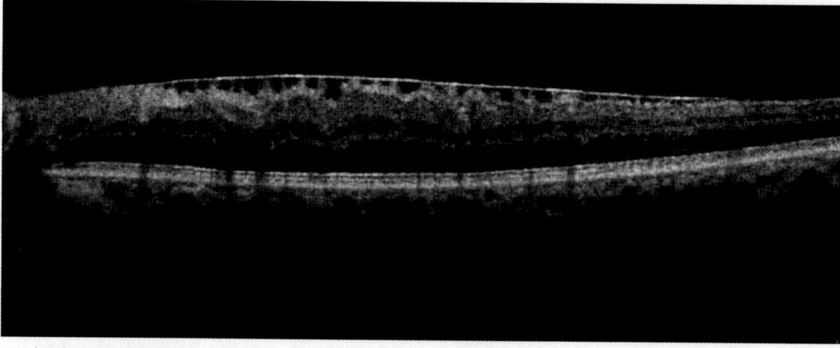

Kimberly Castillo, OD

What to Know: Epiretinal membranes are common age-related diseases. Some ERMs contract leading to horizontal traction and distortion of the macula and consequent vision loss.

Symptoms: Patients may have no complaints (asymptomatic), or complain of metamorphopsia and blurry vision.

Signs: ERM presents with an Abnormal Amsler grid. "Cellophane retinopathy" may be appreciable as a sheen seen over the macula. Foveal depression may look atypical on OCT, or fovea may be lifted/thickened, known as a Macular Pucker.

Treatment/Management: When an ERM becomes symptomatic, it should be treated with vitrectomy with membrane peeling.

~~~CHOROID~~~

CHOROIDAL NEVUS

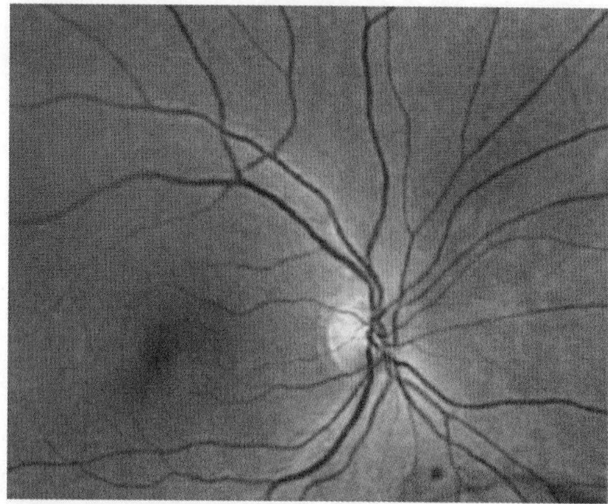

Kimberly Castillo, OD

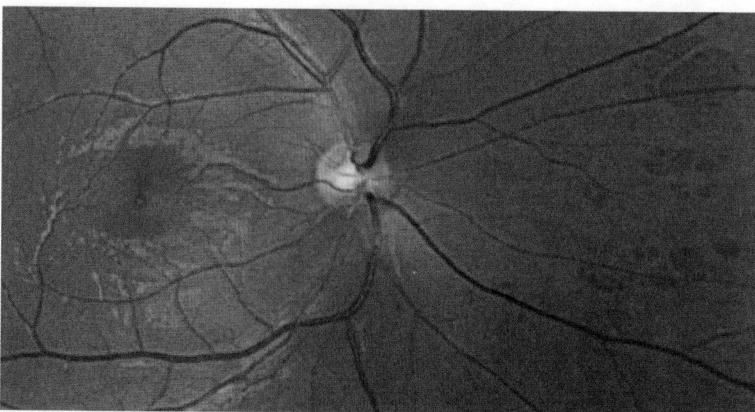

Kimberly Castillo, OD

What to Know: Choroidal Nevi are typically benign, and are similar to freckles. They will disappear with the use of a red-free filter. I remember by thinking *if it's visible with the green then it's in the RPE*. In this case, the nevus will NOT be visible with the green (red-free) filter, and so it is in the choroid, not the RPE.

Symptoms: Asymptomatic.

Signs: A Nevus will appear as a flat, grey-brown spot anywhere in the retina with well demarcated borders. A very small fraction of nevi can grow into choroidal melanomas. These are characteristics for nevi that are at a higher risk: symptoms, close proximity to the optic nerve, change/growth, elevation, overlying orange pigment, and subretinal fluid.

Treatment/Management: Patients should be monitored with fundus photography. The first follow up should be within 3 months. Thereafter, follow up can be every 1-12 months depending on risk level.

CHOROIDAL MELANOMA

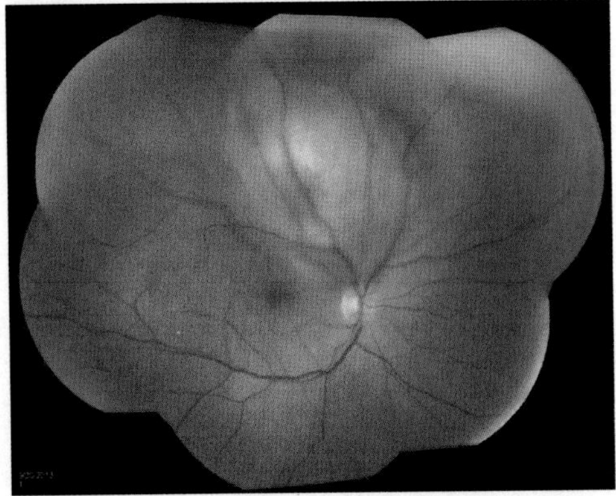

Retina Image Bank. File #10386

What to Know: Choroidal Melanomas are the most common primary intraocular malignancy in adults. Choroidal melanomas can be associated with metastasis, which have a poor prognosis. The most common sites of metastasis include the liver, lung, bone, skin, and CNS (in that order).

Symptoms: Patients may have no complaints (asymptomatic) if the melanoma is located in the periphery. Otherwise patients may complain of blurry vision, metamorphopsia, visual field loss, floaters, and photopsia (flashes of light).

Signs: Choroidal Melanomas present as dome shaped elevations which may or may not be pigmented, may have overlying yellow/orange lipofuscin, borders may be indistinct, and they may have associated serous retinal detachment. Tumors which are most likely to metastasize will have an increased thickness, involve the ciliary body, have a close proximity to the optic nerve, and/or exhibit growth.

Treatment/Management: Patients should see an oncologist for a complete systemic evaluation.

Possible treatments include Plaque Brachytherapy as well as Proton Beam Therapy. The eye may also be enucleated (remove eyeball but leave the EOMs and other orbital content intact) in order to prevent metastasis. It is worth noting that the COMS study showed there is no difference in the 5-year mortality rate for patients who are treated with Brachytherapy or who undergo enucleation in patients who have medium to large sized melanomas. Furthermore, radiation therapy before enucleation does not improve survival rates.

CHOROIDAL METASTASIS

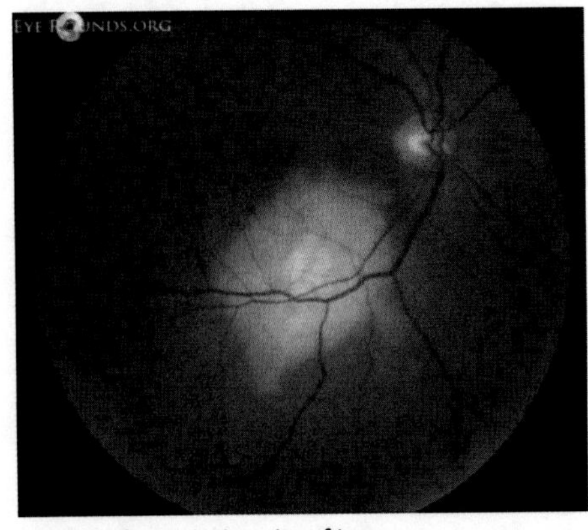

EyeRounds.org University of Iowa

What to Know: Choroidal Metastasis is the most common intraocular malignancy in adults. This occurs when a cancer has spread to the eye from another place in the body. The most common sites of the primary tumor in women is the breast, and the lung in men. Most patients will die within one year of diagnosis.

Signs: Choroidal Metastasis presents with yellow-white elevated lesions with pigmented clumps and possible overlying serous retinal detachment.

Treatment/Management: The underlying cancer should be treated by an oncologist with chemotherapy.

CHOROIDEREMIA

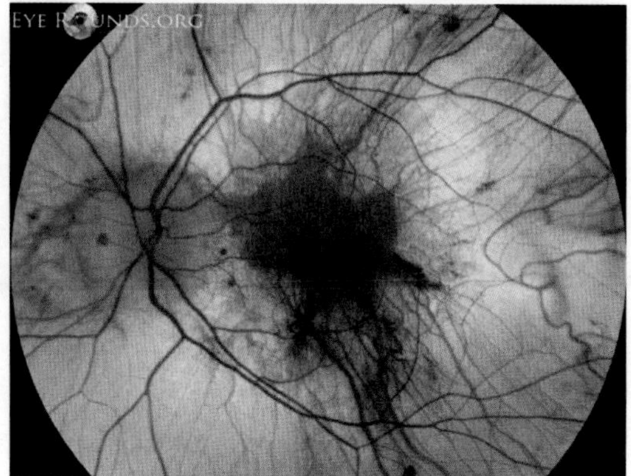

EyeRounds.org University of Iowa

What to Know: Choroideremia has an x-linked recessive inheritance, and so men are affected while women are carriers. It begins to show itself in when the patient is aged 20-30 and progresses to legal blindness by age 50-60.

Symptoms: Patients will complain of night blindness (nyctalopia) and light sensitivity (photophobia).

Signs: Choroideremia presents with peripheral atrophy of the choriocapillaris which reveals the underlying choroidal vessels. It is progressive and spares the macula until late in the disease course.

Treatment/Management: There is no treatment. Patients may benefit from a low vision consult and genetic testing.

CENTRAL AREOLAR CHOROIDAL DYSTROPHY

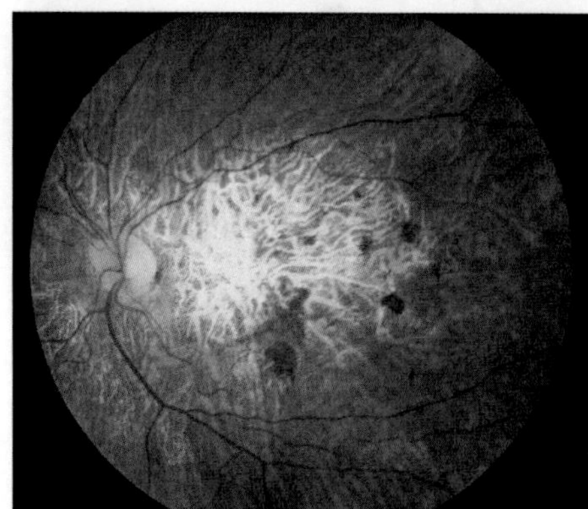
Retina Image Bank. File #7220

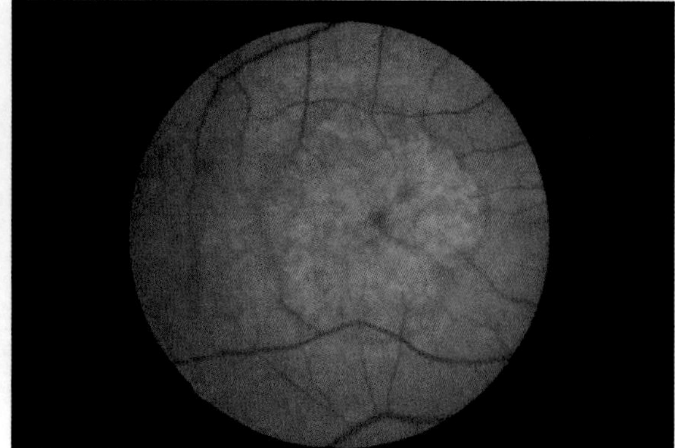
Retina Image Bank. File #23305

What to Know: Central Areolar Choroidal Dystrophy has an autosomal dominant (AD) inheritance. It begins to show itself when the patient is between the age of 30-40, and progresses to severe vision loss by age 60-70.

Symptoms: Patients will complain of blurry vision and central scotoma.

Signs: Early stages will show a hypopigmentation of the macula which will progress to a geographic atrophy with well-defined borders that slowly enlarge and reveal the underlying choroidal vasculature. Vision will decrease from 20/25 to 20/200, this is typically bilateral and symmetric.

Treatment/Management: There is no treatment. Patients may benefit from a low vision consult and genetic testing.

SERPIGINOUS CHOROIDOPATHY

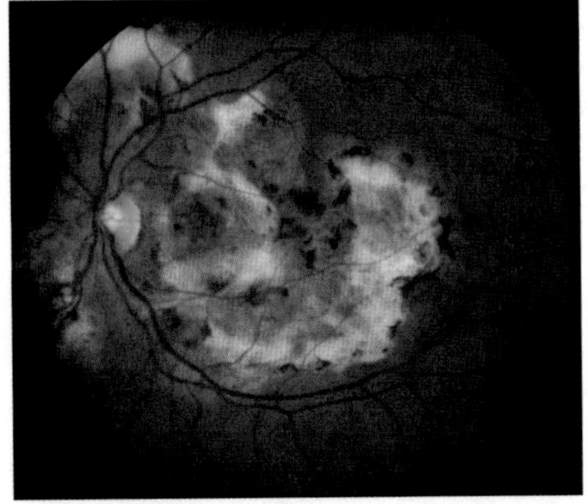

EyeRounds.org University of Iowa

What to Know: Serpiginous Choroidopathy is associated with HLA-B7 and is idiopathic in nature. It is most likely found in 50-60 year old men. Tuberculosis can cause a similar fundus appearance to serpiginous choroidopathy, and should be ruled out.

Symptoms: Patients will complain of central blurry vision or scotoma that may be unilateral or bilateral.

Signs: Serpiginous Choroidopathy is a recurrent disease where lesions will begin at the optic nerve and then extend in a serpentine manner towards the macula. Active lesions will be grey-white in color, while old dormant lesions will atrophy and scar. Choroidal neovascularization (CNV) develops in 25% of cases.

Treatment/Management: Serpiginous Choroidopathy has a chronic and relapsing course and treatment starts with steroids (oral or local) with transition to steroid-sparing immunomodulating medications. CNV is common and can be treated with anti-VEGF injections.

CANDIDIASIS

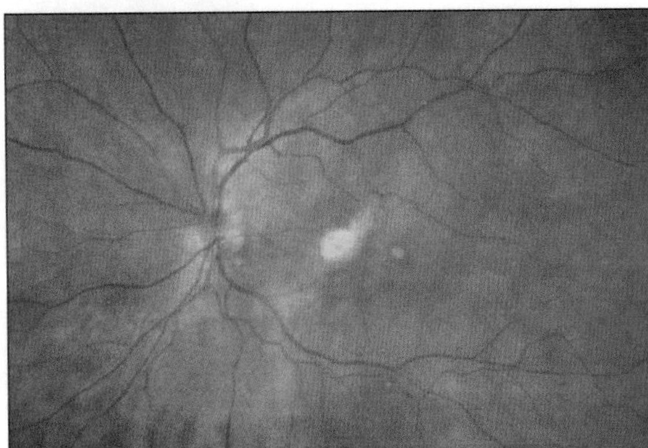

Retina Image Bank. File #27727

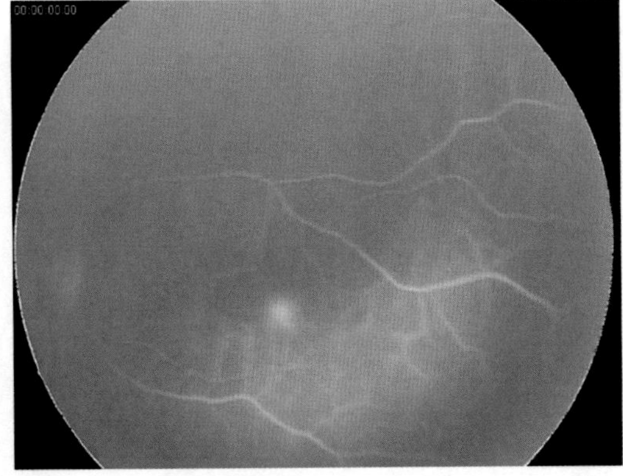

Retina Image Bank. File #11737

What to Know: Candidiasis is caused by a fungal infection of *Candida* and is typically seen in IV drug abusers or in nosocomial (hospital) settings for patients who are chronically sick or immunocompromised.

Symptoms: Patients will complain of bilateral blurry vision, and floaters.

Signs: Candidiasis presents with yellow-white choroidal lesions which will progress into a hazy vitritis with areas that look like "cotton balls." A retinal detachment may occur in late stages.

Treatment/Management: The choroidal lesions should be treated with oral or IV antifungals. If the vitreous is involved, then intravitreal antifungal injections and even vitrectomy are indicated. These patients need to be monitored daily, possibly even hospitalized if they are noncompliant. An infectious disease specialist should be consulted.

CHOROIDAL DETACHMENT

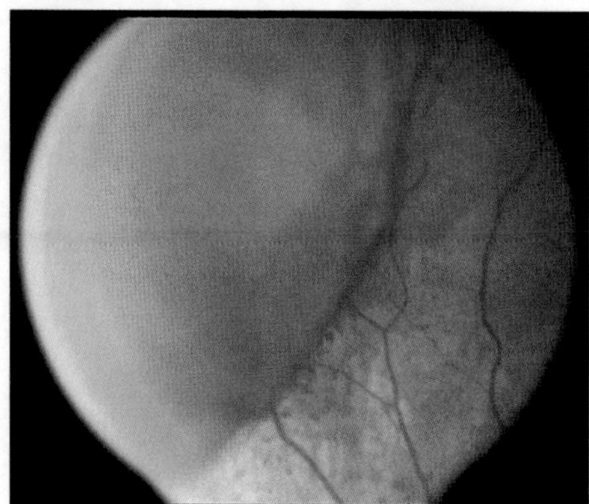
Retina Image Bank. File #5370

<u>What to Know:</u> A choroidal detachment occurs when the choroid is separated from the sclera and will present as a bullous orange-brown peripheral elevation. Both types will look the same on DFE.There are two types of Choroidal Detachments: Serous and Hemorrhagic.

1) **SEROUS CHOROIDAL DETACHMENT aka CHOROIDAL EFFUSION**
    a. **<u>Differences to Know:</u>** Associated with **low** IOP (hypotony) secondary to a puncture wound to the globe. Serous Choroidal Detachments WILL transilluminate.
    b. **<u>Symptoms:</u>** Patients will have no complaints (asymptomatic) if the detachment is peripheral or mild, or complain of severe vision loss if detachments are severe (ie, kissing).
    c. **<u>Treatment/Management:</u>** Treatment is aimed at closing the wound and preventing further decrease of IOP by using any combination of the following: bandage CL, suture, cyanoacrylate glue.
2) **HEMORRHAGIC CHOROIDAL DETACHMENT**
    a. **<u>Differences to Know:</u>** Associated with **high** IOP secondary to hemorrhaging during anterior segment surgery. Because blood is pooling between the choroid and the sclera and there is limited area within the globe, the pressure increases and the anterior chamber narrows as the iris is pushed forwards. Hemorrhagic Choroidal Detachments will NOT transilluminate.
    b. **<u>Symptoms:</u>** Severe pain and rapidly decreased vision with a red and inflamed eye.
    c. **<u>Treatment/Management:</u>** The wound should be closed immediately to prevent further hemorrhaging. A sclerotomy (surgical cutting of the sclera) can be performed to allow drainage of the blood. The patient should be placed on a cycloplegic to prevent synechiae, and ocular hypotensives may also be necessary to reduce the IOP.

BIRDSHOT CHORIORETINOPATHY (VITILIGINOUS CHORIORETINITIS)

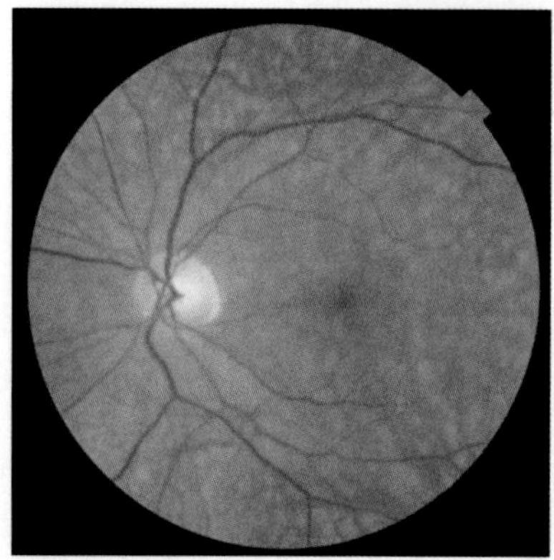
National Vision, Inc.

<u>What to Know:</u> Birdshot Chorioretinopathy is the only White Dot Syndrome discussed in this text. It is a bilateral, chronic chorioretinal inflammatory disease that is typically found in white females aged between 40-60 with HLA-A29.

<u>Symptoms:</u> Patients will complain of blur, photopsia, and nyctalopia.

<u>Signs:</u> Birdshot Chorioretinopathy presents with multiple creamy yellow-white spots in the periphery of the fundus which spare the macula. The spots are less than or equal to the size of the optic disc. Vitritis, retinal vasculitis, and cystoid macular edema may be present. Atrophy and choroidal depigmentation may occur in advanced cases.

<u>Treatment/Management:</u> Birdshot Chorioretinopathy is typically treated with systemic steroids initially with transition to steroid-sparing immunomodulatory medications. Periocular and intravitreal steroids may also be utilized, especially for cystoid macular edema.

~~~VITREOUS~~~

POSTERIOR VITREOUS DETACHMENT (PVD)

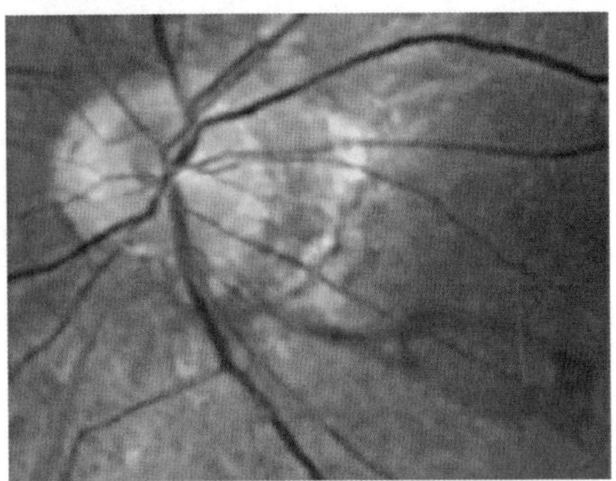
Kimberly Castillo, OD

What to Know: Risk factors include high myopia and old age. A new PVD may be accompanied by a retinal break or detachment, which need to be ruled out. Patients who have a PVD have a reduced risk of getting Tractional Retinal Detachments because the vitreous is no longer attached to the retina, and so cannot tug on the retina and cause a Tractional Retinal Detachment.

Symptoms: Patients will complain of flashes and floaters that move with the eye as it moves and blurry vision that fluctuates with eye movement. It is often located in the temporal visual field and has a sudden onset.

Signs: The presence of a Weiss Ring is diagnostic. It may present as just a vitreous opacity, and may not show any signs. The NBEO will most likely give a picture of a Weiss Ring.

Treatment/Management: An isolated PVD requires no treatment. However, A new PVD could be the precursor for a retinal detachment, and so it should be monitored one, three, and six months after onset. The patient should be educated on the symptoms of retinal detachment and instructed to return immediately if they should develop.

- IF no retinal breaks or detachments are found but...
    - A mild vitreous hemorrhage is present, then monitor at one week as well as the one, three, and six months.
    - A significant vitreous hemorrhage is present, urgent referral to retinal specialist (24 hours) is indicated because of high likelihood of retinal involvement.

VITREOUS HEMORRHAGE

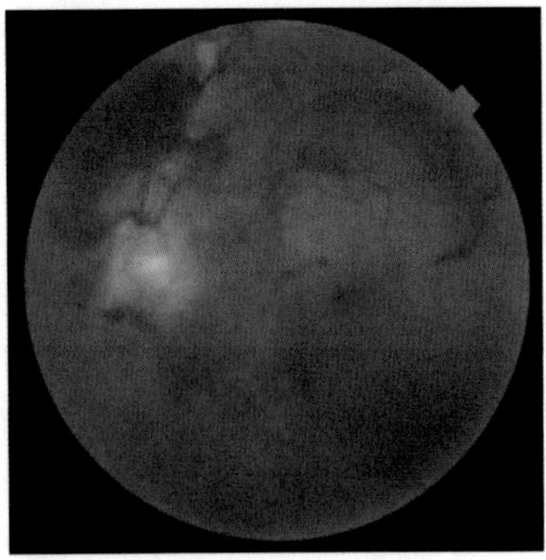
National Vision, Inc.

What to Know: A Vitreous Hemorrhage is exactly what it sounds like; blood in the vitreous. It will typically occur when retinal neovascularization grows into the vitreous. Then the vitreous tugs on and rips the neovascular vessels as well as itself. Now blood can seep into the vitreous.

Symptoms: Patients will complain of painless vision loss, flashes, and floaters (cobwebs, black spots, haze).

Signs: Blood will be visible in the vitreous. A new hemorrhage will present with blood seeping into the vitreous; a longer-standing hemorrhage will appear with blood diffuse throughout the vitreous, obscuring the fundus.

Treatment/Management: If a comorbid retinal tear or break is present, it needs immediate treatment. If not, treat conservatively. Patients should observe bedrest for 2-3 days with their head elevated so that the blood can settle inferiorly. They should avoid anticlotting agents such as aspirin and warfarin so that the hemorrhage is able to clot and heal appropriately. IF the vitreous hemorrhage persists for more than three months, then consider vitrectomy. Any underlying pathology (such as diabetic retinopathy) should be addressed

ASTEROID HYALOSIS

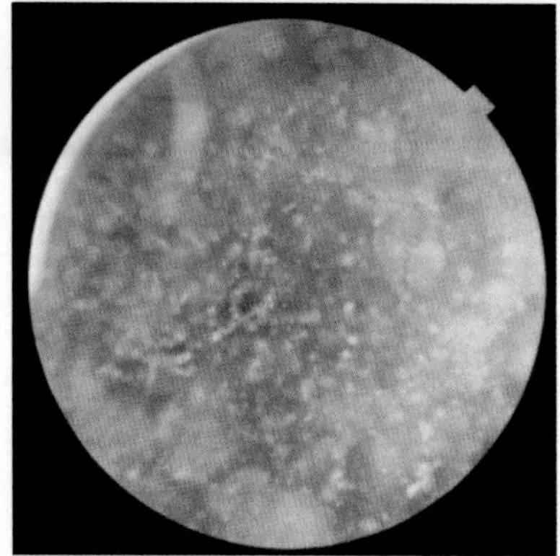

National Vision, Inc.

What to Know: Asteroid Hyalosis is a common degenerative process in which **calcium-phosphate soaps** deposit within the vitreous.

Symptoms: Patients usually have no complaints (asymptomatic). Patients with very severe cases may complain of glare and blurry vision.

Signs: Asteroid Hyalosis looks much more interesting to the examiner than to the patient. It is usually discovered by chance while performing a fundus exam. The first time I saw it I thought that my 20D lens was dirty. It is typically unilateral and appears as yellowish-white "asteroids" in the vitreous obscuring the underlying fundus. The "asteroids" will move with eye movement, but will remain suspended within the vitreous. They do not settle inferiorly.

Treatment/Management: Typically Asteroid Hyalosis requires no treatment. In very severe cases where vision is affected or the doctor is unable to view and treat the fundus, a vitrectomy may be considered. Fluorescein angiography and optical coherence tomography may offer a better fundus examination than indirect ophthalmoscopy.

SYNCHYSIS SCINTILLANS

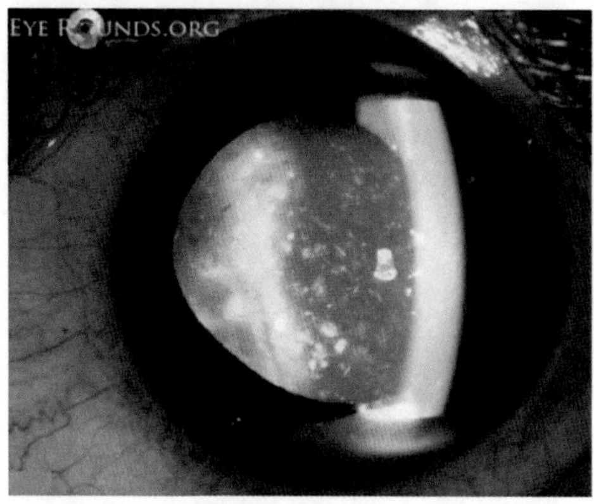

EyeRounds.org University of Iowa

What to Know: Synchysis Scintillans is a rare complication which usually occurs in a blind eye after chronic vitreous hemorrhage, trauma, or uveitis. It consists of **cholesterol crystals** deposited into a liquefied vitreous, usually settling inferiorly (as opposed to asteroid hyalosis which have opacities distributed throughout the vitreous). I included this disease in this book because it is important to be able to distinguish it from Asteroid Hyalosis, and this does seem to be a highly test-able disease.

Symptoms: Patients usually have no complaints (asymptomatic) for this usually occurs in eyes which are already blind.

Signs: Synchysis Scintillans presents with brownish-yellow refractile crystals which will be visible in the vitreous and occasionally the anterior chamber. Since the vitreous is usually liquefied in these patients, the crystals are typically free-floating and will settle inferiorly when the eye is not in motion.

Treatment/Management: Observation.

CHAPTER 4

CONJUNCTIVA / CORNEA / REFRACTIVE SURGERY

The NBEO website states that 33-44 questions will be asked on Conjunctiva / Cornea / Refractive Surgery. Historically they have asked about 38.6 questions, meaning this chapter covers approximately 11% of the material tested on the exam, or roughly 8 cases. In reality almost the same number of questions are asked on Conjunctiva / Cornea / Refractive Surgery as on Retina / Vitreous / Choroid, but this chapter is significantly shorter. And so this chapter may be considered higher yield than the Retina / Vitreous / Choroid chapter. Conjunctiva / Cornea / Refractive Surgery IS included on TMOD.

~~~CONJUNCTIVA~~~

PTERYGIUM

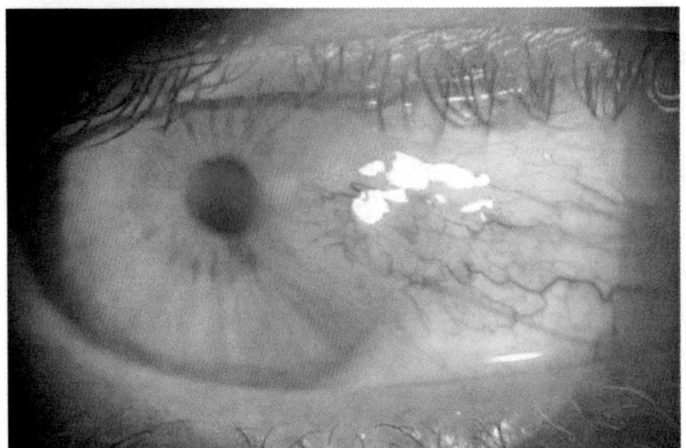

Kimberly Castillo, OD

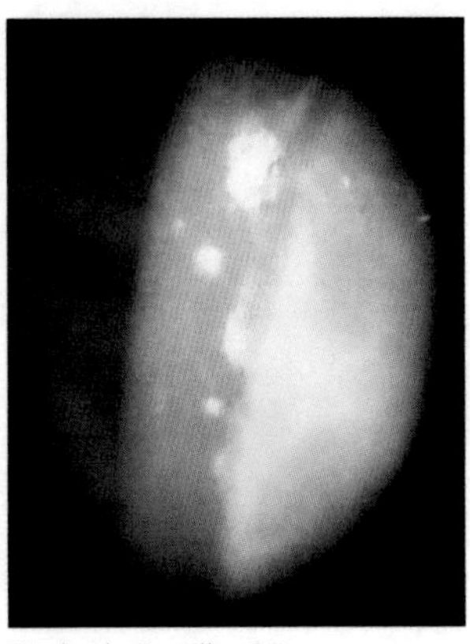

Kimberly Castillo, OD

What to Know: A Pterygium is a fibrovascular growth typically extending from the caruncle across the cornea which destroys Bowman's layer. They are related to chronic exposure to UV light and ocular irritation (dry eye).

Symptoms: Patients may have no complaints (asymptomatic). Possible complaints may include ocular irritation, dry eye, cosmesis, and blurry vision due to induced astigmatism or blockage of the visual axis.

Signs: A fibrovascular growth extending from the caruncle across the cornea will be visible. Stocker's line (iron line at edge of Pterygium, right image) may also be present.

Treatment/Management: Frequently no treatment is necessary. Patients may use artificial tears for comfort, but recommend preservative free artificial tears if used more than QID. Patients should be educated to wear sunglasses to reduce ocular UV exposure. Surgical removal is reserved until Pterygium encroaches across the visual axis/reduces vision. If inflammation is present, treat with a topical NSAID or steroid depending on severity.

PINGUECULA / PINGUECULITIS

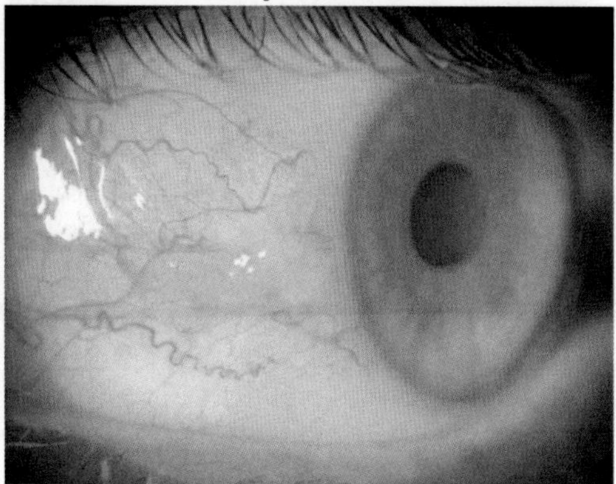

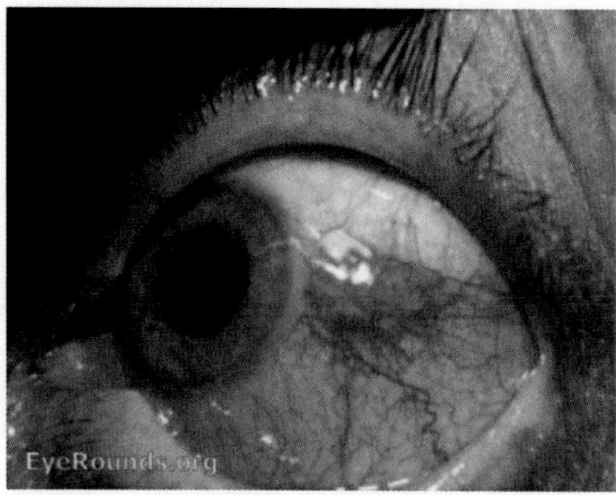

Kimberly Castillo, OD

EyeRounds.org University of Iowa

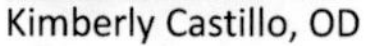

What to Know:

- A **Pinguecula** (left image) is defined by abnormal mounds of collagen at either the temporal or nasal bulbar conjunctiva, never involving the cornea. Typically yellow in nature, they are related to chronic exposure to UV light and ocular irritation (dry eye). After time they can become calcified. A Pinguecula may also be responsible for contact lens intolerance.
- **Pingueculitis** (right image) is defined by inflammation of a Pinguecula, as the name suggests.

Symptoms:

- Patients with a **Pinguecula** may be asymptomatic. Possible complaints may include ocular irritation, dry eye, and cosmesis.
- **Pingueculitis** is defined by an increase in ocular irritation and epiphora.

Signs:

- **Pinguecula**: Yellow mounds of collagen at either the temporal or nasal bulbar conjunctiva, never involving the cornea which can become calcified.
- **Pingueculitis**: Hyperemia (redness) and inflammation of a Pinguecula.

Treatment/Management:

- **Pinguecula**: Frequently no treatment is necessary. Patients may use artificial tears for comfort, but recommend preservative free artificial tears if used more than QID. Patients should be educated to wear sunglasses to reduce ocular UV exposure. Surgical removal may be indicated if ocular irritation is not relieved with use of artificial tears or is unable to wear contact lenses.
- **Pingueculitis**: Treat the inflammation with a topical NSAID or mild steroid depending on severity.

CICATRICIAL PEMPHIGOID

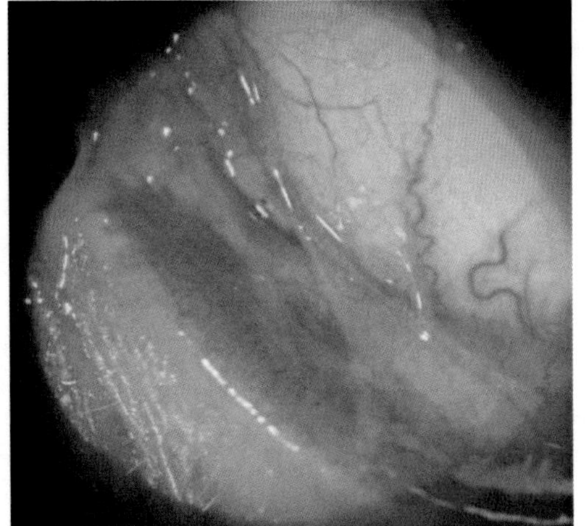
Kimberly Castillo, OD

What to Know: Cicatricial Pemphigoid is typically occurs in women over the age of 60. It is an autoimmune disease of the mucous membranes throughout the body. That being said, it will cause crusting and ulceration of any part of the body which involves mucous membranes: ocular, oral, respiratory, and genital tissues. This is a chronic, progressive disease with a poor prognosis.

Symptoms: Patients will complain of blur, ocular irritation, foreign body sensation, redness, dryness, epiphora, and possibly difficulty breathing (dyspnea).

Signs: Inferior symblepharon (connection of bulbar and palpebral conjunctiva), ankyloblepharon (connection between superior and inferior lids), tightening and foreshortening of the inferior fornix. Other signs include discharge, hyperemia (redness), keratitis, entropion, trichiasis, and keratinization. Given this is a disorder of mucous membranes, it makes sense that it afflicts the mucous membranes of the eyes.

Treatment/Management: Given this is a systemic autoimmune disorder, patients frequently need systemic treatment with steroids or immunosuppressive agents performed by a specialist. Ocular complications should also be addressed. Dry eye can be relieved with use of artificial tears (recommend preservative free if used more than QID) and punctal plugs. If present, treat any corneal defects with antibiotics. Surgery may be required for symblepharon, ankyloblepharon, entropion, and trichiasis.

ERYTHEMA MULTIFORME (EM) / STEVENS-JOHNSON SYNDROME (SJS)

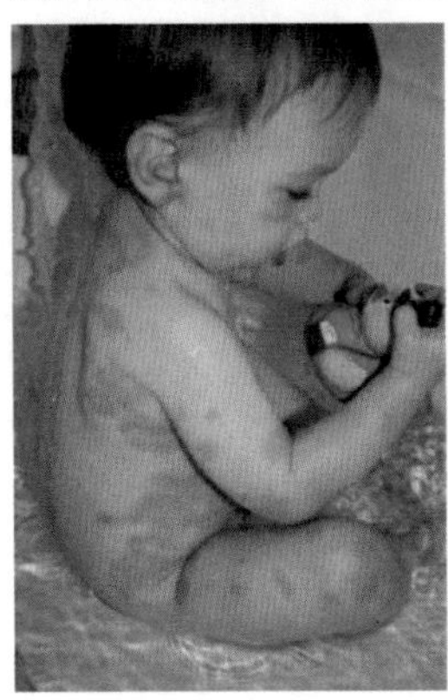
Flicker © Image #2574141467

What to Know: EM and SJS are both type IV hypersensitivity reactions. EM is a more mild and self-limiting than SJS. They may be caused by an infection or a poor reaction to a medication. Less than 5% of cases of EM end in mortality, but mortality could occur in up to 30% of patients with SJS.

Symptoms: Patients may complain of blurry vision, dry eye, headache, malaise, and pain.

Signs: Patients will present with target skin lesions/eruptions. Ocular signs will include symblepharon (connection of bulbar and palpebral conjunctiva), ankyloblepharon (connection between superior and inferior lids), discharge, hyperemia (redness), keratitis, entropion, trichiasis, and keratinization.

Treatment/Management: The dry eye can be relieved with use of artificial tears (recommend preservative free if used more than QID) and punctal plugs. If present, treat any corneal defects with antibiotics. The inflammation can be treated with topical or oral steroids depending on severity. Surgery may be required for symblepharon, ankyloblepharon, entropion, and trichiasis. Scleral lenses can be used in cases of SJS.

SUBCONJUNCTIVAL HEMORRHAGE

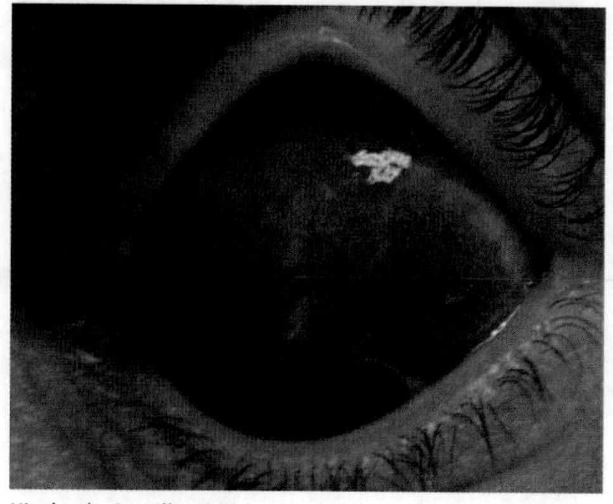

Kimberly Castillo, OD

What to Know: A Subconjunctival Hemorrhage is bleeding underneath the conjunctiva. It is like a bruise, but since the conjunctiva is clear, the blood looks red instead of purple. Possible causes include anything which can increase intraorbital pressure: sneezing, coughing, straining, difficult bowel movement. Other systemic causes include hypertension, aspirin/anticoagulant use, or bleeding disorders.

Symptoms: Patients will complain of a "red eye" with a sudden onset and possibly a dull ache.

Signs: Red blood will be visible underneath the conjunctiva, obscuring the underlying scleral vessels.

Treatment/Management: No treatment is necessary as a Subconjunctival Hemorrhage will spontaneously resolve within 2-3 weeks. Elective use of Aspirin should be discontinued. If recurrent, patients should be referred to their PCP to rule out bleeding disorders.

CONJUNCTIVITIS

SUPERIOR LIMBIC KERATOCONJUNCTIVITIS (SLK)

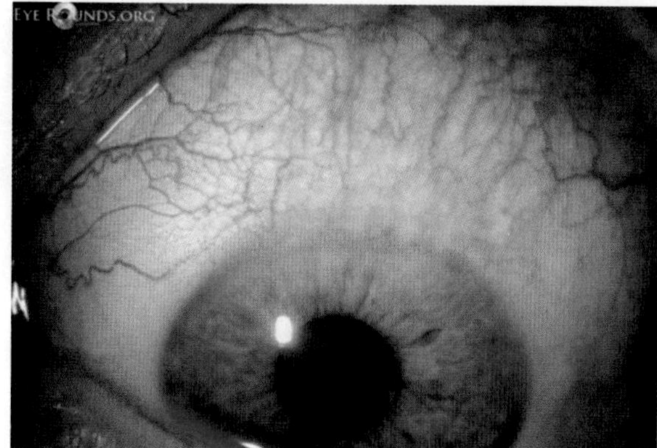

EyeRounds.org University of Iowa

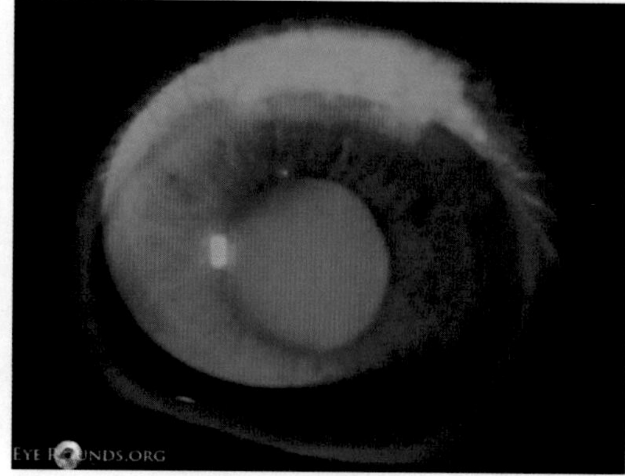

EyeRounds.org University of Iowa

What to Know: SLK occurs when the superior lid chafes on the superior bulbar conjunctiva. The friction can be caused by Thyroid Disease (proptosis causes the globe to push against the lid), dry eye (without proper lubrication, the lid chafes the conjunctiva on blink), Rheumatoid Arthritis, Sjogren's Syndrome, and excessive contact lens wear (plastic in the eye can cause increased friction).

Symptoms: Patients may complain of bilateral foreign body sensation, pain, and burning sensation. Their complaints may outweigh signs.

Signs: SLK presents with Inflammation and hyperemia (redness) of the superior bulbar conjunctiva which will stain with fluorescein. Filaments (mucous strands) may also be present.

Treatment/Management: Treatment for SLK will be aimed at the underlying etiology. If present, appropriately treat the Thyroid Disease, Dry Eye, or excessive contact lens wear. Given that SLK occurs due to friction, the first line of treatment is excessive use of artificial tears (recommend preservative free if using more than QID). Punctal plugs can also be considered. In severe cases, **silver nitrate** can be applied on the afflicted area for 10-20 seconds and then rinsed thoroughly with saline solution followed by 1 week of antibiotic ointment use. If filaments (mucous strands) are present, treat with topical **acetylcysteine**.

ALLERGIC CONJUNCTIVITIS
Symptoms: Patients will complain of **itchy**, watery eyes.
Signs: Allergic conjunctivitis is characterized by the presence of papillae and possible chemosis (conjunctival edema).
Treatment: Allergic Conjunctivitis is treated with topical antihistamines and/or steroids depending on severity.

ALLERGIC CONJUNCTIVITIS

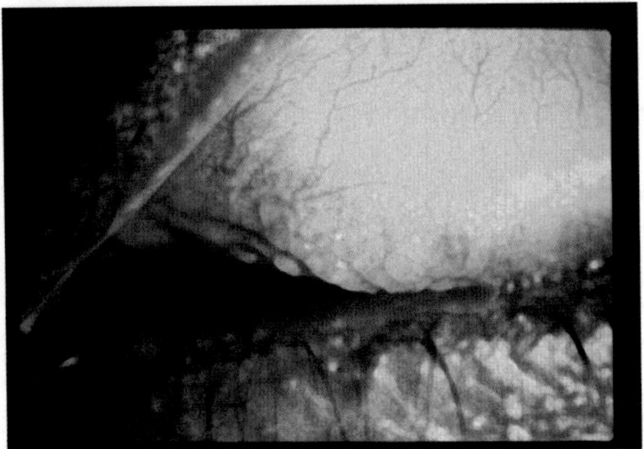

Retina Image Bank. File #12613

What to Know: This is the classic type of Allergic Conjunctivitis. There are two types.

1. Seasonal Allergic Conjunctivitis is the most common type of Allergic Conjunctivitis and it is associated with airborne pathogens such as pollens and hay fever.
2. Perennial Allergic Conjunctivitis occurs year round and it is associated with dust and dander.

ATOPIC CONJUNCTIVITIS

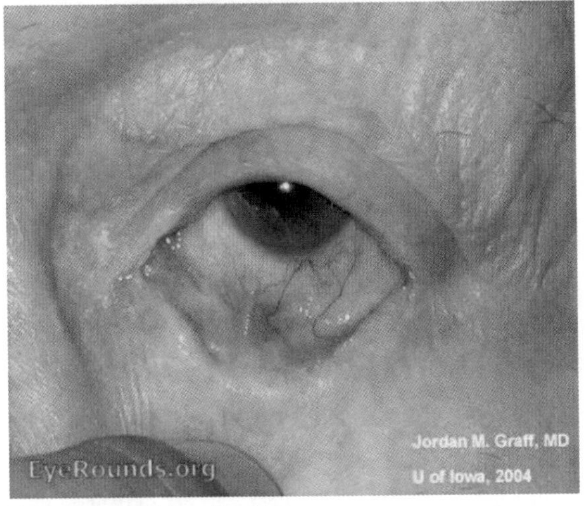

EyeRounds.org University of Iowa

What to Know: Atopic Conjunctivitis is a rare condition associated with atopy (hereditary predilection for allergic diseases such as atopic dermatitis/eczema, allergic rhinitis, and asthma). It is most commonly seen in individuals aged 13-50 years old.

Symptoms: In addition to the symptoms listed in the green "Allergic Conjunctivitis" box above, patients may complain of photophobia and pain.

Signs: In addition to the signs listed in the green "Allergic Conjunctivitis" box above, patients may have eczematous dermatitis of the eyelids, ectropion, trichiasis, madarosis, conjunctival injection and chemosis, corneal staining and erosions, symblepharon, neovascularization, keratoconus, and cataracts. The papillae will be located in the inferior palpebral conjunctiva.

Atopic Conjunctivitis is frequently seen concurrently with Atopic Dermatitis. Dennie's Lines (an extra crease in the inferior lid) are frequently seen with Atopic Dermatitis.

VERNAL CONJUNCTIVITIS

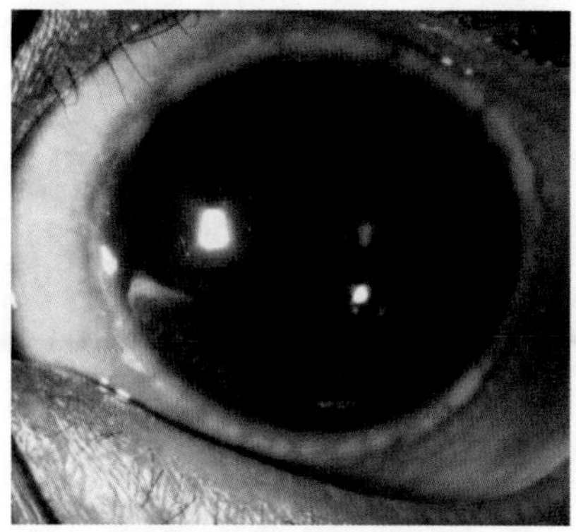

EyeRounds.org University of Iowa

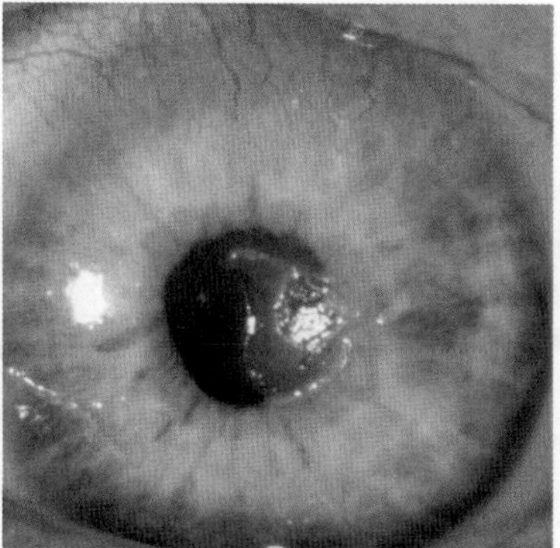

EyeRounds.org University of Iowa

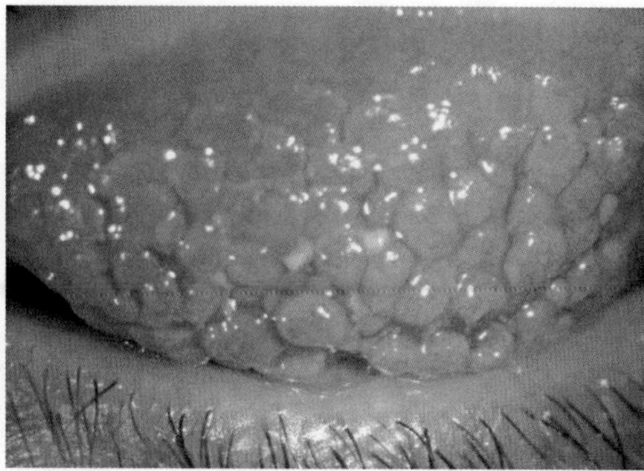

EyeRounds.org University of Iowa

What to Know: Vernal Conjunctivitis is a very rare condition typically seen in boys under the age of 10 who live in hot climates and have a predilection for atopy. It is characterized by seasonal outbreaks which will decrease in severity over time and spontaneously resolve during puberty.

Symptoms: In addition to the symptoms listed in the green "Allergic Conjunctivitis" box above, patients may complain of photophobia and pain.

Signs: In addition to the signs listed in the green "Allergic Conjunctivitis" box above, patients may have a thick ropy discharge, Horner-Trantas dots (collections of eosinophils at the limbus – left picture), and a shield ulcer (superiorly located, sterile, well-delineated, grey infiltrate – center picture). Papillae will manifest as large cobblestones located in the superior palpebral conjunctiva (right picture).

Treatment/Management: Treat the allergic conjunctivitis, and if present, also treat the shield ulcer.

BACTERIAL CONJUNCTIVITIS
Signs: Bacterial conjunctivitis is characterized by the presence of papillae and negative lymphadenopathy. It is more commonly seen in children than adults.
Treatment: Conjunctivitis caused by a bacteria will usually be treated with a topical antibiotic.

BACTERIAL CONJUNCTIVITIS (NON-GONOCOCCAL)

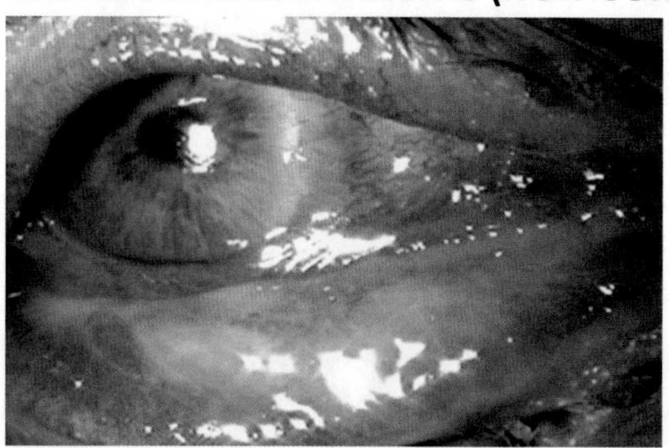

Flicker © Image 32529009371

What to Know: Bacterial Conjunctivitis is most commonly caused by gram positive bacteria (*Staphylococcus aureus, Streptococcus pneumoniae*). This is the most common cause of conjunctivitis in children under 3 years of age.

Symptoms: Symptoms will be acute. Patients will be able to tell you the time of day it started, but not the exact moment. They will frequently have a history of a recent cold, and they will complain of foreign body sensation.

Signs: Bacterial Conjunctivitis presents with mucopurulent discharge, hyperemia (redness), chemosis (swollen conjunctiva), papillae, and lid swelling. There will be NO corneal involvement and NO lymphadenopathy.

GONOCOCCAL CONJUNCTIVITIS

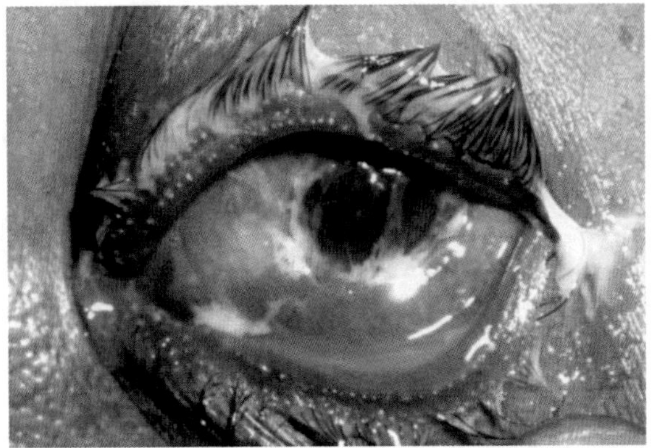
Flicker © Image #5594570699

What to Know: Gonococcal Conjunctivitis is caused by *Neisseria gonorrhoeae*. This is one of the bacteria which can attack the intact corneal epithelium!

Symptoms: Symptoms will be **HYPERACUTE**. The patient will be able to tell you the exact second the conjunctivitis started.

Signs: Gonococcal Conjunctivitis will present with **HYPERACUTE** signs of **SEVERE** mucopurulent discharge, hyperemia (redness), chemosis (swollen conjunctiva), papillae, and lid swelling. Rarely, the patient will also have lymphadenopathy, which is uncommon in bacterial infections (usually lymphadenopathy is only seen in viral infections). **Patients may have signs of corneal ulcers, in which case the bacteria is attacking the corneal epithelium and causing infectious keratitis!**

Treatment/Management: Ceftriaxone should be administered intramuscularly (IM) if the cornea is not involved and intravenously (IV) if the cornea IS involved. In cases where the cornea IS involved, these patients should also be hospitalized. Fluoroquinolones and referral to an infectious specialist should be considered if the patient is allergic to penicillins or cephalosporins.

OPHTHALMIA NEONATORUM (NEWBORN CONJUNCTIVITIS)

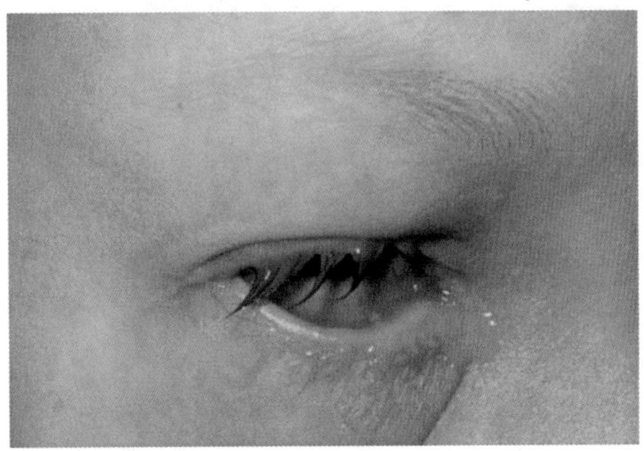
EyeRounds.org University of Iowa

What to Know: Infants may develop a Gonococcal Conjunctivitis within 4 days of birth, also known as Ophthalmia Neonatorum. Note that there are other causes of Ophthalmia Neonatorum, but *Neisseria gonorrhoeae* is the most common cause.

Signs: Ophthalmia Neonatorum will present with **HYPERACUTE** signs of **SEVERE** mucopurulent discharge, hyperemia (redness), chemosis (swollen conjunctiva), papillae, and lid swelling. The patient will also have lymphadenopathy, which is unique to bacterial infections (usually lymphadenopathy is only seen in viral infections). **Patients may have signs of corneal ulcers, in which case the bacteria is attacking the corneal epithelium and causing infectious keratitis!**

Treatment/Management: Historically Silver Nitrate was used as a prophylactic against Ophthalmia Neonatorum, but now erythromycin ointment is used instead. If an active infection develops, then intramuscular (IM) or intravenous (IV) Ceftriaxone should be administered.

CHLAMYDIAL CONJUNCTIVITIS

There are two types of conjunctivitis caused by Chlamydia.

ADULT INCLUSION CONJUNCTIVITIS	**TRACHOMA**
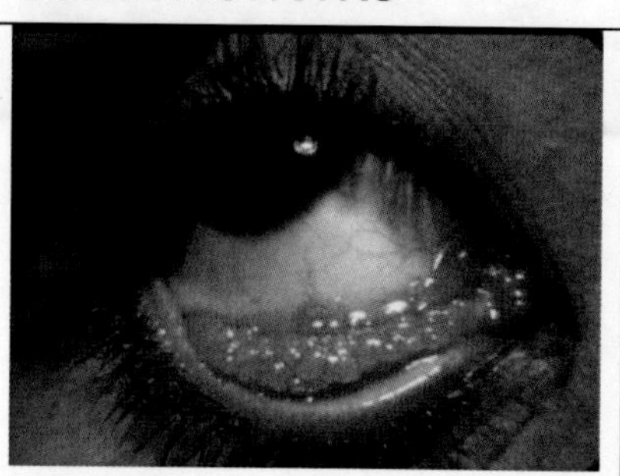 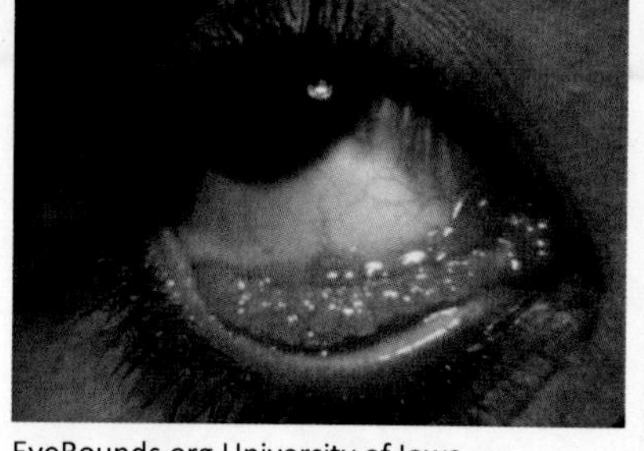 EyeRounds.org University of Iowa	EyeRounds.org University of Iowa 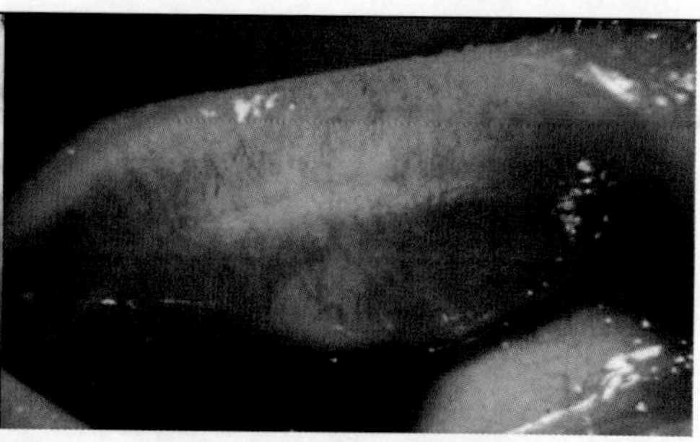 EyeRounds.org University of Iowa
What to Know:	
Both Adult Inclusion Conjunctivitis and Trachoma are considered **chronic** forms of conjunctivitis, meaning it can last for up to 12 months without treatment.	
Caused by serotypes D-K.	Caused by serotypes A-C, Trachoma is the leading cause of preventable blindness in the world, but is not commonly seen in developed countries anymore.
Signs:	
While Chlamydial Conjunctivitis is caused by a bacteria, be sure to look for **follicles** in these patients. Patients may also present with a stringy mucous discharge, and tender, palpable preauricular nodes.	
Look for large follicles located in the **inferior** palpebral conjunctiva.	All of the important signs of Trachoma are located **superiorly**. The follicles will be located in the **superior** palpebral conjunctiva. They may press against the globe and cause indentations along the superior limbus (**Herbert's Pits** – middle picture). After time, the follicles may also cause scarring along the superior palpebral conjunctiva (**Arlt Lines** - right image).
Treatment/Management:	
Given that both Adult Inclusion Conjunctivitis and Trachoma are caused by Chlamydia, they are both treated in the same way. A single dose of oral Azithromycin should be used followed by daily use of oral doxycycline, erythromycin, or tetracycline for 1-2 weeks. Topical antibiotics may also be beneficial. Follow up should occur every 2-3 weeks until resolution. Any of the patient's current sexual partners should also be treated.	

VIRAL CONJUNCTIVITIS
Signs: Viral Conjunctivitis is characterized by the presence of follicles and positive lymphadenopathy.
Treatment: There is no effective treatment for Viral Conjunctivitis for it will self-resolve. Treatment is aimed at alleviating symptoms. Artificial tears can be used for comfort and topical steroids can be used to reduce inflammation.

ADENOVIRAL CONJUNCTIVITIS

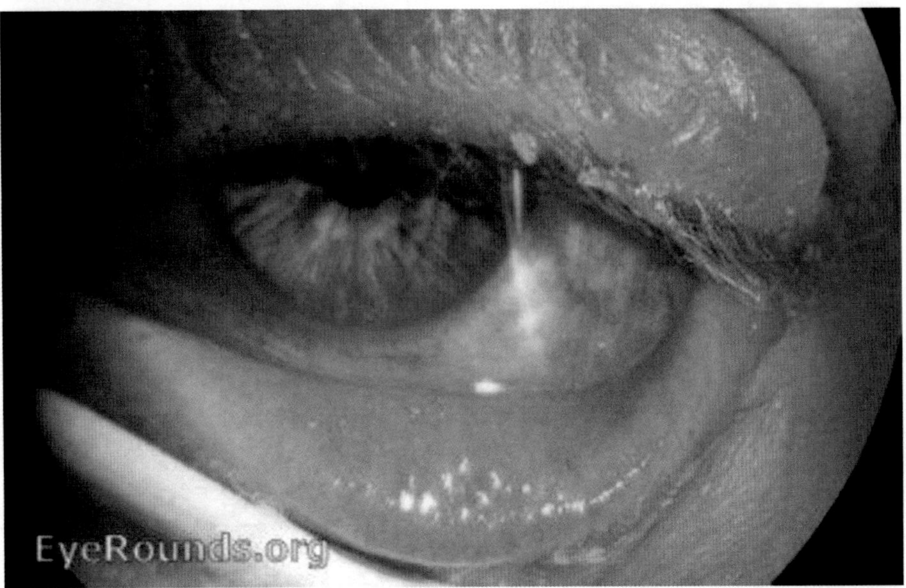

EyeRounds.org University of Iowa

What to Know: Adenoviral Conjunctivitis is the MOST COMMON cause of "pink eye" or viral conjunctivitis. This is highly contagious for up to 14 days and it is transmitted via contact.

Symptoms: Patients will frequently have a history of a recent cold. They will complain of foreign body sensation, itching, burning, or gritty feeling.

Signs will include serous discharge, hyperemia (redness), positive lymphadenopathy, and lid edema. There are three types:

1. Nonspecific: This is the classic and most common type of Adenoviral Conjunctivitis.
2. Epidemic Keratoconjunctivitis (EKC) can be differentiated from the other types based on the presence of subepithelial infiltrates (SEIs), which occur 2-3 weeks after onset of the infection (meaning if SEIs are present, the patient is no longer contagious). EKC is known to cause severe pain.
3. Pharyngoconjunctival fever (aka Swimming Pool Conjunctivitis) can be differentiated from the other types based on the presence of fever and pharyngitis (sore throat).

Treatment: Patients should be followed after 2-3 weeks. They should be educated about the contagious nature of the disease and advised to avoid contact with other people. Recommend that patients clean their bedsheets and towels.

MOLLUSCUM CONTAGIOSUM

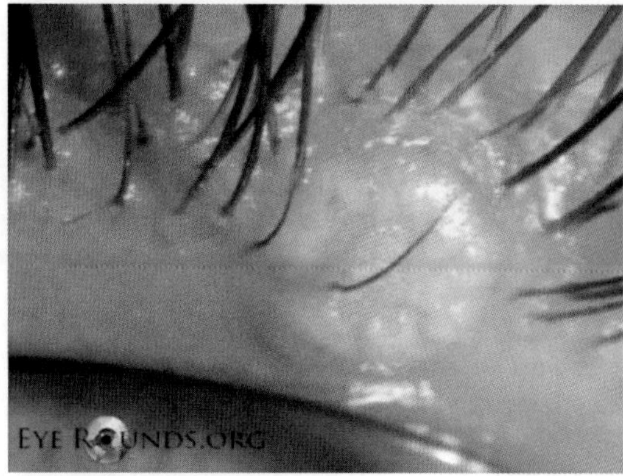

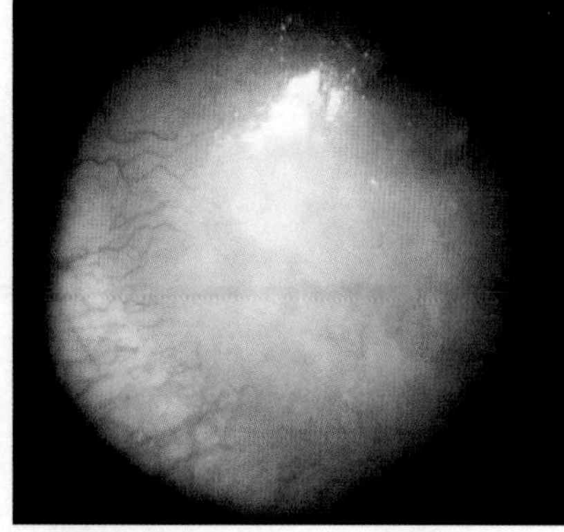

EyeRounds.org University of Iowa Kimberly Castillo, OD

What to Know: Molluscum Contagiosum is caused by the DNA pox virus.

Signs: Molluscum Contagiosum presents with dome shaped umbilicated shiny nodule(s) along the lid margin (left image). If multiple are present, then HIV may be the underlying etiology. Ruptured nodules may lead to pannus (fibrous vascular tissue growth over the cornea – right image), and **chronic conjunctivitis**.

Treatment/Management: The nodules need to be removed by excision, curettage, or cryotherapy (freezing of tissue). Be careful not to spill the contents of the nodule into the eye. These patients should also be referred for HIV testing (Western Blot and ELISA).

CONJUNCTIVAL TUMORS

CONJUNCTIVAL INTRAEPITHELIAL NEOPLASIA (CIN) → SQUAMOUS CELL CARCINOMA

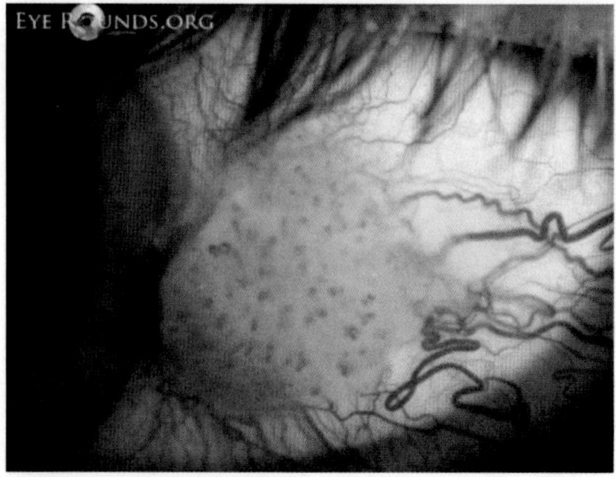

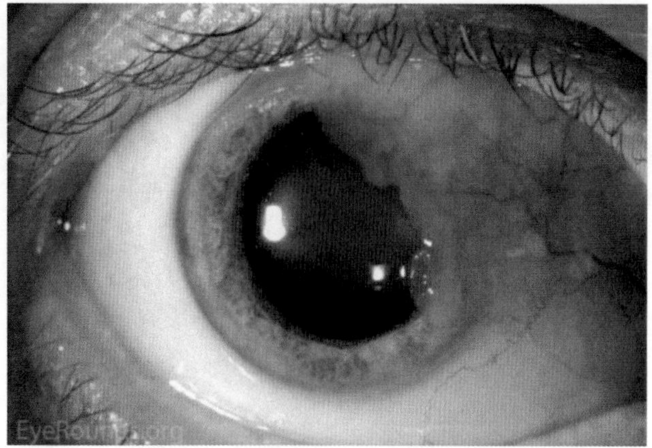

EyeRounds.org University of Iowa EyeRounds.org University of Iowa

What to Know: CIN (left picture) is the precursor to Squamous Cell Carcinoma (right picture). Squamous Cell Carcinoma is the **most common conjunctival malignancy in the US**. Both are most commonly seen in elderly Caucasian males and are usually associated with heavy smoking, UV radiation, and the human papillomavirus (HPV). If present in a patient under the age of 50, suspect HIV. Metastasis and orbital invasion is rare for Squamous Cell Carcinoma, but mortality is as high as 8%.

Symptoms: Patients may complain of ocular irritation, foreign body sensation, and dry eye.

Signs:

- CIN remains limited to just the conjunctival epithelium near the limbus. It appears as white, gelatinous dysplasia (abnormal, precancerous tissue).
- Squamous Cell Carcinoma is a peripapillary, gelatinous lesion with abnormal loops of vessels.

Treatment/Management: Patients should be referred for a medical workup and receive an MRI to rule out orbital invasion. Excision with biopsy, exenteration (complete removal of the globe and all the contents of the eye socket), and radiation may be necessary. If recurrent, topical interferon, Mitomycin C (DNA synthesis inhibitor which stops the growth of cancer cells), or 5-fluorouracil can be considered.

PRIMARY ACQUIRED MELANOSIS (PAM) → MALIGNANT MELANOMA

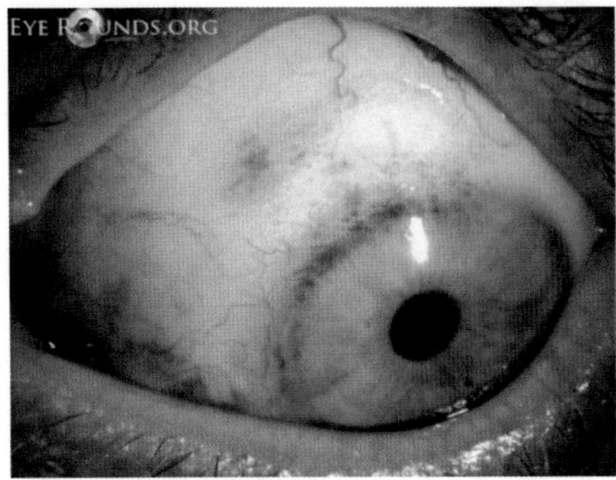

EyeRounds.org University of Iowa

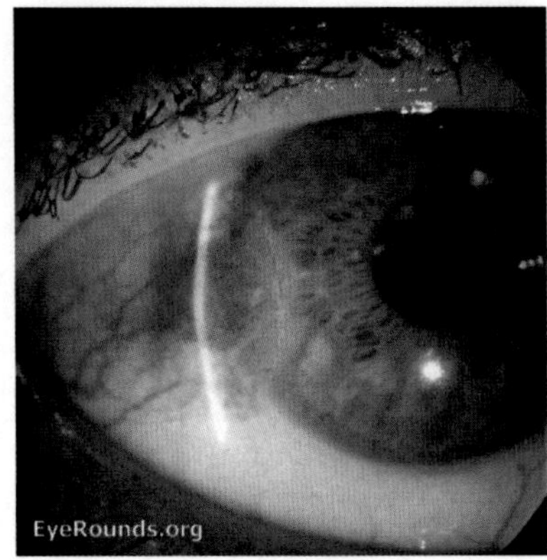

EyeRounds.org University of Iowa

What to Know: PAM precedes approximately 70% of cases of Malignant Melanoma. Both conditions present unilaterally and occur almost exclusively in middle-aged Caucasians.

Signs:

- **PAM** (left image) is characterized by an acquired area of brown, flat pigmentation. The first signs of malignant transformation is elevation of the pigmented area and engorged vascularization to the area.
- **Malignant Melanoma** (right image) is a slowly growing, elevated, pigmented mass which is highly vascularized. The first area of metastasis is the parotid and/or submandibular lymph nodes, which can have up to a 45% mortality rate.

Treatment/Management:

- PAM should be monitored carefully for evidence of malignant transformation with serial photography. If signs of malignancy develop, then treat as Malignant Melanoma.
- Malignant Melanoma should be treated with excisional biopsy, cryotherapy (freezing of tissue), corneal epitheliectomy (removal of the epithelium of a tissue), and exenteration (complete removal of the globe and all the contents of the eye socket) depending on severity. If recurrent, use topical Mitomycin C (DNA synthesis inhibitor which stops the growth of cancer cells). A systemic workup is also indicated.

~~~CORNEA~~~

DRY EYE

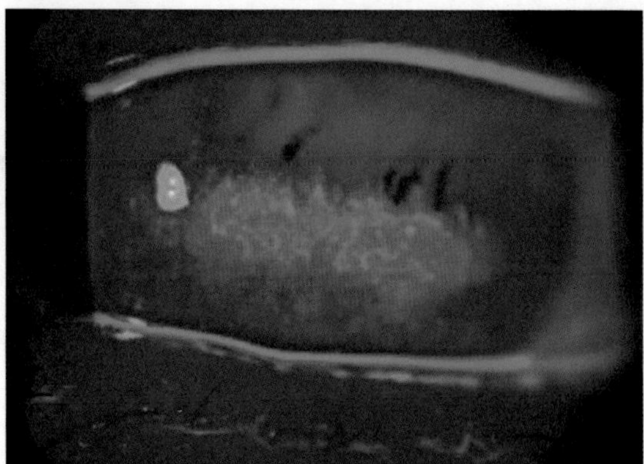

Kimberly Castillo, OD

What to Know: Dry Eye is a very common condition which occurs when a patient has an unstable tear film due to a deficiency of one the three layers (lipid, aqueous, mucin). There are two types of Dry Eye which can be further broken into two subtypes:

1. Aqueous Deficient Dry Eye – reduced production of the lacrimal gland.
    a. Non-Sjogren's Syndrome – lacrimal gland production is reduced due to senile stenosis (age-related narrowing of lacrimal ducts), lacrimal duct blockage (cicatrizing conjunctivitis aka mucous membrane disorder), and reduced corneal sensitivity secondary to contact lens wear or refractive surgery.
    b. Sjogren's Syndrome – **Dry Eye AND Dry Mouth** caused autoimmune disease and exocrine gland dysfunction. Diagnosed individuals also have an increased risk of lymphoma.
2. Evaporative Dry Eye – Excessive evaporation of the tears due to a deficiency of the mucin or lipid layers of the tear film.
    a. Intrinsic Causes – problems with the eyelid anatomy or behavior (MGD, proptosis, lagophthalmos, ectropion, etc.)
    b. Extrinsic Causes – due to issues with diet, prolonged screen time, or drug use (Vitamin A deficiency, topical medications, contact lens wear).

Symptoms: Patients will complain of dry, burning, itching, stinging, tearing, and/or foreign body sensation. Symptoms may be worse at night, when it is windy, or after reading/watching TV. Vision may fluctuate and improve with blink.

Signs: Patients will have superficial punctate keratitis (SPK) on the cornea due to chafing of the lid on the poorly lubricated surface. They will also have a reduced tear break up time (TBUT). A normal TBUT is greater than 10 seconds. The tear meniscus may be less than 0.20 mm, and tear osmolarity may be greater than 316 mOsm/L.

Schirmer's Test may be abnormal. A strip of Whatman #41 is placed in the temporal fornix for five minutes, after which the amount the paper which became wet is measured. Expected findings is greater than 15 mm without anesthesia (reflex + basal tears) and greater than 10 mm with anesthesia (basal tears only). This test has limited usefulness because it has limited repeatability.

Likewise, Phenyl Red Test may also be abnormal. This is performed similarly to the Schirmer's Test. A cotton thread is placed in the temporal fornix for 30 seconds. The expected finding is greater than 10 mm. This test may be more useful than Schirmer's Test because it is less irritating and thus more reproducible.

Treatment/Management: See "Dry Eye" in Chapter 2. Remember that all types of try eye can benefit from the use of Artificial Tears and supplementing the diet with omega-3 fatty acids. Other treatments should be considered based on the type of Dry Eye –

1. Aqueous Deficient Dry Eye: Consider use of punctal plugs, temporary use of steroids, and indefinite use of Lifitegrast (Xiidra) or cyclosporine (Restasis, Cequa).
    a. Non-Sjogren's Syndrome
    b. Sjogren's Syndrome: In addition to other Dry Eye treatments, refer the patient to a rheumatologist if they have complaint of dry mouth and/or joint pain.
2. Evaporative Dry Eye:
    a. Intrinsic Causes: Consider surgery to correct the eyelid abnormality or treat the underlying cause of the proptosis. If the patient has MGD, consider use of lid hygiene, hot compress, Erythromycin, Xiidra, or Restasis.
    b. Extrinsic Causes – Supplement the patient's diet with vitamin A if a deficiency is present. Discontinue use of offending topical medications and/or recommend use of artificial tears. These patients may also benefit from the use of punctal plugs.

EXPOSURE KERATOPATHY

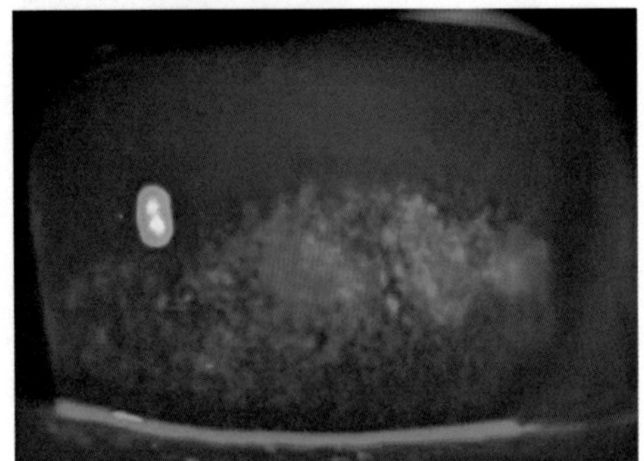

Kimberly Castillo, OD

What to Know: Exposure Keratopathy occurs when the cornea receives mechanical traction. It usually occurs due to an eyelid abnormality which prevents proper eyelid closure: Ectropion, Entropion, Thyroid Eye Disease (EOM inflammation from Hyperthyroidism), Chronic Progressive External Ophthalmoplegia (gradual loss of extraocular motility), Parinaud's Syndrome (inability to voluntarily look in upgaze), Herpes Zoster (secondary lid malfunction), Möbius Syndrome (congenital bilateral inability to abduct past midline), Globe Subluxation (globe trapped behind eyelids), and lagophthalmos.

Symptoms: Patients may complain of ocular irritation with foreign body sensation, burning, and tearing (epiphora).

Signs: Patients present with sectoral hyperemia (redness) with dryness and associated superficial punctate keratitis (SPK) of the inferior cornea. Severe cases may present with a corneal ulcer.

Treatment/Management: The eyelid abnormality should be addressed: tape the eyelids closed at night, partial tarsorrhaphy (sewing together eyelids), eyelid reconstruction, and gold weight eyelid implant. Other treatments are aimed at healing the cornea: preservative free artificial tears up to Q1H, artificial tear ointment QHS, and amniotic membrane graft. If present, the corneal ulcer should be treated as such.

ULTRAVIOLET / THERMAL KERATOPATHY

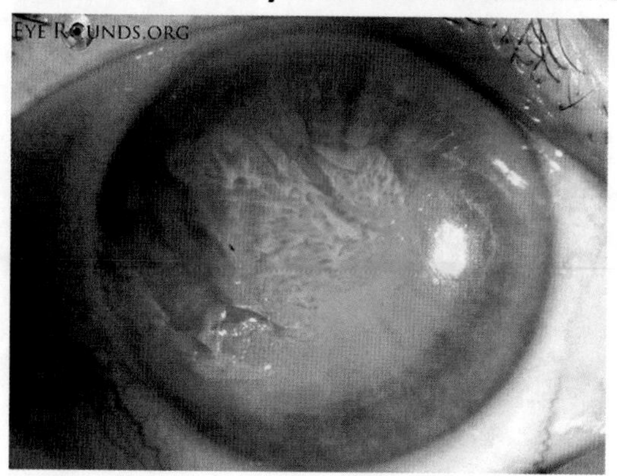

EyeRounds.org University of Iowa

What to Know: UV Keratopathy is caused by prolonged exposure to UV-C light without protective eye wear. Causative activities include skiing, welding, and using sun tanning beds.

Symptoms: Symptoms will occur 6-12 hours after the causative activity. Patients may complain of photophobia and blurry vision with ocular irritation, foreign body sensation, burning, and epiphora.

Signs: Patients present with severe interpalpebral superficial punctate keratitis (SPK).

Treatment/Management: The corneal compromise should be treated with topical antibiotics. The ocular pain should be treated with a topical cycloplegic, an oral NSAID, and a bandage contact lens in severe cases. Patients should be monitored in 24 hours for improvement.

FILAMENTARY KERATITIS

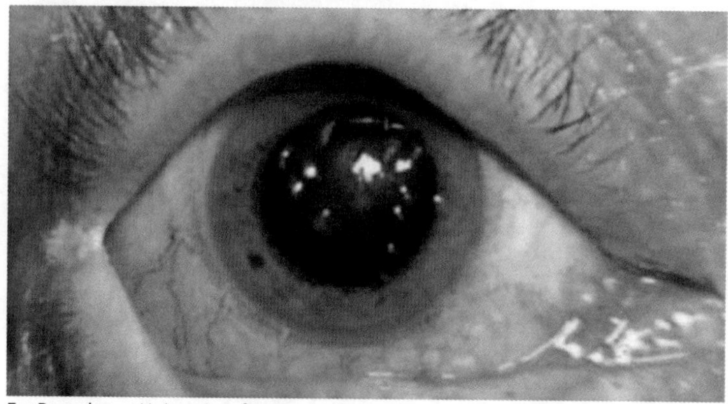

EyeRounds.org University of Iowa

What to Know: Potential causes of Filamentary Keratitis include conditions related to a dry eye, reduced corneal sensitivity, and chafing of the eyelid (dry eye, recurrent corneal erosion, superior limbic keratopathy, neurotrophic keratopathy).

Symptoms: Patients will complain of pain, photophobia, foreign body sensation, and red eye.

Signs: Filaments are made of strands of mucous rolled up with dead epithelial cells, and will stain with fluorescein.

Treatment/Management: Treat the underlying condition. Consider corneal debridement of the filaments. Prescribe preservative free artificial tears up to Q1H, artificial tear ointment QHS, and punctal plugs depending on severity. **May also prescribe Acetylcysteine QID.** For severe symptoms which do not respond to treatment, consider using a soft bandage contact lens.

DELLEN

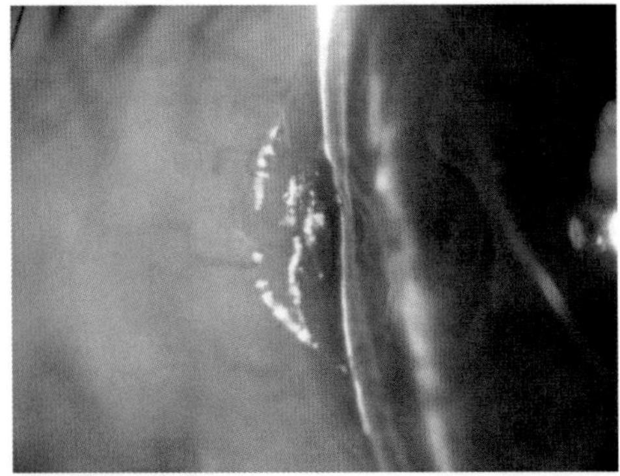
Clinica Rementeria 1

What to Know: Dellen is an area of corneal thinning adjacent to an abnormally raised area. Essentially, the abnormal cornea surface causes an uneven spread of the tear film and some areas of the cornea to dry out, leading to a Dellen. Fluorescein will pool in these areas. Typical causes of an abnormally raised area include pterygium and a filtering bleb (glaucoma treatment).

Symptoms: Patients may be asymptomatic. They may complain of pain, photophobia, epiphora, and blur.

Treatment/Management: The causative raised area should be removed. In the meantime (or if the area cannot be removed) patients should use copious artificial tears Q1H, gels Q1H, and ointments QHS.

THYGESON'S SUPERFICIAL PUNCTATE KERATITIS

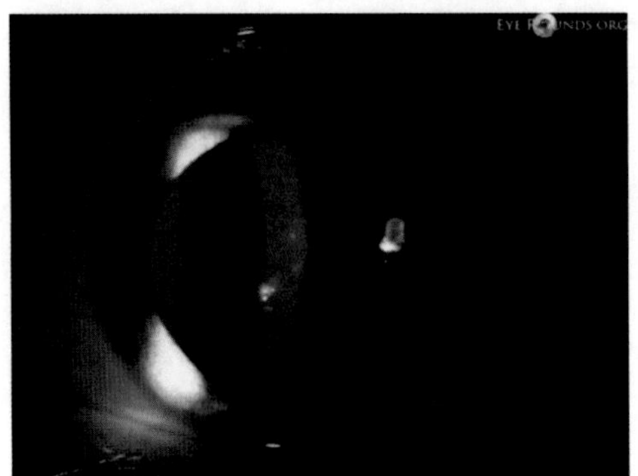
EyeRounds.org University of Iowa

What to Know: Thygeson's Superficial Punctate Keratitis is a chronic, bilateral condition typically seen in 20-30 year olds.

Symptoms: Patients will complain of foreign body sensation, photophobia, and epiphora. Symptoms will often outweigh signs.

Signs: Patients will have central bilateral gray-white stellate or "bread crumb" elevated opacities which will stain with fluorescein.

Treatment/Management: Prescribe preservative free artificial tears up to Q1H and artificial tear ointment QHS. May also consider using a soft bandage contact lens. More severe cases may benefit from a mild topical steroid and/or cyclosporine drops.

PHLYCTENULOSIS / PHLYCTENULE

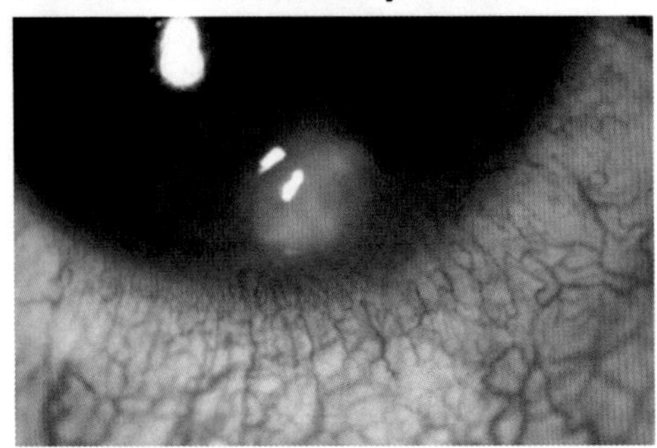
Ento Key 1

What to Know: Phlyctenulosis is caused by a delayed *staphylococcus* hypersensitivity reaction, often associated with Blepharitis and/or Acne Rosacea. In developing countries it is caused by Tuberculosis. Usually it is self-limited, although severe cases may cause blindness.

Symptoms: Patients will complain of pain, irritation, photophobia, and epiphora.

Signs: Patients present with a vascularized white nodule which may be on the conjunctiva or on the cornea near the limbus. They may also present with blepharospasm.

Treatment/Management: Patients should be treated with a topical steroid for the inflammation and an antibiotic for the *staphylococcus* infection. If Blepharitis is present, recommend lid hygiene. If Acne Rosacea is present, then prescribe oral doxycycline or erythromycin. Phlyctenulosis typically resolves within 14 days.

CORNEAL GRAFT REJECTION/FAILURE

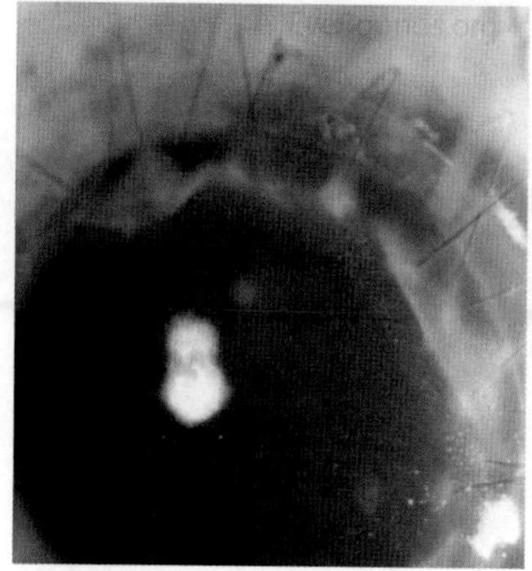

EyeRounds.org University of Iowa

What to Know: Up to 30% of patients reject a corneal graft within one year of surgery. This is an autoimmune response in which the body detects that the graft is foreign and mounts an immune response against it.

Symptoms: Patients will complain of blur, pain, and photophobia.

Signs: Signs of a Corneal Graft Rejection can all be attributed to the autoimmune response: keratic precipitates, corneal edema, conjunctival injection, epithelial rejection line, endothelial rejection line (Khodadoust Line), subepithelial infiltrates, and neovascularization.

Treatment/Management: Treatment is aimed at reducing the inappropriate immune response with steroids (topical, oral, sub-Tenon's) depending on severity. If the patient does not respond to steroids, then an immunosuppressant (cyclosporine) should be considered. Patients should be monitored every 3-7 days and steroids can be tapered very slowly upon signs of improvement.

NEUROTROPHIC KERATOPATHY (NK)

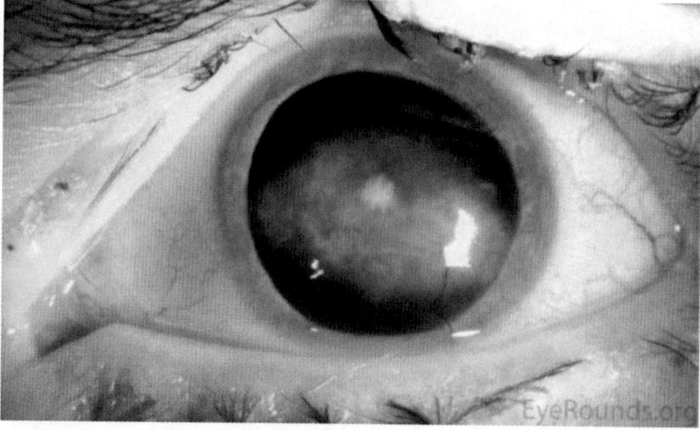

EyeRounds.org University of Iowa

What to Know: Neurotrophic Keratopathy typically occurs secondary to reduced sensitivity of CN5 (V1 branch). Neurotrophic Keratopathy is most commonly caused by prior herpetic corneal (HSK, HZK) infections. The nerve stops sensing that the cornea needs repair, thus disrupting the feedback loop which causes the eye to maintain the quality of the cornea. As a result, the poorly maintained cornea develops an ulcer.

Symptoms: Patient complaints will be less than expected given the signs due to reduced CN5 sensitivity.

Signs: Patients will have reduced corneal sensitivity with epithelial defects which will stain with fluorescein.

Treatment/Management: Due to reduced CN5 sensitivity, these patients will have severely dry corneas. Therefore, prescribe preservative free artificial tears up to Q1H, artificial tear ointment QHS, and punctal plugs depending on severity. If an epithelial defect is present (corneal ulcer), prescribe an antibiotic ointment up to Q2H, and/or topical recombinant human nerve growth factor (Cenegermin). An amniotic membrane can also be used to promote healing.

PETER'S ANOMALY

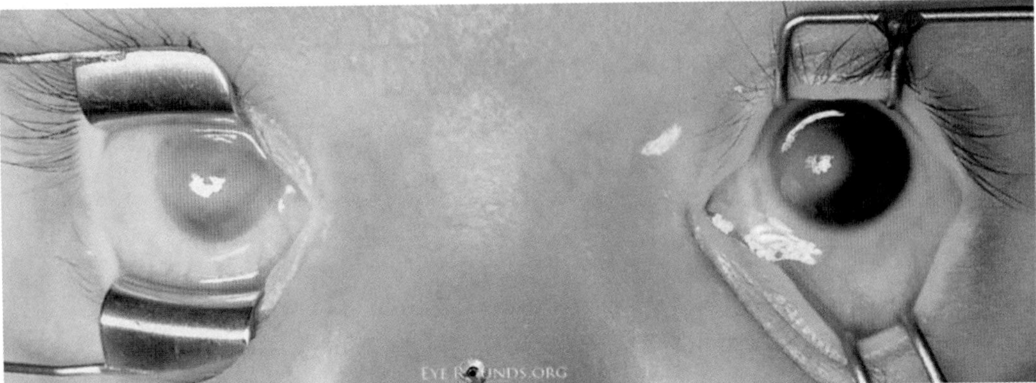

EyeRounds.org University of Iowa

What to Know: Peter's Anomaly is extremely rare and characterized by abnormal development of the corneal endothelium and Descemet's membrane, meaning the cornea is unable to properly maintain its deturgescence. Peter's Plus is coined to distinguish when Peter's Anomaly is associated with skeletal malformations.

Symptoms: Symptoms may range for asymptomatic to complaints of blurred vision.

Signs: Peter's Anomaly presents with central corneal opacities which can range from mild to very severe. Patients may also have comorbid glaucoma, amblyopia, aniridia, and microphthalmos.

Treatment/Management: Patients may require corneal transplant (penetrating keratoplasty, endothelial keratoplasty, or anterior lamellar keratoplasty). If present, treat the glaucoma, amblyopia, and aniridia as such.

INFECTIOUS KERATITIS
Symptoms: Patients will have the same complaints for any type of infectious keratitis: pain, photophobia, discharge, "red eye," and blur.

HERPES ZOSTER

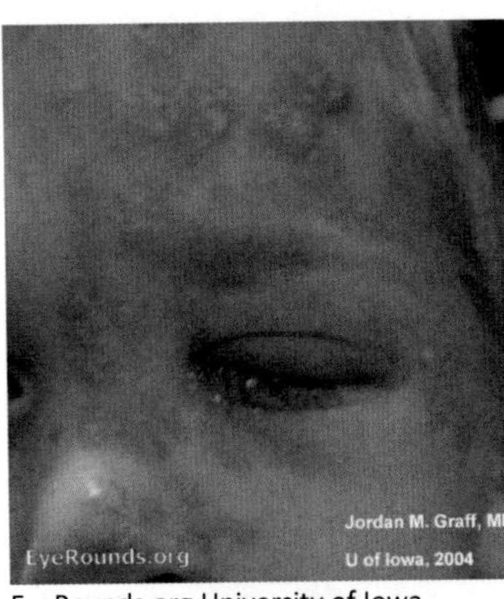

EyeRounds.org University of Iowa

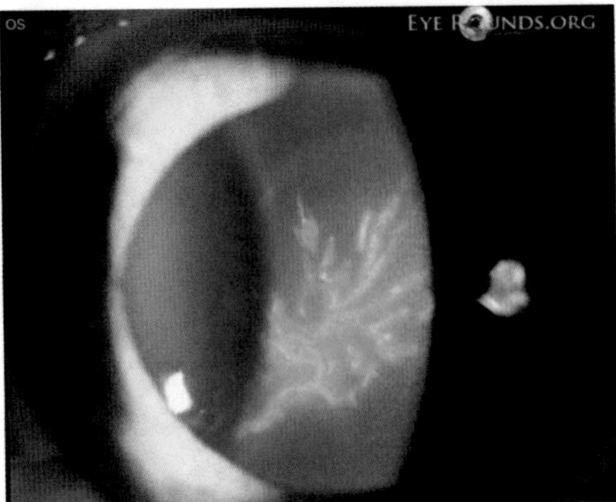

EyeRounds.org University of Iowa

What to Know: Herpes Zoster is caused by the same virus as Chickenpox. After childhood infection, the varicella-zoster virus (VZV) lives dormant in the system until the patient is over the age of 60. Then, it becomes reactivated as Herpes Zoster.

Signs: Patients will have a pustule rash on their face (see right image). Pustule(s) on their nose is called Hutchinson's sign and indicates that there is corneal involvement because CN5 V1 traverses through the cornea before terminating in the nose. Herpes Zoster may cause a variety of ocular signs.

- Epithelial keratitis will initially look similar to superficial punctate keratitis (SPK), but later in the disease course will present as a pseudodendrite (right image) which does not have end bulbs. Epithelial keratitis may last as long as a month.

- Stromal Keratitis will present as anterior stromal infiltrates, disciform keratitis, or peripheral edema. Chronic Stromal Keratitis can lead to corneal scarring (see image under Herpes Simplex Keratitis).
- Interstitial Keratitis is an inflammation of the stroma which may be vascularized. There is no epithelial defect. (See image under Herpes Simplex Keratitis)
- Neurotrophic Keratopathy (see Neurotrophic Keratopathy in this chapter)
- Exposure Keratopathy can occur secondary to lid malfunction due to the Herpes Zoster (see Exposure Keratopathy in this chapter).
- Iritis may be present with transillumination defects, anterior chamber cells and flare, and keratic precipitates.

Treatment/Management: Patients with Herpes Zoster should be initiated with oral antivirals:

- Famciclovir 500mg TID for 7 days
- Acyclovir 800mg 5x/day for 7 days
- Valacyclovir 1000mg TID for 7 days

If an epithelial defect is present, prescribe a topical antibiotic ointment. If Stromal Keratitis or Endotheliitis is present, prescribe topical steroid and cycloplegic. Some patients may require long term treatment with topical steroids to reduce recurrence, in which case they should be monitored for signs of increased IOP. Initial follow up should be at one day. DO NOT prescribe a steroid if there is still an active epithelial keratitis.

HERPES SIMPLEX*

EyeRounds.org University of Iowa

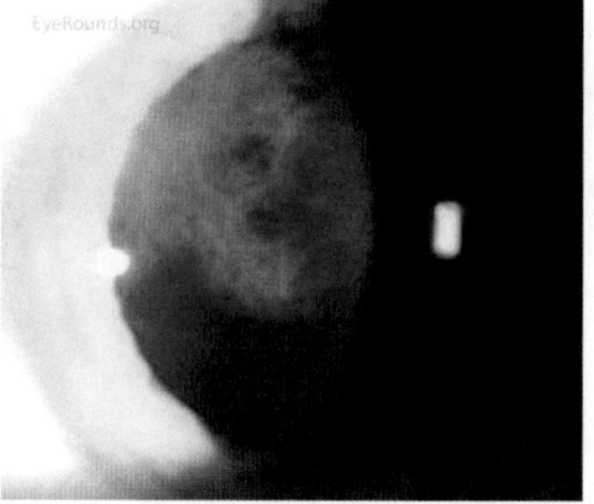

EyeRounds.org University of Iowa

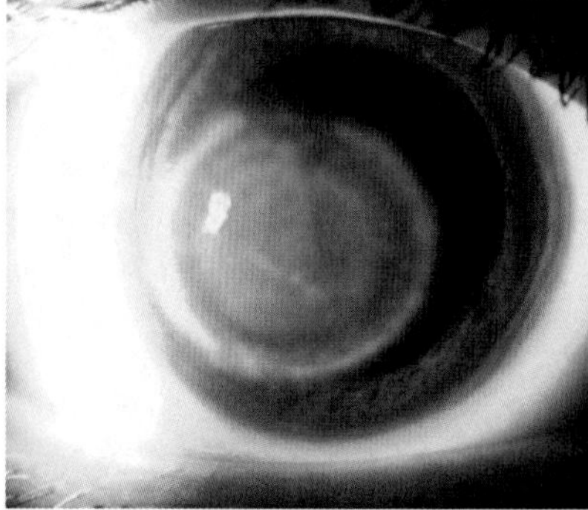

EyeRounds.org University of Iowa

What to Know: Herpes Simplex Keratitis is the leading cause of infectious blindness in the US. It is caused by the HSV1 virus, which resides in the trigeminal ganglion. An infection will occur when the virus gets triggered by an event which compromises the immune system (stress, illness, trauma, UV exposure, etc.).

Signs: Patients may present with pustules on their eyelids. Iritis may be present with transillumination defects, anterior chamber cells and flare, and keratic precipitates. Other signs are classified based on which layer it is found in the cornea.

- Epithelial Keratitis presents as the classic dendrite with end bulbs which stains with Rose Bengal (left image). When a dendrite is present, the infection is said to be active. Early in the disease course the dendrite may look like superficial punctate keratitis (SPK).
- Stromal Keratitis can have two separate presentations:
    - Interstitial Keratitis (middle image) is an inflammation of the stroma which may be vascularized. There is no epithelial defect.

  - Necrotizing Keratitis is also an inflammation of the stroma, but has an associated epithelial defect (ulcer). This has a high risk for corneal melt.
- Endothelial Keratitis/Disciform Keratitis/Endotheliitis (right image): Circular endothelial defect which can lead to corneal edema. Frequently comorbid with uveitis (granulomatous keratic precipitates and anterior chamber reaction).
- Neurotrophic Keratopathy (see Neurotrophic Keratopathy in this chapter)

Treatment/Management: Treatment for HSV depends on where the infection is located in the cornea.

- Epithelial Keratitis (dendrite)
  - Topical drops:
    - Zirgan (ganciclovir) 5x/day
    - Trifluridine (viroptic) 9x/day
  - Oral pills:
    - Famciclovir 250mg TID for 7 days
    - Acyclovir 400mg 5x/day for 7 days
    - Valacyclovir 500mg TID for 7 days
- Stromal and Endothelial Keratitis:
  - Topical steroid to reduce inflammation in conjunction with oral antiviral. If present, treat Uveitis with topical cycloplegic.
- Neurotrophic Keratopathy (see Neurotrophic Keratopathy in this chapter)

Initial follow up should be at one day.

When a patient has an active herpes simplex infection (dendrite), DO NOT use a steroid. A herpes outbreak occurs when the patient's immune system is already compromised and therefore cannot subdue the virus anymore. That said, putting a steroid on top of a herpes infection will add fuel to the fire by further reducing the immune response and cause the infection to become significantly worse very quickly.

FUNGAL KERATITIS

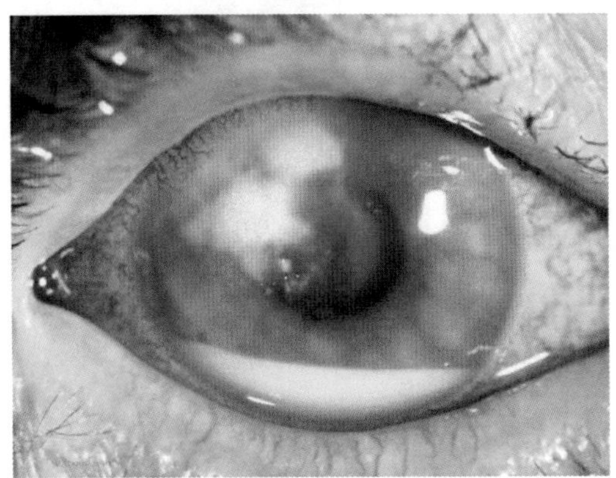

EyeRounds.org University of Iowa

What to Know: A Fungal Keratitis should be suspected when the patient has a history of trauma involving plant matter or fingernails. The most likely involved fungi include *Aspergillus, Candida,* or *Fusarium*.

Signs: Patients will have a stellate infiltrate which will have feathery borders.

Treatment/Management: Given this is a fungal infection, treat with either a topical or systemic anti-fungal. Also consider a topical cycloplegic for comfort. Remember that steroids are contraindicated because they reduce the immune response.

BACTERIAL KERATITIS

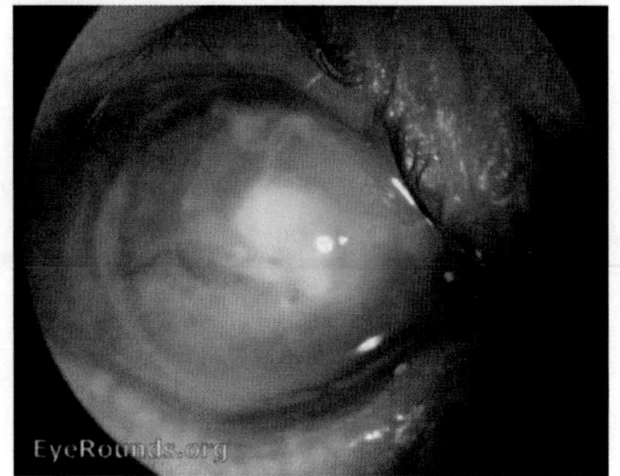
EyeRounds.org University of Iowa

What to Know: Bacteria are the most common cause of Keratitis. The most likely involved bacteria include *Staph aureus, Staph epidermidis, Strep pneumoniae, Pseudomonas aeruginosa,* and *Haemophilus influenzae*.

Signs: Patients will have a well-defined white corneal opacity which may be either an infiltrate (no epithelial defect and so no fluorescein staining) or an ulcer (with epithelial defect which will stain with fluorescein). There will be corneal edema, severe conjunctival injection, anterior chamber cells and flare, and possible hypopyon.

Treatment/Management: Always treat ulcers and infiltrates as bacterial unless there's a high suspicion of a different etiology. Given this is a bacterial infection, treat with a topical antibiotic. Also prescribe a topical cycloplegic for comfort and to prevent the formation of synechiae, especially in cases presenting with hypopyon.

ACANTHAMOEBA/PARASITIC KERATITIS

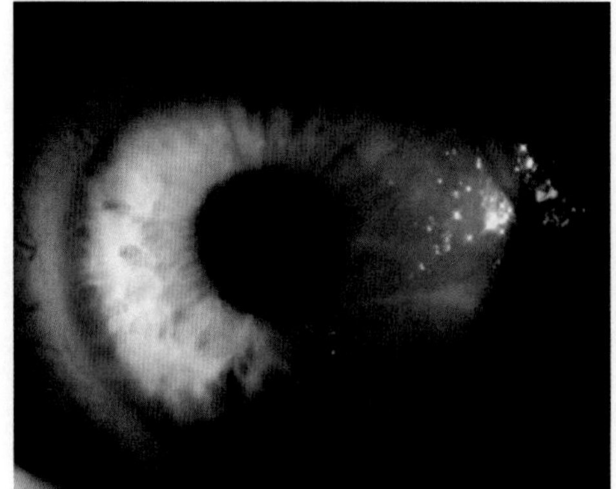
EyeRounds.org University of Iowa

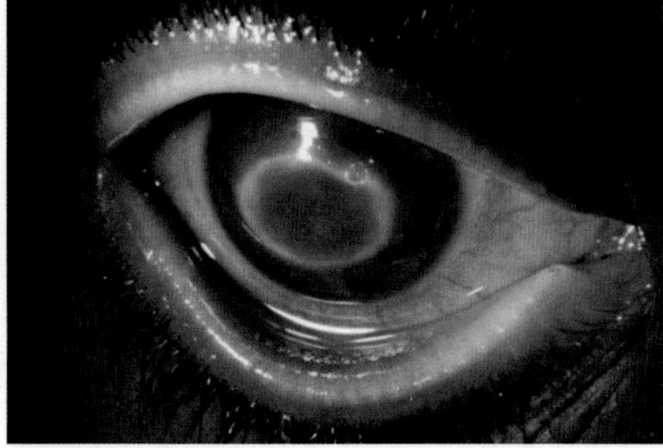
EyeRounds.org University of Iowa

What to Know: Acanthamoeba Keratitis is caused by the parasite *Acanthamoeba*. It is associated with patients who wore their contact lenses while in fresh water environments such as lakes or while they were in a hot tub, or patients who rinse their contact lenses or cases with water.

Symptoms: Patient complaints of pain will be far more severe than signs.

Signs: Early in the disease course the patient will present with mild superficial punctate keratitis (pseudodendrite, left image) which will stain with fluorescein. Frequently this is misdiagnosed as herpes simplex! It will progress slowly, and late stages (at 3-8 weeks) will present with a ring ulcer (right image) and corneal melt. If the patient is not responsive to therapy for Bacterial Keratitis, suspect Acanthamoeba Keratitis.

Treatment/Management: Patients may be initially hospitalized, and they should discontinue contact lens wear. Treatment includes Polyhexamethylene biguanide (PHMD) Q1H, Chlorhexidine Q1H, Propamidine isethionate Q1H, or Dibromopropamidine isethionate ointment. An antifungal may also be used. A topical cycloplegic and oral NSAID may be used for pain. Initially patients should be followed every 1-4 days, then every 1-3 weeks. Treatment will last 3-12 months.

PERIPHERAL ULCERATIVE KERATITIS (PUK)

What to Know: Multiple conditions are associated with PUK.

Symptoms: Patients may be asymptomatic. They may complain of pain, photophobia, epiphora, or blurry vision.

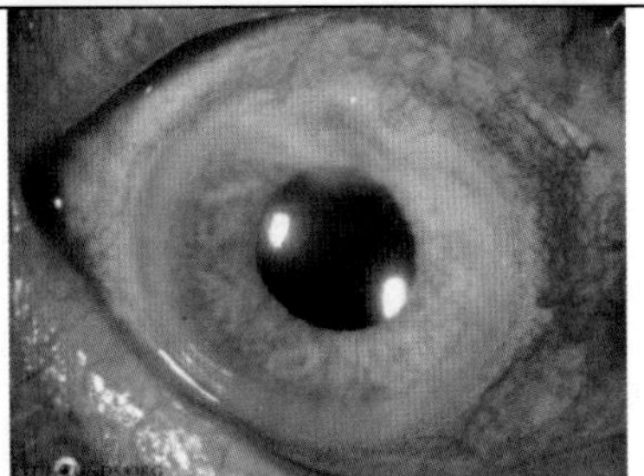

EyeRounds.org University of Iowa

COLLAGEN VASCULAR DISORDER/MARGINAL KERATOLYSIS is caused by autoimmune diseases and presents as an acute PUK with a rapid progression. It usually afflicts only one sector of the cornea and can result in corneal melt. Patients may have an associated scleritis.

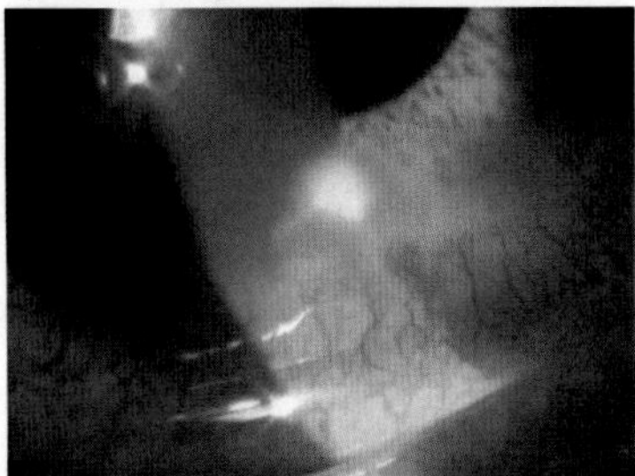

Flicker © Image #332271350480

STAPH MARGINAL KERATITIS is caused by the staph bacteria in the patient's eyelids. The immune response overacts to this bacteria and creates infiltrates along the inferior limbus where the staph bacteria are located.

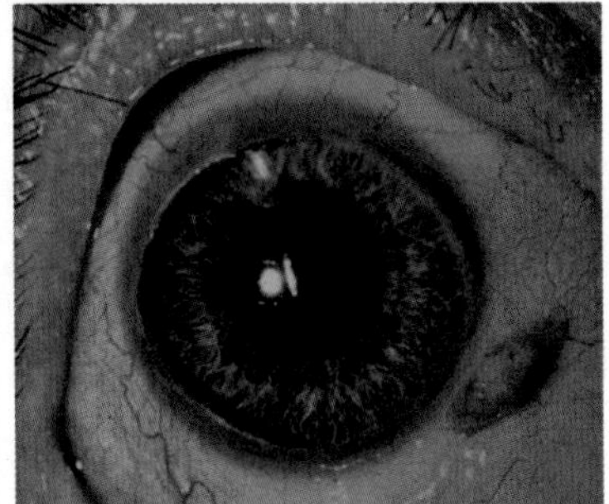

Retina Image Bank. File #24525

MOOREN'S ULCER typically occurs in elderly patients and can present either unilaterally or bilaterally. It is characterized by a **painful** ragged peripheral thinning which will begin in one sector and then spread **circumferentially** around the cornea.

Treatment/Management: Treat the underlying condition. If present, a referral to rheumatology for treatment of the autoimmune disease may be necessary. Patients should use preservative free artificial tears up to Q1H for comfort. Prescribe a topical and/or oral antibiotic if an epithelial defect is present. A topical cycloplegic can also be considered for pain. Also consider a topical collagenase inhibitor (acetylcysteine).

CORNEAL DYSTROPHIES
What to Know: Corneal Dystrophies have a familial inheritance pattern. (You get a dystrophy from your family!) They are typically bilateral, symmetric, central, and have no neovascularization.
Symptoms: Patients may be asymptomatic. They may complain of pain, photophobia, epiphora, or blurry vision.
Signs: A common sign seen in the Corneal Dystrophies is recurrent corneal erosions.
Treatment/Management: If present, treat the recurrent corneal erosion as usual. If central corneal scarring develops, consider phototherapeutic keratectomy (PTK), lamellar keratoplasty (DALK), superficial keratectomy, or penetrating keratoplasty.

ANTERIOR CORNEAL DYSTROPHIES

EBMD/ABMD/MAP-DOT-FINGERPRINT/COGAN'S MICROCYSTIC DYSTROPHY

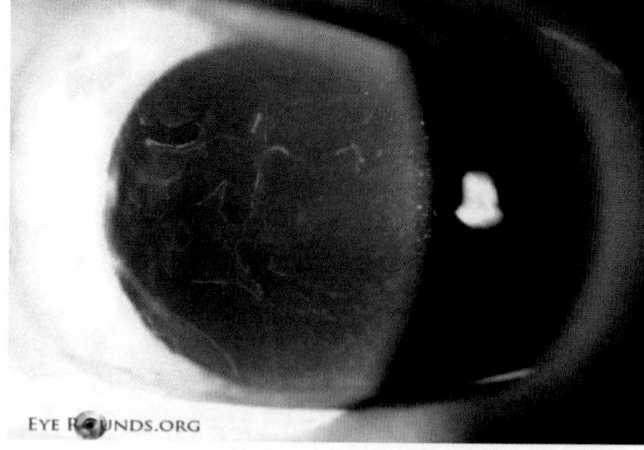

EyeRounds.org University of Iowa

What to Know: EBMD has an AD inheritance pattern and is **the most common anterior corneal dystrophy!** It is more frequently seen in females than males. EBMD is caused by weak hemidesmosomes and excessive basement membrane production which traps the corneal epithelial cells beneath the basement membrane and prevents them from progressing anteriorly.

Signs: Patients will present with subepithelial ridges and lines and intraepithelial microcysts which do not stain. Recurrent corneal erosions occur frequently.

STROMAL CORNEAL DYSTROPHIES

The different types of deposits which are found in each of the stromal dystrophies can be remembered with "Marilyn Monroe Got High in LA." Macular Dystrophy = Mucopolysaccharide deposits, Granular Dystrophy = Hyaline deposits, Lattice Dystrophy = Amyloid deposits.

The staining associated with the stromal dystrophies can be remembered with "General Motors Always Makes Red Lamborghinis." (Yes, yes, I know this is the wrong manufacturer). Granular Dystrophy = Masson's Trichome, Macular Dystrophy = Alcian Blue, Lattice Dystrophy = Congo Red.

MACULAR DYSTROPHY

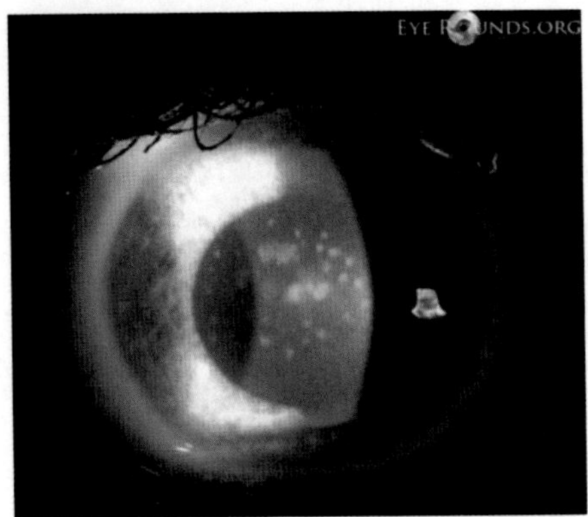

EyeRounds.org University of Iowa

What to Know: Macular Dystrophy is a rare, but severe dystrophy seen in children between the ages of 3-9. **It is the only AR corneal dystrophy!**

Signs: Patients will present with limbus to limbus corneal haze which has scattered gray-white opacities (Mucopolysaccharide deposits) which stain with Alcian Blue. Recurrent corneal erosions occur occasionally.

GRANULAR DYSTROPHY*

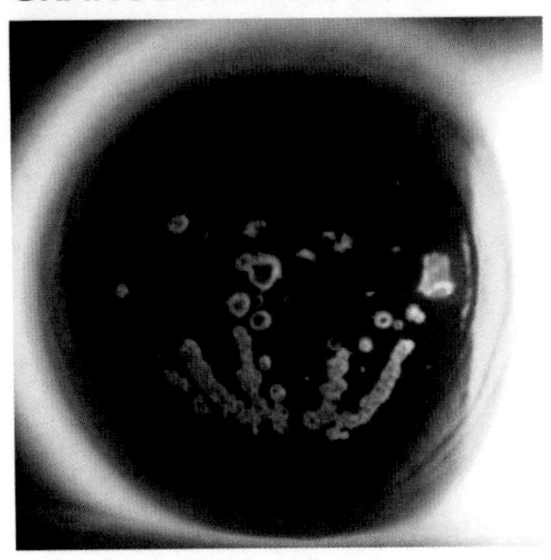

EyeRounds.org University of Iowa

What to Know: Granular Dystrophy has an autosomal dominant (AD) inheritance pattern and is the **most common stromal dystrophy**.

Signs: Patients will present with central snow-flake or bread-crumb like stromal opacities (Hyaline deposits) which stain with Masson's Trichome. Recurrent corneal erosions are rare.

LATTICE DYSTROPHY

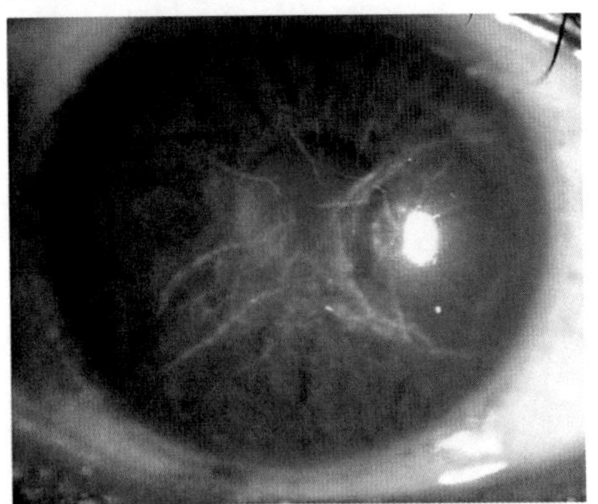

EyeRounds.org University of Iowa

What to Know: Lattice Dystrophy has an autosomal dominant (AD) inheritance pattern and will lead to decreased vision while the patient is in their 30s.

Signs: Patients will present with corneal haze which has refractile branching lines (Amyloid deposits) which stain with Congo Red. Recurrent corneal erosions are common.

POSTERIOR CORNEAL DYSTROPHIES

FUCH'S ENDOTHELIAL DYSTROPHY

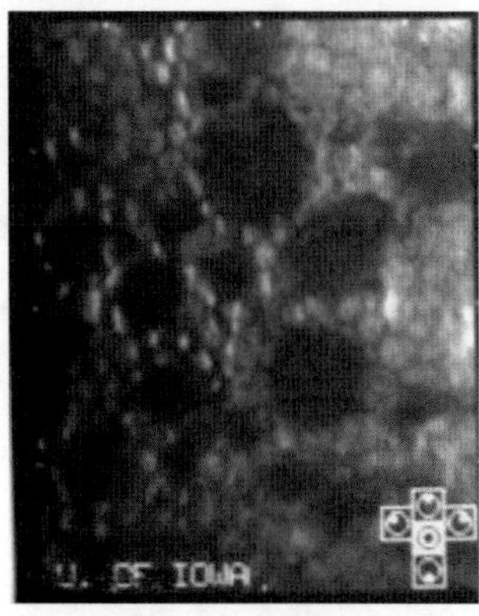

EyeRounds.org University of Iowa

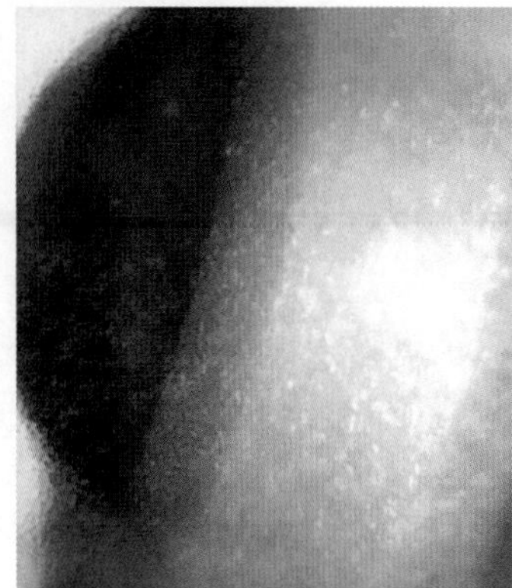

Kimberly Castillo, OD

What to Know: Fuch's Endothelial Dystrophy has an autosomal dominant (AD) inheritance pattern and is most commonly seen in 60 year old females. It is caused by an excrescences of Descemet's Membrane which leads to a decrease in the endothelial cell count (left image). It is a relative contraindication for cataract surgery because it is possible the surgeon may rub the endothelium during the surgery, further reducing the endothelial cell count.

Symptoms: Patients may have blurry vision which is worse in the morning due to increased corneal swelling while the patient is asleep. Remember that the cornea normally swells at night, and so the swelling is even more significant in Fuch's Endothelial Dystrophy.

Signs: The presence of endothelial guttata is diagnostic (right image). Endothelial cells will show pleomorphism (change in cell shape) and polymegathism (increased cell size) due to reduced cell count. The abnormal endothelium can lead to stromal edema which can advance to present epithelial bullae which will stain with fluorescein. It is not associated with recurrent corneal erosions.

Treatment/Management: In addition to the treatment listed in the purple "Corneal Dystrophies" box above, treat corneal edema with topical sodium chloride drops and/or ointment (Muro 128). Patients may consider drying their corneas in the morning with a blow dryer to accelerate the evaporation of the nocturnal edema. Treat bullae as recurrent corneal erosions. Severe cases may require Descemet's Membrane Endothelial Keratoplasty (DMEK, corneal endothelium transplant) or Descemet's Stripping and Automated Endothelial Keratoplasty (DSAEK).

POSTERIOR POLYMORPHOUS DYSTROPHY (PPMD)

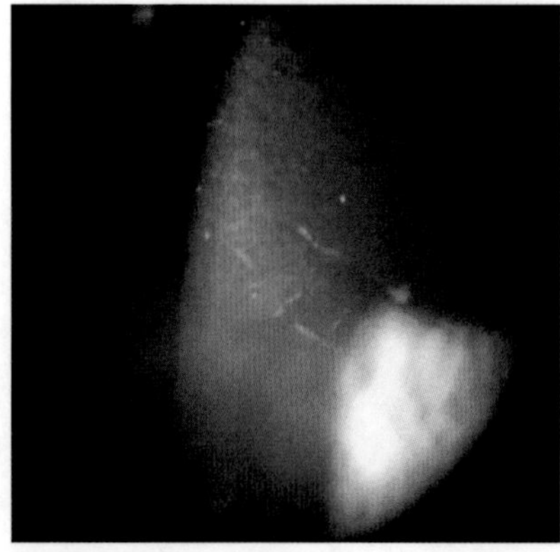

Kimberly Castillo, OD

What to Know: PPMD has an autosomal dominant (AD) inheritance pattern and is most commonly seen in 20-30 year olds. It is characterized by excessive proliferation and migration of the endothelial cells.

Signs: Patients will present with corneal haze which has vesicles and broad bands arranged linearly (train tracks). The migration of the endothelial cells can progress into and block the angle, leading to an increase in IOP. PPMD does not stain with dye due to the endothelial location, and it is not associated with recurrent corneal erosions.

Treatment/Management: In addition to the treatment listed in the purple "Corneal Dystrophies" box above, treat any increased IOP.

CORNEAL DEGENERATIONS
What to Know: Corneal Degenerations do not have a familial inheritance pattern. They are typically unilateral, asymmetric, peripheral, and neovascular.
Symptoms: Patients may be asymptomatic. They may complain of pain, photophobia, epiphora, blurry vision.
TREATMENT: Usually no treatment is recommended unless specified below.

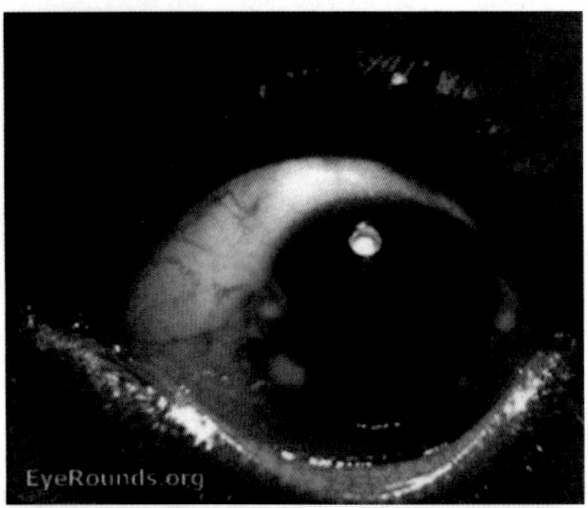

EyeRounds.org University of Iowa

SALZMANN'S NODULAR DEGENERATION

What to Know: Salzmann's Nodular Degeneration is comprised of elevated blue-white nodules in the corneal mid-periphery located at the level of Bowman's Layer. It is caused by chronic corneal inflammation. Typically afflicts elderly women.

TREATMENT is aimed at removing the nodules via superficial keratectomy or Phototherapeutic Keratectomy (PTK).

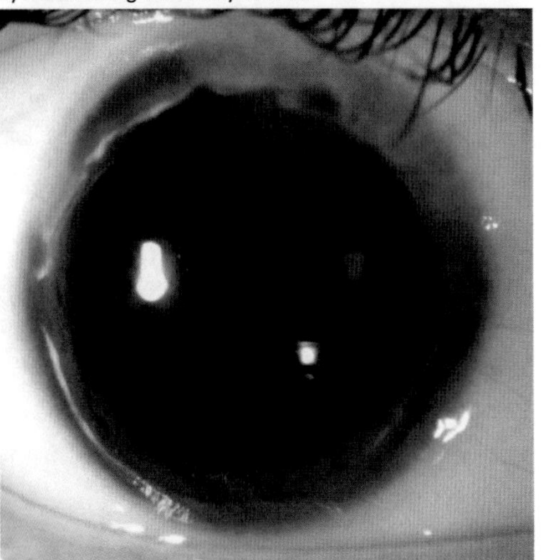

EyeRounds.org University of Iowa

TERRIEN'S MARGINAL DEGENERATION

What to Know: Terrien's Marginal Degeneration begins when the patient is in their 30s. It is a **painless** progressive bilateral thinning of the superior cornea which can lead to progressive against the rule astigmatism. This is usually found in men. I remember this degeneration by thinking that the peripheral cornea appears to be torn in Terrien's Marginal Degeneration.

TREATMENT: Initial treatment is correction of refractive error with glasses. If unsuccessful, consider tectonic or penetrating keratoplasty.

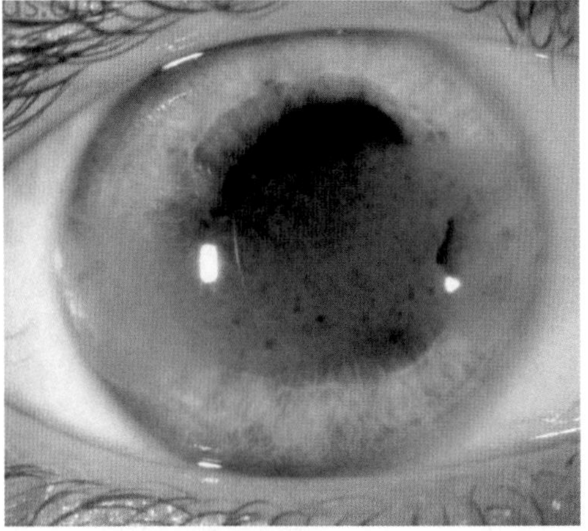

EyeRounds.org University of Iowa

BAND KERATOPATHY

What to Know: Band Keratopathy is typically bilateral and found in Bowman's Layer. It is characterized by inter-palpebral deposits of calcium (Hypercalcemia) or uric crystals (Gout) which gives a "Swiss Cheese" appearance.

TREATMENT is aimed at removing the calcium via superficial keratectomy, ethylenediaminetetraacetic acid (EDTA) chelation, or Phototherapeutic Keratectomy (PTK).

ARCUS SENILIS

What to Know: Arcus Senilis is comprised of bilateral peripheral circumferential deposits of lipid in Bowmen's and Descemet's layers of the cornea. It is a benign finding associated with change. However, if seen in patients under the age of 40, refer for a lipid workup.

Kimberly Castillo, OD

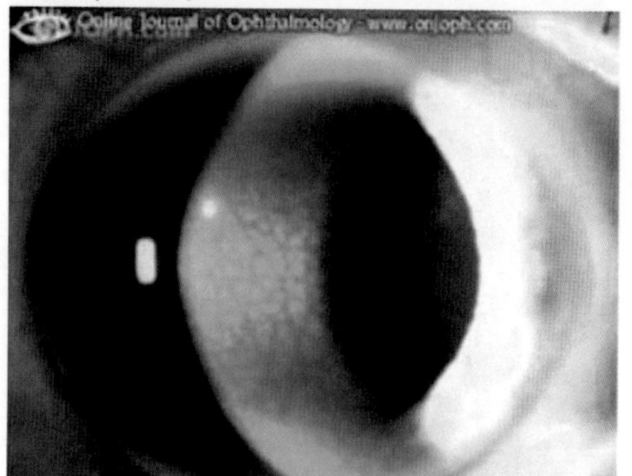

CROCODILE SHAGREEN

What to Know: Crocodile Shagreen is a bilateral opacification with a cracked ice/mosaic pattern located in Bowman's Layer or the Stroma. It is benign and no treatment is necessary.

Atlas of Ophthalmology 2832

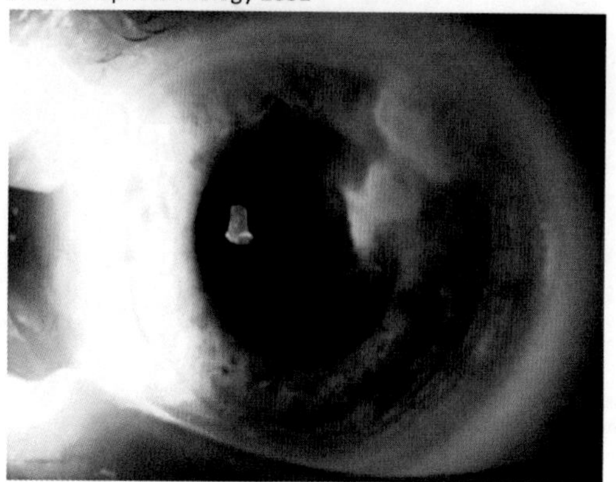

EyeRounds.org University of Iowa

LIPID KERATOPATHY

LIPID KERATOPATHY is characterized by lipid deposits in the stroma which can occur spontaneously (and will have no vascularization) or secondary to Herpes Simplex Virus or Herpes Zoster Virus (and will be vascularized).

TREATMENT is aimed at reducing the inflammation via argon laser photocoagulation (a narrow beam of light is used to shrink or destroy the cancerous cells), needle point cautery, or penetrating keratoplasty (corneal transplant which replaces all the layers of the cornea but retains the peripheral cornea).

CORNEAL ECTASIAS

What to Know: A Corneal Ectasia is defined as a non-inflammatory, abnormal, progressive thinning and distortion of the cornea. Ectasias may be primary, or secondary to refractive surgery. We will discuss two types of ectasias (keratoconus, pellucid marginal degeneration) below.

Symptoms: Patients will complain of gradual blurry vision. If hydrops form, they will complain of pain and tearing.

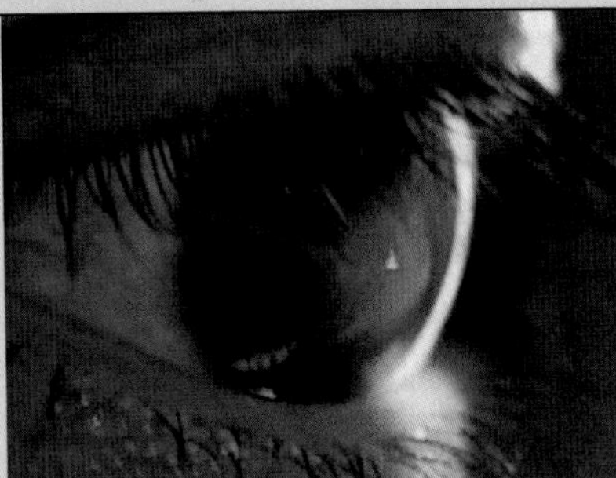

Kimberly Castillo, OD

Signs: Corneal Ectasias are defined as bilateral, asymmetric thinning of the inferior paracentral cornea. All Corneal Ectasias might cause Hydrops (which are ruptures in Descemet's Membrane, pictured to the left)!

Treatment/Management: Acute corneal hydrops should be treated with a cycloplegic for pain and a topical antibiotic ointment (due to compromised epithelium from secondary bullae). Ongoing, corneal hydrops should be treated with sodium chloride ointment (Muro 128) to help dehydrate the cornea.

PELLUCID MARGINAL DEGENERATION

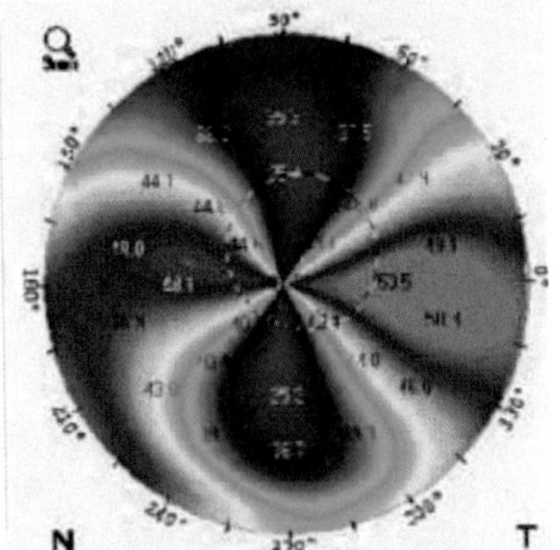

EyeRounds.org University of Iowa

What to Know: I think of Pellucid Marginal Degeneration as being a milder form of keratoconus; some may consider it an early stage of keratoconus. It is also defined as a thinning of the inferior cornea.

Signs: Pellucid Marginal Degeneration will induce against the rule astigmatism and will show as "kissing doves" or "crab claws" on topography. Patients may develop corneal hydrops. Patients will present with ***no*** cone, striae, or scarring.

Treatment/Management: Most cases of Pellucid Marginal Degeneration can be managed with glasses or contacts (soft or RGP). Severe cases may require a corneal transplant. The transplant can be either partial (Deep Anterior Lamellar Keratoplasty aka DALK) or full thickness (Penetrating Keratoplasty).

KERATOCONUS

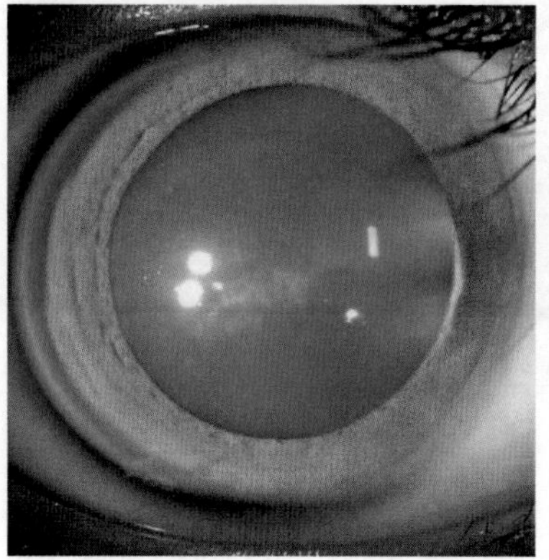
EyeRounds.org University of Iowa

Kimberly Castillo, OD

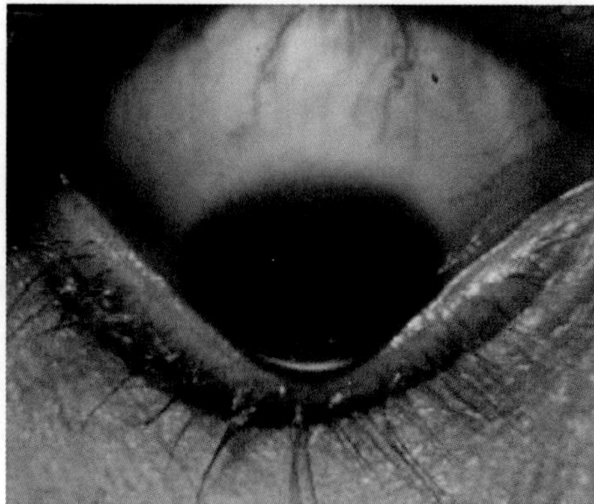
EyeRounds.org University of Iowa

What to Know: Keratoconus is a progressive thinning of the inferior cornea which usually begins when a patient is a teenager. It is associated with eye rubbing (Atopy) and connective tissue disorders: Down's Syndrome (these patients also rub their eyes), Ehlers Danlos Syndrome, Marfan's Syndrome, Osteogenesis Imperfecta, and Turner Syndrome.

Signs: During Keratoconus the paracentral cornea will assume the shape of a cone which will cause progressive irregular astigmatism and a steep cornea (central power >47.25D or greater than 0.90D difference between the two eyes). Early signs include scissor reflex on retinoscopy due to irregularly shaped cornea, egg-shaped mires with keratometry, inferior thinning seen on topography, and Fleischer ring (deposits of iron around the base of the cone in the epithelium, left picture). Late signs include Vogt Striae (stromal folds due to abnormal corneal stretching, middle image), Munson's Sign (lower eyelid bulging on downgaze, right image), and corneal hydrops due to a rupture in Descemet's Membrane.

Treatment/Management: Patients should be educated to avoid rubbing their eyes. Consider corneal crosslinking early to strengthen the cornea and slow progression of the disease. Corneal crosslinking is a surgical procedure which involves exposing the cornea to UV light and vitamin C. This causes the corneal collagen fibrils to form strong chemical bonds with each other, thus strengthening the structure of the cornea. The process of crosslinking occurs naturally with sun exposure and reaches its maximum effect by the time the patient reaches the age of 35. Therefore corneal crosslinking is performed less frequently in older patients. However, any patient showing progression of keratoconus can have corneal crosslinking.

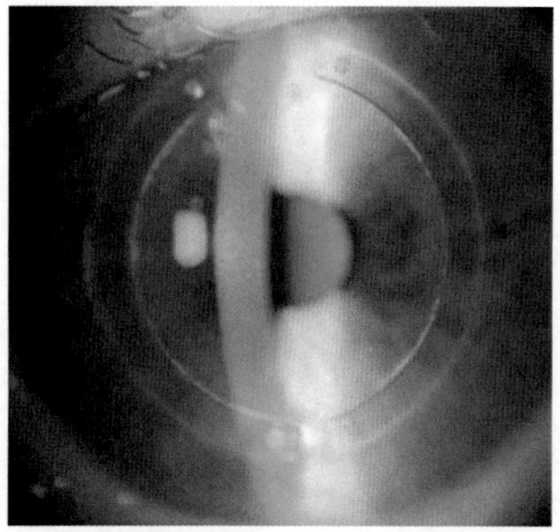
Kimberly Castillo, OD

Contact lenses should be used to correct refractive errors (soft or RGP depending on severity). Intrastromal corneal ring segments (INTACS, see left) can be used as a supportive measure for the cornea (similar to a pushup bra). Consider a corneal transplant in severe cases. The transplant can be either partial (Deep Anterior Lamellar Keratoplasty aka DALK) or full thickness (Penetrating Keratoplasty).

~~~REFRACTIVE SURGERY~~~

What to Know: Surgeons choose which refractive surgery to perform on their patients based on the patient's prescription and corneal presentation. Here is a guideline on choosing surgeries:

- Myopia less than -10.00D and astigmatism less than -4.00D
  - LASIK and SMILE are the first choice surgeries.
  - PRK is considered for patients with thin corneas or active lifestyles.
- Hyperopia less than +4.00D and astigmatism
  - Conductive Keratoplasty
- Astigmatism Only
  - Astigmatic Keratotomy
  - Limbal Relaxing Incisions / Peripheral Corneal Relaxing Incisions are performed at the same time as cataract surgery
- High Refractive Errors
  - Refractive Lens Exchange / Clear Lens Exchange is performed on patients who have presbyopia.
  - Phakic intraocular lens is preferable for patients who do not yet have presbyopia

Symptoms: Common postoperative complaints for any refractive surgery include decreased/fluctuating vision, glare, halos, difficulty with night vision, foreign body sensation, and pain.

Complications: Possible complications from any refractive surgery include residual refractive error and infection.

SURGERIES FOR MILD TO MODERATE MYOPIA AND ASTIGMATISM

LASIK and PRK can be used to treat myopia up to -10.00D and astigmatism up to -4.00D. The higher the prescription, the more severe the possible post-surgical complications.

Symptoms: In addition to the complaints listed in the purple box at the beginning of this section, common postoperative complaints for both LASIK and PRK include starbursts and ghost images.

Complications: In addition to the complications listed in the purple box at the beginning of this section, other complications for both LASIK and PRK include poor night vision, corneal haze and halos, decentration, and regression over time.

PHOTOREFRACTIVE KERATECTOMY (PRK)

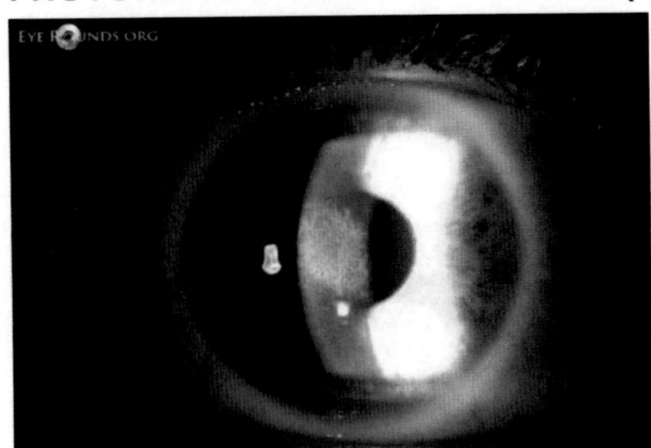

EyeRounds.org University of Iowa

What to Know: PRK is used if the patient's corneas are too thin for LASIK or if they have an active lifestyle which puts them at risk for a dislodged flap (police officers, sky divers). During PRK, the surgeon removes just the outer layer of epithelial cells with alcohol or laser and applies laser to the anterior stroma. Afterwards, the epithelium is allowed to grow back over the stroma. Given that the epithelium needs to regrow, there is a longer recovery time than with LASIK and a higher risk of infection. Another complication may include slow-healing epithelial defects. However, there is no chance of flap complications.

LASER IN-SITU KERATOMILEUSIS (LASIK)

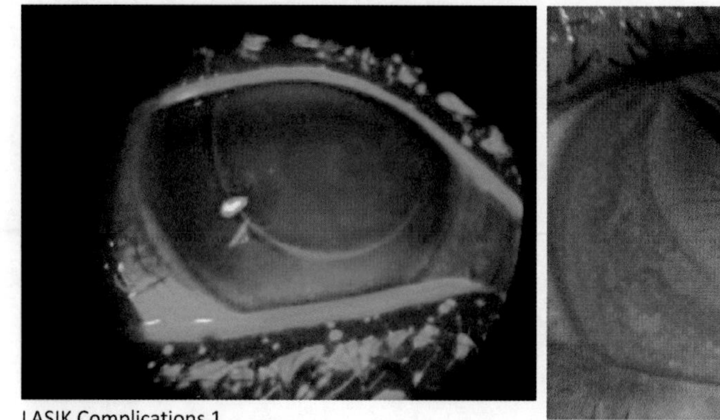
LASIK Complications 1

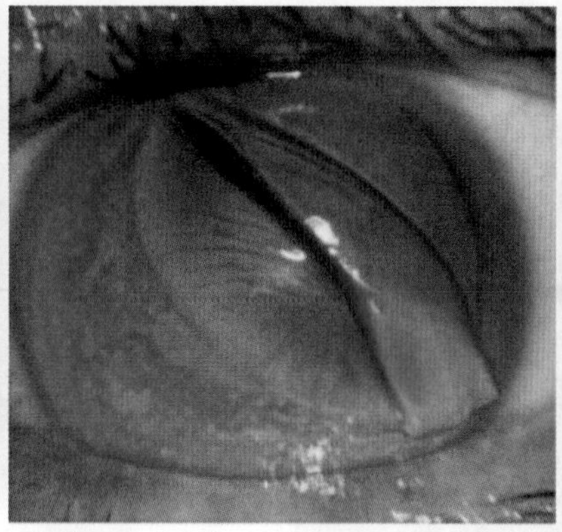
Donelson R. Manley 1

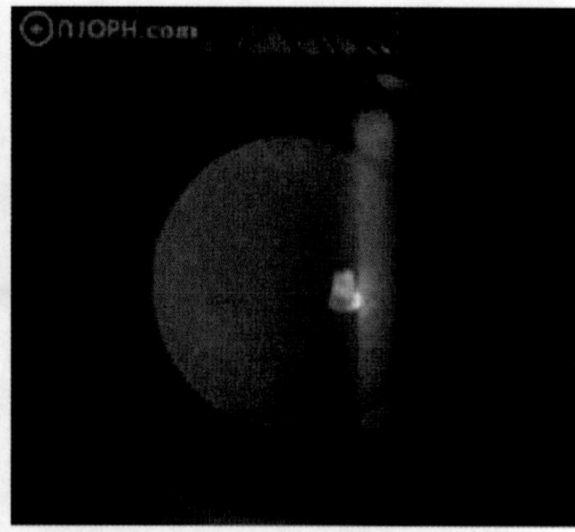

Atlas of Ophthalmology Image #9508

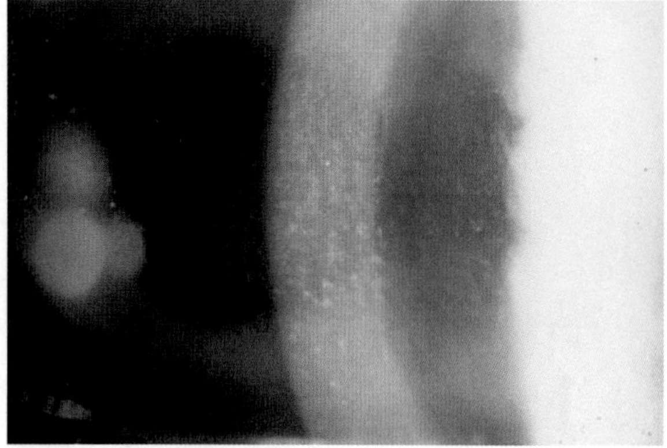
AAO 1

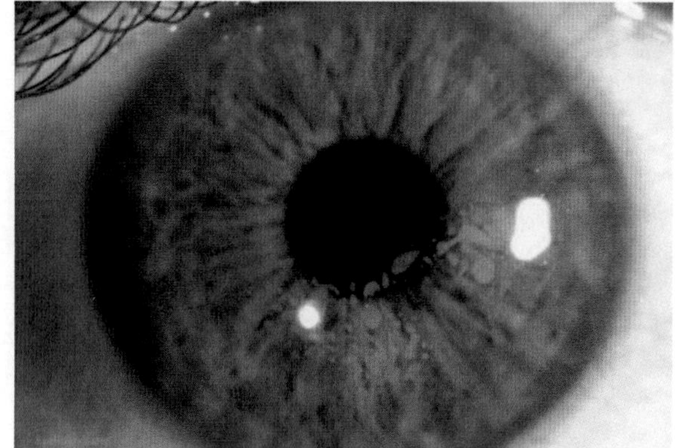
EyeRounds.org University of Iowa

What to Know: LASIK is the first choice refractive surgery for eligible patients. The surgeon uses a laser to cut a flap into the corneal stroma, then another laser is used to remove stromal tissue and flatten the cornea, and finally the flap is laid back down. When calculating if a patient's cornea is thick enough for LASIK, remember they need 250 microns of residual stroma, the flap thickness is 150 microns, and about 15 microns will be removed for each diopter treated.

Complications: Complications which are unique to LASIK include:

- Dry eye due to severing of corneal nerves. This disrupts the feedback loop which allows the brain to sense if the cornea is dry and trigger secretion of basal tears.
- LASIK Scar (top left) may be visible for many years after the surgery.
- Flap Trauma (top middle) is caused by blunt trauma to the eye and can occur many years after the surgery. Must be treated with immediate surgical flap repositioning. A flap which is lost completely must be treated as an epithelial defect.
- Flap Striae (top right) are wrinkles in the flap. Requires urgent surgery to lift and refloat flap.
- Diffuse Lamellar Keratitis aka DLK aka Sands of Sahara (bottom left): Sterile inflammation underneath the flap which occurs within a week after surgery. DLK can have serious consequences and so must be treated aggressively with topical steroids. Severe cases may need to have flap irrigation.
- Epithelial Ingrowth (bottom right) occurs when epithelial cells begin to grow underneath the flap. It originates at the edge of the flap. If severe (dense or threatening vision) then treat with epithelial debridement.
- Keratectasia (removal of too much corneal tissue leading to a weakened, distorted cornea)
- Central Toxic Keratopathy (noninflammatory opacification of the central corneal stroma following LASIK)

SURGERIES FOR MILD TO MODERATE MYOPIA ONLY

RADIAL KERATOTOMY (RK)

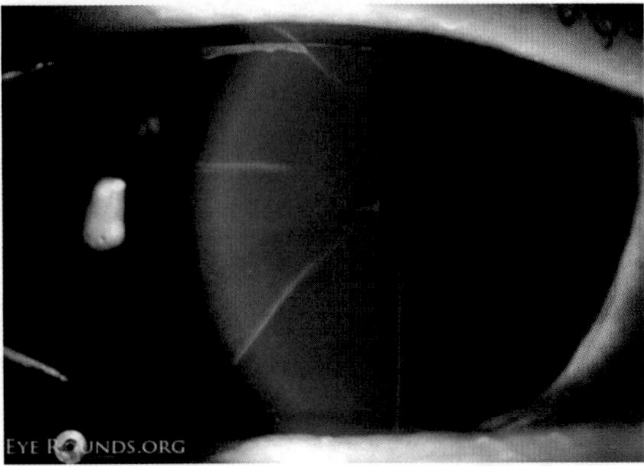

EyeRounds.org University of Iowa

What to Know: RK was historically used to treat myopia up to -10.00D. The higher the prescription, the more severe the possible post-surgical complications. A diamond blade was used to make deep, radial incisions into the stroma. These cuts are known to weaken the cornea, allowing the IOP to push on the cornea and flatten it to correct for myopia. This procedure is rarely performed anymore due to complications.

Symptoms: Postoperatively patients may complain of ghost images, starbursts, and diplopia.

Signs: Possible surgical complications include corneal scarring, perforation, regression, and progression over time (often keratoconus). Dramatic hyperopic shifts are a common complication from the cornea becoming weakened too much and allowing the IOP to over-flatten the cornea.

Treatment/Management: Patients with deformed corneas may benefit from a scleral contact lens.

SURGERIES FOR HYPEROPIA AND ASTIGMATISM

CONDUCTIVE KERATOPLASTY

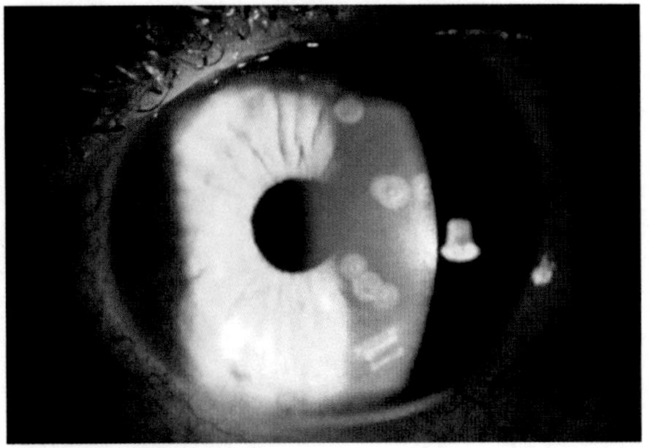

EyeRounds.org University of Iowa

What to Know: Conductive Keratoplasty steepens the central cornea by applying radiofrequency spots around the peripheral cornea. These spots shrink the collagen tissue, and the contraction steepens the central cornea.

Symptoms: See purple box at the beginning of this section.

Complications: In addition to the complications listed in the purple box at the beginning of this section, a significant complication of Conductive Keratoplasty is regression of the refractive error.

Treatment/Management: Conductive Keratoplasty can be repeated to correct regression of refractive error.

SURGERIES FOR PRESBYOPIA

INTRACORNEAL INLAYS

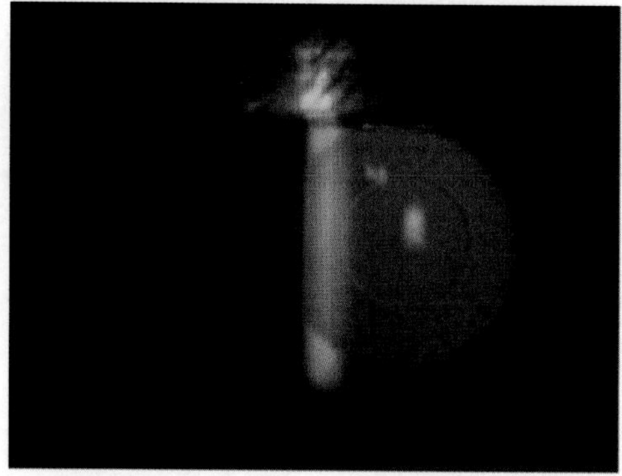

EyeWorld 1

What to Know: Similar to LASIK, a flap is created into the mid stroma, but then a contact lens implant is placed under the flap. Best used to treat hyperopia.

Symptoms/Complications: See purple box at the beginning of this section.

SURGERIES FOR ASTIGMATISM ONLY

ASTIGMATIC KERATOTOMY

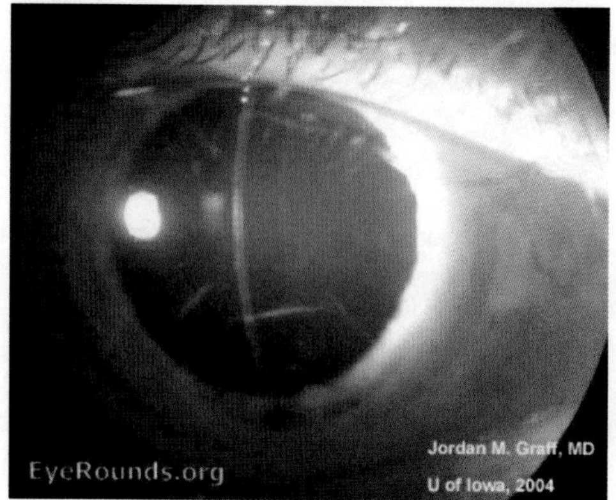

EyeRounds.org University of Iowa

What to Know: Deep incisions are made in the mid-peripheral cornea parallel to the limbus along the steep meridian which flattens it in order to correct for astigmatism. Shown as a horizontal incision in the inferior cornea in the picture above.

Symptoms/Complications: See purple box at the beginning of this section.

LIMBAL RELAXING INCISIONS / PERIPHERAL CORNEAL RELAXING INCISIONS

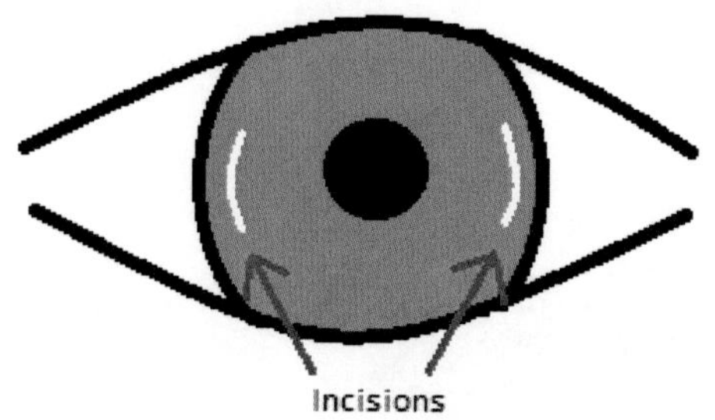

Kimberly Castillo, OD

What to Know: Limbal Relaxing Incisions are commonly performed in conjunction with cataract surgery in order to correct for astigmatism. Incisions are made in the peripheral cornea parallel to the limbus along the steep meridian to flatten it.

Symptoms: Postoperatively patients may complain of ghost images, starbursts, and diplopia.

Signs: Possible surgical complications include corneal scarring, perforation, regression, and progression over time.

SURGERIES FOR HIGH REFRACTIVE ERRORS

What to Know: The two surgeries for high refractive errors are known as the Intraocular Refractive Procedures. They can be considered for patients with myopia greater than -10D, hyperopia greater than +4.00D, or astigmatism greater than -4.00D.

REFRACTIVE LENS EXCHANGE aka CLEAR LENS EXCHANGE	PHAKIC INTRAOCULAR LENS
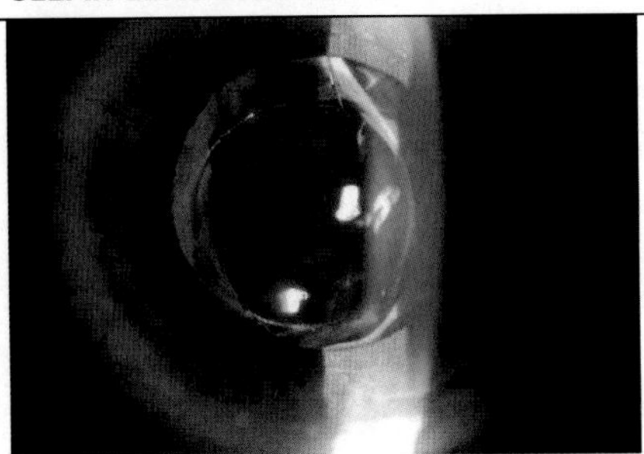 Retina Image Bank. File #7339	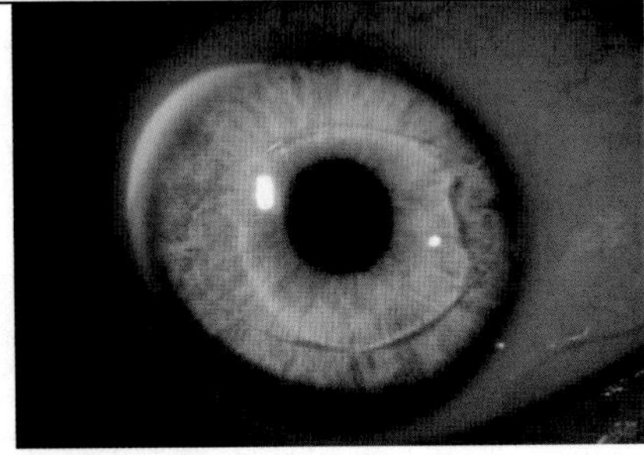 EyeRounds.org University of Iowa
A Refractive Lens Exchange is basically a cataract surgery on an eye with no cataracts. The natural lens is removed and replaced with an implant. Since the natural lens is removed, the patient loses their accommodation.	A Phakic Intraocular Lens surgery entails implanting an artificial lens in either the anterior chamber, posterior chamber, or fixed to the iris. The natural lens is left intact, thereby preserving accommodation.

Possible Complications:

Cataracts, corneal edema, cystoid macular edema, glaucoma, iris damage, posterior capsular opacification, retinal detachment, suprachoroidal hemorrhage, and retained lens material.

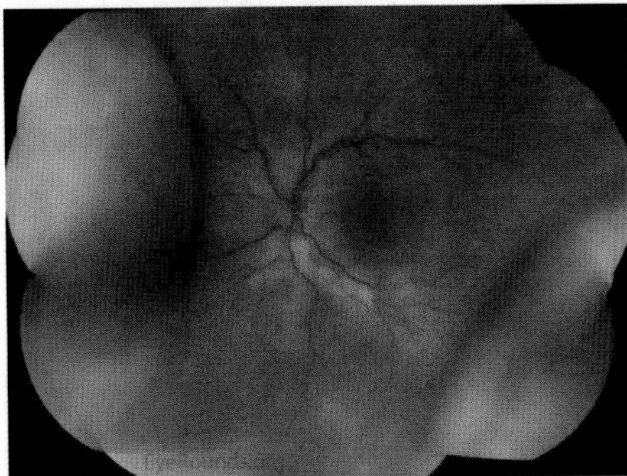

EyeRounds.org University of Iowa

Choroidal effusion (abnormal accumulation of fluid in the suprachoroidal space)

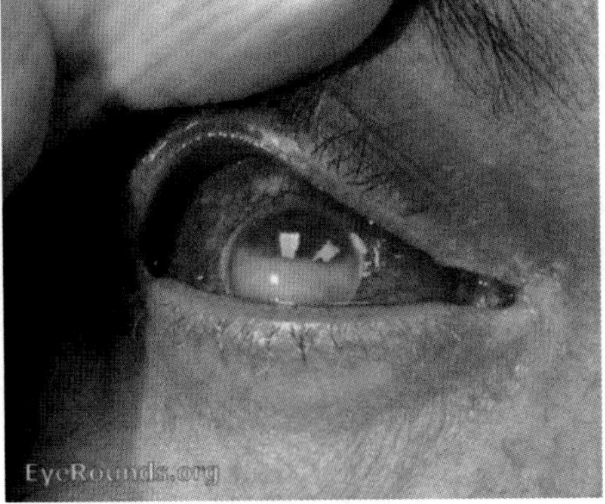

EyeRounds.org University of Iowa

Endophthalmitis (intraocular infection with inflammation seen with hypopyon)

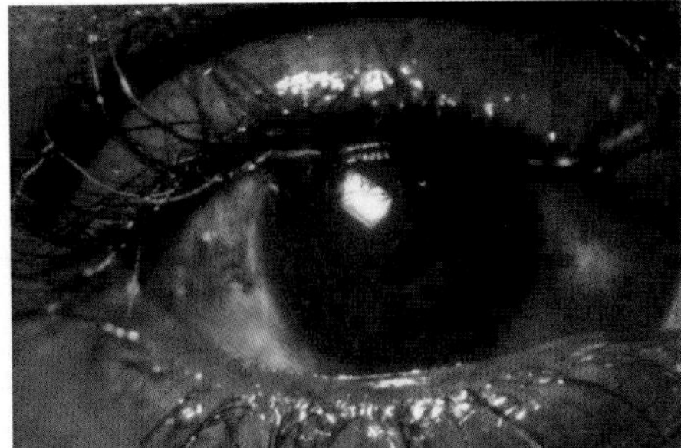

Flicker © Image 5686300673

Iridocyclitis (inflammation of the iris and the ciliary body)

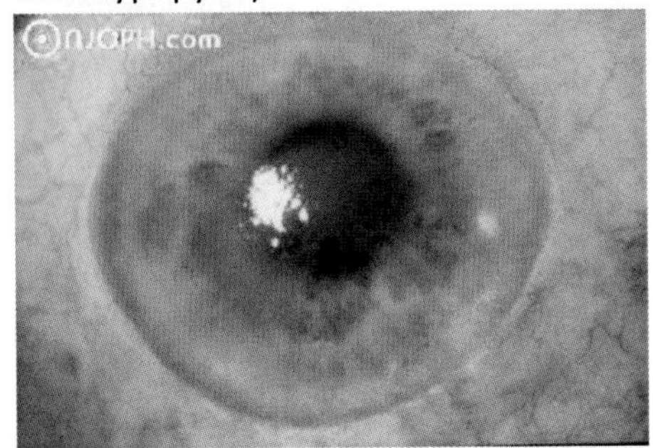

Atlas of Ophthalmology Image #4850

Pupillary Block (pupillary border seals itself off on the lens)

CHAPTER 5
OPTIC NERVE / NEURO-OPHTHALMIC PATHWAYS

The NBEO website states that 28-38 questions will be asked on Optic Nerve / Neuro-Ophthalmic Pathways. Historically they have asked about 30.6 questions, meaning this chapter covers approximately 9% of the material tested on the exam, or roughly 6 cases. This material IS included on TMOD.

~~~OPTIC NERVE~~~

NERVE EDEMA

PAPILLEDEMA

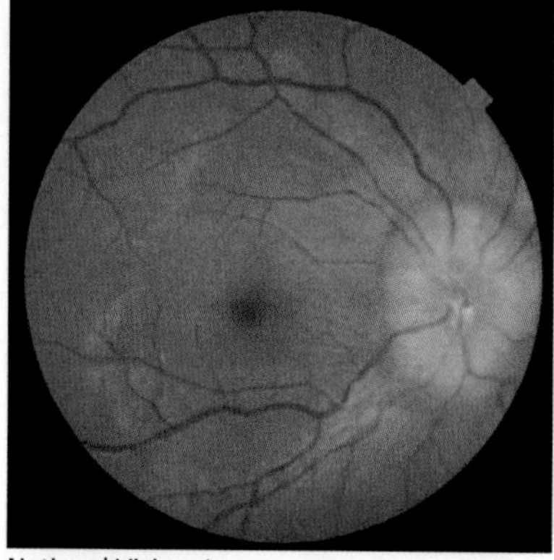

National Vision, Inc.

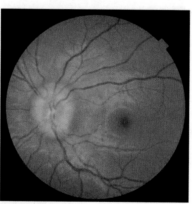

National Vision, Inc.

What to Know: Papilledema is defined by BILATERAL swollen optic nerves secondary to increased intracranial pressure (ICP). Causes of increased ICP include an intracranial mass (including hemorrhage and edema from blunt head trauma), Pseudotumor cerebri (idiopathic intracranial hypertension), inhibition of the arachnoid villi from absorbing cerebral spinal fluid, malignant hypertension, and venous sinus thrombosis. The cranium has a limited amount of space, and so anything which crowds that space causes the intracranial pressure to increase. If the ICP increases too much, then the axoplasmic flow from the optic nerve is halted or reversed. This backflow causes bilateral swollen optic nerves. Papilledema is bilateral because the ICP occurs posterior to the optic chiasm.

Symptoms: Papilledema may initially be asymptomatic. But, patients may complain of blurry vision, headache, nausea, color vision abnormalities (dyschromatopsia), transient vision disturbances, and a reduced affect.

Signs: The biggest sign is bilateral swollen optic nerves. Patients may have an elevated IOP due to increased ICP adding pressure to the back of the globe. Other signs are due to a compressed optic nerve: abnormal color vision, red cap desaturation, loss of spontaneous venous pulsation, and visual field defects including an enlarged blind spot. Retinal folds may be present due to stretching over the edema (Paton's lines).

Treatment/Management: Every case of Papilledema should be suspected as a intracranial mass until proven otherwise. MRI and CT should be performed to rule out a mass. Further testing should be performed to investigate for the underlying etiology (order CBC, fasting blood sugar, ESR, CRP, ANA, and ACE. Measure the patient's blood pressure and refer to neurology. Once identified, the underlying etiology should be treated.

PSEUDOTUMOR CEREBRI (IDIOPATHIC INTRACRANIAL HYPERTENSION)

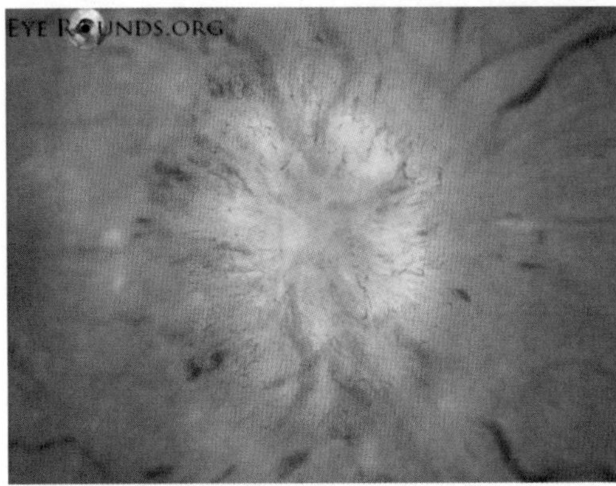

EyeRounds.org University of Iowa

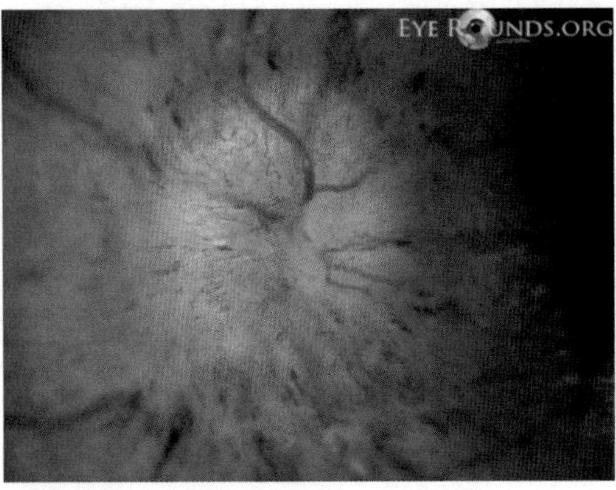

EyeRounds.org University of Iowa

What to Know: Pseudotumor Cerebri most commonly occurs in obese women of childbearing age (crudely known as fat, fertile females). It is idiopathic, as the name suggests, but associations can include Accutane, Nalidixic Acid, Oral Contraceptives, Tetracyclines, and Vitamin A.

Symptoms: Patients may complain of blurry vision, headache, nausea, color vision abnormalities (dyschromatopsia), transient vision disturbances, and a reduced affect.

Signs: There are three criteria required to make a diagnosis of Pseudotumor Cerebri:

1. Papilledema (which by definition is caused by increased ICP).
2. Normal brain MRI/CT
3. High cerebral spinal fluid pressure on lumbar puncture (>200 mmH_20 in nonobese patients, and >250 mm H_20 in obese patients).

Treatment/Management: Treatment is aimed at any possible causative factors. Patients should discontinue any known associated medication, and obese patients should lose weight. Oral acetazolamide should be used to reduce the production of cerebral spinal fluid at the choroidal plexus (although it should be avoided in patients with sulfa allergies). Patients should be followed every three weeks to three months depending on severity and response to treatment.

ARTERITIC AND NONARTERITIC ISCHEMIC OPTIC NEUROPATHY

<table>
<tr><th>Nonarteritic Ischemic Optic Neuropathy (NAION)</th><th>Arteritic Ischemic Optic Neuropathy (AION)</th></tr>
<tr><td>EyeRounds.org University of Iowa</td><td>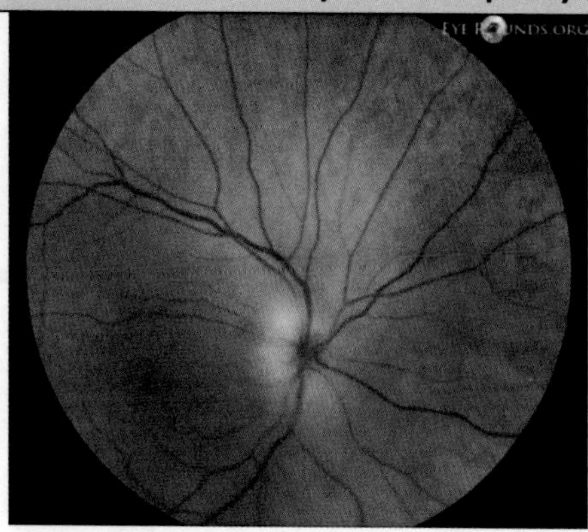
EyeRounds.org University of Iowa</td></tr>
<tr><th colspan="2">What to Know:</th></tr>
<tr><td colspan="2">Both NAION and AION cause disc edema due to ischemia from a blockage of the posterior ciliary artery. They both occur in middle aged patients over the age of 55. I remember which of these is emergent and which is not from this mnemonic: Arteritic is Alarming and NonArteritic is Not Alarming.</td></tr>
<tr><td>NAION is caused by cardiovascular disorders (HTN, DM, Hypercholesterolemia, and smoking). Drugs which cause NAION include Amiodarone, Imitrex, Vardenafil , and Viagra. A long term finding of NAION will be optic nerve pallor.</td><td>AION is caused by Giant Cell Arteritis (GCA), which is characterized by inflammation of both medium and large sized arteries. This is an emergent condition because without treatment patients may lose vision in the fellow eye within 24 hours. The most common visual field defect seen in these patients will be altitudinal.</td></tr>
<tr><th colspan="2">Symptoms:</th></tr>
<tr><td colspan="2">Patients will complain of sudden, painless, unilateral vision loss with abnormal color perception.</td></tr>
<tr><td></td><td>Patients with AION will also complain of amaurosis fugax, headache, malaise, fever, scalp tenderness over the ipsilateral temporal artery, jaw claudication, and weight loss (secondary to the jaw claudication).</td></tr>
<tr><th colspan="2">Signs:</th></tr>
<tr><td colspan="2">Signs include an unilateral swollen optic nerve with an APD, visual field defects, small optic cups (disc at risk).</td></tr>
<tr><th colspan="2">Treatment/Management:</th></tr>
<tr><td colspan="2">Patients should be immediately started on IV steroids for the inflammation. STAT tests should be ordered (CRP and ESR are the two biggies). An ESR is abnormal if it is greater than the age/2 in men and age+10/2 in women. A temporal biopsy should also be ordered, but bear in mind there may be a false negative due to skip lesions.</td></tr>
<tr><td>If testing rules out AION, then patients with NAION can discontinue the steroids and take daily aspirin as prophylaxis.</td><td></td></tr>
</table>

OPTIC NEURITIS

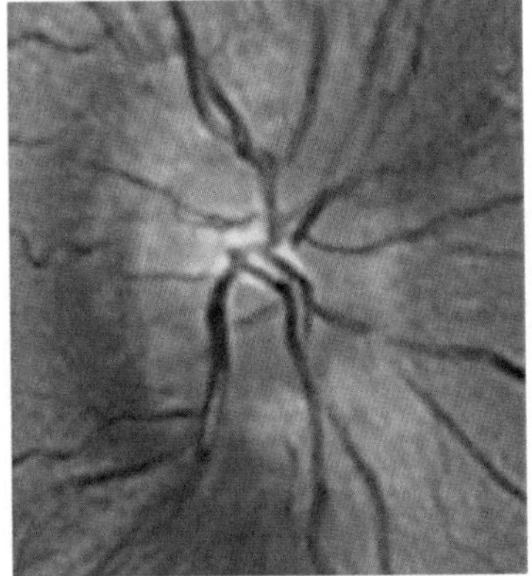
Kimberly Castillo, OD

What to Know: Optic Neuritis is inflammation of the optic nerve and is frequently the first sign of Multiple Sclerosis (MS). If not yet diagnosed, up to 50% of patients will be diagnosed with MS within 10 years of presentation with Optic Neuritis.

Symptoms: Patients will complain of loss of vision which can occur over a few hours to a couple of weeks due to swelling of the optic nerve. They will also experience pain with eye movement as the swelling may compress the EOMs.

Signs: Patients will have an unilateral swollen optic nerve with an APD, unilateral color vision and visual field defects.

In some cases the examiner may not be able to appreciate the swollen nerve because the inflammation is present behind the globe. These cases are known as Retrobulbar Optic Neuritis, and can be confirmed with a MRI of the brain and orbits.

Treatment/Management: All patients with Optic Neuritis should be referred to Neurology and get an MRI to investigate for MS. Due to its inflammatory nature, patients should initially be treated with intravenous (IV) steroids, and then transitioned to oral steroids. Visual resolution may take 1 week. Patients should be followed every 1-6 months depending on severity and response to treatment.

TOXIC OPTIC NEUROPATHY

TOXIC OPTIC NEUROPATHY

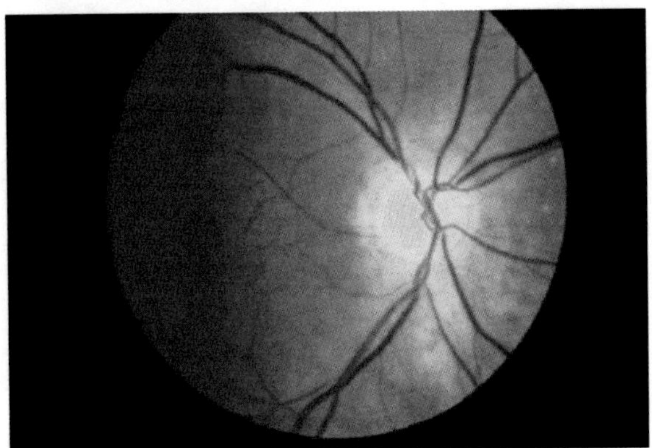
Retina Image Bank. File #15735

What to Know: The most common cause of toxic optic neuropathy is **ethambutol**. Other causes include chloramphenicol, digitalis, isoniazid, streptomycin, lead, malnutrition, and alcohol. Toxic optic neuropathy may cause centrocecal visual field defects.

Symptoms: Patients will complain of an acute onset of reduced vision (as poor as 20/400), visual field loss, and dyschromatopsia (color vision disturbance).

Signs: Patients will present with bilateral optic nerve pallor with swelling, nerve fiber layer defects, and reduced contrast sensitivity. They may have an APD if optic nerve damage is asymmetric.

Treatment/Management: Discontinue use of offending agent. Vision will spontaneously improve within 12 months, but permanent visual changes may occur.

HEREDITARY OPTIC NEUROPATHIES
None of these diseases have an effective treatment. Patients should be referred for genetic counseling and to a low vision specialist.

DOMINANT OPTIC ATROPHY (AKA KJER OR JUVENILE OPTIC ATROPHY)

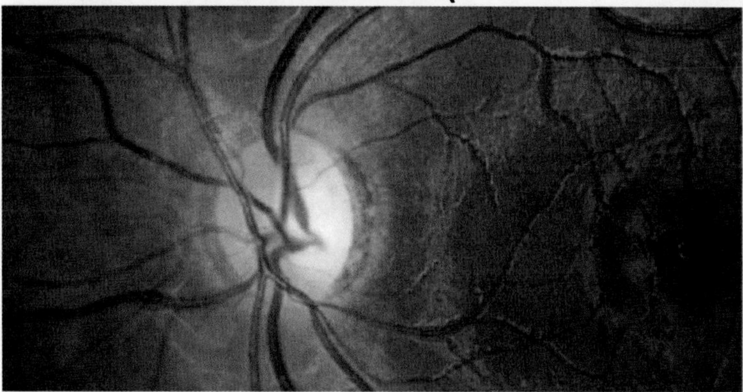

EyeRounds.org University of Iowa

What to Know: Dominant Optic Atrophy is the most common hereditary optic neuropathy. It has an autosomal dominant (AD) inheritance with an onset around the age of 5 years old.

Symptoms: Patients will complain of very slow progressive loss of vision to as poor as 20/800.

Signs: Patients will present with a wedge of temporal pallor

LEBER'S HEREDITARY OPTIC NEUROPATHY

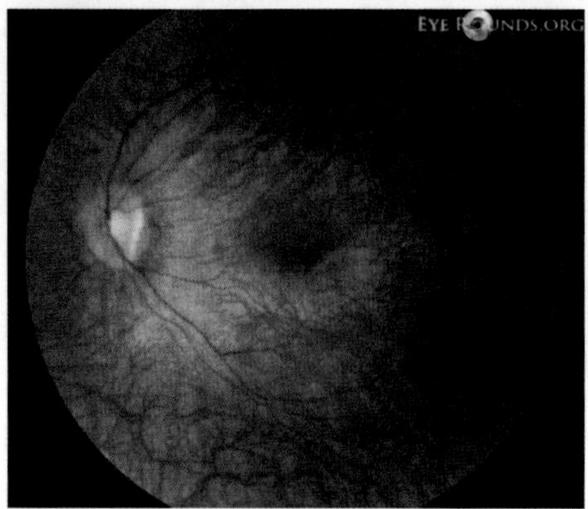

EyeRounds.org University of Iowa

What to Know: Leber's Hereditary Optic Neuropathy is transmitted from mothers to their sons via their mitochondria. Onset of visual changes occurs when the patient is between the age of 20-40.

Symptoms: Patients will complain of severe, acute, painless loss of central vision in one eye which will progress to the second eye within days to months.

Signs: Most of the signs seen with Leber's Hereditary Optic Neuropathy revolve around abnormal blood vessels. Examiners will see optic nerve hyperemia (redness) which can lead to blurring of the disc margins. Dilated capillaries with telangiectasia (engorged, spidery clumping of capillaries) will also be present. The excessive blood in the area leads to swelling of the peripapillary optic nerve fiber layer. This swelling causes optic atrophy which will persist even after the abnormal blood vessels regress.

CONGENITAL OPTIC NEUROPATHIES

OPTIC NERVE HYPOPLASIA

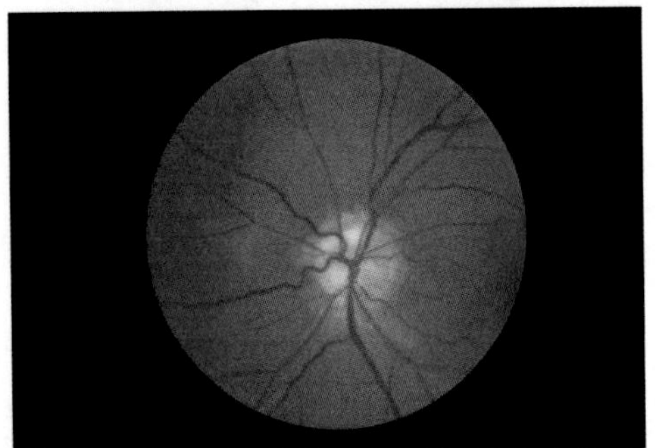

Retina Image Bank. File #12845

What to Know: Optic Nerve Hypoplasia is characterized by a reduced number of optic nerve fibers. It can be unilateral or bilateral and is seen in infants whose mothers either had an endocrine disorder (diabetes mellitus) or abused drugs (quinine, alcohol, LSD) during pregnancy.

Symptoms: Patients will complain of vision loss ranging from mild to as severe as no light perception.

Signs: Optic Nerve Hypoplasia will present with small discs viewed as the "double ring sign." In severe cases patients may have a roving eye and minimal pupillary reaction to light.

Treatment/Management: There is no effective treatment. Patients should be referred to a low vision specialist.

MORNING GLORY SYNDROME

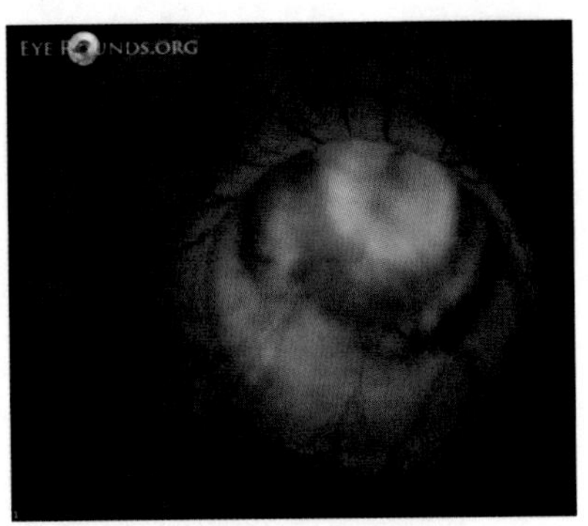

EyeRounds.org University of Iowa

What to Know: Morning Glory Syndrome is very rare. It is typically unilateral and seen in females who have midline facial defects and forebrain conditions.

Symptoms: Patients will complain of severe loss of vision in the afflicted eye(s).

Signs: Morning Glory Syndrome will present as an enlarged funnel shaped optic nerve with overlying glial tissue. Blood vessels leave the nerve in a spoke-like pattern, and the nerve is surrounded by elevated pigment. Patients may develop a secondary serous retinal detachment. Nystagmus and amblyopia may also be present.

Treatment/Management: No effective treatment. Patients should be referred to a low vision specialist.

OPTIC NERVE DRUSEN

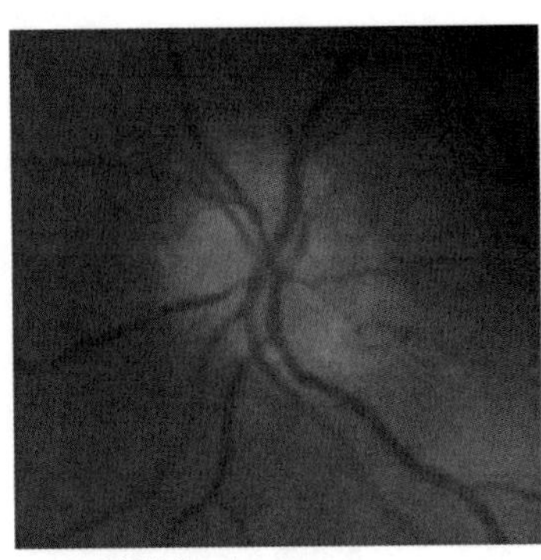

National Vision, Inc.

What to Know: Optic Nerve Drusen is a congenital condition in which hyaline-like material is buried in the nerve fiber layer surrounding the optic nerve.

Symptoms: Patients will be asymptomatic although they may have an enlarged blind spot.

Signs: Optic Nerve Drusen will look like a swollen disc with blurred margins, similar to optic neuritis. An MRI or B-scan needs to be performed to differentiate the two. In the case of Optic Nerve Drusen, the hyaline material may calcify with time and look like refractile clumps.

Treatment/Management: No treatment is necessary once optic nerve edema has been ruled out.

OPTIC NERVE PIT

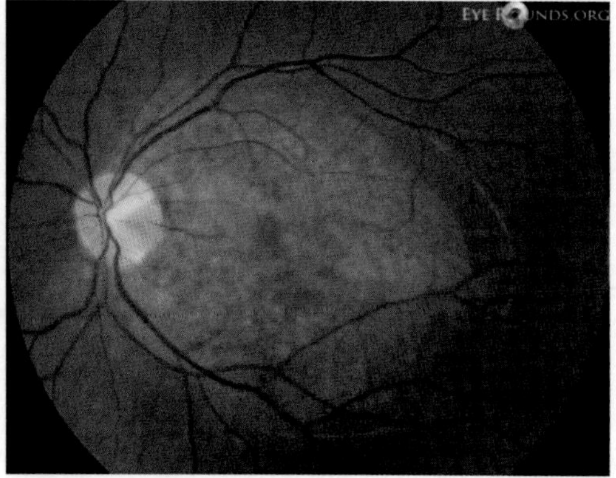

EyeRounds.org University of Iowa

<u>Symptoms:</u> Patients will have no complaints (asymptomatic) unless a serous macular detachment forms.

<u>Signs:</u> An Optic Nerve Pit presents as a **temporal** grey-white depression of the optic nerve which can range from 0.1-0.7 DD in size. It can lead to a serous retinal detachment which can extend from the pit to the macula.

<u>Treatment/Management:</u> Asymptomatic Optic Nerve Pits can be monitored annually. Pits presenting with a serous **retinal** detachment can be initially observed. However, if the pit presents with a serous **macular** detachment, it should be treated with laser photocoagulation (cautery of retinal blood vessels with a laser) and monitored on a monthly interval.

TUMORS

OPTIC NERVE GLIOMA

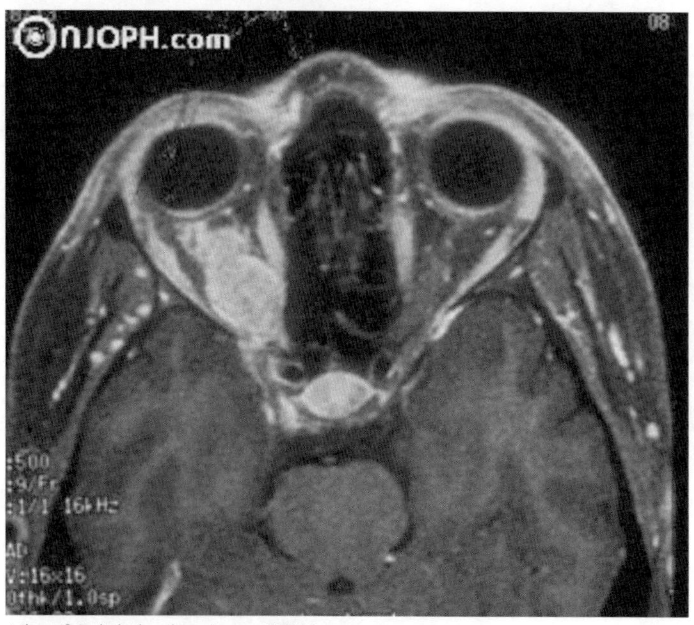

Atlas of Ophthalmology Image #6303

<u>What to Know:</u> There are two types of Optic Nerve Glioma:

1. Glioblastoma Multiforme: Rare malignant form found in adults. It leads to blindness within months and death within a year.
2. Juvenile Pilocytic Astrocytoma: Most common intrinsic neoplasm of the optic nerve typically diagnosed by the time the patient has reached the age of 6. This is frequently associated with Neurofibromatosis Type 1.

<u>Symptoms:</u> Patients will complain of progressive unilateral vision loss with painless proptosis.

<u>Signs:</u> Patients will present with proptosis, APD, disc edema, and enlargement of the optic nerve on CT scan.

<u>Treatment/Management:</u> If the tumor is stable with no vision changes and no cosmetic disturbance, it can be monitored. Otherwise, the tumor needs to be removed via surgical excision, or radiotherapy (use of radiation prior to surgery to reduce the size of the tumor) combined with chemotherapy.

OPTIC DISC MELANOCYTOMA

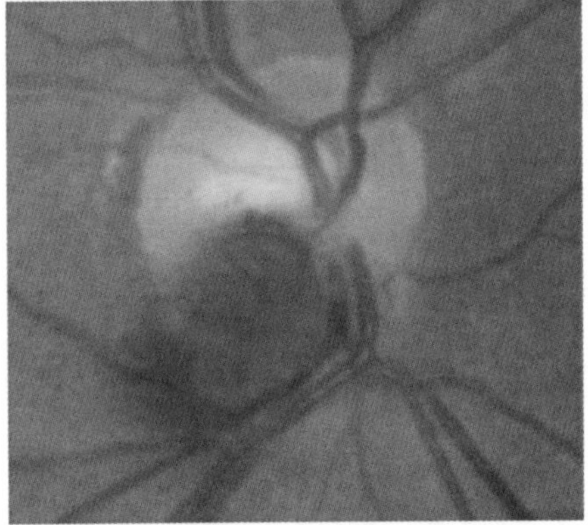

National Vision, Inc.

What to Know: An Optic Disc Melanocytoma is a rare benign neoplasm/tumor usually seen in darkly pigmented 50 year old patients. In extremely rare cases, it may metastasize.

Symptoms: Patients usually have no complaints (asymptomatic).

Signs: An Optic Disc Melanocytoma is a jet-black tumor with fuzzy edges found adjacent to the optic nerve. It may overlap onto the optic disc, and it may appear flat or slightly elevated.

Treatment/Management: Treatment is only necessary if metastasis occurs, then refer to oncologist for treatment of the malignant tumor.

MENINGIOMA

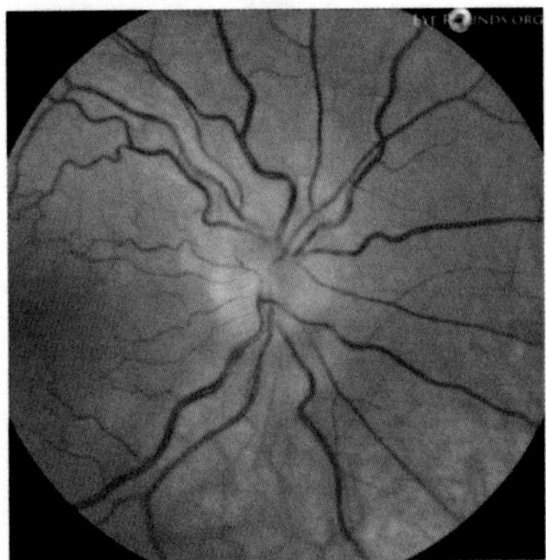

EyeRounds.org University of Iowa

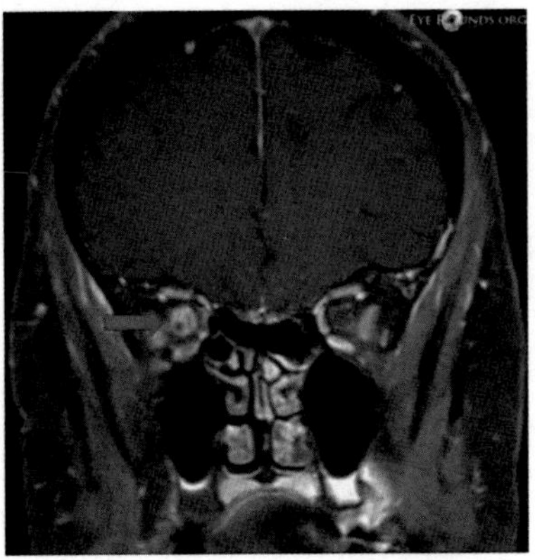

EyeRounds.org University of Iowa

What to Know: Meningiomas are typically seen in middle aged women. They are rare tumors of the optic nerve meninges or optic nerve sheath tissue which are usually benign, but can be malignant.

Symptoms: Patients may complain of progressive unilateral vision loss with painless proptosis and color vision defects.

Signs: Patients may present with an APD, optic nerve edema followed by atrophy, optociliary shunt vessels, and angiomas. The tumor may compress the globe and cause EOM restriction, increased IOP, and metamorphopsia.

Treatment/Management: Treat IOP if increased. Angiomas can be treated with laser photocoagulation (cautery of retinal blood vessels with a laser). Malignant tumors can be treated with radiation, chemotherapy, or surgical excision.

PITUITARY GLAND TUMOR

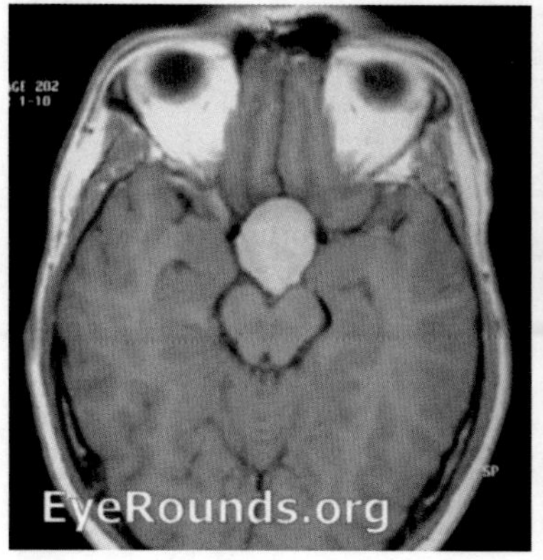

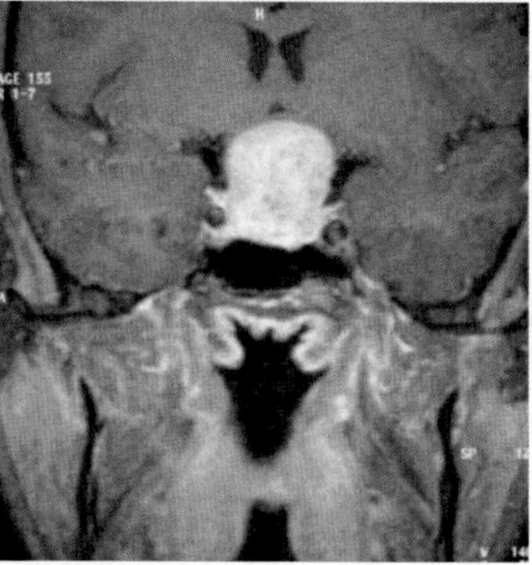

Eyerounds.org University of Iowa

What to Know: The pituitary gland is located inferiorly to the Cavernous Sinus and a tumor at this location will compress the optic nerve at the optic chiasm.

Symptoms: Patients may have no complaints or have reduced vision, headaches, or color vision/visual field defects. They may also have a reduced libido, malaise, or infertility.

Signs: Patients will present with a bitemporal hemianopia on visual fields, optic atrophy, and an APD.

Treatment/Management: Refer to a neurosurgeon for treatment of the tumor with surgery, bromocriptine, radiation, or hormone replacement therapy. A Pituitary apoplexy should be treated with systemic steroids and surgical decompression. Usually these patients have a good prognosis.

~~~NEURO-OPHTHALMIC PATHWAYS~~~

VISUAL PATHWAY LESIONS

What to Know: Visual Pathway Lesions are typically caused either by vascular disorders or tumors (neoplastic). Be sure you know this diagram and what visual field defects are caused by which lesions. Remember that as the lesion moves posteriorly, the visual field defect becomes more homonymous and congruent. Here are some extra bits of testable information to know:

- (B) A Bitemporal Hemianopsia is typically caused a Pituitary Gland Tumor.
- (C) For a Junctional Scotoma, the lesion is located ipsilateral to the central visual field defect and the superior temporal quadrant defect is located on the contralateral side to the lesion.
- (E and F) Use the mnemonic PITS to remember the location of this lesion. A Parietal lobe lesion will cause an Inferior quadrantanopia, while a Temporal lobe lesion will cause a Superior quadrantanopia. Parietal = Inferior, Temporal = Superior.
- (G) A Contralateral Homonymous Hemianopia is usually caused by either a stroke or a tumor:
    - A stroke in this area is caused by a Posterior Cerebral Artery Occlusion. Macular sparing typically occurs because there is a dual blood supply to this region of the brain and usually both sides of the dual blood supply will not be involved in the stroke; therefore, the macula for both eyes will still be intact.
    - Tumors can also cause a Contralateral Homonymous Hemianopia by compressing the Posterior Cerebral Artery. If the tumor is located on either the right or left side, then macular sparing will occur. If the tumor is centered such that it is compressing both the right and left portions of the Posterior Cerebral Artery, then there will be no macular sparing.

Symptoms: Onset may be gradual or acute depending on if the causative factor is a tumor (gradual) or stroke (acute). Therefore, the patient may or may not notice visual field loss.

Signs: Patients will present with a visual field defect with possible reduced acuity and other neurological defects (reduced affect).

Treatment/Management: First check visual fields, then refer to a PCP or neurologist for a CT or MRI. A trip to the ER may be necessary if the patient is experiencing severe symptoms.

Acute vs. Chronic Cranial Nerve Palsies will present differently. Chronic Palsies will present with a spread of comitance (which can be identified with cover test in 9 positions of gaze), increased vertical ranges, and evidence of a space occupying lesion on MRI. Acute Palsies will present with evidence of acute trauma on MRI, and none of the other signs seen in chronic cases.

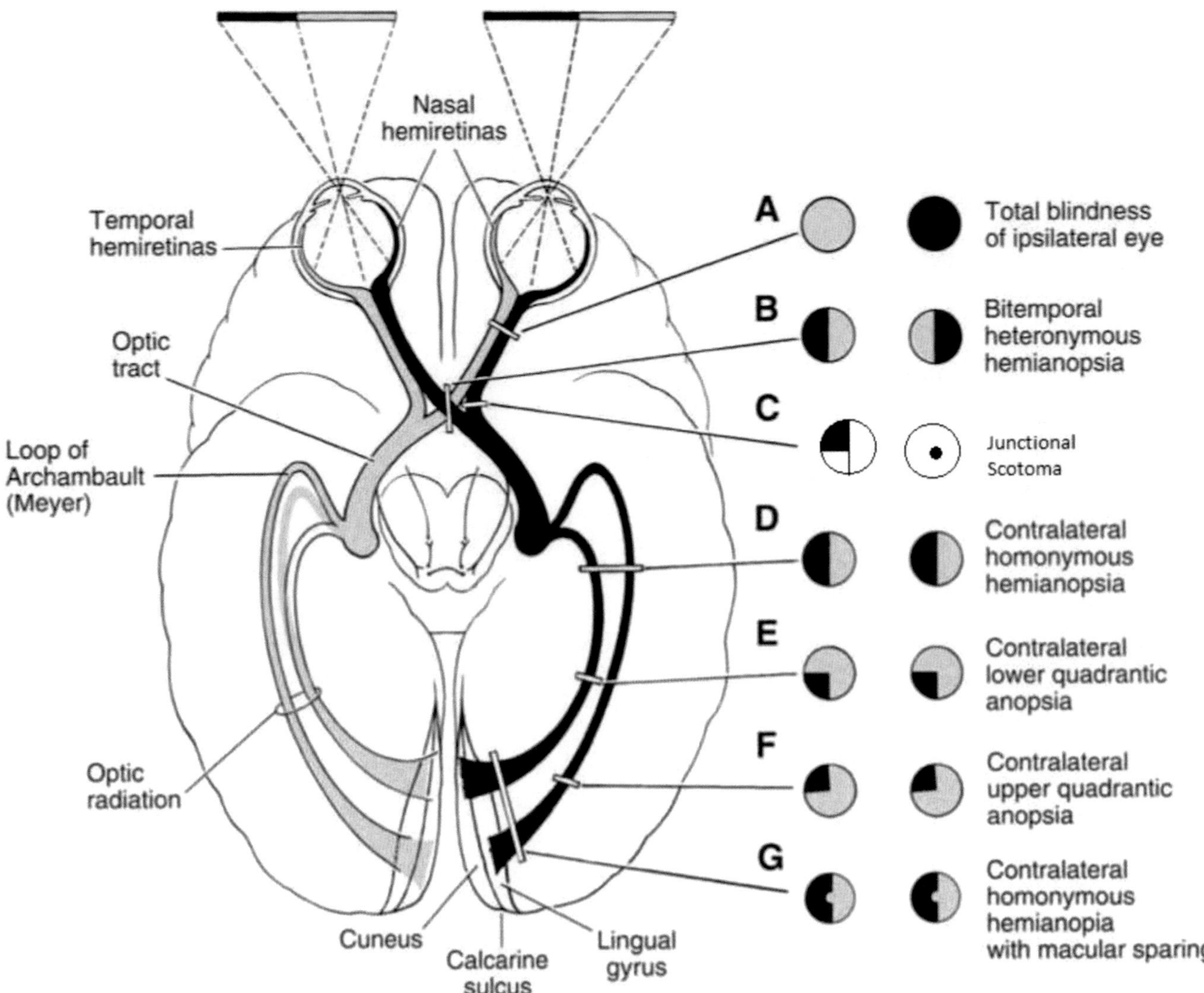

Aibolita 1

The CN II afferent pupillary and saccadic pathway destinations can be remembered with this mnemonic:

- Pupil = Pretectal nucleus
- Saccades = Superior colliculus

The symptoms associated with lesions in Wernicke's or Broca's areas (Aphasias) can be remembered with this mnemonic:

- Wernicke's = Wordy speech/difficulty understanding speech.
- Broca's = Broken speech

The arrangement of the fibers in the optic tract are as follows:

- Superior fibers : Medial
- Inferior fibers : Lateral
- Macular fibers are in the middle

CORTICAL BLINDNESS

What to Know: Cortical Blindness is sudden, bilateral, complete blindness due to extensive damage to the occipital lobe. It can be congenital, caused by cerebrovascular accident (a stroke with bilateral cerebral artery blockage), or **occur within a day of cardiac surgery**.

Symptoms: Patients will complain of complete, sudden, bilateral blindness with possible visual hallucinations. Patients may deny vision loss, which is known as Anton's Syndrome.

Signs: Eye exam will be normal aside for bilateral no light perception. The pupillary light reflex will be present because the occipital lobe is not responsible for the pupillary response. Patients may be able to perceive moving but not stationary objects (Riddoch phenomenon) and maintain the ability to navigate around objects (blind sight).

Treatment/Management: Loss of vision is usually permanent and there is no treatment available. The underlying etiology should be treated.

VETEBROBASILAR INSUFFICIENCY (VERTEBROBASILAR ATHEROTHROMBOTIC DISEASE)

What To Know: Vertebrobasilar Insufficiency occurs when the Vertebrobasilar arterial blood supply to the brain becomes blocked due to a thrombus, emboli, hypertension, or anything which can cause a hypercoagulable state.

Symptoms: Patients may complain of flashes of light (photopsia), bilateral transient visual loss (amaurosis fugax), diplopia, and nystagmus. Systemic symptoms include vertigo (critical complaint), unilateral weakness and sensory loss, and a history of syncope (drop attacks).

Signs: Typically there are no accompanying signs given that this is occurring in the blood vessels supporting the brain. Patients may have homonymous visual field defects due to the issue occurring in the occipital lobe.

Treatment/Management: Treatment is aimed at controlling the hypercoagulable state with prophylactic use of daily aspirin.

HEADACHES

Migraine Headache

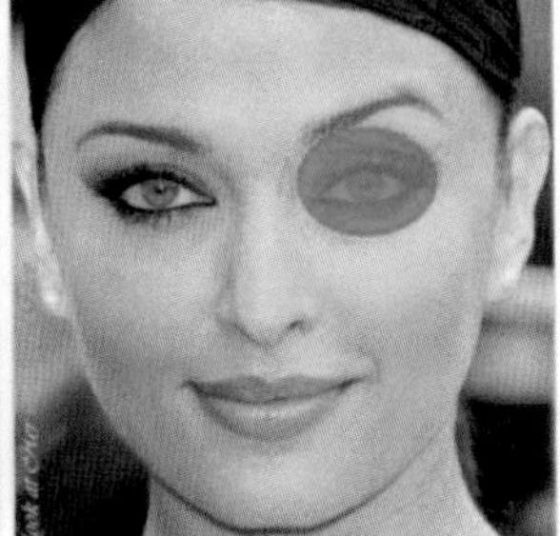
Cluster Headache

Tension/Ocular Headache

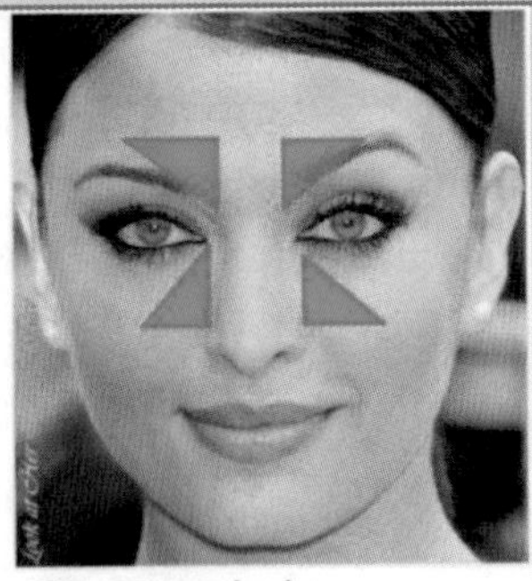
Sinus Headache

Kimberly Castillo, OD

MIGRAINE

Kimberly Castillo, OD

What to Know: Migraines typically last between 4-72 hours. They can occur at any age, they afflict women more than men, and are associated with triggers (stress, foods, alcohol, dehydration, sleep changes, obnoxious noises or lights, fatigue, head trauma, hormone changes, weather changes, etc.). There are three types:

1. Migraine Without Aura (Common Migraine): MOST common type of migraine (80%), which is why they are called Common Migraines. As the name suggests, these are migraines without an aura.
2. Migraine With Aura (Classic Migraine): As the name suggests, these migraines present with an aura that will typically last for less than one hour. The aura typically precedes the headache and presents with visual disruption (spreading scotoma, tunnel vision, blur, altitudinal defect, bright color distortion, squiggly/zig zag lines) which may predominantly affect one side of the patient's visual field.
3. Ocular Migraine: A migraine which presents with an aura without any headache. The aura will last less than an hour and will be characterized by visual disruptions (spreading scotoma, tunnel vision, blur, altitudinal defect, bright color distortion, squiggly/zig zag lines) which may predominantly affect one side of the patient's visual field.

Symptoms: Typically about 30 minutes before onset of the headache, a migraine will present with a prodrome which can include aura (for Migraines With Aura), mood fluctuations, and gastrointestinal upset. Patients will complain of a deep, throbbing headache of the frontal lobe. They will be unilateral and always on the same side for each attack. Patients may have light and/or sound sensitivity as well as nausea which can be severe enough to lead to vomiting. **These patients will want to lie down in a dark, quiet room.**

Signs: No signs will be present.

Treatment/Management: Patients should have an MRI or CT scan to rule out brain tumors. They should avoid triggers. During an attack they will benefit from using NSAIDs, triptans (rizatriptan, sumatriptan), or opioids (codeine, oxycodone). Patients may find immediate relief from resting in a dark, quiet room. FL41 (magenta) tints can be an option to assist with alleviating symptoms as well.

CLUSTER HEADACHE

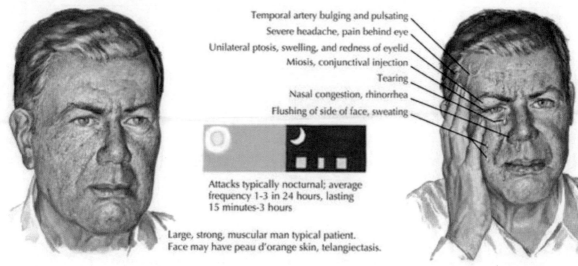

Temporal artery bulging and pulsating
Severe headache, pain behind eye
Unilateral ptosis, swelling, and redness of eyelid
Miosis, conjunctival injection
Tearing
Nasal congestion, rhinorrhea
Flushing of side of face, sweating

Attacks typically nocturnal; average frequency 1-3 in 24 hours, lasting 15 minutes-3 hours

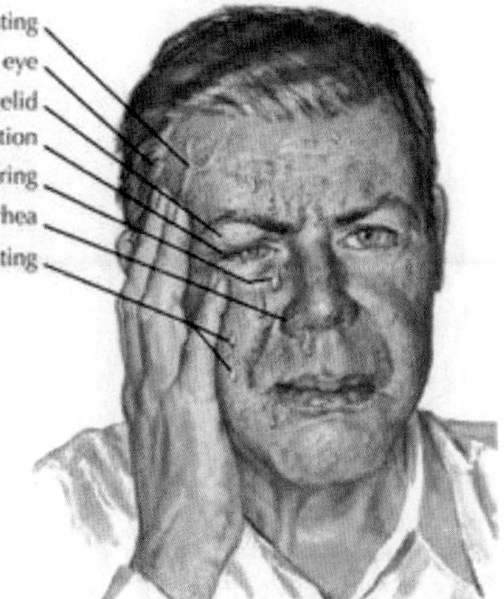

Large, strong, muscular man typical patient. Face may have peau d'orange skin, telangiectasis.

Neupsy Key 1

<u>What to Know:</u> Cluster headaches typically occur in men in their 40s – 50s and may be triggered by alcohol or smoking.

<u>Symptoms:</u> Patients may complain of an excruciating unilateral stabbing headache which is located temporally. **They will become agitated and be unable to hold still.** The attack will last for 10-120 minutes and the patient may have several attacks in a 24-hour period, frequently waking patients up in the middle of the night (around 2:00 am). This will last for several weeks, and then the patient will be headache free for several years until the cycle repeats.

<u>Signs:</u> Patients present with a bulging temporal artery with ipsilateral facial flush, conjunctival injection, epiphora, and rhinorrhea. They may also have Horner's Syndrome (ptosis, miosis, anhydrosis), and the ptosis may not resolve.

<u>Treatment/Management:</u> Patients should have an MRI or CT scan to rule out brain tumors. They should avoid triggers. During an attack they will benefit from an oxygen face mask. Medical therapy may include the triptans (rizatriptan, sumatriptan), calcium channel blockers, lithium, ergotamine, methysergide, oral steroids, NSAIDs. amitriptyline, clonidine, pizotifen, baby aspirin, or codeine.

TENSION/OCULAR HEADACHE

<u>Symptoms:</u> Patients who suffer for Ocular Headaches will complain of a headache which is located as a band across the front of their forehead. It will be worse at the end of the day or after reading or other near activities. These patients will experience relief from the headache when they discontinue the near activity.

<u>Treatment/Management:</u> An Ocular Headache usually occurs when a patient is over-minused, and uncorrected hyperopes and presbyopes. Therefore, these patients will experience relief from the headaches with an updated glasses or contact prescription. The pain from an Ocular Headache can be managed with acetaminophen or an NSAID.

SINUS HEADACHES

What to Know: Sinus headaches occur when the patient's sinuses are either inflamed or congested. Causes may include allergy or a cold.

Symptoms: Patients will complain of a headache located under their cheek bones and/or between their eyebrows, or where their sinuses are located. The location of the headache may move when the patient changes positions.

Treatment/Management: Treatment is aimed at resolving the underlying cause. Allergies should be treated with an oral or nasal antihistamine. The cold should be treated with a nasal rinse, humidifier, hot tea, decongestant, etc. The pain from a Sinus Headache can be managed with acetaminophen or an NSAID.

PUPILS
As you know, pupils are evaluated in both light and dark. You know if the problem is due to a constricted pupil or a dilated pupil based on if the anisocoria is greater in the light or dark. For example, if the anisocoria is greater in the light, this is due to an abnormally dilated pupil. Since the abnormally dilated pupil does not constrict properly in the light and the normal pupil does, there is a greater anisocoria in the light.
Below is a summary of pupils – Abnormal pupil is small (greater anisocoria in dark): • Argyll Robertson Pupil • Horner's Syndrome Abnormal pupil is large (greater anisocoria in light): • Adie's Tonic Pupil • CN3 Palsy (see Chapter 9)

ARGYLL ROBERTSON PUPIL

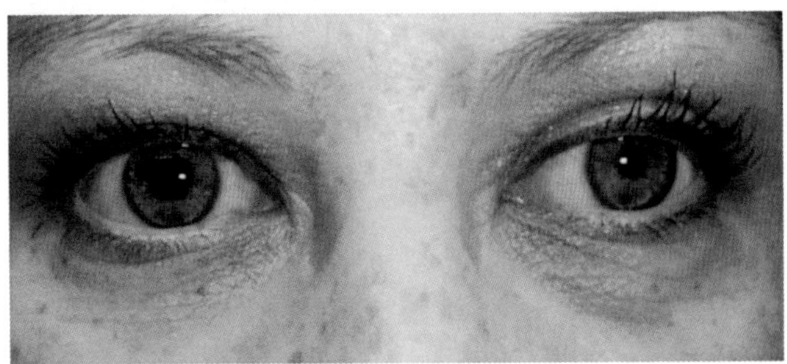
Optometry Times 1

Etsy 1

Signs: An Argyll Robertson Pupil is an abnormally constricted pupil with its accommodative response still present "light-near dissociation."

What to Know: Argyll Robertson Pupils are caused by damage to the Edinger-Westphal nucleus due to Syphilis, which I remember by thinking of sexy argyle socks.

Symptoms: Patients may have no complaints (asymptomatic).

Treatment/Management: Order a VDRL and FTA-ABS to confirm the Syphilis diagnosis. Treatment is aimed at the causative Syphilis with intravenous (IV) penicillin followed by intramuscular (IM) penicillin (or tetracycline in patients with penicillin allergy). The pupil will resolve with Syphilis treatment.

HORNER'S SYNDROME

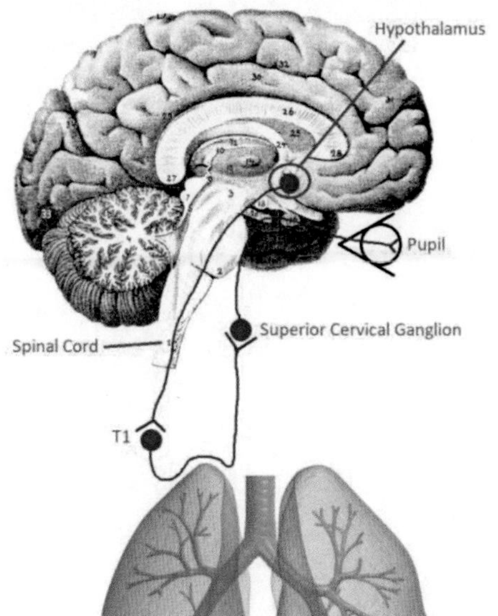

Kimberly Castillo, OD

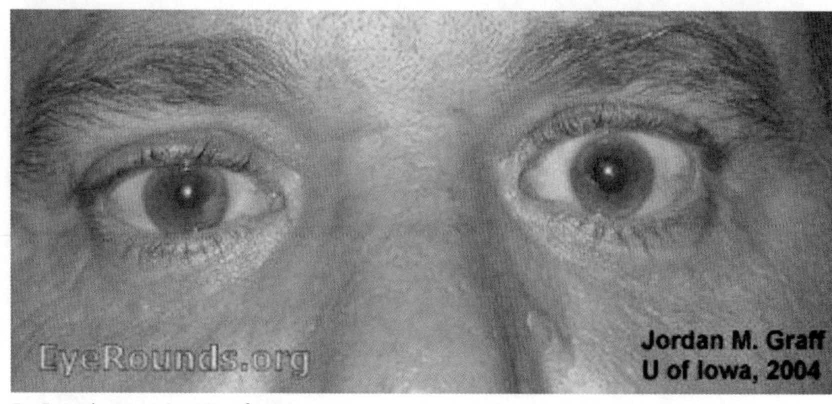

EyeRounds.org University of Iowa

Signs: Horner's Syndrome is defined by the triad of unilateral ptosis (of the superior and inferior lids), miosis, and anhydrosis (inability to sweat, typically seen in preganglionic lesions). This entire triad shows that the sympathetic system is crippled in Horner's Syndrome, allowing the parasympathetic system to overact.

What to Know: Horner's Syndrome is caused by a lesion along the sympathetic pathway (since the sympathetic system is responsible for pupil dilation, this is why the pupil is constricted):

- First Order Neuron (Preganglionic): Hypothalamus → Spinal Cord
  - Caused by a stroke.
- Second Order Neuron (Preganglionic): Spinal Cord → Superior Cervical Ganglion
  - Caused by a Pancoast 's Tumor at the apex of the lung.
- Third Order Neuron (Postganglionic): Superior Cervical Ganglion → Eye and sweat glands
  - Caused by a vascular disorder (migraine, carotid-cavernous fistula)

The examiner can determine if the lesion is pre or post-ganglionic with pharmacological testing. A diagnosis of Horner's Syndrome can be confirmed with application of Apraclonidine because it dilates any Horner's Pupil. A pre vs. post-ganglionic pupil can be differentiated by applying hydroxyamphetamine on another day because it will dilate a pre-ganglionic pupil. Here's a brief summary of pharmacologic testing for Horner's Pupils:

- Apraclonidine dilates any Horner's Pupil.
- Hydroxyamphetamine dilates pre-ganglionic Horner's Pupils.

A Complete Blood Counts (CBC) can also be used to help determine the cause of the Horner's Pupil.

Symptoms: Patients may be asymptomatic or complain of blurry vision and unilateral droopy eyelids.

Treatment/Management: The underlying etiology must be determined and then managed appropriately. Upneeq gtts can be used cosmetically to raise the eyelids. Ptosis surgery may be indicated if visual fields are affected.

ADIE'S TONIC PUPIL

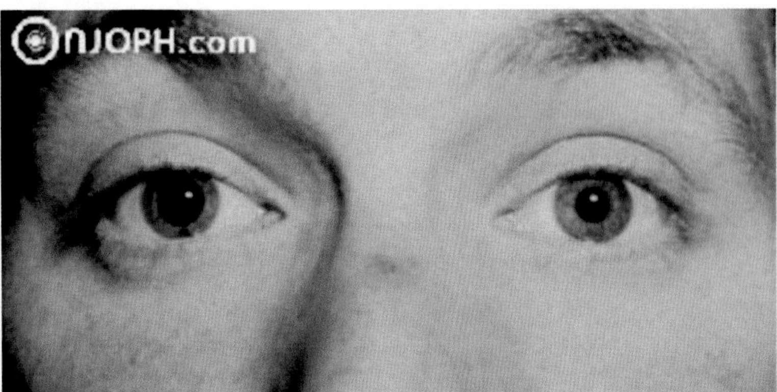

Atlas of Ophthalmology Image #5831

Signs: An Adie's Tonic Pupil is defined as a dilated pupil with an acute onset. The afflicted pupil will have a poor light response and poor accommodation. Patients may also have poor deep tendon reflexes; which I remember by using Tonic to remind me of Tendons. In chronic cases, the abnormal pupil will become constricted with poor light response due to the pupil essentially over compensating for the problem.

What to Know: Adie's Tonic Pupil occurs in the ciliary ganglion, and is most commonly seen in women between 20-40 years old. An Adie's Tonic Pupil is severely deprived of acetylcholine, which is an agent of the parasympathetic system. Given that the parasympathetic system is responsible for pupil constriction, it makes sense that a pupil that is deprived of acetylcholine will be dilated. This is why application of Pilocarpine 0.1% will cause pupil constriction. The Adie's Tonic Pupil is so desperate for acetylcholine, it becomes super sensitive to a cholinergic stimulation and constricts to a diluted concentration of Pilocarpine which would not constrict a normal pupil. An Adie's Tonic Pupil may be idiopathic or caused by surgery, orbital trauma, or a herpes zoster infection.

It is possible for a patient to have a pharmacological cause of an unilateral dilated pupil due to medications such as scopolamine (which is used to treat motion sickness), as well as others. If a pharmacological etiology is suspected, then instill 1% pilocarpine into the dilated eye. If the pupil does not constrict, then the pharmacological etiology is confirmed.

Symptoms: Patients may be asymptomatic or have complaints of blur at near and photophobia.

Treatment/Management: No treatment is necessary for an Adie's Tonic Pupil because it will independently resolve without treatment over the course of several months. If desired, the loss of accommodation can be treated with either a near add or 0.125% Pilocarpine BID-QID. Pilocarpine may also aid in cosmesis as the patients waits for the Adie's Tonic Pupil to resolve.

NON-ORGANIC VISION LOSS

MALINGERING	HYSTERIA / PSYCHOGENIC VISUAL LOSS
What to Know: A patient who is Malingering is a healthy individual who is purposefully pretending to have an ocular condition, usually for financial gain. They will typically be aggressive and combative.	**What to Know:** A patient with Hysteria genuinely believes they have an ocular condition when they actually do not. They will typically be cooperative and indifferent.

Remember that up to 20% of patients who you think are either Malingering or have Hysteria do in fact have an organic condition.

Symptoms: Patients will complain of blur which may be monocular or binocular and range from 20/20 to NLP. They may also complain of metamorphopsia, oscillopsia, and/or diplopia.

Signs: When Malingering or Hysteria is suspected, rely on objective rather than subjective testing:

- Visual Acuity: Present the patient with an isolated 20/10 line. When the patient is unable to read it, act surprised and concerned, and then present them with the 20/15 line. Continue with the charade until the patient is able to read a line.
    - Alternatively, move the patient from 20 to 10 feet away from the acuity chart. Their acuity should now be twice as good as before.
    - Normal near acuities indicate myopia or non-organic vision loss.
- Pupils: A pupil with NLP or "dimmed vision" will have a poor light response and/or an APD.
- Visual Field Testing: Visual Field results will be atypical.
- Worth Four-Dot: If a patient can see all four dots, then their vision is better than hand motion. This can also help differentiate whether or not a patient has diplopia/suppression.
- OKN: If a patient's optokinetic response is intact, then their vision is better than count fingers. It can be tested both unilaterally and bilaterally.
- Mirror Test: Similar concept to the OKN test. Ask a patient to hold their eyes steady looking straight ahead. Then tilt a mirror slowly side to side in front of them. The patient's vision is better than hand motion if their eyes move with the mirror. It can be tested both unilaterally and bilaterally

Treatment/Management: Reassure the patient that all findings from the exam are normal. Possibly obtain an MRI, CT, ERG, or VER. Have the patient return to clinic in 1-2 weeks and advise the patient their vision should have recovered by this time (this will help reassure the hysterical patients). If there is an organic problem, a 1-2 week wait may allow it time to express appreciable signs. Hysterical patients may benefit from a Psychiatric referral.

CHAPTER 6
CONTACT LENSES (CL'S)

The NBEO website states that 17-28 questions will be asked on Contact Lenses. Historically they have asked about 23.6 questions, meaning this chapter covers approximately 7% of the material tested on the exam, or roughly 5 cases. This material is NOT tested on TMOD.

CL FITTING

LOOSE VS. TIGHT FITTING CLS	
Think of the CL as being like a suction cup. A deep, curvy, large suction cup would stick better (tighter fit) than a shallow, flat, small suction cup (looser fit).	
LOOSE/FLAT	**TIGHT**
Excessive CL movement with blink	Minimal CL movement with blink
Poor CL centration	Indentation around limbus
Lens edge bubbles	Injection around limbus
Lens edge stand-off	Corneal edema
Superior eyelid irritation	No comfort complaints
HOW TO ADJUST CL FIT	
Increase sagittal height	Decrease sagittal height
Choose steeper base curve	Choose flatter base curve
Increase diameter	Reduce diameter

Remember that a steep contact lens will create a positive lacrimal lens, which is why you need to add minus to adjust the power on these lenses. Conversely, flat contact lenses will create a negative lacrimal lens, and so you need to add plus to adjust the power on these lenses.

CL EQUATIONS	
Tear Lens	Tear Lens = Base Curve – Keratometry
mm to Diopter Conversion	mm = 337.5 / D
Vertexing Equation	CL Power = Spectacle Power / [1 – (Vertex Distance * Spectacle Power)]
CL Power	CL Power = Diagnostic CL Power + Over Refraction + Lacrimal Lens Power
Residual Astigmatism	Residual Astigmatism=Total astigmatism of the eye – corneal astigmatism
SAM FAP	Steeper Add Minus, Flatter Add Plus
LARS (toric lenses)	Left Add, Right Subtract (add or subtract based on YOUR right vs left).

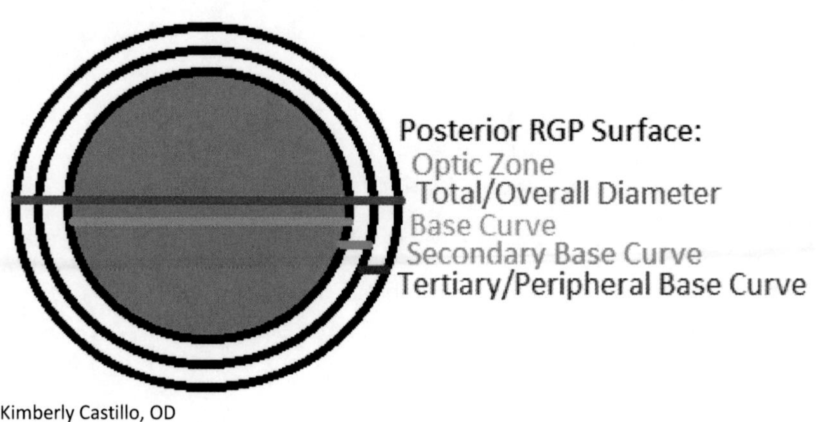

Kimberly Castillo, OD

Flexure occurs when an RGP becomes distorted while it is on the cornea, but assumes its normal shape when it is no longer on the cornea. Therefore, you will measure astigmatism with keratometry or topography when the RGP is on the eye, but when the RGP is off of the eye you will not measure the astigmatism. Flexure is usually caused when the RGP is thin and so its shape is easily contorted.

Warpage occurs when the RGP is distorted both when it is on and off the cornea. You will measure astigmatism with keratometry or topography both when the RGP is on and off of the eye. It can be confirmed with a radiuscope. Warpage is usually caused when the patient excessively rubs the RGP during cleaning.

The **Wetting Angle** can be used to determine how well a contact lens remains wet, or in other words, how likely the contact lens is to stay dry. A low wetting angle (less than 90°) means the contact is able to wet well with an even spread of fluid, while a high wetting angle (above 90°) means the contact does not spread fluid well and will have many dry spots.

RGP FLUORESCEIN PATTERNS	
Dr. Kimberly Castillo, OD	Alignment Fit: Even distribution of fluorescein between the RGP and the cornea with a ring around the perimeter for the edge lift.
Dr. Kimberly Castillo, OD	Flat Fit: Fluorescein will pool around the periphery of the RGP while the center of the lens will touch the cornea with minimal fluorescein present.
Dr. Kimberly Castillo, OD	Steep Fit: Fluorescein will pool in the center with minimal edge left in the periphery.
Dr. Kimberly Castillo, OD	With The Rule Astigmatism: Fluorescein will pool along the top and bottom of the lens with central touch across the 3:00-9:00 band.
Dr. Kimberly Castillo, OD	Against The Rule Astigmatism: Fluorescein will pool along the right and left sides of the lens with central touch across the 12:00-6:00 band.

RGP FITTING GUIDELINES

If an RGP is fit on flat K, it is frequently too tight. Therefore, it is recommended to fit 0.25D flatter than flat K. A low riding plus-RGP can also be raised by lenticulating the lens, which increases the thickness on the edge of the lens. A minus carrier lenticular design on a high plus lens will increase edge thickness (to give the upper lid more to grab and to reduce center mass). A plus carrier lenticular design on a high minus lens will reduce edge thickness.

Front Surface Toric RGPs have a spherical back surface and toricity on the front surface. They are rarely used because it is difficult to stabilize an RGP with a spherical back surface. (However, front surface torics are commonly used on scleral lenses, because they are stabilized by scleral haptics).

Back Surface Toric RGPs have toricity on their back surface/ base curve. They should be used for patients with >2.50D of corneal toricity in order to follow the shape of the cornea and prevent the RGP from rocking due to the irregular surface.

Some patients will have residual astigmatism with Back Surface Toric RGPs. **Bitoric** RGPs can be used in these cases. Bitoric RGPs have toricity on both their front and back surfaces. This allows for the contact to settle appropriately on the cornea without rocking, and to also correct residual astigmatism.

Selecting the proper RGP:

- Spherical RGP
  - <1.00D residual astigmatism
  - <2.50D of corneal astigmatism
- Back surface toric RGP
  - >0.75D residual astigmatism (or approximately half the corneal astigmatism)
  - >1.50D of corneal astigmatism
- Front Surface Toric (F1 Toric): These lenses have a spherical back surface and a toric front surface. They are used on patients with spherical corneas that have too much residual astigmatism. However, Front Surface Toric RGPs are rarely used because it is hard to stabilize them due to the spherical back surface. It is better to fit these patients into toric soft contact lenses.
  - >1.00D residual astigmatism
  - <1.00D corneal astigmatism
- Spherical Power Effect (SPE) Bitoric: These lenses compensate for their toric back surface with a toric front surface, and thus have a combined spherical power. They are used to improve fitting comfort on patients who have a lot of corneal astigmatism but do not need correction for astigmatism in their contact lenses.
  - <0.75D residual astigmatism
  - >1.50D of corneal astigmatism
- Cylinder Power Effect (CPE) Bitoric: These lenses have a toric back surface for proper fitting on a cornea with a lot of toricity, and a front toric surface to correct for residual astigmatism. They have a combined toric power. They are used to improve fitting comfort on patients who have a lot of corneal astigmatism and also need correction for astigmatism in their contact lenses.
  - >0.75D residual astigmatism
  - >1.50D of corneal astigmatism
- **In short, the first step in choosing an RGP is to decide if you want the back surface of the RGP to be toric or not. Make the back surface of the RGP toric if the corneal astigmatism is ≥2.00D. Next you need to decide if you want the front surface to be toric not. If the residual astigmatism after placing the RGP on the eye is ≥1.00D, then make the front surface of the RGP toric.**

FDA Classes of soft contact lenses:

1. Group 1 has low water content and is non-ionic
2. Group 2 has high water content and is non-ionic
3. Group 3 has low water content and is ionic
4. Group 4 has high water content and is ionic
5. Group 5 includes the silicone hydrogels

Nonionic lenses with a low water content are the least likely to develop deposits (Group 1).

CL COMPLICATIONS

GIANT PAPILLARY CONJUNCTIVITIS (GPC)

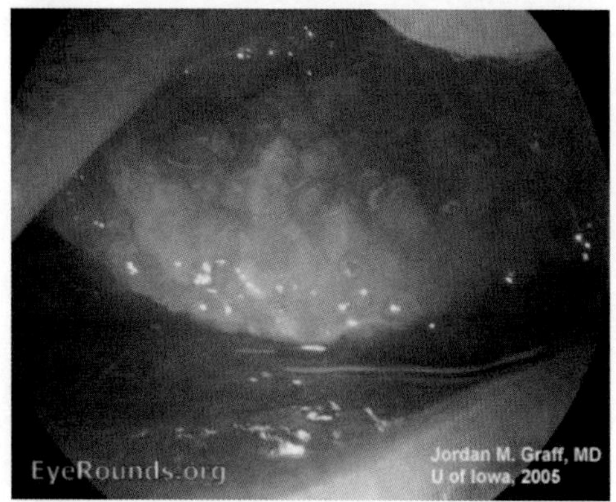

EyeRounds.org University of Iowa

What to Know: GPC is most commonly caused by contact lens over wear. The lids develop an allergic response to the protein deposits in the contact lens.

Symptoms: Patients will complain of itch and irritation with contact lens wear. They will also complain that their contacts move excessively. This is because the GPC bumps cause traction on the contact lens and move it around with blink.

Signs: In addition to very large GPC, patients may have ropy mucous discharge. VA may also be reduced.

Treatment/Management: Given that contact lenses are the most common cause of GPC, consider refitting the patient into a new CL, possibly a daily disposable to reduce protein buildup. The patient should also reduce contact lens wear time and clean the lenses more thoroughly. In severe cases, patients should discontinue CL wear for 1-4 months. Consider prescribing a topical NSAID to reduce the allergic inflammation. Mild steroids should only be used in very severe cases.

INCOMPLETE BLINKING → DRY EYES

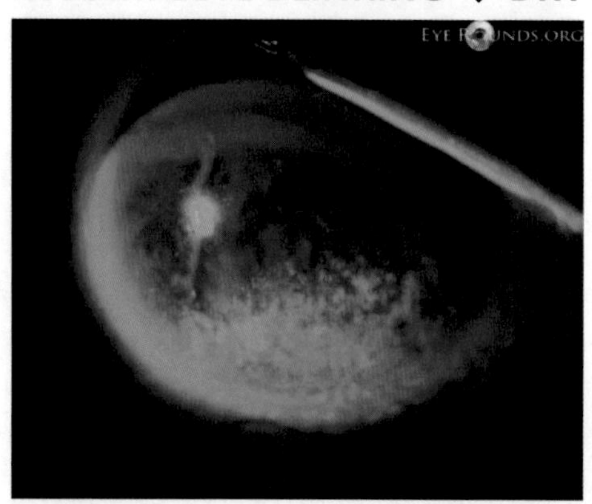

EyeRounds.org University of Iowa

What to Know: Incomplete blinking may occur when patients subconsciously find the contact lens irritating. This particularly occurs in RGP wearers.

Symptoms: Patients may complain of dry eye and epiphora.

Signs: Patients present with interpalpebral superficial punctate keratitis (between 3-9:00) and incomplete closure on blink. If chronic, they may have inflammation and scarring.

Treatment/Management: Discontinue contact lens wear. Use preservative free artificial tears up to Q1H with possible punctal plugs. Refit the patient into a soft contact lens.

CORNEAL NEOVASCULARIZATION

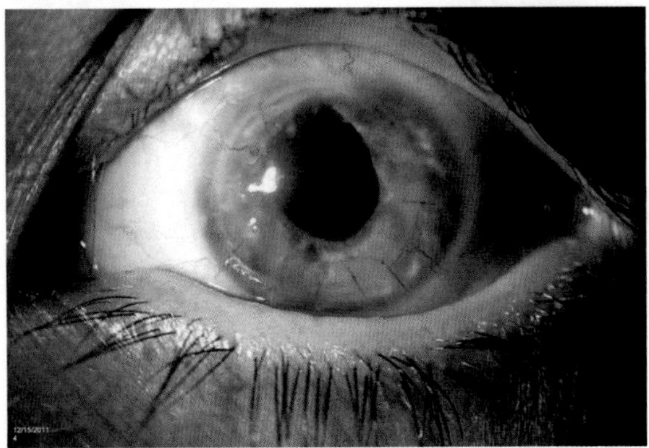

Retina Image Bank. File #7828

What to Know: When a patient has been wearing tight fitting CLs or over wearing their CLs, then corneal hypoxia (oxygen deficiency) occurs. One way the cornea can respond to the lack of oxygen is to grow new blood vessels to the area (neovascularization), thus increasing the available blood supply.

Symptoms: Patients will have no complaints (asymptomatic) until late stages when the patient will notice reduced vision.

Signs: Corneal neovascularization larger than 2mm is considered significant. Usually it is more significant in the superior and inferior regions where the lid covers the cornea (thus further reducing oxygen supply).

Treatment/Management: Patients should discontinue CL use. Prescribe a topical steroid to cause regression of the neovascularization. Severe cases may require argon laser photocoagulation (a narrow beam of light is used to shrink or destroy the neovascular vessels). Refit the patient into a higher Dk/t CL. Educate the patient on proper CL wear time.

CL SOLUTION HYPERSENSITIVITY

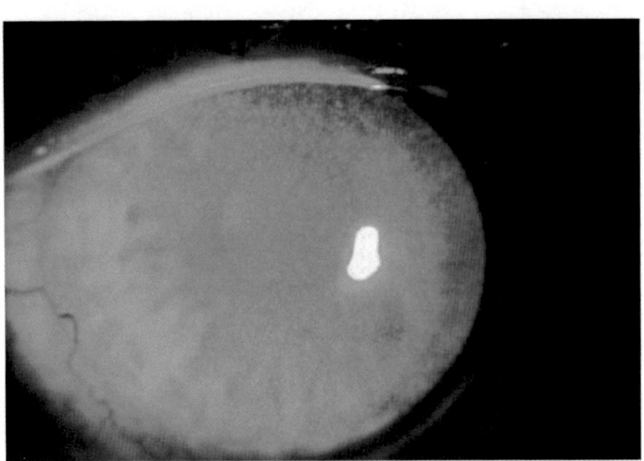

EyeRounds.org University of Iowa

What to Know: Patients may develop an allergic reaction to the preservatives in their contact lens solution.

Symptoms: Patients will complain of ocular discomfort, reduced vision, photophobia.

Signs: Patients will have diffuse punctate epithelial defects which will stain with fluorescein.

Treatment/Management: Patients should switch to a preservative free CL solution (Clear Care, Peroxiclear). They may need to discontinue CL wear until resolution. Consider prescribing topical antibiotics due to compromised epithelium.

CORNEAL INFILTRATES / ULCERS

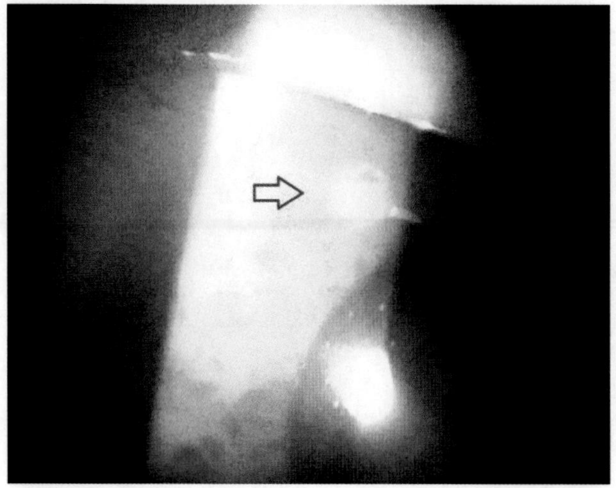
Kimberly Castillo, OD

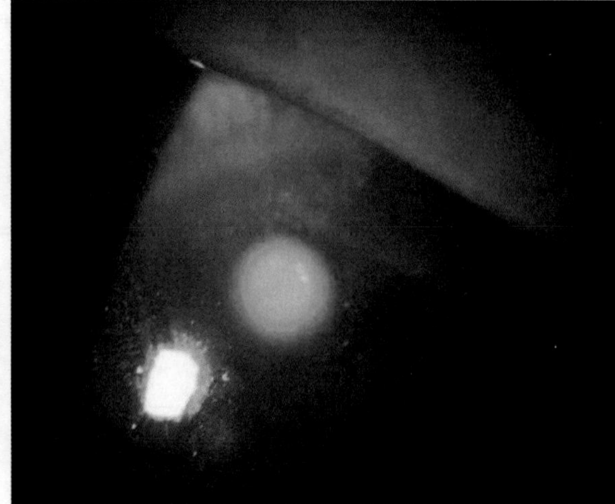
Kimberly Castillo, OD

What to Know: CL over wear can cause proteins to get deposited into the lens. This can subsequently trigger a corneal immune response which will initially present as infiltrates and may progress into an ulcer if the infiltrate breaks the corneal surface. Remember that infiltrates are sterile, they are an accumulation of white blood cells. Also, CL's are not the only causes of Corneal Infiltrates and Ulcers!

Central corneal ulcers are more severe than peripheral ulcers because they are further away from the limbus and blood supply (which aids in healing). Remember a small central corneal ulcer is more severe than a large peripheral corneal ulcer! The bacteria which can aggressively attack an intact cornea include *Pseudomonas, Corynebacterium diphtheria*, *Haemophilus*, *Listeria*, and *Neisseria gonorrhea*. Remember that the most common bacteria to afflict contact lens wearers is Pseudomonas!

Symptoms: Patients will complain of pain and photophobia.

Signs: Infiltrates or ulcers will be present, especially in the superior and inferior regions of the cornea where the lid covers the cornea (and so the most protein deposits accumulate). Remember the difference between infiltrates is that infiltrates have no corneal defect (do not stain with fluorescein) while ulcers do have a corneal defect (stain with fluorescein).

Treatment/Management: Discontinue CL wear. Use oral NSAIDs and preservative free artificial tears up to Q1H for comfort. DO NOT PATCH the eye due to CL wear etiology.

- Corneal Infiltrates: Use topical antibiotic QID.
- Corneal Ulcers: Use topical antibiotic (fluoroquinolone) up to Q1H and a topical cycloplegic for comfort. Severe cases may require oral antibiotics and use of steroids to reduce inflammation after the infection has cleared. Patients should be followed daily for resolution and IOP check.

TIGHT LENS SYNDROME

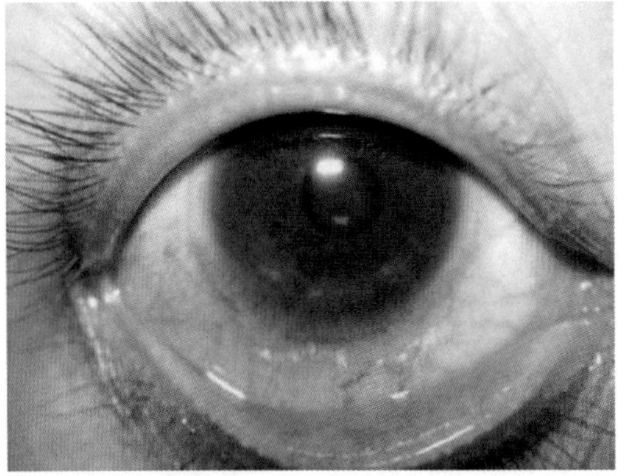

My Health 1

What to Know: Tight Lens Syndrome occurs when a patient is wearing a tight contact lens (as the name suggests). It will be worse if the patient sleeps in their contact lenses, and will develop within 24-48 hours after the patient begins wearing the offending contact lens.

Signs: Patients present with a contact lens which will not move with blink and will indent the conjunctiva, causing a ring which will stain with fluorescein. Patients may present with associated superficial punctate keratitis (SPK), corneal edema, and anterior chamber cells and flare.

Treatment/Management: Patients may be advised to discontinue contact lens wear until signs resolve. If superficial punctate keratitis (SPK) is present, patients should use an artificial tear QID. If cornea edema is present, prescribe a topical steroid. If cells/flare are present, prescribe a topical steroid and cycloplegic. Upon resolution, patients should be fit with a looser contact lens with reduced wear time.

CORNEAL WARPAGE

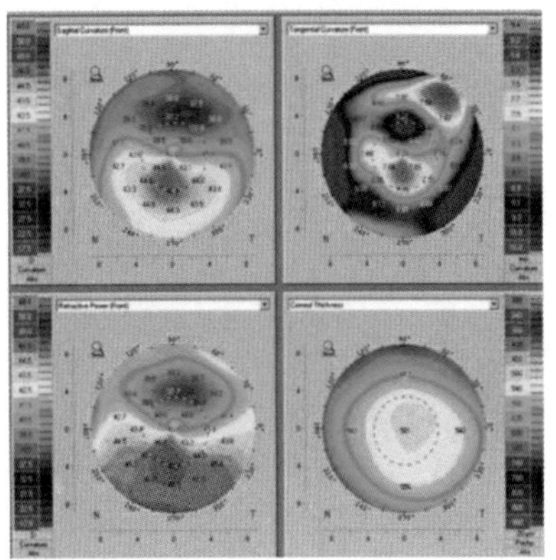

iKnowledge 1

What to Know: Corneal Warpage typically occurs secondary to prolonged RGP wear.

Symptoms: Patients may complain of blur with their glasses which improves with contact lens wear (spectacle blur).

Signs: Patients present with corneal distortion seen with keratometry and topography which resolves with discontinued contact lens wear.

Treatment/Management: Patients need to discontinue contact lens wear for up to 6 weeks to allow the cornea to return to normal. The patient should be alerted that vision may be blurry during this time. Patients may need to discontinue contact lens wear one at a time to allow for clear vision from one eye. After the cornea has stabilized, the patients should be given a new spectacle prescription and refit into a new contact lens.

JELLY BUMPS / MULBERRY SPOTS / LENS CALCULI

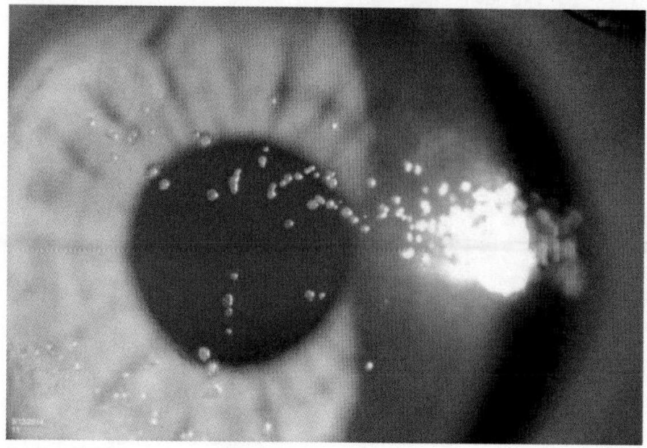

RetinaGallery.com: calhoun16

What to Know: Jelly Bumps occur when proteins or other deposits lodge themselves into the front of a soft contact lens. This occurs due to contact lens over wear and improper contact lens care.

Symptoms: Patients may complain of discomfort with contact lens wear.

Signs: Patients present with gelatinous, focal, irregularly shaped lumps on the front surface of the lens.

Treatment/Management: Patients need to discard the damaged contact lenses because they cannot be salvaged; removal of the Jelly Bumps will cause dimples in the lens. They should be educated on proper contact lens care and wear time.

MUCIN BALLS

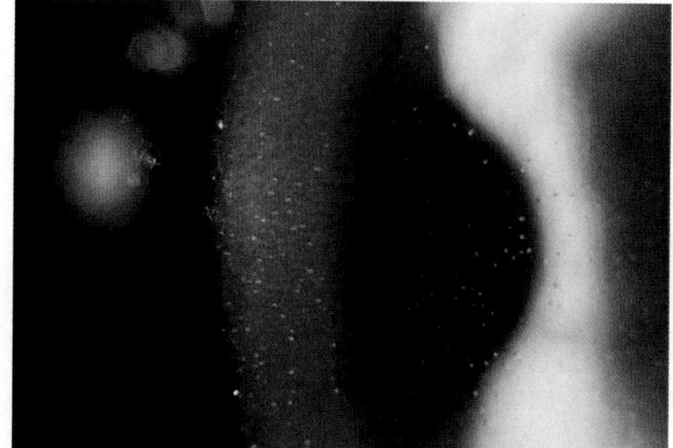

MyAlcon 1

What to Know: Mucin Balls are found with both soft and hard contact lens wearers. They occur when mechanical rubbing of the contact lens stimulates the goblet cells to produce extra mucin which will form balls that embed themselves in the corneal epithelium.

Signs: Mucin Balls do not move with blink while the patient is wearing a contact lens. They will become dislodged with blink after the contact lens is removed, leaving behind dimples in the corneal epithelium in which fluorescein will pool.

Treatment/Management: Mucin Balls rarely require treatment. If the Mucin Balls disrupt clarity of vision, then consider fitting the patient into a steeper contact lens. The tighter fit will reduce the mechanical rubbing of the contact lens. Patients can also reduce contact lens wear time and use contact lens rewetting drops.

CORNEAL MICROCYSTS

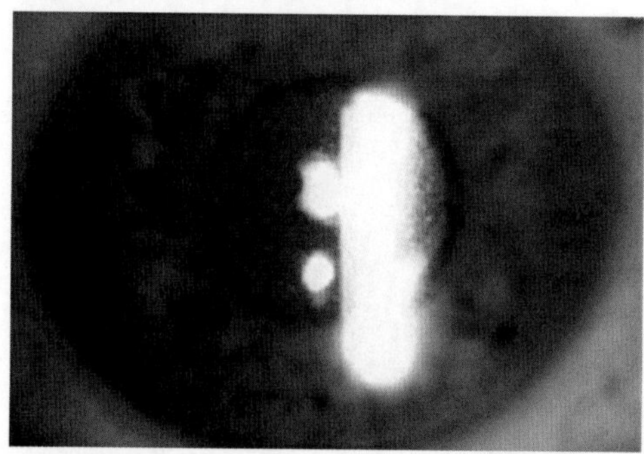

EyeRounds.org University of Iowa

What to Know: Corneal Microcysts are caused by corneal hypoxia (oxygen deprivation) due to contact lens over wear.

Symptoms: Patients may complain of pain if the Microcysts rupture.

Signs: Corneal Microcysts are small, fluid filled, abnormal membranous sacs found in the cornea.

Treatment/Management: Patients should decrease contact lens wear time and be fit into contact lenses with a higher DK/t, or higher oxygen permeability.

DIMPLE VEILING

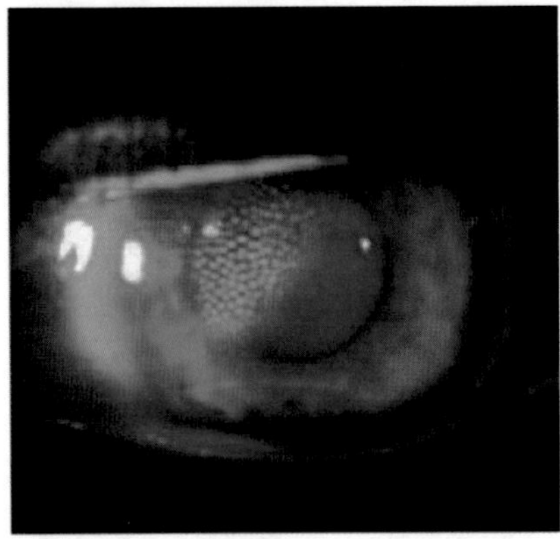
Brighton Vision Center 1

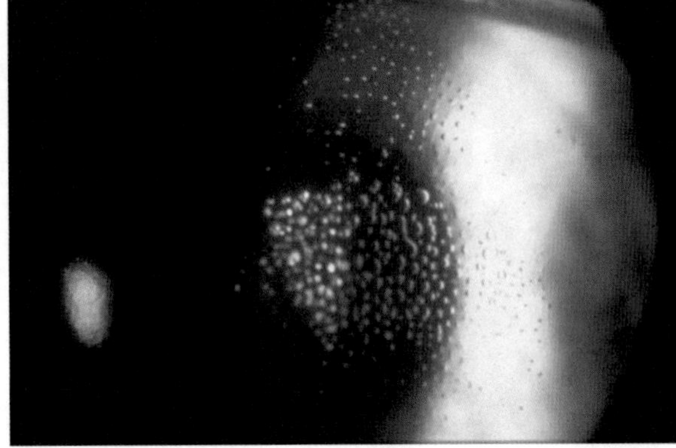
Bausch + Lomb 1

What to Know: Dimple Veiling occurs when bubbles get trapped under an RGP due to a tight contact lens fit, or in patients wearing soft lenses overnight/extended wear. These bubbles imprint dimples into the cornea which will pool with sodium fluorescein when the RGP is removed.

Symptoms: Patients may have no complaints (asymptomatic) or complain of blur, epiphora, and ocular irritation.

Treatment/Management: Patients should be fit into a flatter RGP.

PROTEIN DEPOSITS

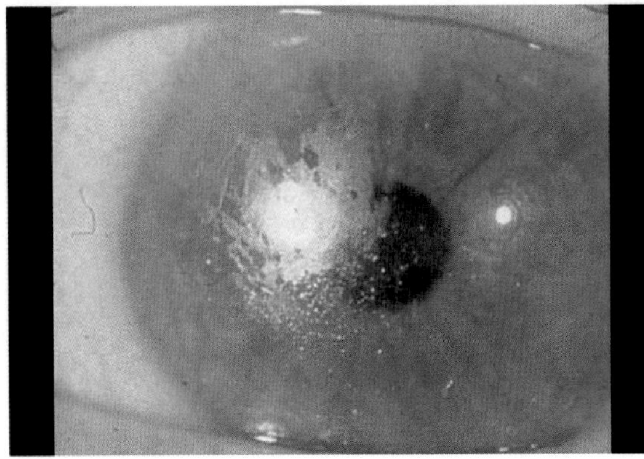
My Alcon 2

What to Know: Protein Deposits occur when denatured proteins accumulate on a hard or soft contact lens. This occurs due to contact lens over wear and improper contact lens care.

Symptoms: Patients may complain of cloudy uncomfortable contact lenses.

Signs: Protein deposits can be visible with the naked eye as a film over the contact lens.

Treatment/Management: Patients need to discard the damaged contact lenses because they cannot be salvaged. They should be educated on proper contact lens care and wear time.

CHAPTER 7
LENS / CATARACT / IOL / PRE- AND POST-OPERATIVE CARE

The NBEO website states that 17-28 questions will be asked on Lens / Cataract / IOL / Pre- And Post-Operative Care. Historically they have asked about 23 questions, meaning this chapter covers approximately 7% of the material tested on the exam, or roughly 5 cases. This material IS included on TMOD.

Cataracts are treated with surgery which removes the natural lens and replaces it with an artificial lens. The most common lens implants used currently are Posterior Chamber Intraocular Lenses (PCIOLs), which are inserted into the capsular bag. Be aware that complications are more likely in patients with pseudoexfoliation syndrome (weakened zonules are most likely to allow the lens to dislocate) or who have a history of using Flomax (intraoperative floppy iris syndrome). There are several types of cataract surgeries.

- **Intracapsular Cataract Extraction (ICCE)** is an older procedure in which a large incision was made into the cornea in order to remove the entire lens and its capsule. No artificial lens was implanted, and so these patients required high plus lenses to compensate. This procedure is not performed anymore.
- **Extracapsular Cataract Extraction (ECCE)** is another older procedure in which a large incision was made into the cornea in order to remove the entire lens. The capsule would remain, in which an IOL would replace the natural lens.
- **Phacoemulsification** is the newest procedure. Ultrasound is used to break up the lens. This allows for a small incision because the lens is sucked out. The eye's IOP will press against the small incision, effectively closing it without the need for sutures.

A possible complication of cataract surgery is transillumination defects of the iris due to mechanical rubbing of the iris with the surgical instruments used during the procedure.

CONGENITAL CATARACTS

What to Know: Congenital Cataracts are present at birth. They can range in severity from having no impact on vision to severe blockage of vision leading to amblyopia and strabismus. Congenital Cataracts are usually idiopathic. They may also be caused by Galactosemia (improper metabolism of galactose), Hypoglycemia (low blood sugar), Hypocalcemia (low blood calcium), Rubella (viral infection), Fabry's Disease (improper buildup of globotriaosylceramide), Lowe Syndrome (aka Oculocerebrorenal Syndrome which is a rare X-linked recessive disorder), and Alport's Syndrome (basement membrane disease).

Signs: Patients may have Leukocoria, Nystagmus, and Strabismus. Below is a description of different types of Congenital Cataracts.

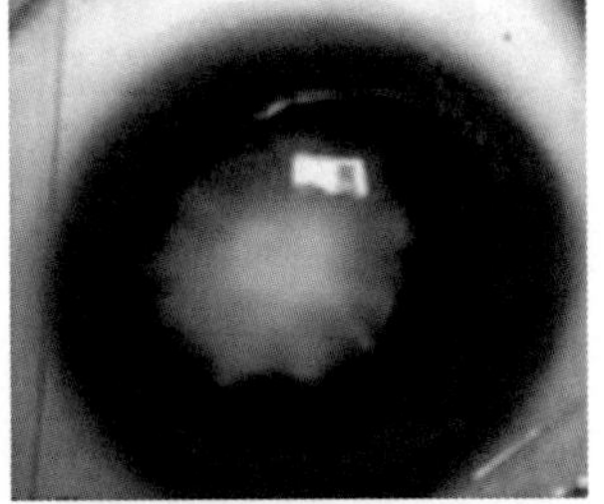

EyeRounds.org University of Iowa

LAMELLAR / ZONULAR CATARACT: **Most common congenital cataract.** Has a "sand dollar" appearance with white opacification surrounding the nucleus.

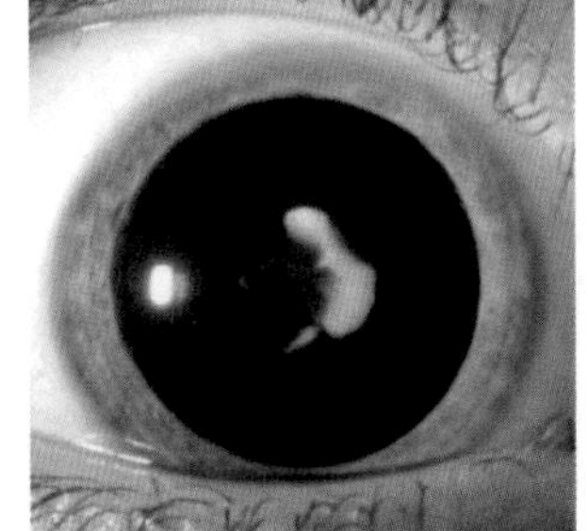

EyeRounds.org University of Iowa

LENTICULAR / NUCLEAR CATARACT: Opacification of the embryonic and possibly fetal nucleus.

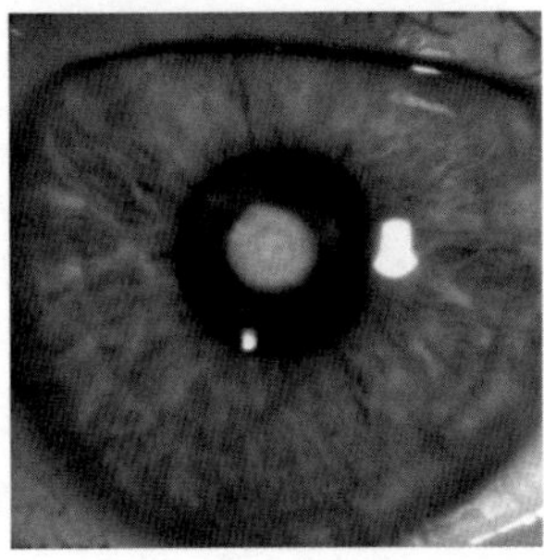

EyeRounds.org University of Iowa

POLAR CATARACTS are opacifications of the lens capsule either the anterior or posterior poles. Anterior Polar Cataracts usually have little impact on vision, while Posterior Polar Cataracts can grow large enough to decrease vision.

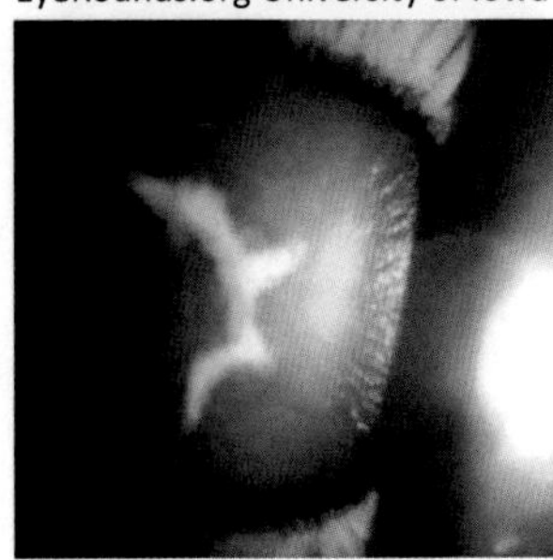

Kimberly Castillo, OD

SUTURAL CATARACTS are opacities located along the Y-sutures which usually have little impact on vision.

Symptoms: Patients may have no complaints (asymptomatic). Babies may be seen rubbing their eyes.

Treatment/Management: Cataract surgery should be performed as soon as possible to prevent development of amblyopia. If amblyopia occurs, then it should be treated as necessary. If present, any underlying disorder should be treated by a pediatrician.

ACQUIRED CATARACTS (AGE RELATED)

What to Know: Acquired Cataracts are caused by age and exposure to UV light over the course of a lifetime.

Symptoms: Patients will complain of gradual blurring of vision, difficulty with night driving, difficulty seeing in low light situations, difficulty with glare, and difficulty with halos around lights.

Signs: Patients will have opacification of the lens. Cataracts DO NOT cause an APD.

Many types of cataracts are age related:

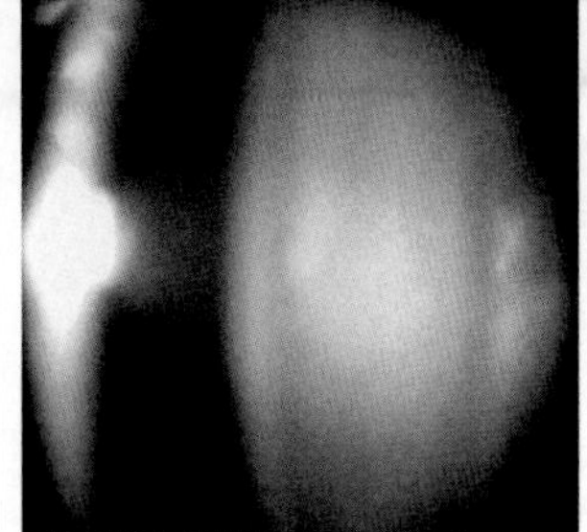
Kimberly Castillo, OD

Nuclear Sclerosis is a change of color (yellow or brown with advanced cases) of the nucleus of the lens. Patients may have a myopic shift (which can be significant), also known as "second sight" as they will be able to read more easily (but they will have increased blur at distance).

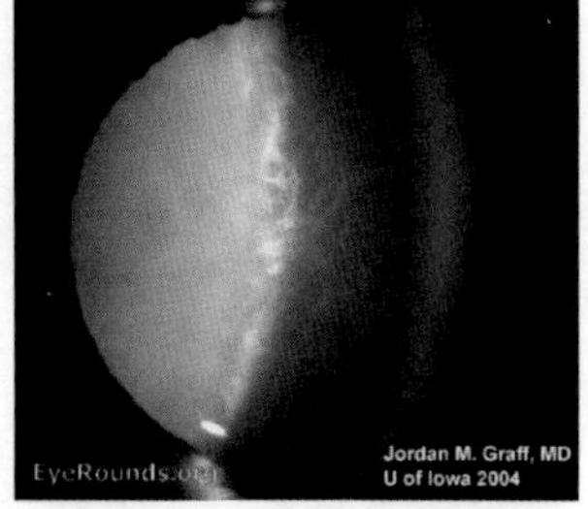

EyeRounds.org University of Iowa

Mature Cataracts have a completely opacified cortex, and so the lens will appear white.

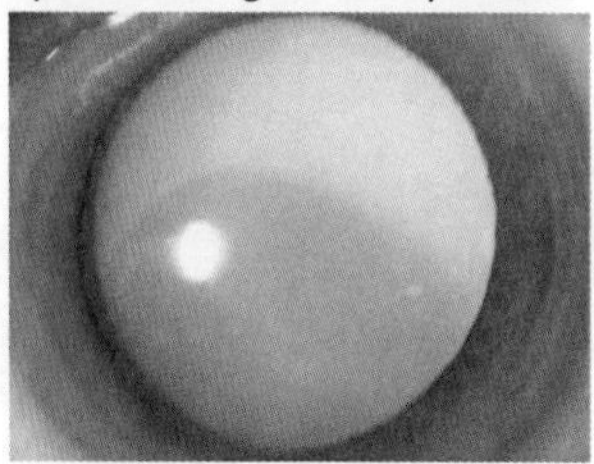
EyeRounds.org University of Iowa

Morgagnian Cataracts have a liquefied, white cortex and an inferiorly displaced nucleus (the nucleus is sinking).

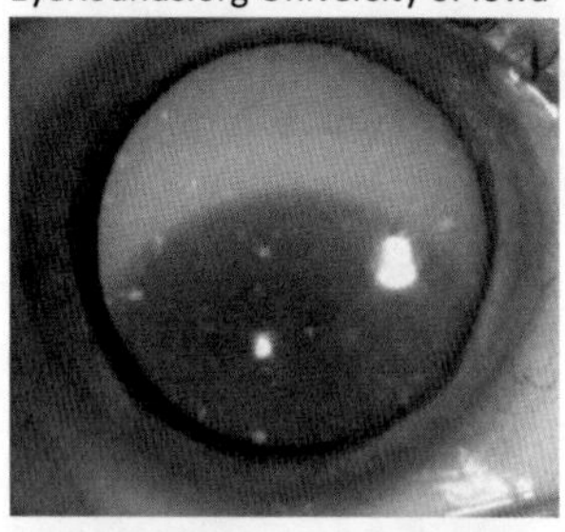
EyeRounds.org University of Iowa

Hypermature Cataracts are advanced Morgagnian Cataracts. The lens shrinks and subsequently the capsule wrinkles. Hypermature Cataracts can lead to either Phacolytic Glaucoma (caused when proteins leak out of the lens) or Phacomorphic Glaucoma (caused when the thickened cataractous lens pushes the iris forward leading to angle closure glaucoma).

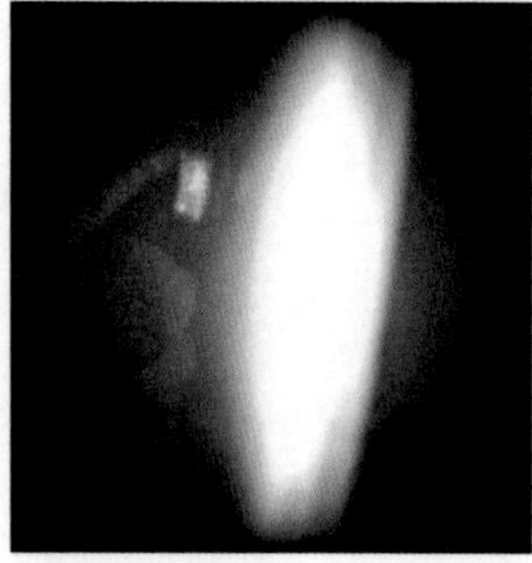
Kimberly Castillo, OD

Cortical Cataracts occur when the cortical fibers liquefy. Since the fibers are situated in a radial pattern, the cataracts will look like spokes. Early signs of Cortical Cataracts are vacuoles. Because the spokes occur peripherally, these cataracts are usually most symptomatic at night when the patient is dilated, and the most common complaint will be glare.

ACQUIRED CATARACTS (NOT AGE RELATED)

Cataracts which are not age related can occur earlier in life than would be expected.

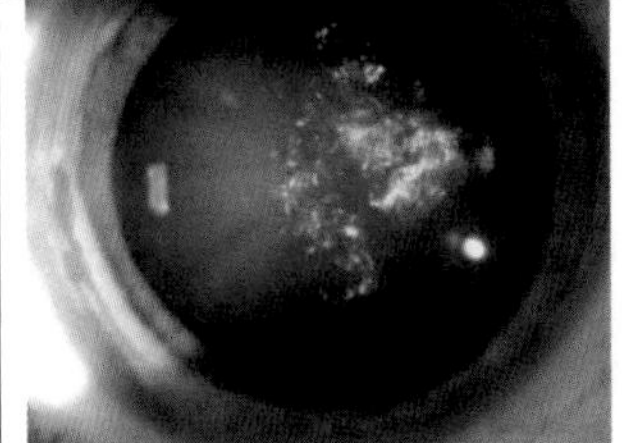

EyeRounds.org University of Iowa

Christmas Tree Cataracts are caused by Myotonic Dystrophy. They present as refractile central cortical crystals.

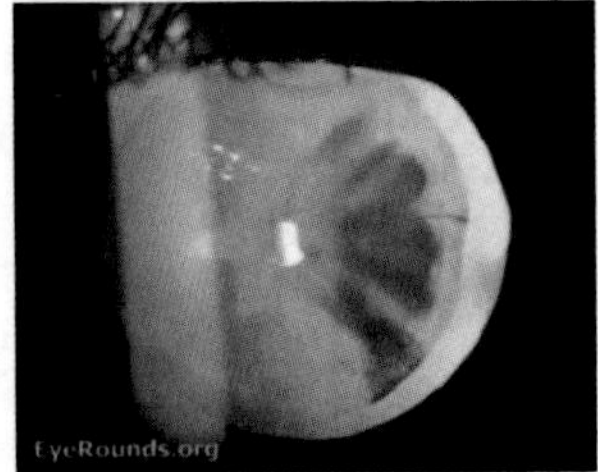

EyeRounds.org University of Iowa

Rosette Cataracts (Traumatic Cataracts) may look similar to Snowflake Cataracts. They are caused by blunt ocular trauma, and can develop within months to years after the trauma occurs.

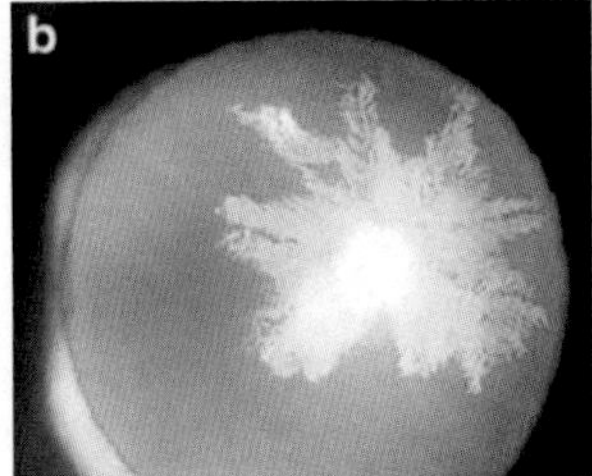

Journal of Medical Case Reports 1

Snowflake Cataracts may look similar to Rosette Cataracts. They are associated with Diabetes and can have a very rapid onset. They are caused by elevated levels of intraocular glucose and lenticular sorbitol, which causes oxidative stress.

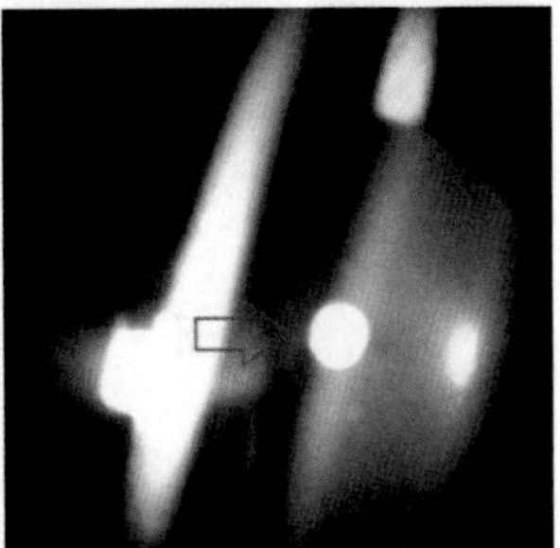

Kimberly Castillo, OD

Subcapsular Cataracts are plaque-like opacities located either at the anterior or posterior (more common) poles of the lens. These cataracts are often associated with Atopic Dermatitis, steroid use, inflammation, trauma, diabetes, or radiation. Given their central location, these cataracts will cause difficulty with reading.

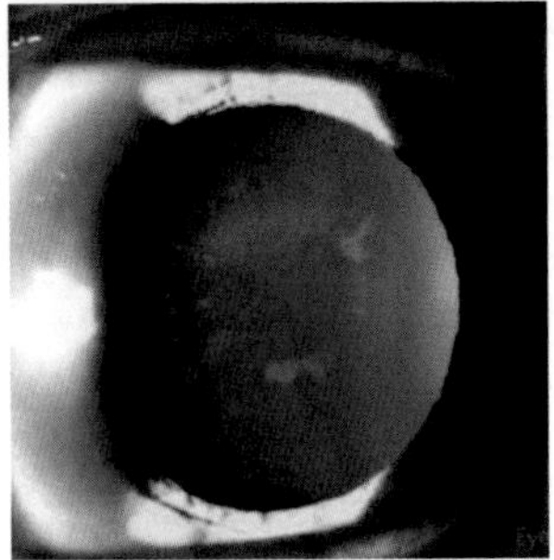

EyeRounds.org University of Iowa

Sunflower Cataracts are associated with Wilson's Disease, which is an abnormal accumulation of copper. (Notice the yellow color of the cataract and remember that copper and sunflowers are yellow).

Treatment/Management: Cataracts are treated with surgery which removes the natural lens and replaces it with an artificial lens. The most common lens implants used currently are Posterior Chamber Intraocular Lenses (PCIOLs), which are inserted into the capsular bag. Be aware that complications are more likely in patients with pseudoexfoliation syndrome (weakened zonules are most likely to allow the lens to dislocate) or who have a history of using Flomax (intraoperative floppy iris syndrome).

POSTERIOR CAPSULAR OPACIFICATION (PCO)

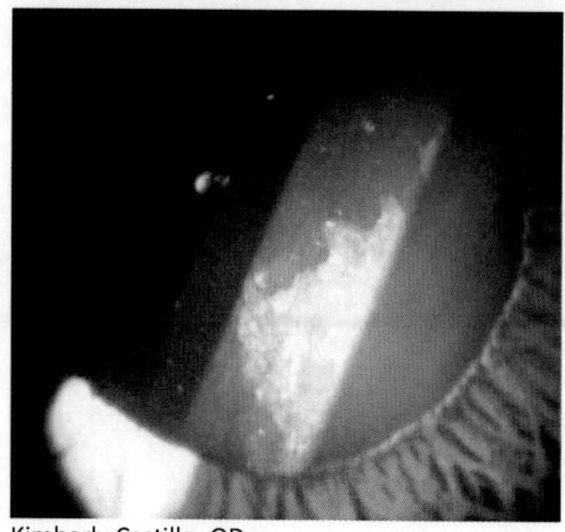
Kimberly Castillo, OD

What to Know: During cataract surgery it is hard to remove every single cell of the natural lens prior to inserting the implant. After the surgery is completed, left over cells on the posterior capsule from the natural lens can begin to grow. The growth of these cells causes a PCO. A PCO can occur between months and years after the cataract surgery. This is a very common complication after cataract surgery (up to 50%).

Symptoms: Patients will complain of gradual blurring of vision, difficulty with night driving, difficulty seeing in low light situations, difficulty with glare, and difficulty with halos around lights.

Signs: Opacification of the posterior lenticular capsule which may manifest as any combination of striae, haze, or Elschnig pearls (transparent clusters of proliferative lens cells – see picture above).

Treatment/Management: YAG Capsulotomy (laser treatment) is performed to remove the proliferated lens cells. This procedure only needs to be performed once. The cells do not grow back again after the YAG Capsulotomy has been completed.

APHAKIC / PSEUDOPHAKIC BULLOUS KERATOPATHY

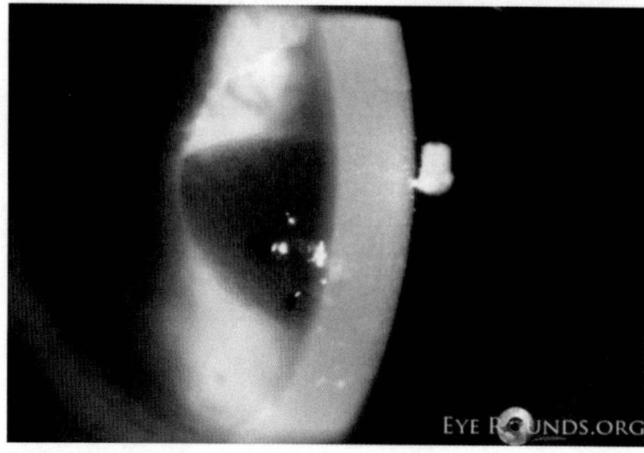

EyeRounds.org University of Iowa

What to Know: Aphakic / Pseudophakic Bullous Keratopathy occurs after cataract surgery.

Symptoms: Patients may complain of blur. They will also have pain with foreign body sensation and photophobia.

Signs: Patients may present with conjunctival hyperemia (redness) and increased IOP. Corneal signs will be due to abnormal endothelial function: edema, bullae (vesicles in the epithelium), guttata (vesicles in the endothelium), and folds in Descemet's membrane (due to stretching from edema)

Treatment/Management: Corneal edema should be treated with topical sodium chloride (Muro 128). If increased, the IOP should be reduced. Bullae will cause epithelial defects, and so it should be treated with an antibiotic ointment. Severe cases may require a full thickness corneal transplant.

ECTOPIA LENTIS

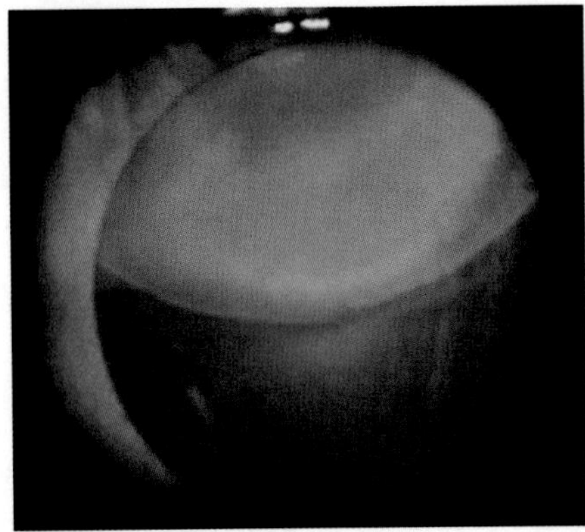
EyeRounds.org University of Iowa

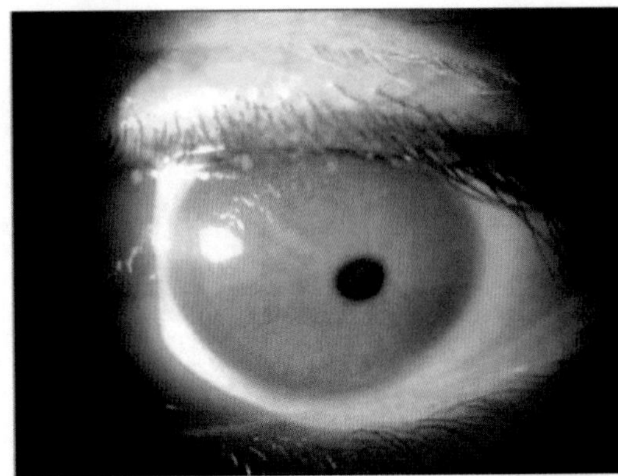
Scielo 1

What to Know: Ectopia Lentis is displacement of the natural lens. The lens may be completely displaced (dislocation/luxation) or only partially displaced (subluxation). Ectopia Lentis may lead to glaucoma.

Symptoms: Patients may have no complaints (asymptomatic). They may also have diplopia, blur, and symptoms similar to angle-closure glaucoma.

Signs:

Presentation can vary based on the cause:

- Blunt trauma is the most common cause of Ectopia Lentis.
- Marfan's Syndrome is the most common heritable (AD) cause of Ectopia Lentis, and the lens dislocation is caused by defective zonules. Remember that Marfan's Syndrome is a connective tissue disorder, which encompasses the lens zonules. **The lens dislocation will typically be bilateral and located up and out** (left picture).
- Homocystinuria is an enzymatic disorder in which there are increased levels of homocysteine in the body. At least 90% of these patients will have a dislocated lens by the time they reach their 30s. The direction of the dislocation will be down and in.
- Ectopia Lentis et Pupillae is a rare, bilateral, AR disorder characterized by a small, slit-like pupil which has limited response to dilation. The pupil will be displaced in the opposite direction of the lens (right picture).
- Other causes include Hyperlysinemia, Microspherophakia (dislocation is inferior and anterior), Sulfite Oxidase Deficiency, and Simple Ectopia Lentis (dislocation is up and out).

Treatment/Management: Treatment includes surgery to remove the dislocated lens. The patient should also have their refractive error corrected, and any underlying disease should be treated as well

CHAPTER 8
GLAUCOMA

The NBEO website states that 16-27 questions will be asked on Glaucoma. Historically they have asked about 21.3 questions, meaning this chapter covers approximately 6% of the material tested on the exam, or roughly 4 cases. This material IS included on TMOD.

GLAUCOMA
Signs that are seen with all forms of glaucoma include: • Increased cup to disc ratio. Normal thickness of the optic nerve rim tissue from thickest to thinnest can be remembered with ISNT (Inferior, Superior, Nasal, Temporal) • Reduced RNFL thickness on OCT. • Splinter (Drance) hemorrhages at the ONH. • Visual field defects will be present. The first field affected will be an inferior nasal paracentral scotoma. Other visual field defects may include arcuate, nasal step, Seidel, and temporal wedge. • **IOP will be increased above 21 in all types of glaucoma EXCEPT for Normal/Low Tension Glaucoma.** If the patient has a thin cornea, GAT will underestimate IOP. If the patient has a thick cornea, then GAT will overestimate IOP. Remember that the average corneal thickness is 550.
Workup for patients with glaucoma should include measurement of IOP with GAT, pachymetry, gonioscopy, fundus photos, OCT of the optic nerve, and 24-2 visual field. Patients should be followed every 3-6 months.
Treatment options for all types of glaucoma are discussed in Chapter Two under "Increased IOP."

OCULAR HYPERTENSION

What to Know: Ocular Hypertension is defined as cases where the patient has increased IOP (above 21 mmHg) but no other signs of glaucoma. Patients with thin corneas are at an increased risk of developing glaucoma.

Symptoms: Ocular Hypertension is asymptomatic.

Treatment/Management: Patients should be monitored closely every 3-6 months for signs of glaucoma; the frequency of testing can be reduced if the patient remains stable for a few years. The Ocular Hypertension Study (OHTS) showed that if the IOP is raised above 24 mmHg, prophylactic use of ocular hypotensive drops reduce the risk of visual field loss by over 50% five years after diagnosis, with the IOP reduced by 20%.

OPEN-ANGLE GLAUCOMA

PRIMARY OPEN ANGLE GLAUCOMA (POAG)*

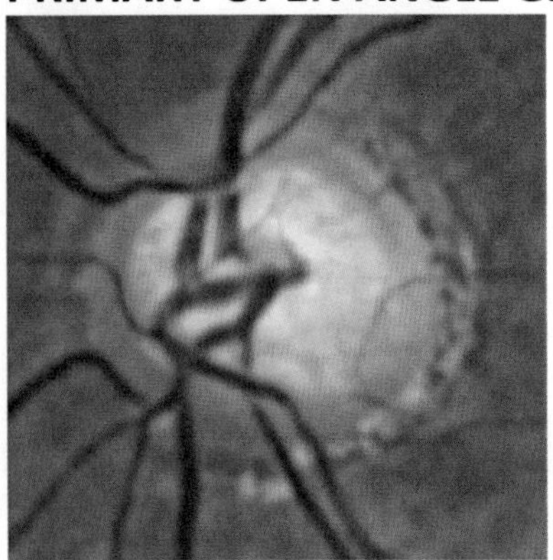

Kimberly Castillo, OD

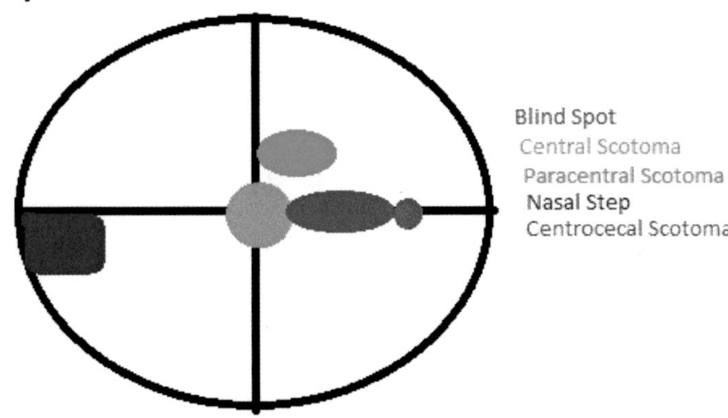

Kimberly Castillo, OD

What to Know: POAG is the most common form of glaucoma. It is glaucoma with an open angle and no underlying cause. POAG is progressive and bilateral. Risk factors include age, family history (first degree: parents, siblings, children), African American heritage, and thin corneas.

Symptoms: POAG will be asymptomatic until end stage, at which point the patient will complain of blurry "dim" vision, constricted visual field defects, difficulty with dark adaptation, and difficulty seeing in dim light.

Signs: See purple box at the beginning of this chapter.

Treatment/Management: See "Increased IOP" in chapter 2.

NORMAL / LOW-TENSION GLAUCOMA

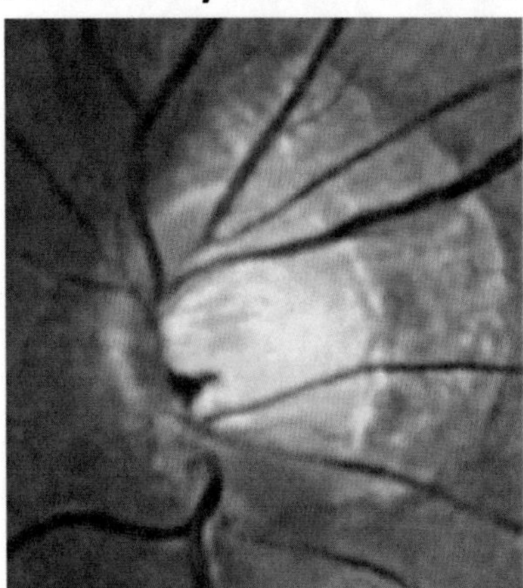

Kimberly Castillo, OD

What to Know: Low Tension glaucoma is virtually the same as POAG EXCEPT that the IOP is below 21mmHg. Splinter (Drance) hemorrhages at the ONH (pictured) are more common in Normal Tension Glaucoma.

Treatment/Management: See "Increased IOP" in chapter 2. Initial goal should be to reduce IOP by 30% from baseline. Further IOP reduction may be necessary if progression occurs. Prognosis is poorer than with POAG.

SECONDARY OPEN-ANGLE GLAUCOMA
Secondary Open-Angle Glaucoma is glaucoma with an open angle which has an underlying cause. Different types of Secondary Open-Angle Glaucoma are discussed below.
Treatment: In addition to the treatment options discussed under "Increased IOP" in Chapter Two, treatment for Secondary Open-Angle Glaucoma will be aimed at addressing the underlying issue.

PSEUDOEXFOLIATION SYNDROME (PXF) → EXFOLIATIVE GLAUCOMA*

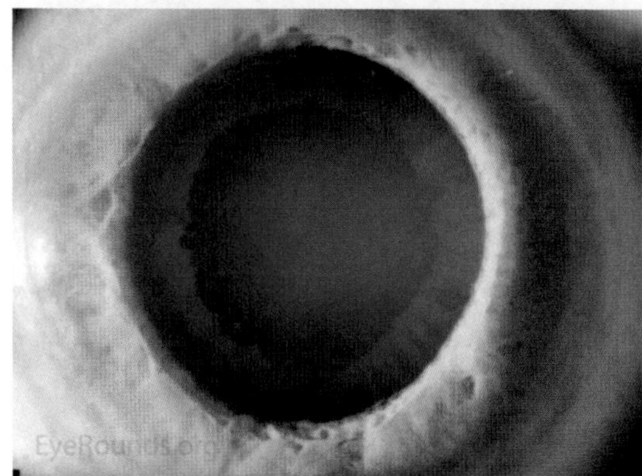

EyeRounds.org University of Iowa

What to Know: PXF is the precursor to Exfoliative Glaucoma; up to 60% of patients with PXF will get Exfoliative Glaucoma. **Exfoliative Glaucoma is the most common secondary glaucoma**. Exfoliative glaucoma can be seen in glass blowers. It is also more common in patients of Scandinavian/Viking ancestry.

Symptoms:

- PXF is asymptomatic.
- Exfoliative Glaucoma will be asymptomatic until late stages when reduced vision and constricted visual fields occur.

Signs:

- PXF: Up to 60% of cases are **bilateral**. A target pattern of exfoliative material will be seen on the anterior lens capsule, which will be more easily visualized on dilation. Patients will have a loss of the pupillary ruff. White exfoliative material will be present throughout the anterior chamber including the trabecular meshwork, zonules, iris, pupillary margin, and anterior hyaloid. Peripupillary transillumination defects will also be present.
- Exfoliative Glaucoma: In addition to the signs found with PXF, patients will have an increased IOP and the other signs seen with glaucoma. The increased IOP occurs due to blockage of the trabecular meshwork by the exfoliative material.

Treatment/Management:

- IOP should be monitored every 6-12 months for patients with PXF. No treatment is necessary until IOP increase occurs. See "Increased IOP" in chapter 2.
- IOP is difficult to control in Exfoliative glaucoma. Furthermore, glaucoma can develop rapidly (within months), and so patients should be monitored every 3 months. Treatment includes topical ocular hypotensives, SLT/ALT, and guarded filtration procedure.
- Cataract extraction requires special precautions due to risk of complications secondary to weakened zonules.

PIGMENT DISPERSION SYNDROME (PDS) → PIGMENTARY GLAUCOMA*

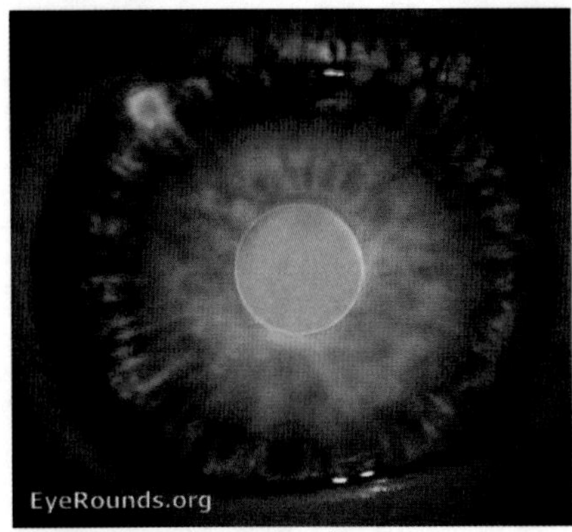

EyeRounds.org University of Iowa

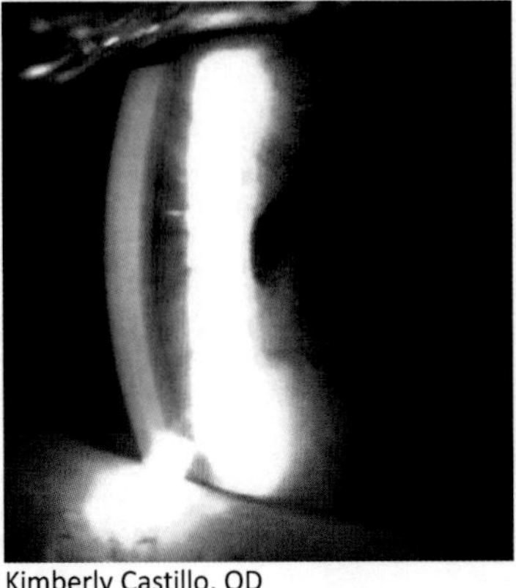
Kimberly Castillo, OD

Kimberly Castillo, OD

What to Know: Pigment Dispersion Syndrome is the precursor to Pigmentary Glaucoma; up to 50% of patients with PDS will get Pigmentary Glaucoma. PDS typically occurs in 20-50 year old myopic Caucasian men.

Symptoms: Patients with both PDS and Pigmentary Glaucoma may be asymptomatic. Some patients may complain of blurry vision or halos after exercise. Excessive movement can increase the iris-zonule chafing and release pigment, which can cause a transient increase of IOP and a subsequent mildly hazy cornea. Patients with end-stage Pigmentary Glaucoma may complain of blurry "dim" vision and constricted visual field defects.

Signs:

- Pigment Dispersion Syndrome: With PDS the **iris is backbowed** such that it rubs on the lens zonules. This mechanical rubbing causes release of pigment from the posterior surface of the iris, which can be appreciated as **mid-peripheral iris transillumination defects**. The pigment then becomes deposited on the endothelium (**krukenberg spindle**), trabecular meshwork, and anterior to Schwalbe's Line (which is known as Sampaolesi's Line). IOP may vary greatly throughout the day (>5 mmHg) based on the release of pigment.
- Pigmentary Glaucoma: In addition to the signs found with PDS, patients will have an increased IOP and the other signs seen with glaucoma.

Treatment/Management:

- Pigment Dispersion Syndrome: Monitor annually for signs of Pigmentary Glaucoma.
- Pigmentary Glaucoma: See "Increased IOP" in chapter 2. An LPI can be considered because it may help stabilize the pressure between the anterior and posterior chambers.

STEROID INDUCED GLAUCOMA

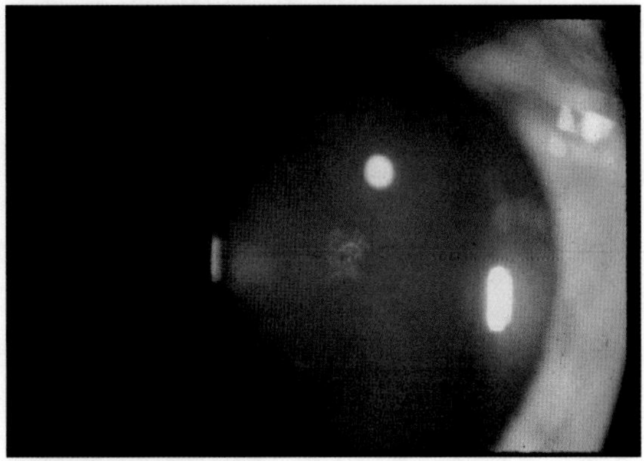

Cogan Collection, NEI/NIH

What to Know: IOP can increase due to the use of ocular steroids.

Symptoms: Steroid Induced Glaucoma will be asymptomatic until end stage, at which point the patient will complain of blurry "dim" vision and diminished visual field defects.

Signs: Patients present with an increased IOP 4 or more weeks after the initiation of steroid therapy. Chronic Steroid Induced Glaucoma (pictured above) can cause posterior subcapsular cataracts and other signs of glaucoma (ONH cupping, thinned RNFL, and abnormal visual fields).

Treatment/Management: Discontinue/taper steroid use. If IOP does not return to normal, then reduce IOP (see "Increased IOP" in Chapter 2). If IOP has a dramatic spike, then consider paracentesis (allowing outflow of aqueous from the globe by penetrating the cornea near the limbus with a needle) for urgent treatment.

UVEITIS – GLAUCOMA – HYPHEMA SYNDROME (UGH SYNDROME)

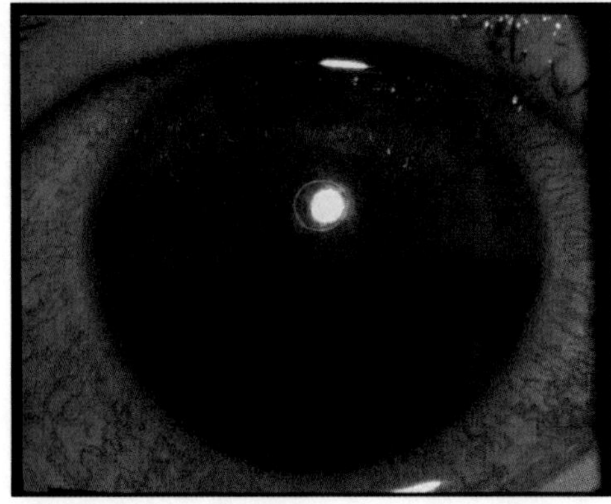

Cogan Collection, NEI/NIH

What to Know: UGH syndrome occurs when a one piece IOL is accidentally placed in the sulcus allowing for the IOL haptic to rub on underside of the iris during pupil movements.

Symptoms: Patients will complain of reduced vision, pain, and photophobia. They may complain of reduced visual fields in late stages.

Signs: This disease is named after it's signs. Uveitis (anterior chamber cells and flare), glaucoma (increased IOP, ONH cupping, RNFL loss), and hyphema (blood in the anterior chamber) will all be present.

Treatment/Management: Treat each of the independent problems. The iris needs to be immobilized with a topical cycloplegic (Atropine), the inflammation needs to be reduced with a topical steroid, and the IOP needs to be reduced (see "Increased IOP" in chapter 2). Surgery may be necessary to remove or reposition the IOL.

INFANTILE GLAUCOMA

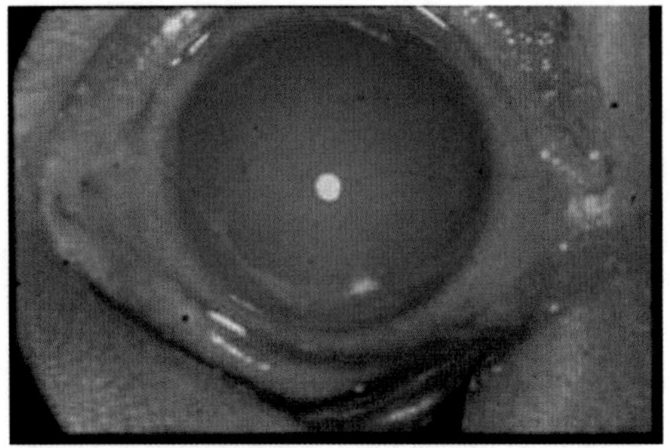

Cogan Collection, NEI/NIH

What to Know: Infantile/Congenital Glaucoma is bilateral 70% of the time and is seen in males 65% of the time. The difference between Infantile and Congenital Glaucoma is the age of onset:

- Infantile Glaucoma presents between 3 months – 3 years.
- Juvenile Glaucoma presents between 3 – 35 years of age.

One third of cases are primary, another third are secondary, and the last third have systemic associations.

- Primary cases are hereditary. Usually the angle is not formed correctly during development.
- Secondary cases are lens-induced or caused by tumors, trauma, or steroids.
- Systemic associations include: aniridia, persistent primary vitreous, nanophthalmos, rubella, neurofibromatosis, mucopolysaccharidoses, and a variety of syndromes (Sturge-Weber syndrome, Marfan's, Weill Marchesani, Lowe's).

Symptoms: Babies will show evidence of photophobia.

Signs: See purple box at the beginning of this chapter. Additional signs can all be traced back to an increased IOP during development, which stretches out the globe (buphthalmos). Therefore, the patient will have an increased corneal diameter (>12mm) and an increased axial length (with subsequent myopia which can lead to amblyopia). This ocular stretching can lead to Haab's striae (breaks in Descemet's membrane perpendicular to the limbus) and subsequent edema of the corneal stroma.

Treatment/Management: See "Increased IOP" in chapter 2. Usually treatment for Congenital Glaucoma is surgical because it is caused by abnormal anatomy, although topical drops can be used as well. With treatment the cup to disc ratio may return to normal. Amblyopia should be treated/avoided with prescription of glasses and patching.

INFLAMMATORY GLAUCOMA

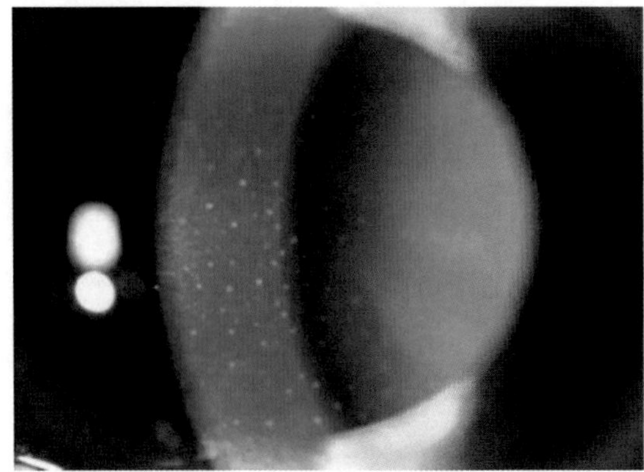

Jaypee Journals 1

What to Know: Inflammatory Glaucoma is related to uveitis. There are two types:

1) Acute Inflammatory Glaucoma which occurs during active inflammation/uveitis. It is usually due to trabeculitis, more common in infectious etiology (HSV, HZV, toxoplasmosis, etc) and improves with steroid treatment.
2) Chronic Inflammatory Glaucoma is caused by chronic trabecular meshwork damage and/or Peripheral Anterior Synechiae (PAS) formation and becomes difficult to treat with higher rates of medical and surgical failures.

Symptoms: Patients may have similar complaints as those with uveitis: reduced vision, pain, photophobia, and epiphora.

Signs: Patients present with uveitis (severe anterior chamber reaction with possible keratic precipitates) as well as the other signs of glaucoma (ONH cupping, thinned RNFL, abnormal visual fields).

Treatment/Management: See "Increased IOP" in chapter 2. Also treat the uveitis as usual with a topical steroid and cycloplegic. The prognosis is poorer than with POAG.

LENS-INDUCED GLAUCOMA

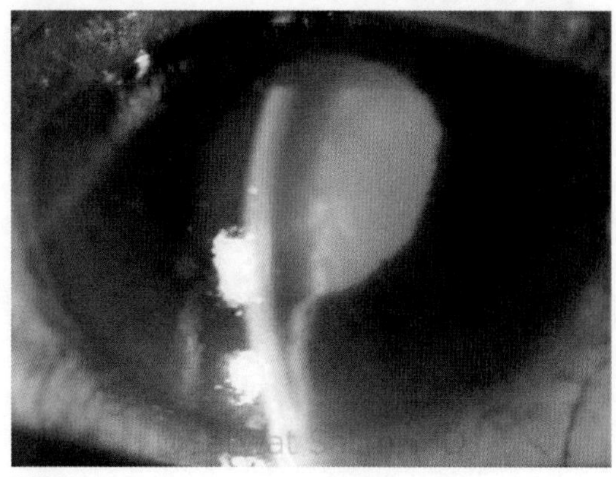

AAO2

What to Know: There are five types of Lens-Induced Glaucoma.

1. **Lens Particle Glaucoma** occurs when part of the natural lens is liberated into the anterior chamber during cataract surgery or penetrating trauma. The liberated lens particles clog the trabecular meshwork, preventing outflow, and increasing IOP.
2. **Phacoanaphylaxis** is an advanced form of Lens Particle Glaucoma. After a latent period, a granulomatous inflammatory response develops against the liberated lens particles. Now inflammation as well as lens particles clog the trabecular meshwork, preventing outflow, and increasing IOP.
3. **Ectopia Lentis** (luxation/dislocation and subluxation) can induce glaucoma, most commonly with an anteriorly displaced lens which can cause pupillary block. Additionally, the angle structures can become damaged and inflamed during the dislocation, further causing increased IOP.

Hypermature Cataracts are advanced Morgagnian Cataracts. Hypermature Cataracts can cause glaucoma via two mechanisms:

4. **Phacolytic Glaucoma** is caused when **proteins leak out of the lens** into the anterior chamber and are subsequently ingested by macrophages. Remember that "lytic" refers to cell rupture, and so in this case the lens cells rupture. The proteins and macrophages clog the trabecular meshwork, preventing aqueous outflow, thereby increasing IOP and leading to secondary glaucoma.
5. **Phacomorphic Glaucoma** occurs when the thickened cataractous lens pushes the iris forward and **causes angle closure glaucoma**. Remember that "morph" refers to a change in shape, and so in this case the glaucoma is caused by a change in the shape of the lens.

Symptoms: Patient complaints will be similar to those of angle closure glaucoma: nausea with possible vomiting, pain around eyes, frontal headache, photophobia, and blurry vision with halos around lights. Late stages may have constricted visual fields.

Signs: Signs may include anterior chamber cells and flare, peripheral anterior synechiae, ciliary injection, and increased IOP. Patients may have other signs of glaucoma as well (ONH cupping, thinned RNFL, abnormal visual fields).

Treatment/Management: The inflammation needs to be treated with a topical steroid and cycloplegic. See "Increased IOP" in chapter 2. Definitive treatment includes removal of the natural lens.

ANGLE RECESSION GLAUCOMA

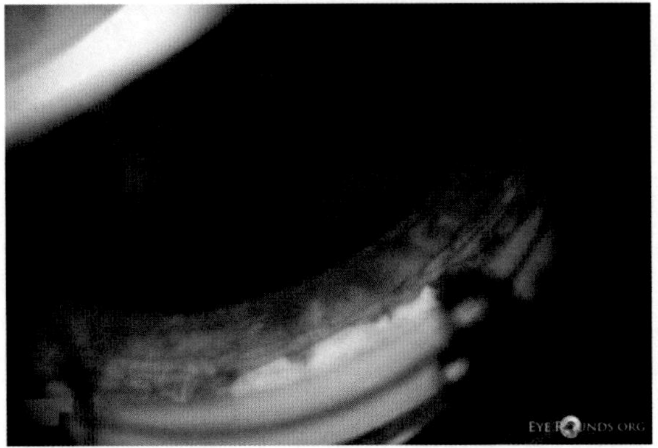

EyeRounds.org University of Iowa

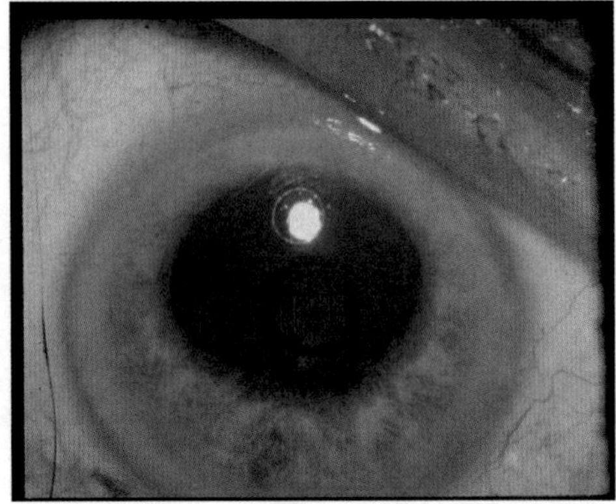

Cogan Collection, NEI/NIH

What to Know: Angle Recession Glaucoma usually occurs after blunt ocular trauma/hyphema, but can develop within months to years after the traumatic event.

Symptoms: Patients usually have no complaints.

Signs: Patients present with an uneven iris insertion and broadened ciliary body band (left image) on gonioscopy. The cause of the glaucoma is due to trabecular meshwork damage, and the risk factor for developing glaucoma depends on the extent of the angle recession; those with more than 50% angle recession are at highest risk. Patients may have other signs of ocular trauma: iris sphincter tears, cataracts, vossius ring (right image). Patients may have other signs of glaucoma as well (ONH cupping, thinned RNFL, abnormal visual fields).

Treatment/Management: See "Increased IOP" in chapter 2. Typically SLT and ALT are not effective for Angle Recession Glaucoma; the patient may require surgery instead. After a traumatic event has healed, if angle recession is still present on gonio, then the patient needs to be monitored at least annually to watch for progression to glaucoma.

POSNER-SCHLOSSMAN SYNDROME / GLAUCOMATOCYCLITIC CRISIS

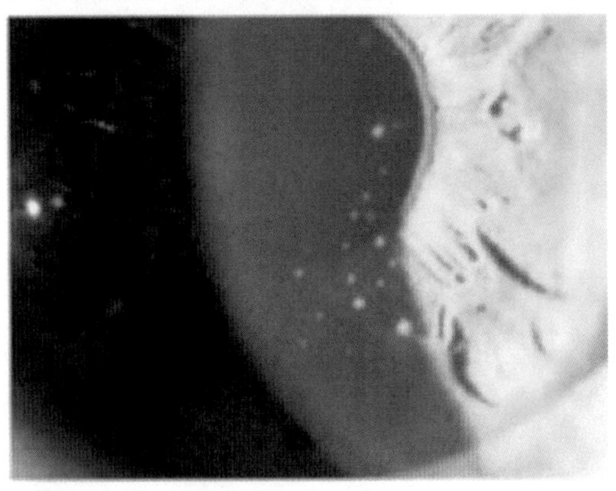

AAO 3

What to Know: Posner-Schlossman Syndrome is caused by trabeculitis.

Symptoms: Patients will complain of pain, blurry vision, and halos around lights. They may also have nausea, vomiting, and a frontal headache depending on the severity of the IOP increase.

Signs: Patients present with recurrent attacks of increased IOP (up to 60 mmHg). The trabeculitis will cause a mild anterior chamber reaction of cells/flare. They will have an OPEN angle with NO synechiae.

Treatment/Management: If the IOP is dramatically increased consider paracentesis (allowing outflow of aqueous from the globe by penetrating the cornea near the limbus with a needle). Prescribe a topical hypotensive and possibly a systemic CAI. The inflammation can be treated with a topical steroid or an oral NSAID. Patients are followed every 1-7 days depending on their response to the therapy.

<table>
<tr><th colspan="2">ANGLE CLOSURE GLAUCOMA</th></tr>
<tr><th colspan="2">PRIMARY ANGLE CLOSURE GLAUCOMA</th></tr>
<tr><th>ACUTE</th><th>CHRONIC</th></tr>
<tr><td> 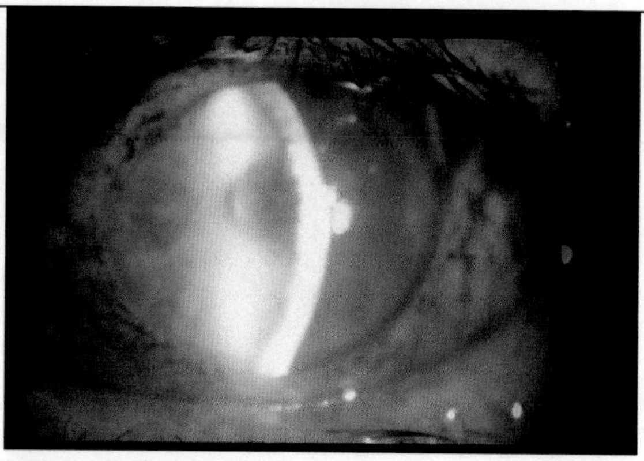Retina Image Bank File #8195</td><td> 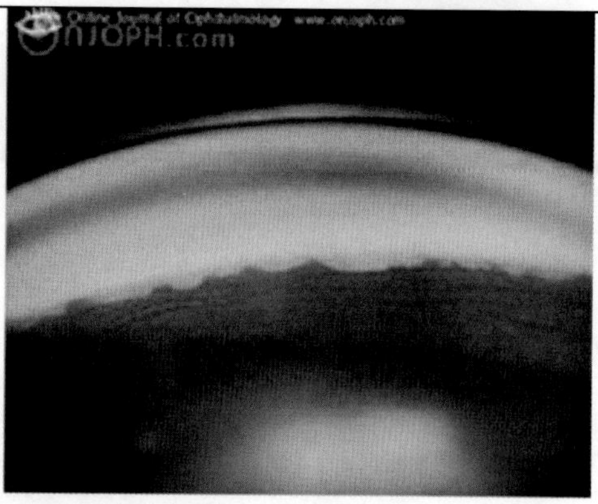Atlas of Ophthalmology Image #4638</td></tr>
<tr><td colspan="2"><u>What to Know:</u> Angle Closure Glaucoma can be either acute or chronic. After a patient has been dilated (dark adaptation, pharmacological), the iris may become apposed to the lens when attempting to constrict, thus creating a seal between the anterior and posterior chambers. Now that the aqueous cannot flow into the anterior chamber, it will back up in the posterior chamber and IOP will increase causing the iris to bow forward and the angle to close. Now aqueous cannot flow out of the trabecular meshwork, and the IOP will increase even further. Angle Closure Glaucoma is most commonly found in hyperopes because they have a shorter eyeball. The reduced axial length pushes all of the ocular structures closer together, thus causing the angles to narrow.</td></tr>
<tr><td>Acute Angle Closure Glaucoma will present unilaterally.</td><td>Chronic Angle Closure Glaucoma occurs when a patient has multiple subclinical attacks of Acute Angle Closure Glaucoma or prolonged Acute Angle Closure Glaucoma.</td></tr>
<tr><td><u>Symptoms:</u> Patients will complain of nausea with possible vomiting, pain around eyes, frontal headache, and blurry vision with halos around lights (caused by corneal edema and bullae).</td><td><u>Symptoms:</u> Patients will be asymptomatic until late stages when they will complain of reduced vision and constricted visual fields.</td></tr>
<tr><td><u>Signs:</u> IOP will be increased significantly, angle will be closed, and pupil will be mid-dilated. Patients will have corneal edema with bullae because increased IOP interferes with the ability of the endothelium to maintain corneal deturgescence.</td><td><u>Signs:</u> Patients will have broad areas of peripheral anterior synechiae (PAS) seen on gonioscopy and narrow angles. They will also have the other signs of glaucoma.</td></tr>
<tr><td colspan="2">After the iris and cornea have been apposed for a long time, they may stick together forming synechiae.</td></tr>
<tr><td><u>Treatment/Management:</u>
1. Initial treatment for Acute Angle Closure Glaucoma is aimed at breaking the attack (separate the iris from the lens) and urgently reducing IOP. The attack can be broken with indentation gonioscopy. The IOP can be reduced topically by following the ABC method: Alpha Agonist, Beta Blocker, and Carbonic Anhydrase Inhibitor (dorzolamide). The round of drops should be administered every fifteen minutes and each drop should be separated by five minutes. An IV osmotic or acetazolamide can also be employed. Side effects</td><td><u>Treatment/Management:</u>
Treatment for Chronic Angle Closure Glaucoma is aimed at reducing IOP and preventing future angle closure. IOP can be difficult to control due to PAS. Laser iridoplasty can be used to prevent the formation of new PAS. A peripheral iridotomy or iridectomy should be performed bilaterally to stabilize the IOP between the anterior and posterior chambers, and prevent future attacks. The patient may also need to chronically use topical medications to lower IOP if surgical efforts are not successful.</td></tr>
</table>

of acetazolamide include a myopic shift, depression, a metallic taste, aplastic anemia, and metabolic acidosis. Topical steroids can also be used to reduce inflammation. Prostaglandins usually take about two weeks to start showing significant reduction of IOP, and so they are not the first line of treatment for an Acute Angle Closure Attack. 2. Once the pressure has been stabilized and the cornea is clear, a laser peripheral iridotomy (LPI) or iridectomy should be performed bilaterally to prevent future attacks. Pilocarpine is often used prior to surgery to pull the iris taught and allow the surgeon to work more precisely.	

IRIDOCORNEAL ENDOTHELIAL (ICE) SYNDROME

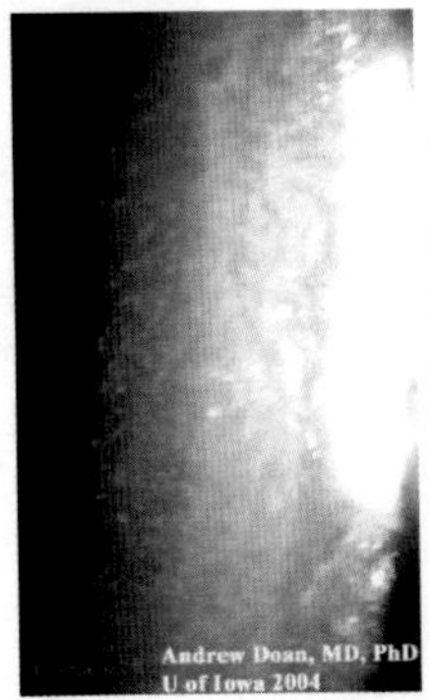

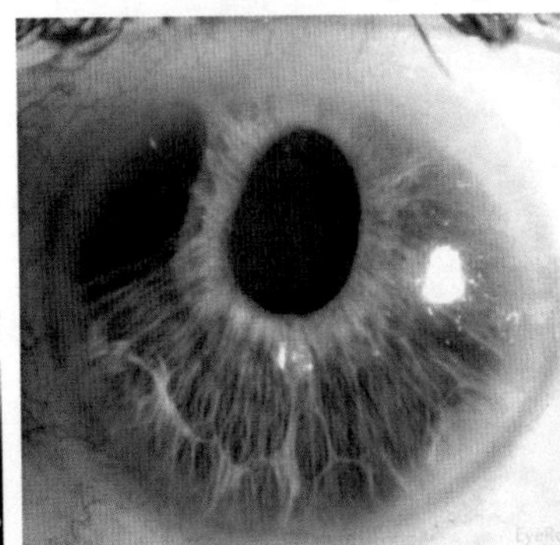
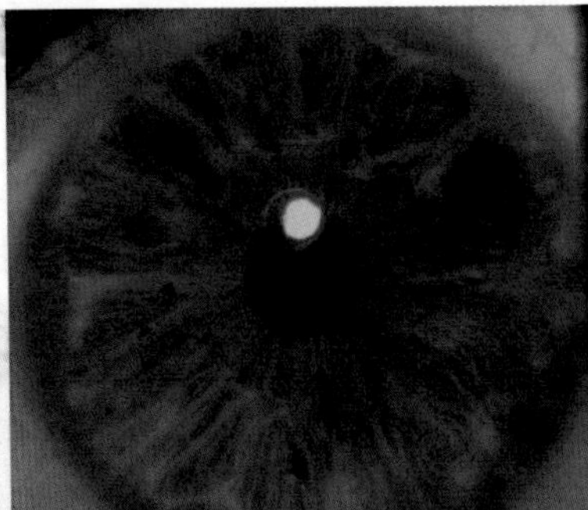
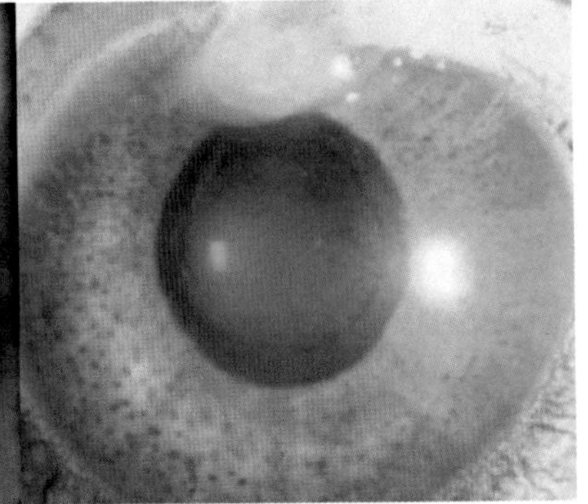

EyeRounds.org University of Iowa   Cogan Collection, NEI/NIH   Atlas of Ophthalmology Image #2742

What to Know: ICE syndrome occurs when the corneal endothelium proliferates across the anterior chamber angle, causing contraction of the iris and secondary angle closure glaucoma. It most frequently occurs in women.

Symptoms: Initially patients will be asymptomatic. As iris changes occur in late stages, patients may complain of blur and monocular diplopia.

Signs: Patients present with a deep anterior chamber, a "beaten bronze" appearance of the corneal endothelium (left image), corneal edema (due to endothelial defects), and peripheral anterior synechiae. There are three types of characteristic iris changes, listed below from best to worst prognosis.

1. Essential Iris Atrophy (second image from left): **Severe** iris thinning causing **holes** and a distorted/displaced pupil (corectopia).
2. Chandler Syndrome (third image from left): **Mild** iris thinning causing a distorted/displaced pupil (corectopia).
3. Iris Nevus / Cogan-Reese Syndrome (right image) is characterized by pigmented iris nodules.

Treatment/Management: See "Increased IOP" in chapter 2. Patients may benefit from surgical treatment options. The corneal edema can be treated with a topical hypertonic (sodium chloride, Muro 128), but severe cases may require a corneal transplant. Patients should be followed every 1-3 months.

RUBEOSIS IRIDIS → NEOVASCULAR GLAUCOMA

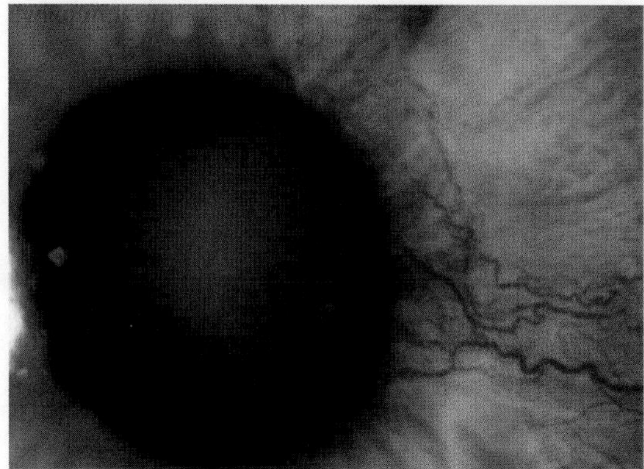
EyeRounds.org University of Iowa

What to Know: Rubeosis Iridis is the precursor to Neovascular Glaucoma. The disease process transfers from Rubeosis Iridis to Neovascular Glaucoma when the IOP increases. Both are caused by any retinal disease which leads to release of VEGF. When the retinal disease is severe enough, the VEGF will penetrate all the way to the iris, thereby initiating neovascularization of the iris. The neovascularization of the iris begins at the pupillary border and grows towards the angle. Retinal diseases which can lead to Rubeosis Iridis and Neovascular Glaucoma can include diabetic retinopathy, ocular ischemic syndrome, retinopathy of prematurity, sickle cell retinopathy, and vein occlusions. However, the most common offenders are proliferative diabetic retinopathy and ischemic central retinal vein occlusions.

Symptoms:

- Rubeosis Iridis: asymptomatic.
- Neovascular Glaucoma: Patient complaints will be similar to those who have Angle Closure Glaucoma (photophobia, malaise, pain, blur, "red eye").

Signs:

- Rubeosis Iridis: The most important sign seen in Rubeosis Iridis is radial neovascularization of the iris.
- Neovascular Glaucoma: Eventually the neovascularization will grow into the angle. The fibrovascular tissue will grow across the angle, thereby pulling it closed and raising the IOP. The examiner will see narrowed angles with neovascularization. Stromal edema may cause the cornea to appear hazy; the endothelium is unable to maintain deturgescence due to the increased IOP.

Treatment/Management:

- Rubeosis Iridis: Inflammation of the iris can be treated with steroids and cycloplegics. The retinal ischemia also needs to be treated with anti-VEGF injections and laser photocoagulation (cautery of retinal blood vessels with a laser) can also be used if the cornea is clear (a cloudy cornea will disrupt the laser beam and prevent the accuracy necessary while performing laser photocoagulation). If the cornea is cloudy then use peripheral cryotherapy (freezing of tissue).
- Neovascular Glaucoma: Like Angle Closure Glaucoma, Neovascular Glaucoma needs to be treated with urgency. In addition to the treatment options for Rubeosis Iridis, the IOP needs to be reduced in patients who have Neovascular Glaucoma. See "Increased IOP" in chapter 2. If the cornea is hazy then consider peripheral cryotherapy (freezing of tissue) instead of laser photocoagulation (cautery of retinal blood vessels with a laser).

PLATEAU IRIS CONFIGURATION / SYNDROME

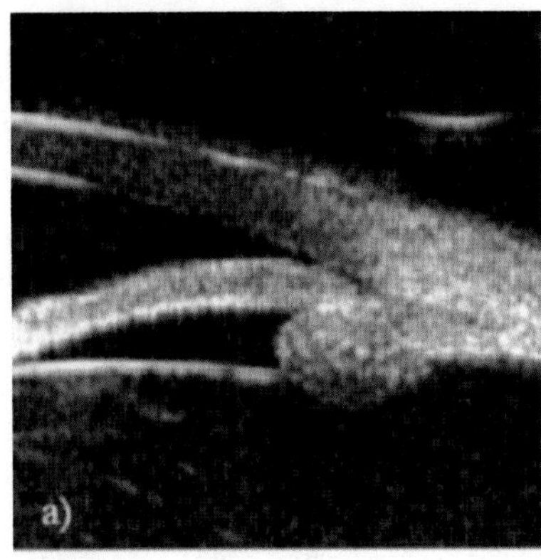

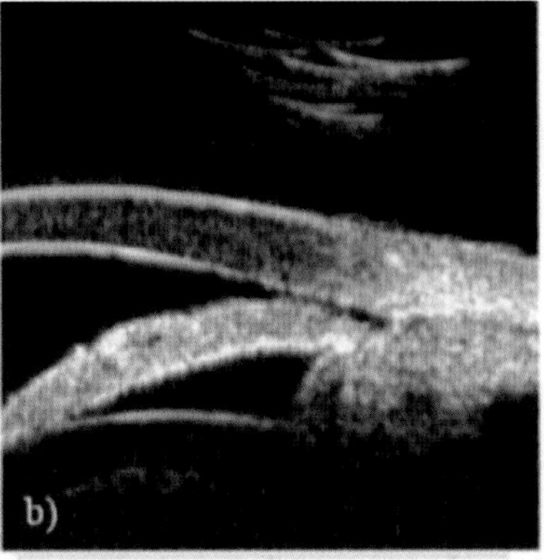

Openi 1

What to Know: Plateau Iris Configuration is defined by a flat iris which is sharply convex in the periphery due to anteriorly rotated ciliary processes. It is defined as Plateau Iris Syndrome when angle closure with an increased IOP occurs.

Symptoms: Patients have no complaints unless angle closure occurs, in which case they will have the same complaints as those who have Angle Closure Glaucoma (nausea with possible vomiting, pain around eyes, frontal headache, photophobia, and blurry vision with halos around lights)

Signs: Plateau Iris Syndrome will initially present the same as Angle Closure Glaucoma. However, after an LPI the IOP will still increase with dilation due to the iris configuration, and this is diagnostic.

Treatment/Management: Surgical options to consider for patients with Plateau Iris Syndrome include iridectomy and argon laser iridoplasty or gonioplasty.

AQUEOUS MISDIRECTION SYNDROME / MALIGNANT GLAUCOMA

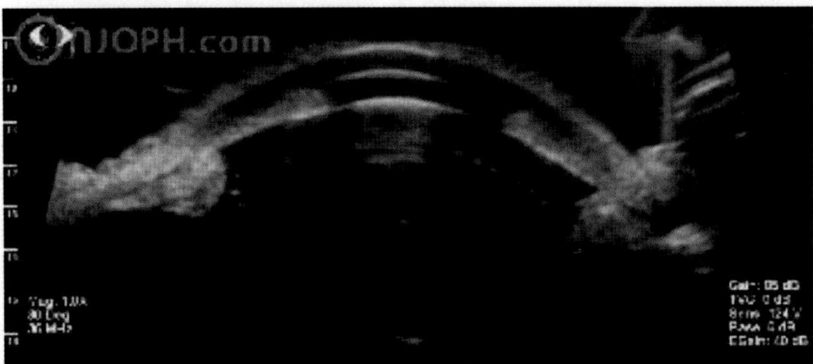

Atlas of Ophthalmology Image #8916

What to Know: Malignant Glaucoma occurs when the ciliary body rolls anteriorly causing the aqueous humor to be misdirected posteriorly and pool in Berger's Space. Accumulation of aqueous in the posterior chamber causes the anterior chamber structures to be displaced anteriorly and cause angle closure glaucoma.

Symptoms: Patients may complain of a red painful eye and photophobia.

Signs: Patients present with an extremely high IOP with a very shallow anterior chamber.

Treatment/Management: Initial treatment is aimed at breaking the angle closure attack. Topical atropine should be utilized; pupillary dilation will cause the zonules to contract and pull the lens back into its appropriate position. The IOP should be reduced by using all topical medications available for treating increased IOP which are not contraindicated. Oral or IV acetazolamide and an osmotic can also be employed.

If medical treatment is unsuccessful at breaking the attack, then consider surgical options: laser peripheral iridotomy (LPI) to equalize the pressure between the anterior and posterior chambers, or vitrectomy/lensectomy to reduce ocular crowding.

GLAUCOMA TREATMENT COMPLICATION

BLEBITIS

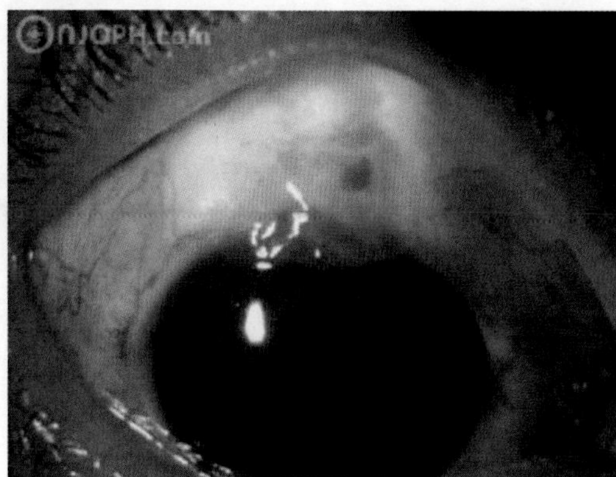

Atlas of Ophthalmology Image #8252

What to Know: A filtering bleb used to treat glaucoma may become infected within days to years after the surgery is completed. The infection may highly resemble Endophthalmitis.

Symptoms: Patients may complain of a painful red eye with mucous discharge, blurry vision, and photophobia.

Signs: Patients present with a white, inflamed bleb with concurrent anterior chamber reaction (which may include hypopyon) and possible vitritis.

Treatment/Management: Treatment includes topical antibiotics Q1H to treat the infection. The anterior chamber reaction should be treated with a topical cycloplegic. Steroids should be introduced after 24 hours to treat the inflammation. Patients should be followed daily until the infection resolves, and they may require hospitalization to ensure compliance.

CHAPTER 9
ACCOMMODATIVE / VERGENCE / OCULOMOTOR CONDITIONS

The NBEO website states that 20-25 questions will be asked on Accommodative / Vergence / Oculomotor Conditions. Historically they have asked about 20.6 questions, meaning this chapter covers approximately 6% of the material tested on the exam, or roughly 4 cases. This material is NOT tested on TMOD.

When discussing Accommodative and Vergence conditions, one must be familiar with Morgan's Expecteds:

Test	Expected Finding
Distance lateral phoria	1 exophoria
Near lateral phoria	3 exophoria
AC/A ratio	4:1 +/-2
BO at Distance	9/19/10
BI at Distance	7/4
BO at Near	17/21/11
BI at Near	13/21/13
Near Point of Convergence (NPC)	Break 5, Recovery 7
NRA	+2.50
PRA	-3.00
Minimum amplitude of accommodation	A = 15 – ¼(Age)
Monocular Accommodative Facility	11 cycles per minute (cpm)
Binocular Accommodative Facility	11 cycles per minute (cpm). If the patient reports seeing double, then they have failed the test and have a vergence dysfunction.
Monocular Estimation Method (MEM)	Normal: Plano to +0.75D (small lag of accommodation) Abnormal: +1.00D or more (aka high, large lag of accommodation) OR any minus (aka low, lead of accommodation)

I remember some of these by noticing that it is normal to be a little exophoric at both distance and near (but it is never normal to be esophoric). Also notice that the break for vergence amplitudes (except BI at Distance) is about 20.

Positive Fusional Vergence (PFV) can be tested directly with BO prism or indirectly with Plus (positive) lenses. PFV measures convergence. Negative Fusional Vergence (NFV) can be tested directly with BI prism or indirectly with minus (negative) lenses. NFV measures divergence.

The way in which plus lenses interact with the visual system can be difficult to conceptualize. You know that a plus lens will relax accommodation, and so by definition will stimulate divergence. However, if the patient's eyes want to remain focused on the same point in space as before the plus lens was introduced, then they need to engage their convergence again in order to maintain a single image. Naturally, the opposite can be said of minus lenses. This can be remembered as "BIM BOP" Base In Minus, Base Out Plus. Or Base In prisms behave similarly to Minus lenses, and Base Out prisms behave similarly to Plus Lenses.

It is important to be able to perform a case analysis in order to answer questions on these cases. These are the steps I follow while analyzing a case:

1. First look at the patient's NPC. If it is reduced, then the patient has Convergence Insufficiency.
2. Next look at Amplitude of accommodation. If it is reduced, then the patient has Accommodative Insufficiency. If the accommodation becomes worse with time, then the patient has Ill-Sustained Accommodation.
3. Now look at AC/A ratio, cover test, and accommodative facility, as described in the table below:

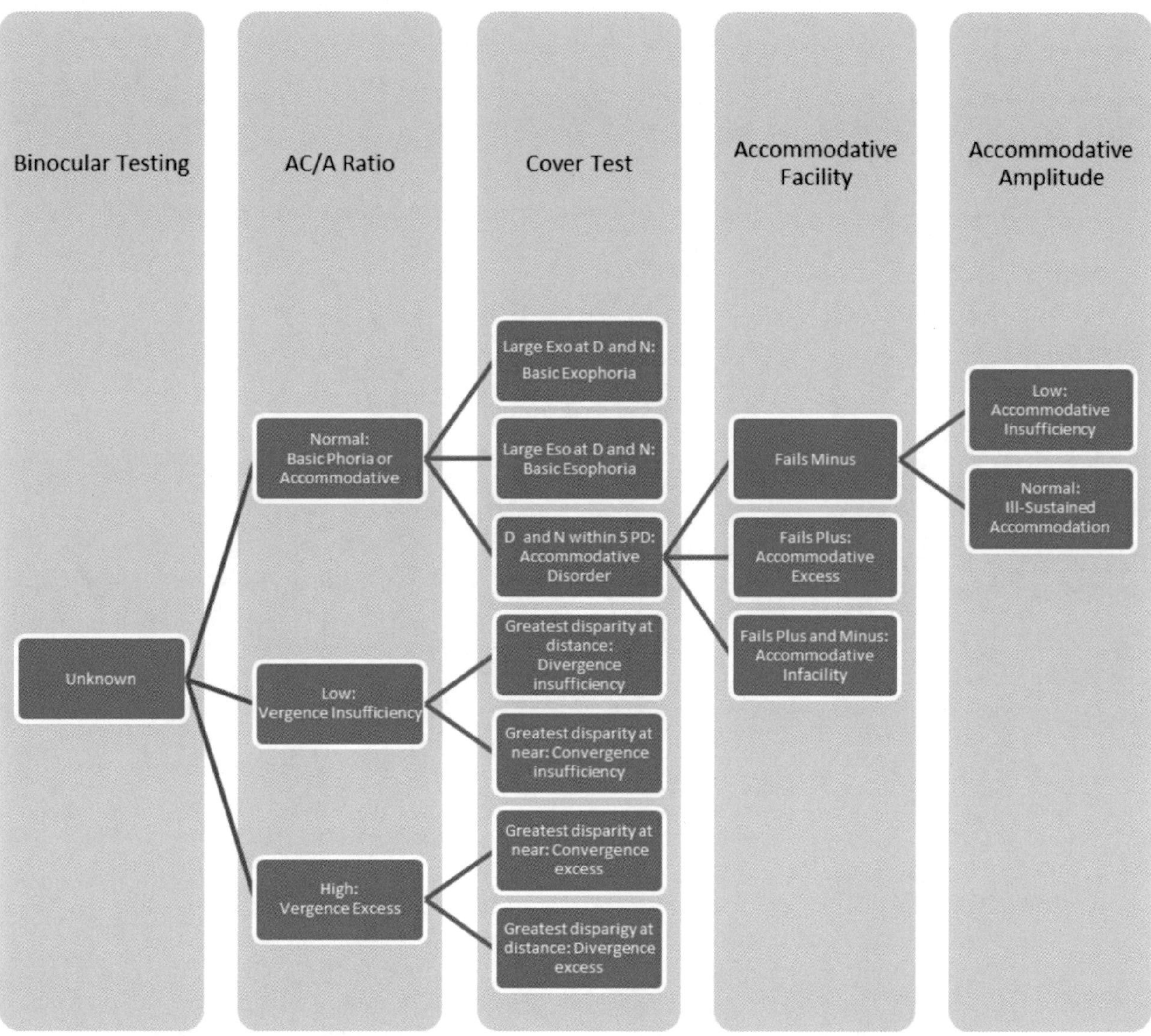

~~~VERGENCE~~~

SIGNS OF VERGENCE CONDITIONS

Patients with vergence disorders will have some similar characteristics. Their stereopsis, accommodative amplitudes, and monocular accommodative facilities will be normal. Remember any Excess Vergence Disorder will have a high AC/A ratio, while any Insufficient Vergence Disorder will have a low AC/A ratio. Furthermore, if the vergence disparity is greatest at distance, then the problem is at distance (divergence); while if the vergence disparity is greatest at near, then the disparity is at near (convergence). Below is a summary of the differences between the various accommodative conditions.

Condition	Cover Test	AC/A Ratio	NPC	Vergence Amplitude	Vergence Facility	Binocular Accommodative Facility	NRA and PRA	Monocular Estimation Method
Basic Exophoria	Equal exo at D&N	Normal	Normal	Low BO at D and N		Fails +	Low NRA	Low
Basic Esophoria	Equal eso at D&N			Low BI at D and N		Fails –	Low PRA	High
Convergence Insufficiency	Exo > N	Low	Receded	Low BO		Fails +	Low NRA	Low
Convergence Excess	Eso > N	High	Normal	Low BI		Fails –	Low PRA	High
Divergence Insufficiency	Eso > D	Low		Low BI at D		Normal: Remember accommodation is not engaged with distance viewing.		
Divergence Excess	Exo > D	High		Low BO at D and Low BI at N				

This is a quick way to summarize this table. This summary does not account for MEM findings:

- Basic Exophoria
  - Increased exo-posture which is about equal at distance and near.
  - Difficulty with Plus Lenses
  - Difficulty with Base Out Prisms
- Basic Esophoria
  - Increased eso-posture which is about equal at distance and near.
  - Difficulty with Minus Lenses
  - Difficulty with Base In Prisms
- Convergence Insufficiency
  - Reduced NPC
  - Increased exo-posture at near
  - Difficulty with Plus Lenses
  - Difficulty with Base Out Prisms
- Convergence Excess
  - Increased eso-posture at near
  - Difficulty with Minus Lenses
  - Difficulty with Base In Prisms
- Divergence Insufficiency
  - Increased eso-posture at distance
  - Difficulty with Base In Prisms
- Divergence Excess
  - Increased exo-posture at distance
  - Difficulty with Base Out Prisms

Either Sheard's Criterion or Percival's Criterion can be used to determine the amount of prism which should be prescribed for a patient with a vergence condition. Both criteria can be used for either exo-postures or eso-postures; however, Sheard's Criterion is best used for exo-postures, and Percival's Criterion is best used for eso-postures.

Percival's Criterion is based on vergence ranges. It states:
Prism needed = 1/3 Greater Vergence Range – 2/3 Lesser Vergence Range

Sheard's Criterion states:
Prism needed = 2/3 phoria – 1/3 compensating vergence

BASIC EXOPHORIA

What to Know: Patients with Basic Exophoria will have nearly the same amount of exophoria at distance and near (within 5 PD).

Symptoms: Patient complaints will sound the same as those with Basic Esophoria. They may complain of blur and diplopia at near. At near they may complain of asthenopia, headaches, diplopia, and poor concentration.

Signs: Patients will have difficulty converging due to their exophoric posture, and so they will have difficulty with BO prisms and Plus Lenses because they ask the vergence system to converge. Remember from BIM BOP that BO and Plus lenses place similar demands on the vergence system. These patients will have a low MEM (lead of accommodation) because their accommodative system is working in overdrive in an attempt to make up for the poor convergence.

Treatment/Management: If myopia is present, prescribe corrective lenses for not only will they give clear vision, but they will also aid in ocular alignment. If the patient has +1.50 or greater hyperopia it may be wise to wait to prescribe spectacles until after vision therapy has been initiated because plus lenses will increase the deviation. BI prisms may also be prescribed, although they are not frequently necessary if vision therapy is employed. Vision therapy should be aimed at increasing convergence ranges with the use of BO prisms.

BASIC ESOPHORIA

What to Know: Patients with Basic Esophoria will have nearly the same amount of esophoria at distance and near (within 5 PD).

Symptoms: Patient complaints will sound the same as those with Basic Exophoria. They may complain of blur and diplopia at distance. At near they may complain of asthenopia, headaches, diplopia, and poor concentration.

Signs: Patients will have difficulty diverging due to their esophoric posture, and so they will have difficulty with BI prisms and Minus Lenses because they ask the vergence system to diverge. Remember from BIM BOP that BI and Minus lenses place similar demands on the vergence system. These patients will have a high MEM (lag of accommodation) because their accommodative system is relaxing as an attempt to simulate divergence.

Treatment/Management: If hyperopia is present, prescribe as much plus as possible. BO prisms may also be prescribed to relieve symptoms of diplopia. Vision therapy should be aimed at increasing divergence ranges with the use of BI prisms.

CONVERGENCE INSUFFICIENCY

What to Know: Convergence Insufficiency is defined by a reduced near point of convergence. **Convergence Insufficiency is the only vergence or accommodative condition with a reduced near point of convergence.**

Symptoms: Patients may complain of difficulty reading with asthenopia, headaches, blurry vision, and diplopia. Words may appear to move around on the page and the patient may become sleepy while reading.

Signs: The name convergence insufficiency tells you that the problem is located at near and the AC/A will be low. **The most significant finding is the patient will have a reduced NPC.** Since these patients cannot converge, they will have an exophoria which is greater at near than at distance. Since a BO lens is asking the patient to converge, findings with BO lenses will be low. Plus lenses stimulate convergence during Binocular Accommodative Facility testing, and so patients will perform poorly with plus lenses (they may even report diplopia). MEM will be low because the accommodative system is working so hard to simulate convergence, the patient may appear to even have a lead of accommodation.

Treatment/Management: First, any ametropia should be fully corrected for myopes and under corrected for hyperopes. Patients should undergo vision therapy with an emphasis on training convergence using BO prism and plus lenses. Patients who are unresponsive to Vision Therapy may benefit from reading glasses with BI prism. In very rare cases, patients may require strabismus surgery.

CONVERGENCE EXCESS

What to Know: I like to break down the word to help me figure out what is the problem. Convergence refers to near problems, and excess means the patient is overdoing the problem (and they will have a high AC/A ratio). In other words, these patients will have relatively normal binocular posture at distance, but as they shift to near gaze they converge too much ending up with an abnormal eso-posture.

Symptoms: Patients may complain of difficulty reading with asthenopia, headaches, blurry vision, diplopia, and difficulty concentrating. Words may appear to move around on the page and the patient may become sleepy while reading.

Signs: Patients will have a high AC/A ratio because this is an "Excess" problem. **They will be more esophoric at near than distance by greater than 5 PD.** Due to their esophoria, patients will have difficulty diverging at near to a "normal" near binocular posture, and so they will have difficulty with BI prisms and Minus Lenses because they ask the vergence system to diverge. Remember from BIM BOP that BI and Minus lenses place similar demands on the vergence system. These patients will have a high MEM (lag of accommodation) because their accommodative system is relaxing as an attempt to simulate divergence.

Treatment/Management: Release a glasses prescription with as much plus as possible as well as a near add. Prisms are rarely necessary to add to the spectacle prescription because a near add is so effective due to the high AC/A ratio. Vision therapy should be aimed at increasing divergence ranges at near with the use of BI prisms and Minus lenses.

DIVERGENCE INSUFFICIENCY

What to Know: Divergence Insufficiency is the least common vergence condition. If we were to break down the name of this condition, "divergence" indicates that the problem is at distance, and "insufficiency" indicates that the patient does not diverge enough (and that the patient will have a low AC/A ratio).

Symptoms: Patients may complain of diplopia and asthenopia with prolonged distance activities which is worse at the end of the day.

Signs: Patients present with an esophoria which will be larger at distance than at near by at least 5 PD with a low AC/A ratio. Given that these patients do not like to diverge at distance, they will struggle with BI prism at distance. Since this is a problem with distance, all near tests will be normal (NPC, accommodative facility, NRA/PRA, and MEM).

Treatment/Management: Patients should be prescribed as much plus as possible, bearing in mind that spectacle lenses will have minimal therapeutic effect given that this is a distance issue, and so does not tap into the AC/A system. BO prisms can be prescribed for distance activities only, although these patients may tolerate BO prism at near as well because their positive fusional convergence can compensate. Vision therapy should be aimed at increasing divergence ranges at distance with the use of BI prisms and Minus lenses.

DIVERGENCE EXCESS

What to Know: If we were to break down the name of this condition, "divergence" indicates that the problem is at distance, and "excess" indicates that the patient is diverging too much (and that the patient will have a high AC/A ratio).

Symptoms: Parents may complain of one eye turning out, and **children may close one eye in bright light**.

Signs: Patients present with an exophoria which will be larger at distance than at near by at least 5 PD with a high AC/A ratio. Given that these patients do not like to converge at distance, they will struggle with BO prism at distance. Since this is a problem with distance, all near tests will be normal (NPC, accommodative facility, NRA/PRA, and MEM).

Treatment/Management: Correct for any myopia and only hyperopia over +1.50D because minus will reduce distance divergence, especially due to the high AC/A seen in these patients. Patients may respond well to extra minus at distance with a near add. Prism is rarely prescribed for these patients because vision therapy is so successful and lenses are so effective given the high AC/A ratio. Vision therapy should be aimed at decreasing divergence ranges at distance with the use of BO prisms and Plus lenses.

~~~ACCOMMODATION~~~

SIGNS OF ACCOMMODATIVE CONDITIONS

What to Know: Patients with accommodation disorders will have some similar characteristics. Their cover test will be unpredictable. Other findings will be normal: AC/A ratio, NPC, vergence facility, and stereopsis. Below is a summary of the differences between the various accommodative conditions.

<table>
<tr><th>Condition</th><th>Vergence Amplitude</th><th>Accommodative Amplitude</th><th>Accommodative Facility (Monocular and Binocular)</th><th>NRA and PRA</th><th>Monocular Estimation Method (MEM)</th></tr>
<tr><td>Accommodative Insufficiency</td><td rowspan="2">BO blur at near may be low</td><td>Low</td><td rowspan="2">Fails –</td><td rowspan="2">Low PRA</td><td rowspan="2">High</td></tr>
<tr><td>Ill-Sustained Accommodation</td><td rowspan="3">Normal</td></tr>
<tr><td>Accommodative Excess</td><td>BI blur at near may be low</td><td>Fails +</td><td>Low NRA</td><td>Low</td></tr>
<tr><td>Accommodative Infacility</td><td>BI and BO blur at near may be low</td><td>Fails + and –</td><td>Low NRA and PRA</td><td>Normal</td></tr>
</table>

This is a quick way to summarize this table. This summary does not account for MEM findings:

- Accommodative Insufficiency
  - Reduced Amplitude of Accommodation
  - Difficulty with Minus Lenses
  - Difficulty with Base Out Prisms
- Accommodative Excess
  - Difficulty with Plus Lenses
  - Difficulty with Base In Prisms
- Ill-Sustained Accommodation
  - Findings get worse with time
  - Difficulty with Minus Lenses
  - Difficulty with Base Out Prisms
- Accommodative Infacility
  - Difficulty with both + and Minus Lenses
  - Difficulty with both BI and BO Prisms

Treatment/Management: Vision therapy techniques for accommodative conditions should be aimed at increasing the flexibility and speed of accommodation: practice alternating fixation from distance to near, and practice alternating fixation through plus and minus lenses. Vision therapy should begin monocularly and progress to binocular.

ACCOMMODATIVE INSUFFICIENCY

What to Know: Accommodative Insufficiency occurs when the patient cannot accommodate enough. It presents very similarly to presbyopia.

Symptoms: All symptoms will be associated with near tasks, which all require accommodation. Patients will have blur, headaches, and eyestrain with reading. They will get tired and have trouble maintaining attention with near tasks.

Signs: **Accommodative Insufficiency is the only vergence or accommodative condition with a reduced amplitude of accommodation.** Other abnormal findings will all be due to the fact that these patients have trouble accommodating. Vergence amplitudes will show a low BO blur at near because BO lenses ask the patient to converge, and increasing convergence is paired with increasing accommodation. These patients will also have a low PRA and struggle with minus lenses during monocular and binocular accommodative facility because minus lenses require the patient to accommodate to maintain a clear image. The examiner will detect a high MEM (large lag) because these patients are unable to crank in their accommodation to their target.

ILL-SUSTAINED ACCOMMODATION

What to Know: Patients with Ill-Sustained Accommodation will have difficulty maintaining accommodation. During initial testing their accommodation will be normal, but it will decline with prolonged testing. These patients will present similarly to those with Accommodative Insufficiency with the exception that their accommodation will initially appear normal until it declines with further stress.

Symptoms: Patients may complain of difficulty with near tasks which will become more difficult the longer they engage in the activity. Complaints will include blur and eyestrain with reading. They will get tired and have trouble maintaining attention with near tasks.

Signs: Patients with Ill-Sustained Accommodation will have a normal amplitude of accommodation on initial testing which will reduce with repeated testing. Other abnormal findings will all be due to the fact that these patients have increased difficulty accommodating with prolonged stress of their accommodative system. Vergence amplitudes will show a low BO blur at near because BO lenses ask the patient to converge, and increasing convergence is paired with increasing accommodation. These patients will also have a low PRA and struggle with minus lenses during monocular and binocular accommodative facility because minus lenses require the patient to accommodate to maintain a clear image. The examiner will detect a high MEM (large lag) because these patients are unable to crank in their accommodation to see their target.

ACCOMMODATIVE EXCESS / ACCOMMODATIVE SPASM

What to Know: Accommodative Excess occurs when the patient's natural lens is in a constant state of accommodation (their ciliary muscles are constantly engaged). In other words, these patients are unable to relax their accommodation, even when looking at distance. It can be induced by prolonged reading or stress.

Symptoms: Patients may complain of asthenopia and headache with near activities, as well as blurry vision at distance.

Signs: Patients with Accommodative Excess have difficulty with plus lenses because plus lenses ask the accommodative system to relax, and relaxation is exactly what the system is unable to achieve in Accommodative Excess. Therefore, patients will have difficulty with plus lenses during both monocular and binocular accommodative facility testing, and they will also have a low NRA. Given that these patients are excessively accommodating, their MEM will be low, or will show a lead of accommodation. Cycloplegic refraction will force that accommodative system to relax and will reveal a significant degree of hyperopia.

Treatment/Management: The Accommodative Spasm needs to be broken. Patients should be prescribed their full cycloplegic refraction/try to push plus in order to relax the accommodative system. If resistant, a mild topical cycloplegic can be prescribed to break the spasm. If the patient has a significant esophoria or esotropia at near, they should also be prescribed an add for reading.

ACCOMMODATIVE INFACILITY

What to Know: Patients with Accommodative Infacility have difficulty with shifting the focus of their accommodation. They will have normal accommodative ranges, but transitioning from distance to near gaze or vice versa will prove difficult.

Symptoms: Patients may complain of blurred distance vision after prolonged reading (difficulty relaxing accommodation). Similarly, patients may complain of blurry near vision after prolonged distance viewing (difficulty engaging accommodation).

Signs: Patients with Accommodative Infacility will show difficulty with testing which engages and relaxes accommodation. **They will struggle with both plus and minus lenses during the accommodative facility testing.** They will also have a low NRA and a low PRA. Patients may also have low BI and BO vergence amplitudes because these are related to accommodation. All other findings will be normal.

~~~OCULOMOTOR~~~

Bear in mind the actions of each EOM when considering their palsies. If a nerve is affected, then its associated muscles will no longer be able to perform its normal actions. The nerves with their associated muscles and actions are described below:

- CN 3
    - Medial Rectus: ADuction
    - Superior Rectus: Elevation, Intorsion, Adduction (listed from primary to tertiary actions)
    - Inferior Rectus: Depression, Extorsion, Adduction (listed from primary to tertiary actions)
    - Inferior Oblique: Extorsion, Elevation, Abduction (listed from primary to tertiary actions)
- CN 4
    - Superior Oblique: Intorsion, Depression, Abduction (listed from primary to tertiary actions)
- CN6
    - Lateral Rectus: ABduction

The way I like to think of this is that when a patient has a CN3 palsy, their eye will not be able to move very much at all because CN3 innervates most of the EOMs (their eye will be located down and out). A patient with a CN6 palsy will be unable to ABduct (their eye will be towards their nose) but there will be no vertical component. This is unlike a patient who has a CN4 palsy, who will also be unable to ABduct (their eye will be turned towards their nose), but there will also be a vertical component (they will be unable to depress their eye, and so it will be elevated).

CRANIAL NERVE VI PALSY

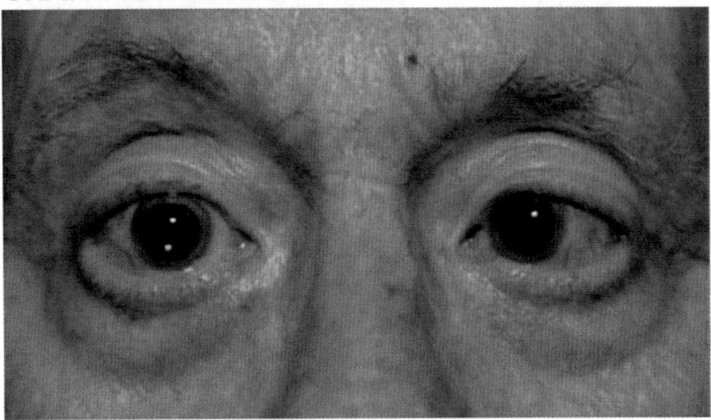

EyeRounds.org University of Iowa

What to Know: CN6 innervates the LR and is at higher risk for damage due to compressive **tumors** because of its pathway from the brain stem to the LR. Other causes could include vascular disorders (hypertension, diabetes) and trauma.

Symptoms: Patients may complain of horizontal diplopia.

Signs: Patients will present with esotropia with inability to abduct the involved eye.

Treatment/Management: Manage the underlying etiology. The patient may require a referral for an MRI and neurosurgery if a tumor is present. Diplopia can be managed with patching or prisms. Consider strabismus surgery for a longstanding, stable cases. CN6 palsy from a vascular disorder typically spontaneously resolves

CRANIAL NERVE III PALSY

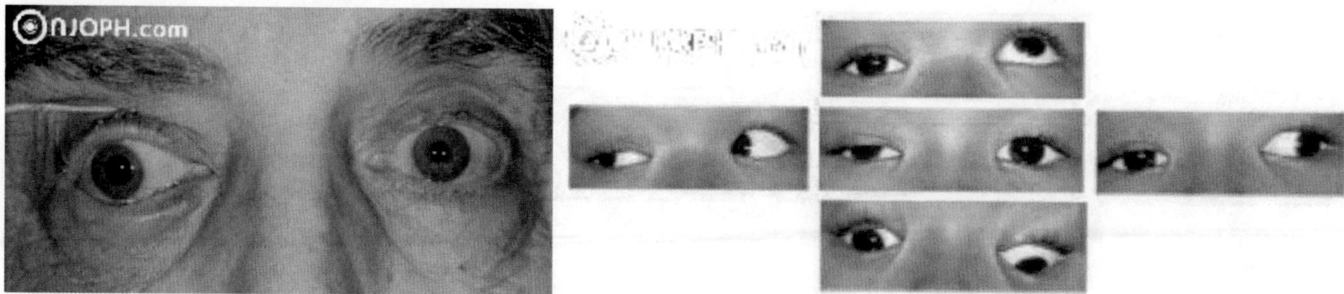

Atlas of Ophthalmology Image #5830 Atlas of Ophthalmology Image #5132

What to Know: Remember that CN3 innervates the SR, IR, MR, IO, the levator muscle, and the iris sphincter. Also, the pupillary fibers are located towards the outer layers of the nerve, which is why they are more susceptible to compressive lesions. Blood vessels travel in the middle of the nerve, which is why pupil-sparing palsies are usually related to microvascular conditions.

Symptoms: Patients will complain of diplopia and ptosis.

Signs: Given the innervation of CN3, the patient's eye will be located down and out with limited motility, and they will also have a complete ptosis (notice the patient's right lid is being elevated in the picture above to allow for viewing of the globe). When a patient presents with a CN3 palsy, it is incredibly important to determine if it is pupil involving or pupil sparing. If the patient has a blown (dilated) pupil, then the etiology is likely compressive (aneurysm or tumor) and requires emergent treatment. If the pupil is not involved, then the etiology is likely microvascular or ischemic (diabetes, hypertension). Fortunately, most cases are pupil sparing.

Treatment/Management:

- If the pupil is involved, refer the patient for an emergent MRI to investigate a tumor or aneurysm. Neurosurgery may be required.
- If the pupil is spared, the patient should be followed closely for a week. The underlying systemic disease should be managed.

ABERRANT REGENERATION OF CRANIAL NERVE III

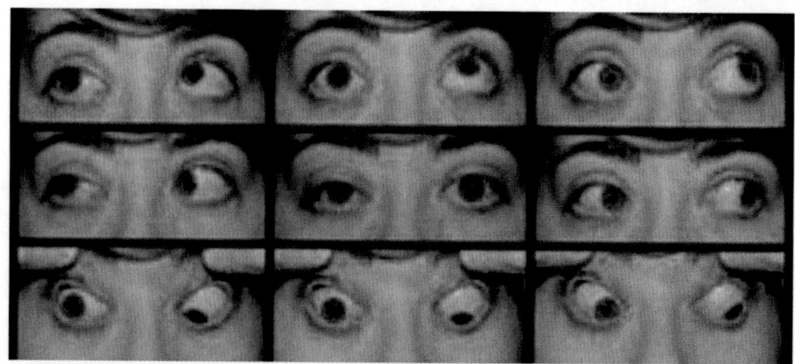

EyeRounds.org University of Iowa

What to Know: Aberrant Regeneration of CN3 occurs after a CN3 Palsy. As the nerve regenerates, it may innervate the wrong muscle, typically the lateral rectus.

Symptoms: Patients may complain of diplopia and ptosis (same as with CN3 Palsy)

Signs: Patients present with eyelid-gaze dyskinesis (eyelid retraction on downgaze or adduction, aka the pseudo-Graefe phenomenon), and pupil-gaze dyskinesis (pupil constriction on downgaze or adduction).

Treatment/Management: Treatment is aimed at reducing symptoms of diplopia with prisms or unilateral occlusion. If the patient shows stability with no improvement after 6 months, then consider strabismus surgery.

CRANIAL NERVE IV PALSY

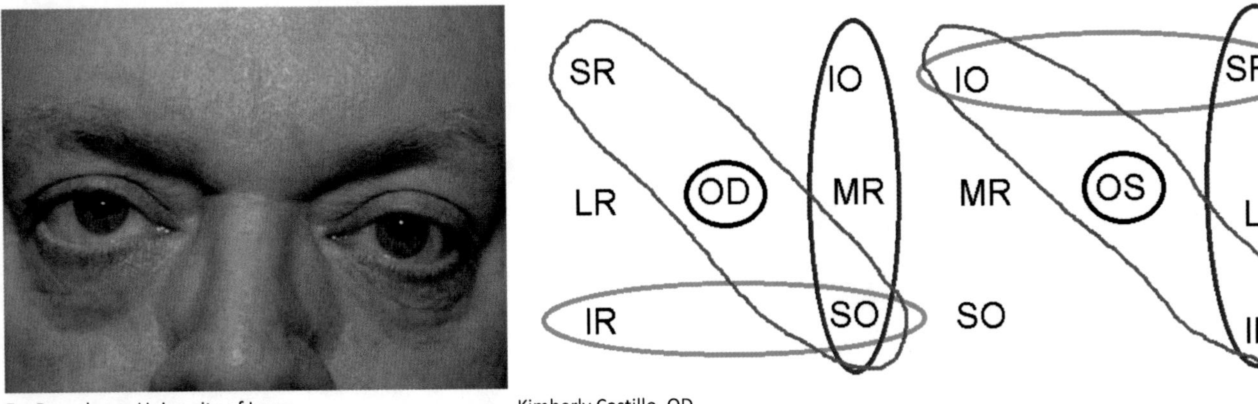

EyeRounds.org University of Iowa Kimberly Castillo, OD

What to Know: CN4 innervates the SO and is a long, thin nerve, placing it at higher risk for damage due to **trauma**. Other causes could include vascular disorders (hypertension, diabetes) and tumors.

Symptoms: Patients will complain of diplopia.

Signs: The affected eye will be located in and up with a possible torsional component. **The patient will frequently compensate for the palsy by tilting their head towards the contralateral side**. The affected muscle can be determined by using the Parks-Three-Step test (see top right picture):

1. Perform cover test in primary position. If right hypertropia present, circle the RIR, RSO, LIO, and LSR.
2. Perform cover test with head turned to the right and left. Circle the muscles for the gaze with the worst deviation. Right head turn = left eye gaze = circle left muscles.
3. Perform cover test with head tilted to the right and left and identify direction with largest deviation. Circle the muscles as you observe the patient. For example, if head tilt is worse to the right, circle the RSR, RSO, LIO, and LIR.

The muscle which is circled three times is the affected muscle. In this example it is the RSO, which matches the patient pictured above. Be sure to note that when performing Parks-Three-Step your result will nearly always be an oblique.

Treatment/Management: Manage the underlying etiology. The patient may require a referral for an MRI and neurosurgery if a tumor is present. Diplopia can be managed with patching or prisms. Consider strabismus surgery for a longstanding deviation with a head tilt.

NYSTAGMUS

What to Know: Nystagmus can be either congenital, acquired, or physiologic. It will usually have a "null point" or a direction of gaze in which the Nystagmus slows or stops compared to other gazes.

Symptoms:

- **Congenital Nystagmus** is asymptomatic because it has been present since birth and so the brain has adapted and these patients do not know anything else.
- Patients with **Acquired Nystagmus** will complain of oscillopsia and blurry vision.
- **Physiologic Nystagmus** is normal and so patients will not have any complaints.

Signs: There are a variety of different types of Nystagmus.

- Congenital Nystagmus:
    - Efferent/Motor/Infantile Nystagmus is typically horizontal and due to an oculomotor condition which presents itself by the fourth month of life.
    - Latent Nystagmus occurs when one eye is occluded with the fast phase away from the occluded eye (temporally). These patients have no Nystagmus (and better vision) with binocular viewing.
    - Spasmus Nutans presents with a triad of horizontal Nystagmus, head nodding, and head turning (torticollis). It will present itself within the first year of life and then spontaneously resolve by the age of 5.
- Acquired Nystagmus:
    - Drug-Induced nystagmus is vertical (**downbeat**) and caused by anticonvulsants such as carbamazepine and phenytoin.
    - Internuclear Ophthalmoplegia is caused by a lesion to the medial longitudinal fasciculus (MLF). It will lead to poor adduction with jerk nystagmus of the abducting eye. Patients will have no difficulty looking toward the lesion, but poor adduction and nystagmus will occur when the patient is looking away from the lesion.
    - One-And-A-Half Syndrome occurs when there is a lesion of the MLF and CN6 Nucleus (Paramedian Pontine Reticular Formation). Both eyes will be unable to look past midline towards the direction of the lesion. Only the contralateral eye will be able to look away from the lesion, but with nystagmus. In other words, the only horizontal movement the patient will be able to perform will be nystagmus of the contralateral eye while looking away from the lesion. Convergence will still be intact.
    - Convergence-Retraction: When a patient attempts an upward saccade their eyes will converge and their globes will retract. This is typically associated with a pineal tumor.
    - Downbeat Nystagmus is most prominent when the patient is looking down and to the right or left. This is a vertical nystagmus with a down fast phase. This is typically associated with an Arnold-Chiari malformation (brain tissue extends into the spinal canal).
    - Gaze Evoked Nystagmus will have a null point in primary gaze and a jerk nystagmus in the direction of gaze. This is typically associated with alcohol consumption.
    - See Saw: One eye rises and intorts while the other descends and extorts, then the progression alternates. The lesion is typically located in the chiasm and parasellar region.
    - Upbeat Nystagmus is present in primary gaze and worsens on superior gaze. It is typically associated with a lesion of the brainstem.
    - Peripheral Vestibular Nystagmus is horizontal with a rotary component. This will be caused by an condition of the peripheral vestibular system (inner ear disease or CN8 disruption), which explains why patients may also complain of deafness, tinnitus, and vertigo. The fast phase will be away from the affected side while the slow phase will be towards the affected side.
- Physiologic Nystagmus is a normal presentation.
    - End-Point: Nystagmus which occurs when a patient is looking in an extreme gaze.
    - Optokinetic: Nystagmus which is induced by an OKN drum or a moving striped pattern. The fast phase will be in the opposite direction which the striped pattern is moving.
    - Rotational: Nystagmus which is induced after a patient has been rotating.
    - Caloric: Nystagmus which is induced by dropping water into the patient's ear. The direction of the fast phase can be remembered with COWS (cold opposite, warm same).

Treatment/Management:

- **Congenital Nystagmus** should be treated by maximizing vision with refraction, treating any comorbid amblyopia, prescribing prism for head turn, and considering muscle surgery for large head turn.
- Patients with **Acquired Nystagmus** should be referred for a brain MRI to rule out brain tumors or lesions, and the underlying etiology should be treated.
- **Physiologic Nystagmus** requires no treatment because it is a normal finding.

MYASTHENIA GRAVIS

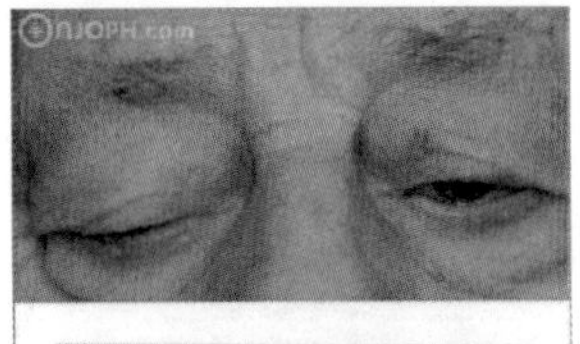

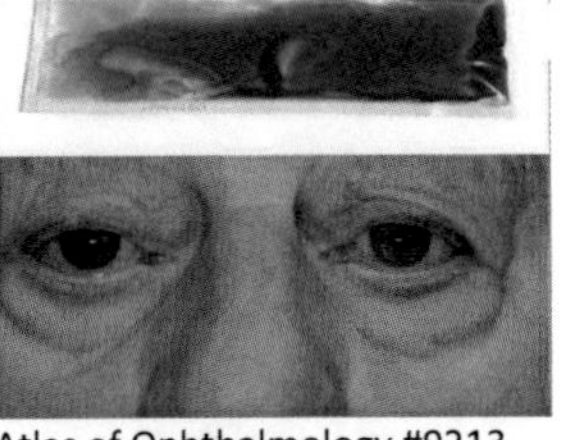

Atlas of Ophthalmology #9213

What to Know: Myasthenia Gravis is an autoimmune disease which causes muscle weakness due to a deficiency of acetylcholine at the neuromuscular junction. It is most commonly seen in women.

Symptoms: Patients will complain of ptosis and diplopia which is worse at the end of the day or when the patient is tired. They may also become easily fatigued with exercise.

Signs: Patients will have ptosis after prolonged upgaze which will improve after 2 minutes of ice application (Ice Pack Test, pictured above) or injection of Edrophonium (Tensilon Test). Their orbicularis muscle will also be weakened (poor eyelid closure), such that the patient will be unable to resist when the examiner attempts to pry open their eyes. Patients may also have little to no facial expression and difficulty swallowing and/or breathing.

Treatment/Management: Treatment depends on severity. Mild cases require no treatment. Prism can be prescribed for diplopia. If the case is disrupting the patient's activities of daily life, then prescribe an oral anticholinesterase such as Pyridostigmine. For persistent cases, consider systemic steroids. Patients who have difficulty swallowing or breathing should be hospitalized for immediate support.

CHRONIC PROGRESSIVE EXTERNAL OPHTHALMOPLEGIA (CPEO)

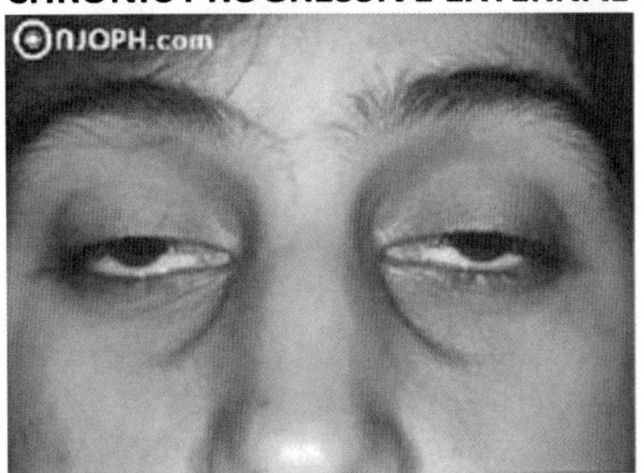

Atlas of Ophthalmology 5031

What to Know: In cases of CPEO all of the extraocular muscles slowly lose their motility.

Symptoms: Patients will complain of bilateral loss of ocular motility and ptosis. It is usually symmetrical.

Signs: Patients will present with reduced ocular motility and ptosis. There are several causes, two of which are discussed below.

- Myotonic Dystrophy is the **most common type of muscular dystrophy** seen in adults characterized by a progressive weakening of the muscles. Ocular findings include Christmas Tree Cataracts.
- Kearns-Sayre Syndrome (Mitochondrial DNA) is defined by a triad of findings: cardiac conduction defects, pigmentary retinopathy, and CPEO.

Treatment/Management: There is no effective treatment. Concurrent exposure keratopathy can be treated with artificial tears and ointment PRN (recommend preservative free if used more than QID). Ptosis surgery can be considered, but be mindful of increased risk for exposure keratopathy. Patients with Kearns-Sayre Syndrome should be referred to cardiology and may require a pacemaker.

PARINAUD'S (DORSAL MIDBRAIN) SYNDROME

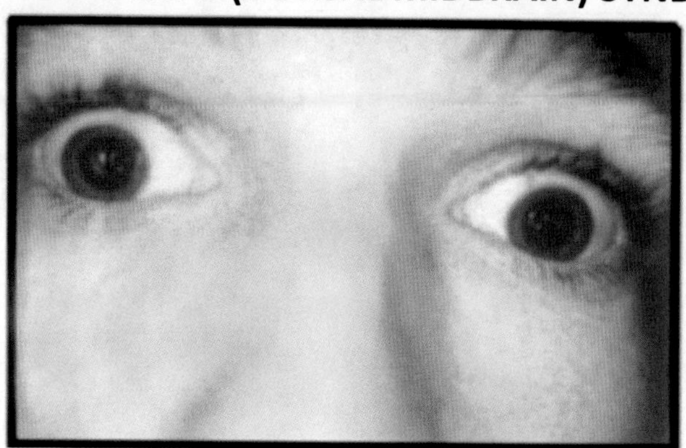

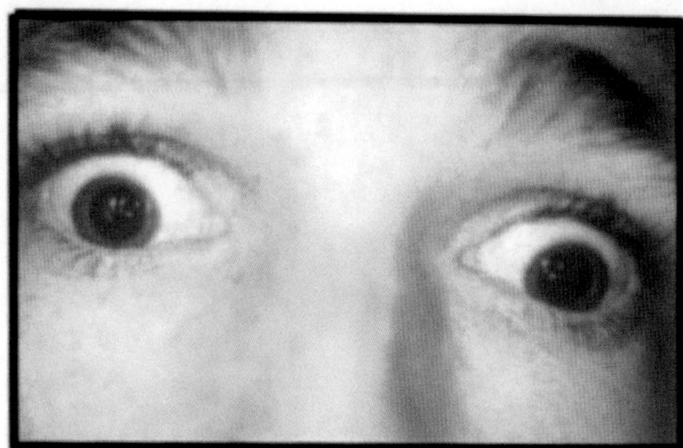

Miriam 1

What to Know: Parinaud's Syndrome is typically caused by a Pineal tumor of the upper brain stem. It is typically seen in young men.

Signs: Patients will be unable to voluntarily look in upgaze. However, given the paresis is supranuclear, Bell's phenomenon will be intact and the patient will have negative forced ductions test. Pupils will respond to accommodation but not to light (light-near dissociation).

Treatment/Management: There is no effective treatment. Concurrent exposure keratopathy can be treated with artificial tears and ointment PRN (recommend preservative free if used more than QID). Refer the patient to neurosurgery for evaluation and possible tumor removal.

CHAPTER 10
AMETROPIA

The NBEO website states that 11-22 questions will be asked on Ametropia. Historically they have asked about 18.6 questions, meaning this chapter covers approximately 5% of the material tested on the exam, or roughly 4 cases. This material is NOT tested on TMOD.

Ametropia is expected to change over a patient's lifetime by the following trends:

- Infants and the elderly typically have Against the Rule Astigmatism. All other patients typically have With the Rule Astigmatism.
- Myopia is expected to increase at the rate of -0.50D each year until the age of 14.
- Ametropia should remain stable between 20-40 years of age.
- Presbyopia begins while the patient is in their 40s. Uncorrected Hyperopes are more likely to show signs of presbyopia at a younger age because they have to accommodate to achieve clear distance vision, and then accommodate further to achieve clear near vision.

Pinhole testing can be completed to determine if the patient's vision is reduced due to a refractive error or pathology. If the patient can achieve 20/20 with pinhole, then they have a refractive error which can be corrected with glasses or contacts. If the patient cannot achieve 20/20 with pinhole, then this indicates that their vision is reduced due to ocular pathology.

Axial ametropia is caused by a change in the axial length of the eye (remember that 24 mm is normal. 1mm of change in axial length corresponds in 3.00D of ametropia). Refractive ametropia is more common and is caused by a cornea which is too steep or too flat. According to **Knapp's Law**, axial ametropia is best corrected with spectacles while refractive ametropia is best corrected with contact lenses. I remember this by thinking that contact lenses sit on the cornea, and refractive ametropia is due to an condition with the cornea. Meanwhile, spectacles sit a distance away from the globe, and axial ametropia is due to a change in the distance of the axial length.

While performing retinoscopy, remember to subtract the dioptric power of your working distance from your gross findings in order to calculate your net findings. This is how to calculate the dioptric power of your working distance: Power = 100 / Working Distance.

The goal of refraction is to place the far point of the eye at the secondary focal point of the lens. An object located at the far point will form a clear image on the retina with no accommodation. The far point for hyperopes is behind the cornea, which is why they are corrected with plus lenses. The far point for myopes is in front of the eye, which is why they are corrected with minus lenses. The far point for emmetropes is at infinity which is why they do not require spectacle correction.

The range of clear vision without spectacle correction expected in any patient is the difference between their near point and their far point.

- Far Point = 100 / Distance Spectacle Prescription
- Near Point = 100 / (Distance Spectacle Prescription + Amplitude of Accommodation)

Complete presbyopes cannot accommodate and so their Far Point is equal to their Near Point.

If clarity of vision improves when a patient moves their glasses down their nose, thereby increasing vertex distance, they want extra plus in their spectacle prescription. Conversely, If clarity of vision improves when the patient pushes their glasses up their nose, thereby decreasing vertex distance, they want more minus in their prescription.

Egger's Rule states that a patient's spherical prescription should only change by 0.25D for each line of reduced visual acuity, as described by the chart below:

Visual Acuity	Expected Spherical Prescription (Absolute Value)
20/20	Plano
20/25	0.25
20/30	0.50
20/40	0.75
20/50	1.00
20/60	1.25
20/70	1.50
20/80	1.75
20/100	2.00
20/150	2.25
20/200	2.50
20/400	2.75

There are several methods by which to calculate a patient's add:

- Age:
    - 35 to 45 = +1.00
    - 45 to 50 = +1.50
    - 50 to 55 = +2.00
    - Over 55 = +2.50 or higher
- Add at 40 cm = 15 – age/4. The add at 80 cm (intermediate) is half which is calculated for 40 cm.
- (NRA + PRA)/2
- Fused Cross Cylinder: The add is determined based upon when both the horizontal and vertical lines are equally clear.

When determining how much add to prescribe a patient, bear in mind that they should keep half of their accommodation in reserve for the given working distance. This is the equation for determining the add necessary for any working distance:

- Add = Dioptric Demand of the Working Distance – (Accommodative Amplitude / 2)
- Example: A patient has an amplitude of accommodation of 1.00D and wants glasses set for 50cm.
    - The dioptric demand of 50cm = 100/50, which is +2.00D. This can be plugged into the above equation: Add = +2.00 – (1.00/2), or the add should be +1.50.

There are four types of Hyperopia.

1. **Manifest Hyperopia** is measured with manifest refraction.
2. **Latent Hyperopia** is the difference between the hyperopia found with the Manifest and Cycloplegic refractions.
    - If a child has latent hyperopia but only complains about difficulty with near vision, then prescribe their full cycloplegic distance refraction for reading only. They do not need correction for distance because they do not difficulty with distance vision. But, prescribing their cycloplegic distance refraction for near will allow them to use a normal amount of accommodation to achieve clarity of near vision.
3. **Facultative Hyperopia** is the amount of hyperopia which can be compensated for with accommodation.
4. **Absolute Hyperopia** is the residual hyperopia when the patient is engaging all of their accommodation.

Hyperopic shifts can be caused by cortical cataracts, temporary low blood sugar (ex. DM1 patient starting insulin), or diseases which cause elevation of macular structures.

Possible causes of **myopic shifts** include nuclear sclerotic cataracts and high blood sugar in diabetic patients because both of these increase the density of the lens. Scleral buckles can also cause a myopic shift because they squeeze the globe, thus causing an increase in axial length. Medications which can cause a myopic shift include NSAIDs, Diamox, and Topamax.

There are three types of myopia.

1. **Inherited Myopia**: There is a genetic component to myopia, and children are at greater risk depending on if one or both parents are myopic and the severity of myopia in both parents.
2. **Pseudomyopia:** Hyperopes accommodate to allow themselves to see clearly. However, occasionally they will accommodate too much, making them effectively myopic.
3. **Night/Nocturnal Myopia:** In dark conditions patients may not have enough stimuli to allow the visual system to accurately determine how much it needs to accommodate to see clearly. Therefore, the patient may over accommodate, making them effectively myopic for the given situation.

There are seven types of astigmatism.

1. With the Rule Astigmatism: The axis is at 180 +/- 30 degrees.
2. Against the Rule Astigmatism: The axis is at 90 +/- 30 degrees.
3. Oblique Astigmatism: The axis is at 45 +/- 15 degrees OR the axis is at 135 +/- 15 degrees.
4. Irregular Astigmatism: The major and minor axis are **not** 90 degrees apart. This is typically seen with pathology.
5. Simple Astigmatism: The patient has plano spherical power accompanied with astigmatism. They can have Simple Hyperopic Astigmatism (SHA) where one axis is located behind the retina and the other axis is located on the retina. Or they can have Simple Myopic Astigmatism (SMA) where one axis is located in

front of the retina and the other axis is located on the retina.

6. Compound Astigmatism: Both the major and minor axis will be located either in front (Compound Myopic Astigmatism aka CMA) of or behind (Compound Hyperopic Astigmatism aka CHA) the retina.
7. Mixed astigmatism: One axis is located in front of the retina while the other is located behind the retina.

Oblique Astigmatism causes the most blur, Against the Rule Astigmatism causes the second most blur, and With the Rule Astigmatism causes the least amount of blur.

The amount of astigmatism expected in a patient's glasses prescription can be estimated from the keratometry findings by using **Javal's Rule** which states that the expected amount of Spectacle Astigmatism is equal to the Corneal Astigmatism plus 0.50D MORE astigmatism at axis 090.

Spherical Equivalence needs to be maintained during refraction by adding or subtracting sphere as the cylinder changes. It can be calculated with the following equation:

- Spherical Equivalent = (Cylinder Power / 2) + Sphere Power.

A **Jackson Cross Cylinder** will have a spherical equivalency of zero. An example would be +1.50 – 3.00 x 180.

Astigmatism can also be determined using the **Astigmatic Dial.** The axis can be calculated with **The Rule of 30** by asking the patient which set of lines appear clearest. Multiply the lowest number by 30.

- Example: The patient states the 3:00-9:00 lines are clearest.
    - 3 * 30 = 90. The axis for this patient is 090.

The Astigmatic Dial Test is performed by the following steps:

1. Fog the patient to 20/50.
2. Align the axis with the set of lines the patient finds darkest and clearest.
3. Add minus cylinder until all the lines of the dial appear equally clear. You have now found the cylinder power and axis of the prescription.
4. Add minus spherical lenses to find the endpoint.

Binocular Balance can only be performed on patients who have equal acuities between their two eyes because its goal is to equalize accommodation between the two eyes.

This is how to transpose from Plus Cylinder to Minus Cylinder:

- Add the Sphere and Cylinder Powers of the original prescription. This becomes your new Sphere Power.
- Change the sign of the Cylinder Power. This is your new Cylinder Power.
- Add or subtract the axis by 90, be sure not to go over 180. This is your new Axis.

CHAPTER 11
LIDS / LASHES / LACRIMAL SYSTEM / OCULAR ADNEXA / ORBIT

The NBEO website states that 11-22 questions will be asked on Lids / Lashes / Lacrimal System / Ocular Adnexa / Orbit. Historically they have asked about 18.6 questions, meaning this chapter covers approximately 5% of the material tested on the exam, or roughly 4 cases. This material IS included on TMOD.

~~~LIDS / LASHES~~~

DERMATOCHALASIS

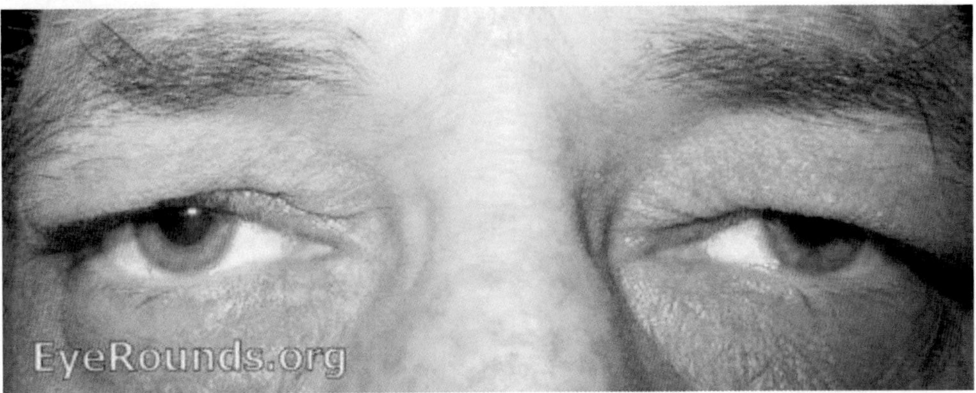

EyeRounds.org University of Iowa

What to Know: Dermatochalasis occurs when skin becomes laxative with age.

Symptoms: Patients will complain of heavy eyelids and reduced superior visual field.

Signs: Patients will present with loose skin which weighs down the superior lid and induces ptosis. They will show superior visual field defects which will improve when the superior lid is taped, thus relieving the weight of the laxative skin.

Treatment/Management: Treatment is blepharoplasty (surgical removal of excessive eyelid tissue).

ECTROPION

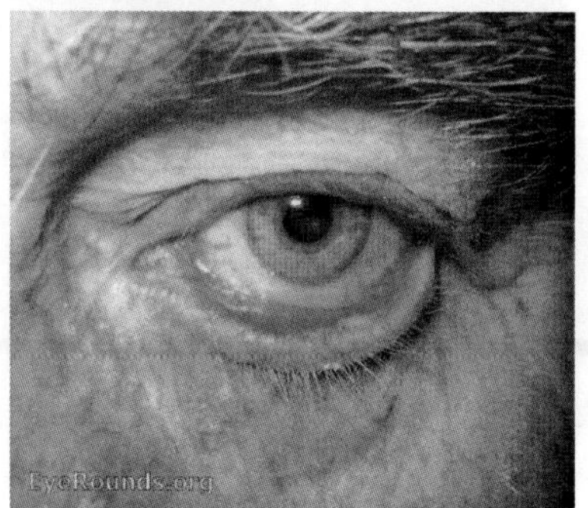
EyeRounds.org University of Iowa

What to Know: Ectropion is defined as outward rolling, particularly of the lower lid. Causes include age/involutional (eyelid laxity), trauma, and Bell's Palsy.

Symptoms: Patients may have no complaints (asymptomatic) or complain of chronic epiphora with ocular irritation.

Signs: Patients will present with an eyelid which is not apposed to the globe. They may also have signs of inferior exposure keratopathy.

Treatment/Management: The malpositioned eyelid can be treated with surgery to tighten the lateral tarsal strip. Any concurrent exposure keratopathy should be treated as such. If the cause is Bell's Palsy, then the Ectropion will resolve spontaneously.

ENTROPION

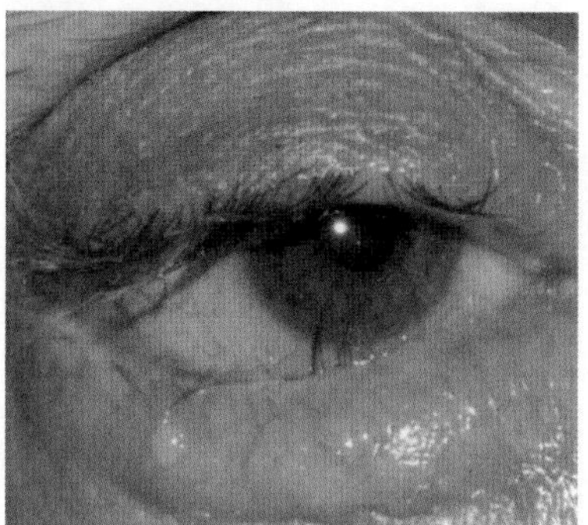
EyeRounds.org University of Iowa

What to Know: Entropion is an inward rolling of the eyelid. The most common cause of Entropion is involution (structural changes) with age.

Symptoms: Patients may complain of ocular irritation, foreign body sensation, and epiphora.

Signs: The eyelid will be rolled inward. The patients may have exposure keratopathy, abrasions, and/or trichiasis (mechanical rubbing of the eyelashes on the globe).

Treatment/Management: If corneal epithelial compromise exists, prescribe a topical antibiotic ointment as a preventative measure. The abnormal position of the eyelid can be addressed with tape temporarily and surgery permanently.

TRICHIASIS

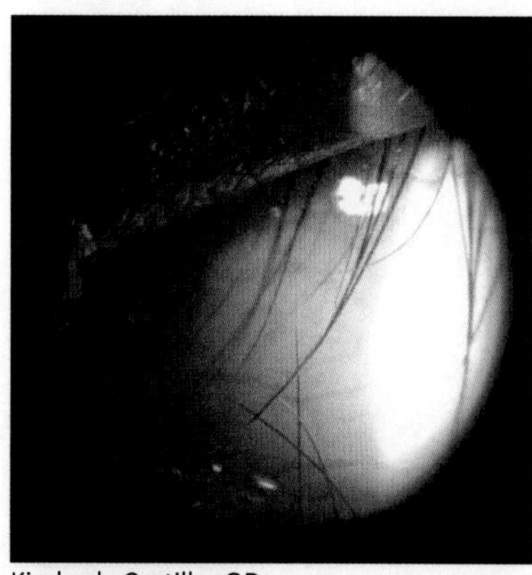
Kimberly Castillo, OD

What to Know: Trichiasis is defined as misdirected eyelashes which mechanically rub the globe. Usually it is idiopathic or caused by Entropion.

Symptoms: Patients may complain of ocular irritation, foreign body sensation, and epiphora.

Signs: Patients will present with misdirected eyelashes which may rub the globe and cause superficial punctate keratitis (SPK), abrasions, injection, and possible corneal scarring in chronic cases.

Treatment/Management: First line treatment of Trichiasis is eyelash epilation (removal with forceps). In chronic cases the eyelashes can be permanently removed surgically with cryotherapy (freezing of tissue), cautery, or electrolysis. If corneal epithelial compromise exists, prescribe a topical antibiotic ointment as a preventative measure.

BLEPHAROSPASM

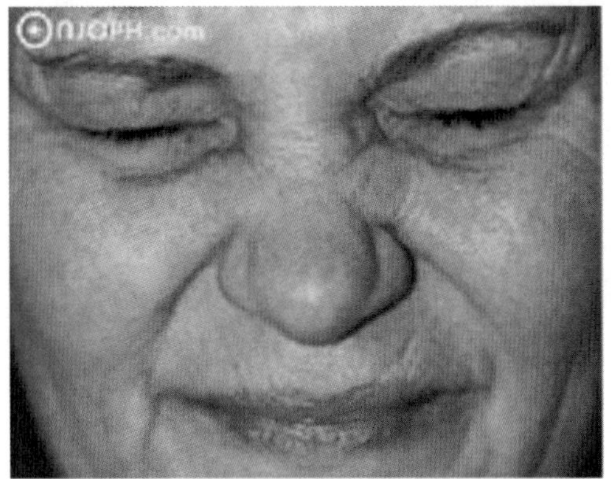
Atlas of Ophthalmology 5033

What to Know: Blepharospasm is idiopathic bilateral uncontrollable closure of the eyelids. When severe, Blepharospasm can render the patient functionally blind.

Signs: Patients will present with uncontrollable contracture of the orbicularis oculi and surrounding facial muscles. The contracture will be so severe that the examiner will be unable to pry the eyelids open. Frequently the spasms will be absent during sleep.

Treatment/Management: Botox injections can be performed every 12 weeks. Remember that Botox causes flaccid paralysis, and so its mechanism is to relax the overactive muscles.

BELL'S PALSY

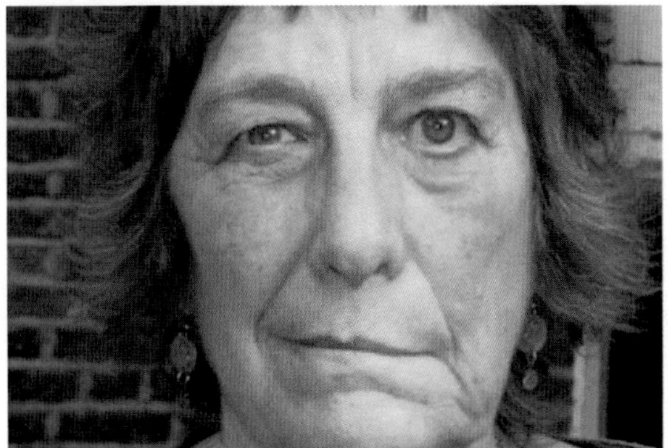
Susan Salvo 1

What to Know: Bell's Palsy is flaccid paralysis of the lower motor neuron of CN7, affecting the entire ipsilateral side of the face. Bell's Palsy is most commonly idiopathic, but possible causes include neural inflammation and herpes simplex. Onset will be acute with signs and symptoms developing over 24 hours. Conversely, remember that a stroke will cause a supranuclear lesion, which will affect the lower contralateral side of the face.

Symptoms: In addition to unilateral flaccid paralysis of an acute onset, patients will complain of unilateral epiphora, dry eye, drooling, and an inability to close one eye.

Signs: Remember that CN7 is responsible for movement of the facial muscles, closure of the eyelids, and ocular and oral secretions. All of these functions may be impaired depending on severity. Bell's reflex will still be present (the globe will roll backwards with lid closure, which is a normal finding). Given that the globe rolls backwards with Bell's reflex and exposes the inferior portion of the globe, the patient may have inferior exposure keratoconjunctivitis from rubbing their head on their pillow while sleeping.

Treatment/Management: Bell's Palsy will typically spontaneously improve within 4 months with complete resolution within one year of onset. If neural inflammation is suspected, consider an oral steroid. If herpes simplex is suspected, consider an oral antiviral. The poor eyelid closure needs to be addressed. The patient can tape their eyelid shut while sleeping. If chronic, the patient may benefit from a gold weight implant to aid with eyelid closure. During the day the patient should lubricate their eye with preservative free artificial tears up to Q1H as well as an artificial tear ointment QHS (for further protection from nocturnal mechanical rubbing). Patients should be followed every 6 weeks.

FLOPPY EYELID SYNDROME

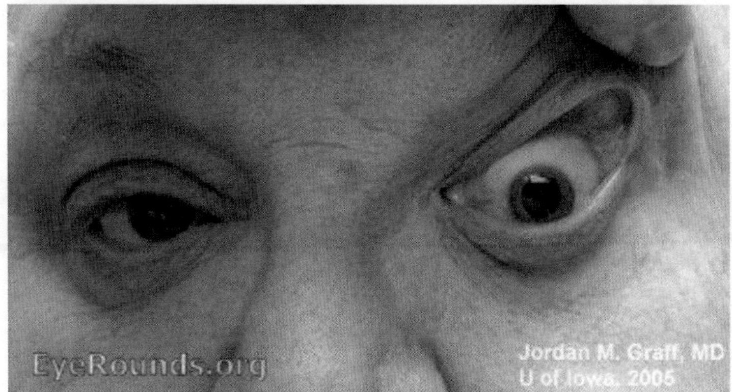

EyeRounds.org University of Iowa

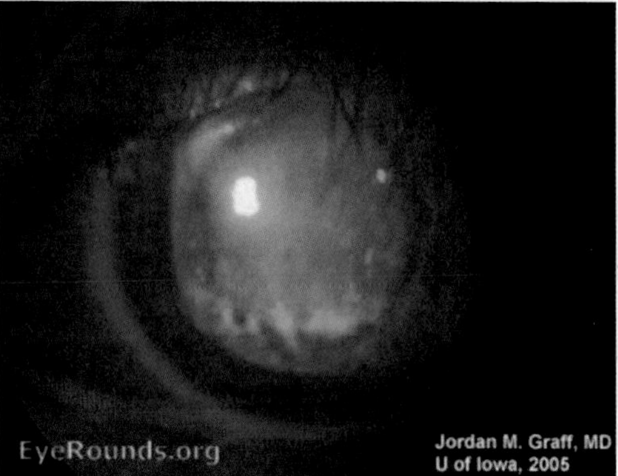

EyeRounds.org University of Iowa

What to Know: Floppy Eyelid Syndrome occurs when there is excessive eyelid laxity, allowing for spontaneous eyelid eversion. It is typically seen in overweight men, and it is frequently a sign of sleep apnea.

Symptoms: Patients may complain of chronically red, irritated eyes with discharge. The symptoms will frequently be worse in the morning.

Signs: Patients will present with eyelids which are extremely easy to evert. Given that the eyelid may evert due to mechanical pillow rubbing during sleep, the patient may have exposure keratoconjunctivitis of the inferior cornea and conjunctiva (the globe rolls backwards due to Bell's reflex during sleep, thereby exposing the inferior portion of the globe). The palpebral conjunctiva also becomes exposed and irritated during this spontaneous eversion, and so it may present with papillae. Frequently surgery is required as a definitive treatment.

Treatment/Management: Patients should be referred to rule out sleep apnea (remember that sleep apnea can be fatal). The poor eyelid closure needs to be addressed. The patient can tape their eyelid shut or wear an eye shield while sleeping. During the day the patient should lubricate their eye with preservative free artificial tears up to Q1H as well as an artificial tear ointment QHS (for further protection from nocturnal mechanical rubbing). If corneal or conjunctival compromise is present, then prescribe a topical antibiotic ointment as a preventative measure.

XANTHELASMA

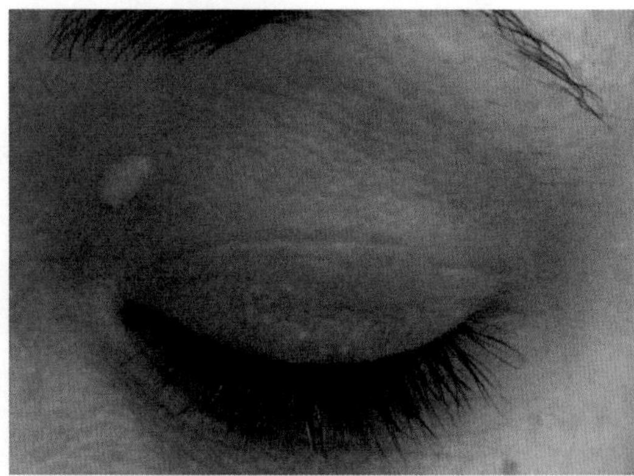

Kimberly Castillo, OD

What to Know: Xanthelasma is typically seen in elderly patients.

Symptoms: Patients will complain of poor cosmesis.

Signs: Xanthelasma presents as creamy yellow plaques found in the superior nasal eyelids. I think of them as being deposits of fat/lipid because they are seen in patients with hyperlipidemia (particularly if the patient is under 40, like with Arcus).

Treatment/Management: Treatment is not necessary and so is only performed to improve cosmesis. The plaques can be removed with excision or carbon dioxide laser treatment. Xanthelasma has a tendency for recurrence, especially in patients with hyperlipidemia.

MEIBOMIAN GLAND DYSFUNCTION (MGD)*

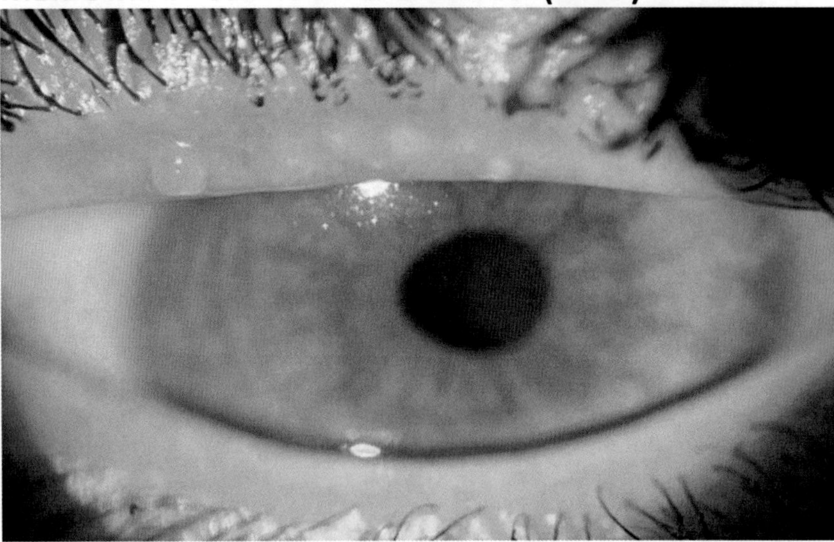

Kimberly Castillo, OD

What to Know: MGD is a very common condition which causes clogging of the meibomian glands along the eyelid margins. MGD causes Intrinsic Evaporative Dry Eye (see Cornea in Chapter 4) due to abnormal lipid production causing increased tear evaporation.

Symptoms: Symptoms for MGD are the same as those for dry eye. Patients will complain of dry, burning, itching, stinging, tearing, and/or foreign body sensation. Symptoms may be worse at night, when it is windy, or after reading/watching TV. Vision may fluctuate and improve with blink. Patients with MGD may complain of crusting of their eyes in the morning.

Signs: Patients may present with the "toothpaste sign" in which thick sebaceous material expresses from the afflicted glands. Inspissation, or frothy tears, may also be present. Patients may also have red, inflamed lid margins with madarosis (loss of eyelashes). See "Dry Eye" in Chapter 2 for more signs of Dry Eye.

Treatment/Management: First line of treatment for MGD is lid hygiene and hot compress. Also consider prescribing Erythromycin to treat the bacterial infection. Artificial Tears and supplementing the diet with omega-3 fatty acids can also help. Newer therapies available include Intense Pulsed Light (IPL) and Radio Frequency (RF).

BLEPHARITIS*

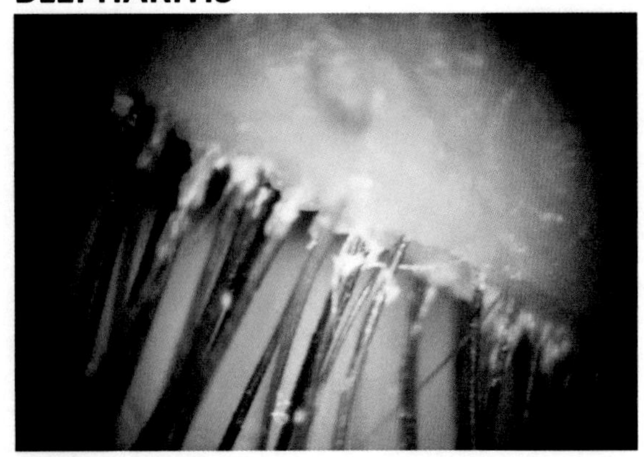

Kimberly Castillo, OD

What to Know: Blepharitis is a very common condition which is caused by inflammation of the sebaceous glands due to *Staphylococcus* infection. It can be either anterior or posterior with Anterior Blepharitis afflicting the glands of Zeis and Moll and Posterior Blepharitis afflicting the Meibomian glands. Blepharitis causes Intrinsic Evaporative Dry Eye (see Cornea in Chapter 4) due to abnormal lipid production causing increased tear evaporation.

Symptoms: Symptoms for Blepharitis are the same as those for dry eye. Patients will complain of dry, burning, itching, stinging, tearing, and/or foreign body sensation. Symptoms may be worse at night, when it is windy, or after reading/watching TV. Patients may note crusting on the base of their eyelashes. Vision may fluctuate and improve with blink.

Signs: Patients may present with flaking on their eyelashes. They may also have red, inflamed lid margins with madarosis (loss of eyelashes). See "Dry Eye" in Chapter 2 for more signs of Dry Eye.

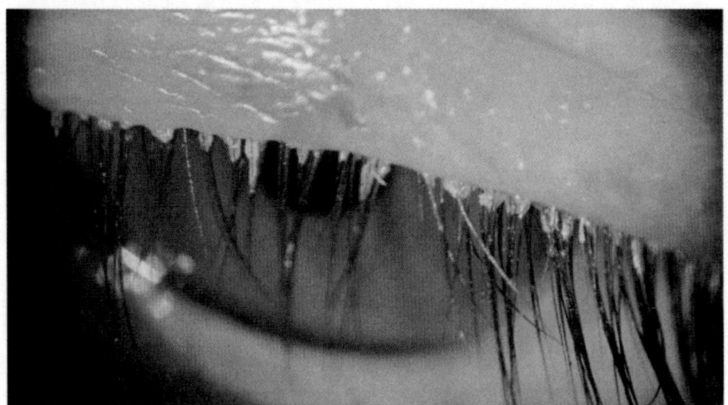

Kimberly Castillo, OD

Demodicosis (aka Demodex, see picture to the left) is a common type of Blepharitis caused by the parasite ***Demodex folliculorum.*** It presents with triangular globs of waste at the base of the patient's eyelashes called collarets.

Treatment/Management: First line of treatment for Blepharitis is lid hygiene and hot compress. Also consider prescribing Erythromycin to treat the bacterial infection. Artificial Tears and supplementing the diet with omega-3 fatty acids can also help. Newer therapies available include Intense Pulsed Light (IPL) and Radio Frequency (RF). Demodex can also be treated with Xdemvy gtts.

PEDICULOSIS / PHTHIRIASIS*

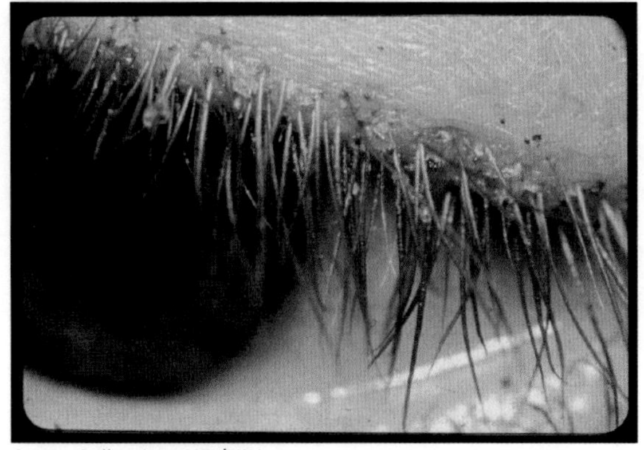

Cogan Collection, NEI/NIH

What to Know: Pediculosis is caused by an eyelash infection of lice (*Phthirus pubis*). If this presents in children, then suspect sexual abuse.

Symptoms: Patients will complain of burning and itching.

Signs: Patients will present with several signs at the base of their eyelashes: burrowing lice, spots of dried blood (from bites), tiny brown deposits (feces), and white/translucent nits (eggs). Patients may also have positive preauricular lymphadenopathy.

Treatment/Management: The lice need to be removed with jeweler's forceps. An antibiotic ointment (Erythromycin) should be used for two weeks to smother the lice. Patients should be instructed to thoroughly wash their towels and linens. Lice shampoos **are NOT** approved for ocular use. The patient's sexual partner should also be treated.

It is considered a sign of sexual abuse if a child presents with Pediculosis given this is typically sexually transmitted. As optometrists we are mandated reporters, and so we must notify authorities if we suspect a child is being abused.

HORDEOLUM

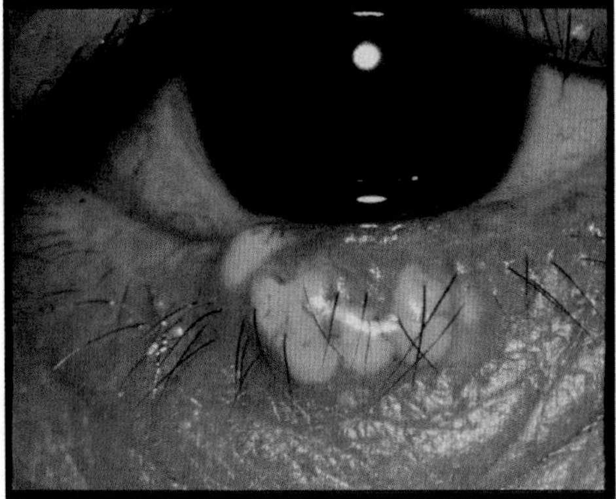
Cogan Collection, NEI/NIH

<u>What to Know:</u> The laymen's term for a Hordeolum is "stye." It is essentially a pimple of the eyelid, or an infection of a sebaceous gland.

<u>Symptoms:</u> For a Hordeolum I think of "horrible" because patients will complain of associated pain and eyelid tenderness. A Hordeolum is also horrible because it may possibly progress into Preseptal Cellulitis.

<u>Signs:</u> The eyelid will also be red and hot, and a pustule or "white cap" may also be visible.

<u>Treatment/Management:</u> The first line of treatment is hot compress for 10-15 minutes as frequently as possible, paired with mechanical vertical massage and lid hygiene. If persistent, prescribe a topical antibiotic ointment or a topical steroid-antibiotic ointment.

CHALAZION

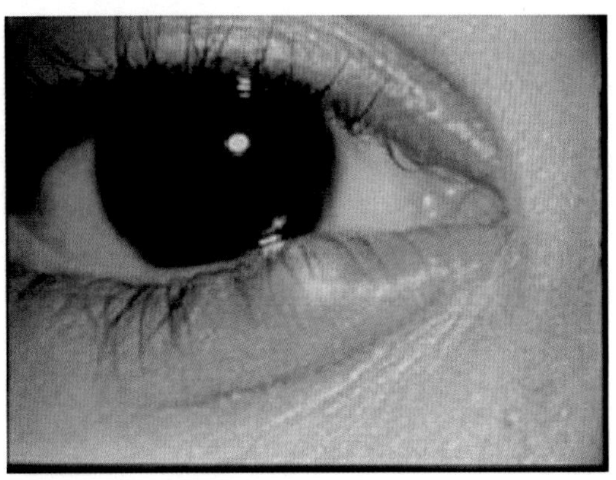
Cogan Collection, NEI/NIH

<u>What to Know:</u> A Chalazion is a sterile inflammation of a sebaceous gland.

<u>Symptoms:</u> Patients will complain of a painless bump on their eyelid.

<u>Signs:</u> Patients will present with a nontender bump on their lid which is not red.

<u>Treatment/Management:</u> The first line of treatment is hot compress for 10-15 minutes as frequently as possible, paired with mechanical vertical massage and lid hygiene. If the Chalazion persists for a month, then remove it via biopsy. A very new option for breaking up a Chalazion is Radio Frequency (RF) therapy. **If the Chalazion is recurrent in the same location, then suspect sebaceous gland carcinoma and refer for biopsy.**

SEBACEOUS GLAND CARCINOMA

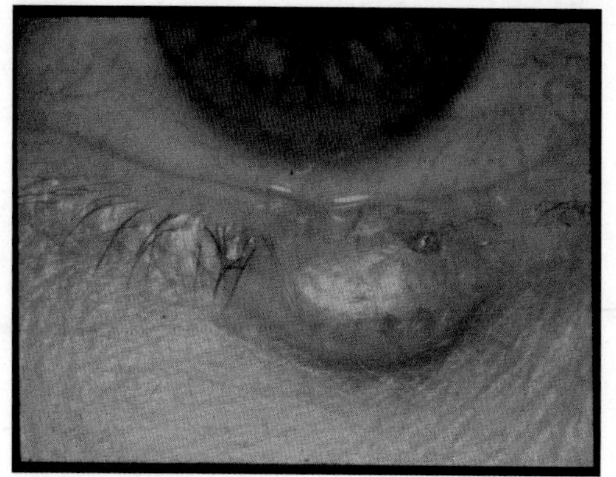
Cogan Collection, NEI/NIH

What to Know: Sebaceous Gland Carcinoma should be suspected when a patient presents with a recurring Chalazion in the same location or chronic unilateral blepharitis. It is rare but highly malignant and is most frequently found in women between the ages of 50-70. Risk factors for mortality include tumors greater than 2cm, superior and inferior lid involvement, and a duration of more than 6 months.

Signs: Patients present with a yellow, hard tumor (usually located on the superior eyelid), madarosis (loss of eyelashes), and possible poliosis (white eyelashes). The tumor causes destruction of the sebaceous cells near the caruncle and may present with lymphadenopathy (which indicates malignancy).

Treatment/Management includes full thickness excision with biopsy.

BASAL CELL CARCINOMA

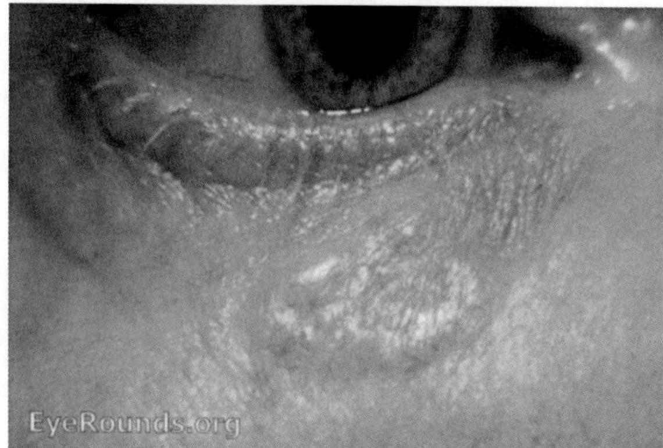

EyeRounds.org University of Iowa

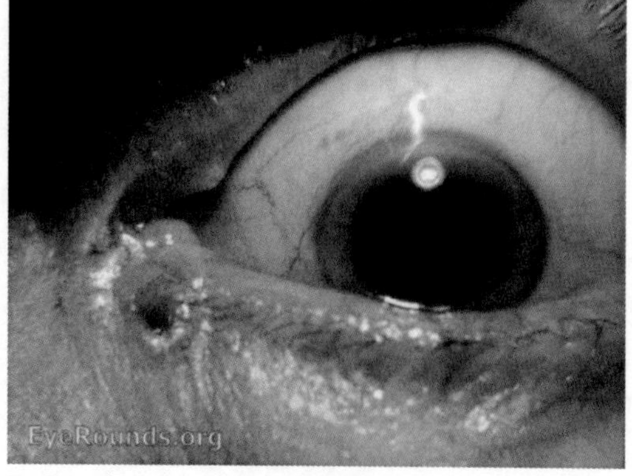

EyeRounds.org University of Iowa

What to Know: Basal Cell Carcinoma occurs most frequently on the inferior eyelid / sun exposed areas of the skin. It is found in older Caucasian patients. Basal Cell Carcinoma is the most common malignant eyelid tumor, but it rarely metastasizes. Remember the order of layers of the epidermis from most superficial to most deep are Stratum corneum, Stratum lucidum, Stratum granulosum, Stratum spinosum, and Stratum basale. Basal Cell Carcinoma occurs due to excessive proliferation of the Stratum basale. Note that it is normal for cell division to occur in the Stratum basale (the deepest layer of the epithelium), which is why Basal Cell Carcinoma is the most common malignant eyelid tumor and why it rarely metastasizes (cell division should occur at this layer).

Signs: Basal Cell Carcinoma can present as a pearly umbilicated nodule (left image) which can progress to include central ulcerative telangiectasia ("rodent ulcer," right image). I remember that "rodent ulcers" are associated with Basal Cell Carcinoma by thinking that rodents/rats are found in the basement.

Treatment/Management includes full thickness excision with biopsy. Patients should be advised to use sun protection.

ACTINIC KERATOSIS → SQUAMOUS CELL CARCINOMA

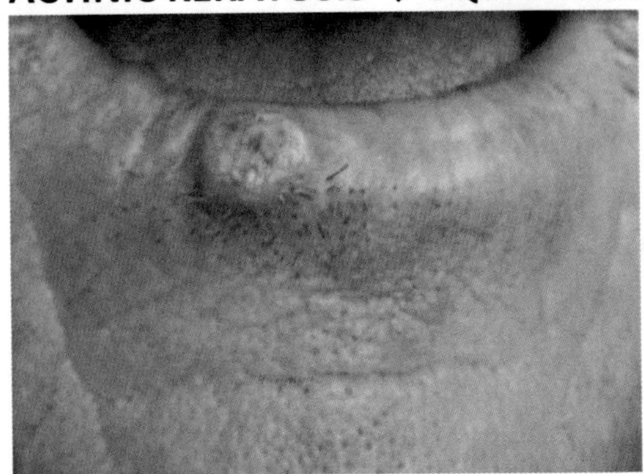

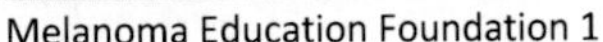
Melanoma Education Foundation 1

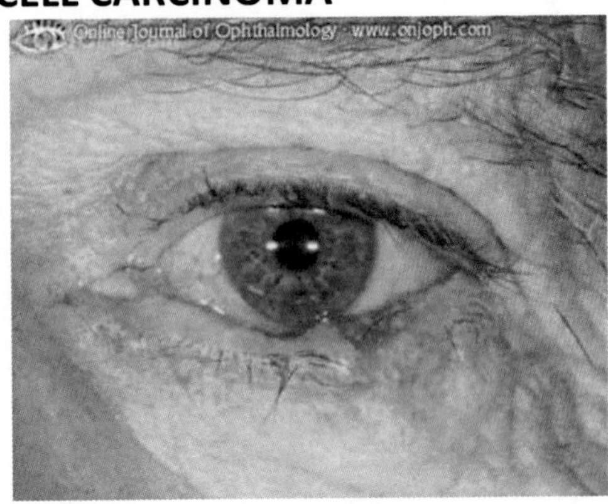

Atlas of Ophthalmology 2607

What to Know: Actinic Keratosis is the precursor for Squamous Cell Carcinoma. Both occur most frequently on the inferior eyelid / sun exposed areas of the skin. They are found in older Caucasian patients. Actinic Keratosis is the most common precancerous skin lesion, and Squamous Cell Carcinoma is the second most common malignant eyelid tumor. Remember the order of layers of the epidermis from most superficial to most deep are Stratum corneum, Stratum lucidum, Stratum granulosum, Stratum spinosum, and Stratum basale. Squamous Cell Carcinoma occurs due to excessive proliferation of the Stratum spinosum. Note that it is normal for cell division to occur in the Stratum basale (the deepest layer of the epithelium), but not in the Stratum spinosum. This explains why Squamous Cell Carcinoma is more invasive than Basal Cell Carcinoma (cell division should not occur at the Stratum spinosum).

Signs:

- Actinic Keratosis presents as a scaly, round erythematous (redness due to dilated capillaries) lesion.
- Squamous Cell Carcinoma presents as a scaly, erythematous, ulcerated plaque which may be flat or slightly elevated.

Treatment/Management for both includes full thickness excision with biopsy. Cryotherapy (freezing of tissue) can be used as further treatment once diagnosis has been confirmed. Patients should be advised to use sun protection.

MALIGNANT MELANOMA

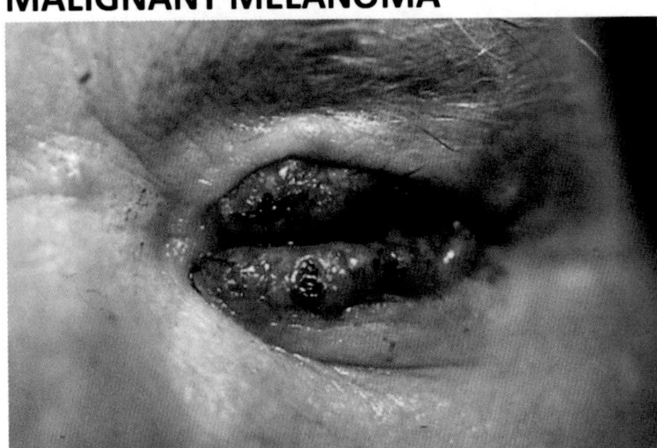
Retina Image Bank. File #2856

What to Know: While Malignant Melanoma is rare, it is the most lethal primary skin tumor. Prognosis is based on the thickness and depth of the lesion.

Signs: Patients present with pigmented, elevated, lesions with irregular borders. Malignant Melanoma is caused by abnormal proliferation of melanocytes. Remember that melanocytes contain pigment, which explains why Malignant Melanoma presents as a pigmented lesion.

Treatment/Management includes full thickness excision with biopsy. Severe cases may require orbital Exenteration with neck dissection. Patients should be advised to use sun protection and referred to dermatology for an evaluation.

CAPILLARY HEMANGIOMA

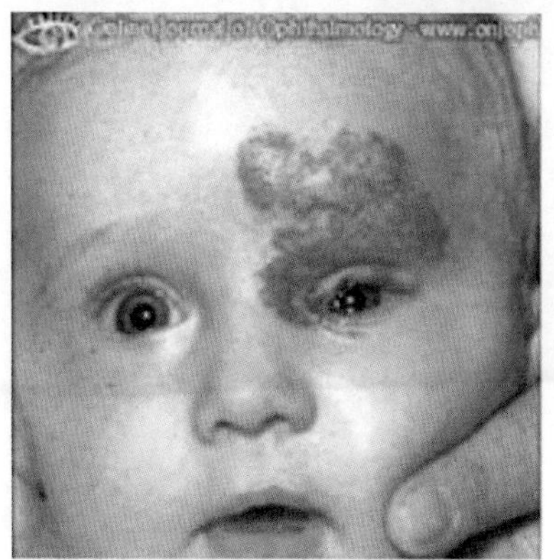

Atlas of Ophthalmology 2842

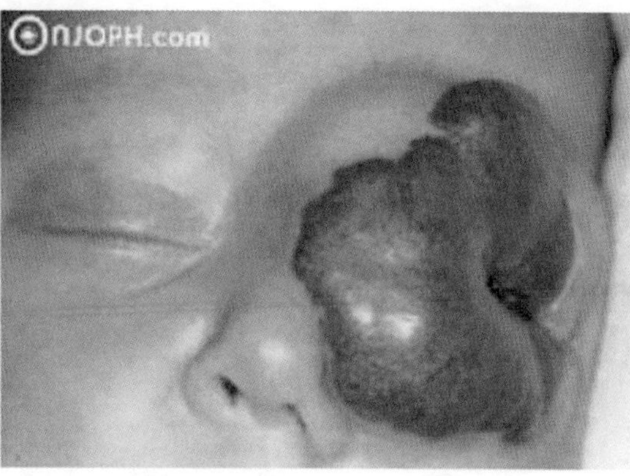

Atlas of Ophthalmology 5028

What to Know: Capillary Hemangiomas are the **most common benign orbital tumors in children**. Be sure to differentiate them from Cavernous Hemangiomas, which are the most common benign orbital tumors in adults. I remember this by thinking that Capillaries are smaller than Caverns, and children are smaller than adults.

Signs: Capillary Hemangiomas usually present themselves in the first month of life as a superficial vascular lesion (strawberry nevus) with rapid growth. They may cause amblyopia if they block the visual axis or press on the cornea and induce astigmatism.

Treatment/Management: Capillary Hemangiomas will spontaneously involute (resolve/disappear) by the time the patients turns 10.

~~~LACRIMAL SYSTEM~~~

CANALICULITIS

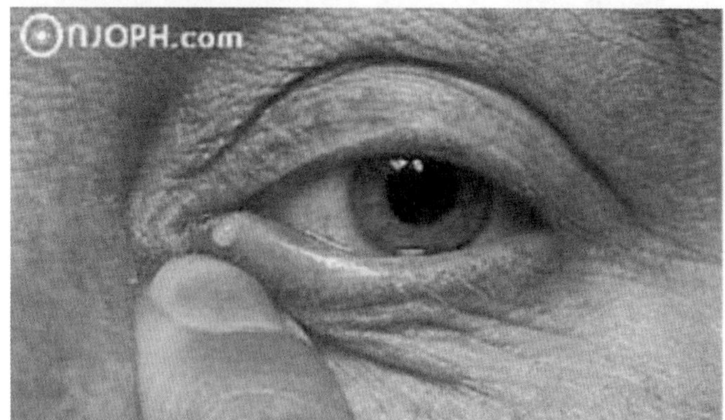

Atlas of Ophthalmology #6201

What to Know: Canaliculitis is an inflammation of the duct connecting the punctum and lacrimal sac (canaliculus) which is caused most frequently by an infection of *Actinomyces israelii*. *Actinomyces israelii* is unique to Canaliculitis.

Symptoms: Patients may complain of a red tender punctum with epiphora.

Signs: Patients present with a red puncta which is rolled away from the globe (pouting puncta) due to lid swelling. It will express white discharge and have concretions in the canaliculus.

Treatment/Management should initially include removal of the concretions via expression. Once achieved, perform irrigation of the canaliculi with an antibiotic solution and prescribe oral antibiotics. Patients can also aid drainage with warm compress and lid massage. Cases which do not respond to treatment may require surgery: curettage (scraping away unwanted material), canaliculotomy (removal of the posterior wall of the canaliculi), or marsupialization (cutting and suturing a slit allowing free drainage). Patients should be followed every 5-7 days.

NASOLACRIMAL DUCT OBSTRUCTION

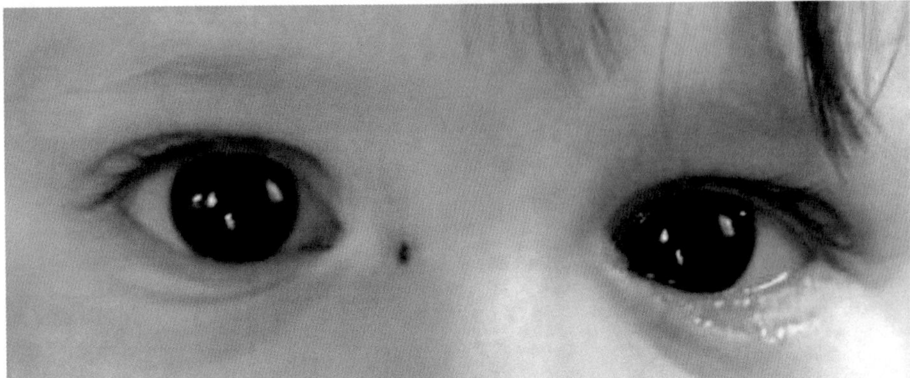

Kimberly Castillo, OD

What to Know: There are two types of Nasolacrimal Duct Obstructions:

- Congenital Nasolacrimal Duct Obstructions are caused by an imperforate membrane over the valve of Hasner.
- Acquired Nasolacrimal Duct Obstructions are most commonly seen in women and are caused by involutional stenosis (age related narrowing of the nasolacrimal duct).

Symptoms: Patients may complain of epiphora and crusting of the eyelids.

Signs: Patients with an Acquired Nasolacrimal Duct Obstruction should be evaluated with the Jones tests to prove whether or not the nasolacrimal duct is blocked.

- Jones 1 Test: Apply copious amounts of topical fluorescein to the afflicted eye. Wait five minutes. Have the patient insert a cotton tipped applicator inside the ipsilateral nostril. If fluorescein is present on the applicator, then the nasolacrimal duct is patent (open) and the test is considered positive.
- Jones 2 Test: Dilate and irrigate the affected side. If the fluid beings to flow out the nose, the patient tastes the saline, or begins to swallow, then the nasolacrimal duct is patent (open) and the test is considered positive. Jones 2 Test can also clear a Nasolacrimal Duct Obstruction and so also serves as a therapeutic procedure.

Treatment/Management:

- Congenital Nasolacrimal Duct Obstructions should spontaneously resolve by the child's first birthday. To aid the process, parents should apply digital massage to the nasolacrimal duct BID-QID. If the obstruction does not resolve by the child's first birthday, then nasolacrimal duct probing may be necessary to clear the blockage.
- Acquired Nasolacrimal Duct Obstructions may be cleared with dilation and irrigation, which may need to be repeated. If unsuccessful, then prescribe a topical antibiotic/steroid. Severe cases may require surgery: silicone intubation, dacryoplasty, or dacryocystorhinostomy.

DACRYOCYSTITIS

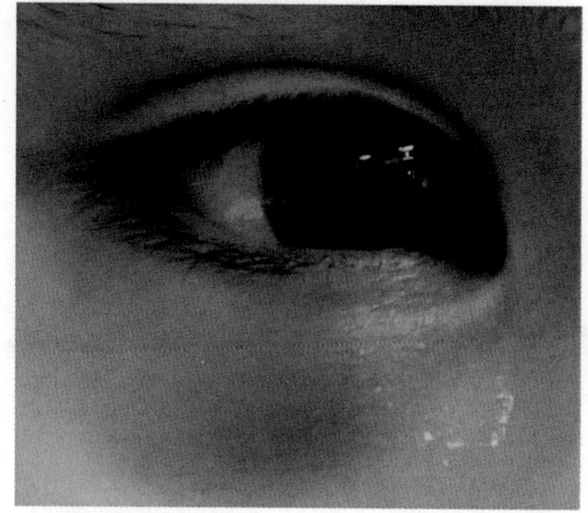

Kimberly Castillo, OD

What to Know: Dacryocystitis is an infection of the lacrimal sac below the medial canthal tendon. It is caused by *Streptococcus pneumoniae* in adults and *Haemophilus influenza* in children.

Symptoms: Patients may complain of a red tender medial eyelid with epiphora.

Signs: Patients may present with a fever. They will also have a red, swollen lacrimal sac which will express mucopurulent discharge with palpation. Patients may have a comorbid conjunctivitis.

Treatment/Management: **Do not *probe* the nasolacrimal duct if the patient is having an acute infection because this can spread the infection!** Patients should be advised to use warm compress regularly. Prescribe oral or IV antibiotics depending on severity. If conjunctivitis is present, prescribe a topical antibiotic. Once the infection has resolved, the patient may benefit from a dacryocystorhinostomy. Patients should be followed daily until they show signs of improvement.

DACRYOADENITIS

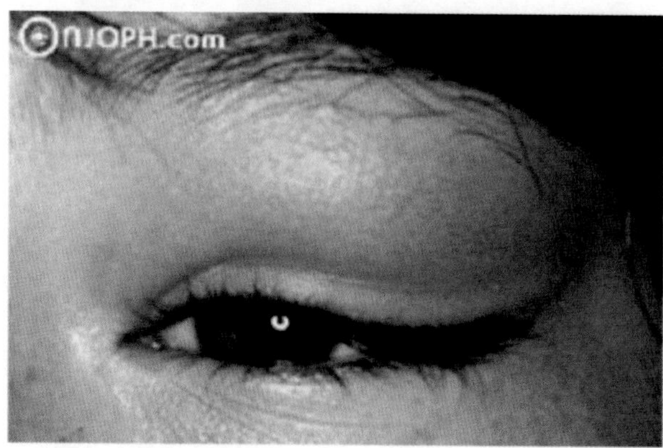

Atlas of Ophthalmology 5843

What to Know: Dacryoadenitis is defined as inflammation of the lacrimal gland. It can either be acute (due to infection) or chronic (more common, due to an inflammatory disorder).

Symptoms: Patients may complain of a red, swollen, painful superior eyelid, particularly the temporal section. Acute Dacryoadenitis will be more painful than Chronic Dacryoadenitis.

Signs: Patients present with a "S-shaped ptosis" in which the temporal region of the superior eyelid displays more ptosis due to a swollen lacrimal gland.

- Acute: Patients may also have a fever and preauricular lymphadenopathy.
- Chronic: Patients may also have restricted EOM movement.

Treatment/Management:

- Acute: Patients should be prescribed oral or intravenous (IV) medications depending on the suspected etiology (bacterial or viral). They may require surgical excision.
- Chronic: The underlying inflammatory disorder should be identified and treated.

~~~OCULAR ADNEXA~~~

CONTACT DERMATITIS

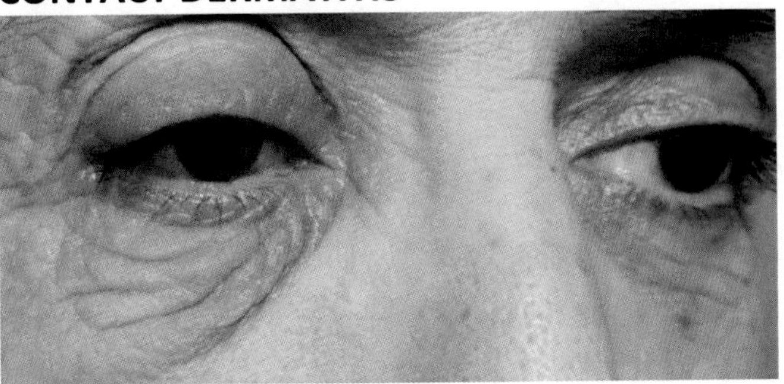

Kimberly Castillo, OD

What to Know: Contact Dermatitis occurs when a patient touches an allergen with their hands and then rubs their eyes, thus transferring the allergen to the skin around their eyes.

Symptoms: Patients will complain of itchy uncomfortable lids with possible foreign body sensation.

Signs: Patients will present with a crusting/flaking erythematous (redness of skin secondary to capillary dilation) rash with associated edema.

Treatment/Management: First line treatment is to identify and avoid the allergen. It may be necessary to refer the patient for allergy testing. The inflammation can be treated with cold compress and a topical steroid cream. The allergic reaction can be treated with an oral antihistamine. If the rash is crusting and weeping, then a topical antibiotic ointment can be prescribed.

ACNE ROSACEA / OCULAR ROSACEA

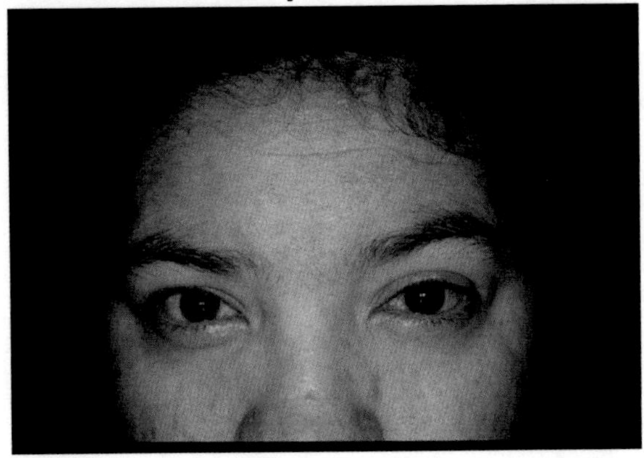

Retina Image Bank. File #8039

What to Know: Acne Rosacea is a degenerative autoimmune/idiopathic inflammatory disorder in which the patient gets acne with pustules which persists into adulthood. It predominately occurs in women. Inflammatory episodes can be caused by triggers including spicy food, alcohol, caffeine, stress, and sunlight.

Symptoms: Ocular complaints may include foreign body sensation, dry eye, and redness of the eyelids/eyeballs.

Signs: Patients will present with telangiectasia (engorged, spidery clumping of capillaries), pustules (acne), and erythema (redness of skin secondary to capillary dilation) on the cheeks, forehead, and nose. Patients may also have signs of dry eye as well as corneal neovascularization. These patients are more likely to develop a recurrent Chalazion due to the inflammatory nature of the disease.

Treatment/Management: Patients should be advised to avoid any triggering agent. The dry eye and Chalazion should be treated with lid hygiene and/or artificial tears. Oral doxycycline or tetracycline should be prescribed to treat the systemic pathology (these medications can be substituted with erythromycin if patient allergies are a contraindication). Patients may also benefit from topical steroids to treat the inflammation.

~~~ORBIT~~~

GLOBE SUBLUXATION

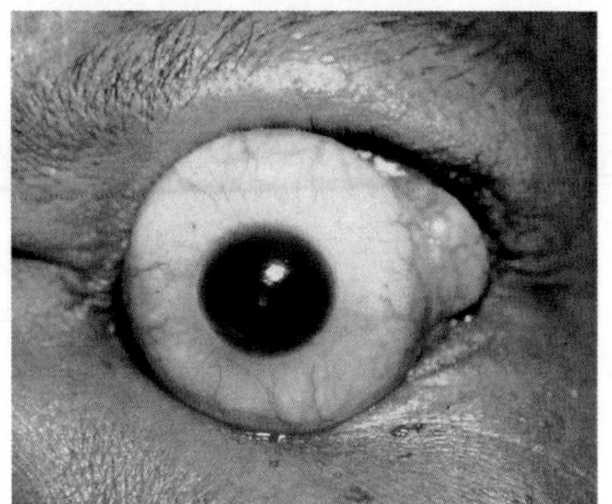
iKnowledge 2

What to Know: The etiology of Globe Subluxation can be spontaneous, voluntary, or traumatic. It has a higher risk in patients who have proptosis (Graves' Disease). Manipulation of the eyelids can cause the globe to move forward, then when the patient blinks the lids contract and become trapped behind the globe.

Symptoms: Patients may be asymptomatic. They may be anxious and complain of pain and blurry vision (due to inability to blink).

Signs: Extreme proptosis of the globe will be present with secondary topical trauma including corneal abrasions and exposure keratopathy. Patients may also have blepharospasm and optic neuropathy due to a stretched optic nerve.

Treatment/Management: Apply a topical anesthetic and ask the patient to relax. Patients may require sedation or anesthesia to relax. Manually reposition the globe by having the patient look down and pulling the upper eyelid while depressing the globe. Patients should be advised to avoid triggers, and any underlying condition should be treated (Graves' Disease). Surgery may be required in severe cases including tarsorrhaphy (sewing together the eyelids) or orbital decompression (removal of one or more walls of the orbit).

DERMOID CYST / ORBITAL DERMOID

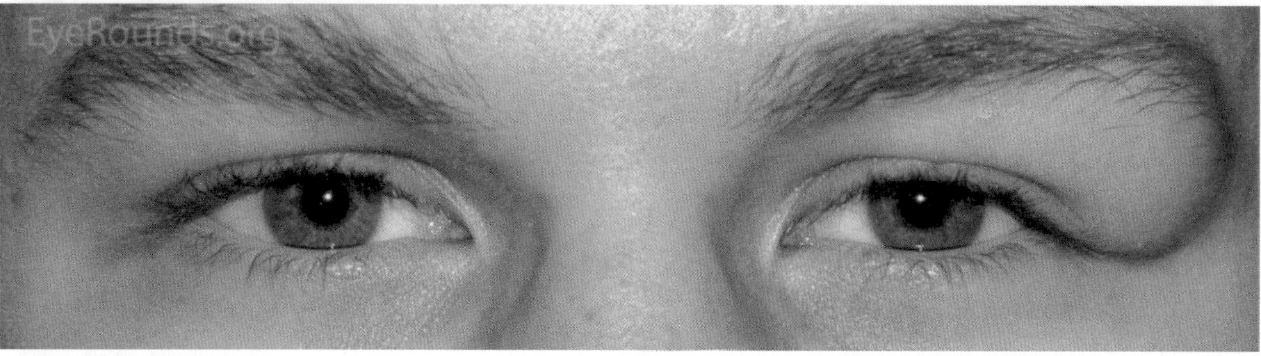

EyeRounds.org University of Iowa

What to Know: A Dermoid Cyst is the **most common pediatric orbital tumor**. It is **benign** and will typically present itself during infancy or by the time the child is 10 years old.

Symptoms: Patients may complain of diplopia, ptosis, and proptosis.

Signs: A Dermoid Cyst is most commonly located superior-temporally at the zygomaticofrontal suture (pictured). They are painless, smooth, palpable choristomas comprised of a fibrous wall which encases sebaceous glands, sweat glands, and hair follicles. A Dermoid Cyst is basically normal tissue in an abnormal location.

Treatment/Management: The only treatment option is complete surgical excision.

PRESEPTAL CELLULITIS

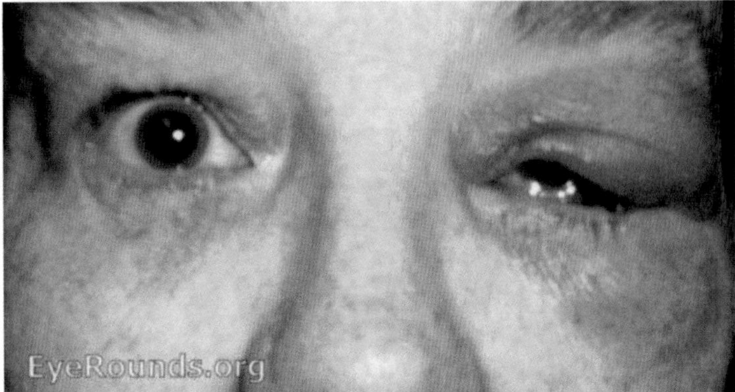

EyeRounds.org University of Iowa

What to Know: Preseptal Cellulitis is an infection of the eyelid which is located anterior to the orbital septum. It frequently is caused by a Hordeolum which spreads. Common offending bacteria include *Staph aureus* and *Haemophilus influenzae*.

Symptoms: Patients will complain of a red, tender eyelid. They won't feel sick.
Signs: Preseptal Cellulitis involves the entire eyelid. It will be red with edema. Significantly, there will be no pain with EOM movement and no reduced vision.

Treatment/Management: Patients will require oral antibiotics to treat the infection and prevent it from spreading. Severe cases may require IV antibiotics. Topical antibiotics should be used if there is evidence of corneal epithelial compromise. Patients should be followed daily until the infection shows improvement.

ORBITAL CELLULITIS*

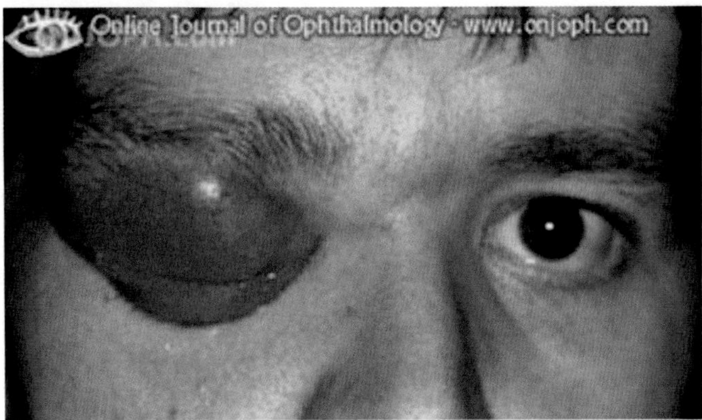

Atlas of Ophthalmology 3411

What to Know: Orbital Cellulitis is an infection located posterior to the orbital septum. It frequently occurs secondary to an Ethmoid sinus infection. Common causative bacteria include *Staph, Strep,* and *Haemophilus influenzae*. The region behind the orbital septum has direct access to the brain, and so Orbital Cellulitis can be fatal if the infection spreads intracranially. Patients who are diabetic or have a compromised immune system are at a higher risk of developing mucormycosis (fungal infection).
Symptoms: Patients will feel ill with a fever. They will have reduced vision, headache, diplopia. They will also have red, swollen, tender eyelids.

Signs: Eyelids will be swollen shut on the affected side. Patients will have proptosis, limited painful EOM movement, conjunctival injection and chemosis, and an APD with color vision defects (due to optic nerve compression). Patients may also present with a subperiosteal abscess.

Treatment/Management: Given that this is a severe bacterial infection, patients should be hospitalized and treated with intravenous (IV) antibiotics followed by oral antibiotics. Topical antibiotics should be used if there is evidence of corneal epithelial compromise. Patients should be followed daily. If present, the subperiosteal abscess should be surgically drained by an oculoplastic surgeon. If mucormycosis is suspected, patients should be given emergent IV antifungal treatment. Patients who are diabetic or have a compromised immune system are at a higher risk of developing mucormycosis (fungal infection). Any underlying medical disorder should be treated.

THYROID EYE DISEASE / GRAVES' DISEASE

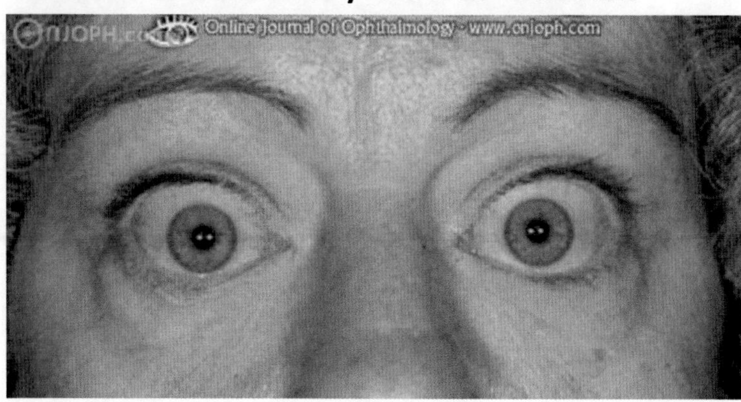

Atlas of Ophthalmology 2645

What to Know: Graves' Disease is most commonly caused by **HYPER**thyroidism, and **smoking is the biggest risk factor.** It afflicts women more than men 8:1.

Signs: Patients will present with bilateral or unilateral proptosis with upper lid retraction, lid lag on downgaze (von Graefe sign), inability to close the eyelids completely (lagophthalmos), reduced blinking, superior limbic keratoconjunctivitis (SLK), diplopia, dry eye, and exposure keratopathy. The EOMs (but **NOT** the tendons) may become inflamed, causing a positive forced-duction test and diplopia. The first EOM to become involved is the inferior rectus, followed by the medial rectus, superior rectus, lateral rectus, and finally the obliques. Given that the inferior rectus is usually involved first, patients are most likely to have limited upgaze. The optic nerve may be compressed, leading to reduced visual acuity, reduced color vision, and visual field defects.

Treatment/Management: An MRI and CT scan should be obtained to confirm diagnosis. The underlying Thyroid disease should be managed by an endocrinologist. Complications due to eyelid abnormalities (SLK, dry eye, exposure keratopathy) should be treated as such. Diplopia can be addressed with prism. Optic neuropathy secondary to inflammation should be treated with oral steroids and possible orbital decompression (removal of one of the walls of the orbit) depending on severity. Once the patient's condition has stabilized for several months, consider surgery for eyelid retraction and diplopia.

NEUROBLASTOMA

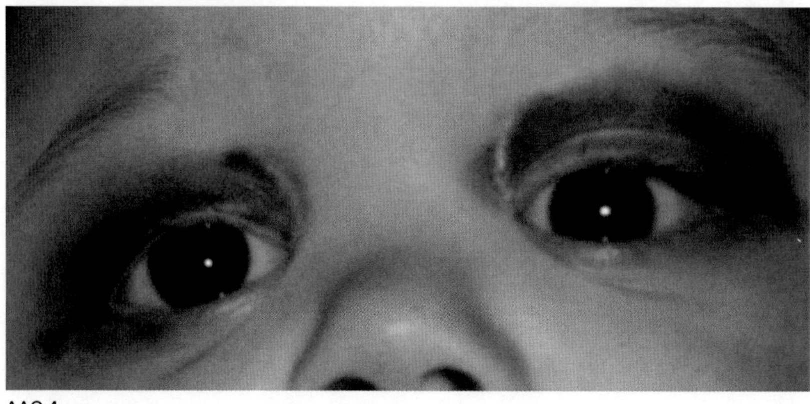

AAO 4

What to Know: A Neuroblastoma is the most common **pediatric metastatic tumor**, and will present itself by the time the child is 10 years old. The most common location of the primary tumor is the neuroblasts of the abdomen.

Signs: Patients will present with an acute onset of unilateral or bilateral superior orbital mass, proptosis, and eyelid ecchymosis (bruising aka "raccoon eyes.") On Orbital CT there will be evidence of bony erosion.

Treatment/Management: Patients should be referred for an oncology evaluation. Treatment includes chemotherapy and radiotherapy (use of radiation prior to surgery to reduce the size of the tumor).

RHABDOMYOSARCOMA / EMBRYONAL SARCOMA

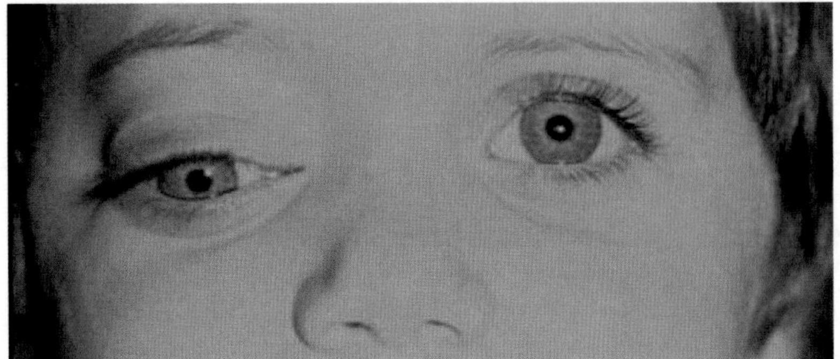
Retina Image Bank. File #12755

What to Know: Rhabdomyosarcoma is **the most common pediatric soft tissue malignancy AND the most common primary pediatric orbital malignancy**. It is typically seen in 7 year old males. Rhabdomyosarcoma most frequently afflicts the superonasal orbit and it arises from undifferentiated mesenchyme.

Signs: Patients will present with an acute onset of unilateral proptosis with eyelid discoloration and edema. Signs that the sinus is involved include headaches, sinusitis (nasal sinus inflammation most commonly caused by *Strep pneumonia* or *H. influenza*), and epistaxis (nose bleeding).

Treatment/Management: Patients need to receive an emergent diagnosis via biopsy and should receive an oncology consult to investigate any associated systemic findings. Treatment includes chemotherapy, radiotherapy (use of radiation prior to surgery to reduce the size of the tumor), and surgery.

CAVERNOUS HEMANGIOMA*

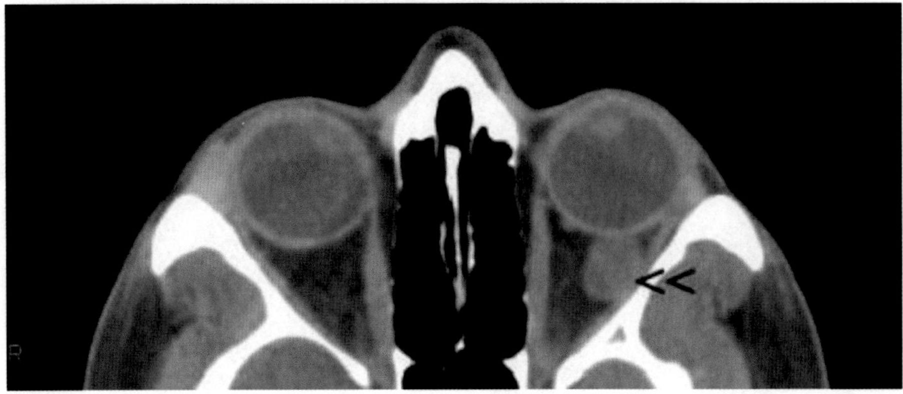
EyeRounds.org University of Iowa

What to Know: Cavernous Hemangiomas are the most common **benign orbital tumors in adults**. Be sure to differentiate them from Capillary Hemangiomas, which are the most common benign orbital tumors in children. I remember this by thinking that Capillaries are smaller than Caverns, and children are smaller than adults. It typically occurs in 40-60 year old women and leads to optic nerve compression. “Cavernous Hemangioma” is actually a misnomer, for these are actually vascular hamartomas (vascularized benign growth of the local tissue).

Symptoms: Patients will complain of painless progressive blurry vision and possible diplopia.

Signs: Patients will present with slowly progressive unilateral proptosis with compressive optic neuropathy leading to reduced VA and color vision defects. Mechanical pressure on the globe may cause choroidal folds and induced hyperopia (due to reduced axial length). CT scan will show a well-defined intraconal mass which does not invade surrounding structures but may displace them.

Treatment/Management: Patients need a complete surgical excision.

ORBITAL PSEUDOTUMOR

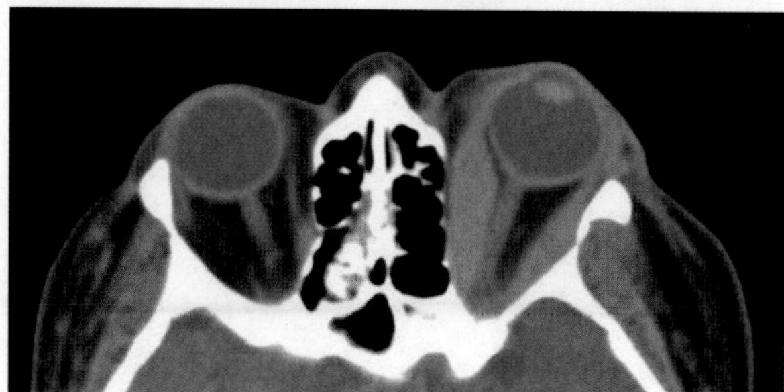

EyeRounds.org University of Iowa

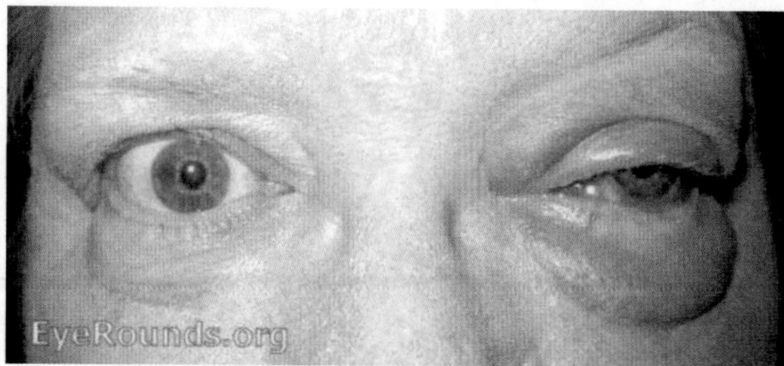

EyeRounds.org University of Iowa

What to Know: Orbital Pseudotumor is a unilateral inflammation of literally any of the tissues within the orbit. Orbital Pseudotumor is an idiopathic disease which can be chronic, recurrent, or acute. It is the second most common cause of exophthalmos.

Symptoms: Symptoms will have an **acute "explosive" onset**. Patients will complain of pain, swollen eyelids, and blur.

Signs: Orbital Pseudotumor will cause **unilateral** inflammation of any of the tissues in the orbit: EOMs, **tendons**, sclera, lacrimal gland, orbital fat, and optic nerve sheath. Given this inflammation will cause crowding within the orbit, the patient will also have proptosis and limited EOM movement (with positive forced ductions) due to tethering the EOMs. The mechanical pressure on the globe can shorten the axial length and induce hyperopia as well as cause increased IOP. Patients may also present with chemosis and iritis.

Treatment/Management: Given the inflammatory nature of Orbital Pseudotumor, patients are treated with oral and topical steroids. If patients do not have a significant improvement within 48 hours of initiating steroid treatment, then another diagnosis should be considered.

CHAPTER 12
SYSTEMIC HEALTH

The NBEO website states that 11-22 questions will be asked on Systemic Health. Historically they have asked about 18.3 questions, meaning this chapter covers approximately 5% of the material tested on the exam, or roughly 4 cases. This material IS included on TMOD.

It is hard to predict what the NBEO will include in "Systemic Health" because it is such a broad category, and so I am left with my best guess. I have decided to include in this chapter systemic diseases which cause a myriad of ocular complications. Instead of discussing these diseases multiple times in separate chapters based on their many ocular complications, I am going to do a comprehensive discussion of all their conditions in this chapter.

HYPERTENSION

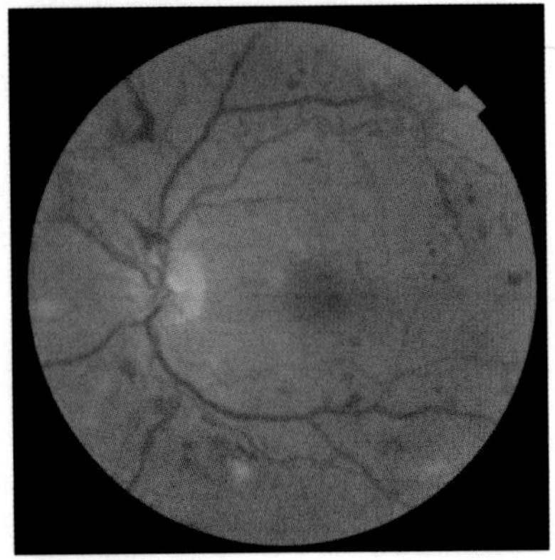
National Vision, Inc.

Hypertension is the most common systemic health disease in America with increasing prevalence in individuals over 60 years of age. It is defined as a blood pressure greater than 140/90. There is a variety of risk factors, but some include consumption of salt and an African American descent.

Among the many ways blood pressure rises includes when arteries become lined with plaque. The plaque reduces the real estate in which the blood has to move, which increases the pressure and speed at which blood travels through the blood vessel. This process is not unlike squeezing a hose so that the water shoots out more quickly. Given that hypertension is caused by plaque inside the blood vessels, it is not surprising that hypertension has a high association with artery occlusions. The plaque which causes the hypertension also provides the source for the emboli.

After an artery has been subjected to high pressure for a long time, it becomes stretched out, and this is the mechanism behind how arteries become engorged during hypertension. These engorged arteries can compress neighboring veins, creating an environment for a thrombus to form within the vein. Given that hypertension creates the environment necessary for thrombi to form within veins, it is not surprising that hypertension is highly associated with vein occlusions as well.

Hypertension causes challenges on the heart and kidneys over time.

Hypertension is treated with diet, exercise, and medications designed to reduce blood pressure.

DIABETES MELLITUS

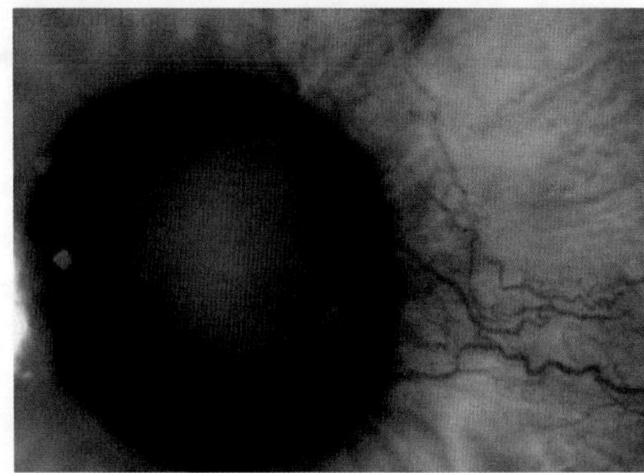

EyeRounds.org University of Iowa

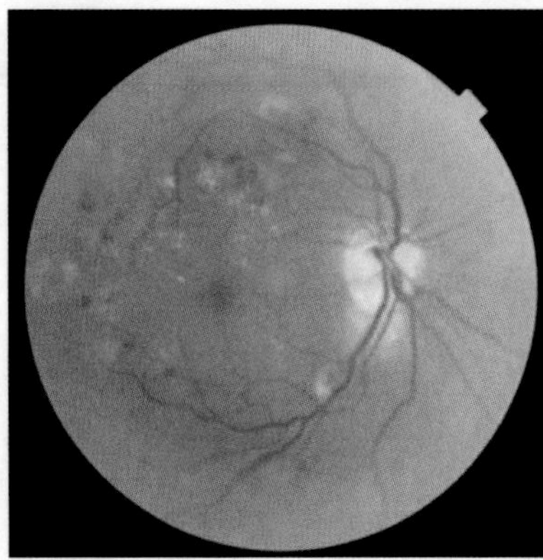

National Vision, Inc.

What to Know: Diabetes Mellitus is an endocrine disorder associated with reduced production of insulin in the pancreas, and so these patients are unable to absorb sugars from their blood into their cells. Meaning, these patients have an increased blood sugar level, making their blood like molasses. Because it is hard to move around molasses blood, these patients will accrue damage to their blood vessels, specifically loss of pericytes. As this process occurs, the patient may have a breakdown of the blood-retinal barrier, and this is why they get diabetic retinopathy.

Diabetes Mellitus tends to run in families, and patients tend to be obese. Also, diabetes may occur as a side effect of prolonged use of systemic steroids.

There are two types of Diabetes Mellitus:

1. Type 1 (Juvenile Onset) typically has an onset before the patient turns 40. It is associated with damage to the beta cells of the pancreas, leading to a reduction in the production of insulin.
2. Type 2 (Adult Onset) typically has an onset after the patient turns 40. It occurs when the pancreas gives up making insulin.

Symptoms: Patients may complain of polyuria (increased urination), polydipsia (increased thirst), and polyphagia (increased hunger).

Signs: Systemic signs may include an A1C above 6.0, blood sugar above 100, kidney and liver failure, and congestive heart failure. Peripheral neuropathy will prevent patients from feeling cuts or ulcers on their feet, and so they will get infected. Spreading infections may require the patient to get an amputation, and this is why Diabetes Mellitus is the leading cause of non-traumatic amputations in the United States.

The biggest risk factor for developing diabetic retinopathy is the duration which the patient has had the disease. Other ocular complications include rubeosis iridis and neovascular glaucoma, retinal artery occlusions, optic nerve hypoplasia, subcapsular cataracts, snowflake cataracts, and orbital cellulitis. Cranial nerve palsies may include cranial nerves 3, 4, and 6.

Treatment/Management: Diabetes Mellitus can be managed with diet and exercise. Pharmacological treatment includes Metformin (first choice drug), Glipizide, Pioglitazone, Rosiglitazone, and Insulin replacement. Beta-Blockers should be avoided in patients who have Diabetes Mellitus.

Ocular complications should be treated as such (see each specific section for a thorough discussion). Patients should have a CEE within 5 years of diagnosis with diabetes and annually thereafter.

SYPHILIS

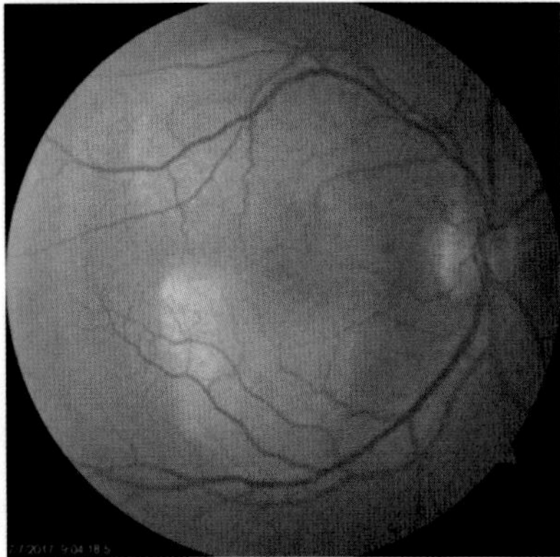

Retina Image Bank. File #27345

What to Know: Syphilis is caused by an infection of the spirochete *Treponema pallidum*. It is spread by either congenital transmission from mother to child, or sexual intercourse.

Signs:

Acquired Syphilis is a great masquerader because its disease course has three stages with distinctive presentations in each:

1. Primary Syphilis is characterized as a chancre which occurs at the site of infection after a 2-4 week incubation period.
2. Secondary Syphilis occurs 6-8 weeks after the chancre and is characterized by mucous membrane lesions. **This is the stage in which ocular manifestations occur:**
    a. Granulomatous Panuveitis is the major finding. Pan means all, so it is uveitis of the entire eye – anterior, intermediate, and posterior segments.
    b. Retinal findings include a salt and pepper fundus, yellow-white chorioretinal lesions, flame shaped hemorrhages, vascular sheathing, papillitis, and possible neuroretinitis.
    c. Anterior segment findings include Argyle Robertson Pupil, episcleritis, and scleritis.
3. 40% of cases progress to Tertiary Syphilis, and typically manifests in patients who have not been treated. It occurs after a latent period which can last several years, and is characterized by cardiovascular and CNS disease.

Congenital Syphilis is defined by Hutchinson's triad:

1. Peg shaped incisors
2. Interstitial keratitis (non-ulcerating inflammation of the corneal stroma without involvement of either the epithelium or endothelium)
3. Deafness

Treatment/Management: Tests that should be run for Syphilis can distinguish an active case (RPR and VDRL) from a latent case (FTA-ABS).

Regarding treatment, the first thing that should come to mind for both acquired and congenital Syphilis is **IV Penicillin G**. Tetracycline can be used instead if the patient is allergic to penicillin. Immunocompromised patients may require long-term prophylactic treatment with tetracycline or doxycycline. If anterior uveitis is present, it should be treated with the usual steroid and cycloplegic.

HUMAN IMMUNODEFICIENCY VIRUS (HIV)

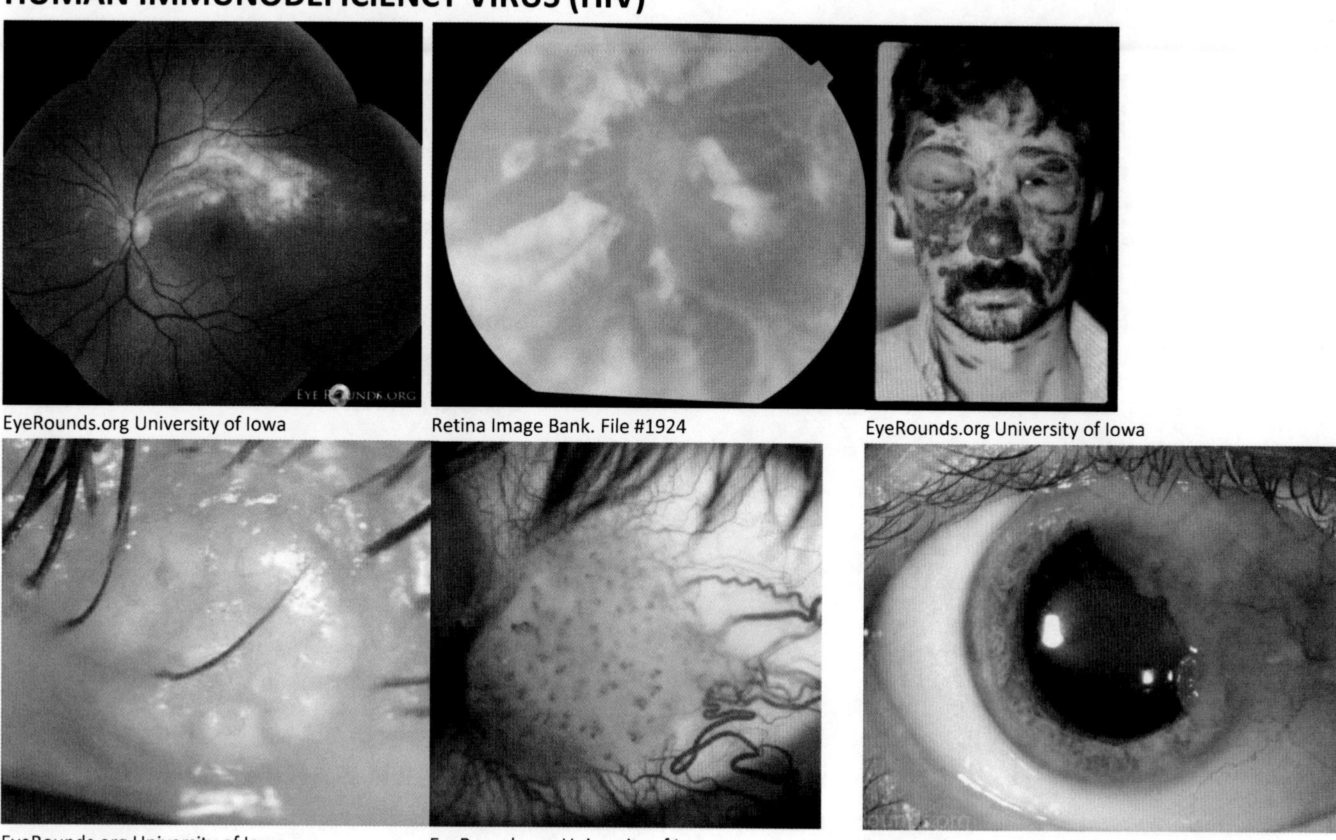

EyeRounds.org University of Iowa | Retina Image Bank. File #1924 | EyeRounds.org University of Iowa

EyeRounds.org University of Iowa | EyeRounds.org University of Iowa | EyeRounds.org University of Iowa

What to Know: HIV is a sexually transmitted disease which cripples the immune system, causing the patients to become immunocompromised. When a patient is initially infected they will show signs of the flu, after which the virus will lay dormant for months to years before progressing into AIDS.

Signs: There are many signs (systemic and ocular) which are associated with HIV.

- **Cytomegalovirus (CMV**, top left picture): If a patient has CMV, you should immediately associate it with HIV because this is the most common opportunistic retinal infection found in these patients. Usually asymptomatic, but may have unilateral or bilateral blurry vision with floaters.
- **Progressive Outer Retinal Necrosis Syndrome (PORN**, top middle picture) is caused by the Herpes Zoster Virus and occurs in patients with HIV (as well as other immunocompromised patients). The compromised immune system allows the opportunistic HIV to behave aggressively, necrotizing (killing) the retinal flesh. Patients will complain of unilateral blurry vision. The first sign will be a minimal anterior uveitis and vitritis followed by yellow-white retinal infiltrates. Next will be a rapid full-thickness retinal necrosis which will have early involvement of the macula. Vitreous inflammation with retinal detachments will occur in the late stages.
- **Kaposi's Sarcoma** (top right picture) presents as a deep purple plaque which may be flat or elevated. It may cause recurrent subconjunctival hemorrhages, entropion, trichiasis, and corneal scarring. It may

present on the conjunctiva, eyelid, or anywhere on the face. Kaposi's Sarcoma is frequently seen in HIV positive patients and can be highly malignant in this population. Patients may have no complaints (asymptomatic) or complain of ocular irritation.

- **Molluscum Contagiosum** (bottom left picture) is caused by the DNA pox virus. It presents with a dome shaped umbilicated shiny nodule along the lid margin. If multiple are present, then HIV may be the underlying etiology. Ruptured nodules may lead to pannus (fibrous vascular tissue growth over the cornea), and **chronic conjunctivitis.**
- **Conjunctival Intraepithelial Neoplasia (CIN**, bottom middle picture) → **Squamous Cell Carcinoma** (bottom right picture): CIN is the precursor to Squamous Cell Carcinoma. Squamous Cell Carcinoma is the **most common conjunctival malignancy in the US**. Both are most commonly seen in elderly Caucasian males and are usually associated with heavy smoking, UV radiation, and HPV. If present in a patient under the age of 50, suspect HIV. Metastasis and orbital invasion is rare for Squamous Cell Carcinoma, but mortality is as high as an 8%. Patients may complain of ocular irritation, foreign body sensation, and dry eye. CIN remains limited to just the conjunctival epithelium near the limbus. It appears as white, gelatinous dysplasia (abnormal, precancerous tissue). Squamous Cell Carcinoma is a peripapillary, gelatinous lesions with abnormal loops of vessels.
- Patients may also suffer from other opportunistic infections.

Treatment/Management: If you suspect that a patient has HIV, they should be referred for testing (Western Blot and ELISA). Patients who have HIV are generally treated with a cocktail of drugs, also known as antiretroviral therapy (HAART). If a HIV-positive patient presents with new ocular signs, their HAART therapy may need to be adjusted. If patients with HIV need treatment for an ocular viral disease, they will most benefit from topical, oral, intravenous (IV), or intravitreal injections and implants.

- **Kaposi's Sarcoma**: If present in HIV positive patients, then the Kaposi's Sarcoma will spontaneously resolve with a change in HAART HIV treatment. Otherwise, patients may benefit from excision, cryotherapy (freezing of tissue), chemotherapy, or irradiation.
- **Progressive Outer Retinal Necrosis Syndrome (PORN):** Given the viral origin, PORN should be treated with anti-virals (oral, IV, and intravitreal injections). If inflammation is present, then topical steroids should be considered. Any subsequent retinal detachments should be treated surgically.
- **Cytomegalovirus (CMV)**: The name of this disease tells you the treatment. Given that Cytomegalovirus is a virus, it needs to be treated like a viral infection of the retina. Given this occurs in immunocompromised patients, treatment should be aggressive. Antiviral intravenous (IV) and intravitreal injections should be considered. If the disease course improves, the patient may be switched to oral antivirals. Also, these patients' HAART therapy may need to be adjusted to prevent recurrence. An intravitreal antiviral implant can be considered as prophylaxis against recurrence. If present, treat any retinal detachments surgically.
- **Molluscum Contagiosum:** The nodules will resolve with initializing or adjusting the patient's HAART therapy.
- **Conjunctival Intraepithelial Neoplasia (CIN)**: Patients should be referred for a medical workup and receive an MRI to rule out orbital invasion. Excision with biopsy, exenteration (complete removal of the globe and all the contents of the eye socket), and radiation may be necessary. If recurrent, topical interferon, Mitomycin C (DNA synthesis inhibitor which stops the growth of cancer cells), or 5-fluorouracil can be considered.

SARCOIDOSIS

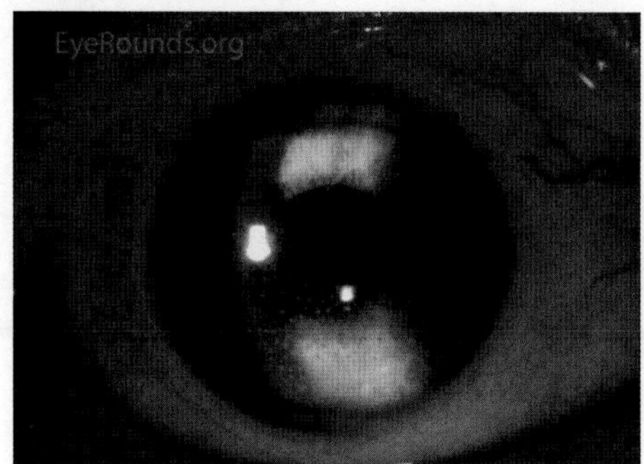

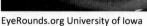

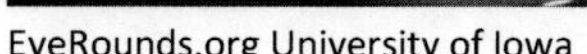
EyeRounds.org University of Iowa

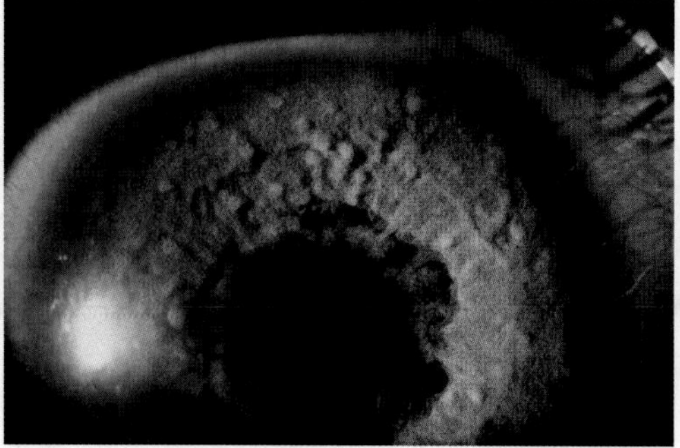
Retina Image Bank. File #6220

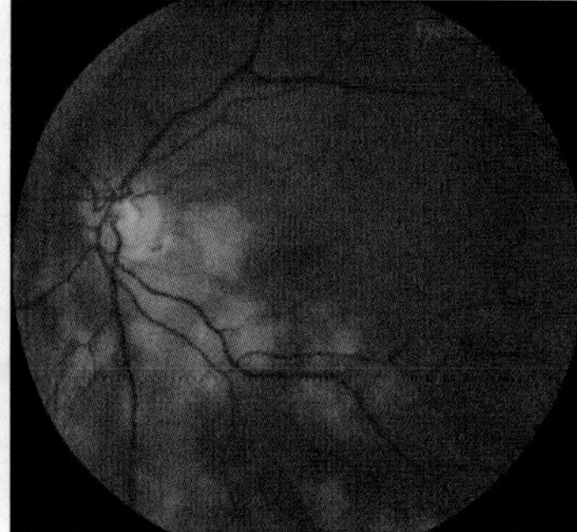
EyeRounds.org University of Iowa

What to Know: Sarcoidosis is an idiopathic disease which causes noncaseating (not cheesy) granulomas (Tuberculosis presents with caseating granulomas). The granulomas may be present on the lungs, eyes, and skin. Ocular complications are typically seen in 20-30 year old African Americans. Remember that idiopathic diseases are most likely autoimmune in nature. Sarcoidosis is knowns as the "great masquerader" because it causes a large variety of signs and so can be easily misdiagnosed.

Symptoms: Patients may complain of bilateral blurry vision with photophobia and pain secondary to uveitis.

Signs: Ocular signs include granulomatous panuveitis (pan means all, so it uveitis of the entire eye – anterior, intermediate, and posterior segments) with large mutton-fat keratic precipitates (left image) and iris Koeppe/Busacca nodules (central image). Retinal vasculitis (right image) presents as candle wax drippings, vitreous snowballs, or string of pearls. Late complications include disc/retinal neovascularization (with a sea-fan appearance) and epiretinal membrane. Additional ocular complications include inflammation of the conjunctiva, eyelids, and lacrimal system; band keratopathy; cataracts; and glaucoma.

Treatment/Management:

It is important to remember that serum ACE will be elevated in these patients. I remember this by "Sarc-ACE." Also remember that chest radiography should be run on these patients looking for lung granulomas, and this is the most useful diagnostic test. Sarcoidosis will present with a negative PPD test, while Tuberculosis will present with a positive PPD test.

The inflammation should be treated with steroids: oral or Sub-Tenon's injections. The anterior uveitis should be treated with a topical steroid and cycloplegic. Any neovascularization can be treated with laser photocoagulation (cautery of retinal blood vessels with a laser).

Patients should be monitored every 1-7 days depending on severity. Chronic treatment with steroids should be monitored every 3-6 weeks.

GARDENER'S SYNDROME

Gardener's Syndrome is typically diagnosed when the patient is in their 20s and will lead to colon cancer by the time the patient is in their 50s. Ocular findings may include multiple bilateral CHRPEs. Systemic findings may include polyps throughout the colon, soft tissue tumors (neurofibromas, cysts), and skeletal hamartomas.

TUBERCULOSIS (TB)

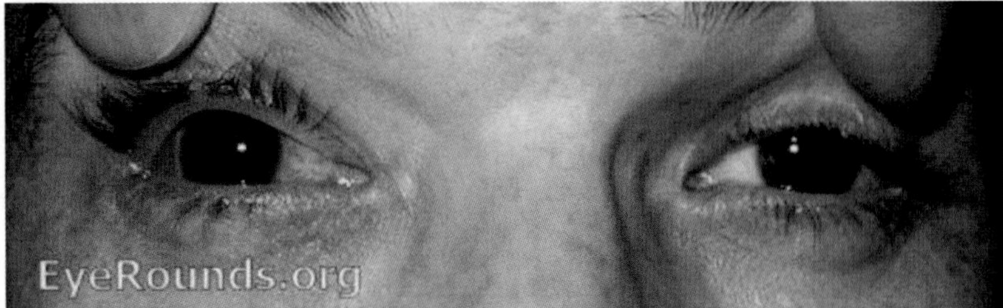

EyeRounds.org University of Iowa

What to Know: TB is caused by *Mycobacterium tuberculosis*, which is an obligate aerobe. It is transmitted via air droplets and unpasteurized milk.

Signs: Systemic findings include caseating (cheesy) granulomas typically seen on the lungs. Since TB is caused by an obligate aerobe, it makes sense that the granulomas would be found on the lungs. Other systemic signs include a chronic cough, night sweats, and fever.

TB can cause anterior, intermediate, or posterior uveitis with Anterior Granulomatous Uveitis being the most common ocular sign. Intermediate uveitis includes vitritis, and posterior vitritis includes Periphlebitis (inflammation of the tissues surrounding veins).

Other ocular findings include conjunctivitis with lymphadenopathy, cystoid macular edema, papilledema, phlyctenulosis, interstitial keratitis, episcleritis, and scleritis.

Treatment/Management: If TB is suspected, testing should include PPD and chest radiograph, both of which will be abnormal. If a patient has an active infection, then they should be treated with all of the TB medications:

- Medications specific to active TB infections:
  - Ethambutol may cause bilateral optic neuritis.
  - Pyrazinamide
- Medications for both latent and active TB infections
  - Rifampin is known to cause pink and orange tears/urine. Rifampin can be used independently from the other TB medications in order to treat latent TB.
  - Isoniazid may cause optic neuritis.

PREECLAMPSIA/ECLAMPSIA

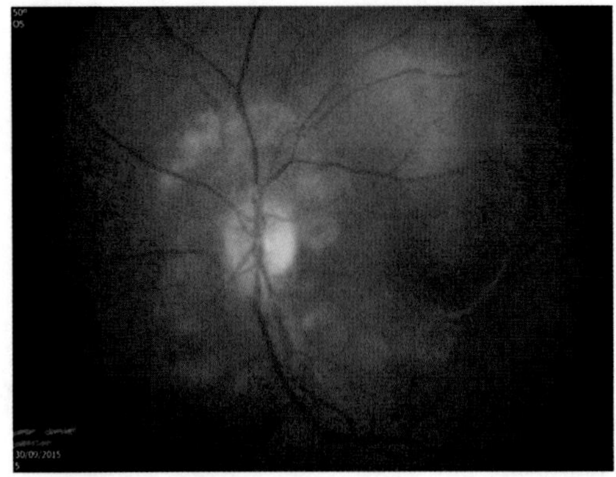

Retina Image Bank. File #26174

What to Know: Pregnant women may develop gestational hypertension towards the end of their pregnancy. In preeclampsia the mother has a sudden spike of blood pressure which reduces blood supply (aka oxygen and nutrients) to the fetus. Retinal edema can also be seen in preeclampsia. If it progresses, the mother may start having seizures or go into a coma – when this happens it is considered Eclampsia.

Symptoms: Patients may complain of blurry vision/scotomas from the edema, and headaches from the increased blood pressure.

Signs: Ocular findings of mothers affected with Pre-Eclampsia/Eclampsia are similar to hypertensive retinopathy; narrowing of blood vessels, intraretinal hemorrhages, cotton wool spots, hard exudates, and disc edema. Pre-eclampsia/eclampsia can also present with Elschnig spots (focal chorioretinal atrophy), neovascularization, and serous retinal detachments.

Babies of these mothers may be born with ocular findings including Retinopathy of Prematurity (ROP), optic nerve head pallor, and retinopathy.

Treatment/Management: Induce labor and reduce blood pressure. Signs usually resolve post-partum.

LEUKEMIC RETINOPATHY

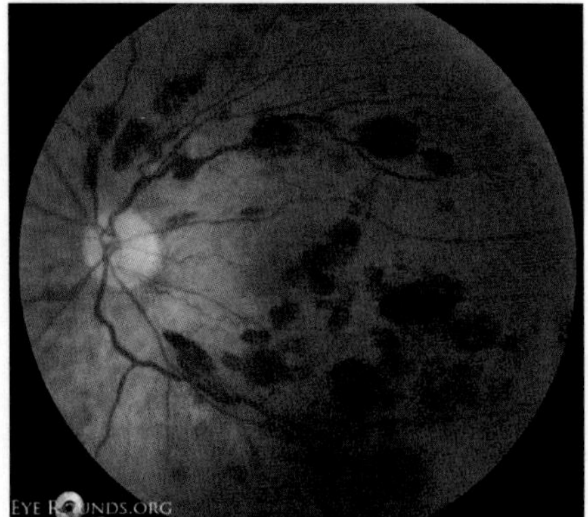

EyeRounds.org University of Iowa

Leukemic Retinopathy occurs secondary to leukemia and is characterized by roth spots (intraretinal hemorrhages with a white center or lymphocytic embolus). Other signs include dilated/tortuous vessels, venous beading/vascular sheathing, and cotton wool spots. Patients can have concurrent CRVO. It will resolve as the leukemia resolves.

ACNE ROSACEA

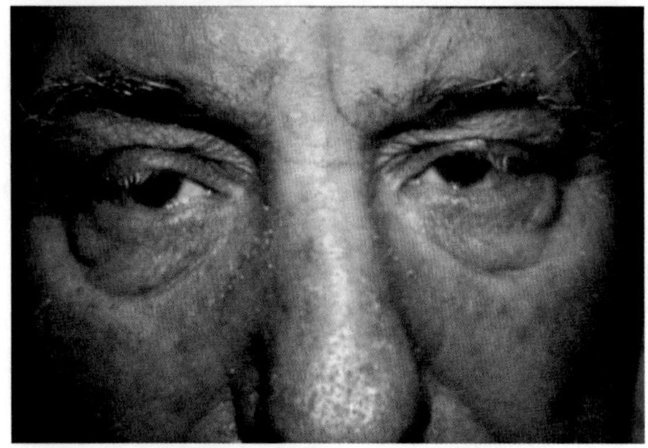

EyeRounds.org University of Iowa

What to Know: Acne Rosacea is an inflammatory disorder.

Symptoms: Patients may complain of acne which persists into adulthood. Their face may also flush in response to triggers such as working out, alcohol, and spicy foods.

Signs: Patients may present with flushing of the face with pustules (acne) which persist into adulthood primarily located on the cheeks, chin, and nose. Patients may also present with rhinophyma (a large, bulbous, lumpy, red, nose). Ocular signs may include dry eye, episcleritis, phlyctenules (nodular corneal inflammation), corneal pannus (growth of find blood vessels), and iritis. Given that Acne Rosacea is an inflammatory disease, the ocular signs seen are generally caused by inflammation.

Treatment/Management: Treatment includes oral tetracycline, doxycycline, or erythromycin.

SYSTEMIC LUPUS ERYTHEMATOSUS (SLE) and CHLOROQUINE / HYDROXYCHLOROQUINE (PLAQUENIL) TOXICITY

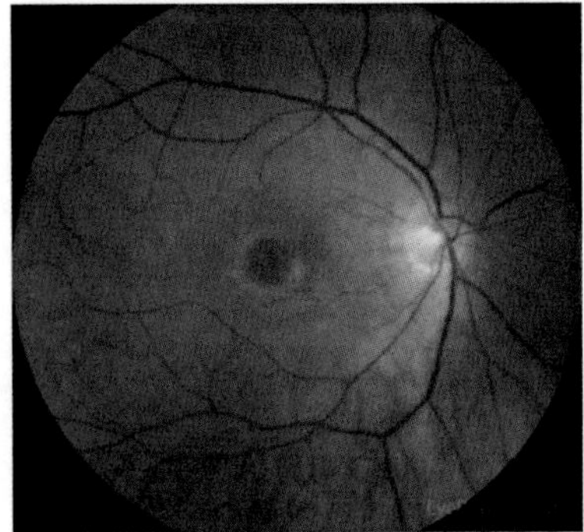

EyeRounds.org University of Iowa

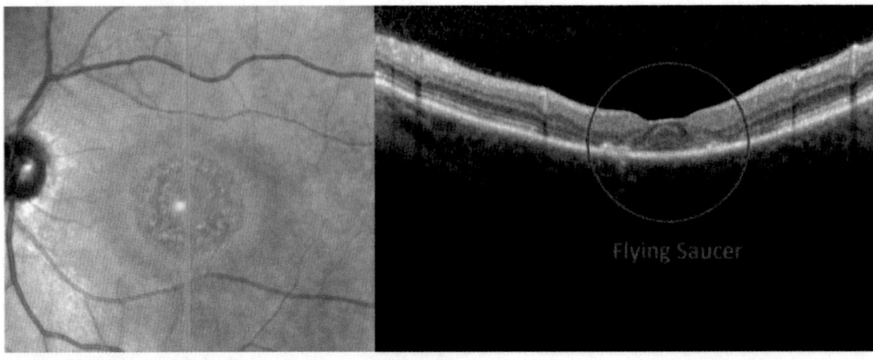

EyeRounds.org University of Iowa

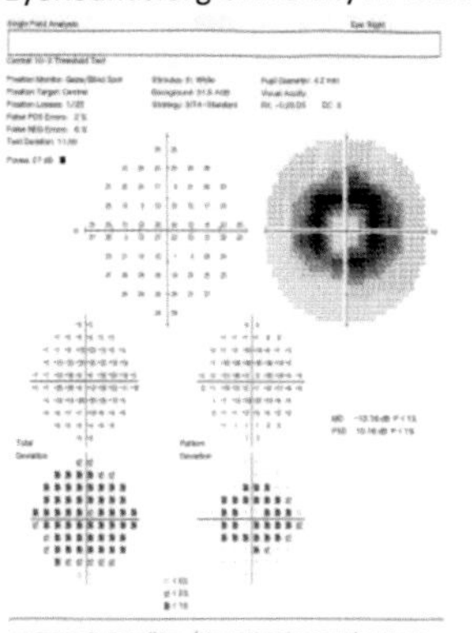

EyeRounds.org University of Iowa

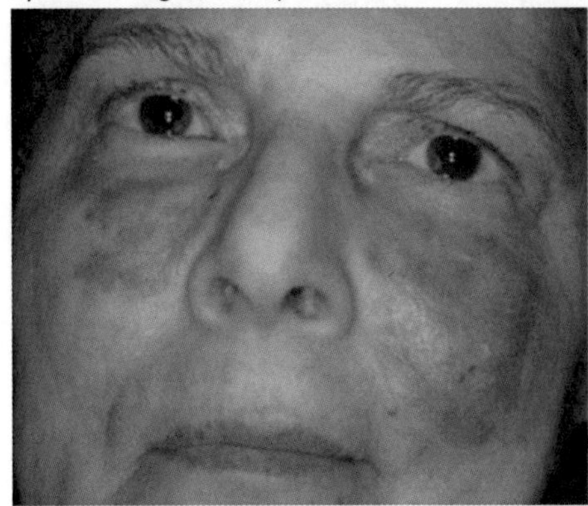

Cogan Collection, NEI/NIH

What to Know: SLE is an autoimmune disease which will have a positive ANA test, and Plaquenil is used to treat SLE. Below are the Plaquenil doses which may cause toxicity/maculopathy:

- Chloroquine: 3mg/kg/day for 5 years (300 grams, total cumulative dose)
- Hydroxychloroquine: 6.5mg/kg/day for 5 years (700 grams, total cumulative dose). The daily dose should not exceed 400 mg.

Symptoms:

- SLE: Patients may complain of photophobia and dry eye.
- Plaquenil Toxicity: Patients may complain of blur, abnormal color vision, and difficulty adjusting to lighting changes.

Signs:

- SLE: Ocular signs may include recurrent episcleritis, peripheral keratitis, and dry eye. Systemic signs may include a butterfly malar rash, renal disorders, arthritis, seizures, and hemolytic anemia.
- Plaquenil Toxicity: Bullseye maculopathy, "flying saucer" on OCT with loss of foveal light reflex, and visual field defects including scotomas.

Treatment/Management:

When the patient initially starts taking Plaquenil they should undergo baseline testing. Then screening for toxicity should begin 5 years later and be repeated every 6-12 months. Testing should include: 10-2 Visual Field, Multifocal ERG, Spectral Domain OCT, and Color Vision. Discontinue use of Plaquenil if toxicity develops.

FABRY'S DISEASE

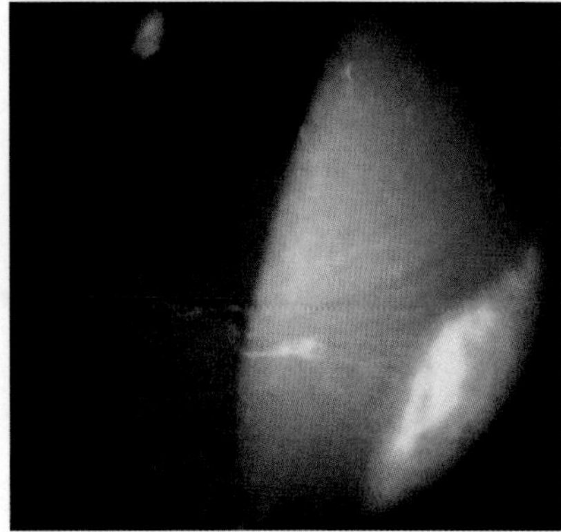

Kimberly Castillo, OD

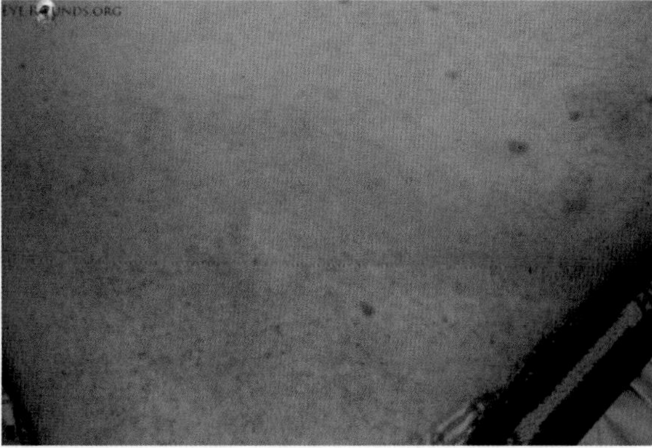

EyeRounds.org University of Iowa

What to Know: Fabry's Disease is an X-Linked AR disorder of lysozyme storage most frequently seen in males. It will frequently lead to death due to cardiovascular or renal/kidney complications.

Symptoms: Patients may complain of extreme pain in their small joints.

Signs: Ocular signs may include corneal verticillata/whorl keratopathy (left image), wedge-shaped posterior subcapsular cataracts, nystagmus, CN3 Palsy, and conjunctival and vascular tortuosity. Systemic signs include telangiectasia (engorged, spidery clumping of capillaries: right image), renal/kidney disease, and hypertrophic cardiomyopathy.

Treatment/Management: Patients should be treated with Enzyme Replacement Therapy (ERT). If renal disease occurs, treat with diuretics, dialysis, or kidney transplant depending on severity. Cardiovascular treatment can vary widely depending on the specific case. Treatment may include lifestyle changes, reducing blood pressure, and surgery.

THYROID DISEASE

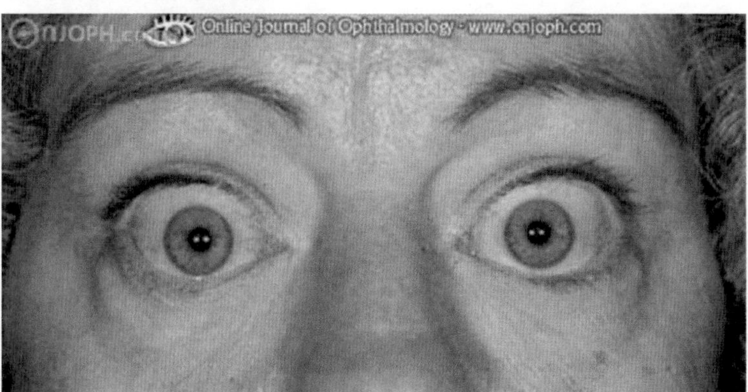

Atlas of Ophthalmology Image #2645

Thyroid disease occurs when the feedback mechanism between T3, T4, and TSH is disrupted. Patients with hyperthyroidism will have an overactive metabolism, and so they tend to be skinny. Hyperthyroidism can lead to Grave's Disease/Thyroid Eye Disease. Patients with hypothyroidism have a slowed metabolism, and so they tend to be overweight. Hypothyroidism can cause Hashimoto's Disease.

NEUROFIBROMATOSIS (NF)

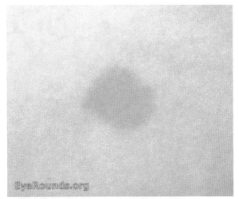

EyeRounds.org University of Iowa

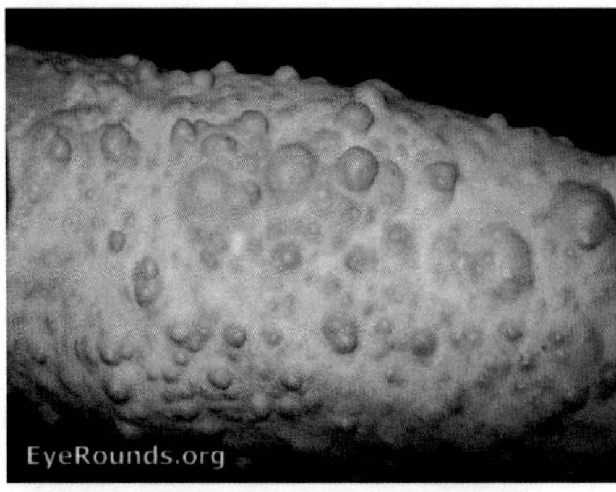

EyeRounds.org University of Iowa

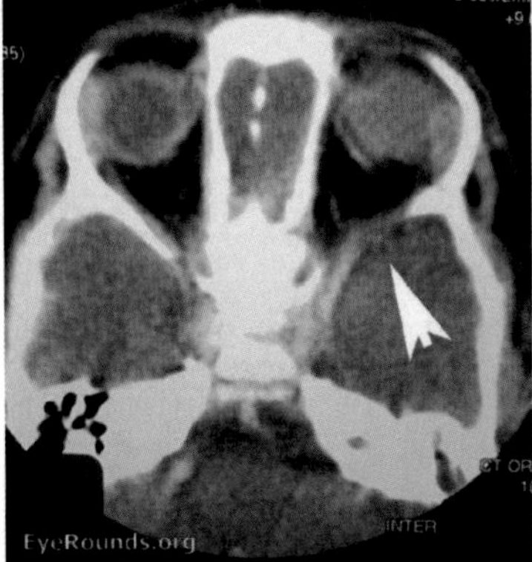

EyeRounds.org University of Iowa

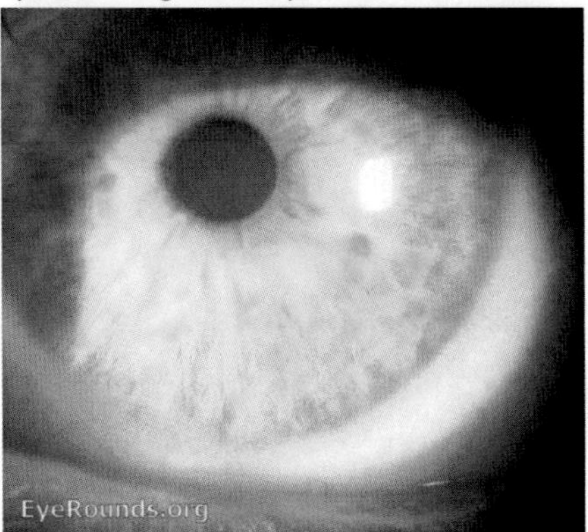

EyeRounds.org University of Iowa

What to Know: NF displays an AD inheritance. It is a neuro-oculo-cutaneous syndrome (phakomatoses) characterized by the abnormal vascularized benign growth of local tissue (hamartomas). There are two types: NF-1 and NF-2. We are only going to discuss NF-1 because it is more common, and NF-2 does not have any ocular complications.

Signs: There is a list of seven diagnostic criteria for NF-1, but below I've listed the classic findings which are unique to NF-1 and will most likely be included in a case if this were tested on Part 2.

1. Six or more cafe-au-lait spots (large, flat, brown, "freckles." See top left image).
2. Neurofibromas (asymptomatic tumors of a nerve cell sheath. See top right image).
3. Optic nerve glioma (tumor of the optic nerve glial cells. See bottom left image) which may lead to pulsating proptosis.
4. Lisch nodules (melanocytic hamartomas of the iris. See bottom right image).

Other signs include glaucoma and cataracts.

Treatment/Management: Patients should get routine eye exams to monitor for ocular complications and any findings should be treated as such. Neurofibromas can be surgically removed, although they have a high rate of recurrence. Patients should also be referred for genetic counseling.

RHEUMATOID ARTHRITIS (RA)

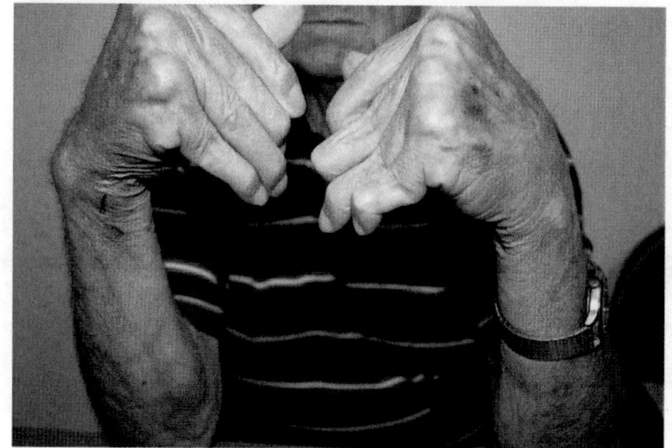

Flicker © Image #9212534322

What to Know: RA is an autoimmune disease most frequently seen in women between the ages of 30-50.

Symptoms: Patients may complain of joint pain.

Signs: RA usually presents as bilateral, symmetrical, deforming, inflammatory polyarthritis (arthritis involving at least five joints) of the hands. Systemic complications include septic arthritis, carpal tunnel syndrome, pulmonary nodules/fibrosis, multifocal neuropathy, and secondary amyloidosis. RA is the most common cause of scleritis (scleromalacia perforans). Other ocular complications include blue sclera, dry eye, and ulcerative keratitis. Diagnosis can be confirmed with a positive Rheumatoid Factor (RF) test.

Treatment/Management: Treatment is aimed at reducing the inflammation with systemic steroids and NSAIDS, and reducing the autoimmune response with immunosuppressive medications. Ocular manifestations may also be treated as needed.

JUVENILE RHEUMATOID ARTHRITIS (JRA)

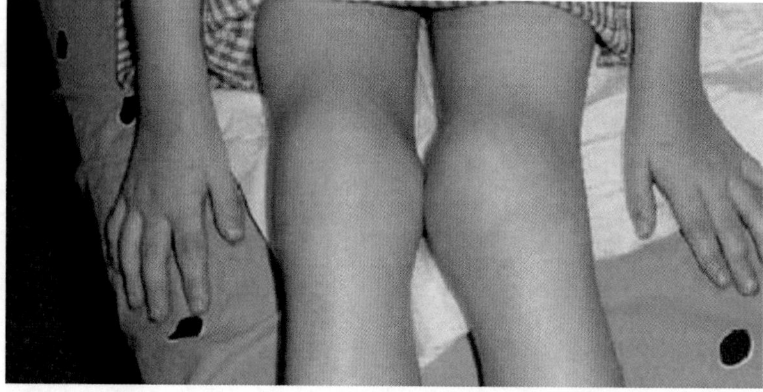

Medical Observer 1

What to Know: JRA is the most common cause of recurrent uveitis in children and is typically seen in females under the age of 8.

Symptoms: Patients may complain of joint pain in the lower extremities and recurrent uveitis with photophobia.

Signs: JRA is the most common cause of chronic/recurrent bilateral, non-granulomatous, anterior uveitis in children. Other ocular signs may include band keratopathy and early cataract formation. Systemic findings will include inflammation of multiple joints, particularly the sacroiliac joints (the joint in the pelvis between sacrum and ilium bones). Testing will find a positive ANA and a negative RF.

Treatment/Management: Patients should be treated with steroids to reduce inflammation. If they develop steroid resistance, then consider methotrexate.

TUBEROUS SCLEROSIS (BOURNEVILLLE'S DISEASE)

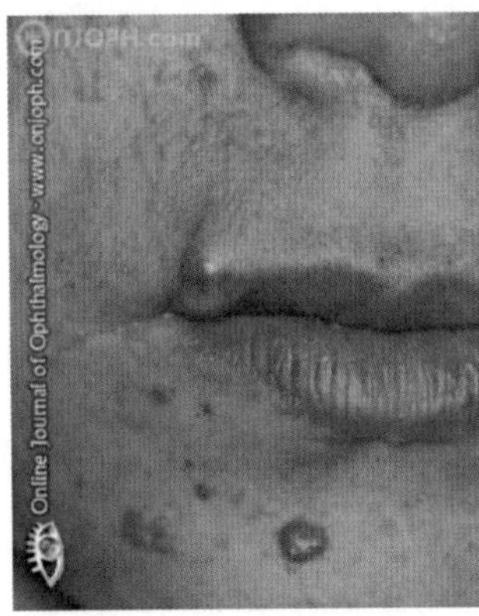

Atlas of Ophthalmology 1812

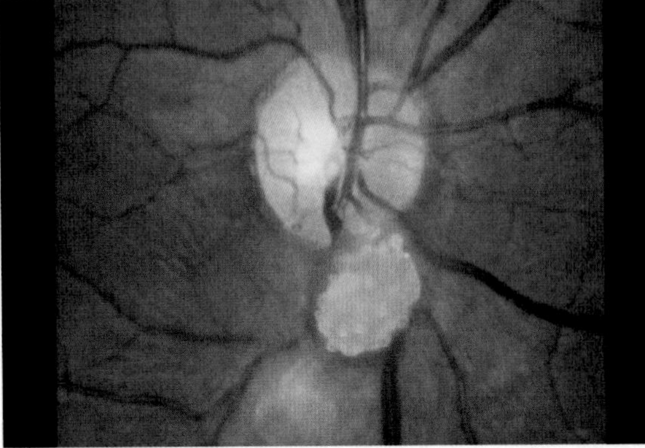

Retina Image Bank. File #3486

What to Know: An autosomal dominant (AD) disease, Tuberous Sclerosis is identified by a triad of findings: seizures, mental retardation, and adenoma sebaceum (a papular malar rash). Mortality rate is 75% by the age of 20 in these individuals.

Signs: The main ocular sign is an elevated mulberry-like lesion adjacent to the optic nerve.

Treatment/Management: These patients should be managed by a neurologist with regular MRIs.

VOGT-KOYANAGI-HARADA SYNDROME (VKH SYNDROME)

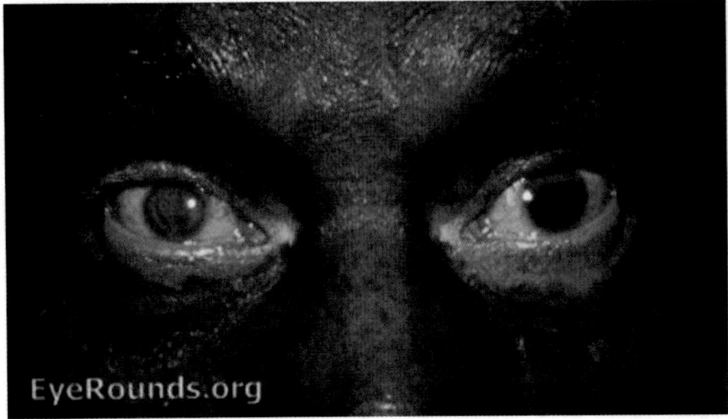

EyeRounds.org University of Iowa

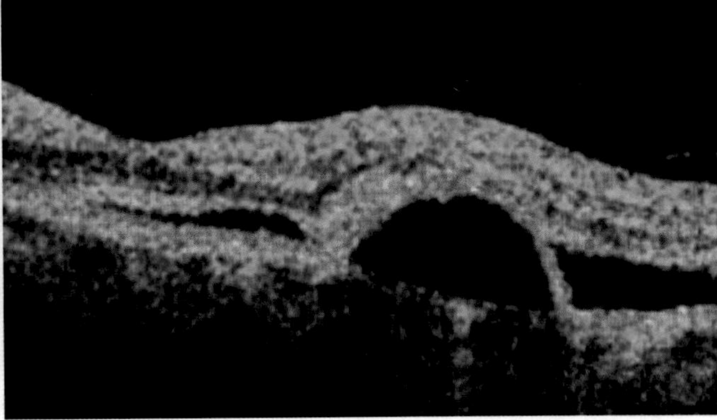

EyeRounds.org University of Iowa

What to Know: Typically seen in Hispanic and Japanese patients, VKH Syndrome is an autoimmune disease.

Symptoms: Before ocular signs develop, patients will experience a prodrome including a headache, stiff neck, vertigo, tinnitus, and deafness. Ocular symptoms will include blur with pain and photophobia secondary to anterior uveitis.

Signs: Patients will present with bilateral panuveitis (affecting anterior and posterior segments), which can be chronic and severe. Retinal findings include exudates and serous/exudative detachments. In late stages, patients may experience tinnitus, hearing loss, vitiligo, poliosis, and/or alopecia (whitening of the skin, whitening of the hair, loss of hair/baldness).

Treatment/Management: The inflammation should be treated with steroids: oral, topical, or Sub-Tenon's injections. The anterior uveitis should be treated with a topical steroid and cycloplegic.

BECHET'S DISEASE

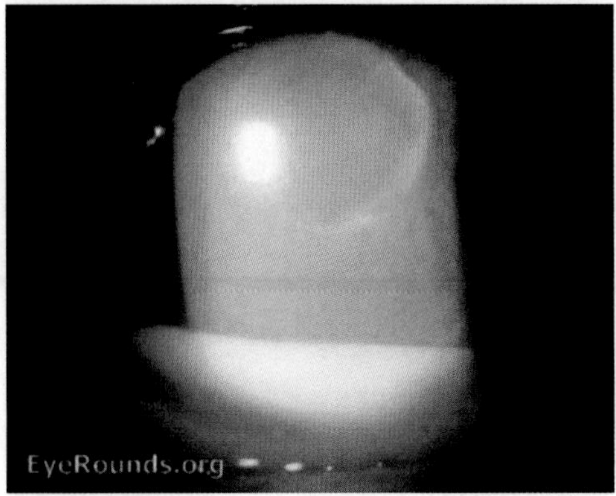

EyeRounds.org University of Iowa

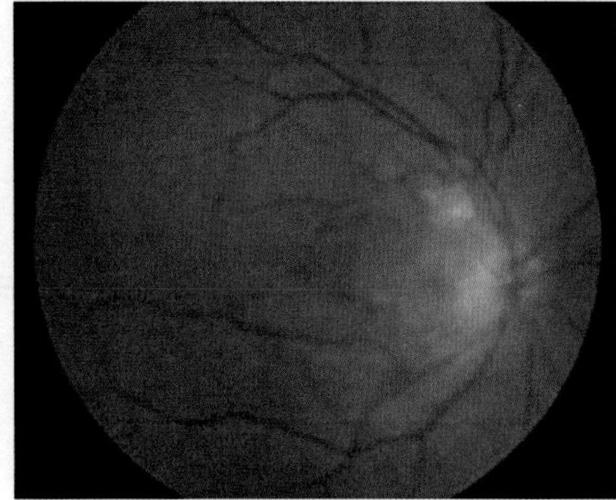

EyeRounds.org University of Iowa

What to Know: Bechet's Disease is found in Asians and Mediterraneans with either HLA-B5 or HLA-B12. Relapses of this disease are common.

Symptoms: Patients will complain of photophobia and pain from uveitis. Patients will also have blur and a red eye.

Signs: Bechet's Disease is a systemic disease defined by a triad:

1. Oral ulcers
2. Genital ulcers
3. Bilateral nongranulomatous uveitis

Hypopyon is a classic finding. Uveitis will be both anterior and posterior and will include severe vitritis. Retinal findings include vasculitis with associated hemorrhages. Patients will also have macular and disc edema with ischemic optic neuropathy in late stages.

Treatment/Management: Given the inflammatory nature of this disease, treatment includes topical, oral, and sub-Tenon's steroids. Treat the anterior uveitis with the typical topical steroid and cycloplegic.

MYOTONIC DYSTROPHY

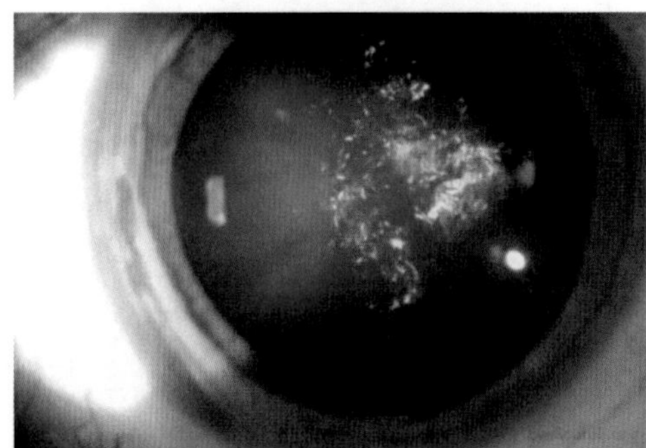

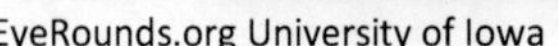

EyeRounds.org University of Iowa

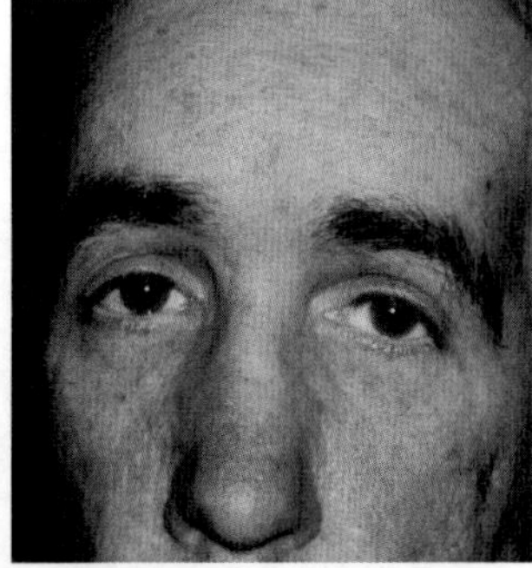

Cogan Collection, NEI/NIH

What to Know: Myotonic Dystrophy has an AD inheritance, it is the **most common muscular dystrophy**, and it occurs while the patient is in their 30s-60s. After voluntary movement, patients will have a delayed relaxation of their muscles.

Symptoms: Patients may complain of difficulty walking, talking, and relaxing their grasp.

Signs: Ocular signs include **Christmas Tree Cataracts** (refractile central cortical crystals, left image), reduced IOP, bilateral optic atrophy, and pigmentary retinopathy. They will also have weakness of the ocular muscles: Chronic

Progressive External Ophthalmoplegia (right image), bilateral ptosis, obiclularis oculi weakness, miotic pupils, and lid lag.

Systemic signs include musclar dystrophy which is worse in the morning, wasting of the temporalis muscle, cardiomyopathy, testicular atrophy due to hypogonadism, frontal baldness, pulmonary disease, and mental deteriation.

Treatment/Management: Patients should be advised to exercise and prevent contractures. Ocular surgeries may be indicated for EOM and/or cataract complications.

WILSON'S DISEASE

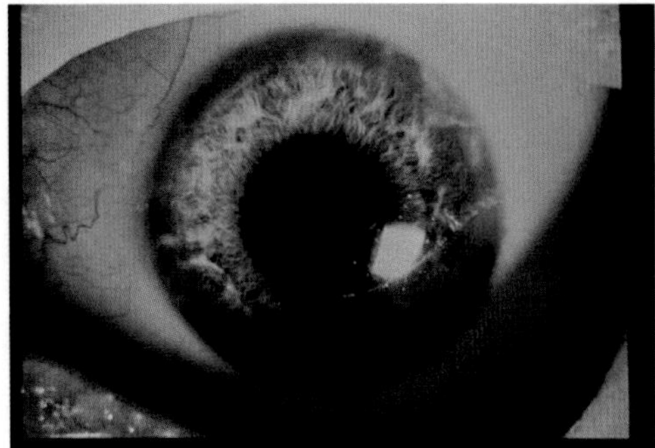

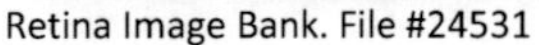

Retina Image Bank. File #24531

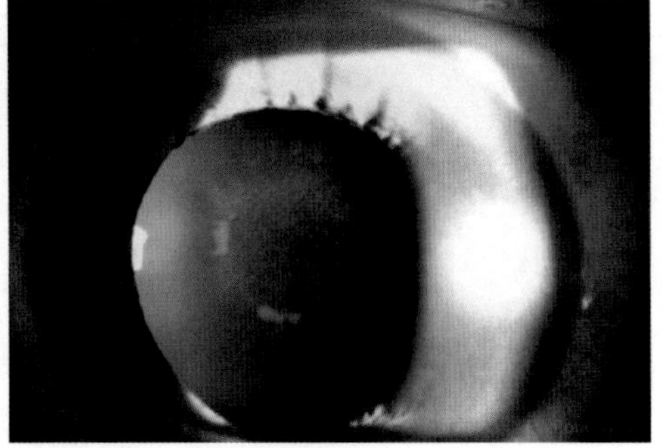

EyeRounds.org University of Iowa

What to Know: Wilson's Disease is characterized by an abnormal accumulation of copper in the body and afflicts patients between the ages of 5-40.

Symptoms: Patients will rarely have ocular complaints.

Signs which are unique to Wilson's Disease include a Kayser-Fleischer ring (circumferential corneal deposition of copper at the level of Descemet's Membrane, left image) and a Sunflower Cataract (right image). Systemic signs may include neurologic or psychiatric problems, cirrhosis (chronic liver disease), or renal/kidney disease.

Treatment/Management: Fortunately the ocular conditions usually require no treatment. Systemic management include lifelong trientine, zinc, and/or D-penicillamine supplementation. If present, cirrhosis may require a transplant. Renal disease may require diuretics, dialysis, or kidney transplant depending on severity.

ALBINISM

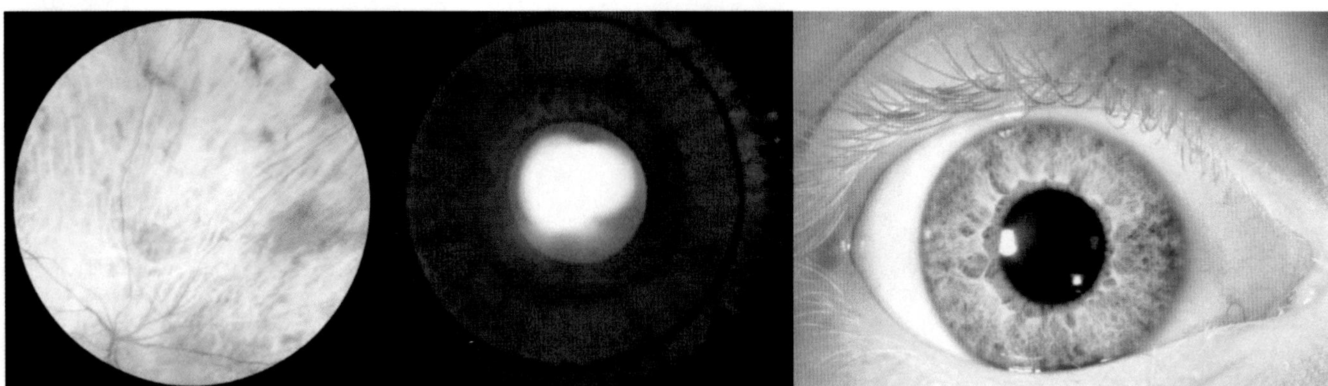

National Vision, Inc. EyeRounds.org University of Iowa EyeRounds.org University of Iowa

There are two types of albinism:

1. **Ocular Albinism:** As the name suggests, these are cases where only the eyes are involved. These

patients will appear normal exteriorly, but will have blue eyes (even patients of African descent). Ocular Albinism has an X-Linked Autosomal Recessive inheritance pattern. **These patients have a decreased number of melanosomes in their eyes, but each melanosome that is present has a normal level of melanin.**

2. **Oculocutaneous Albinism:** As this name suggests both the eyes and skin are involved in these individuals. It has an autosomal recessive (AR) inheritance pattern. **These patients have a decreased level of melanin in all of their melanosomes.**

Symptoms: Patients may complain of blur and photophobia.

Signs: Patients will present with high refractive errors with concurrent nystagmus, strabismus, and reduced stereopsis. Patients will have transillumination defects and a hypopigmented fundus. Patients will have a BCVA which ranges from 20/40 to 20/400.

Treatment/Management: There is no effective treatment. Management can include referring the patient to hematology to rule out lethal variants of Albinism, referral to a genetic counselor, and referral to a low vision specialist. Patients will benefit from using sunglasses and sunscreen.

MARFAN'S SYNDROME

Marfan's Syndrome is an AD disorder of connective tissues caused by a mutation on chromosome 15 (fibrillin gene). Patients with Marfan's Syndrome typically have a tall stature with long limbs. Patients with Marfan's Syndrome often have an increased intelligence. All complications are associated with deterioration of connective tissues. Ectopia Lentis is caused by weakened, **stretched** lens zonules (with an up and out dislocation of the lens). Keratoconus is caused by a thinned cornea. The globe becomes elongated causing myopia and **retinal detachments (which are the most severe ocular complication)**. Systemic connective tissue complications include cardiovascular pathology (mitral valve prolapse, aortic aneurysm). They should be urgently referred to a cardiologist due to possible cardiac complications.

PARINAUD OCULOGLANDULAR CONJUNCTIVITIS / CAT-SCRATCH DISEASE / TULAREMIA

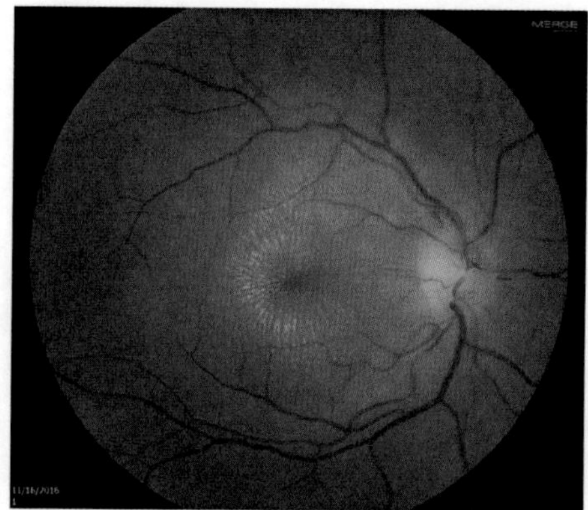

Retina Image Bank. File #26972

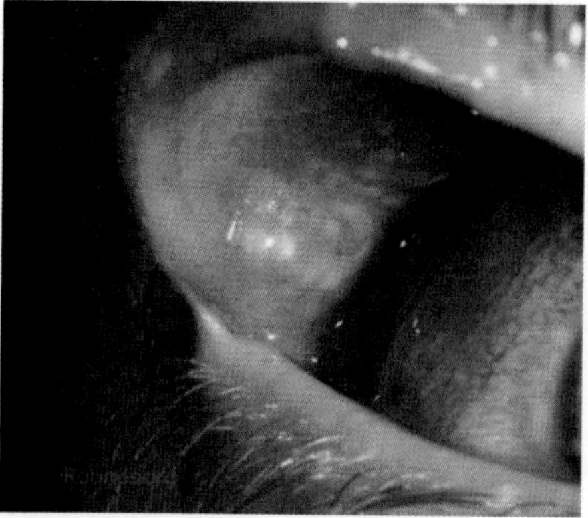

EyeRounds.org University of Iowa

What to Know: Parinaud Oculoglandular Conjunctivitis and Cat-Scratch Disease are virtually synonymous for each other. Cat-Scratch Disease occurs when a cat actually scratches or licks the patient's eyeball, causing a *Bartonella henselae* infection. Tularemia presents similarly to Cat-Scratch Disease with the difference being that it is associated with rabbit contact.

Symptoms: Patients may complain of painless unilateral vision loss. If the anterior segment is involved, they may complain of a red eye with foreign body sensation and mucopurulent discharge.

Signs: Ocular signs include Neuroretinitis (swollen optic nerve head with an associated APD, visual field defects, and macular star. See left image), and a peripapillary exudative retinal detachment with vitreous cells in later stages. Patients may also have granulomas on the palpebral conjunctiva (right image). Systemic findings may include a rash, blisters, loss of appetite, positive lymphadenopathy, and fever.

Treatment/Management: Patients can use warm compress to soothe painful lymph nodes. Cat-Scratch disease typically resolves spontaneously within 6 weeks, but patients may benefit from azithromycin. Patients with Tularemia may benefit from oral tobramycin or gentamicin.

ALCOHOLISM

Patients who drink alcohol obtain most of their calories from the alcohol, leading to a nutritional deficit. Ocular signs of Chronic Alcoholism include optic nerve pallor, and up and downbeat nystagmus due to nerve hydrocephalus (fluid on the brain) and demyelination. Systemic signs of Chronic Alcoholism include renal/kidney disease, vitamin B1 (thiamine) deficiency, and hepatitis. Abnormal blood tests associated with hepatitis include decreased B1 levels and increased alanine transaminase (ALT) levels. Chronic vitamin B1 deficiency can cause Wernicke's Encephalopathy which presents with a classic triad of ataxia (inability to control body movements), ophthalmoplegia (inability to control EOMs), and confusion. Wernicke's Encephalopathy is reversible with vitamin B1 supplementation. Korsakoff Syndrome may cause permanent cognitive changes (even with vitamin B1 supplementation) including with confabulation (memory blackouts), amnesia (loss of memory), apathy (indifference), poor communication, and loss of intuition.

ANAPHYLAXIS / ANAPHYLACTIC SHOCK

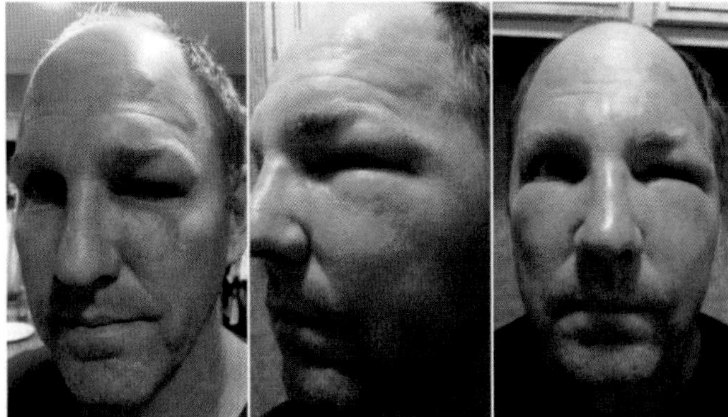

Flicker © Image #21939757361

What to Know: Anaphylaxis is a rare, acute, extreme Type I Hypersensitivity reaction which can be fatal. Classic causes include medications, foods (such as peanuts), and bee stings.

There are four types of hypersensitivity reactions:

- Type I: Anaphylactic (IgE, histamine)
- Type II: Cytotoxic (IgG, IgM)

- Type III: Immune-complex-mediated (Ag-Ab complex)
- Type IV: Delayed or cell-mediated (T-lymphocyte)

Symptoms: Patients may complain of difficulty breathing, runny nose, pain with swallowing, chest pain, GI upset, and dizziness.

Signs: Patients present with angioedema (swelling of the eyelids, conjunctiva/chemosis, lips, tongue), bronchospasms with stridor (closing of the respiratory pathways and associated wheezing), itchy urticaria (hives), and blood vessel dilation. As the patient becomes oxygen deprived, their skin may appear blue. This can progress from hypoxia (oxygen deprivation), to anoxia (complete oxygen deprivation), and finally death.

Treatment/Management: These patients require emergent care. They should be treated with an EpiPen (epinephrine) and sent to the hospital. CPR may be required.

EHLERS-DANLOS SYNDROME

Ehlers Danlos Syndrome is a rare autosomal dominant (AD) connective tissue disorder caused by a deficiency of hydroxylysine. It will cause connective tissues to become too flexible leading to joint dislocation, easy bruising, translucent skin, and dilation and rupture of blood vessels. Ocular complications may include angioid streaks, blue sclera, megalocornea, Ectopia Lentis, keratoconus. Serious cardiology findings include mitral valve prolapse, and aortic aneurysms.

OTHER SYSTEMIC CONDITIONS

Systemic diseases which affect adrenocortical levels include Addison's and Cushing's diseases:

- Addison's is defined by decreased adrenocortical levels.
- Cushing's is defined by increased adrenocortical levels.

The symptoms for Pheochromocytoma include pain, palpitations, pallor, and perspiration. These patients have hypertension, which leads to severe headaches.

It is important to know which drugs can and cannot be used with pregnant women:

- DO NOT use Fluoroquinolones, Aminoglycosides, Sulfonamides, or Tetracyclines with pregnant patients.
- Penicillin, Azithromycin, and Cephalosporin are okay for use with pregnant patients.

Drugs which reduce blood clotting include Aspirin, Clopidogrel, Dipyridamole, NSAIDs, and Warfarin.

Cardiovascular Disease is the leading cause of death in the United States.

The most common cancers in the US for men and women from most to least common:

- Men: prostate, lung, colon
- Women: breast, lung, colon

The most common cancers to cause death in the US for men and women from most to least common:

- Men: lung, prostate, colon
- Women: lung, breast, colon

CHAPTER 13
EMERGENCIES / TRAUMA

The NBEO website states that 11-22 questions will be asked on Emergencies / Trauma. Historically they have asked about 18.3 questions, meaning this chapter covers approximately 5% of the material tested on the exam, or roughly 4 cases. This material IS included on TMOD.

SYMPATHETIC OPHTHALMIA

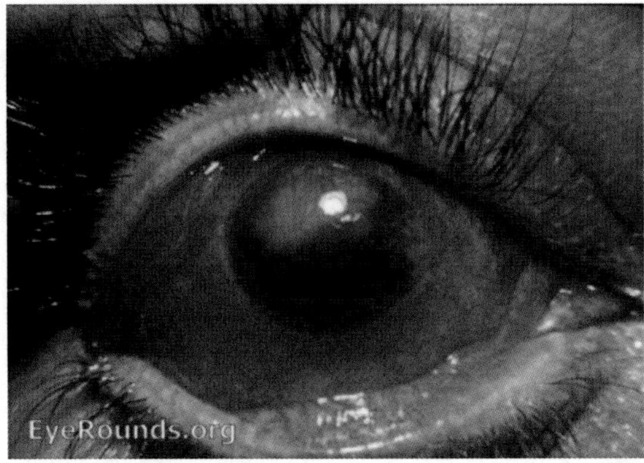

EyeRounds.org University of Iowa

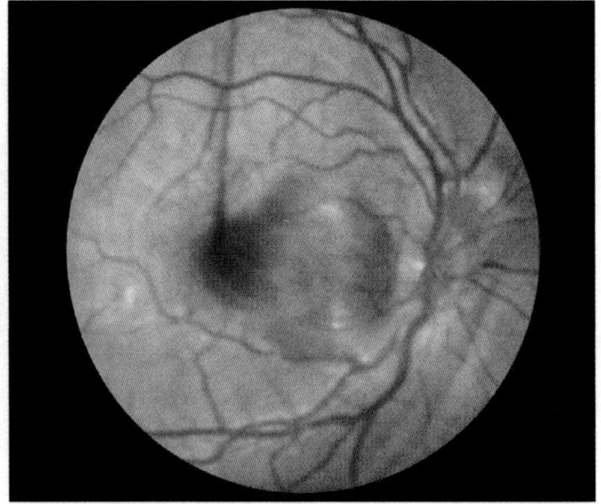

Retina Image Bank. File #1643

What to Know: In Sympathetic Ophthalmia the "exciting eye" has undergone a penetrating ocular injury or intraocular surgery. Typically within three months (or any time after the surgery) a ***bilateral*** reaction can develop, with the response less severe in the "sympathizing eye." This is an autoimmune disease.

Symptoms: Patients will complain of bilateral blur with pain and photophobia secondary to uveitis.

Signs: Patients will present with bilateral anterior granulomatous uveitis. As part of the autoimmune response, lymphocytes gather in the choroid, presenting as mid-peripheral multifocal infiltrates. Serous retinal detachments and vitritis will overlie the infiltrates.

Treatment/Management: Blind eyes with no hope of recovery should be enucleated prophylactically at the time of injury to prevent Sympathetic Ophthalmia from developing.

Prognosis is good (with final vision better than 20/60) if treatment is aggressive. The immune response should be suppressed with steroids: topical, oral, Sub-Tenon's injections, or slow release intravitreal implants. Steroids may be needed long term to prevent recurrence. The anterior uveitis should be treated with a topical steroid and cycloplegic.

ANTERIOR SEGMENT TRAUMA
Symptoms: Patients will complain of pain, epiphora, photophobia, and blurry vision if the visual axis is involved.
Evaluation for anterior segment trauma should always include investigation for a full-thickness wound with the use of Seidel's Sign.
Treatment for trauma to the front of the eye is aimed at preventing infection (due to a compromised cornea) and reducing pain. To prevent infection, a topical antibiotic should be prescribed. If a fungal infection is possible (when plant matter is the suspected offender), then prescribe a topical antifungal. A topical ointment can be considered in either case to aid with lubrication of the eye and provide an additional barrier between the eye and the air. Depending on the patient's needs, ointments are frequently used only at night because they blur vision. To treat the pain, topical NSAIDs can be prescribed. Patients may appreciate patching or a bandage contact lens for comfort, but DO NOT use these options if a fungal infection is possible. If loose, hanging epithelium is present, it should be debrided (removed).

IRIDODIALYSIS / CYCLODIALYSIS

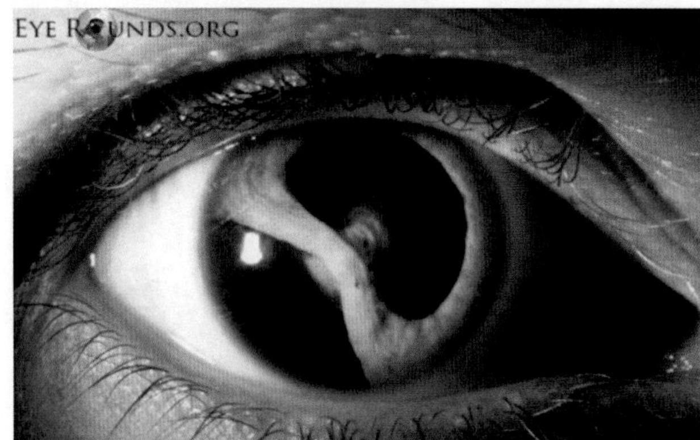

EyeRounds.org University of Iowa

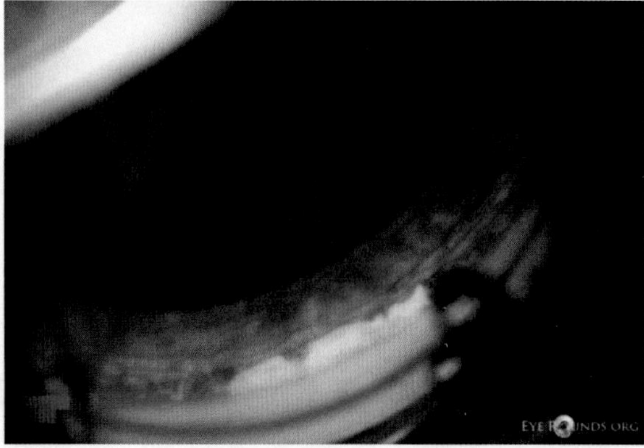
EyeRounds.org University of Iowa

What to Know: Iridodialysis and Cyclodialysis are both caused by penetrating globe injuries or blunt trauma.

Symptoms: Patients may have no complaints (asymptomatic) or complain of monocular diplopia if a large disinsertion is present.

Signs: Remember the order of the angle structures (from posterior to anterior): iris, ciliary body, scleral spur, trabecular meshwork, Schlemm's Canal, Schwalbe's line (mnemonic: I Can't See This Stupid Line). Notice that the name of the disinsertion is patterned after the name of the most anterior structure which is still attached.

- Iridodialysis (left image) is defined as a separation of the iris from the ciliary body.
- Cyclodialysis (right image) is defined as a separation of the ciliary body from the scleral spur.

Patients may also develop glaucoma or hypotony (low IOP) due to damage to the angle affecting inflow/outflow of aqueous humor.

Treatment/Management: Observe if there are no symptoms or complications. Patients may benefit from using sunglasses. If the patient complains of monocular diplopia, then consider an opaque contact lens with an artificial pupil or surgical correction. If present, treat the hypotony or glaucoma as such.

FOREIGN BODY

Kimberly Castillo, OD

What to Know: A Foreign Body is defined as a particle which gets trapped within the cornea or conjunctiva. The particle may be dirt, metal, glass, or plant matter among other things. Patients will sometimes have a history of ocular trauma.

Symptoms: Patients will complain of pain on blink in addition to the other symptoms listed under "Symptoms" in the purple box at the beginning of this section.

Signs: Patients will present with a foreign body which may be embedded in the cornea or conjunctiva. The foreign body may be loose and move with blink, causing tracking on the cornea which will stain with fluorescein. The patient may secrete mucous in response to the ocular irritation.

Treatment/Management: See "Treatment" in the purple box at the beginning of this section. Before attempting to remove the foreign body, determine if it has caused a full thickness penetration by looking for Seidel's Sign. Also be sure to flip the superior lid and check the palpebral conjunctiva for an embedded foreign body. It may be possible to flush out the foreign body using eye wash. Otherwise, remove the foreign body with a spud or cotton-tipped applicator. If the foreign body leaves behind a rust ring, it may be removed with an algerbrush. If the rust ring is located deep in the cornea, it may be necessary to wait a couple of days for it to rise to the surface before attempting to remove it. Follow the patient daily if the rust ring is still present, and every 3-5 days otherwise.

CONJUNCTIVAL/CORNEAL LACERATION

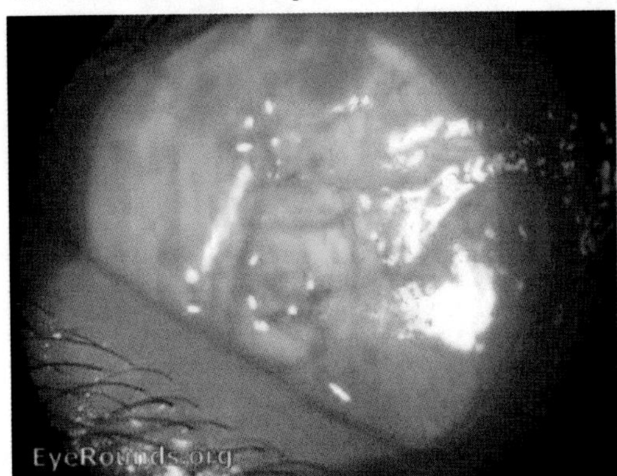

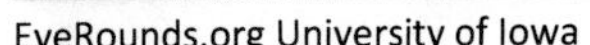

EyeRounds.org University of Iowa

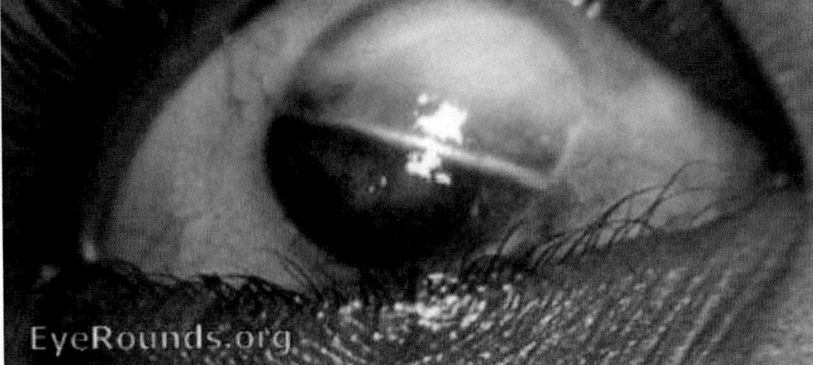

EyeRounds.org University of Iowa

What to Know: A Laceration is a cut across the anterior globe. Patients will sometimes have a history of ocular trauma.

Symptoms: Patients will complain of pain, epiphora, photophobia, and foreign body sensation depending on the location of the laceration.

Signs: The Laceration will stain with fluorescein. Evidence of rolled up or loose skin may be present. The laceration may be deep enough to show exposed white sclera.

Treatment/Management: See "Treatment" in the purple box at the beginning of this section. Rarely Lacerations will require surgical repair.

CHEMICAL BURN*

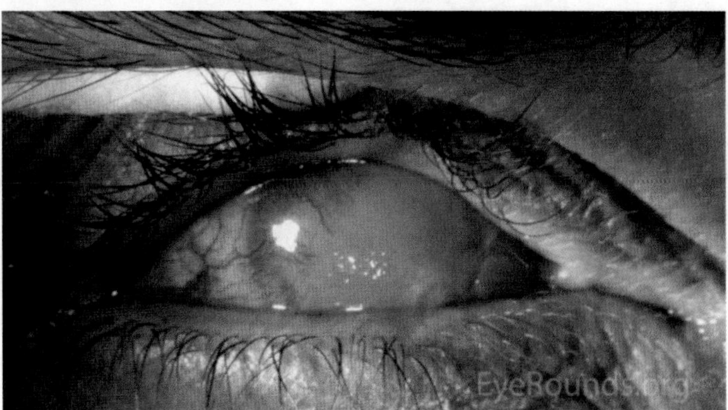

EyeRounds.org University of Iowa

What to Know: Chemical Burns occur when patients get either an acid or a base into their eyes. **Burns from bases are more severe than burns from acids** because bases penetrate and damage the lipid layers. If you are trying to differentiate an acid vs. base, bear in mind that bases taste bitter and acids have a zesty flavor. You need to know which common household items are acids or bases:

Common Household Acids	Common Household Bases
• Vinegar • Citric Acid • Battery Acid • Pool cleaner	• Soaps • Ammonia • Windex • Bleach • Drain cleaner

Symptoms: Patients will complain of pain, photophobia, foreign body sensation, and blurry vision.

Signs: A white cornea has a very poor prognosis because it indicates the blood vessels have been damaged, thereby reducing oxygen flow to the cornea which is imperative for proper healing. Injection is a good sign, for this means the blood vessels are still intact and can still aid in the healing process. IOP may increase.

Treatment/Management: Chemical Burns are ocular emergencies. Patients require immediate copious irrigation with saline solution. Monitor the pH until it reaches neutral. Evert the lids and sweep the fornices with a cotton tip applicator for any trapped offending agents. Once a neutral pH has been achieved use preservative free artificial tears Q1H. Since the epithelium has been compromised, use topical antibiotics QID. Consider oral antibiotics in severe cases. A topical cycloplegic or pressure patch can be used for pain. If present, treat the increased IOP. Severe cases may require topical steroids to reduce inflammation. Patients may require debridement (removal) of loose epithelial tissue, or surgery to remove more severe complications such as symblepharon.

CORNEAL ABRASION

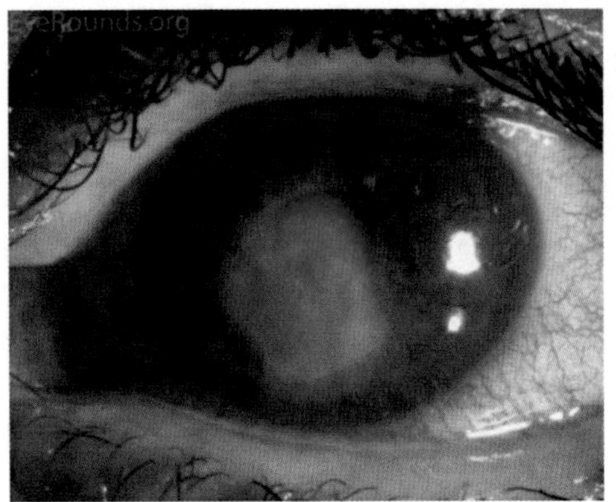

EyeRounds.org University of Iowa

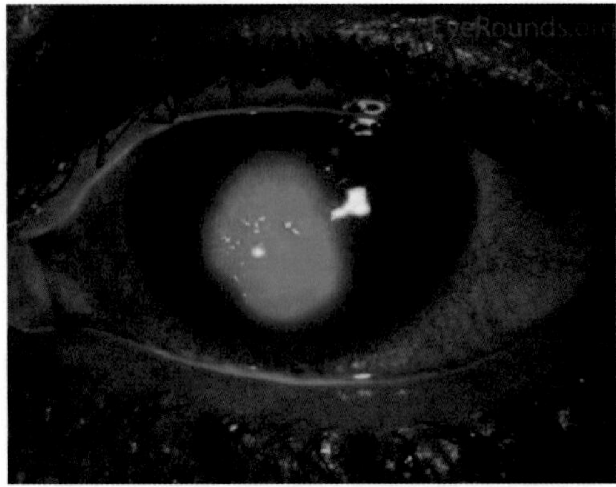
EyeRounds.org University of Iowa

<u>What to Know:</u> Corneal abrasions are caused by trauma.

<u>Symptoms:</u> Patients will complain of pain, photophobia, epiphora, and foreign body sensation. They will have a history of recent trauma.

<u>Signs:</u> Patients will have an epithelial defect which will stain with fluorescein.

<u>Treatment/Management:</u> Since the epithelium has a defect, the patient will be at an increased risk for infection. Therefore, prescribe a topical antibiotic QID. Consider a topical NSAID and/or a cycloplegic for pain. A bandage contact lens or a patch can also be considered for large abrasions. However, **a patch is contraindicated** in contact lens wearers and cases where a fungal infection is possible (when the trauma was caused by finger nails or plant matter).

RECURRENT CORNEAL EROSION

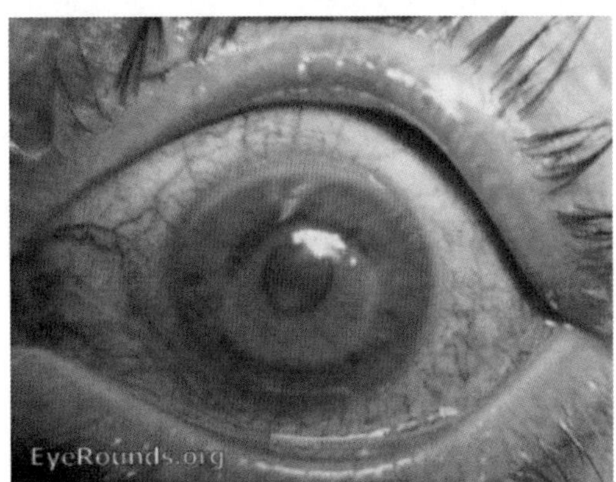

EyeRounds.org University of Iowa

<u>What to Know:</u> Recurrent Corneal Erosions are typically caused by corneal dystrophies (like EBMD) or occur within three months after a Corneal Abrasion. The cornea swells a little bit over night and the epithelium sticks to the palpebral conjunctiva. When the patient wakes up and opens their eyes, the palpebral conjunctiva rips off the epithelium.

<u>Symptoms:</u> Patients will complain of recurrent pain, foreign body sensation, and photophobia **in the morning**.

<u>Signs:</u> Patients will have a corneal epithelial defect, most likely inferior, which will stain with fluorescein. Evidence of EBMD may be present.

<u>Treatment/Management:</u> Since the epithelium has a defect, the patient will be at an increased risk for infection. Therefore, prescribe a topical antibiotic QID. Consider an artificial tear, or a topical NSAID and/or a cycloplegic for pain. A bandage contact lens or a patch can also be considered for large abrasions. However, **a patch is contraindicated** in contact lens wearers. A topical hypertonic ointment (Muro 128) can be used QHS for three months to help repair the corneal hemidesmosomes. The hypertonic solution will dehydrate the cornea and prevent it from swelling at night. It takes three months for the cornea to replace its hemidesmosomes. An amniotic membrane can also be considered.

HYPHEMA

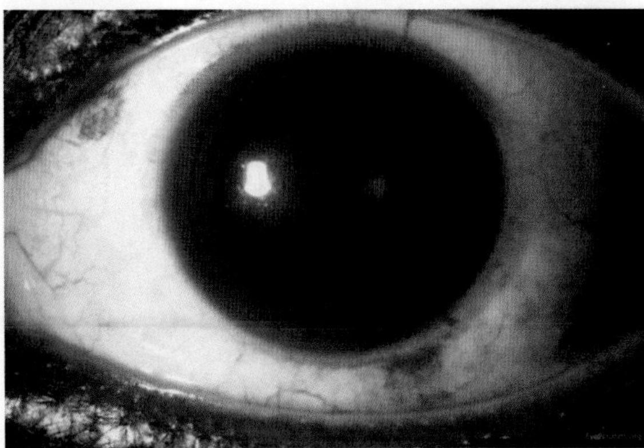
EyeRounds.org University of Iowa

What to Know: A Hyphema is defined as blood in the anterior chamber. A Microhyphema is when the blood has not settled, and so is only visible as red cells floating in the anterior chamber. A total 100% Hyphema is coined an 8-ball Hyphema.

Trauma is the most common cause of Hyphema (80%), which is why it is included in this chapter. However, **a Hyphema may occur spontaneously secondary to HSV, iris tumors, iris lesions, or iris neovascularization.**

Symptoms: Patients may complain of pain, photophobia, reduced vision, and "red eye."

Signs: The examiner will see blood in the anterior chamber which may be visible as red cells on conical beam. Patients may have an increased IOP if the blood is blocking too much of the trabecular meshwork. If the cause is due to trauma, then the patient may have other signs of trauma including subconjunctival hemorrhage, angle recession and iris sphincter tears, iridodonesis (vibration or agitated motion of the iris with eye movement), iridodialysis (a separation of the iris from the ciliary body), or cyclodialysis (a separation of the ciliary body from the scleral spur). Rubeosis may be visible if the hyphema is secondary to neovascularization.

Treatment/Management: The first goal when treating a Hyphema is to stop the bleeding. Other goals include reducing inflammation, preventing the formation of posterior synechiae, and reducing IOP. Patients should be confined to bedrest with bathroom privileges or minimal movement to reduce risk of minor trauma. They should keep their head elevated to allow the blood to pool inferiorly and wear a shield (not a patch) to keep the eye protected. Consider hospitalizing children to ensure compliance.

Attempts to stop bleeding include discontinuing the use of anti-coagulants such as aspirin and use of topical Atropine or Scopolamine. It is important to immobilize the iris because it can cause a re-bleed when it moves; this also helps alleviate pain, and prevent the formation of posterior synechiae. The associated inflammation can be treated with topical steroids, and increased IOP can be treated with topical drops. If the patient shows no improvement, then consider surgical evacuation.

Patients should be followed daily for the first week, and upon improvement the frequency can be reduced. If the hyphema occurs secondary to trauma, the patient should return four weeks after the traumatic event for gonioscopy and a dilated exam. DO NOT perform gonioscopy during the initial exam, but DO perform Goldman tonometry.

HYPOTONY → PHTHISIS BULBI

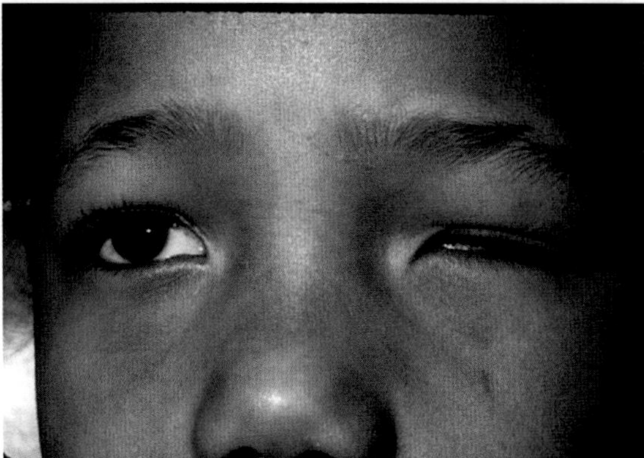

Retina Image Bank. File #10818

What to Know: Hypotony is defined as an IOP below 6 mmHg and is caused by excessive outflow or reduced production of aqueous humor. Causes of excessive outflow include surgery and trauma, while causes of reduced production include medications and uveitis that has shut down the ciliary body.

Symptoms: Patients may be asymptomatic. They may complain of mild to severe pain, reduced vision, and epiphora.

Signs: Patients may present with an IOP which is below 6 mmHg. Patients may have a shallow anterior chamber and a hyperopic shift due to shortening of the axial length (remember pressure provides structure for the eye); corneal edema and folds; aqueous cells and flare; retina, macula, and disc edema; tortuosity of the retinal vasculature; and a positive Seidel sign if trauma/surgery is causative.

Phthisis Bulbi is end-stage. The eye will be 2/3 its normal size and have no vision due to intraocular disorganization and calcification of the retina, cornea, and lens. The patient may also present with hemorrhaging and inflammation.

Treatment/Management: Treatment is aimed at managing the underlying etiology. If an open wound is present, then it needs to be treated with a topical antibiotic and closed with a bandage contact lens, pressure patch, cyanoacrylate glue, or sutures. If the etiology is pharmacological, then the medication should be discontinued. Uveitis should be treated with a topical steroid and cycloplegic. If present, edema should be treated with topical sodium chloride (Muro 128).

If the case has progressed to Phthisis Bulbi, treatment is aimed at preventing pain and improving cosmesis. Painful eyes can be treated with topical steroids, cycloplegics, and enucleation (remove eyeball but leave the EOMs and other orbital content intact). Cosmesis can be managed with a cosmetic shell or enucleation with a prosthetic eye.

RUPTURED GLOBE / PENETRATING INJURY / INTRAOCULAR FOREIGN BODY*

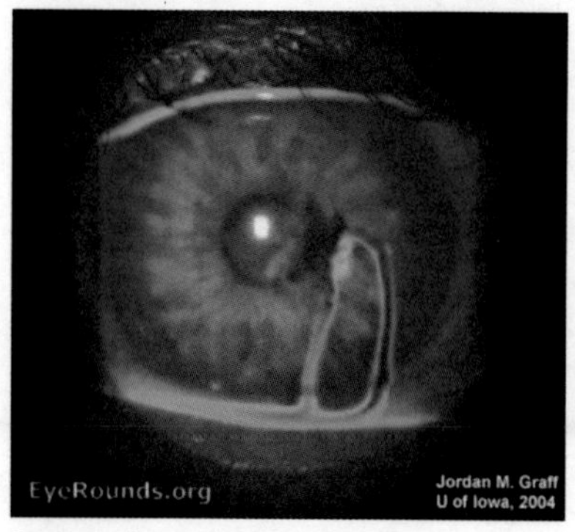
EyeRounds.org University of Iowa

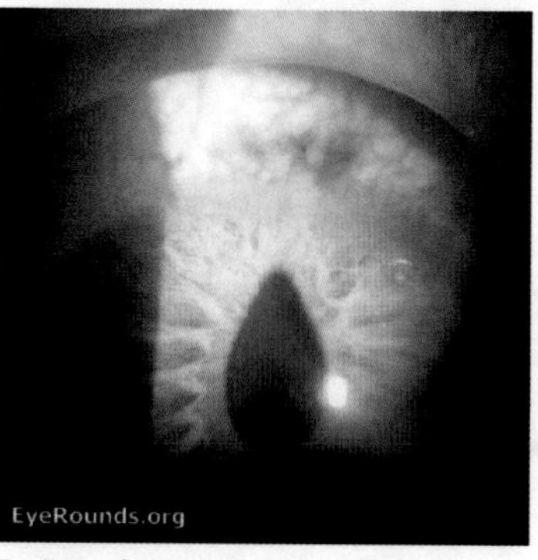
EyeRounds.org University of Iowa

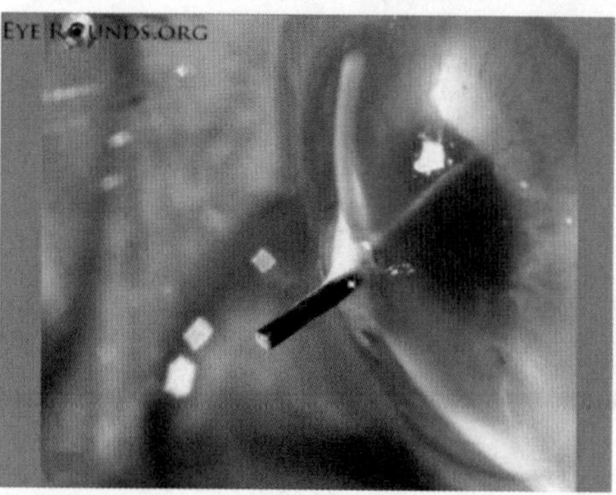
EyeRounds.org University of Iowa

What to Know: A full-thickness penetrating injury to the eyeball will cause an open globe.

Signs: The most important sign will be a positive Seidel's sign (left image). Patients may also have a reduced IOP, transillumination defects, and a peaked pupil (the pupil is displaced towards the location of the injury due to pressure differences, middle image). If the penetrating injury involves the cornea, then the most likely finding will be a shallow anterior chamber as the aqueous humor will escape through the wound. Other signs of ocular trauma may be present as well.

Treatment/Management: This is an ophthalmic emergency. Once an open globe is suspected, further examination should be paused. The patient should be referred for immediate treatment and possible surgery by an ophthalmologist. Shield the eye to prevent anything new from getting inside until the patient gets to the ophthalmologist. DO NOT PATCH for this may lower IOP even further. Imaging may be performed to identify if a foreign body is inside the globe. If there is reason to think the foreign body is metal perform a CT scan because an MRI will cause a metal foreign body to move around within the eye and wreak havoc. IV antibiotics and steroids should be initiated within 6 hours of injury. A tetanus shot may also be indicated.

POSTERIOR SEGMENT TRAUMA

CHOROIDAL RUPTURE

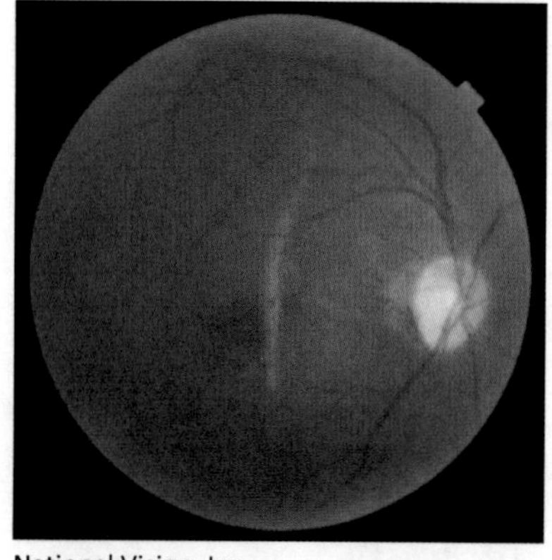
National Vision, Inc.

What to Know: Choroidal ruptures are tears through the choroid, Bruch's membrane, and RPE which occur after blunt trauma.

Symptoms: Patients may be asymptomatic unless the macula is involved.

Signs: Patients may present with a white streak which is concentric to the optic disc. With time it may scar over and become pigmented. Neovascularization may also grow with time.

Treatment/Management: The only treatment option is to address the neovascularization if/when it grows with laser or anti-VEGF injections.

COMMOTIO RETINAE

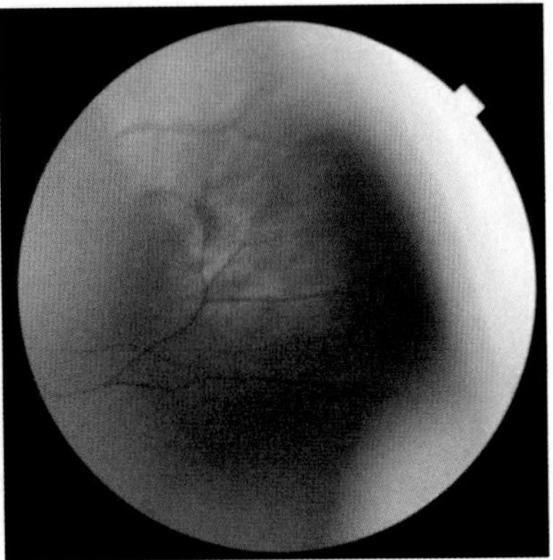

National Vision, Inc.

What to Know: The easiest way to think of Commotio Retinae is that it is a bruise of the retinal photoreceptors after blunt trauma. When the macula is involved, this is termed "Berlin's Edema."

Symptoms: Patients may be asymptomatic unless the macula is involved.

Signs: Patients may present with greyish white, flat areas of the retina, and possible loss of vision/visual field defects. The severity of the whitening does not correlate with the severity of vision loss.

Treatment/Management Like a bruise, Commotio Retinae will usually self-resolve. It may lead to permanent vision loss of the macula is involved.

CHORIORETINITIS SCLOPETARIA

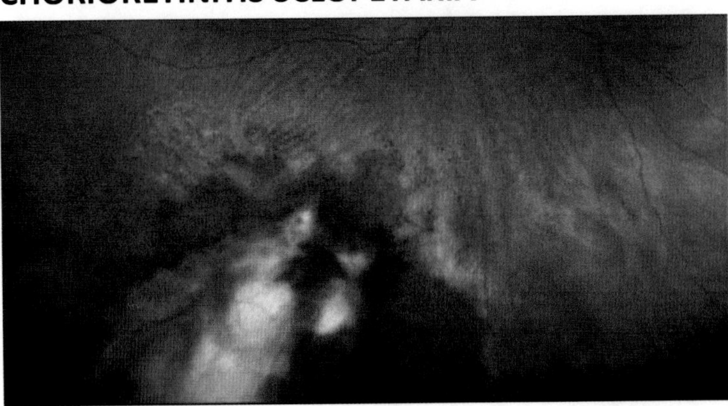

Retina Image Bank. File #27627

What to Know: Chorioretinitis Sclopetaria occurs when a high-velocity projectile passes through the orbit without contacting the globe. Resulting shock waves cause trauma to the retina and choroid.

Symptoms: Patients may be asymptomatic unless the macula is involved.

Signs: Patients may present with retinal and choroidal rupture leaving bare sclera visible. With time this will scar over with fibrous tissue and retinal detachments may occur.

Treatment/Management: Treatment is only indicated to surgically fix any subsequent retinal detachments.

PURTSCHER'S RETINOPATHY

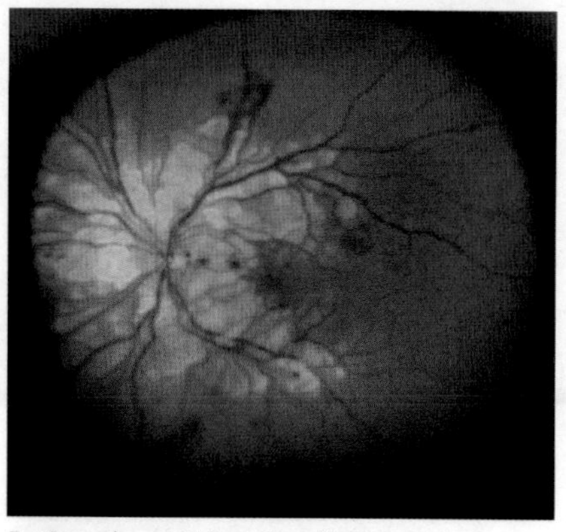

What to Know: If you see a case where the patient has a recent history of receiving CPR, immediately think of Purtscher's Retinopathy. It is caused by compression injury to the chest.

Symptoms: Patients may complain of sudden vision loss after a compressive chest injury.

Signs: Patients may present with multiple cotton wool spots and large areas of retinal whitening, hemorrhages, visual field loss, and possibly ONH edema with an APD.

Treatment/Management: There is no recommended treatment. Vision may recover in 50% of patients.

TRAUMATIC OPTIC NEUROPATHY

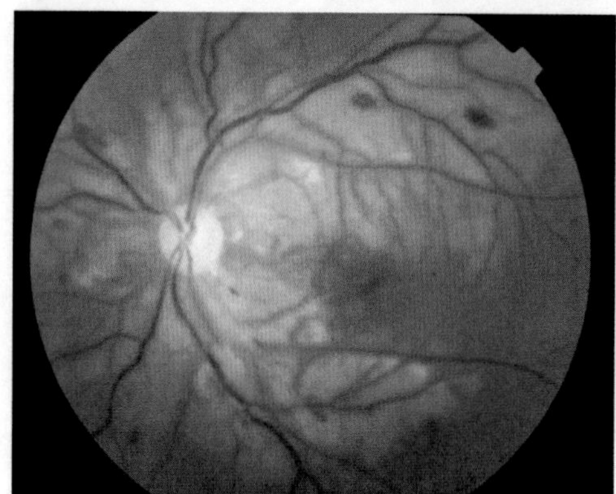

Retina Image Bank. File #2161

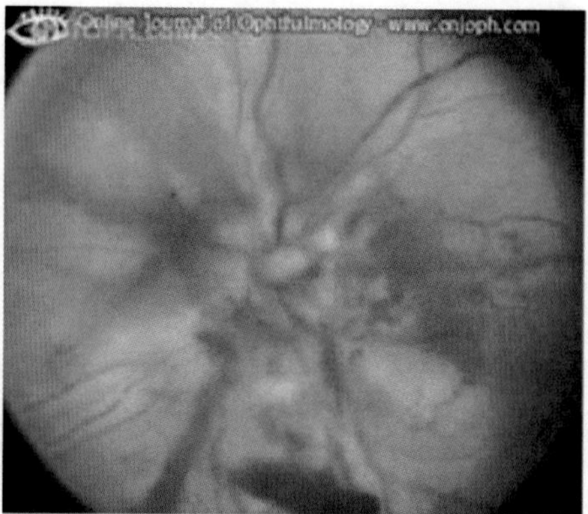

Atlas of Ophthalmology 3274

What to Know: Direct or indirect trauma to the head or eyes can damage the anatomy of the optic nerve.

Symptoms: Patients will complain of sudden vision loss which may be as severe as light perception.

Signs: Immediately after the trauma the optic nerve may appear normal, but will present with an APD. After several days or weeks, the nerve will become pale (left image). In cases of deceleration injuries, the optic nerve may become disconnected from its attachment to the globe (aka Optic Nerve Avulsion, right image).

Treatment/Management: First patients should be evaluated for life threatening injuries with a MRI or CT scan. Visual fields should also be assessed in these patients. Vision will spontaneously improve in mild to moderate cases. However, in severe and very severe cases, the prognosis is poor. Intravenous (IV) followed by oral steroids can be considered in cases with poor prognosis, and orbital compression can be considered to relieve pressure on the nerve.

SHAKEN BABY SYNDROME

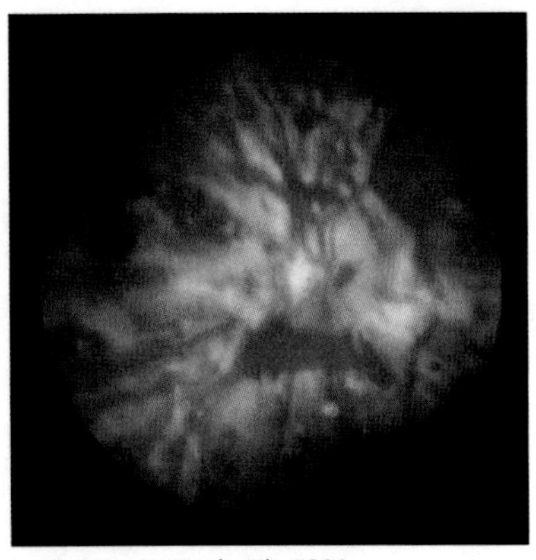
Retina Image Bank. File #801

What to Know: Shaken Baby Syndrome occurs when a parent shakes a baby causing acceleration/deceleration injuries (most likely after the parent becomes frustrated because the baby won't stop crying). It usually occurs in children less than one year old, and may lead to severe mental disability. The mortality rate is up to 25-30%.

Signs: Babies will present with a typical triad:

1. Subdural hematoma
2. Cerebral edema (brain swelling)
3. Multilayered retinal hemorrhages

Other ocular signs may include an inability to track with their eyes, periocular bruising, and subconjunctival hemorrhage. Other behavioral signs may include change in affect, mood, and appetite. Other systemic findings may include a new history of seizures and multiple bone/skull fractures.

Treatment/Management: Physicians are mandated reporters and so are legally required to report cases of child abuse. Refer to a pediatric physician for treatment of systemic complications and provide supportive treatment to any ocular complications.

ORBIT TRAUMA

RETROBULBAR HEMORRHAGE / ORBITAL COMPARTMENT SYNDROME*

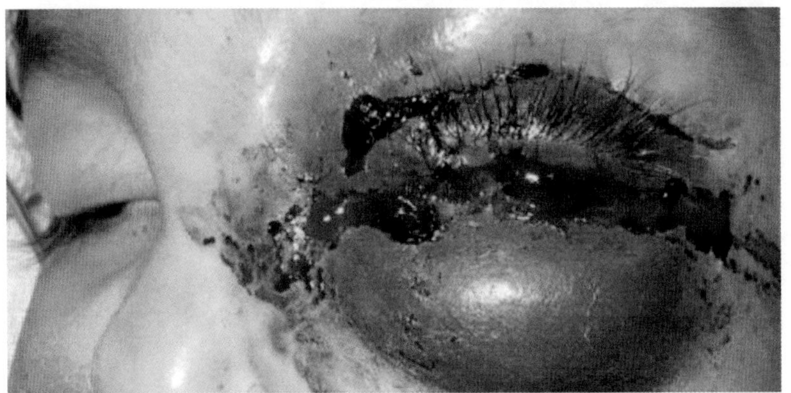
EyeRounds.org University of Iowa

What to Know: A Retrobulbar Hemorrhage occurs within three hours after surgery or trauma to the orbit. As the name suggests, a hemorrhage pools behind the orbit.

Symptoms: Patients will complain of blur, pain, and possible color vision changes.

Signs are all associated with crowding of the orbit due to the hemorrhage consuming too much real estate. Patients will present with proptosis, limited ocular movement, "rock hard" eyelids which are hard to open, severe subconjunctival hemorrhage, compressed optic nerve, and increased IOP. There will also be vascular congestion and disc edema.

Treatment/Management: This is an ocular emergency!! A surgeon needs to perform an emergent canthotomy and cantholysis (incision and disinsertion) of the lateral canthal tendon. If IOP is increased, it should also be treated with topical medications. A CT scan should also be performed to rule out further orbital complications.

CAVERNOUS SINUS SYNDROMES

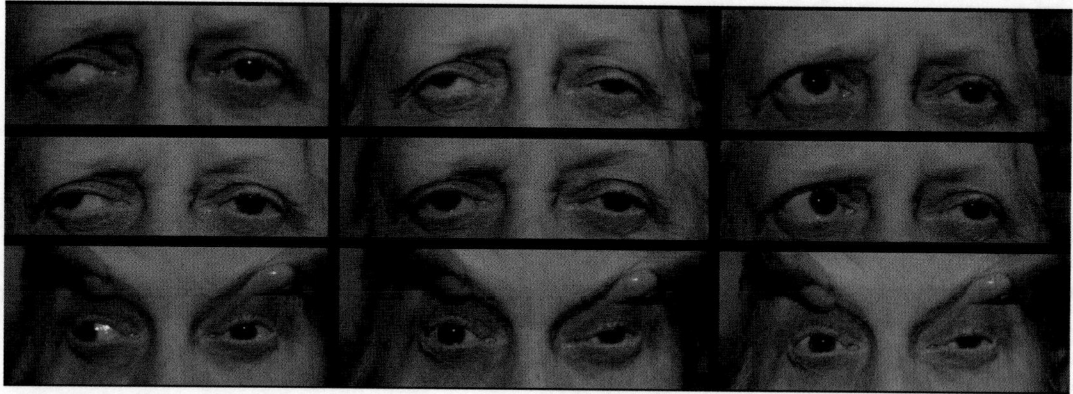

EyeRounds.org University of Iowa

Signs: Bear in mind which nerves pass through the Cavernous Sinus: CN 3, 4, 6, VI, V2. Given these are virtually all of the nerves which innervate the eye, a patient with an condition affecting the Cavernous Sinus will have limited to no ocular motility, ptosis, loss of accommodation, and limited light reaction (blown pupil). The CN5 involvement (V1, V2) will cause facial numbness/loss of sensitivity in the areas of these branches. IOP may also be elevated, and proptosis may also be present.

Symptoms: Patients will complain of pain, diplopia, numb face, and a droopy eyelid.

What to Know: There are multiple etiologies which can disrupt the Cavernous Sinus including tumors and aneurysms. Two of these etiologies are discussed below:

- Carotid-Cavernous Fistula typically occurs in 20-40 year old males who have been in a recent car accident. Head trauma will damage the Cavernous Sinus. Given that the ocular veins drain out of the Cavernous Sinus, the damage will block their pathway, and so blood backs up into the ocular structures. As a result the globe and surrounding structures will become engorged with blood, the IOP will increase, the patient will be able to hear an ocular bruit, and you will be able to visualize a pulsatile proptosis.
- Mucormycosis/Zygomycosis is a fungal infection of the Cavernous Sinus typically seen in diabetic patients who have ketoacidosis or a reduced immune system. Presentation will be acute with an associated bloody nose. Mucormycosis/Zygomycosis is an emergency because it can be fatal.

Treatment/Management:

- Carotid-Cavernous Fistulas will frequently resolve spontaneously with the aid of ipsilateral carotid massage. IV antibiotics may also be required.
- Mucormycosis/Zygomycosis is an emergency which requires immediate hospitalization with IV antifungal treatment.

ORBITAL BLOW-OUT FRACTURE

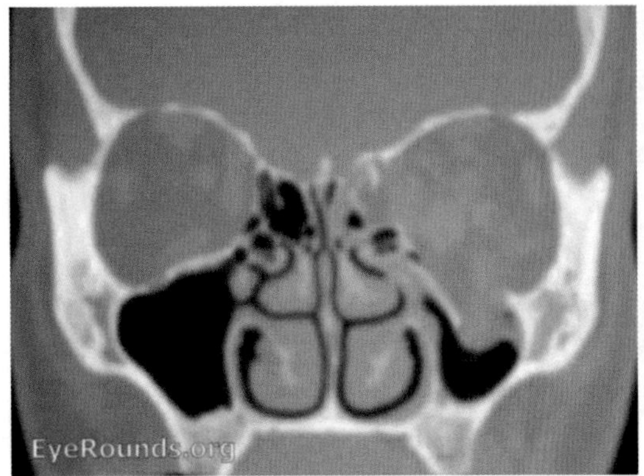

EyeRounds.org University of Iowa

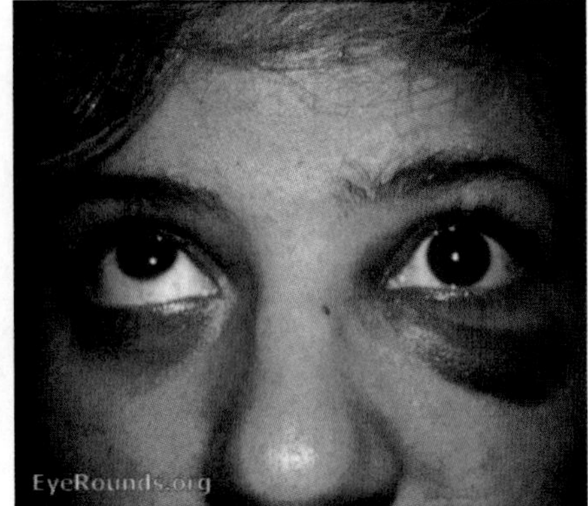

EyeRounds.org University of Iowa

What to Know: Orbital Blow-Out Fractures are caused by blunt trauma, and the most common location of the fracture is the posterior medial floor of the maxillary bone because this is the weakest point of the orbit.

Symptoms: Patients will complain of pain with eye movement, diplopia, local tenderness, crepitus (sound of bone traction on bone), and reduced sensation/numbness/hypesthesia of the inferior eyelid of the afflicted eye due to CN5 V2 involvement.

Signs: Patients will have restricted upgaze in the afflicted eye due to a trapped/tethered inferior rectus. The globe may sink into the maxillary sinus, presenting as an enophthalmos.

Treatment/Management: Patients should be advised to avoid blowing their nose! A CT scan should be performed to confirm and locate the location of the fracture. Orbital surgery should be performed to repair the orbital floor within one day to one week depending on severity and extent of muscle entrapment. Prescribe prophylactic oral antibiotics and nasal decongestants. Swelling should be managed with regular cold compress of the lids and possible prescription of oral steroids depending on severity. Patients should be followed in 24 hours.

CHAPTER 14
EPISCLERA / SCLERA / ANTERIOR / UVEA

The NBEO website states that 11-22 questions will be asked on Episclera / Sclera / Anterior / Uvea. Historically they have asked about 16.3 questions, meaning this chapter covers approximately 5% of the material tested on the exam, or roughly 4 cases. This material IS included on TMOD.

~~~EPISCLERA~~~

EPISCLERITIS

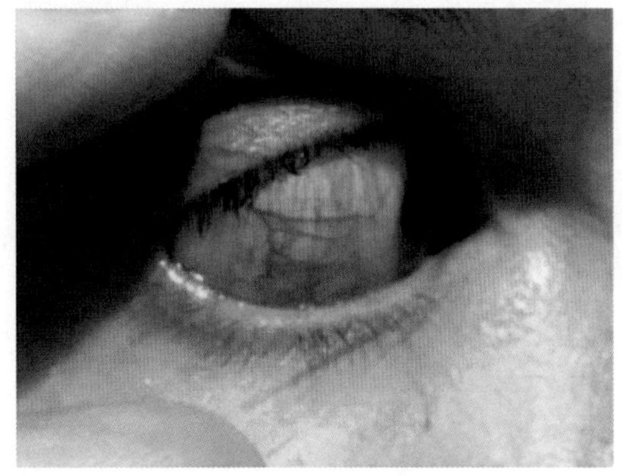

Kimberly Castillo, OD

What to Know: Episcleritis is **most frequently idiopathic**, but may be caused by **collagen vascular diseases** (rheumatoid arthritis, rosacea, atopy), gout, thyroid disease, herpes zoster, tuberculosis, or syphilis. It may be recurrent and/or bilateral especially if an underlying etiology is involved.

Symptoms: Patients may be asymptomatic or have complaints of mild tenderness.

Signs: Episcleritis has an acute onset of sectoral or diffuse hyperemia (redness) which will blanch with topical phenylephrine. This makes sense because phenylephrine is a vasoconstrictor and Episcleritis is located more superficially than Scleritis. It is usually unilateral but may be bilateral in more severe cases.

Treatment/Management: Patients should be reassured because mild cases will resolve spontaneously. Episcleritis can also be treated with a topical vasoconstrictor (naphazoline) and artificial tears. Severe cases should be treated with a topical steroid or oral NSAID. If an underlying etiology is suspected, refer for a systemic workup.

~~~SCLERA~~~

SCLERITIS

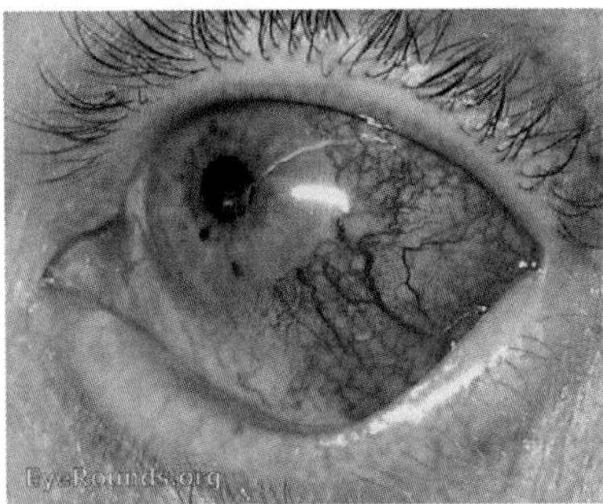
EyeRounds.org University of Iowa

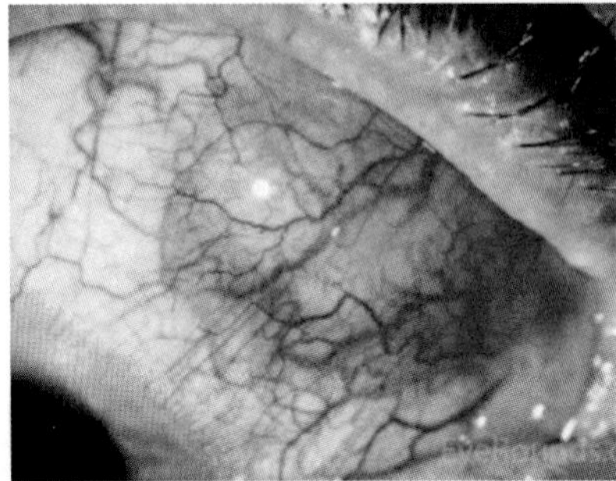
EyeRounds.org University of Iowa

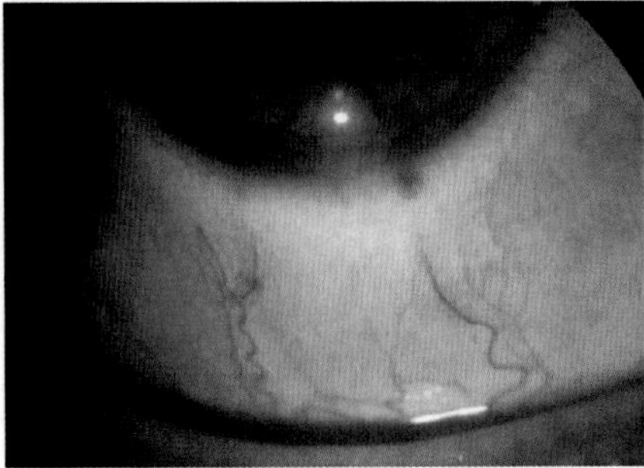
EyeRounds.org University of Iowa

What to Know: Scleritis is **most frequently idiopathic**, but may be caused by **collagen vascular diseases** (rheumatoid arthritis, ankylosing spondylitis, polyarteritis nodosa, lupus, relapsing polychondritis, Wegener's granulomatosis), gout, leprosy, herpes zoster, tuberculosis, or syphilis. Scleritis can be divided into four types.

- Non-Necrotizing (not flesh eating). More common than Necrotizing.
  - Diffuse: **Most common** type of scleritis (60% of cases). See left picture.
  - Nodular: Represents 25% of cases. See center picture.
- Necrotizing (flesh eating). Less common than Non-Necrotizing (fortunately!!).
  - Without inflammation (aka Scleromalacia Perforans): Represents 10% of Scleritis. **ASYMPTOMATIC(!!)** and associated with Rheumatoid Arthritis.
  - With inflammation: Least common (5% of cases), but **most severe**.

Symptoms: Scleromalacia Perforans is asymptomatic! All of the other types of Scleritis will present with photophobia and a severe deep, boring pain, tearing, and/or blurry vision.

Signs: Significant hyperemia (redness) with a thinned sclera causing a blue hue (see right picture). May have a nodule, chemosis, edema, and associated uveitis. The globe may be tender with palpation. Scleritis will NOT blanch with topical phenylephrine because the blood vessels involved are too deep to be affected by the topical vasoconstrictor.

Treatment/Management:

- Non-Necrotizing Scleritis: Treat with oral NSAIDs or steroids depending on severity. Immunosuppressive agents may be necessary. If present, the underlying etiology should be treated. Sub-Tenon's steroid injections are contraindicated.
- Necrotizing Scleritis: Treat the same as with Non-Necrotizing Scleritis. Additional management may be required due to risk for perforation. Patients should wear glasses or eye shields to protect the thinned sclera. If perforation occurs, scleral patch grafting may be indicated.

~~~ANTERIOR / UVEA~~~

ENDOPHTHALMITIS*

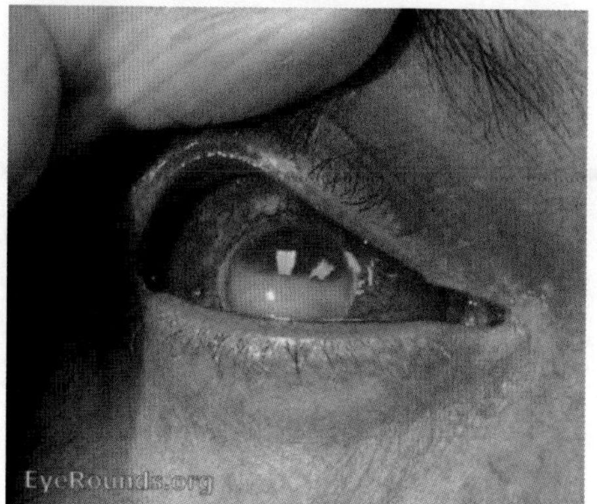
EyeRounds.org University of Iowa

What to Know: Endophthalmitis is a very serious infection which typically occurs after intraocular surgery, but can also occur after penetrating ocular trauma. It is most commonly caused by a *Staph epidermidis* infection.

Symptoms: Patients will complain of postoperative decreased vision and pain of an acute onset.

Signs: Hypopyon is a hallmark finding. Patients will have a severely reduced VA (20/800). Other findings include proptosis, vitritis, chemosis (conjunctival swelling), hyperemia (redness), and corneal edema. Signs of penetrating ocular injury may also be present (Seidel's Sign).

Treatment/Management: Endophthalmitis is considered an ocular emergency, and the patient may need to be hospitalized. Given this is a bacterial infection, patients should be treated aggressively with antibiotics (intravitreal injection, topical, and possibly systemic). The inflammation should also be aggressively treated with steroids (topical Q1H around the clock). Immediate pars plana vitrectomy is indicated if endophthalmitis occurs after cataract surgery OR if the patient is Light Perception only. If Endophthalmitis occurs after a penetrating ocular injury, or if the patient shows no improvement with treatment, then vitrectomy may be considered.

ANIRIDIA

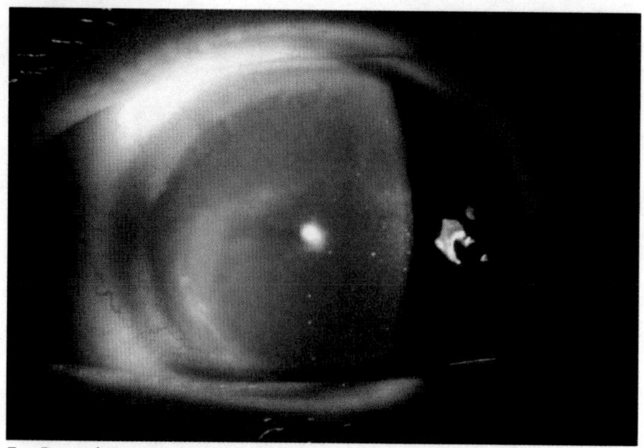
EyeRounds.org University of Iowa

What to Know: Aniridia is a hereditary disorder in which the patient is born without an iris.

Symptoms: Infants may show signs of photophobia and parents my complain that the pupil looks "dilated."

Signs: Patients will present with a bilateral loss of their iris with only an iris stump visible. The main complications to look out for in these patients are Wilms tumor (the most common kidney cancer in children) and glaucoma. They may also have cataracts, dry eye, reduced vision, nystagmus, strabismus, and amblyopia.

Treatment/Management: If present, the glaucoma should be treated by reducing IOP, and it will very likely require the surgical treatments. The patient should be screened regularly for Wilms Tumor with ultrasonography until the age of 16. The photophobia can be treated with a painted contact lens. Any comorbid cataracts should be removed via surgery. Also consider treatment for the dry eye, amblyopia, and strabismus.

IRIS NEVUS

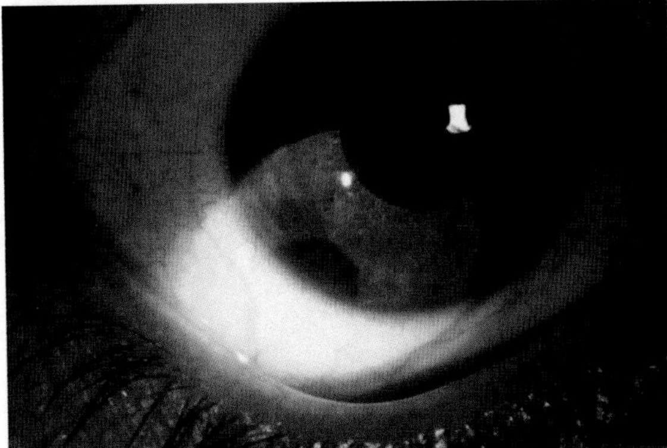

EyeRounds.org University of Iowa

What to Know: An Iris Nevus is a proliferation of iris stromal melanocytes.

Symptoms: Asymptomatic.

Signs: An Iris Nevus is like a freckle. Typically they will be flat, less than 3 mm in diameter, and benign. An Iris Nevus may disrupt the iris anatomy, and thus cause pupillary distortion.

Treatment/Management: An iris nevus should be followed periodically with serial photography to monitor for any signs of melanoma (elevation, growth, and abnormal vasculature).

IRIS MALIGNANT MELANOMA

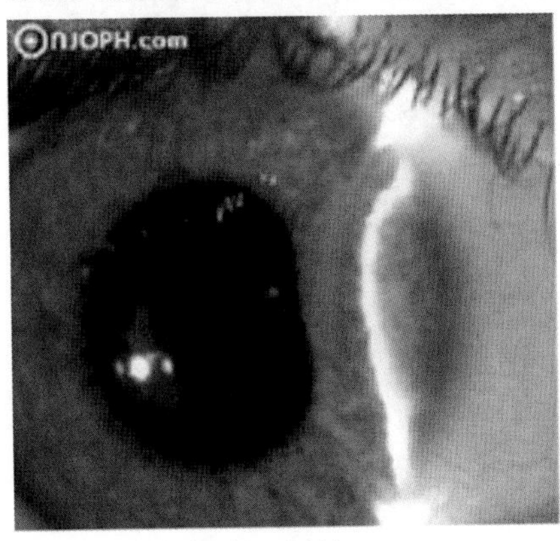

Atlas of Ophthalmology 5441

What to Know: An Iris Malignant Melanoma is defined by the abnormal proliferation of melanocytes. It is most commonly found in fair-skinned patients who have blue/green irises in their 50s-60s. Prognosis is good, only 4-5% metastasize within 10 years.

Symptoms: Asymptomatic.

Signs: Patients may present with a growing, elevated, vascularized, brown lesion which may be responsible for secondary glaucoma.

Treatment/Management: Given that an Iris Malignant Melanoma is a cancer, it should be treated with chemotherapy, radio therapy, iridectomy, or enucleation (remove eyeball that leaves the EOMs and other orbital content intact) in serious cases. If present, treat the glaucoma.

UVEITIS
What to Know: There are two types of uveitis: granulomatous and nongranulomatous. They can be differentiated based on the presence (granulomatous, seen as mutton-fat keratic precipitates in the eyes) or absence (nongranulomatous) of granulomas.
Treatment/Management: Uveitis is treated with topical steroids to reduce the inflammation and a cycloplegic to immobilize the iris. You want to immobilize the iris to relieve the patient's photophobia and also to prevent the formation of synechiae. Patients should be followed every 1-14 days depending on severity and response to treatment. Be careful to watch for an increased IOP in steroid responders. After resolution, the patient will need to have a slow taper from the steroid to prevent rebound inflammation. If the patient is presenting with their first episode of mild, unilateral, nongranulomatous uveitis, then the etiology is assumed to be idiopathic and no further testing is indicated. However, cases which are bilateral, granulomatous, and/or recurrent warrant extra testing to rule out other causes.

GRANULOMATOUS UVEITIS

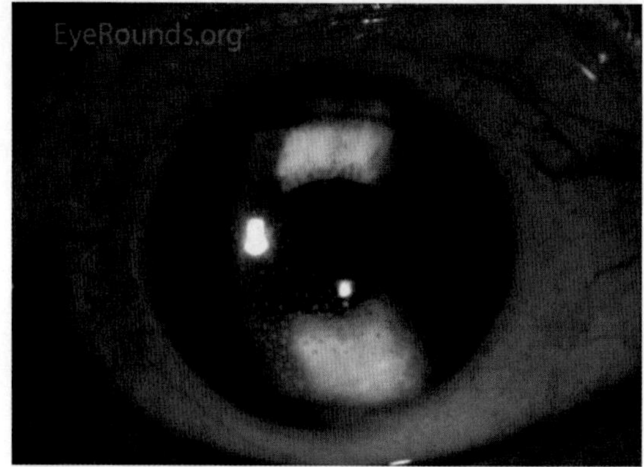

EyeRounds.org University of Iowa

What to Know:

Granulomatous Uveitis is typically **bilateral** and has several causes:

- Systemic (each of these are discussed in detail in Chapter 12): Sarcoidosis, Syphilis, Tuberculosis, Vogt-Koyanagi-Harada (VKH) Syndrome.
- Ocular: Lens-induced, Sympathetic Ophthalmia (see Chapter 13), Wegener's Granulomatosis (inflammation of the blood vessels), and Birdshot Choroidopathy (see Chapter 3).

Symptoms: Patients will complain of reduced vision, pain, photophobia, and epiphora.

Signs: Cells/Flare will be present in the anterior chamber (critical). Granulomatous Keratic Precipitates may also be present on the endothelium.

Treatment/Management: See the purple "Uveitis" box above. Patients with recurrent, bilateral, granulomatous uveitis should be tested to determine any systemic causes. They should get a chest radiograph to investigate for Tuberculosis or Sarcoidosis. Tuberculosis will have a positive PPD test while Sarcoidosis will not. Sarcoidosis will have positive serum ACE testing. Syphilis will have a positive RPR, VDRL, and FTA-ABS. Once the systemic finding is determined, it should be treated as such.

NONGRANULOMATOUS UVEITIS

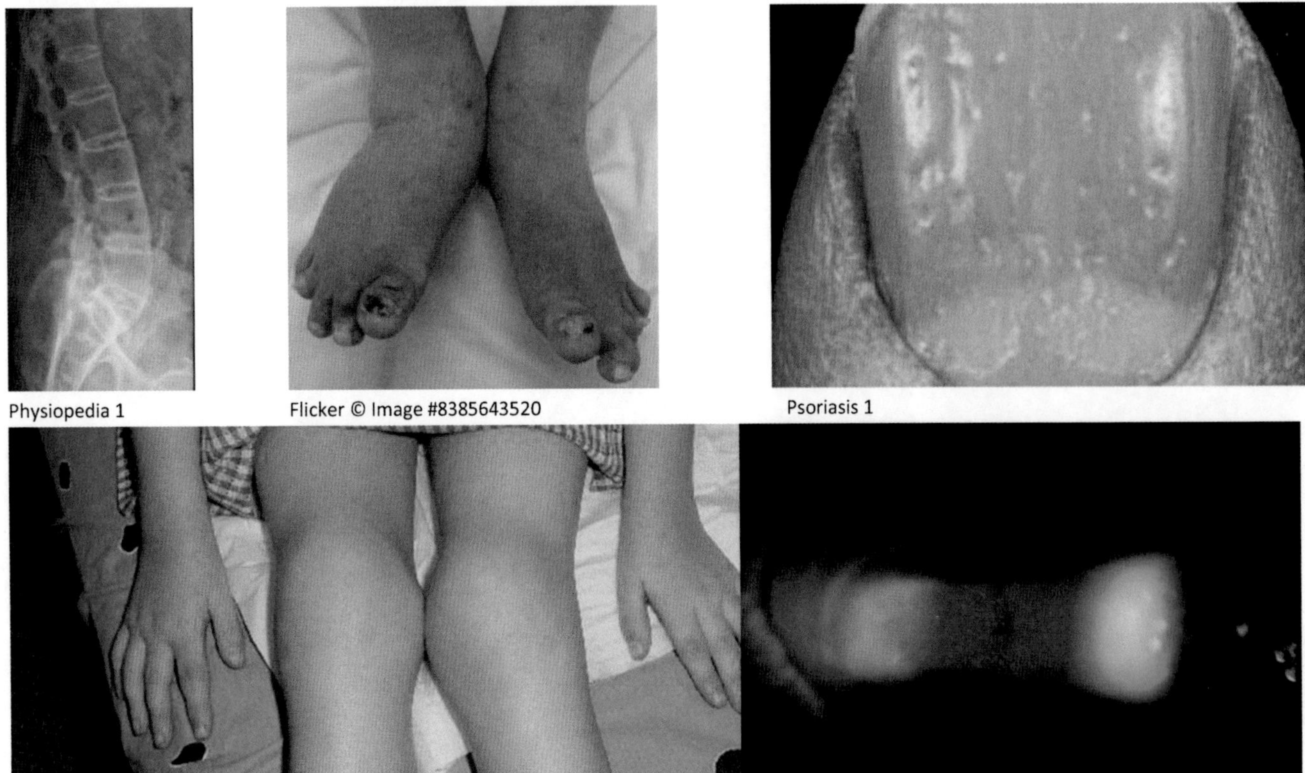

Physiopedia 1 Flicker © Image #8385643520 Psoriasis 1

Medical Observer 1 Keeler 1

Symptoms: Patients will complain of reduced vision, pain, photophobia, and epiphora.

Signs: Cells/Flare will be present in the anterior chamber (critical, see bottom right image). Stellate Keratic Precipitates may also be present on the endothelium.

What to Know:

Nongranulomatous Uveitis is caused by the following diseases:

- Idiopathic: this is the most common cause of uveitis (up to 50%). It is typically **unilateral**.
- HLA-B27: Usually HLA-B27 associated uveitis is **bilateral**. If any of these are suspected, consider testing the patient for HLA-B27:
  - Ankylosing Spondylitis is characterized by a stiff, painful lower back after exercise. On x-ray the vertebrae will have a "bamboo spine" appearance (top left image). "Spondylitis" should help you remember "spine." If suspected, then a spinal x-ray is warranted.
  - Crohn's Disease is a subset of Inflammatory Bowel Disease which afflicts the entire gastrointestinal tract. Uveitis is more common in Crohn's Disease than Ulcerative Colitis. Given that Crohn's Disease can afflict both the superior and inferior portions of the GI tract, I remember that Crohn's disease is more common in the eyes because both are located superiorly to Ulcerative Colitis. Other findings include skip lesions and cobblestone mucosa. If suspected, the patient should be referred for a colonoscopy.
  - Psoriatic Arthritis is characterized by "sores" of the skin (erythematous rash, top middle picture), arthritis of the phalanges (fingers and toes), and nail pitting (top right picture). If suspected, observe the patient's hands or feet for signs and ask about pain on movement.

    - Reiter's Syndrome (Reactive Arthritis) has a classic triad of uveitis, urethritis, and polyarthritis (remembered as "can't see, can't pee, can't climb a tree.") If suspected, ask the patient about joint pain and pain on urination.
    - Ulcerative Colitis is a subset of Inflammatory Bowel Disease which afflicts only the colon (large intestine), or the most inferior portion of the GI tract. If suspected, the patient should be referred for a colonoscopy.
- Juvenile Rheumatoid Arthritis (JRA) is the most common cause of uveitis in children, is typically **bilateral**, and seen in females. 90% of cases are pauciarticular (afflict large joints, see bottom left image). If present, testing will be RF negative and ANA positive.
- Lyme Disease is caused when a patient gets infected with *Borrelia burgdorferi* after a tick bite. There is usually a "bullseye" lesion at the site of the bite, and it takes 1-3 months after the bite occurs for systemic findings to present themselves: encephalitis (inflammation of the brain), meningitis (inflammation of the brain and spinal cord), and uveitis. If suspected, order a Lyme titer and ELISA.
- Glaucomatocyclitic Crisis (Posner-Schlossman Syndrome): **Unilateral** mild, **acute**, recurrent uveitis with markedly elevated IOP which is usually self-limiting.
- Fuch's Heterochromic Iridocyclitis is usually **unilateral** and **chronic.** Findings include low grade inflammation presenting as small stellate keratic precipitates, abnormal anterior chamber vessels, and very mild heterochromia. Frequently patients will develop cataracts.

Treatment/Management: See the purple "Uveitis" box above. Glaucomatocyclitic crisis will require treatment to reduce IOP. Systemic antibiotics are required for Lyme Disease.

CHAPTER 15
AMBLYOPIA / STRABISMUS

The NBEO website states that 6-17 questions will be asked on Amblyopia / Strabismus. Historically they have asked about 14.6 questions, meaning this chapter covers approximately 4% of the material tested on the exam, or roughly 3 cases. This material is NOT tested on TMOD.

~~~AMBLYOPIA~~~

AMBLYOPIA

What to Know: It is important for the brain to receive a clear image from the eyes during development of the visual system in order for the brain to learn how to "talk" with the eyes. If the brain does not receive a clear image from the eyes, then it may never learn to see clearly out of the affected eye(s). Contrast sensitivity may also be reduced. The type of amblyopia a patient has is named after the causative factor. There are four types of amblyopia listed below from most to least common:

- Strabismic: When a child has strabismus, the brain may respond to the diplopia by suppressing or "turning off" the deviated eye. If the brain refuses to acknowledge an eye, then it will never learn to see clearly from that eye.
- Anisometropic: When a child has a large difference in refractive error between their two eyes, the eye with the worse refractive error is at risk for developing amblyopia because the brain would rather use the better seeing eye. The anisometropia is amblyogenic if the patient has >3D of myopia, >1D of hyperopia, or >1.5D of astigmatism.
- Isometropic: Both eyes have an extreme refractive error with isometropic amblyopia. The isometropia is amblyogenic if the patient has >8D myopia, >5D hyperopia, or >2.50D astigmatism.
- Deprivation: Deprivation amblyopia occurs when an anatomical structure blocks light from entering the eye. Examples include congenital cataracts, ptosis, corneal opacity, and retinal conditions such as Hemangioma. Usually this will result in very severe amblyopia.

Symptoms: The patient may have no complaints because they have never experienced anything else. But it is possible they may complain of blurry vision.

Signs: The patient will have decreased vision (even with pinhole) with no signs of an organic condition. It is important to perform a DFE on these patients in order to rule out retinal causes of the reduced vision. Visual acuity will improve with single letter testing due to the crowding phenomenon, but it will decrease significantly in dim illumination (neutral-density filter effect). Patients will have reduced stereopsis and contrast sensitivity. They may have comorbid strabismus and nystagmus.

Treatment/Management: See amblyopia in Chapter 2.

~~~STRABISMUS~~~

HYPERTROPIA

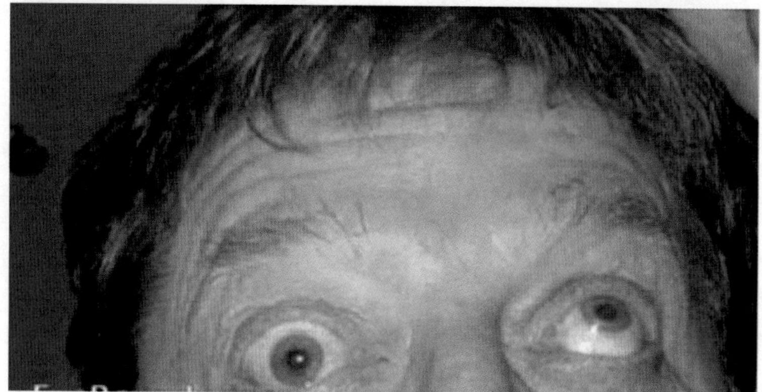

EyeRounds.org University of Iowa

What to Know: A vertical deviation is typically defined by the elevated eye. It may be congenital (idiopathic) or acquired (nerve or muscle condition).

Symptoms vary based on onset. If it is congenital, then it may be asymptomatic. If it is acquired, symptoms may include diplopia, head tilt, asthenopia, and headaches.

Signs: A vertical tropia will be seen on cover test. If congenital, the patient may have comorbid amblyopia. The patients may have reduced stereopsis and abnormal EOM movement.

Treatment/Management: If present, treat the underlying etiology. The first step in treating strabismus should be to correct any associated refractive error. If the strabismus is present in children, utilize patching (occlusion or Atropine) in order to reduce risk for amblyopia. Vision therapy can also be considered. Severe cases may require strabismus surgery.

MÖBIUS SYNDROME

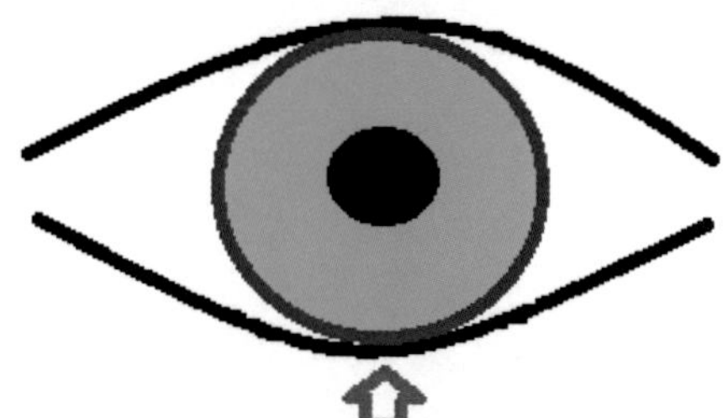

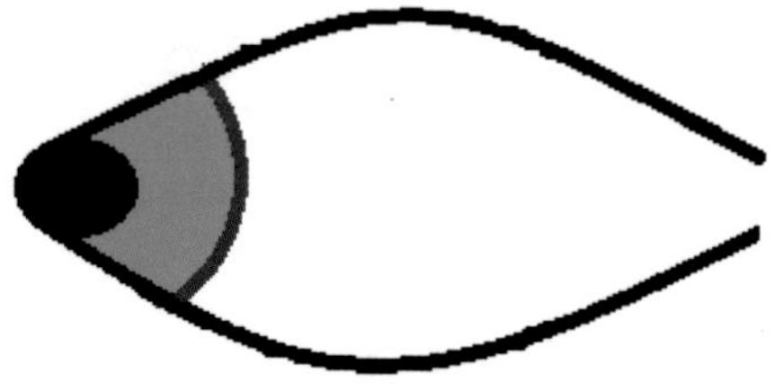

Kimberly Castillo, OD

What to Know: Möbius Syndrome is a congenital bilateral inability to abduct past midline due to aplasia (failure to develop or function normally) of the CN VI and VII nuclei.

Signs: Given that CN VII is also affected, patients will have reduced facial movement (mask-like facies) due to bilateral disruption of the facial nerve. They may also have epiphora and exposure keratopathy.

Treatment/Management: If present, treat the exposure keratopathy. Surgical intervention of the EOMs may also be indicated.

BROWN'S SYNDROME

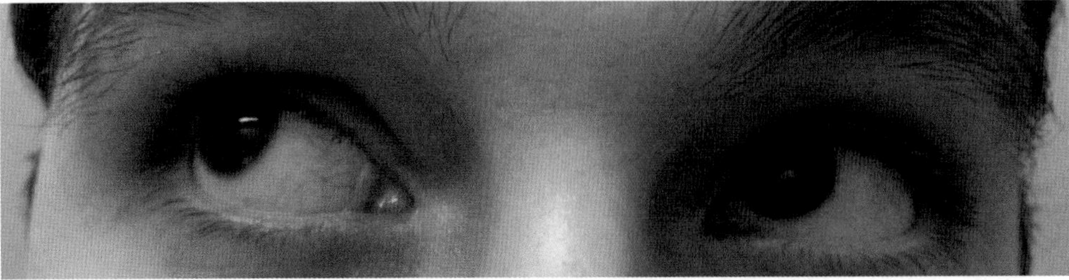

Kimberly Castillo, OD

What to Know: Brown's Syndrome is a congenital (idiopathic, more frequent) or acquired (inflammation, surgery, trauma) disorder in which the patient is unable to elevate their eye during adduction due to a superior oblique or trochlea condition. They will be able to look downward during adduction.

Symptoms: Patients may notice diplopia during right or left superior gaze.

Signs: Patients may present with abnormal EOM movement in which the patient will be unable to elevate the affected eye during adduction. Patients may have an associated head tilt.

Treatment/Management: Usually treatment is not necessary. If acquired secondary to inflammation, patients may benefit from steroids (oral or injected near trochlea). If the patient has an abnormal head tilt, then muscle surgery may be required.

DUANE'S RETRACTION SYNDROME

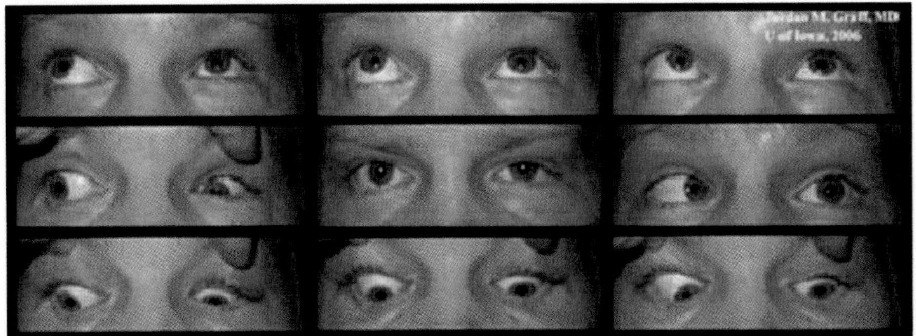

EyeRounds.org University of Iowa

What to Know: Duane's Retraction Syndrome is a congenital hypoplasia (underdevelopment) or agenesis (failure to develop) of the abducens nerve (CN VI) with reduced action of the lateral muscle. There are three types of Duane's Retraction Syndrome:

- Type 1: Limited Abduction (Notice one D for Type 1)
- Type 2: Limited Adduction (Notice two Ds for Type 2)
- Type 3: Limited Abduction and Adduction (Notice three Ds for Type 3)

Symptoms vary based on onset.

Signs: In addition to the limited adduction, the globe may retract during adduction (hence Duane's RETRACTION syndrome) with narrowing of the palpebral fissure due to co-contraction of the lateral and medial rectus muscles. Patients may have amblyopia, the leash phenomenon (upshoots or downshoots), or an associated head tilt.

Treatment/Management: Usually treatment is not necessary. If present, correct any refractive error and treat the amblyopia. If the patient has an abnormal head tilt, then muscle surgery may be required.

ESOTROPIA

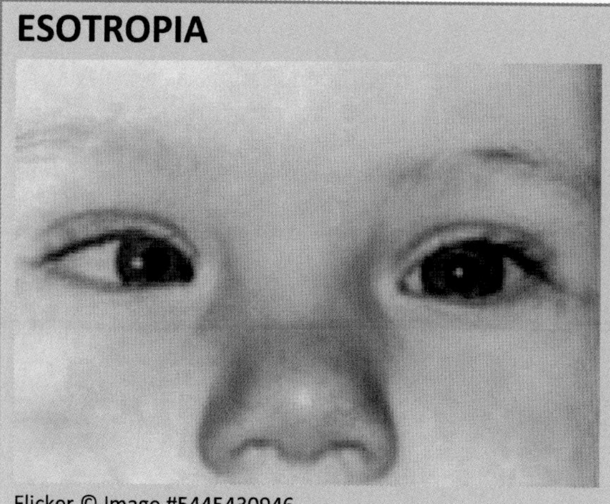

Flicker © Image #5445430946

What to Know: Esotropia is more common than Exotropia in infants (however, exotropia is more common worldwide). Here is a summary of the different types of Esotropia:

1. Congenital/Infantile <6mo old
2. Accommodative. Caused by an accommodative condition. The patient will rub or close an eye during near tasks. There are three types of Accommodative Esotropias:
   a. Refractive: Characterized by increased hyperopia
   b. Non-Refractive: Characterized by accommodative excess
   c. Mixed: Characterized by both increased hyperopia and accommodative excess
3. Non-Accommodative. There are three types:
   a. Early onset >6mo old
   b. Divergence Insufficiency
   c. Decompensated (the eyes give up)
4. Sensory caused by organic blocking of the retina (such as a congenital cataract)
5. Consecutive, which occurs after surgery.

Treatment: Base OUT prisms can be prescribed for esotropia. However, base IN prisms are used during vision therapy exercises. Surgical treatment would include a medial rectus recession of the affected eye.

CONGENITAL/INFANTILE ESOTROPIA

What to Know: Infantile Esotropia will have a large angle of deviation (greater than 35 PD) which is about equal at distance and near fixation and will **manifest before the patient is 6 months old**.

Signs: The horizontal deviation will most likely be visible without needing to perform cover test. The angle of deviation will be about equal at distance and at near. Amblyopia will be present if the patient does not alternate fixation. The patient may have an associated inferior oblique overaction (as it tries to compensate for the eso deviation), latent nystagmus, and abnormal EOM movement. There may be reduced local/global stereopsis. There is no accommodative component to Congenital Esotropia.

Treatment/Management: Hyperopia greater than +2.00D should be corrected. Utilize patching (occlusion or Atropine) in order to reduce risk for amblyopia. Strabismus surgery should be performed before the child is 2 years old. Surgical intervention may help improve stereopsis.

ACCOMMODATIVE ESOTROPIA*

What to Know: Up to 55% of all Esotropias have an accommodative component. Accommodative Esotropia is usually intermittent due to the variable nature of accommodation. It usually **manifests when the child is around 2 years old**. There are three types.

- Refractive: High hyperopia (greater than +4.75D) with a normal AC/A ratio. The angle of deviation will be about equal at distance and at near.
- Non-Refractive: The patient will have a normal refractive error but a high AC/A ratio. The angle of deviation will be larger at near than at distance.
- Mixed: The patient will have a moderate to high refractive error as well as a high AC/A ratio.

Symptoms: **The patient will rub or close an eye during near tasks** and may also complain of diplopia.

Signs: Esotropia will be visible with uncorrected cover test and will improve with correction. Amblyopia will only develop if the strabismus becomes constant. The patient may also have reduced stereopsis.

Treatment/Management: The first line of treatment for Accommodative Esotropia is to prescribe glasses for full time wear. Children under 6 should be given full cycloplegic refraction, and patients over 6 should be prescribed as much as they will tolerate. No further treatment is necessary if the patient is corrected within 8PD. If the patient has residual esotropia and a high AC/A ratio, prescribe an add of at least +2.50 in exudative bifocals with the line at the lower pupillary border. If none of these methods correct the esotropia within 10PD, then strabismus surgery may be required.

NON-ACCOMMODATIVE ESOTROPIA

What to Know: A Non-Accommodative Esotropia will **NOT** improve with correction of refractive error or prescription of a near add. It may have an **acute onset**.

Symptoms: Patients may initially complain of diplopia. However, in longstanding cases the body will learn to adapt to the diplopia (suppression, anomalous correspondence).

Signs: There are three types.

- Early Onset appears the same as Infantile Esotropia, except the onset will be **after 6 months of age** and before 2 years of age. Typically the strabismus will be constant and alternating.
- Divergence Insufficiency: Strabismus which is worse at distance than at near and can be either constant or intermittent.
- Decompensated Esotropia occurs when a patient can no longer compensate for their esotropia with Negative Fusional Vergence (NFV). Basically, the NFV gets tired and gives up trying to compensate for the Esotropia. This will typically occur in patients who are greater than 7 years old. The strabismus can be either constant or intermittent.

Treatment/Management: Consider referring patients to rule out a neurologic etiology. Correct any refractive error, prescribe base out prism, recommend vision therapy. Surgery is only indicated in severe cases.

SENSORY ESOTROPIA

What to Know: Sensory Esotropia occurs when an organic ocular condition blocks and decreases vision. Possible causes include cataracts, corneal scars, ptosis, macular scars, optic atrophy, and uncorrected refractive error.

Symptoms: Patients or parents my complain of an eye turn.

Signs: Patients will have a constant, unilateral esotropia with an associated poor acuity ranging from 20/60 to light perception.

Treatment/Management: Visual prognosis is poor, and so treatment is for cosmesis only (to align the eyes).

CONSECUTIVE ESOTROPIA

What to Know: Consecutive Esotropia occurs after strabismus surgery to correct exotropia. The surgeon overshoots and instead of ending with aligned eyes, the patient now has an esotropia.

Symptoms: Patients may complain of diplopia and asthenopia.

Treatment: Prisms may be required to place the image in a suppression zone.

PROMINENT EPICANTHAL FOLDS

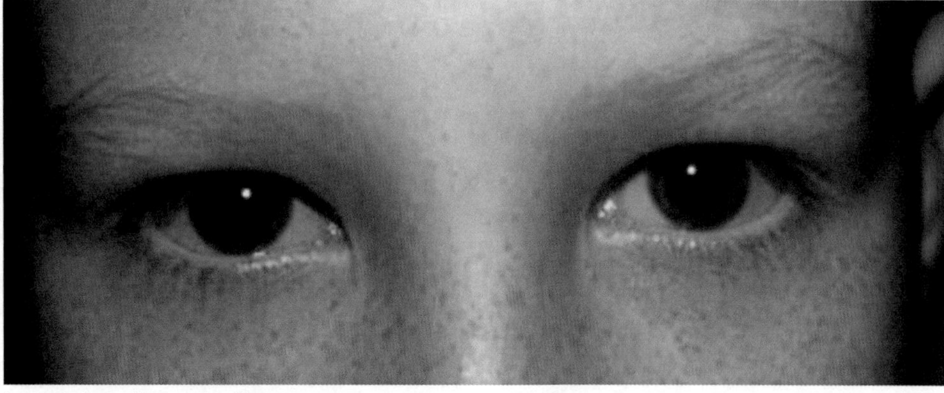

EyeRounds.org University of Iowa

What to Know: Patients (usually Asians and patients with Down's Syndrome) may have Prominent Epicanthal Folds which may be confused with Esotropia.

Symptoms: Patients or parents my complain of an eye turn.

Signs: If Prominent Epicanthal Folds are suspected, pinch the skin across the nose to pull it away from the globe. This may make it easier to appreciate normal fixation. Patients will also have no esodeviation on cover test.

Treatment/Management: No treatment is necessary. In fact, it is most important to properly diagnose and NOT treat for Esotropia.

EXOTROPIA

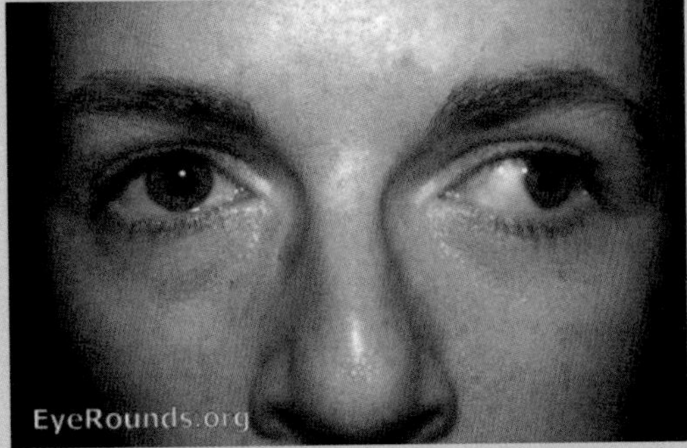

EyeRounds.org University of Iowa

What to Know: Exotropia is more common than Esotropia worldwide (however, Esotropia is more common in infants). Here is a summary of the different types of exotropia:

1. Intermittent. These patients will close an eye with sun exposure. There are three types:
    a. Basic
    b. Divergence Excess
    c. Convergence Insufficiency
2. Congenital/Infantile <1 year old
3. Decompensated (the eyes give up)
4. Sensory caused by organic blocking of the retina (such as a congenital cataract)
5. Consecutive, which occurs after surgery.

Treatment: The first step to treating any Exotropia is to correct the refractive error. If present, treat the amblyopia. Base IN prisms can be prescribed for exotropia. However, base OUT prisms are used during vision therapy exercises. In severe cases, surgical treatment would include a lateral rectus recession of the affected eye.

INTERMITTENT EXOTROPIA*

What to Know: Intermittent Exotropia is an outward eye turn which can be triggered by anxiety, excessive fatigue, inattention, bright lights, and poor health. **Intermittent Exotropia is the most common type of exodeviation**.

Symptoms: **Children may close the deviated eye during exposure to the sun**. Mature patients may experience asthenopia, headaches, diplopia, photophobia, and difficulty reading.

Signs: Exotropia will be appreciated on cover test. Since Intermittent Exotropia manifests with alternating fixation, amblyopia is rare. There are three types:

- Basic Exotropia occurs in children around the age of 2.
- Divergence Excess Exotropia typically occurs in older patients and is characterized by a larger angle of deviation at distance than at near.
- Convergence Insufficiency typically occurs in older patients and is characterized by a larger angle of deviation at near than at distance.

Treatment/Management: If the treatment described in the green "Exotropia" box above is unsuccessful, consider strabismus surgery.

CONGENITAL/INFANTILE EXOTROPIA

What to Know: Congenital Exotropia manifests before the patient is one year old.

Signs: Usually Congenital Exotropia is constant, but it alternates and so amblyopia is unlikely because both eyes get a chance to fixate. The patients will have normal accommodation and their refractive error will be unremarkable based on age norms.

Treatment/Management: See the green "Exotropia" box above.

DECOMPENSATED EXOTROPIA

What to Know: Decompensated Exotropia occurs when a patient can no longer compensate for their exotropia with Positive Fusional Vergence (PFV). Basically, the PFV gets tired and gives up trying to compensate for the Exotropia. This will typically occur in patients with early presbyopia. The strabismus can be either constant or intermittent.

Symptoms: Patients may complain of diplopia and asthenopia.

Signs: Exotropia will be appreciated on cover test.

Treatment/Management: See the green "Exotropia" box above.

CONSECUTIVE EXOTROPIA

What to Know: Consecutive Exotropia occurs after strabismus surgery to correct esotropia. The surgeon overshoots and instead of ending with aligned eyes, the patient now has an exotropia.

Symptoms: Patients may complain of diplopia and asthenopia.

Treatment/Management: Prisms may be required to place the image in a suppression zone.

SENSORY EXOTROPIA

What to Know: Sensory Exotropia occurs when a congenital organic ocular condition results in decreased vision. Possible causes include cataracts, corneal scars, ptosis, macular scars, optic atrophy, and uncorrected refractive error.

Symptoms: Patients or parents may complain of an eye turn.

Signs: Patients will have a constant, unilateral exotropia with an associated poor visual acuity

Treatment/Management: Visual prognosis is poor, and so treatment is for cosmesis only (to align the eyes).

PATTERN

Treatment: Strabismus surgery may be indicated in severe cases.

A-PATTERN

Signs: Patients will have strabismus which displays a larger exo-posture in downgaze than upgaze by at least 10PD. In other words, their eyes will have their best alignment when the patient is looking upwards. Patients may present with a chin-down position to help reduce diplopia.

V-Pattern

Signs: Patients will have strabismus which displays a larger exo-posture in upgaze than downgaze by at least 10PD. In other words, their eyes will have their best alignment when the patient is looking downwards. Patients may present with a chin-up position to help reduce diplopia.

X-Pattern

Signs: Patients will have exotropia which displays a larger deviation in upgaze as well as downgaze by at least 10PD. In other words, their eyes will have their best alignment when the patient is looking in primary position.

TESTING FOR STRABISMUS

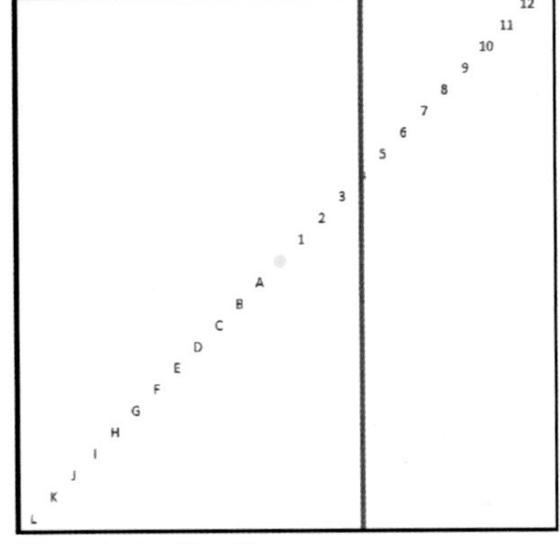

Kimberly Castillo, OD

MADDOX ROD TESTING

The patient is asked to hold the red lens over their right eye. When the striations of the Maddox Lens are oriented vertically, the patient is being evaluated for horizontal deviations. When the striations of the Maddox Lens are oriented horizontally, the patient is being evaluated for vertical deviations. Remember that Maddox Rod testing cannot differentiate phorias from tropias.

- For both vertical and horizontal deviations, if the patient states that the red line goes through the white light, then they are ortho.
- For horizontal deviations, if the patient states the red line goes through one of the letters on the left side of the card, then the patient is said to have a crossed (or exo) deviation. I remember this by noticing that there is an "x" in exo, which represents a cross. Likewise, if the patient states the line goes through one of the numbers on the right side of the card, they have an uncrossed (or eso) deviation.
- For vertical deviations, the red line will be located in the opposite direction as the deviation. For example, patients with hyper deviations will state the red line goes through one of the letters below the light, and for hypo deviations the patient will state the red line goes through one of the numbers above the white light.

HERING-BIRLSCHOWSKI AFTERIMAGE TEST

Cross Response Right Esotropia Right Exotropia

Kimberly Castillo, OD

The flash of a camera is used to produce either a horizontal or vertical afterimage, both with a break in the middle to protect the fovea. A horizontal afterimage is created in the normal eye and a vertical afterimage is created in the turned eye. The patient will see the afterimage whether his/her eyes are open, closed, straight, or turned. The afterimage will create a pattern which can have different indications:

- Cross response: A symmetrical cross with the central gaps superimposed indicates a normal bifoveal correspondence (if eccentric fixation is excluded). Any eso or exo-deviation with normal retinal correspondence (NRC) still gives a symmetrical cross response.
- Asymmetrical crossing: In case of abnormal retinal correspondence (ARC) the horizontal and vertical lines are separated. Amount of separation depends on the angle of condition. Right ESOtropia sees the vertical afterimage displaced to the left; Right EXOtropia sees the vertical afterimage displaced to the right.
- Single line with a gap indicates suppression in the fellow eye.

BAGOLINI LENS TEST

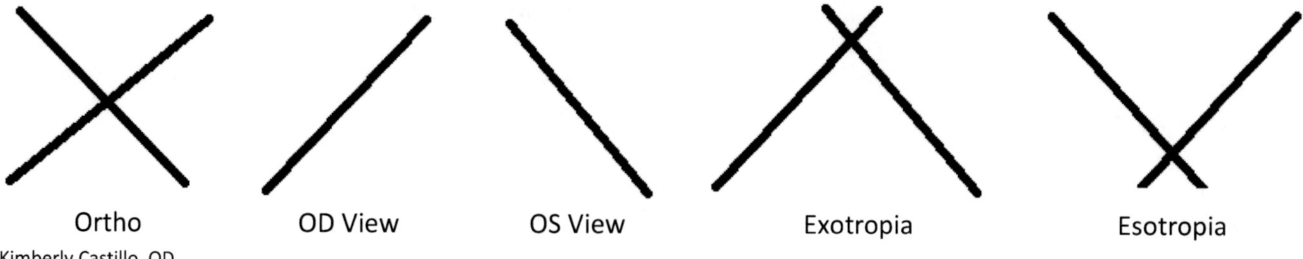

Ortho OD View OS View Exotropia Esotropia

Kimberly Castillo, OD

A patient looks through a pair of glasses which have plano, clear lenses with striations which don't affect the patient's vision or accommodation. The striations are placed at 45 degrees OD and 135 degrees OS. If the patient is ortho with normal retinal correspondence, then they will see a perfect "x." The "OD View" above represents what the patient will see if s/he is suppressing his/her left eye (and therefore only viewing out of the right eye). The "OS View" above represents what the patient will see if s/he is suppressing his/her right eye (and therefore only viewing out of the left eye). If the patient has exotropia, they will view a teepee (above), and if the patient has esotropia, they will view a "V" (above).

CHAPTER 16
PUBLIC HEALTH

The NBEO website states that 15-17 questions will be asked on Public Health. Historically they have asked about 13.3 questions, meaning this chapter covers approximately 4% of the material tested on the exam. This material is NOT tested on TMOD. The NBEO website states that these topics will be tested in Public Health: "epidemiology, biostatistics and measurement, environmental vision, health care policy and administration."

EPIDEMIOLOGY

Epidemiology studies how diseases spread throughout a society.

The CDC Guidelines to handwashing state: "Wet your hands with clean, running water (warm or cold), turn off the tap, and apply soap. Lather your hands by rubbing them together with the soap. Be sure to lather the backs of your hands, between your fingers, and under your nails. **Scrub your hands for at least 20 seconds**."

Prevalence is the number of cases of a disease that are present in a particular population at a given time. For example, about 30.3 million people have Diabetes in the United States.

Incidence refers to the number of new cases that develop in a given period of time. For example, about 1.5 million people are diagnosed with Diabetes each year in the United States.

NATIONAL ELECTRONIC INJURY SURVEILLANCE SYSTEM (NEISS)

The NEISS study analyzes product and non-product related injuries to determine if a product needs to be recalled.

- NEISS evaluated ocular injuries in patients over the age of 65 between 2001-2007. It found that most injuries occurred in males (64%) and at home (70%). The cause of the ocular injury was usually chemicals (22%) or cutting tools used during construction (21%).
- NEISS evaluated ocular injuries which occurred in children between 1997-2006. It found that 62% of affected patients were boys, and 15% of affect children were under the age of 2. 45% of the injuries were due to abrasions or contusions, 12% were due to conjunctivitis, 9% due to foreign bodies, and 7% were due to chemical burns.
- NEISS evaluated ocular injuries associated with aerosol containers between 1997-2009. It found that 55% of injuries occurred in patients under the age of 18 using spray paint.

BIOSTATISTICS AND MEASUREMENT

Measurement with Biostatistics allows researchers to analyze their data. These equations are low yield.

Precision / Positive Predictive Value is the probability that people who test positive for a disease actually have the disease. It can be calculated by the following equation:

- Precision = True Positives / Everyone who tested positive
- Precision = True Positives / (True Positives + False Positives)

Negative Predictive Value is the probability that people who test negative for a disease actually DO NOT have the disease. It can be calculated by the following equation:

- Negative Predictive Value = True Negatives / Everyone who tested negative
- Negative Predictive Value = True Negatives / (True Negatives + False Negatives

Sensitivity is the proportion of people who have a disease and test positive for the disease. It can be calculated by the following equations:

- Sensitivity = True Positives / Actual Positives
- Sensitivity = True Positives / (True Positives + False Negatives)

Specificity is the proportion of people who do NOT have the disease and test negative for the disease. It can be calculated by the following equations:

- Specificity = True Negatives / Actual Negatives, OR
- Specificity = True Negatives / (True Negatives + False Positives)

The **False-Positive Rate** is the proportion of people who DO NOT have the disease but test positive. It can be calculated by the following equations:

- False Positive Rate = False Positives / Actual Negatives
- False Positive Rate = False Positives / (True Negatives + False Positives)
- False Positive Rate = 1 - Specificity

The **False-Negative Rate** is the proportion of people who HAVE the disease but test negative. It can be calculated by the following equations:

- False Negative Rate = False Negatives / Actual Positives
- False Negative Rate = False Negatives / (True Positives + False Negatives)
- False Negative Rate = 1 - Sensitivity

Accuracy describes how closely your findings represent reality. It can be calculated by the following equations:

- Accuracy = Everyone who tested **correctly** / Everyone who tested
- Accuracy = (True Positives + True Negatives) / (True Positives + True Negatives + False Negatives + False Positives)

A test which has **Reliability** is highly repeatable with the same results. A test which has **Validity** measures what it is supposed to measure (a test which is supposed to detect dry eye actually detects dry eye).

ENVIRONMENTAL VISION

CORNING PHOTOCHROMIC FILTER LENSES (CPF)

CPF lenses filter out blue/short light in order to relieve patients with glare and light sensitivity. Possible causes of photophobia include albinism, aniridia, aphakia/pseudophakia, cataracts, macular degeneration, and retinitis pigmentosa.

Color Rendering Index indicates if a light source will make objects appear natural. A score of 100 is the most natural while 1 is the least natural.

ELECTROMAGNETIC SPECTRUM

Gamma Rays	X-Rays	UV Rays	Visible Light						IR	Radar	FM	TV	AM
longest													shortest
10^ -14 m			400 nm					700 nm					10^4 m

Kimberly Castillo, OD

- Visible light: 400 – 750 nm
- UVA: 320 – 400 nm
- UVB 290 – 320 nm
    - Associated with Cortical Cataract formation according to the Chesapeake Bay Study.
- UVC: 100 – 290 nm
    - Associated with Ultraviolet / Thermal Keratopathy.
    - Patients who are recovering from Photorefractive Keratometry (PRK) are at a risk for UV Exposure because they do not have an epithelium.

UV Index Scale															
Low		Moderate			High		Very High		Extreme		Very Extreme				
UV Index 1	UV Index 2	UV Index 3	UV Index 4	UV Index 5	UV Index 6	UV Index 7	UV Index 8	UV Index 9	UV Index 10	UV Index 11	UV Index 12	UV Index 13	UV Index 14	UV Index 15	UV Index 16
No Protection Required		Protection Required					Extra Protection Required								

Kimberly Castillo, OD

UV Index is used to indicate how much harmful UV radiation will reach the Earth's surface on any given day. The amount of UV radiation which reaches the Earth's surface depends on the cloud layer, the elevation of the sun in the sky (the highest radiation levels occur at noon), and the amount of ozone is in the stratosphere. 90% of the radiation will reach the Earth's surface on days with a thin, high cloud layer. Meanwhile, 30% of the radiation will reach the Earth's surface on days with a dense, low cloud layer. At night the UV index is 0 because the sun is not shining light onto the Earth's surface. When the skies are clear at high elevations in the tropics, the UV index can be as high as 16.

UV TRANSMISSIBILITY OF DIFFERENT LENS MATERIALS

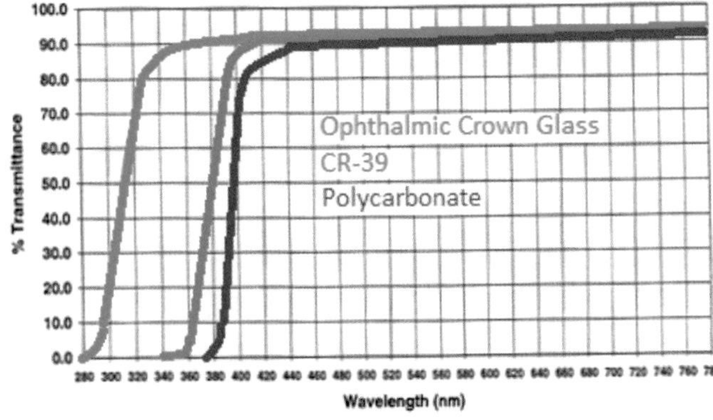

Kimberly Castillo, OD

Crown Glass allows the most UV light to pass, therefore providing the least protection from UV light. Polycarbonate allows the least UV light to pass, and so provides the most protection from UV light. CR-39 only gives partial protection to UV light.

GRADING OF UV RADIATION

- Eye-Sun Protection Factor (E-SPF) is assigned to a lens material to indicate the total UV radiation which will enter the eye. It like the SPF seen on sunscreen where the higher the number, the more sun protection is provided. It can be calculated with the following formula:
  - E-SPF = Irradiance with No Lens / Irradiance with Lens
- FUBI Eye Protection Factor (EPF) indicates how effective a pair of sunglasses is at protecting eyes from UV radiation. A perfect EPF score is 100.

RADIATION INJURIES

- Optical Radiation Injuries typically occur after a patient has been welding. The onset can be anywhere from 30 minutes – 24 hours depending on the intensity of the offending radiation. This is why patients should wear eye shields while welding.
- Infrared (IR) Radiation Injuries typically occur in patients who work in the iron, steel, or glass making industries, and is due to damage accumulating over 15-20 years. YAG lasers also emit IR light. IR injuries are usually more permanent than UV injuries and will cause sub-capsular cataracts.

BRAYER ABRASION VALUE

Two lenses, one with and the other without coatings, are exposed to oscillating aluminum zirconia (sand) for a set period of time, after which the amount of haze present on the lenses is measured. The amount of haze on the lens with coatings and without coatings is expressed as a ratio. A ratio of 1 means the coating has an equivalent abrasion resistance as uncoated CR-39. A ratio of 5 means the coating has 5x less abrasion resistance than an uncoated CR-39. Industry standard is a ratio of 4.

HEAVY METALS TESTING

Some occupations expose patients to high levels of heavy metals which puts them at risk for metal poisoning. These occupations may include mining, firing ranges, radiator repair shops, and construction work. Examples of offending heavy metals include lead, arsenic, cadmium, chromium, and mercury. If you suspect that a patient has been exposed to heavy metals, you can order a metals panel to confirm diagnosis.

ANSI STANDARDS

ANSI Z80.3-2001: Nonprescription Sunglasses and Fashion Eyewear

- Prescription must be virtually plano.
- Glasses may deform but not ignite when placed in a 200°C oven for 15 minutes.
- Lenses must have no visible pits, scratches, grayness, water marks, bubbles, or local aberrations when placed 12 inches from a 40-watt incandescent clear lamp.
- Luminous Transmittance must follow these guidelines:
  - Cosmetic/Light Sunglasses must transmit more than 40%
  - General Purpose/ Medium to Dark Sunglasses can transmit as low as 8%
  - Special Purpose / Very Dark and Strongly Colored Sunglasses can transmit as low as 3%
- Color Transmittance for traffic signals must follow these guidelines:
  - Red 8%
  - Yellow and Green 6%
  - Special Purpose / Very Dark and Strongly Colored Sunglasses should not be worn while driving.

UV Blocking of Contact Lenses. ANSI divides contact lenses into two categories.

- Class I Blocker must absorb at least 90% UVA and 99% UVB
- Class II Blocker must absorb at least 70% of UVA and 95% of UVB

ANSI Z87.1-2010: Safety Glasses

- Drop Ball Test: When a 1 inch, 2.4 ounce steel ball is dropped from 50 inches onto the lens, the lens must not fracture or break.
- Penetration Test: When a 1.56 ounce needle is dropped from 50 inches onto the lens, the lens must not

fracture or break.

- Minimum lens thickness
    - Spectacles must be at least 3.00 mm, or 2.5 mm if the patient has a prescription of at least +3.00D
    - Glass Goggles must be at least 3.00 mm
    - Non Glass Goggles must be at least 1.27 mm
    - Face Shields must be at least 1.00 mm
- Luminous transmission must be at least 85%.
- Glasses frame and lenses must be at least 33mm high and 40mm wide.
- No piece shall detach from the inner surface.
- No lens will fracture.
- No penetration of the rear surface will occur.
- No lens will be knocked loose of the frame.

ANSI Z80.1-2010: Power Tolerances (this material may be considered part of Ophthalmic Optics, but I wanted to keep all of the ANSI Standards together).

- Sphere Power
    - Less than +/- 6.50D: Tolerance is +/-0.13D
    - Greater than +/- 6.50D: Tolerance is 2% of Sphere Power
- Cylinder Power
    - Less than 2.00D: Tolerance is +/-0.13D
    - 2.00-4.50D: Tolerance is +/-0.15D
    - Greater than 4.50D: Tolerance is 4% of Cylinder Power
- Cylinder Axis
    - Less than 0.25D: Tolerance is +/-14 degrees
    - 0.25-0.50D: Tolerance is +/-7 degrees
    - 0.75D-1.00D: Tolerance is +/-5 degrees
    - 1.25D-1.50D: Tolerance is +/-3 degrees
    - Greater than 1.50D: Tolerance is +/-2 degrees

HEALTH CARE POLICY AND ADMINISTRATION

Health Care Administration deals with the logistics of running a hospital.

Health Care Policy deals with how a society manages healthcare including funding of services (universal healthcare, insurance, or out of pocket), funding of research (public or private), staffing of medical facilities, and promoting a healthy global community.

When a new drug is being tested, it will go through four phases of clinical trials:

1. Phase 1: Tests the drug's safety on healthy people.
2. Phase 2: Tests the drug's **efficacy** (the ability to produce a desired or intended result) on a small group of sick people. It includes a test group and a control group.
3. Phase 3: Tests the drug's efficacy on a large group of sick people and determines adverse reactions.
4. Phase 4: Evaluates marketing for the drug.

CHAPTER 17
OPHTHALMIC OPTICS

The NBEO website states that 6-17 questions will be asked on Ophthalmic Optics. Historically they have asked about 12.6 questions, meaning this chapter covers approximately 4% of the material tested on the exam, or roughly 3 cases. Ophthalmic Optics is NOT tested on TMOD.

The Boxing System

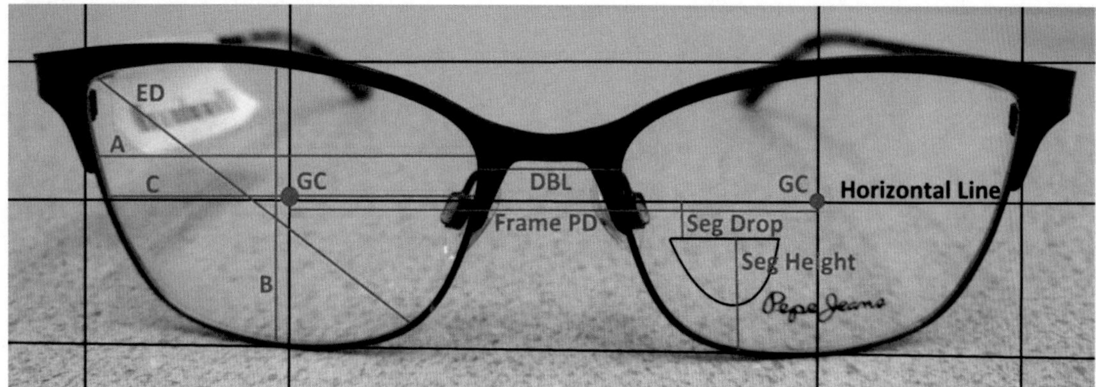

Kimberly Castillo, OD

The Boxing System refers to several important measurements which can be used to describe the size and shape of a lens. Remember that it is necessary to add 0.50mm to the length of the visible lens to account for the lens bevel.

- A Measurement: the longest horizontal length of the lens.
- B Measurement: the longest vertical length of the lens.
- C Measurement: the length of the lens along the Horizontal Line.
- Horizontal Line/Datum Line: line which runs through the vertical center of the lens.
- Geometrical Center (GC): point which lies in the middle of the Horizontal Line. This is the physical center of the lens.
- Distance Between Lenses (DBL) / Bridge Size: The narrowest distance between the two lenses.
- Frame PD / Geometric Center Distance (GCD): The distance between the two Geometric Centers.
    - Frame PD = A Measurement + DBL
- Effective Diameter (ED): The longest line which can be drawn through the lens, usually oriented diagonally.
- Segment Height: distance from the top of the bifocal/trifocal segment to the very bottom of the lens.
- Segment drop: distance from the Horizontal Line to the top of the Segment Height.

LENS MATERIAL CHARACTERISTICS

<table>
<tr><th>Material</th><th>n</th><th>Pros</th><th>Cons</th></tr>
<tr><td>CR-39 (Plastic)</td><td>1.498</td><td>Light</td><td>Thick and easily scratches</td></tr>
<tr><td>Crown Glass</td><td>1.523</td><td>Scratch resistant</td><td>Thick, heavy, and shatters easily</td></tr>
<tr><td>Trivex</td><td>1.53</td><td rowspan="2">Safe</td><td>Thick and expensive</td></tr>
<tr><td>Polycarbonate</td><td>1.586</td><td rowspan="2">Scratches and have a lot of chromatic aberrations.</td></tr>
<tr><td>High Index Plastic</td><td>1.54 – 1.66</td><td>Thin and light</td></tr>
</table>

ABERRATIONS

There are six types of common lenticular aberrations.

- **Spherical Aberrations** occur because marginal rays of light bend more than central rays of light.
- **Radial/Oblique Astigmatism** occurs when light rays enter the lens obliquely. It can be reduced by selecting the Tscherning Ellipse.
- **Coma** results when an object is off the axis of the lens.
- **Chromatic Aberration** is what we are utilizing during the red/green duochrome test. When doing this test, if the patient says the red side is clearer, add minus. When they say the green side is clearer, add plus (RAM-GAP). This test can be done on color blind patients because it utilizes the difference in wavelengths between the different colors. Short, blue wavelengths refract/bend more readily than long/red wavelengths. As the Abbe Value increases, so does the Chromatic Aberrations. Chromatic Aberrations can be decreased by decreasing the vertex distance and increasing pantascopic tilt.
- **Curvature of Field/Power Error** occurs because the effective power of the lens varies from the center to the periphery. This is why movie theaters will curve the periphery of their screens, to ensure the image is clear all the way to the edge of the image. Power Error can be accommodated for in spectacles by adjusting the base curve.

Spherical Aberrations and Coma are usually not problems because both of these deal with marginal rays of light, which are blocked out by the pupil. Aspheric lenses can also be used to reduce aberrations, and they are applied to progressive lenses. Aspheric lenses are also desirable because they are thinner and flatter, providing better cosmesis and comfort.

FRAME AND LENS SELECTION

General guidelines should be kept in mind while selecting frames and lenses.

- High Myopes and Hyperopes should be fit into small, round, fames. Lenses should have a high refractive index.
- You are required to recommend polycarbonate for Children, Firefighters, and Policemen. They should also avoid rimless frames.
- Frames for a Progressive Lens should have a large B measurement and pantascopic tilt.

There are several types of Progressive Lenses which should be recommended in different circumstances.

- **Standard progressive lenses** are the traditional progressive with no specialty design. They will require a larger lens size.
- **Computer progressive lenses** aka Near Variable Focus Lenses are designed for people who spend at least 4 hours per day on the computer. The top of the lens is used for the computer, and the reading portion of the lens is used for reading. They can reduce visual eyestrain.
- **Premium progressive lenses** have a wide channel with reduced peripheral aberrations.
- **Short corridor progressive lenses** have a short channel between the distance and reading prescriptions to allow for a short frame/lens size.
- **Transition progressive lenses** are progressives with the transition coating on them so that they go dark outside and remain clear inside.

INDUCED ASTIGMATISM IN MINUS CYLINDER

Frame fitting which induces astigmatism will also increase astigmatic lens distortions.

- **Face Form Tilt**
  - Minus lenses induce astigmatism along axis 090.
  - Plus lenses induce astigmatism along axis 180.
- **Pantoscopic Tilt**: The bottom of the lens is closer to the face than the top of the lens.
  - Minus lenses induce astigmatism along axis 180.
  - Plus lenses induce astigmatism along 090.
- **Retroscopic Tilt** is the opposite of Pantoscopic Tilt. The top of the lens is closer to the face than the bottom of the lens.

MEASURING HEIGHTS OF BIFOCALS, TRIFOCALS, AND PROGRESSIVE ADDITION LENSES

- Bifocals: measure from the lower lid to the very bottom of the lens.
- Trifocals: measure from the lower edge of the pupil to the very bottom of the lens.
- Progressive Addition Lenses (PALs): measure from the center of the pupil to the very bottom of the lens.

ADJUSTING FRAMES

- If the left lens is higher than the right lens, then the glasses are misaligned. Bend the right temple arm down. This will allow the left lens to fall into place. The opposite is true if the right lens is higher than the left lens.
- To increase Pantoscopic Tilt, increase the angle by bending both temples down. This will effectively lower the lens. Patients who wear Progressive Addition Lenses benefit from increased Pantoscopic Tilt because it brings the add portion of the lens closer to their eye, thereby increasing the reading area. The opposite applies when you decrease Pantoscopic tilt.
- If one lens is closer to the face than the other, then the glasses are misaligned. The temples need to be straightened.
- If the glasses slide down the patient's nose, the glasses need to be fit tighter. Bend down the temple tips, bend in the nose pads, and/or bend in the temples.
- If the glasses touch the patient's cheeks or are sitting too low on the patient's face, raise the frame by narrowing the nose pads or by reducing pantascopic tilt.
- If the glasses are too far away from the patient's face, they need to be brought inwards. Increase face form, expand the bridge, or widen the nose pads. The opposite is true if the glasses are too close to the patient's face.

MAGNIFICATION/MINIFICATION

Increase Magnification	**Increase Minification**
Increase Plus Power	Decrease Plus Power
Increase center thickness	Decrease center thickness
Steepen base curve	Flatten base curve
Increase vertex distance of a plus lens	Increase vertex distance of a minus lens
Decrease vertex distance of a minus lens	Decrease vertex distance of a plus lens

FIELD OF VIEW

As a lens becomes more plus, the Field of View decreases. Conversely, as a lens becomes more minus, the Field of View increases. Also, as the vertex distance increases, the Field of view decreases.

REFLECTANCE AND TRANSMITTANCE

Reflectance refers to how much light is reflected off a lens and therefore does not pass through the lens. Transmittance refers to how much light is allowed to pass through the lens. Here are the relevant equations:

- Reflectance = $[(n_2 - n_1)/(n_2 + n_1)]^2$

- Transmittance of One Surface = 1 – Reflectance
- Total Transmittance = Surface 1 Transmittance * Surface 2 Transmittance * Material Transmittance
    - Notice these are MULTIPLIED!!

PRENTICE'S RULE:

- Induced Prism = distance patient is looking away from the optical center in cm * lens power in diopters
    - aka Δ = dF

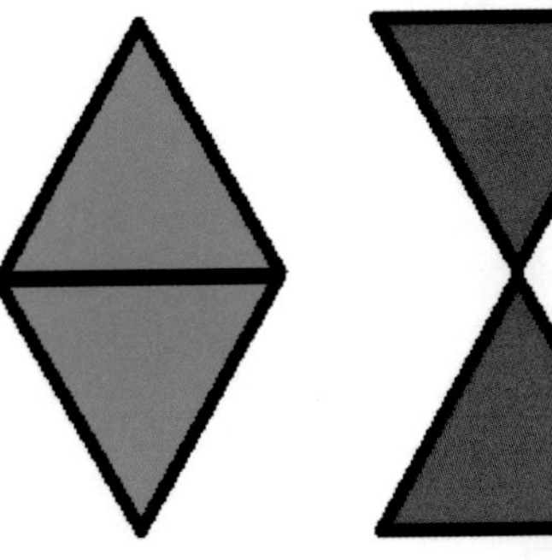

Kimberly Castillo, OD

Imagine that a plus lens is made of two prisms connected at their bases and a minus lens is made of two prisms connected at their apex. Now you can see that if a patient is wearing a plus lens and looks above the optical center, the induced prism will be base down. Meanwhile, if a patient is wearing a minus lens and looks above the optical center, the induced prism will be base up.

Prism Imbalance: When the induced prism has the same base value, then the prism values are subtracted. When the induced prism has opposite base values, then the values are added. With prism imbalance we are looking for the difference between how much each eye is deviated from each other by a prism. When both eyes are being deviated by prism in the same direction, the Prism Imbalance is going to be just the difference in the size of the prism.

- Example: OD 3BU Prism, OS 1BU Prism. Both eyes are being deviated downwards. The difference between how much each eye is being deviated is 2PD.
- Example: OD 3BU Prism, OS 1BD Prism. The eyes are being deviated in opposite directions. The right eye is being deviated downwards and the left eye is being deviated upwards. Therefore, the difference between how much the eyes are being deviated is 4PD.

Ways to compensate for vertical prism imbalance include prescribing contact lenses, prescribing separate distance and reading glasses, using different segment heights between the two lenses, or utilizing slab off prism. Notice that progressive lenses are not a way to compensate for vertical prism imbalance because they will still have induced vertical imbalance.

SLAB OFF PRISM induces BU prism by removing material from the 90 degree meridian of the lower portion of the lens. It is applied to only one lens, that which is the least plus (or most minus) because these lenses tend to have more material available to remove in the periphery and because the most minus lens will induce the most base down prism (which will be compensated for with the BU prism).

IMAGE JUMP

Image Jump occurs when a patient looks from distance into the add power of their lens. Their perceived image may appear to "jump" due to the induced prism of the bifocal segment. It can be calculated using Prentice's Rule based on the add power (F) and type of bifocal (d). These are the distances for three types of bifocals:

- Flat Top 28: 0.50cm
- Executive: 0.00cm
- Round: radius of the round segment in centimeter

CHAPTER 18
PERCEPTUAL FUNCTION / COLOR VISION

The NBEO website states that 6-17 questions will be asked on Perceptual Function / Color Vision. Historically they have asked about 12.6 questions, meaning this chapter covers approximately 4% of the material tested on the exam, or roughly 3 cases. This material is NOT tested on TMOD.

~~~PERCEPTUAL FUNCTION~~~

When light reflects off of the cornea, it will create four different **Purkinje Images:**

Image	Source of Reflection	Intensity	Size	Image Characteristics
I	Anterior cornea	**Brightest**	Small	Virtual, Upright
II	Posterior cornea	Bright	Very Small	Virtual, Upright
III	Anterior lens	Faint	**Largest**	Virtual, Upright
IV	Posterior lens	**Faintest**	**Smallest**	**Real, Inverted**

There are a variety of filters which are used in optometry.

- **Neutral Density Filters** transmit all wavelengths of light. They reduce the amount of light which passes through equally for all wavelengths, and so they do not change color perception. Neutral Density Filters can be used to measure APDs. Neutral Density Filters of increasing intensity are placed over the good eye until the examiner no longer sees the APD.
    - The **Pulfrich Phenomenon** is associated with Neutral Density Filters. The filter is placed over one eye while the patient views a pendulum. When the filter is placed over the right eye, the patient will perceive the pendulum as moving counterclockwise. When the filter is placed over the left eye, the patient will perceive the pendulum as moving clockwise.
- **Broad Band Filters** transmit a large range of wavelengths of light.
- **Narrow Band Filters** transmit a small range of wavelengths of light.
- **Long-Pass Filters** transmit only long wavelengths of light.
- **Blue Blockers** are amber colored and prevent short wavelengths of light from transmitting. They can help patients who have complaints about glare sensitivity.
    - Blue light from a screen can disrupt circadian rhythms/sleep cycles.
- **Interference Filters** transmit only one wavelength of light.

Below are some terms which are associated with Perceptual Function.

- **Spatial Vision** is measured with Visual Acuity and Contrast Sensitivity. It is related to the patient's ability to resolve details.
- **Temporal Vision** is measured with Critical Flicker Fusion Frequency (CFF). It is related to the patient's ability to detect motion. CFF is measured by presenting a flickering light to the patient and increasing the speed of the flashes. When the patient reports that the light no longer appears to flicker, this is said to be their High Temporal Resolution Limit. It is measured in hertz where one cycle/second equals one hertz.
- **Photopic vision** is what we use during the day. It utilizes our cones in order to perceive color and fine details due to its low temporal summation. I associate this system with color by remembering that photos are printed in color. It is not very effective in low light settings.
- **Scotopic vision** utilizes our rods at night to resolve objects during low light situations. It is very sensitive to light because of its high spatial summation. However, this means that it is not ideal for detecting fine details.
- **Mesopic** situations stimulate both Photopic and Scotopic vision. An example would be driving at night.
- The **Parvocellular Pathway** is involved with identifying an object. It is said to be the "what" pathway, is mostly located in the macula, resolves fine detail and contrast sensitivity, and has small receptor fields.
- The **Magnocellular Pathway** is involved with detecting motion. It is said to be the "where" pathway, is located in the temporal retina, does not resolve fine details, and has large receptor fields.
    - The Magnocellular Pathway is used to detect the appearance of an object, and the Parvocellular Pathway is used to identify an object.
- **Kollner's Rule** states that peripheral retinal pathology results in blue/yellow color defects, and optic nerve pathology results in red/green color defects. A notable exception to this rule is glaucoma which is an optic nerve disease which initially presents with blue/yellow color defects, followed by red/green defects.
- **Masking** occurs when one stimulus becomes less visible in the presence of a different stimulus.
- The **Troxler Effect** occurs when an object appears to fade from a patient's vision. This occurs when the retina is presented with the same stimuli for a prolonged period of time. The photoreceptors need a visual variance in order to be stimulated. When they are not presented with a visual variance, they are no longer being stimulated, and so the object appears to fade from their vision. Microsaccades are used to counter the Troxler Effect. They keep the eye moving, and this movement provides visual variance.
- The **Broca-Sulzer Effect** describes that flashes for a duration of 50-100 ms (which is above our threshold) is perceived as being brighter than shorter or longer flash durations. This is associated with providing our photoreceptors with optimal visual variance.
- The **Brucke-Bartley Effect** describes how flickering light appears brighter than steady light. This is because flickering light provides more visual variance to stimulate our photoreceptors.
- The **Stiles-Crawford Effect** describes how perpendicular light rays will appear brighter than those which are not. This is because photoreceptors best collect light from rays which strike them perpendicularly. Photoreceptors will actually orient themselves in order to collect perpendicular light.
- **Phosphenes** are the flashes of light a patient perceives when they rub their eyeballs.
- **Maxwell's Spot** describes how the pigmented macula will absorb blue wavelengths. Therefore, if a patient is looking at a purple light source (which is comprised of red and blue wavelengths), they will see

a red spot in the middle of the light because the macula absorbs blue wavelengths.

- **Blue Arcs of the Retina** are seen when a patient is in a dark room. The blue arcs appear to streak from a light source towards the blind spot.
- **Moore's Lightning Streaks**: When the vitreous syneresis pulls on the peripheral retina it will cause the perception of vertical flashes of light, or "lightning."

CONTRAST SENSITIVITY

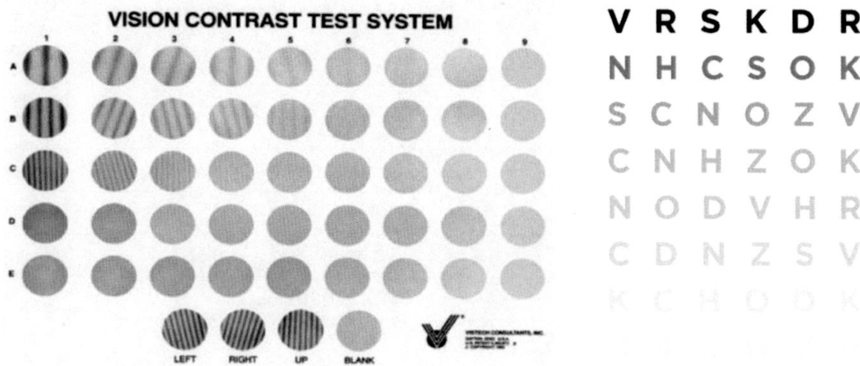

University of Calgary 1 All About Vision 1

Contrast is usually described on a range from 0-1, with 0 being the least contrast and 1 being the most contrast. This can also be represented as a percent, with 100% being the most contrast.

Spatial frequency plays a role in contrast sensitivity. The higher the spatial frequency, the lower the perceived contrast. Cycles/Degree can be converted to Snellen Acuity by dividing the Cycles/Degree by 30. The result is the reduced Snellen Fraction.

- Example: 30 cycles/degree = 30/30, or 1. 20/20 = 1. Therefore, 30 cycles/degree = 20/20.
- Example: 60 cycles/degree = 60/30, or 2. 20/10 = 2. Therefore, 60 cycles/degree = 20/10.
- Example: 15 cycles/degree = 15/30, or 0.5. 20/40 = 0.50. Therefore, 15 cycles/degree = 20/40.

Patients who have optic neuritis may complain of poor vision, but have 20/20 acuity. Their complaints are usually due to loss of contrast sensitivity.

The Snellen Visual Acuity test has virtually 100% contrast. Therefore, contrast sensitivity can be measured with the Vistech Chart/Arden Plate Test (left image) or the Pelli Robson Test (right image).

Patients with loss of contrast sensitivity will benefit from bright lighting and filters.

~~~COLOR VISION~~~

Most of the questions in this chapter will likely be about color vision because it is the most clinically relevant.

Color vision anomalies are typically defined as either congenital or acquired. Congenital anomalies are usually bilateral, symmetrical, red/green, and seen in males. They are X-linked recessive, and so males inherit color vision anomalies from their mothers who are carriers. Approximately 5% of males are affected with color vision anomalies. Acquired anomalies are usually asymmetrical and are associated with pathology.

This table describes the different types of color anomalies:

Anomaly	Deficiency	Pigment
Green Weak	Deutan	Chlorolabe
Red Weak	Protan	Erythrolabe
Blue/Yellow Confusion	Tritan	Cyanolabe
No color perception	Rod Monochromat	Rhodopsin

The Dichromats do not have their respective photopigments and have "nope" as their suffix. Trichromats have all their photopigments, but their perception of color is shifted on the spectrum. Reds will appear very dim to Protanopes but will not appear dim to Deuteranopes.

I remember which photopigment belongs to which deficiency from a story I created which was inspired by *The Little Mermaid.*

- Protan, Erythrolabe, red weak: Arielle is the protagonist, she has red hair, and she has everything in her cave.
- Tritan, Cyanolabe, blue/yellow: King Triton's staff is yellow and swims in the cyan sea.
- Deutan, Chlorolabe, green weak: It is their duty to live among the green coral.

Dichromats may benefit from wearing an X-Chrom contact lens. This is a red contact lens worn over one eye which creates color disparity between the two eyes and shifts the color absorption curve and the color confusion lines towards normal color vision helping the patient distinguish between reds and greens. A variant on this management is the patient can carry a red filter which they can hold over an eye when they need help distinguishing colors.

Achromatopsia/Rod Monochromatism is very rare, and as the name suggests, is defined as a patient who lacks cones. It has an autosomal recessive (AR) inheritance pattern. Since cones are responsible for foveal vision, these patients have a reduced vision of 20/200 or worse. Other signs may include severe photophobia, poor/no color vision, eccentric viewing, pendular nystagmus, a central scotoma, and a normal appearing fundus. Diagnosis should be confirmed with ERG which will show normal rod function but will lack any cone response.

COLOR VISION TESTING

Kimberly Castillo, OD

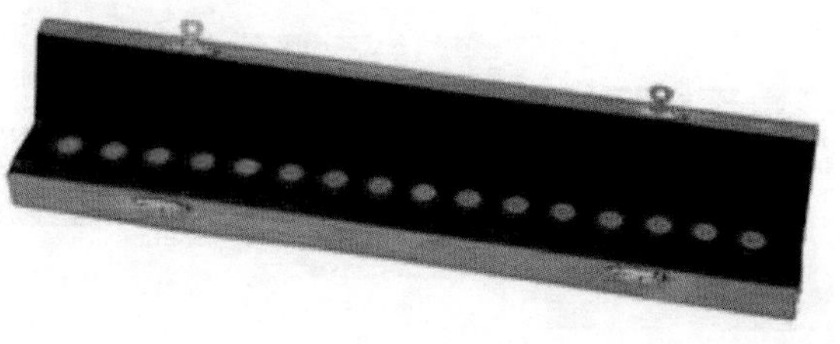

ProTech Ophthalmics 1

Green: 546nm
Red: 670nm
Mixture Field
Test Field
Yellow: 590nm

Kimberly Castillo, OD

There are several methods of measuring color vision, and they are each useful for different reasons. Color vision testing should be performed with a Macbeth Illuminant C lamp or daylight. Testing can be done binocularly to screen for congenital color vision anomalies, or monocularly to screen for acquired color vision anomalies.

- **Ishihara or HRR Plates** (left image) are quick and easy to use and are the most frequently utilized test. They are best at picking up red/green deficiencies because they do not have many blue/yellow plates. They do not distinguish between Deutan and Protan deficiencies. All patients should be able to distinguish the first plate of the Ishihara test.
- **Farnsworth D-15** (middle image) consists of 15 caps which the patient is asked to arrange in order based on their hues. Their results are placed on a graph for interpretation. This test can distinguish between Deutan, Protan, and Tritan defects. Disadvantages include that this test is time consuming and does not distinguish between dichromats and anomalous trichromats.
- The **Nagel Anomaloscope** (right image) is the only color vision test which can distinguish a dichromat from an anomalous trichromat. The patient looks through an eyepiece to view a split field with the yellow Test Field on the bottom and a Red/Green Mixture Field on the top. The patient can adjust the radiance/brightness of the yellow Test Field and the amount of red and green in the Mixture Field. Their goal is to make the top and bottom of the split field look the same. The table below displays the general settings each type of color vision condition will set the Nagel Anomaloscope.

Color Vision Anomaly	Mixture Field (0=green, 73=red)	Test Field
Normal	45	17
Protanope	Mixture Field 73 (Red), Test Field 0. Mixture Field 0 (green), Test Field 87.	
Deuteranope	0-73 looks the same	17
Protanomalous Trichromate	>45 (more red)	10
Deuteranomalous Trichromate	<45 (more green)	17

CHAPTER 19
LOW VISION

The NBEO website states that 6-17 questions will be asked on Low Vision. Historically they have asked about 12.3 questions, meaning this chapter covers approximately 4% of the material tested on the exam, or roughly 3 cases. This material is NOT tested on TMOD.

Definition of **Legal Blindness**:

- Patient's best corrected visual acuity is 20/200 or worse in the better seeing eye. In other words, the patient is unable to read the 20/100 line with their better seeing eye, OR
- Visual field is less than 20 degrees in the better seeing eye.

1M is equal to 20/20 and subtends 5 arcminutes. Newspaper print is 1M at 40cm.

The equation to convert from M-Notation to Snellen-Notation is as follows:

- Test distance / M letter size = 20ft / Snellen letter size

There are two main tests used to measure **distance visual acuity**. Typically the tests are performed at 4, 2, or 1 meters to allow for easy math to convert to Snellen-Notation:

The **Kestenbaum Equation** allows you to estimate the near add a patient will require to read print at 1M (standard print). It states that the inverse of their distance acuity is the estimated near add.

- Example: A patient's BCVA is 20/100.
- Estimated Near Add = 100/20, which is +5.00D.

The equation for determining the distance in centimeters at which a patient needs to hold reading material for clear vision with a given add is Distance = 100 / Add Power. This equation assumes the patient is using no accommodation.

- Example: A patient requires a near add of +5.00
- Distance = 100/5, which is 20cm.

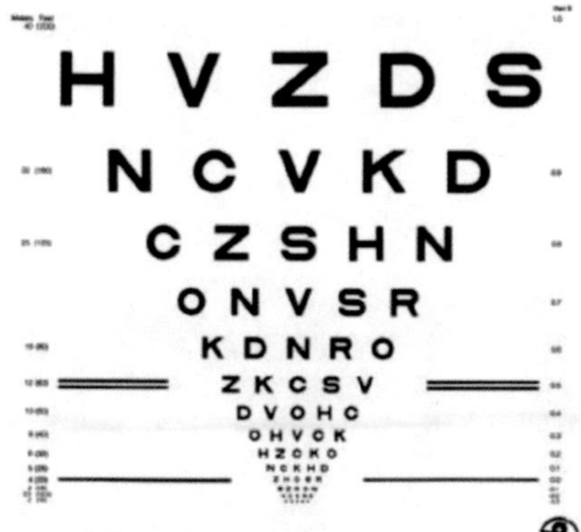

Flicker © Image #7544734768

The **ETDRS** test is expensive and typically used by low vision specialists. Its benefits are that it lights up to provide consistent contrast, it is mobile on wheels so that the examiner can move it to any testing distance, and it has an equal number of letters on each line.

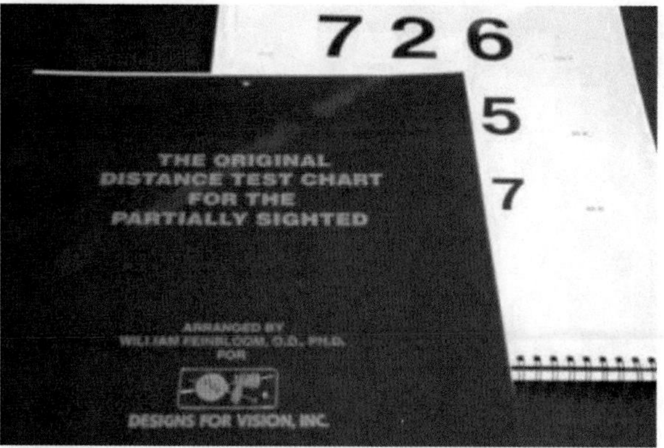

PRCVI 1

The **Feinbloom Chart** is smaller than the ETDRS, less expensive, and so more commonly found in general practices. The examiner holds the chart, walks it to any distance, and flips the pages until the best acuity is attained.

There are three tests which are typically used to measure contrast sensitivity:

University of Calgary 1

VISION CONTRAST TEST SYSTEM

University of Calgary 1

The **Vistech Contrast Sensitivity Chart** utilizes sign waves gratings.

All About Vision 1

The **Pelli-Robson Contrast Sensitivity Chart** is for **distance** testing at 1 meter and utilizes Sloan Letters of the same size with contrast sensitivity reducing after each triplet.

Eye Care and Cure 1

The **Mars Contrast Sensitivity Chart** is for **near** testing at 40 centimeters and utilizes Sloan Letters of the same size.

Art of Optics 1

Patients with low vision may also have increased glare sensitivity, which can be measured with the **Brightness Acuity Test (BAT)**. The patient's acuity is measured while they hold the BAT over the eye which is being measured. If the patient has increased glare sensitivity, like from a cataract, then their BCVA will be reduced during this test.

A patient's **Just Noticeable Difference (JND)** can be calculated by dividing the denominator of their best visual acuity by 100.

- Example: A patient's best visual acuity is 20/200.
- JND = 200/100, which 2.00D.

There are three tests which are used to measure central visual field (VF):

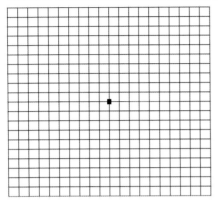

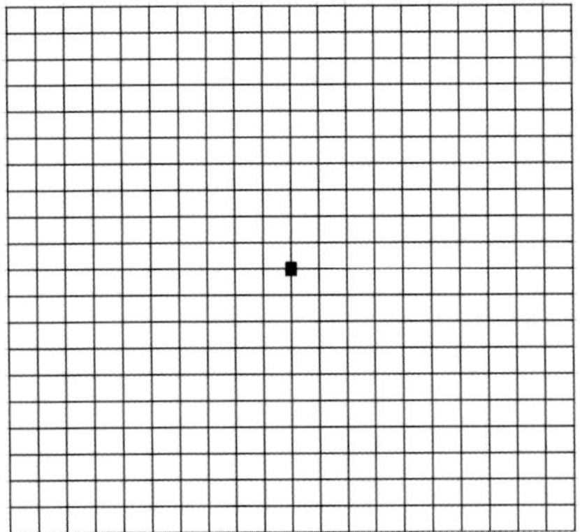

Kimberly Castillo, OD

The **Amsler Grid** is used to measure central scotomas as well as metamorphopsia. It is tested unilaterally. The patient is asked to look at the central dot and to report if any lines are missing or wavy. This test is quick and easy to perform, and is most commonly used in general practice.

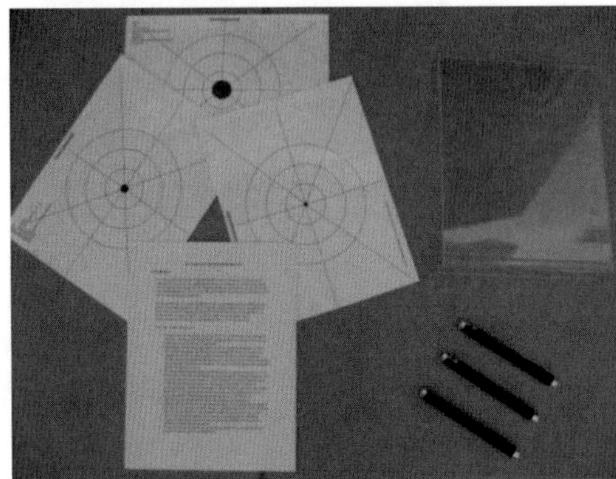

Mattingly Low Vision 1

The **Central California Visual Field Test** can be performed monocularly or binocularly. The patient fixates on a chart while the examiner shines a laser through the chart. This test is considered to be more informative than the Amsler Grid, and is typically used by low vision specialists.

Openi 2

The **Tangent Screen** is used to measure a magnified view of the patient's central visual field. The patient is asked to fixate on the center target while the examiner moves a target from the periphery towards the center. The patient reports when they can first see the target. The VF should be larger when measured at 2 vs. 1 meter. If it is the same size or smaller, this is evidence of malingering.

Keplerian Telescope	**Galilean Telescope**
Positive ocular lens	Negative ocular lens
Positive objective lens	Positive objective lens
Power can be much greater than 4x	Power only up to 4x
Inverted image	Upright image
Exit pupil outside the telescope	Exit pupil inside the telescope
Longer and heavier	Short and light
I remember that the Keplerian Telescope has both a positive ocular and objective lens by thinking that the "K" looks like a distorted "+" sign. I remember that a Galilean Telescope has a negative ocular lens by imagining the horizontal line in the "G" is a "–" sign.	
Telescopes are marked with a set of numbers, which may appear as 4x25. These markings are the magnification (4x) and the objective lens diameter (25mm).	

Exit Pupil

- Exit Pupil Size = diameter of the objective lens in mm / magnification

A **Telemicroscope** is a telescope which is being used for near viewing. Telemicroscopes require the use of a reading cap because they have a high accommodative demand. A reading cap provides an add power to reduce accommodative demand.

- Dioptric Power of Reading Cap Needed = 1 / working distance in cm

When a Reading Cap is added to a telescope, it changes the overall power and magnification of the system, which can be calculated.

- Overall Dioptric Power = Dioptric Power of Reading Cap * Telescope Magnification
- Overall Magnification = Overall Dioptric Power / 4

Magnification

- Telescope Magnification = – (Power of the Ocular Lens / Power of the Objective Lens)
  - Don't forget the negative sign!!
- Distance magnification = current distance BCVA / desired distance BCVA
- Near magnification = (current near BCVA / desired near BCVA) * dioptric power of the working distance
- Relative Distance Magnification = Original Distance / New Distance
- Relative Size Magnification = New object size / Original object size

Low Vision Devices

- Distance Viewing Devices
  - **Hand Held Telescopes** are used for spot viewing distance objects (scoreboard at a sports game).
  - **Center Fit Spectacle Mounted Telescopes** are attached to the patient's glasses and are used for prolonged distance viewing (watching a movie).
  - **Bioptic Telescopes** are mounted to the patient's glasses and are used for spot viewing while driving. Patients must receive thorough training in order to use this device.
- Near Viewing Devices
  - **High Plus Readers** are reading glasses with a high add power. They require BI prism due to their high convergence demand.
    - BI Prism For Each Eye = Dioptric Power of the Lens + 2D
    - Example: Lens Power OD and OS is +8.
    - Prism = 8+2, meaning each eye requires 10BIΔ
  - **Hand Held Magnifiers** DO NOT require the patient to wear a near add, but the patient must learn how to hold the device at the proper working distance. Hand Held Magnifiers are usually used for spot reading (food labels). These are not ideal for patients with hand tremors.
  - A **Collimating Magnifier** is a plus lens with an object placed at its focal point. This setup will create parallel light, and so the patient will not require accommodation (or a near add) in order to view objects with a Collimating Magnifier. When calculating the magnification of a Collimating Magnifier, the distance is assumed to be 25 cm.
    - Magnification = Dioptric Power of the Lens/4
  - **Stand Magnifiers require the patient to wear a near add** because the object is placed within the focal length of the lens. They provide stable viewing, and are used for continuous reading (books). Usually Stand Magnifiers have a reduced field of view. Given that the object is placed within the focal length of the lens, these devices use **Conventional Magnification**.

- Conventional Magnification = (Dioptric Power of the Lens/4) +1

- **Telemicroscopes / Spectacle Mounted Magnifiers** are attached to the patient's glasses to allow for intermediate viewing. These have poor cosmesis and are heavy.
- **CCTV** is an electronic magnifier which consists of a camera, monitor, and moveable table. It can maintain contrast sensitivity and provide magnification without peripheral distortion. Patients without accommodation will require an add to use a CCTV. It utilizes relative size magnification.

CHAPTER 20
VISUAL AND HUMAN DEVELOPMENT

The NBEO website states that 0-6 questions will be asked on Visual and Human Development. Historically they have asked about 5 questions, meaning this chapter covers approximately 2% of the material tested on the exam, or roughly 1 case. The NBEO website states, "Items pertaining to visual and human development may appear in cases in other categories." Meaning, there may not be just one case dedicated to Visual and Human Development. This material is NOT tested on TMOD.

CONGENITAL ANOMALIES

Babies may be born with genetic defects.

- Down's Syndrome (Trisomy 21) is the **most common chromosomal anomaly**. It occurs when patients have three copies of chromosome 21. Patients will have mental retardation, a flat face, prominent epicanthal folds (with possible misdiagnosis for strabismus), and a higher risk for keratoconus due to eye rubbing.
- Edward's Syndrome is trisomy 18. Ocular findings include esotropia, cataract, optic nerve hypoplasia, juxtapapillary coloboma, retinal dysplasia.
- Klinefelter's Syndrome occurs in males who have two X and one Y chromosome (XXY). Ocular findings include microphthalmia, cataracts, and malformed pupils.
- Turner's Syndrome occurs in females who have only one X chromosome (XO). Ocular findings include strabismus and amblyopia.

Infections that affect the baby during gestation can cause birth defects. Very frequently these babies will be born with loss of hearing and mental retardation in addition to ocular anomalies.

- Chickenpox (Varicella and Parvovirus B19): Ocular findings that can occur when the baby is infected with Chickenpox during the first half of the pregnancy include cataracts and Chorioretinitis.
- Cytomegalovirus (CMV): Babies who are infected with CMV may have a low birth weight in addition to chorioretinal lesions. For more about CMV see HIV in Chapter 12.
- Rubella: Ocular findings that can occur when the baby is infected with Rubella during the first trimester include cataracts and retinopathy.
- Toxoplasmosis: Babies typically get infected with Toxoplasmosis when their mother comes into contact with cat feces or undercooked meat while she is pregnant. Toxoplasmosis is caused by the parasite *Toxoplasmosis gondii.* Birth defects may include cataracts, chorioretinal lesions, strabismus, and optic atrophy. For more information, see Toxoplasmosis in Chapter 3.

The mother's health may affect the baby. If the mother is afflicted with the following conditions, there will be outcomes for the baby:

- Diabetes: If the mother's blood sugar runs high, the baby may have a significantly increased birth weight. The increased access to blood sugar will cause the baby to grow faster and be born abnormally large, causing the need for a C-section. Ocular findings may include sectorial optic nerve hypoplasia, and abnormal iris vasculature which will resolve spontaneously by the age of two weeks.
- Preeclampsia: The baby may be born with ocular anomalies if the mother develops Preeclampsia. Preeclampsia is defined as maternal hypertension which develops during the second half of the pregnancy and will resolve post-partum. Babies of these mothers may be born with ocular findings including Retinopathy of Prematurity (ROP), optic nerve head pallor, and retinopathy. For more information see Preeclampsia/Eclampsia is Chapter 3.
- Thyroid Disease: If the mother's thyroid is not stable the baby may have low birth weight, reduced cognitive function, and may be a stillborn. The mother's diet may affect the baby.
- Fetal Alcohol Syndrome (Pictured Right): Alcohol consumption during pregnancy is the leading cause of mental retardation. It can also cause facial abnormalities including a small head, smooth/thin philtrum (upper lip), low nasal bridge, small palpebral fissure, underdeveloped jaw, short nose, and flat midface. This is why expecting mothers are not supposed to drink alcohol.
- Folic Acid Deficiency: If the mother has a folic acid deficiency the baby may be born prematurely with neural tube defects.
- Malnourishment: If the mother is malnourished then the baby will be born with a low birth weight.
- Tobacco: Nicotine is a vasoconstrictor and so it will reduce blood flow to the baby. This may cause the baby to be stillborn, a premature delivery with low birth weight, and increases the risk for sudden infant death syndrome (SIDS).

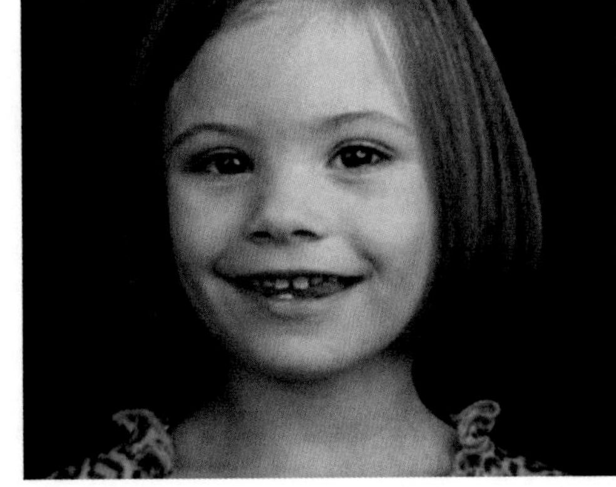
Recovery.org 1

BIRTH

- A full term pregnancy is defined as 40 weeks. The average birth weight is 3400 grams.
- A premature pregnancy occurs when the baby is born at or before 37 weeks.
- Babies who are born weighing <5.5 lbs and/or at <35 weeks gestation are at the highest risk of delays in development.

Birth Weight		
Normal	3400 grams	7.5 lbs
Low Birth Weight	1500-2500 grams	3.3-5.5 lbs
Very Low Birth Weight	1000-1499 grams	2.2-3.4 lbs
Extremely Low Birth Weight	<1000 grams	<2.2 lbs

APGAR SCORE

An infant is assigned an APGAR Score within 5 minutes after birth, and it will be on a scale from 1-10 with 10 being the healthiest. The score will be based on five criteria which comprise the acronym APGAR: Appearance (skin color), Pulse, Grimace (reflex), Activity, and Respiration. Most babies achieve a score of 7 or above, and this is normal. A score of 4-6 indicates the baby needs help breathing, and a score of 1-3 indicates the baby needs emergent lifesaving intervention.

COLOBOMAS

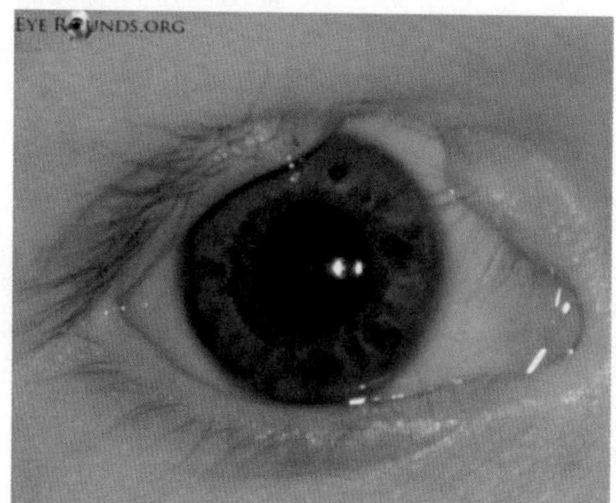

EyeRounds.org University of Iowa

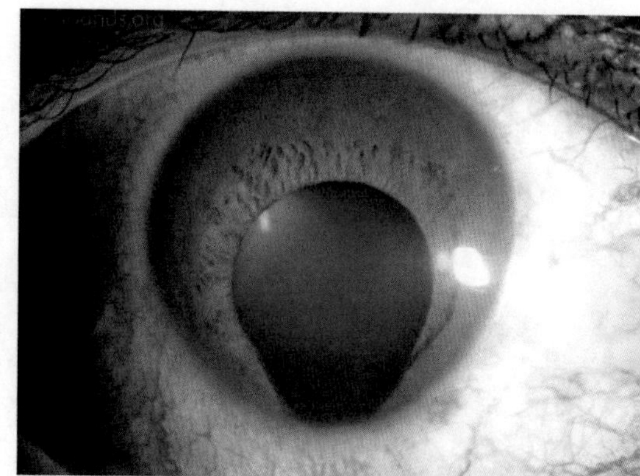

EyeRounds.org University of Iowa

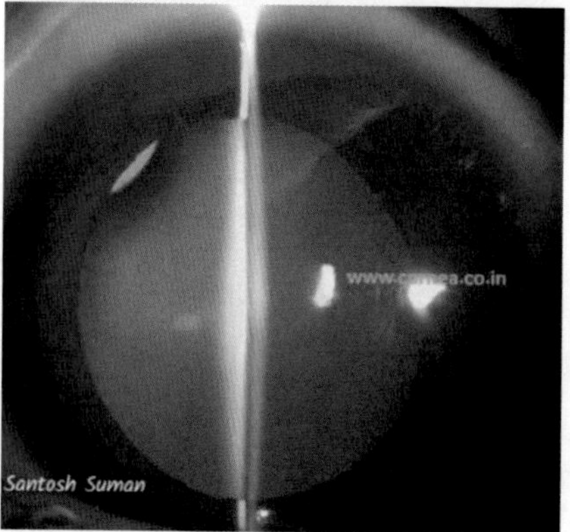

Cornea Eye Hospital 1

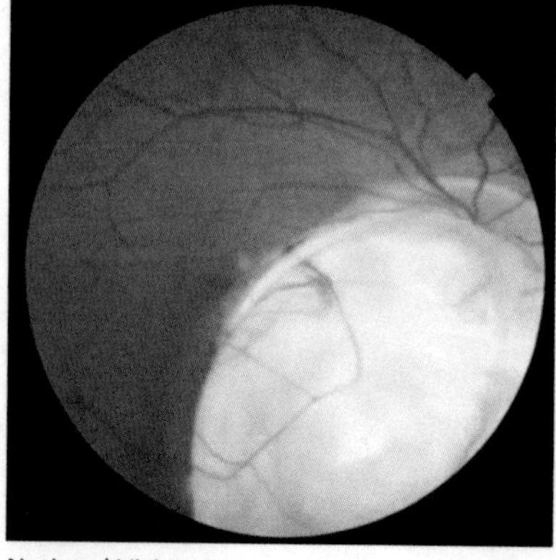

National Vision, Inc.

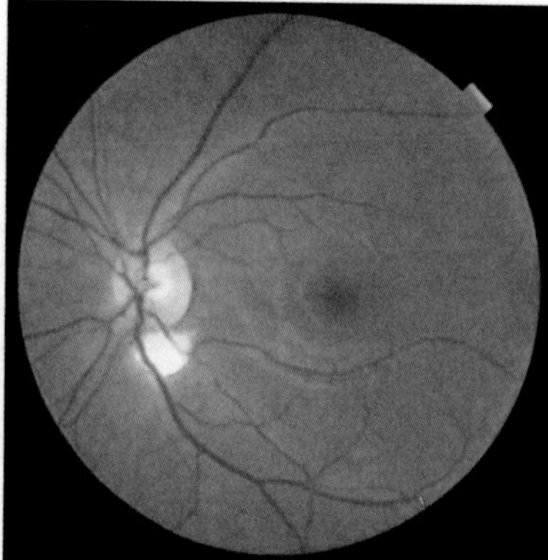

National Vision, Inc.

What to Know: A coloboma is a congenital defect which can be seen in the eyelid, iris, lens, choroid/retina (including the macula), and optic nerve. Multiple colobomas are usually seen in the same patient, and they are frequently comorbid with other systemic conditions. I have divided them into two categories:

1. Eyelid Colobomas are caused by abnormal eyelid development and are usually located superonasally. These are frequently comorbid with iris colobomas. (see top left image)
2. Global Colobomas (a term I created) include all of the other ocular colobomas, which affect the globe of the eye. They are usually located inferonasally and are associated with microphthalmia. The different types of Global Colobomas include iris colobomas (top right image), lens colobomas (bottom left image), retinal/choroid colobomas (bottom middle image), and optic nerve colobomas (bottom right image). Global Colobomas are caused by an incomplete closure of the embryonic fissure. The embryonic fissure begins closing at the equator and closes anteriorly and posteriorly at the same time, with the poles closing last. Meaning, if a lens coloboma is present, an iris coloboma is likely present as well because the iris is located closer to the anterior pole than the lens and so closes later. Furthermore, if a choroid/retinal coloboma is present, an optic nerve coloboma will likely be comorbid because it is closer to the posterior pole. Here is some more information about the specific Global Colobomas:

a. The term "lens coloboma" is a bit of a misnomer because the lens material is present, but the lens zonules are missing (ciliary body coloboma). The lens will look like it is misshapen because the missing zonules are not applying tension to the lens.

b. In the case of a choroid/retinal coloboma, only the glial tissue is present with no underlying RPE or choroid. These patients are at an increased risk for retinal detachments.

Colobomas are associated with **CHARGE Syndrome** which is defined as a collection of findings: Coloboma, Heart conditions, Atresia choana (congenital blockage of the nasal passage), Retarded growth, Genital conditions, and Ear conditions.

Symptoms: Patients will have reduced vision with Global Colobomas and dry eye with Eyelid Colobomas.

Treatment/Management depends on which structure is involved:

- Eyelid: Refer to an oculoplastic surgeon for eyelid reconstruction and use artificial tears for lubrication in the meantime.
- Iris: Treatment is aimed at cosmetics. Fit the patient with prosthetic contact lenses with a painted iris.
- Lens: It is important to correct the patient for refractive error early so as to avoid amblyopia. If this cannot be achieved with glasses or contacts, consider a clear lens exchange.
- Choroid/Retina: Monitor regularly. Treat any retinal detachments which may present themselves and educate the patient to seek immediate attention if they have symptoms of a retinal detachment.

EXPECTED CHILDHOOD MILESTONES/DEVELOPMENT

*Low Yield

- 3 months: The child should be able to lift their head and chest while they are lying on their stomach.
- 4 months: The child should be able to recognize familiar faces and start babbling.
- 6 months: The child should be able to roll over, sit independently, and be able to grasp objects. The child should recognize their caregivers and feel uncomfortable around strangers.
- 9 months: The child should begin to crawl.
- 12 months: The child should begin to walk and should start experiencing separation anxiety. They should be able to say single words.
- 15 months: The child should be able to build a two block tower, throw objects, and turn book pages.
- 18 months: The child should know a few words.
- 2 years: The child should be able to run, climb stairs, build a 6 block tower, scribble, eat independently, and be toilet trained. Hand dominance should be established. They should have a vocabulary of 50 words and be able to combine 2-3 words.
- 3 years: The child should be able to hop, be able to manipulate small objects, and throw a ball 10 feet. They should have a 900 word vocabulary and be able to produce 3-5 word sentences.
- 5 years: The child should be able to copy simple shapes and have a mature pencil grip.
- 6 years: The child should know their right from left. They should be able to build loyal friendships.
- 7 years: The child should be able to hold fluid, elaborate conversations.

BEHAVIORAL ANOMALIES

- Autism is most commonly seen in boys and usually presents itself once the patient has reached the age of three. These patients will have poor intellectual development but may have amazing intellectual gifts. Other signs may include compulsive behavior, social disconnect, and poor language skills. Ocular findings include strabismus, oculomotor deficits, and poor contrast sensitivity.
- Asperger's Syndrome describes a form of Autism in which the patients are highly functional.
- ADHD stands for Attention Deficit Hyperactivity Disorder. These patients have difficulty remining focused.

INDIVIDUALS WITH DISABILITIES EDUCATION ACT (IDEA)

The IDEA Law guarantees everyone will receive a free public education, including those with developmental delays/disabilities. It applies to children ages 3-21.

Children under the age of 3 with developmental disabilities who are not receiving the developmental support they need at home should be referred to **ECI (early childhood intervention)**. Developmentally disabled children ages 3-21 should be referred to the **local school district**.

~~~ CHILDHOOD EYE EXAMS~~~

Children should get eye exams in their first year of life, at 3 years of age, before starting school, and annually thereafter.

EXPECTED OCULAR MILESTONES

Most of the interesting milestones occur at 6 months. I would focus on knowing the milestones at birth, 4-6 months, and 3-5 years.

- Infant: VA 20/400. The child should be able to fixate on a person's face.
- 1 month: VA 20/300. The child should develop binocular alignment and pupil response should be swift.
- 3 months: The child should have coordinated head-eye movements.
- 4 months: VA 20/150. Smooth pursuits, saccades, color vision, and accommodation should be adult-like.
- 6 months: VA 20/50. OKN response becomes symmetric. NPC is to the nose. Stereopsis is present.
- 3 – 5 years: VA 20/20. Contrast sensitivity becomes adult like.

METHODS OF MEASURING VISUAL ACUITY

There are several methods for measuring visual acuity in children. Objective methods are used until the child can respond to subjective methods.

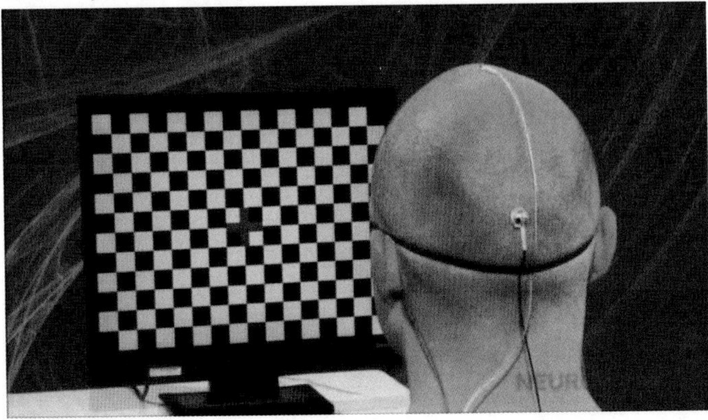

VEP 1

Visual Evoked Potential (VEP): When testing for VEP, the child is connected to electrical diodes which measure the electrical impulses on the scalp over the occipital lobe while the child is being exposed to various visual stimuli. It is the most objective method for measuring visual acuity in children; however, it is rarely used clinically because it is expensive and time consuming.

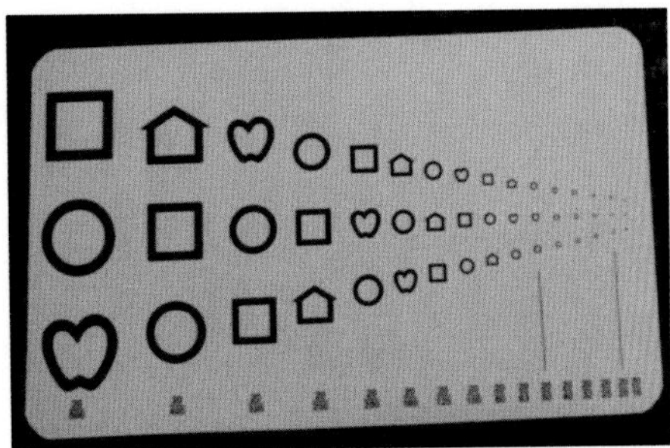

Kimberly Castillo, OD

Visionary 1

Kimberly Castillo, OD

- Lea Symbols (Left Image) are available for both distance and near testing and are well standardized.
- Tumbling E's require the child to have an ability to communicate laterality and directionality which can be hard for them.
- Broken Wheel (Middle Image): Ask the child which car has broken wheels. This is a child-friendly version of the Tumbling C's.
- Allen Figures (Right Image) are not standardized and do not have consistent critical details and so should be avoided.

Perkins 1

Pinterest 2

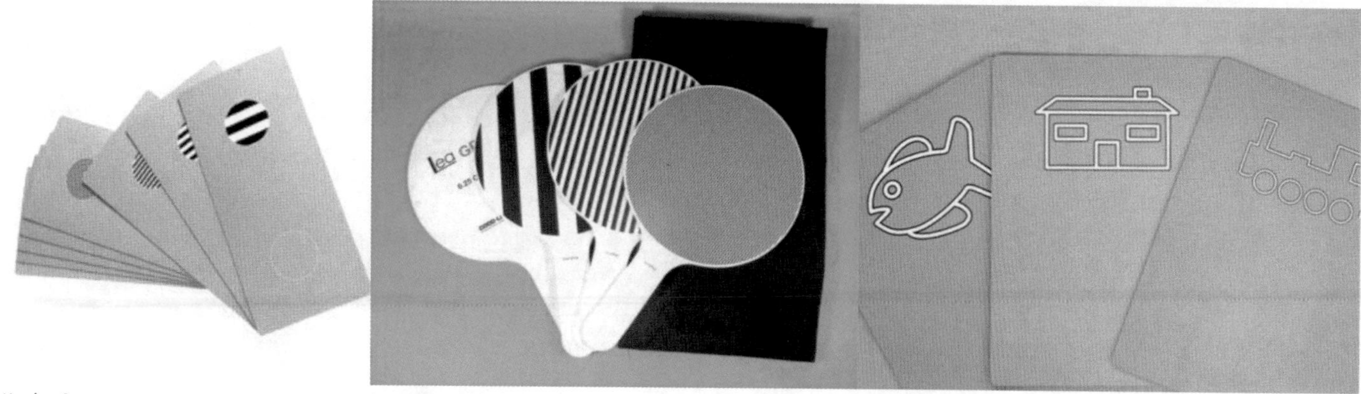

Keeler 2 Low Vision 253300 Akriti 1033

Preferential Looking (PL): PL operates on the assumption that a child would prefer to look at a pattern than a plain stimulus. If a child is presented simultaneously with a plain and a striped image, the child will choose to look at the striped image. There are a few methods of measuring VA in children using this concept:

- Forced-choice PL (FPL): FPL is an objective method for measuring visual acuity in children, but is also expensive and only measures near acuity. (Top left image)
- Teller Acuity Cards have a peep hole so the examiner can hide his/her face and have established age appropriate norms. However, they are large and difficult to transport. (Top right image)
- Keeler Acuity Card is similar to the Teller Acuity Card but the targets are circles instead of squares. (Bottom left image).
- Lea Grating Paddles are the most portable and affordable. However, the examiner's face is not covered and so can be distracting from the intended targets. (Bottom middle image).
- Cardiff Acuity Test (CAT): Contains pictures instead of lines as seen in the other forms of VA testing with Preferential Looking. The pictures provide a more interesting target but the tests are less effective at detecting refractive error. (Bottom right image)

RETINOSCOPY IN CHILDREN

- Mohindra Technique: The child is not dilated and monocularly fixates on a dimmed retinoscope 50 cm away. The exam room is completely darkened. The correction factor for the lens that neutralizes the eye is +0.75 for children under two years of age and +1.25 for children over the age of two.
- Cycloplegic Retinoscopy: The child is dilated during a regular distance retinoscopy exam. This allows the examiner to determine the full amount of hyperopia present in the child, but not the child's normal refractive status. It is the gold standard on all children before the age of 5.

EXPECTED REFRACTIVE ERRORS

Emmetropization is a process where infants are born with a high refractive error which should shift towards Plano by the time the child is 8 years old. However, the majority of the change in refractive error occurs in the first 18 months of life, which is a critical period for visual development. After the age of 8 the child's prescription is expected to change by -0.50D every year until they are a teenager. The average refractive error seen in infants is +2.00D. Below are guidelines of when to prescribe based on age and refractive error:

Age	Myopia	Astigmatism	Hyperopia
<1 year old	Over -5.00	Over -4.00	<2 years old: Over +5.00
1-3 years old	Over -3.00	Over -1.50 oblique or -2.50 ATR or WTR	
3-5 years old	Over -1.00	Over -1.50	>2 years old: Over +3.00
>6 years old	Full	Full	

VISUAL INFORMATION PROCESSING

Visual information Processing refers to how the brain processes information it receives. It can be measured with the Test of Visual Perceptual Skills Test (TVPS Test). It checks seven categories of visual perception:

1. **Visual Discrimination**: Can the patient tell the difference between two similar, but different objects?
2. **Visual Memory:** Can the patient remember details of an image they have seen?
3. **Spatial Relationships**: Can the patient discern the distance and orientation objects are from each other?
4. **Form Constancy**: Can the patient recognize an object is the same thing even if it is positioned differently or a different size?
5. **Sequential Memory**: Can the patient remember the order in which objects are lined up?
6. **Figure Ground**: Can the patient distinguish objects from a cluttered background? Think of *Where's Waldo* and *I Spy*.
7. **Visual Closure**: Can the patient visually complete an unfinished drawing? See image to the right. The patient must be able to visually connect the lines in order to appreciate the image of a cloud with lightning bolt.

Kimberly Castillo, OD

There are three types of **Visual-Spatial Orientation.**

1. **Directionality**: Can the patient identify right and left in their environment?
2. **Laterality**: Can the patient identify their own right and left?
3. **Bilateral integration**: Is the patient able to use both the right and left sides of their body at the same time?

TESTS OF OCULAR MOTILITY

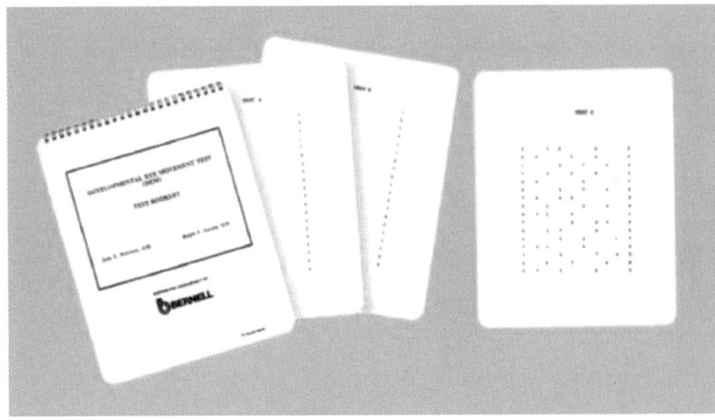

Science Direct 1

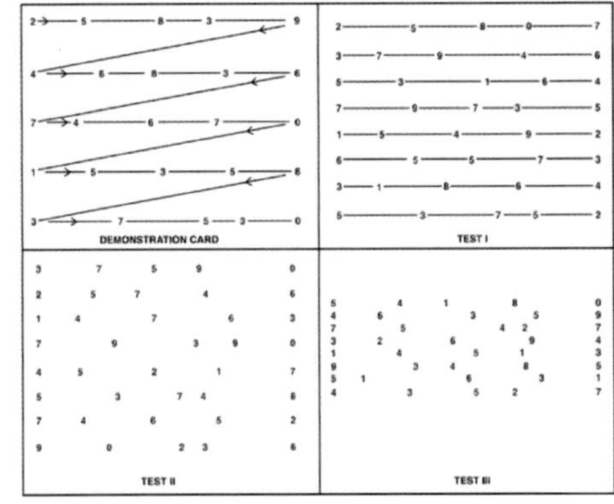

Topend Sports 1

- **DEM (Development Eye Movement)** tests saccades (left picture). The patient's vertical vs. horizontal times for reading the test are compared as a ratio. The lower the ratio, the better the patient performed. Patients can be categorized by one of four types.
  - TYPE I: Normal performance with a low ratio.
  - TYPE II: Reduced horizontal time compared to vertical time, indicating an oculomotor dysfunction. These patients will have a high ratio score.
  - TYPE III: Increased horizontal and vertical times giving rise to a low/normal ratio. These patients do not have on ocular motility condition. Instead, they have poor automaticity. In other words, they have difficulty processing and naming numbers.

- TYPE IV: Combination of Types II and III.

- **King-Devick** tests saccades (right picture). It is usually used as a quick way to determine if a patient has a concussion. The only catch is that the test must be done prior to the suspected concussion as a baseline. King-Devick is mostly used on football teams. At the beginning of the season the players take the test for baseline and then it is utilized if they have an injury.
- **NSUCO** tests both saccades and smooth pursuits. For saccades the patient is asked to look back and forth between two points on command. The examiner looks to see if the patient has accurate saccadic motion or if they have under/over shooting. For pursuits the patient is asked to track a target doing rotations and the examiner evaluates to see if the patient is able to track smoothly and accurately.
  - **Saccadic Suppression:** During saccades the brain momentarily suppresses both eyes to prevent the perception of objects moving.
- **Wold Sentence Copy Test** is a oculomotor test. The patient is given a minute to copy a sentence as fast as possible. The examiner makes analysis of how easily and accurately the patient performed the task.
- **Readalyzer/Visagraph** objectively records eye movements using an infra-red sensor. The patient wears goggles with the sensor, reads a passage, and is then asked comprehension questions. The Readalyzer/Visagraph can give a playback of where the eyes were looking during the test to give direct feedback as to how the patient's eyes are moving while reading.

DEVELOPMENTAL TESTS

- The **Denver II Developmental Screening Test (DDST)** is designed to evaluate general development in children up to the age of six. It evaluates four categories of development:
  - Language: Does the patient verbalize at an age-appropriate level?
  - Fine Motor: Can the patient manipulate small objects?
  - Gross motor: Can the patient crawl, walk, run, jump, etc at an age appropriate level?
  - Social Skills: Does the patient respond appropriately to his/her environment? Examples are smiling, responding when spoken to, showing appropriate emotions for the situation.
- The **Developmental Test of Visual Perception (DTVP-3)** is used to assess children ages 4-12.
  - The test covers five main categories:
    - **Eye-Hand Coordination:** Can the child precisely draw straight and round lines?
    - **Copying**: Can a child copy/draw a specific picture?
    - **Figure-Ground**: Can the patient distinguish objects from a cluttered background?
    - **Visual Closure**: Can the patient visually complete an unfinished drawing? See image to the right. The patient must be able to visually connect the lines in order to appreciate the image of a cloud with lightning bolt.
    - **Form Constancy**: Can the patient recognize an object is the same thing even if it is positioned differently or a different size?

Kimberly Castillo, OD

  - These five categories are then analyzed to create three composite scores:
    - **Visual-Motor Integration** which includes Eye-Hand Coordination and Copying.
    - **Motor Reduced Visual Perception** which includes Figure-Ground, Visual Closure, and Form Constancy.
    - **General Visual Perception** combines all five categories.
- The **Test of Visual Motor Skills** evaluates fine motor skills while copying a design. The patient copies 39 different designs, and are graded based on nine types of possible errors:

    - Incorrect Closures
    - Incorrect Angles
    - Line Quality
    - Line Lengths
    - Line Connections
    - Modification of Size or Part
    - Addition or Deletion of a Part
    - Rotation or Reversal
    - Shape Overlap Error
- The **BEERY-VMI Developmental Test of Visual-Motor Integration** is aptly named, for it check for difficulties with Visual-Motor Integration in children ages 2-18. The child will copy 24 different shapes. There are also two supplemental tests which can be administered based on the examiner's discretion:
    - Visual Perception
    - Motor Coordination
- The **Motor-Free Visual Perception Test** is designed to assess visual perception independent of motor ability.

CHAPTER 21
LEGAL ISSUES / ETHICS

The NBEO website states that 5-6 questions will be asked on Legal Issues / Ethics. Historically they have asked about 5.6 questions, meaning this chapter covers approximately 2% of the material tested on the exam. This material is NOT tested on TMOD. The NBEO website states that these topics will be tested under Legal Issues / Ethics: "licensure and governmental regulation of optometry, standards of professional ethics, doctor-patient relationship, professional liability."

DOCTOR-PATIENT RELATIONSHIP

The **Federal Patient's Bill of Rights** includes:

- Patients should be able to choose their providers in order to guarantee they receive quality healthcare.
- Patients should receive accurate, easily understood information so that they can make informed healthcare decisions.
- Patients have the right to actively participate in decisions regarding their healthcare. If the patient is unable to make decisions, they have the right to be represented by family or a guardian.
- Patients should be able to trust that their healthcare provider will follow HIPAA and protect their identifiable health information.
- **Patients are required to make a good faith effort to pay for their medical care.**

Informed Consent includes:

- The provider is required to explain the diagnosis/problem.
- The provider is required to explain the treatment/management for the diagnosis/problem.
- The provider is required to describe both the possible risks and benefits of the proposed treatment/management.
- The provider is also required to describe alternative treatment options for the diagnosis/problem.
- A surrogate or guardian can give consent for a patient who is a child or who does not have the mental capacity to make informed decisions.
- A provider is **NOT** required to always obtain signed consent from the patient.

Optometrists must release a spectacle prescription to the patient whether or not there has been a change in the prescription.

STANDARDS OF PROFESSIONAL ETHICS

During a job interview you cannot ask the interviewee about their religion, race, sex, disability, marital/family status, birthplace, or age. You CAN ask them why the left/are leaving their prior employment.

It is not ethical to make derogatory comments about your colleagues.

Ownership of Patient Records

- Optometrists are required to keep thorough records of all their patients.
- Patients have a right to view and obtain copies of their medical records, but they do not own their medical records. Doctors can withhold release of the records until the patient initiates some payment for services rendered.
- Regarding when a doctor leaves a practice:
  - All partners in a practice have joint legal ownership of all patient records, even for patients who they have not managed.
  - Independent contractors have legal ownership of patient records for only patients who they managed.
  - Employees have no legal ownership to any of the patient records.

PROFESSIONAL LIABILITY

It is the responsibility of an optometrist to train their staff to properly triage phone calls. If a staff member does not schedule an emergent appointment appropriately and the patient permanently loses their vision or dies before their appointment, then the doctor is responsible.

Important Terms:

- **Autonomy**: Patients have a right to make their own decisions
- **Beneficence**: helping others. Beneficence sounds like "benefit," and others benefit when you help them.
- **Good Samaritan Law**: Protects any person who tries to provide healthcare during an emergency when they are not obligated to help. It protects the Good Samaritan from being liable for any poor outcomes from their help.
- **Justice**: Equal treatment of similar cases and fair distribution of goods and services.
- **Medical Tribunal System**: A system which decides if a claim has merit or enough evidence to proceed as a lawsuit.
- **Nonmaleficence**: Providers should "do no harm." I remember this is the definition by thinking "maleficence" reminds me of Maleficent, the antagonist in *Sleeping Beauty*, who was evil. "Non" is no. So breaking down this word is No-Evil, or do no harm.
- **Punitive Damages**: Fines/Damages designed to punish an optometrist for terrible patient care.
- **Statute of Limitations**: The maximum time parties have to initiate legal action.
- **Tort Reform**: Caps/limits the fines/damages that may be awarded during lawsuits.

LICENSURE AND GOVERNMENTAL REGULATION OF OPTOMETRY

HIPAA is designed to preserve the patient's right to privacy.

- If a provider wants to freely disclose and discuss medical information, they must remove all the patient's identifying information. This Protected Health Information (PHI) includes 18 identifiers:
    1. Patient's Name
    2. Account Number
    3. Social Security Number
    4. Health Plan Beneficiary Number
    5. Email Address
    6. Certificate/License Numbers
    7. Phone Number
    8. Vehicle Identifiers (VIN, License Plate Number)
    9. Medical Record Number
    10. Internet Protocol Address Numbers
    11. Full Face Picture
    12. Device Identifiers And Serial Numbers
    13. Fax Number
    14. URL's
    15. Address
    16. Biometric Identifiers
    17. Date of Birth
    18. Any other unique identifying code, number, or characteristic.
- HIPAA only applies to Health Care Providers, Plans, and Clearinghouses.
- Exceptions to HIPAA
    - Providers can share medical information with the patient's friends and family with the patient's consent.
    - Providers can share medical information in order to collect payment from an insurance company or other payer.
    - Providers can report an epidemic to a government agency which tracks outbreaks.

CONTACT LENS LAWS

- A contact lens prescription must be released to the patient after the fitting is completed regardless of if the patient requests the prescription.
- A contact lens prescription must be valid for at least one year unless there is a medical indication for a sooner expiration date.
- Contact Lenses can be prescribed by optometrists, ophthalmologists, and opticians depending on state laws.
- A third party seller of contact lenses is required to verify the contact lens prescription. Once contacted, an optometrist has 8 business hours to verify the prescription. If the optometrist does not respond to the request within the 8 hours, this is considered "passive verification" and the third party seller can fill the contact lens prescription. Regarding HIPAA, this verification is required for treatment, and so the optometrist does not need to get permission from the patient to release this medical information.

Stark Law: Optometrists are prohibited from referring a Medicare/Medicaid patient to a doctor who is their family or with whom they have a financial relationship.

Rules regarding referrals:

- The optometrist should know that the specialist they refer the patient to is competent to treat the patient.
- When making a referral, the optometrist should provide the patient's medical history information.
- It is illegal for optometrists to receive a kickback/money for making a referral in many states.
- Specialists do not have to send patients back to the referring optometrist. In other words, specialists are allowed to steal patients from the referring optometrist.
- Optometrists are NOT responsible for the patient's treatment after they have made the referral.

Antitrust Laws are intended to maintain the free market economy and thereby protect consumers.

- Optometrists are not allowed to engage in price-fixing by collaborating to set their fees. Each office must independently set their own fees.
- Optometrists cannot join forces to boycott a specific supplier or business.

APPENDIX

Clinical Correlations

Causes of **Angioid Streaks** can be remembered with PEPSI: Pseudoxanthoma Elasticum, Ehlers Danlos, Paget's, Sickle Cell Disease, Idiopathic.

Causes of **blue sclera** include Minocycline, Ehlers Danlos Syndrome, Rheumatoid Arthritis, and Scleritis.

Causes of exudative retinal detachments include Central Serous Retinopathy, VKH Syndrome, Optic Pits, Morning-Glory Syndrome, and Coats Disease.

Causes of **bull's eye maculopathy** can include Chloroquine, Hydroxychloroquine, Progressive Cone Dystrophy, Stargardt's Disease, and Thioridazine.

Causes of **keratoconus** (which looks like a cone of the cornea), include Down's Syndrome, Ehlers Danlos Syndrome, Marfan's Syndrome, Osteogenesis Imperfecta, and Turner Syndrome.

Causes of **Lens Subluxation** include blunt trauma, Marfan's Syndrome, Homocystinuria, Ectopia Lentis et Pupillae, Hyperlysinemia, Microspherophakia, Sulfite Oxidase Deficiency, and Simple Ectopia Lentis.

Causes of **macular thickening** may include chronic intraocular inflammation, intraocular surgery, intraocular tumor, BRVO, best's disease, retinitis pigmentosa, and neuroretinitis. Rhegmatogenous retinal detachments do **NOT** cause macular thickening.

Causes of **Nyctalopia** include Thioridazine Retinopathy, Retinitis Pigmentosa, Gyrate Atrophy, Enhanced S-Cone Syndrome/Goldmann-Favre Syndrome, and Choroideremia.

Causes of **papillae** include allergies, bacteria, and idiopathic.

Causes of **photophobia** include albinism, aniridia, aphakia/pseudophakia, cataracts, macular degeneration, and retinitis pigmentosa.

Causes of **Cystoid Macular Edema (CME)** can be remembered with the DEPRIVENS mnemonic: Diabetes,

Epinephrine, Pars Planitis, Retinitis Pigmentosa, Irvine-Gass, Vein Occlusion, E2-prostaglandin, Nicotinic acid and Niacin, and surgery.

Both Unilateral and Bilateral swollen nerves can be caused by Sarcoidosis, TB, Syphilis, and Lupus. Causes of **premature/early cataracts** include Atopic Dermatitis, Diabetes, Myotonic Dystrophy, Trauma, and Wilson's Disease.

Differentials for swollen nerves can be categorized based on if the swelling is unilateral or bilateral.

- Unilateral swollen nerves (papillitis) is caused due to complications anterior to the optic chiasm:
    - Vascular (Diabetes, Central Retinal Vein Occlusions)
    - Ischemic (NAION, AION)
    - Compressive (Thyroid)
    - Optic Disc Drusen
- Bilateral swollen nerves (papilledema) is caused by increased intracranial pressure.
    - Hypertension
    - Idiopathic Intracranial Hypertension
        - This is caused by Accutane, Idiopathic, Nalidixic Acid, Oral Contraceptives, Tetracyclines, and Vitamin A.

Causes of **Pseudotumor Cerebri** include Accutane, Idiopathic, Nalidixic Acid, Oral Contraceptives, Tetracyclines, and Vitamin A.

Causes of retinal **neovascularization** and subsequent tractional retinal detachments include diabetic retinopathy, ocular ischemic syndrome, retinopathy of prematurity, sickle cell retinopathy, and vein occlusions.

Causes of **transillumination defects** include pigment dispersion syndrome, pseudoexfoliation syndrome, albinism, herpetic uveitis, trauma, and PCIOL intraocular surgery.

Causes of **whorl keratopathy** include Amiodarone, Chloroquine, Hydroxychloroquine, Fabry's Disease, Indomethacin, and Tamoxifen.

Causes of hypopyon include Bechet's Disease, VKH Syndrome, Endophthalmitis, Bacterial Keratitis, and Blebitis. Retinoblastoma may cause a pseudohypopyon.

Bacteria which can invade the intact corneal epithelium include *Corynebacterium diphtheria*, *Haemophilus*, *Listeria*, *Neisseria gonorrhea*, and *Pseudomonas aeruginosa*.

Risk Factors for retinal breaks include high myopia, lattice degeneration, aphakia/pseudophakia, and trauma.

The diseases which are associated with HLA-B27 include Ankylosing Spondylitis, Inflammatory Bowel Disease, Crohn's Disease, Ulcerative Colitis, Psoriatic Arthritis, and Reiter's Syndrome (Reactive Arthritis).

Drugs which cause NAION include Amiodarone, Imitrex, Vardenafil , and Viagra.

Practice Questions

CASE 1

Demographics
48 year-old Hispanic male; sales manager
Chief Complaint
Patient is here for an annual eye exam.
History Of Present Illness
Character/Signs/Symptoms: Patient is having trouble reading small print on his phone.
Location: both eyes
Severity: moderate
Nature Of Onset: gradual
Duration: slowly getting worse over two years
Frequency: whenever he is looking at his phone
Exacerbations/Remissions: none
Relationship To Activity Or Function: worse in low light settings
Accompanying Signs/Symptoms: headaches when he uses his phone for too long
Secondary Complaints/Symptoms none

Patient Ocular History
unremarkable (last comprehensive eye exam was 15 years ago)
Family Ocular History
Mother: cataracts
Father: unremarkable
Patient Medical History
unremarkable (last physical exam 20 years ago)
Medications Taken By Patient
None
Patient Allergy History
NKDA
Family Medical History
Mother: diabetes
Father: unremarkable

Review Of Systems
Constitutional/General Health: denies
Ear/Nose/Throat: denies
Cardiovascular: denies
Pulmonary: denies
Endocrine: denies
Dermatological: denies
Gastrointestinal: denies
Genitourinary: denies
Musculoskeletal: denies
Neurologic: denies
Psychiatric: denies
Immunologic: denies
Hematologic: denies

Mental Status
Orientation: oriented to time, place, and person.
Mood: appropriate
Affect: slow

Clinical Findings
Habitual Rx: none
Entering Acuities:
OD Distance 20/20- Near 20/70
OS Distance 20/20 Near 20/70
Manifest Refraction:
OD: +0.75 DS Add +1.25; VA distance 20/20, VA near 20/20
OS: +0.50 DS Add +1.25; VA distance 20/20, VA near 20/20
Amplitude of Accommodation: 3D
Pupils: PERRL, negative APD
EOMs: full, no restrictions OU
Confrontation Fields: full to finger counting OD, OS
Slit lamp
Lids/lashes/adnexa: unremarkable OD, OS
Conjunctiva: pinguecula OD, OS
Cornea: clear OD, OS
Anterior chamber: deep and quiet OD, OS
Iris: normal OD, OS
Lens: yellow OD, OS
Vitreous: clear OD, OS

IOPs: 16 mmHg OD; 16 mmHg OS via applanation tonometry @ 4:10 p.m.
Fundus OD
See Image 1

Fundus OS
See Image 2
Blood Pressure: 222/125 right arm, sitting
Pulse 71 bpm, regular

Image 1

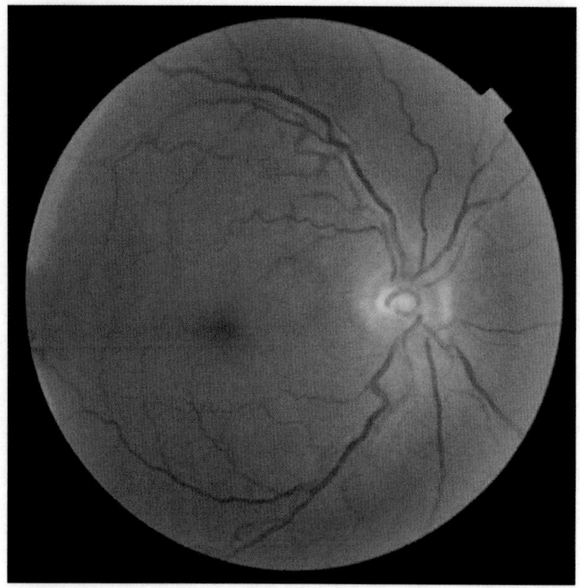

National Vision, Inc.

Image 2

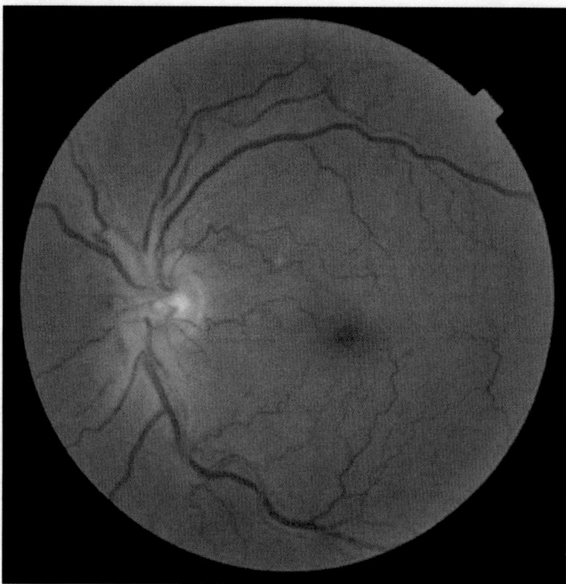

National Vision, Inc.

1. What is the MOST LIKELY diagnosis of the above patient's retinal condition?
    a) Interferon Retinopathy
    b) Venous Stasis
    c) Diabetic retinopathy
    d) HIV Retinopathy
    e) Malignant hypertensive retinopathy
2. What is the BEST treatment for the patient's retinal condition?
    a) Refer the patient for a non-urgent physical examination.
    b) Refer the patient for emergent reduction of high blood pressure.
    c) Refer the patient for a carotid Doppler.
    d) Refer the patient for panretinal laser photocoagulation.
    e) Refer the patient for adjustment of HIV medication
    f) No treatment is necessary.
3. IF the patient's retinal condition was unilateral, what should you suspect?
    a. Venous Stasis
    b. Ocular Ischemic Syndrome
    c. Central Retinal Artery Occlusion
    d. Central Retinal Vein Occlusion
    e. Carotid artery obstruction

4. This patient is at greatest risk for which of the following?
    a. Heart attack
    b. Loss of visual field
    c. Opportunistic infection
    d. Rubeosis Iridis
    e. Hyperglycemia
5. What is the BEST management for this patient's chief complaint?
    a) Release manifest refraction for full time wear.
    b) Release a prescription for reading glasses only
    c) Release a prescription for distance glasses only
    d) Recheck the refraction after the patient's retinal condition has stabilized
    e) The patient does not need glasses.

CASE 2

Demographics
60 year-old Caucasian male; retired army officer
Chief Complaint
Blurry vision at both distance and near
History Of Present Illness
Character/Signs/Symptoms: Patient is having trouble reading street signs and menus in restaurants.
Location: both eyes
Severity: mild
Nature Of Onset: gradual
Duration: slowly getting worse over the last year
Frequency: constant
Exacerbations/Remissions: none
Relationship To Activity Or Function: worse in low light settings
Accompanying Signs/Symptoms: none
Secondary Complaints/Symptoms: Difficulty driving at night due to glare from oncoming headlights.

Patient Ocular History
Herpes Simplex infection OD 5 years ago, resolved
Posterior Vitreous Detachment 15 years ago
Patient was punched in one eye 48 years ago. He does not remember which eye.
Family Ocular History
Mother: cataracts
Father: macular degeneration
Patient Medical History
high cholesterol
Medications Taken By Patient
Atorvastatin
Patient Allergy History
NKDA
Family Medical History
Mother: unremarkable
Father: high cholesterol

Review Of Systems
Constitutional/General Health: denies
Ear/Nose/Throat: denies
Cardiovascular: high cholesterol
Pulmonary: denies
Endocrine: denies
Dermatological: denies
Gastrointestinal: denies
Genitourinary: denies
Musculoskeletal: denies
Neurologic: denies
Psychiatric: denies
Immunologic: denies
Hematologic: denies
Mental Status
Orientation: oriented to time, place, and person.
Mood: appropriate
Affect: appropriate
Clinical Findings
Habitual Rx:
OD: -3.00 -1.00 x095 Add +1.75; VA distance 20/30-, VA near 20/40
OS: -2.75 -0.50 x105 Add +1.75; VA distance 20/40, VA near 20/40
Manifest Refraction:
OD: -3.75 -1.00 x095 Add +2.25; VA distance 20/20, VA near 20/20
OS: -3.75 -0.50 x105 Add +2.25; VA distance 20/20, VA near 20/20
Pupils: PERRL, negative APD
EOMs: full, no restrictions OU
Confrontation Fields: full to finger counting OD, OS
Slit lamp
Lids/lashes/adnexa: unremarkable OD, OS
Conjunctiva: clear OD, OS
Cornea: arcus OD, OS
Anterior chamber: deep and quiet OD, OS
Iris: normal OD, OS

Lens: clear OD, OS
Vitreous: Posterior Vitreous Detachment OD, OS
IOPs: 25 mmHg OD; 26 mmHg OS via GAT @ 9:00 a.m.
Fundus OD
C/D: 0.70H/ 0.70V
Macula: normal
Posterior pole: unremarkable
Periphery: unremarkable
Fundus OS
C/D: 0.80H/0.80V
Macula: normal
Posterior pole: unremarkable
Periphery: unremarkable
Blood Pressure: 123/82 right arm, sitting
Pulse 71 bpm, regular

Image 1

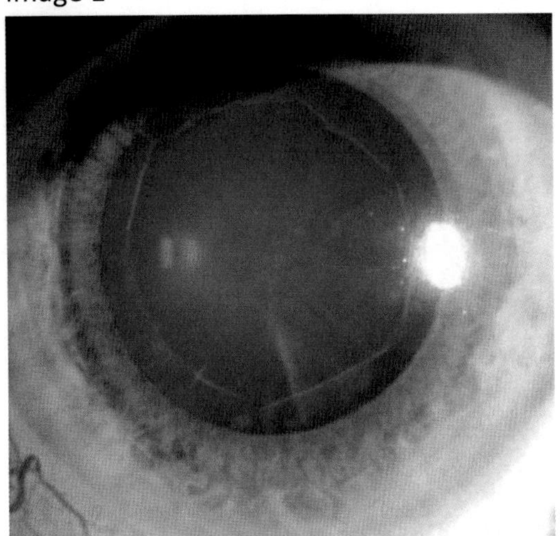

EyeRounds.org University of Iowa

6. Which of the following is another sign you would expect to see with this patient?
   a) Exfoliative Material in the Trabecular Meshwork
   b) Cataracts
   c) Krukenberg Spindle
   d) Broadened Ciliary Body Band
   e) None of the above
7. What is a possible complication for this patient based on the anterior segment findings? (SELECT THREE)
   a) Iridodonesis
   b) Acute Angle Closure
   c) Fluctuating IOP's
   d) Rosette Cataracts
   e) Photophobia
8. What is the MOST LIKELY cause of the patient's increased IOPs?
   a) Primary Open Angle Glaucoma
   b) Ocular Hypertension
   c) Exfoliative Glaucoma
   d) Pigmentary Glaucoma
   e) Angle Recession Glaucoma

9. Which of these is the BEST treatment option for the patient's increased IOPs?
    a) Prescribe Timolol BID
    b) Prescribe Latanoprost QHS
    c) Refer the patient for cataract surgery
    d) Recommend Artificial Tears QID
    e) Monitor every three months
10. Which of the following is a relative contraindication for cataract surgery?
    a) Diabetes
    b) Medical history of Flomax
    c) Fuch's Endothelial Dystrophy
    d) Pseudoexfoliation Syndrome
    e) All of the above

CASE 3

Demographics
26 year-old Hispanic female; maid
Chief Complaint
Patient complains of painful right eye.
History Of Present Illness
Character/Signs/Symptoms: Pain, redness, photophobia, tearing, difficulty opening right eye.
Location: right eye
Severity: severe
Nature Of Onset: Acute onset when she accidentally spilled bleach in her eye while working.
Duration: 2 hours
Frequency: constant. This is the first occurrence.
Exacerbations/Remissions: none
Relationship To Activity Or Function: none
Accompanying Signs/Symptoms: none
Secondary Complaints/Symptoms none

Patient Ocular History
unremarkable
Family Ocular History
Mother: cataracts
Father: cataracts
Patient Medical History
unremarkable
Medications Taken By Patient
None
Patient Allergy History
Seasonal, pollen
Family Medical History
Mother: hemorrhoids
Father: GERD

Review Of Systems
Constitutional/General Health: denies
Ear/Nose/Throat: denies
Cardiovascular: denies
Pulmonary: denies
Endocrine: denies
Dermatological: denies
Gastrointestinal: denies
Genitourinary: denies
Musculoskeletal: denies
Neurologic: denies
Psychiatric: denies
Immunologic: denies
Hematologic: denies

Mental Status
Orientation: oriented to time, place, and person.
Mood: anxious
Affect: appropriate

Clinical Findings
Habitual Rx: none
Entering Acuities:
OD Distance 20/200
OS Distance 20/20
Pupils: PERRL, negative APD
EOMs: full, no restrictions OU
Confrontation Fields: Unable to assess due to patient cooperation OD, OS
Slit lamp
Lids/lashes/adnexa: unremarkable OD, OS
Conjunctiva: See Image 1 OD, clear OS
Cornea: See Image 1 OD, clear OS
Anterior chamber: deep and quiet OD, OS
Iris: flat and intact OD, OS
Lens: clear OD, OS
Vitreous: clear OD, OS
IOPs: 22 mmHg OD; 18 mmHg OS via GAT @ 3:00 p.m.
Blood Pressure: 119/75 right arm, sitting
Pulse 71 bpm, regular

Image 1

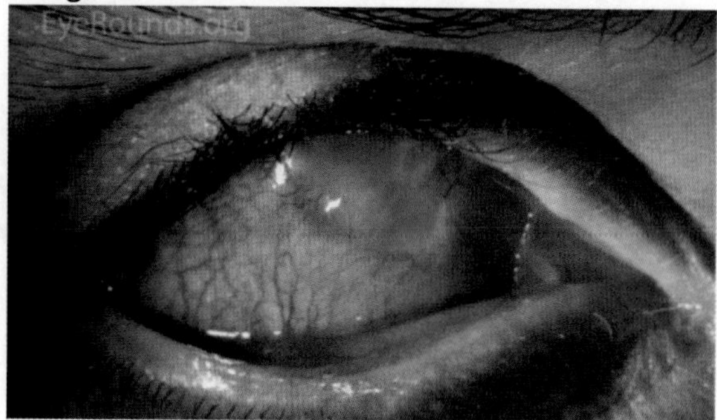

EyeRounds.org University of Iowa

11. Which of the following household items is an acid:
    a) Vinegar
    b) Bleach
    c) Ammonia
    d) Windex
    e) Drain cleaner
12. What is the most appropriate INITIAL treatment option:
    a) Copious irrigation with a basic solution
    b) Copious irrigation with an acid solution
    c) Copious irrigation with a saline solution
    d) Instillation of a beta blocker
    e) Sweep the fornices to measure the pH
13. Which of the following would be CONTRAINDICATED for this patient?
    a) Instillation of Atropine
    b) Instillation of Ciprofloxacin
    c) Instillation of Timolol
    d) Instillation of artificial tears
    e) Instillation of Pilocarpine
14. Which of the following signs indicates a poor prognosis for a chemical burn?
    a) Engorged conjunctival blood vessels
    b) Photophobia
    c) White cornea
    d) Increased IOP
    e) Acid based burn
15. When should you follow up with this patient?
    a) One day
    b) One week
    c) Two weeks
    d) One month
    e) No follow up necessary

CASE 4

Demographics
8 year-old Caucasian male who lives in the desert
Chief Complaint
Patient complains of itchy, painful, watery eyes
History Of Present Illness
Location: both eyes
Severity: severe
Nature Of Onset: Acute
Duration: Every episode lasts at least a month. It has been getting better every year.
Frequency: Occurs every spring
Exacerbations/Remissions: none
Relationship To Activity Or Function: none
Accompanying Signs/Symptoms: photophobia
Secondary Complaints/Symptoms none

Patient Ocular History
Itchy, painful, watery eyes every spring
Family Ocular History
Mother: myopia
Father: unremarkable
Patient Medical History
Asthma
Medications Taken By Patient
Symbicort Inhaler PRN
Patient Allergy History
Pollen, Dander, Dust, Penicillin
Family Medical History
Mother: unremarkable
Father: unremarkable

Review Of Systems
Constitutional/General Health: denies
Ear/Nose/Throat: denies
Cardiovascular: denies
Pulmonary: asthma
Endocrine: denies
Dermatological: denies
Gastrointestinal: denies
Genitourinary: denies
Musculoskeletal: denies
Neurologic: denies
Psychiatric: denies
Immunologic: denies
Hematologic: denies
Mental Status
Orientation: oriented to time, place, and person.
Mood: appropriate
Affect: appropriate

Clinical Findings
Habitual Rx: none
Entering Acuities:
OD Distance 20/20-
OS Distance 20/20
Pupils: PERRL, negative APD
EOMs: full, no restrictions OU
Confrontation Fields: full to finger counting OD, OS
Slit lamp
Lids/lashes/adnexa: thick ropy, green discharge OD, OS
Conjunctiva: cobblestone papillae. See Image 1 OD, OS
Cornea: white, elevated bumps around the limbus. See Image 2 OD, OS
Anterior chamber: deep and quiet OD, OS
Iris: flat and intact OD, OS
Lens: clear OD, OS
Vitreous: clear OD, OS
IOPs: 16 mmHg OD; 16 mmHg OS via GAT @ 4:10 p.m.
Fundus OD
C/D: 0.30H/ 0.30V
Macula: normal
Posterior pole: unremarkable
Periphery: unremarkable
Fundus OS

C/D: 0.30H/0.30V
Macula: normal
Posterior pole: unremarkable

Periphery: unremarkable
Blood Pressure: 110/70 right arm, sitting
Pulse 71 bpm, regular

Image 1

Atlas of Ophthalmology 4908

Image 2

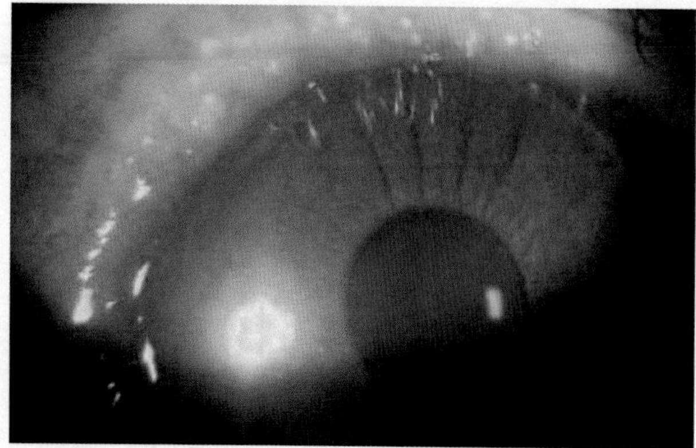

EyeRounds.org University of Iowa

16. What is the MOST LIKELY diagnosis of the patient's chief complaint?
    a) Seasonal Allergic Conjunctivitis
    b) Atopic Conjunctivitis
    c) Perennial Allergic Conjunctivitis
    d) Vernal Conjunctivitis
    e) Bacterial Conjunctivitis
17. Which of the following is another classic sign you could possibly see with this patient?
    a) Symblepharon
    b) Shield ulcer
    c) Keratoconus
    d) Cataracts
    e) Uveitis
18. Which of the following should be included in the patient education for the above case?
    a. The patient should cease having episodes when he reaches puberty
    b. This is a lifelong condition that he will have to always manage
    c. This is highly contagious and so the patient needs to stay home from school
    d. The patient is cleared to go to school for he is not contagious
    e. Both A and D
    f. Both B and D
19. What is the BEST treatment for the patient's chief complaint?
    a) Topical Cephalosporin QID
    b) Topical Azithromycin QID
    c) Artificial Tears QID
    d) Pataday QD
    e) No treatment necessary

20. This patient returns a week later stating that your chosen treatment option from question #19 isn't helping. Which of the following options should you now consider?
    a. Hospitalize the patient for around the clock IV antibiotics
    b. Reassure the patient he will get better spontaneously
    c. Topical Lotemax QID
    d. Topical Dorezol QID
    e. Artificial Tears Q1H

CASE 5

Demographics
25 year-old Caucasian female; stay at home mom
Chief Complaint
Patient complains of transient color vision changes.
History Of Present Illness
Character/Signs/Symptoms: Patient complains of color vision changes that last for less than a minute
Location: both eyes
Severity: moderate
Nature Of Onset: gradual, transient
Duration: slowly getting worse over the last four months
Frequency: once a day
Exacerbations/Remissions: headache worse when bending over
Relationship To Activity Or Function: none
Accompanying Signs/Symptoms: headaches, blurry vision, transient paresthesia in her arms
Secondary Complaints/Symptoms none

Patient Ocular History
Unremarkable
Family Ocular History
Mother: unremarkable
Father: unremarkable
Patient Medical History
Unremarkable. Patient has not had a physical in 7 years because she does not have health insurance.
Medications Taken By Patient
Birth control pills
Patient Allergy History
NKDA
Family Medical History
Mother: hypertension
Father: hyperlipidemia

Review Of Systems
Constitutional/General Health: overweight
Ear/Nose/Throat: denies
Cardiovascular: denies
Pulmonary: denies
Endocrine: denies
Dermatological: denies
Gastrointestinal: denies
Genitourinary: denies
Musculoskeletal: denies
Neurologic: denies
Psychiatric: denies
Immunologic: denies
Hematologic: denies
Mental Status
Orientation: oriented to time, place, and person.
Mood: appropriate
Affect: slow

Clinical Findings
Habitual Rx: none
Entering Acuities:
OD Distance 20/30
OS Distance 20/30
Manifest Refraction:
OD: +0.25 -0.50 x 180; VA distance 20/30
OS: +0.25 -0.50 x 180; VA distance 20/30
Pupils: PERRL, negative APD
EOMs: full, no restrictions OU
Confrontation Fields:
OD inferior temporal defect
OS inferior temporal defect
Slit lamp
Lids/lashes/adnexa: unremarkable OD, OS
Conjunctiva: clear OD, OS
Cornea: clear OD, OS
Anterior chamber: deep and quiet OD, OS
Iris: flat and intact OD, OS
Lens: clear OD, OS

Vitreous: clear OD, OS
IOPs: 16 mmHg OD; 16 mmHg OS via GAT @ 4:10 p.m.
Fundus OD
Optic nerve: See Image 1
Macula: normal
Posterior pole: unremarkable
Periphery: unremarkable

Fundus OS
Optic Nerve: See Image 2
Macula: normal
Posterior pole: unremarkable
Periphery: unremarkable
Blood Pressure: 120/80 right arm, sitting
Pulse 71 bpm, regular
Cerebrospinal Fluid Pressure: 210 mmH_2O

Image 1

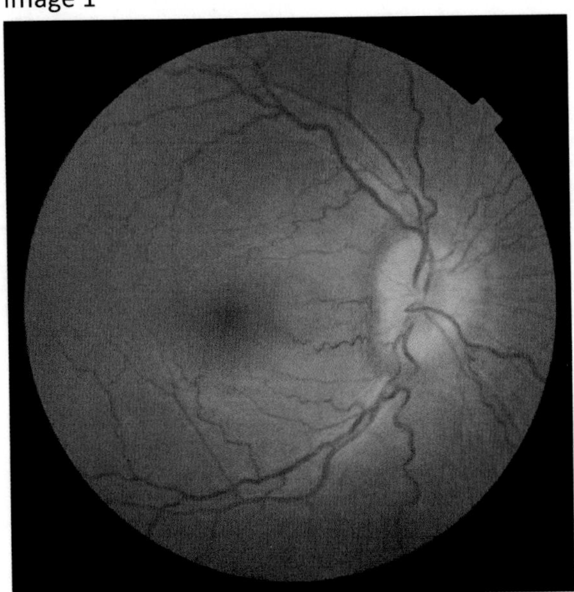

National Vision, Inc.

Image 2

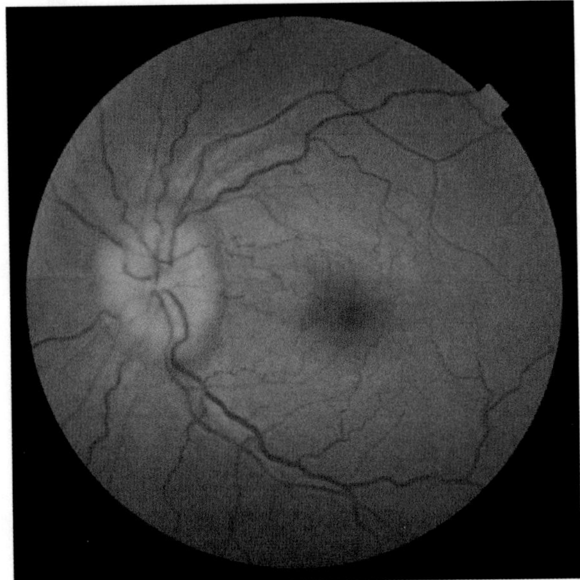

National Vision, Inc.

21. With the given information, what is the MOST APPROPRIATE diagnosis for the patient's chief complaint?
    a) Pituitary Gland Tumor
    b) AAION
    c) Optic Neuritis
    d) Papilledema
    e) Pseudotumor Cerebri
22. The patient's MRI is found to be unremarkable. What is the MOST LIKELY diagnosis of the patient's chief complaint?
    a) Pituitary Gland Tumor
    b) AAION
    c) Optic Neuritis
    d) Papilledema
    e) Pseudotumor Cerebri

23. Which of the following should be considered in the treatment for this patient? (SELECT THREE)
    a) Surgery to remove the tumor
    b) Lose weight
    c) IV Steroids
    d) Discontinue use of birth control pills
    e) Diamox 1000mg po QD
24. Which of the following is the definition of INCREASED Cerebrospinal fluid pressure for a patient who is obese?
    a) >80
    b) >120
    c) >150
    d) >200 mmH_2O
    e) >250 mmH_2O
25. Which of the following would indicate a tumor of the left optic tract?

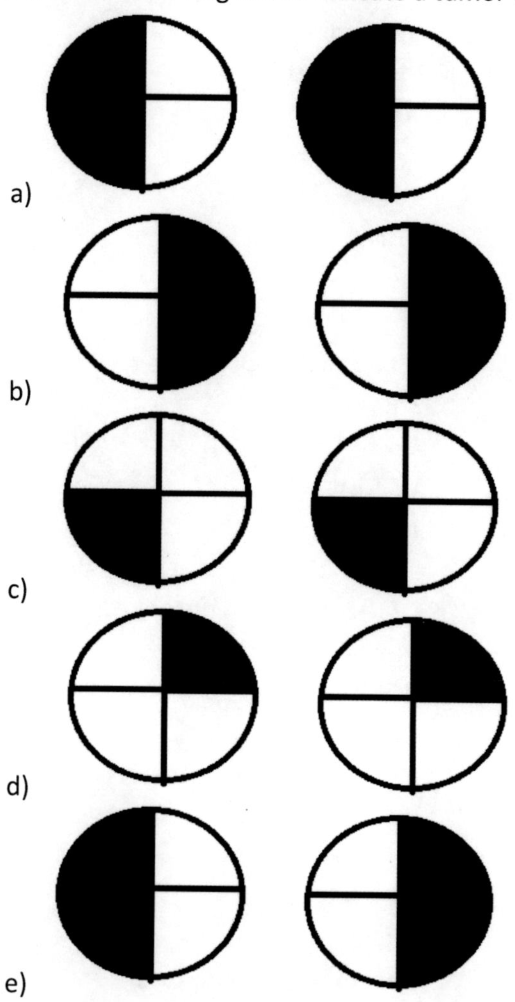

CASE 6

Demographics
8 year-old Hispanic male; student
Chief Complaint
The patient complains of asthenopia with diplopia which is worse towards the end of the day
History Of Present Illness
Character/Signs/Symptoms: Horizontal diplopia with both eyes open only. The patient can't tell which image is real.
Location: both eyes
Severity: moderate
Nature Of Onset: gradual
Duration: slowly getting worse over three years
Frequency: starts after 30 minutes of reading
Exacerbations/Remissions: worse when the patient reads/taking naps helps.
Relationship To Activity Or Function: reading, using the computer
Accompanying Signs/Symptoms: headaches/falls asleep easily when reading
Secondary Complaints/Symptoms: none

Patient Ocular History
Unremarkable, this is his first eye exam
Family Ocular History
Mother: unremarkable
Father: unremarkable
Patient Medical History
unremarkable
Medications Taken By Patient
None
Patient Allergy History
NKDA
Family Medical History
Mother: unremarkable
Father: unremarkable

Review Of Systems
Constitutional/General Health: denies
Ear/Nose/Throat: denies
Cardiovascular: denies
Pulmonary: denies
Endocrine: denies
Dermatological: denies
Gastrointestinal: denies
Genitourinary: denies
Musculoskeletal: denies
Neurologic: denies
Psychiatric: denies
Immunologic: denies
Hematologic: denies
Mental Status
Orientation: oriented to time, place, and person.
Mood: appropriate
Affect: appropriate

Clinical Findings
Habitual Rx: none
Entering Acuities:
OD Distance 20/30 Near 20/30
OS Distance 20/30 Near 20/30
Manifest Refraction:
OD: +2.25 DS; VA distance 20/20, VA near 20/20
OS: +2.25 DS; VA distance 20/20, VA near 20/20
Pupils: PERRL, negative APD
EOMs: full, no restrictions OU
Cover Test
Distance: 15 exophoria
Near: 12 exophoria
Confrontation Fields: full to finger counting OD, OS

Accommodative System
Amplitude of Accommodation: 13D
AC/A: 4:1
Binocular Accommodative Facility +/-2.00: 3 cpm, difficulty with (+)

NRA: +0.75D
PRA: -3.00D
MEM: -0.25D

Vergence System
NPC: Break 5, Recovery 7
Vergences:
Negative fusional convergence (NFC): Far 7/4; Near 12 / 22 / 15
Positive fusional convergence (PFC): Far x/8/4; Near x/10/8

Slit lamp
Lids/lashes/adnexa: unremarkable OD, OS
Conjunctiva: clear OD, OS
Cornea: clear OD, OS
Anterior chamber: deep and quiet OD, OS
Iris: flat and intact OD, OS
Lens: clear OD, OS
Vitreous: clear OD, OS
IOPs: 16 mmHg OD; 16 mmHg OS via GAT @ 4:10 p.m.
Fundus OD
C/D: 0.30H/ 0.30V
Macula: normal
Posterior pole: unremarkable
Periphery: unremarkable
Fundus OS
C/D: 0.30H/0.30V
Macula: normal
Posterior pole: unremarkable
Periphery: unremarkable
Blood Pressure: 123/82 right arm, sitting
Pulse 71 bpm, regular

26. Which of the following is the BEST diagnosis for this patient's chief complaint?
    a. Accommodative Excess
    b. Ill Sustained Accommodation
    c. Basic Exophoria
    d. Convergence Insufficiency
    e. Divergence Excess
27. Which of the following BEST supports your diagnosis for the patient's chief complaint?
    a. Cover test findings
    b. Vergence facility testing
    c. Accommodative Facility testing
    d. NRA/PRA findings
    e. MEM findings
28. Which of the following would be the BEST spectacle prescription for this patient?
    a. OD: +2.25; OS +2.25; No Add
    b. OD: +1.25; OS +1.25; No Add
    c. OD: +2.25; OS +2.25; +1.00 Add
    d. OD: +1.25; OS +1.25; +1.00 Add
    e. Wait to prescribe lenses until after Vision Therapy has been initiated.
29. What types of lenses should be utilized to train the eyes during vision therapy? (PICK TWO)
    a. Base In
    b. Base Out
    c. Minus
    d. Plus

30. What type of prism could you consider including in this patient's spectacle prescription?
    a. Base In
    b. Base Out
    c. Base Up
    d. Base Down

CASE 7

Demographics
21 year-old Caucasian female; student
Chief Complaint
Patient complaints of a red eye
History Of Present Illness
Character/Signs/Symptoms: The affected eye is painful, and the patient has photophobia
Location: OS
Severity: severe
Nature Of Onset: Patient was woken up this morning with the pain
Duration: Started this morning
Frequency: This is the first occurrence
Exacerbations/Remissions: none
Relationship To Activity Or Function: Patient throws her contacts away every six months, sleeps in them, and never removes them during the six month period. She cleans her contacts with a multipurpose solution.
Accompanying Signs/Symptoms: The patient states that she does not like to remove her contact lenses because her eyes hurt when she removes them. She also states that glasses cause her headaches because of their weight, even with the thinnest, lightest possible frames and lenses.
Secondary Complaints/Symptoms none

Patient Ocular History
unremarkable
Family Ocular History
Mother: unremarkable
Father: unremarkable
Patient Medical History
Acne Rosacea
Medications Taken By Patient
Birth control, Doxycycline
Patient Allergy History
Vigamox
Family Medical History
Mother: hemorrhoids
Father: GERD

Review Of Systems
Constitutional/General Health: denies
Ear/Nose/Throat: denies
Cardiovascular: denies
Pulmonary: denies
Endocrine: denies
Dermatological: acne rosacea
Gastrointestinal: denies
Genitourinary: denies
Musculoskeletal: denies
Neurologic: denies
Psychiatric: denies
Immunologic: denies
Hematologic: denies
Mental Status
Orientation: oriented to time, place, and person.
Mood: appropriate
Affect: appropriate

Clinical Findings
Habitual Spectacle Rx:
OD: -8.00 -0.75 x 175; VA distance 20/20
OS: -8.50 -0.25 x 005; VA distance 20/50
Pupils: PERRL, negative APD
EOMs: full, no restrictions OU
Confrontation Fields: full to finger counting OD, OS
Slit lamp
Lids/lashes/adnexa: unremarkable OD, OS
Conjunctiva:
OD: clear
OS: red and injected
Cornea:
OD: clear
OS: See Image 1 and Image 2
Anterior chamber: deep and quiet OD, OS

Iris: flat and intact OD, OS
Lens: clear OD, OS
Vitreous: clear OD, OS
IOPs: 16 mmHg OD; 16 mmHg OS via GAT @ 4:10 p.m.
Fundus OD
C/D: 0.30H/ 0.30V
Macula: normal
Posterior pole: unremarkable
Periphery: unremarkable
Fundus OS
C/D: 0.30H/0.30V
Macula: normal
Posterior pole: unremarkable
Periphery: unremarkable
Blood Pressure: 123/82 right arm, sitting
Pulse 71 bpm, regular

Image 1

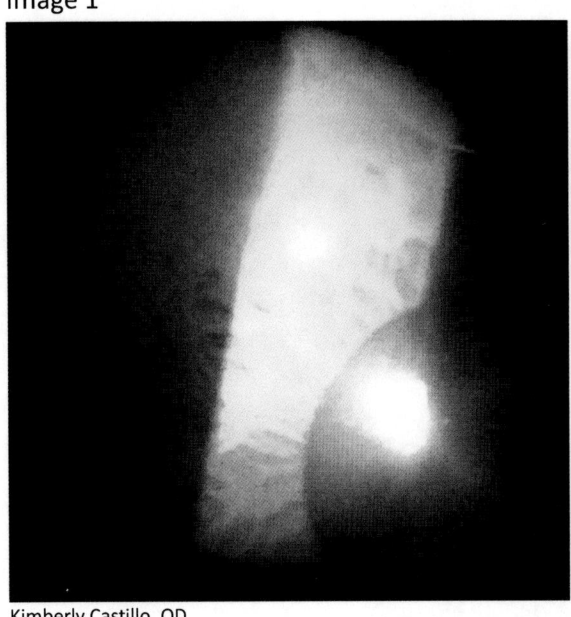

Kimberly Castillo, OD

Image 2

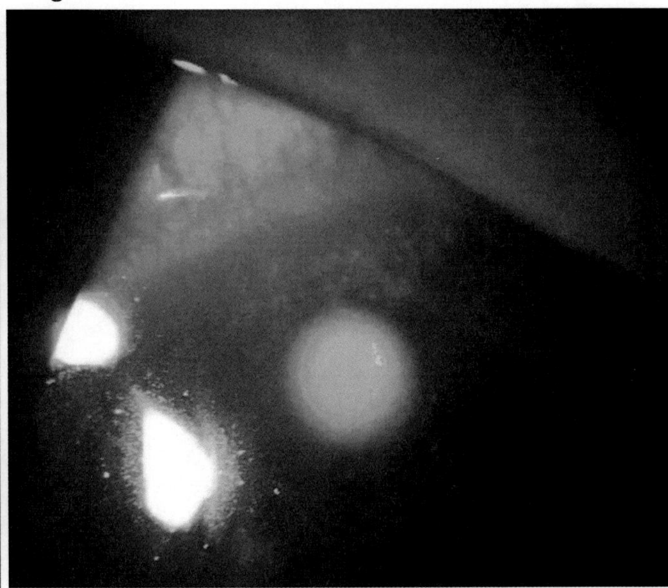

Kimberly Castillo, OD

31. What is the MOST LIKELY diagnosis of the patient's chief complaint?
    a) Corneal infiltrate
    b) Corneal ulcer
    c) Neovascularization
    d) Tight Lens Syndrome
    e) Hypersensitivity to the contact lens solution
32. What is the MOST LIKELY etiology of the patient's chief complaint?
    a. Immune response to the proteins lodged in the contact lens
    b. Bacteria attacking the cornea
    c. A contact lens which is too steep for the patient's cornea
    d. A contact lens which is too flat for the patient's cornea
    e. Allergic response to the preservatives in the patient's contact lens solution
33. Which of the following is the MOST COMMON bacteria to cause corneal ulcers?

a) Pseudomonas aeruginosa
b) Staph aureus
c) Haemophilus
d) Listeria
e) Acanthamoeba

34. What is the BEST initial treatment for the patient's chief complaint? SELECT TWO
    a) Lotemax gt OS QID x7 days
    b) Durezol gt OS QID x7 days
    c) Vigamox gt OS Q2H x7 days
    d) AzaSite gt OS QID x7 days
    e) Pataday QD
    f) Patch the eye for comfort
    g) Change contact lens solution to ClearCare
    h) Discontinue contact lens wear
35. After the patient's chief complaint is fully resolved, what change should be considered in the patient's contact lens fit?
    a) Refit into a flatter contact lens
    b) Refit into a steeper contact lens
    c) Refit into a contact with a higher DK/t
    d) Discontinue contact lens wear indefinitely
    e) No change necessary

CASE 8

Demographics
78 year-old Caucasian male; retired ski instructor
Chief Complaint
Patient complains of blurry vision both distance and near
History Of Present Illness
Character/Signs/Symptoms: Patient states he can't see anything.
Location: both eyes
Severity: severe
Nature Of Onset: gradual
Duration: slowly getting worse over five years
Frequency: constant
Exacerbations/Remissions: none
Relationship To Activity Or Function: none
Accompanying Signs/Symptoms: none
Secondary Complaints/Symptoms: The patient is having trouble with night driving because oncoming headlights at night completely wash out his vision. He complains that "headlights are becoming brighter these days."

Patient Ocular History
Unremarkable, last eye exam 15 years ago
Family Ocular History
Mother: unknown, adopted
Father: unknown, adopted
Patient Medical History
Diabetes
Medications Taken By Patient
Metformin
Patient Allergy History
NKDA
Family Medical History
Mother: unknown, adopted
Father: unknown, adopted

Review Of Systems
Constitutional/General Health: denies
Ear/Nose/Throat: denies
Cardiovascular: denies
Pulmonary: denies
Endocrine: Diabetes
Dermatological: denies
Gastrointestinal: denies
Genitourinary: denies
Musculoskeletal: denies
Neurologic: denies
Psychiatric: denies
Immunologic: denies
Hematologic: denies
Mental Status
Orientation: oriented to time, place, and person.
Mood: appropriate
Affect: appropriate

Clinical Findings
Habitual Rx: none
Entering Acuities:
OD Distance 20/200; Near 20/200
OD Distance 20/200; Near 20/200
Manifest Refraction:
OD: -5.00 DS Add +2.50; VA distance 20/100, VA near 20/100
OS: -5.00 DS Add +2.50; VA distance 20/100, VA near 20/100
Pupils: PERRL, negative APD
EOMs: full, no restrictions OU
Cover Test
Distance: 1 exophoria
Near: 3 exophoria
Confrontation Fields: full to finger counting OD, OS
Slit lamp
Lids/lashes/adnexa: Dermatochalasis OD, OS
Conjunctiva: senile plaque OD
Cornea: arcus OD, OS
Anterior chamber: deep and quiet OD, OS

Iris: flat and intact OD, OS
Lens
OD: See Image 1
OS: Similar to Image 1
Vitreous: clear OD, OS
IOPs: 16 mmHg OD; 16 mmHg OS via GAT @ 4:10 p.m.

Fundus OD
Unable to assess due to blurry views
Fundus OS
Unable to assess due to blurry views
Blood Pressure: 123/82 right arm, sitting
Pulse 71 bpm, regular

Image 1

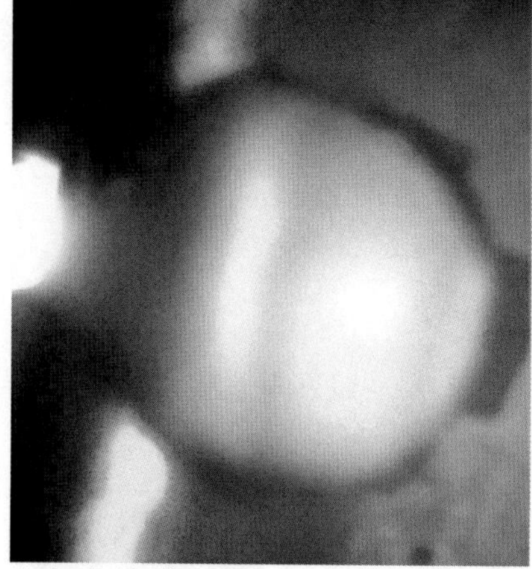

Kimberly Castillo, OD

Image 2

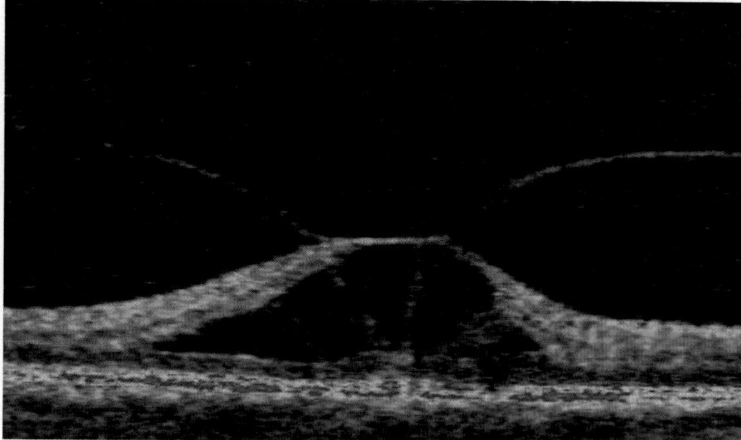

EyeRounds.org University of Iowa

36. What is the MOST LIKELY cause of this patient's reduced BCVA?
    a. Refractive error
    b. Diabetic Retinopathy
    c. Nuclear Sclerosis
    d. Snowflake Cataract
    e. Posterior Polar Cataract
37. What is the MOST LIKELY cause of this patient's secondary complaint?
    a. Uncorrected refractive error
    b. Dermatochalasis
    c. Nuclear Sclerosis
    d. Brighter headlights on cars
    e. Posterior Polar Cataract

Questions 38 and 39 refer to the patient's three month follow up post cataract surgery.

38. The patient's BCVA is 20/50 OD. See image 2 for OCT findings. What is the MOST LIKELY cause of the patient's reduced BCVA?
    a. Cystoid Macular Edema
    b. Irvine-Gass syndrome
    c. Epiretinal Membrane
    d. Pigment Epithelial Detachment
    e. Retinoschisis

39. What would be the MOST APPROPRIATE management for this patient's reduced BCVA?
    a. Ketorolac gt QID
    b. Acular LS gt QID OD
    c. Durezol gt QID OD
    d. Refer the patient for vitrectomy with membrane peel
    e. Refer the patient for pneumatic retinopexy
    f. Refer the patient for Cryotherapy
40. What is a possible complication if a patient delays cataract surgery for too long?
    a. Phacolytic Glaucoma
    b. Intraoperative Floppy Iris Syndrome
    c. Lens subluxation
    d. Posterior capsular opacification
    e. There are no possible complications from delaying cataract surgery

CASE 9

Demographics
25 year-old Hispanic male; accountant
Chief Complaint
Patient is here for an annual eye exam.
History Of Present Illness
Character/Signs/Symptoms: Patient complains of blurry vision at distance.
Location: both eyes
Severity: mild
Nature Of Onset: gradual
Duration: has gradually gotten worse since last eye exam one year ago
Frequency: Notices it most while trying to read street signs.
Exacerbations/Remissions: Squinting helps
Relationship To Activity Or Function: worse in low light settings
Accompanying Signs/Symptoms: none
Secondary Complaints/Symptoms: The patient states that his eyes have been very itchy for the last two months.

Patient Ocular History
unremarkable
Family Ocular History
Mother: unremarkable
Father: unremarkable
Patient Medical History
Asthma
Medications Taken By Patient
None
Patient Allergy History
Pollen, dander, seasonal
Family Medical History
Mother: unremarkable
Father: unremarkable

Review Of Systems
Constitutional/General Health: denies
Ear/Nose/Throat: denies
Cardiovascular: denies
Pulmonary: asthma
Endocrine: denies
Dermatological: denies
Gastrointestinal: denies
Genitourinary: denies
Musculoskeletal: denies
Neurologic: denies
Psychiatric: denies
Immunologic: denies
Hematologic: denies
Mental Status
Orientation: oriented to time, place, and person.
Mood: appropriate
Affect: appropriate

Clinical Findings
Habitual Rx:
OD: -2.25 -0.50 x010; VA distance 20/25-, VA near 20/20
OS: -2.75 -1.00 x170; VA distance 20/20-1, VA near 20/20
Manifest Refraction:
OD: -2.50 -0.75 x010; VA distance 20/20, VA near 20/20
OS: -2.75 -1.25 x170; VA distance 20/20, VA near 20/20
Pupils: PERRL, negative APD
EOMs: full, no restrictions OU
Confrontation Fields: full to finger counting OD, OS
Slit lamp
Lids/lashes/adnexa:
OD: See Image 1 OD
OS: similar to Image 1
Conjunctiva: clear OD, OS
Cornea: 1+ SPK OD, OS
Anterior chamber: deep and quiet OD, OS
Iris: flat and intact OD, OS

Lens: clear OD, OS
Vitreous: clear OD, OS
IOPs: 16 mmHg OD; 16 mmHg OS via GAT @ 4:10 p.m.
Fundus OD
C/D: 0.30H/ 0.30V
Macula: normal
Posterior pole: unremarkable
Periphery: unremarkable
Fundus OS
C/D: 0.30H/0.30V
Macula: normal
Posterior pole: unremarkable
Periphery: unremarkable
Blood Pressure: 123/82 right arm, sitting
Pulse 71 bpm, regular

Image 1

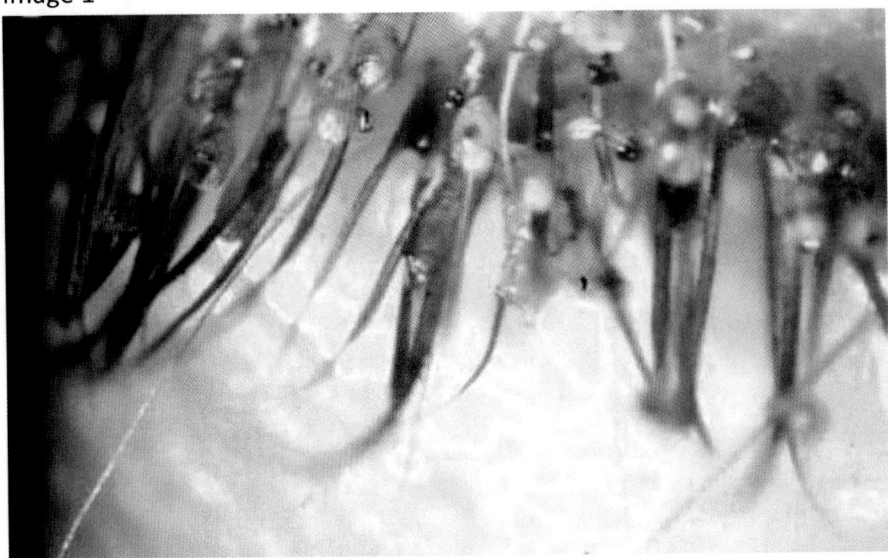

Atlas of Ophthalmology 2774

41. What is the MOST APPROPRIATE diagnosis for the patient's secondary complaint?
    a. Uncorrected refractive error
    b. Allergic conjunctivitis
    c. Meibomian Gland Dysfunction
    d. Demodicosis
    e. Pediculosis
42. What is the MOST LIKELY etiology of the patient's secondary complaint?
    a. Myopia
    b. *Staph aureus*
    c. Seasonal allergy
    d. Demodex folliculorum
    e. Phthirus pubis
43. What should be included in the patient's education regarding his secondary complaint? (SELECT TWO)
    a. His current sexual partner should also be treated
    b. This should be monitored with an annual eye exam
    c. He should expect this will happen on a seasonal basis
    d. Be sure to clean all sheets and towels
    e. Without treatment this can lead to severe visual loss

44. What is the MOST APPROPRIATE treatment for this patient's secondary complaint? (SELECT TWO)
    a. Remove lice with jeweler's forceps
    b. Scrub lids with lice shampoo
    c. Topical erythromycin ointment
    d. Artificial tears QID
    e. Topical Pataday QD
45. What should you consider if a child presents with this eyelid condition?
    a. All the children in the patient's class at school should be tested
    b. Educate the child to avoid eye rubbing
    c. Refer the patient to the centers for disease control and prevention (CDC)
    d. The child should not attend school for two weeks
    e. Child abuse

CASE 10

Demographics
57 year-old Filipino male; postal worker
Chief Complaint
Patient complains of blurry vision.
History Of Present Illness
Location: Both eyes
Severity: moderate
Nature of Onset: Has gotten significantly worse over the last two weeks
Duration: two years
Frequency: constant
Exacerbations/Remissions: none
Relationship To Activity Or Function: none
Accompanying Signs/Symptoms: none
Secondary Complaints/Symptoms: The patient states that he has been extra thirsty lately, and so has been subsequently drinking more and urinating more.

Patient Ocular History
Unremarkable
Family Ocular History
Mother: unremarkable
Father: unremarkable
Patient Medical History
Unremarkable
Medications Taken By Patient
None
Patient Allergy History
NKDA
Family Medical History
Mother: unremarkable
Father: unremarkable

Review Of Systems
Constitutional/General Health: Overweight
Ear/Nose/Throat: denies
Cardiovascular: denies
Pulmonary: denies
Endocrine: denies
Dermatological: denies
Gastrointestinal: denies
Genitourinary: denies
Musculoskeletal: denies
Neurologic: denies
Psychiatric: denies
Immunologic: denies
Hematologic: denies
Mental Status
Orientation: oriented to time, place, and person.
Mood: appropriate
Affect: appropriate

Clinical Findings
Habitual Rx: none
BVA
OD: 20/50 Distance
OS: 20/30 Distance
Pupils: PERRL, negative APD
EOMs: full, no restrictions OU
Confrontation Fields:
Full to finger counting OD, OS
Slit lamp
Lids/lashes/adnexa: unremarkable OD, OS
Conjunctiva: clear OD, OS
Cornea: clear OD, OS
Anterior chamber: deep and quiet OD, OS
Iris: flat and intact OD, OS
Lens: clear OD, OS
Vitreous: clear OD, OS
IOPs: 16 mmHg OD; 16 mmHg OS via GAT @ 4:10 p.m.
Blood Pressure: 115/79 right arm, sitting
Pulse 71 bpm, regular
Fundus OD
See Image 1
Fundus OS
See Image 2

Image 1

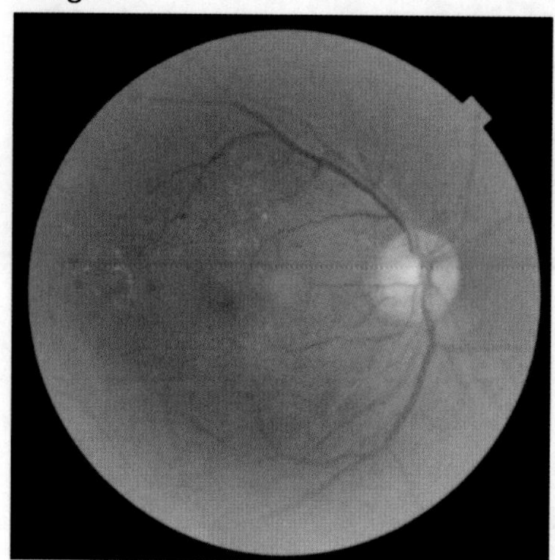

National Vision, Inc.

Image 2

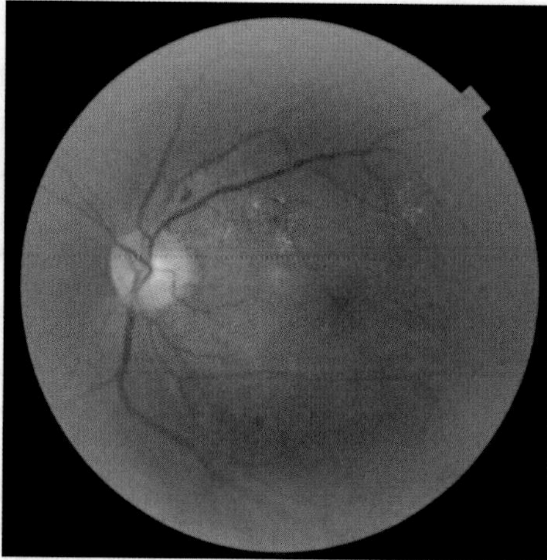

National Vision, Inc.

46. What is the MOST LIKELY diagnosis for the patient's chief complaint?
    a. Central Retinal Vein Occlusion
    b. Hypertensive Retinopathy
    c. Diabetic Retinopathy
    d. Ocular Ischemic Syndrome
    e. Venous Stasis
47. What is the highest risk factor for diabetic retinopathy?
    a. Poorly controlled diabetes
    b. Duration which the patient has had diabetes
    c. Age
    d. Family history
    e. Ethnicity
48. What is the prognosis for Ocular Ischemic Syndrome?
    a. Excellent, the patient is expected to make a full recovery with proper treatment
    b. Treatment should stop the progression, but the patient will not regain lost vision
    c. Poor, OIS is slowly progressive and will lead to blindness
    d. Fatal in 40% of patients after five years
49. What is the medical term for increased thirst?
    a. Polyuria
    b. Polydipsia
    c. Polyphagia
    d. Polymegathism
    e. Pleomorphism
50. Which of the following BEST describe the blood panels seen in diabetic patients? (SELECT TWO)
    a. A1C greater than 6.0
    b. A1C greater than 6.5
    c. Fasting blood sugar above 100
    d. Fasting blood sugar above 150
    e. Fasting blood sugar above 200

CASE 11

Demographics
10 year-old Chinese female; student
Chief Complaint
Blurry vision
History Of Present Illness
Character/Signs/Symptoms: Patient is having trouble seeing the board at school.
Location: both eyes
Severity: moderate
Nature Of Onset: gradual
Duration: slowly getting worse since last eye exam one year ago.
Frequency: Whenever looking at the board at school.
Exacerbations/Remissions: Squinting helps
Relationship To Activity Or Function: worse in low light settings
Accompanying Signs/Symptoms: none
Secondary Complaints/Symptoms none

Patient Ocular History
unremarkable
Family Ocular History
Mother: high myopia
Father: unremarkable
Patient Medical History
unremarkable
Medications Taken By Patient
None
Patient Allergy History
NKDA
Family Medical History
Mother: unremarkable
Father: unremarkable

Review Of Systems
Constitutional/General Health: denies
Ear/Nose/Throat: denies
Cardiovascular: denies
Pulmonary: denies
Endocrine: denies
Dermatological: denies
Gastrointestinal: denies
Genitourinary: denies
Musculoskeletal: denies
Neurologic: denies
Psychiatric: denies
Immunologic: denies
Hematologic: denies
Mental Status
Orientation: oriented to time, place, and person.
Mood: appropriate
Affect: appropriate

Clinical Findings
Habitual Rx:
OD: -3.50 -0.75 x009; Distance 20/30, Near 20/20
OS: -4.00 -1.00 x171; Distance 20/40, Near 20/20
Manifest Refraction:
OD: -4.50 -1.00 x009; VA distance 20/20, VA near 20/20
OS: -5.50 -1.00 x171; VA distance 20/20, VA near 20/20
Pupils: PERRL, negative APD
EOMs: full, no restrictions OU
Confrontation Fields: full to finger counting OD, OS
Slit lamp
Lids/lashes/adnexa: unremarkable OD, OS
Conjunctiva: clear OD, OS
Cornea: clear OD, OS
Anterior chamber: deep and quiet OD, OS
Iris: flat and intact OD, OS
Lens: clear OD, OS
Vitreous: clear OD, OS
IOPs: 16 mmHg OD; 16 mmHg OS via GAT @ 4:10 p.m.

Blood Pressure: 100/70 right arm, sitting
Pulse: 65 bpm, regular
Fundus OD
C/D: 0.30H/ 0.30V
Macula: normal
Posterior pole: unremarkable
Periphery: unremarkable
Fundus OS
C/D: 0.30H/0.30V
Macula: normal
Posterior pole: unremarkable
Periphery: unremarkable
OD: -3.50 -0.75 x009; Distance 20/30, Near 20/20
OS: -4.00 -1.00 x171; Distance 20/40, Near 20/20

51. Which of the following is the MOST APPROPRIATE diagnosis for this patient's chief complaint?
    a. Simple Myopia
    b. Simple Myopic Astigmatism
    c. Compound Myopic Astigmatism
    d. Mixed Astigmatism
52. Which of the following is the MOST APPROPRIATE spectacle prescription for this patient?
    a) OD: -4.50 -1.00 x009
       OS: -5.50 -1.00 x171
    b) OD: -3.50 -0.75 x009
       OS: -4.00 -1.00 x171
    c) OD: -4.00 -0.75 x009
       OS: -4.00 -1.00 x171
    d) OD: -4.50 -1.00 x009
       OS: -4.00 -1.00 x171
    e) OD: -4.00 -0.75 x009
       OS: -4.75 -1.00 x171
53. Which is the correct way to write this patient's HABITUAL prescription in Plus (+) Cylinder form?
    a) OD: -4.25 +0.75 x099
       OS: -5.00 +1.00 x081
    b) OD: -4.50 +1.00 x099
       OS: -5.50 +1.00 x081
    c) OD: -4.25 +0.75 x009
       OS: -5.00 +1.00 x171
    d) OD: -5.50 +1.00 x099
       OS: -6.00 +1.00 x081
    e) OD: -4.00 +0.75 x099
       OS: -4.75 +1.00 x081
54. Where would you expect to see the light converge with no prescription for this patient?
    a. In front of her retina at both axis 009 and 171
    b. In front of her retina at axis 009 and behind the retina at axis 171
    c. In front of her retina at axis 009 and on the retina at axis 171
    d. Behind her retina at both axis 009 and 171
    e. Behind her retina at axis 009 and in front of the retina at axis 171

55. This patient is viewing the astigmatic dial with no prescription. Which set of lines will she perceive as clearest?
    a. 2:00-8:00
    b. 3:00-9:00
    c. 4:00-10:00
    d. 6:00-12:00
    e. None of the above

CASE 12

Demographics
33 year-old Caucasian female; 5th grade teacher
Chief Complaint
Patient states she woke up this morning with "pink eye"
History of Present Illness
Character/Signs/Symptoms: Patient reports associated mild irritation
Location: left eye
Severity: moderate
Nature of Onset: acute, began this morning
Duration: a few hours
Frequency: this is the first occurrence
Exacerbations/Remissions: none
Relationship To Activity Or Function: none
Accompanying Signs/Symptoms: none
Secondary Complaints/Symptoms none

Patient Ocular History
High myopia
Family Ocular History
Mother: unremarkable
Father: unremarkable
Patient Medical History
Acne Rosacea
Medications Taken By Patient
None
Patient Allergy History
Tetracycline
Family Medical History
Mother: high cholesterol
Father: GERD

Review of Systems
Constitutional/General Health: denies
Ear/Nose/Throat: denies
Cardiovascular: denies
Pulmonary: denies
Endocrine: denies
Dermatological: acne rosacea
Gastrointestinal: denies
Genitourinary: denies
Musculoskeletal: denies
Neurologic: denies
Psychiatric: denies
Immunologic: denies
Hematologic: denies
Mental Status
Orientation: oriented to time, place, and person.
Mood: appropriate
Affect: appropriate

Clinical Findings
BVA
OD: 20/20
OS: 20/20
Pupils: PERRL, negative APD
EOMs: full, no restrictions OU
Confrontation Fields: full to finger counting OD, OS
Slit lamp
Lids/lashes/adnexa: No discharge visible OD, OS
Conjunctiva:
OD See Image 1
OS Clear
Cornea: clear OD, OS
Anterior chamber: deep and quiet OD, OS
Iris: flat and intact OD, OS
Lens: clear OD, OS
Vitreous: clear OD, OS
IOPs: 16 mmHg OD; 16 mmHg OS via GAT @ 4:10 p.m.
Blood Pressure: 108/60 right arm, sitting
Pulse 71 bpm, regular
Fundus OD
C/D: 0.10H/ 0.10V
Macula: normal
Posterior pole: unremarkable

Periphery: unremarkable
Fundus OS
C/D: 0.10H/0.10V
Macula: normal

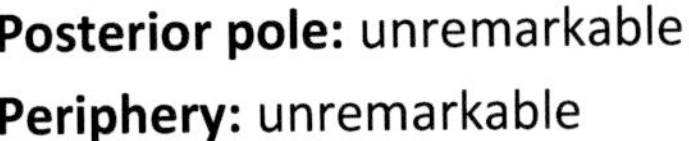
Posterior pole: unremarkable
Periphery: unremarkable

Image 1

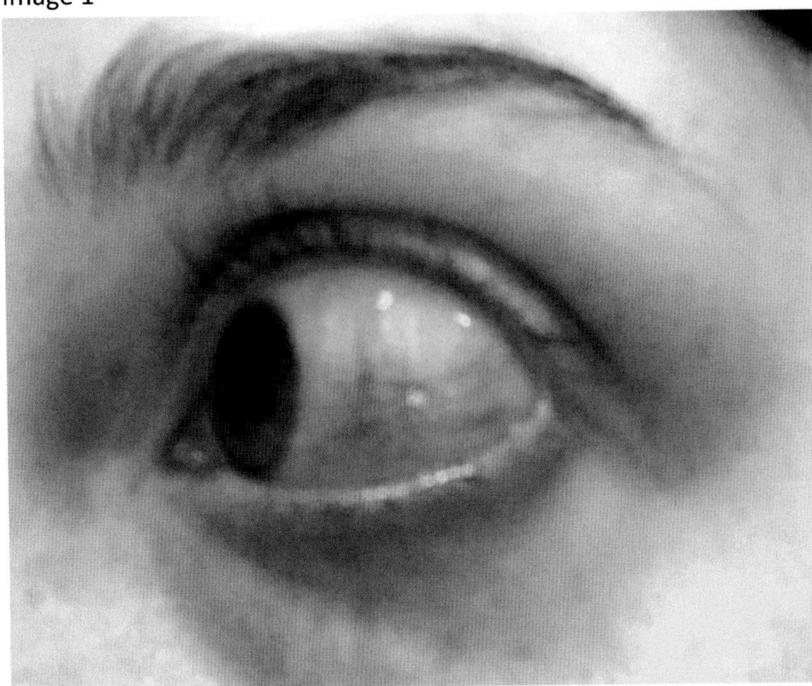

Kimberly Castillo, OD

56. What is the MOST LIKELY diagnosis for the patient's chief complaint?
    a. Ocular Rosacea
    b. Episcleritis
    c. Scleritis
    d. Allergic conjunctivitis
    e. Viral conjunctivitis
57. What is the MOST LIKELY etiology for the patient's chief complaint?
    a. Rosacea
    b. Rheumatoid arthritis
    c. Atopy
    d. Thyroid disease
    e. Idiopathic
58. What is the MOST APPROPRIATE treatment for this patient's chief complaint? SELECT TWO
    a. Oral Doxycycline
    b. Oral Erythromycin
    c. Oral Ibuprofen
    d. Topical Lotemax
    e. Topical naphazoline
    f. Artificial tears

This patient returns two months later with another episode of her chief complaint.

59. What is now the MOST LIKELY etiology for the patient's chief complaint?
    a. Rosacea
    b. Rheumatoid Arthritis
    c. Atopy
    d. Thyroid disease
    e. Idiopathic
60. Which of the following is now the MOST APPROPRIATE treatment for this patient's chief complaint?
    a. Oral Doxycycline
    b. Oral Erythromycin
    c. Oral Ibuprofen
    d. Topical Lotemax
    e. Topical naphazoline
    f. Artificial tears

CASE 13

Demographics
4 year-old African American male; preschooler
Chief Complaint
The patient's parents have noticed that his left eye will turn in.
History of Present Illness
Character/Signs/Symptoms: The patient rubs his left eye when he is coloring.
Location: left eye
Severity: moderate
Nature of Onset: Started one and a half years ago
Duration: One and a half years, slowly getting worse.
Frequency: 2-3 times per day
Exacerbations/Remissions: none
Relationship To Activity Or Function: worse when coloring
Accompanying Signs/Symptoms: none
Secondary Complaints/Symptoms none

Patient Ocular History
Unremarkable, first eye exam
Family Ocular History
Mother: unremarkable
Father: unremarkable
Patient Medical History
Unremarkable
Medications Taken By Patient
None
Patient Allergy History
NKDA
Family Medical History
Mother: unremarkable
Father: unremarkable

Review of Systems
Constitutional/General Health: denies
Ear/Nose/Throat: denies
Cardiovascular: denies
Pulmonary: denies
Endocrine: denies
Dermatological: denies
Gastrointestinal: denies
Genitourinary: denies
Musculoskeletal: denies
Neurologic: denies
Psychiatric: denies
Immunologic: denies
Hematologic: denies
Mental Status
Orientation: oriented to time, place, and person.
Mood: appropriate
Affect: appropriate

Clinical Findings
Habitual Rx: none
Entering Acuities:
OD Distance 20/20 Near 20/20
OS Distance 20/20 Near 20/20
Manifest Refraction:
OD: +1.00 DS; VA distance 20/20, VA near 20/20
OS: +1.00 DS; VA distance 20/20, VA near 20/20
Pupils: PERRL, negative APD
EOMs: full, no restrictions OU
Confrontation Fields: unable to test due to patient compliance
Cover Test
Distance
2 esotropia sc
Orthophoric cc
Near
15 esotropia sc
10 esophoric cc
Vergence System
NPC: TTN
Accommodative System
AC/A: 8/1
Monocular Accommodative Facility: 3 cpm

Stereoacuity (Random dot): 100"
Slit lamp
Lids/lashes/adnexa: unremarkable OD, OS
Conjunctiva: clear OD, OS
Cornea: clear OD, OS
Anterior chamber: deep and quiet OD, OS
Iris: flat and intact OD, OS
Lens: clear OD, OS
Vitreous: clear OD, OS
IOPs: 16 mmHg OD; 16 mmHg OS via NCT @ 4:10 p.m.
Blood Pressure: 100/60 right arm, sitting
Pulse 62 bpm, regular
Fundus OD
C/D: 0.30H/ 0.30V
Macula: normal
Posterior pole: unremarkable
Periphery: unremarkable
Fundus OS
C/D: 0.30H/0.30V
Macula: normal
Posterior pole: unremarkable
Periphery: unremarkable

61. What is the MOST LIKELY cause of the patient's chief complaint?
    a. Congenital Esotropia
    b. Early Onset Esotropia
    c. Refractive Esotropia
    d. Non-Refractive Esotropia
    e. Mixed Esotropia
62. Which of the following should be included in your exam for this patient?
    a. Color vision testing
    b. NSUCO
    c. Test of Visual Information Processing Skills (TIPS)
    d. Von Graefe Phorias
    e. Cycloplegic refraction
63. Prominent epicanthal folds are most likely seen in which of the following patient populations? (SELECT TWO)
    a. Caucasians
    b. Asians
    c. Down's Syndrome
    d. Fetal Alcohol Syndrome
    e. Turner's Syndrome
64. Based on the information provided, which of the following would be the MOST APPROPRIATE spectacle prescription for this patient?
    a. +0.50 DS OU for full time wear
    b. +1.00 DS OU for reading only
    c. +1.00 DS OU for full time wear
    d. +1.00 DS OU Add +2.50 standard bifocal for full time wear
    e. +1.00 DS OU Add +2.50 executive bifocal for full time wear

65. After writing a spectacle prescription as described in question 64, the patient's chief complaint is still not resolved. Which of the following should be the next treatment considered?
    a. Prescribe Base Out prism
    b. Prescribe Base In prism
    c. Vision therapy focusing on Base Out prism
    d. Vision therapy focusing on Base In prism
    e. Strabismus surgery

CASE 14

Demographics
68 year-old Caucasian male; retired truck driver
Chief Complaint
Blurry vision distance and near.
History of Present Illness
Character/Signs/Symptoms: Patient thinks his glasses are no longer "strong enough."
Location: distance and near OD, OS
Severity: moderate
Nature Of Onset: gradual
Duration: slowly getting worse over two years
Frequency: constant
Exacerbations/Remissions: none
Relationship To Activity Or Function: none
Accompanying Signs/Symptoms: none
Secondary Complaints/Symptoms none

Patient Ocular History
Unremarkable
Family Ocular History
Mother: unremarkable
Father: unremarkable
Patient Medical History
Has smoked 1 pack of cigarettes/day for 50 years
Medications Taken By Patient
None
Patient Allergy History
NKDA
Family Medical History
Mother: unremarkable
Father: unremarkable
Review of Systems
Constitutional/General Health: denies
Ear/Nose/Throat: denies
Cardiovascular: denies
Pulmonary: denies
Endocrine: denies
Dermatological: denies
Gastrointestinal: denies
Genitourinary: denies
Musculoskeletal: denies
Neurologic: denies
Psychiatric: denies
Immunologic: denies
Hematologic: denies
Mental Status
Orientation: oriented to time, place, and person.
Mood: appropriate
Affect: appropriate
Clinical Findings
Habitual Rx:
OD: -3.50 DS Add +2.50; VA distance 20/70, VA near 20/70
OS: -3.75 DS Add +2.50; VA distance 20/70, VA near 20/70
Manifest Refraction:
OD: -3.25 DS Add +2.50; VA distance 20/70, VA near 20/70
OS: -3.50 DS Add +2.50; VA distance 20/70, VA near 20/70
Pupils: PERRL, negative APD
EOMs: full, no restrictions OU
Confrontation Fields: full to finger counting OD, OS
Slit lamp
Lids/lashes/adnexa: capped glands OD, OS
Conjunctiva: clear OD, OS
Cornea: 1+ SPK OD, OS
Anterior chamber: deep and quiet OD, OS
Iris: flat and intact OD, OS
Lens: 1+ NSC OD, OS
Vitreous: clear OD, OS
IOPs: 16 mmHg OD; 16 mmHg OS via GAT @ 4:10 p.m.
Blood Pressure: 115/79 RAS @ 4:15 p.m.
Pulse 80 bpm, regular
Fundus OD: See Image 1
Fundus OS: Similar to Image 1

Image 1

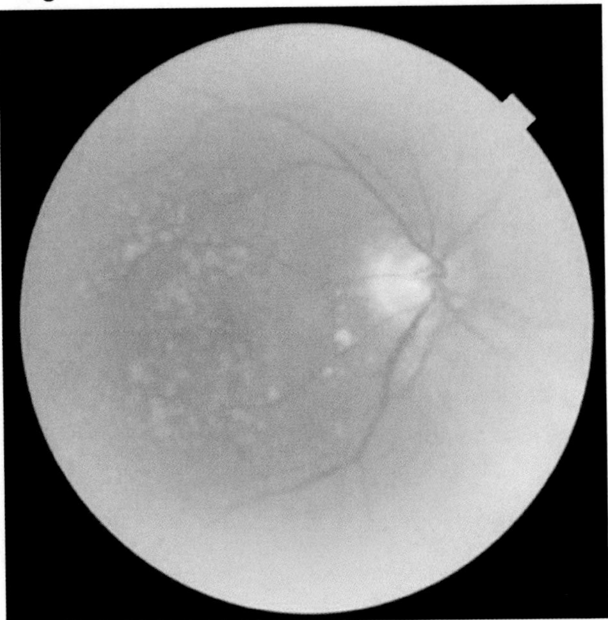

National Vision, Inc.

66. What is the MOST LIKELY cause of the patient's reduced BCVA OU?
    a. Meibomian Gland Dysfunction
    b. Nuclear Sclerotic Cataracts
    c. Familial Dominant Drusen
    d. Age Related Macular Degeneration
    e. Stargardt Disease
67. This patient has which of the following risk factors for his retinal findings? (SELECT THREE)
    a. High cholesterol
    b. Age
    c. Sun exposure
    d. Positive family history
    e. Caucasian ethnicity
68. What should be included in the education for this patient?
    a. Avoid smoking
    b. Increase exercise
    c. The patient should return to 20/20 vision with treatment
    d. A change in glasses prescription will improve the patient's vision
    e. The patient should consider getting genetic testing
69. Which of the following is the MOST APPROPRIATE treatment for this patient's retinal findings?
    a. Focal Laser Photocoagulation
    b. Lucentis Injections
    c. AREDS-1 vitamins
    d. AREDS-2 vitamins
    e. Both C and D

f. No treatment is necessary

70. Which of the following would you expect to find for a patient with Best's Disease?
    a. Normal ERG and EOG
    b. Normal ERG, Abnormal EOG
    c. Abnormal ERG, Normal EOG
    d. Abnormal ERG and EOG

CASE 15

Demographics
23 year-old Indian female; student
Chief Complaint
Patient complains of "pink eye."
History of Present Illness
Character/Signs/Symptoms: Patient's eyes have been red and irritated with a green discharge.
Location: both eyes
Severity: moderate
Nature Of Onset: acute
Duration: Getting worse over the last three months
Frequency: Constant
Exacerbations/Remissions: Eyes are crusty in the morning when she wakes up.
Relationship To Activity Or Function: None
Accompanying Signs/Symptoms: Tender, palpable preauricular nodes
Secondary Complaints/Symptoms: None

Patient Ocular History
Unremarkable
Family Ocular History
Mother: unremarkable
Father: unremarkable
Patient Medical History
Patient had a recent cold two months ago
Medications Taken By Patient
Birth Control Pills
Patient Allergy History
Doxycycline
Family Medical History
Mother: unremarkable
Father: unremarkable

Review of Systems
Constitutional/General Health: denies
Ear/Nose/Throat: denies
Cardiovascular: denies
Pulmonary: denies
Endocrine: denies
Dermatological: denies
Gastrointestinal: denies
Genitourinary: denies
Musculoskeletal: denies
Neurologic: denies
Psychiatric: denies
Immunologic: denies
Hematologic: denies
Mental Status
Orientation: oriented to time, place, and person.
Mood: appropriate
Affect: appropriate

Clinical Findings
Habitual Rx: none
Entering Acuities:
OD Distance 20/20- Near 20/20
OS Distance 20/20- Near 20/20
Manifest Refraction:
OD: +0.25 DS; VA distance 20/20, VA near 20/20
OS: +0.25 -0.25 x 003; VA distance 20/20, VA near 20/20
Pupils: PERRL, negative APD
EOMs: full, no restrictions OU
Confrontation Fields: full to finger counting OD, OS
Cover Test
Distance: 1 exophoria
Near: 3 exophoria
Slit lamp
Lids/lashes/adnexa: unremarkable OD, OS
Conjunctiva:
OD: See Image 1
OS: Similar to Image 1
Cornea: clear OD, OS
Anterior chamber: deep and quiet OD, OS
Iris: flat and intact OD, OS

Lens: clear OD, OS
Vitreous: clear OD, OS
IOPs: 16 mmHg OD; 16 mmHg OS via GAT @ 4:10 p.m.
Blood Pressure: 115/79 RAS @ 4:15 p.m.
Pulse 71 bpm, regular
Fundus OD
C/D: 0.30H/ 0.30V
Macula: normal
Posterior pole: unremarkable
Periphery: unremarkable
Fundus OS
C/D: 0.30H/0.30V
Macula: normal
Posterior pole: unremarkable
Periphery: unremarkable

Image 1

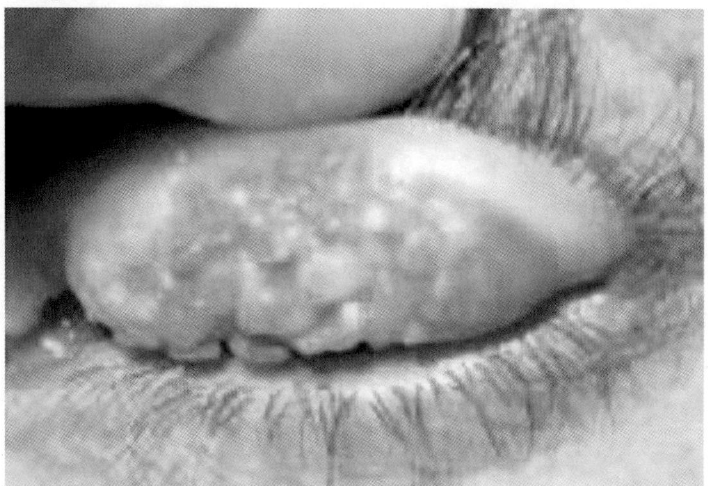

EyeRounds.org University of Iowa

71. What is the MOST LIKELY cause of the patient's chief complaint?
    a. Viral Conjunctivitis
    b. Bacterial Conjunctivitis
    c. Inclusion Conjunctivitis
    d. Atopic Conjunctivitis
    e. Trachoma
72. Which of the following is true regarding the patient's chief complaint?
    a. It is the most common cause of preventable blindness in the world
    b. It is the most common type of conjunctivitis
    c. It is most commonly seen in adults
    d. It is most commonly seen in children
    e. It is most commonly associated with the seasons
73. Which of the following is a possible late complication for the patient's chief complaint?
    a. Subepithelial infiltrates
    b. Arlt Lines
    c. Dennie's Line
    d. No complications are expected
    e. None of the above

74. Which of the following is the MOST APPROPRIATE treatment for this patient's chief complaint? (SELECT TWO)
    a. Tetracycline OU QID for two weeks
    b. Tobradex OU QID for two weeks
    c. Lotemax OU QID for two weeks
    d. Pataday OU QD
    e. Azithromycin PO, single dose
    f. Artificial tears PRN
    g. Erythromycin PO QID for two weeks
75. When should you plan on following up with this patient for her chief complaint?
    a. One day
    b. One week
    c. Two weeks
    d. One month
    e. One year

CASE 16

Demographics
56 year-old Caucasian male; Reporter
Chief Complaint
Patient states that he cannot see out of his left eye.
History of Present Illness
Location: left eye
Severity: severe
Nature Of Onset: Patient could not see out of his left eye when he woke up this morning.
Duration: Today
Frequency: This if the first occurrence
Exacerbations/Remissions: none
Relationship To Activity Or Function: none
Accompanying Signs/Symptoms: The patient mentions that he gets headaches on his left temple and has trouble chewing his food.

Patient Ocular History
Unremarkable
Family Ocular History
Mother: unremarkable
Father: unremarkable
Patient Medical History
Hypertension
Medications Taken By Patient
Lisinopril
Patient Allergy History
NKDA
Family Medical History
Mother: Hypertension
Father: Hypertension
Review of Systems
Constitutional/General Health: denies
Ear/Nose/Throat: denies
Cardiovascular: denies
Pulmonary: denies
Endocrine: denies
Dermatological: denies
Gastrointestinal: denies
Genitourinary: denies
Musculoskeletal: denies
Neurologic: denies
Psychiatric: denies
Immunologic: denies
Hematologic: denies
Mental Status
Orientation: oriented to time, place, and person.
Mood: appropriate
Affect: appropriate
Clinical Findings
Habitual Rx:
OD: -6.00 DS
OS: -6.50 -1.00 x 145
Add +2.00 OU
BVA
OD: 20/20 distance and near
OS: NLP
Pupils: PERRL, positive APD
EOMs: full, no pain or restrictions OU
Confrontation Fields:
OD: full to finger counting
OS: Superior Hemianopsia
Slit lamp
Lids/lashes/adnexa: unremarkable OD, OS
Conjunctiva: clear OD, OS
Cornea: clear OD, OS
Anterior chamber: deep and quiet OD, OS
Iris: flat and intact OD, OS
Lens: clear OD, OS
Vitreous: clear OD, OS
IOPs: 16 mmHg OD; 16 mmHg OS via GAT @ 4:10 p.m.
Blood Pressure: 125/87 RAS @ 4:15 p.m.
Pulse 80 bpm, regular
Fundus OD
See Image One
Fundus OS
See Image Two

Image 1

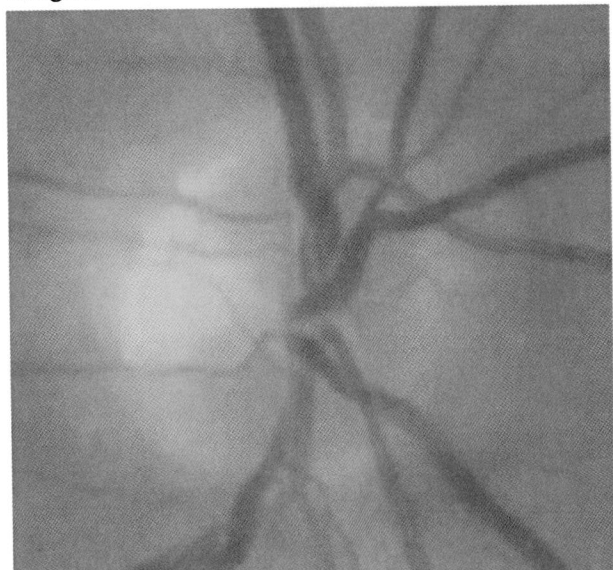

National Vision, Inc.

Image 2

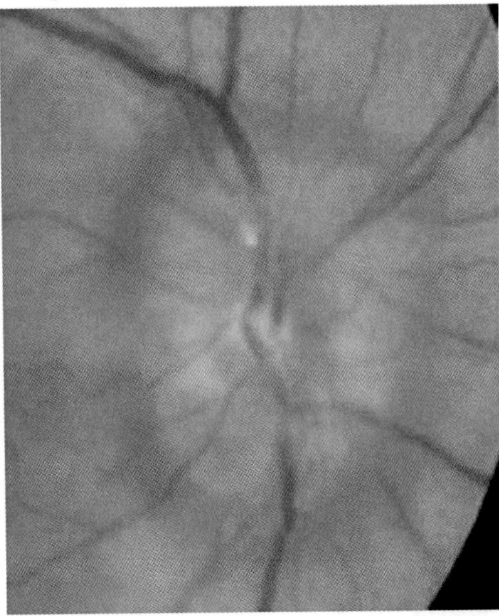

Retina Image Bank 638

76. Which of the following is the MOST LIKELY diagnosis for the patient's chief complaint?
    a. Nonarteritic Ischemic Optic Neuropathy
    b. Arteritic Ischemic Optic Neuropathy
    c. Optic Neuritis
    d. Branch Retinal Artery Occlusion
    e. Central Retinal Artery Occlusion
77. Which of the following in this patient's case history is a risk factor for his chief complaint?
    a. Spectacle Prescription
    b. Hypertension
    c. Optic Nerve Appearance
    d. Occupation
    e. Family history
78. Which of the following tests should be ordered for this patient? (SELECT TWO)
    a. ESR
    b. CRP
    c. BUN
    d. MRI
    e. OCT
    f. Lipid Panel
    g. Fluorescein Angiography
79. Which of the following is the MOST APPROPRIATE INITIAL treatment for this patient?
    a. Emergent IV Steroids
    b. Intravitreal steroids every two weeks
    c. Acetazolamide PO TID
    d. Hyperventilation into a paper bag
    e. No treatment is necessary

80. Optic Neuritis is MOST COMMONLY associated with which of the following?
    a. Giant Cell Arteritis
    b. Multiple Sclerosis
    c. Increased Intracranial Pressure
    d. Optic Nerve Meningioma
    e. Hypertension

CASE 17

Demographics
31 year-old Filipino female; Nurse
Chief Complaint
Blurry vision at distance.
History of Present Illness
Location: both eyes
Severity: mild
Nature Of Onset: gradual
Duration: slowly getting worse over the last 12 months.
Frequency: Constant
Exacerbations/Remissions: none
Relationship To Activity Or Function: worse in low light settings
Accompanying Signs/Symptoms: The patient is inquiring about what type of corrective lens will give her the clearest vision possible.
Secondary Complaints/Symptoms: none

Patient Ocular History
Unremarkable
Family Ocular History
Mother: unremarkable
Father: unremarkable
Patient Medical History
Unremarkable
Medications Taken By Patient
None
Patient Allergy History
NKDA
Family Medical History
Mother: unremarkable
Father: unremarkable

Review of Systems
Constitutional/General Health: denies
Ear/Nose/Throat: denies
Cardiovascular: denies
Pulmonary: denies
Endocrine: denies
Dermatological: denies
Gastrointestinal: denies
Genitourinary: denies
Musculoskeletal: denies
Neurologic: denies
Psychiatric: denies
Immunologic: denies
Hematologic: denies
Mental Status
Orientation: oriented to time, place, and person.
Mood: appropriate
Affect: appropriate

Clinical Findings
Habitual Rx:
OD: -4.25 -3.75 x090; VA distance 20/20-, VA near 20/20-
OS: -3.00 -4.00 x090; VA distance 20/20-, VA near 20/20-
Manifest Refraction:
OD: -4.25 -3.75 x090; VA distance 20/20-, VA near 20/20-
OS: -3.00 -4.00 x090; VA distance 20/20-, VA near 20/20-
Keratometry:
OD: 44.50 @090; 46.50 @180
OS: 44.00 @090; 44.00 @180
Pupils: PERRL, negative APD
EOMs: full, no restrictions OU
Confrontation Fields: full to finger counting OD, OS
Slit lamp
Lids/lashes/adnexa: unremarkable OD, OS
Conjunctiva: clear OD, OS
Cornea: clear OD, OS
Anterior chamber: deep and quiet OD, OS
Iris: flat and intact OD, OS
Lens: clear OD, OS
Vitreous: clear OD, OS

IOPs: 10 mmHg OD; 9 mmHg OS via GAT @ 5:12 p.m.
Blood Pressure: 117/71 RAS @ 5:04 p.m.
Pulse 63 bpm, regular
Fundus OD
C/D: 0.32H/ 0.20V
Macula: normal
Posterior pole: unremarkable
Periphery: unremarkable
Fundus OS
C/D: 0.20H/0.20V
Macula: normal
Posterior pole: unremarkable
Periphery: unremarkable

Image 1

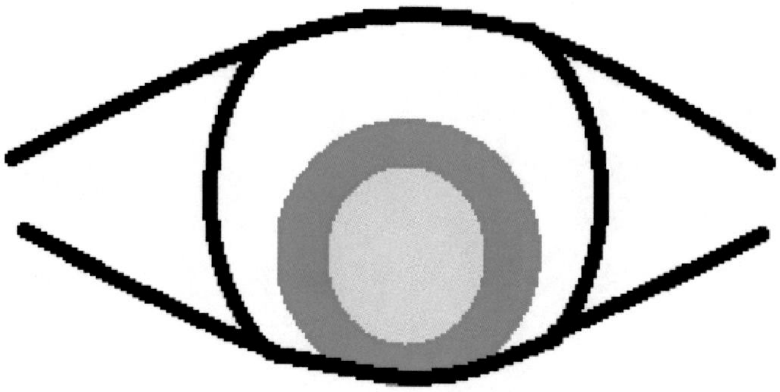

Kimberly Castillo, OD

Image 2

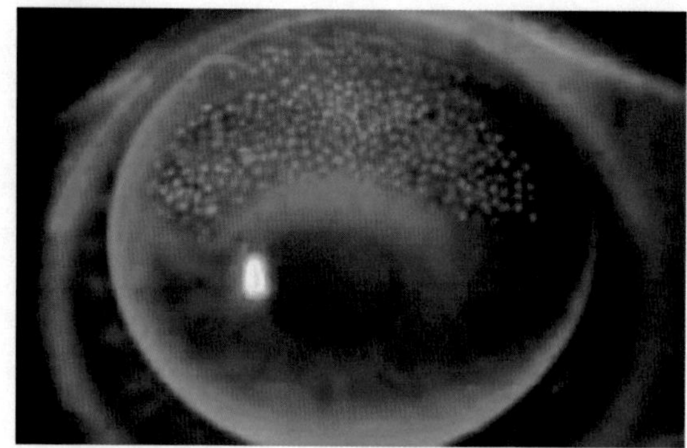

Bausch + Lomb 2

81. Which of the following would be the best RGP design for this patient's right eye?
    a. Spherical
    b. Back Surface Toric
    c. Front Surface Toric
    d. Spherical Power Effect Bitoric
    e. Cylinder Power Effect Bitoric
82. Which of the following would be the best power for an RGP in this patient's right eye?
    a. -4.25 DS
    b. -6.00 DS
    c. -4.25 -3.75 x090
    d. -4.00 -3.75 x090
    e. -4.00 -1.25 x090
83. See Image 1 for the NaFL pattern for the first trial lens you put on this patient. Which of the following changes could you consider for this lens? (SELECT THREE)
    a. Choose a steeper base curve
    b. Choose a flatter base curve
    c. Increase the diameter
    d. Reduce the diameter
    e. Increase the sagittal height
    f. Decrease the sagittal height

84. This patient returns one year later for her annual eye exam. She is happy with her RGP lenses and has not observed any changes in her vision in the past year. See Image 2 for your slit lamp findings. What is the MOST LIKELY cause of the findings seen in Image 2?
    a. Jelly Bumps
    b. Mucin Balls
    c. Corneal Microcysts
    d. Dimple Veiling
    e. Protein Deposits
85. Which of the following is the MOST APPROPRIATE management for the patient's finding in Image 2?
    a. The patient needs to be educated on proper contact lens care
    b. The patient need to be educated to avoid sleeping in her contact lenses
    c. The patient needs to be fitted into a flatter RGP
    d. The patient needs to be fitted into a steeper RGP
    e. The patient needs to throw away and replace her damaged RGP

CASE 18

Demographics
40 year-old Hispanic female; stay at home mom
Chief Complaint
Patient complains that her vision has rapidly decreased.
History of Present Illness
Character/Signs/Symptoms: Patient is having trouble seeing both distance and near.
Location: both eyes
Severity: moderate to severe
Nature Of Onset: gradual
Duration: slowly getting worse over the last four months.
Frequency: constant
Exacerbations/Remissions: none
Relationship To Activity Or Function: worse when driving at night when there are oncoming headlights.

Patient Ocular History
Unremarkable
Family Ocular History
Mother: unremarkable
Father: unremarkable
Patient Medical History
Diabetes Mellitus, last A1C 9.0
Medications Taken By Patient
Insulin
Patient Allergy History
NKDA
Family Medical History
Mother: Diabetes Mellitus
Father: Diabetes Mellitus

Review of Systems
Constitutional/General Health: denies
Ear/Nose/Throat: denies
Cardiovascular: denies
Pulmonary: denies
Endocrine: Diabetes Mellitus
Dermatological: denies
Gastrointestinal: denies
Genitourinary: denies
Musculoskeletal: denies
Neurologic: denies
Psychiatric: denies
Immunologic: denies
Hematologic: denies
Mental Status
Orientation: oriented to time, place, and person.
Mood: appropriate
Affect: appropriate

Clinical Findings
Habitual Rx:
OD: -1.50 DS; VA distance 20/50, VA near 20/50
OS: -2.00 DS; VA distance 20/50, VA near 20/50
Manifest Refraction:
OD: -3.00 DS; VA distance 20/40, VA near 20/50
OS: -5.00DS; VA distance 20/40, VA near 20/50
Pupils: PERRL, negative APD
EOMs: full, no restrictions OU
Confrontation Fields: full to finger counting OD, OS
Cover Test
Distance: 1 exophoria
Near: 3 exophoria
Slit lamp
Lids/lashes/adnexa: unremarkable OD, OS
Conjunctiva: clear OD, OS
Cornea: clear OD, OS
Anterior chamber: deep and quiet OD, OS
Iris: flat and intact OD, OS
Lens:
OD: See Image 1
OS: Similar to Image 1
Vitreous: clear OD, OS
IOPs: 16 mmHg OD; 16 mmHg OS via GAT @ 4:10 p.m.

Blood Pressure: 115/79 RAS @ 4:15 p.m.
Pulse 71 bpm, regular
Fundus OD
C/D: 0.30H/ 0.30V
Macula: normal
Posterior pole: unremarkable
Periphery: unremarkable
Fundus OS
C/D: 0.30H/0.30V
Macula: normal
Posterior pole: unremarkable
Periphery: unremarkable

Image 1 Image 2

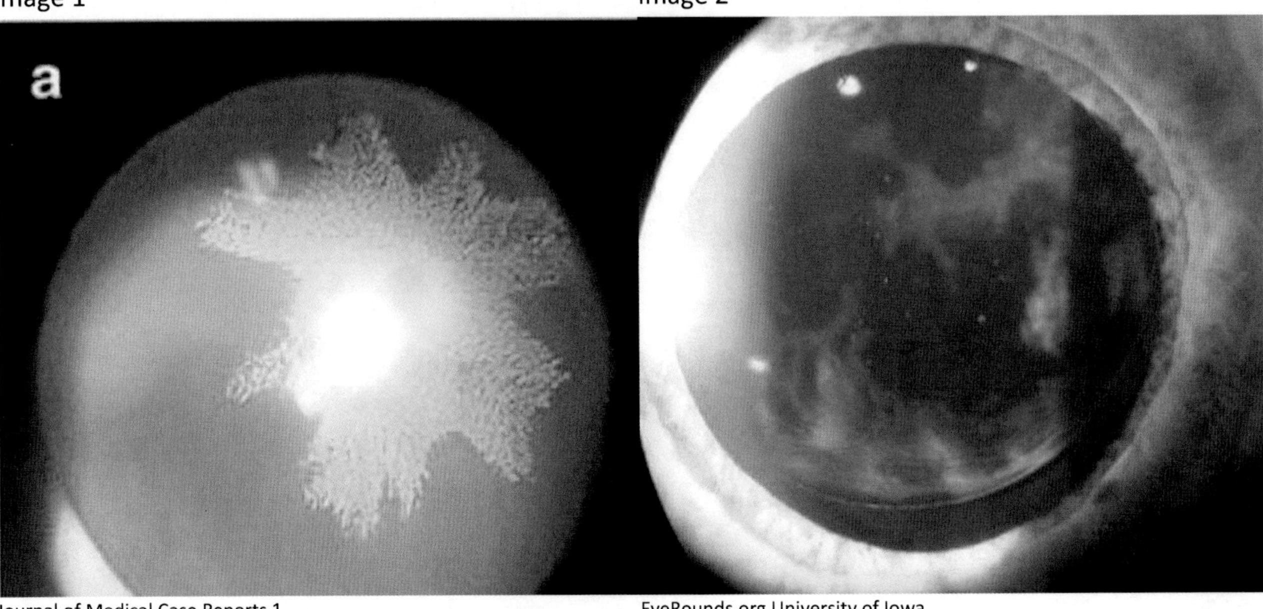

Journal of Medical Case Reports 1 EyeRounds.org University of Iowa

86. What is the MOST LIKELY cause of this patient's chief complaint?
    a. Cortical Cataracts
    b. Rosette Cataracts
    c. Snowflake Cataracts
    d. Posterior Subcapsular Cataracts
    e. Sunflower Cataracts
87. What is the MOST LIKELY etiology for this patient's chief complaint?
    a. Steroid use
    b. Lifetime exposure to the sun
    c. Blunt ocular trauma
    d. Wilson's Disease
    e. Diabetes
88. What is the MOST APPROPRIATE treatment for this patient's chief complaint?
    a. Release an updated spectacle prescription
    b. Refer to endocrinologist to manage diabetes
    c. Refer to primary care physician to manage Wilson's Disease
    d. Refer for cataract surgery
    e. Educate patient to stop using steroids

Questions 89 and 90 Refer to a DIFFERENT PATIENT.

89. A DIFFERENT patient with a history of cataract surgery in both eyes comes to your clinic complaining that it appears his cataracts have "come back." See Image 2 for your slit lamp findings. What is the MOST LIKELY cause of this patient's complaint?
    a. Posterior Capsular Opacification
    b. Posterior Subcapsular Cataracts
    c. Anterior Subcapsular Cataracts
    d. Nuclear Sclerotic Cataracts
    e. Pseudoexfoliation Syndrome
90. What is the most appropriate management for this patient's chief complaint?
    a. Refer for YAG Capsulotomy
    b. Refer for Laser Peripheral Iridotomy
    c. Refer for Selective Laser Trabeculoplasty
    d. Refer for Cataract Surgery
    e. Prescribe Latanoprost QHS

CASE 19

Demographics
55 year-old Caucasian female; paralegal
Chief Complaint
Patient states that her vision is blurry
History of Present Illness
Location: OD
Severity: moderate
Nature Of Onset: gradual
Duration: slowly getting worse since this morning
Frequency: constant
Exacerbations/Remissions: none
Relationship To Activity Or Function: Patient is seeing halos around lights as well
Accompanying Signs/Symptoms: The patient feels nauseous and is experiencing a deep headache behind her eyes
Secondary Complaints/Symptoms: none

Patient Ocular History
Unremarkable
Family Ocular History
Mother: unremarkable
Father: unremarkable
Patient Medical History
Asthma
Medications Taken By Patient
None
Patient Allergy History
NKDA
Family Medical History
Mother: unremarkable
Father: unremarkable

Review of Systems
Constitutional/General Health: denies
Ear/Nose/Throat: denies
Cardiovascular: denies
Pulmonary: Asthma
Endocrine: denies
Dermatological: denies
Gastrointestinal: denies
Genitourinary: denies
Musculoskeletal: denies
Neurologic: denies
Psychiatric: denies
Immunologic: denies
Hematologic: denies
Mental Status
Orientation: oriented to time, place, and person.
Mood: appropriate
Affect: appropriate

Clinical Findings
BVA
OD: 20/60
OS: 20/20
Pupils:
OD: Not responsive to light, see Image 1
OS: Round and reactive to light
EOMs: full, no restrictions OU
Confrontation Fields: full to finger counting OD, OS
Slit lamp
Lids/lashes/adnexa: unremarkable OD, OS
Conjunctiva: clear OD, OS
Cornea:
OD: See Image 1
OS: Clear
Anterior chamber:
Shallow and quiet OD, OS
Van Herick Angles:
OD: 0
OS: 1
Iris: flat and intact OD, OS
Lens: clear OD, OS
Vitreous: clear OD, OS
IOPs: 45 mmHg OD; 16 mmHg OS via GAT @ 4:10 p.m.

Blood Pressure: 115/79 RAS @ 4:15 p.m.
Pulse 75 bpm, regular
Fundus OD
C/D: 0.30H/ 0.30V
Macula: normal
Posterior pole: unremarkable
Periphery: unremarkable
Fundus OS
C/D: 0.30H/0.30V
Macula: normal
Posterior pole: unremarkable
Periphery: unremarkable

Image 1

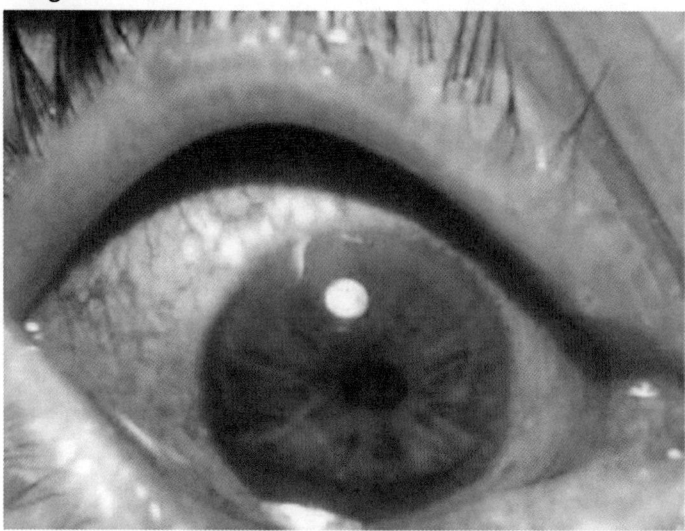

EyeRounds.org University of Iowa

91. What is the MOST LIKELY cause of this patient's chief complaint?
    a. Glaucomatocyclitic Crisis
    b. Acute Angle Closure Glaucoma
    c. Plateau Iris Syndrome
    d. Aqueous Misdirection Syndrome
    e. Malignant Glaucoma
92. Which of the following spectacle prescriptions would be MOST LIKELY for this patient's OD?
    a. +6.00 DS
    b. +1.00 DS
    c. Plano
    d. -1.00 DS
    e. -6.00 DS
    f. -0.25 -4.00 x045
93. Which of the following should be considered in the INITIAL treatment for this patient? (SELECT THREE)
    a. Indentation Gonioscopy
    b. Topical Latanoprost every 15 minutes
    c. Topical Timolol every 15 minutes
    d. Topical Brimonidine every 15 minutes
    e. Oral Acetazolamide

94. Which of the following is the MOST APPROPRIATE treatment once the IOP has been stabilized?
    a. Laser Peripheral Iridotomy (LPI)
    b. Iridectomy
    c. YAG Capsulotomy
    d. Selective Laser Trabeculoplasty
    e. Topical Prostaglandin
95. The patient's chief complaint would be MOST LIKELY to occur after which of the following activities?
    a. Watching a matinee showing of a movie
    b. Snowboarding
    c. Watching a solar eclipse
    d. Reading on a computer for a prolonged period of time
    e. This patient's chief complaint is not associated with any activity

CASE 20

Demographics
66 year-old Caucasian female; retired
Chief Complaint
Patient is here for an annual eye exam.
History of Present Illness
Character/Signs/Symptoms: Patient is having trouble reading his computer.
Location: both eyes
Severity: moderate
Nature Of Onset: gradual
Duration: slowly getting worse over the last year
Frequency: whenever he is looking at his computer
Exacerbations/Remissions: none
Relationship To Activity Or Function: worse in low light settings
Accompanying Signs/Symptoms: horizontal double vision
Secondary Complaints/Symptoms: none

Patient Ocular History
Unremarkable
Family Ocular History
Mother: unremarkable
Father: unremarkable
Patient Medical History
Diabetes Mellitus
Medications Taken By Patient
None
Patient Allergy History
NKDA
Family Medical History
Mother: unremarkable
Father: unremarkable

Review of Systems
Constitutional/General Health: denies
Ear/Nose/Throat: denies
Cardiovascular: denies
Pulmonary: denies
Endocrine: Diabetes Mellitus
Dermatological: denies
Gastrointestinal: denies
Genitourinary: denies
Musculoskeletal: denies
Neurologic: denies
Psychiatric: denies
Immunologic: denies
Hematologic: denies
Mental Status
Orientation: oriented to time, place, and person.
Mood: appropriate
Affect: appropriate

Clinical Findings
Habitual Rx:
OD: -1.00 -0.50 x090 Add +1.75; VA distance 20/20, VA near 20/30
OS: -1.00 -0.50 x090 Add +1.75; VA distance 20/20, VA near 20/30
Manifest Refraction:
OD: -1.00 -0.50 x090 Add +2.50; VA distance 20/20, VA near 20/20
OS: -1.00 -0.50 x090 Add +2.50; VA distance 20/20, VA near 20/20

Pupils: PERRL, negative APD
EOMs: Unable to abduct OS. See Image 1
Cover Test: Right Esotropia
Confrontation Fields: full to finger counting OD, OS
Slit lamp
Lids/lashes/adnexa: unremarkable OD, OS
Conjunctiva: clear OD, OS
Cornea: clear OD, OS
Anterior chamber: deep and quiet OD, OS
Iris: flat and intact OD, OS
Lens: clear OD, OS

Vitreous: clear OD, OS
IOPs: 16 mmHg OD; 16 mmHg OS via GAT @ 4:10 p.m.
Blood Pressure: 115/79 RAS @ 4:15 p.m.
Pulse 60-100 bpm, regular
Fundus OD
C/D: 0.30H/ 0.30V
Macula: normal
Posterior pole: unremarkable
Periphery: unremarkable
Fundus OS
C/D: 0.30H/0.30V
Macula: normal
Posterior pole: unremarkable
Periphery: unremarkable

Image 1

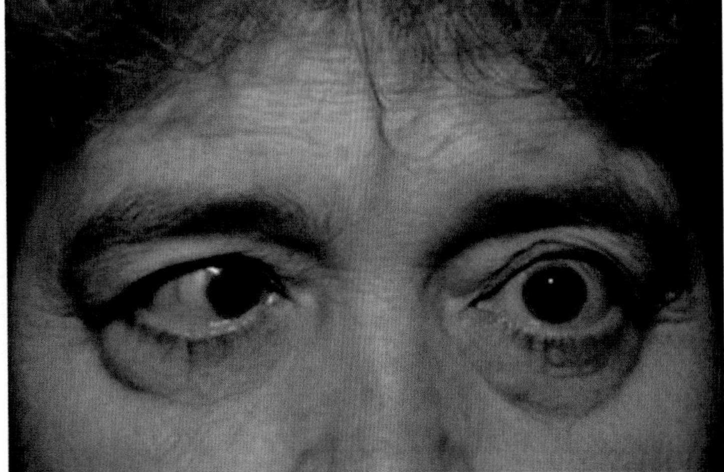

EyeRounds.org University of Iowa

96. Which diagnosis is the MOST LIKELY cause of this patient's diplopia?
    a. Esotropia
    b. Exotropia
    c. Cranial Nerve 3 Palsy
    d. Cranial Nerve 4 Palsy
    e. Cranial Nerve 6 Palsy
97. Which of the following should you include in your initial workup for this patient?
    a. 24-2 Humphrey Visual Field
    b. Double Maddox Rod Test
    c. Forced Ductions
    d. Parks 3-step
    e. Tensilon Test
    f. None of the Above
98. Which of the following is the MOST COMMON etiology for this patient's diplopia?
    a. Aneurysm
    b. Compressive Tumor
    c. Congenital muscle weakness
    d. Decompensated strabismus
    e. Head Trauma
    f. Microvascular Disease

99. Which of the following is the MOST APPROPRIATE management for this patient's diplopia?
    a. Monitor, this is longstanding
    b. Monitor, this should spontaneously resolve
    c. Prescribe prism
    d. Refer for an MRI
    e. Refer for strabismus surgery
    f. Refer for vision therapy
100. If a DIFFERENT PATIENT has Third Nerve palsy and the pupil is NOT involved, what can be concluded?
    a. The etiology is likely due to a microvascular disease
    b. The patient has an APD
    c. The patient likely has a compressive tumor
    d. The patient likely has an aneurysm of the posterior communicating artery
    e. No conclusion can be made, further testing is necessary

CASE 21

Demographics
8 year-old Hispanic male; student
Chief Complaint
Blurry vision at near
History of Present Illness
Location: both eyes
Severity: moderate
Nature Of Onset: gradual
Duration: six months
Frequency: constant
Exacerbations/Remissions: worse at the end of the day
Relationship To Activity Or Function: worse whenever he tries to read
Accompanying Signs/Symptoms: headaches after reading for 15 minutes
Secondary Complaints/Symptoms: none

Patient Ocular History
Unremarkable, first eye exam
Family Ocular History
Mother: unremarkable
Father: unremarkable
Patient Medical History
Unremarkable
Medications Taken By Patient
None
Patient Allergy History
NKDA
Family Medical History
Mother: unremarkable
Father: unremarkable

Review of Systems
Constitutional/General Health: denies
Ear/Nose/Throat: denies
Cardiovascular: denies
Pulmonary: denies
Endocrine: denies
Dermatological: denies
Gastrointestinal: denies
Genitourinary: denies
Musculoskeletal: denies
Neurologic: denies
Psychiatric: denies
Immunologic: denies
Hematologic: denies
Mental Status
Orientation: oriented to time, place, and person.
Mood: appropriate
Affect: appropriate

Clinical Findings
Habitual Rx: none
Entering Acuities:
OD Distance 20/25 Near 20/25
OS Distance 20/20 Near 20/20
Manifest Refraction:
OD: +0.75 -0.50 x175; VA distance 20/20, VA near 20/20
OS: +0.50 DS; VA distance 20/20, VA near 20/20
Cycloplegic Refraction:
OD: +2.25 -0.50 x180; VA distance 20/20, VA near 20/30
OS: +2.00 DS; VA distance 20/20, VA near 20/30
Pupils: PERRL, negative APD
EOMs: full, no restrictions OU
Confrontation Fields: full to finger counting OD, OS
Cover Test
Distance: 1 exophoria
Near: 3 exophoria
Vergence System
NPC: TTN
Vergences:
Negative fusional convergence (NFC): Far 7/4; Near 12 / 22 / 15
Positive fusional convergence (PFC): Far 9/19/10; Near 13/21/13

Stereoacuity (Random dot): 20"
Accommodative System
AC/A: 4/1
Amplitude of Accommodation: 14
Binocular Accommodative Facility: 12 cpm
Slit lamp
Lids/lashes/adnexa: unremarkable OD, OS
Conjunctiva: clear OD, OS
Cornea: clear OD, OS
Anterior chamber: deep and quiet OD, OS
Iris: flat and intact OD, OS
Lens: clear OD, OS
Vitreous: clear OD, OS
IOPs: 16 mmHg OD; 16 mmHg OS via GAT @ 4:10 p.m.
Blood Pressure: 115/79 RAS @ 4:15 p.m.
Pulse 65 bpm, regular
Fundus OD
C/D: 0.30H/ 0.30V
Macula: normal
Posterior pole: unremarkable
Periphery: unremarkable
Fundus OS
C/D: 0.30H/0.30V
Macula: normal
Posterior pole: unremarkable
Periphery: unremarkable

101. What is the spherical equivalent for this patient's right eye based on the MANIFEST REFRACTION?
    a. +0.25 DS
    b. +0.50 DS
    c. +0.75 DS
    d. +1.75 DS
    e. +2.00 DS
102. Which of the following is the MOST APPROPRIATE diagnosis for this patient's chief complaint?
    a. Hyperopia
    b. Accommodative Infacility
    c. Accommodative Insufficiency
    d. Accommodative excess
    e. Ill-Sustained Accommodation
103. This patient presents with how much LATENT hyperopia in his left eye?
    a. +0.50 DS
    b. +1.00 DS
    c. +1.50 DS
    d. +2.00 DS
    e. +2.50 DS
    f. This patient has no latent hyperopia
104. Which of the following would be the MOST APPROPRIATE prescription for this patient?
    a. OD: +0.75 -0.50 x180 / OS: +0.50 DS for full time wear
    b. OD: +0.75 -0.50 x180 / OS: +0.50 DS for reading only
    c. OD: +1.50 -0.50 x180 / OS: +1.25 DS for full time wear
    d. OD: +1.50 -0.50 x180 / OS: +1.25 DS for reading only
    e. OD: +2.25 -0.50 x180 / OS: +2.00 DS for full time wear
    f. OD: +2.25 -0.50 x180 / OS: +2.00 DS for reading only

105. Which of the following is an example of a Jackson Cross Cylinder?
    a. +1.00 -0.50 x180
    b. +1.00 -1.00 x180
    c. +1.00 -1.50 x180
    d. +1.00 -2.00 x180
    e. +1.00 -2.50 x180

CASE 22

Demographics
49 year-old Caucasian female; receptionist
Chief Complaint
Patient states that she cannot close her left eye.
History of Present Illness
Character/Signs/Symptoms: Patient is unable to move the entire left side of her face.
Location: left side of face
Severity: severe
Nature Of Onset: started while driving to work this morning.
Duration: Four hours
Frequency: Constant
Exacerbations/Remissions: None
Relationship To Activity Or Function: None
Accompanying Signs/Symptoms: None
Secondary Complaints/Symptoms: None

Patient Ocular History
Unremarkable
Family Ocular History
Mother: unremarkable
Father: unremarkable
Patient Medical History
Unremarkable
Medications Taken By Patient
None
Patient Allergy History
NKDA
Family Medical History
Mother: unremarkable
Father: unremarkable

Review of Systems
Constitutional/General Health: denies
Ear/Nose/Throat: denies
Cardiovascular: denies
Pulmonary: denies
Endocrine: denies
Dermatological: denies
Gastrointestinal: denies
Genitourinary: denies
Musculoskeletal: denies
Neurologic: denies
Psychiatric: denies
Immunologic: denies
Hematologic: denies
Mental Status
Orientation: oriented to time, place, and person.
Mood: appropriate
Affect: appropriate

Clinical Findings
Habitual Rx: none
Entering Acuities:
OD Distance 20/20- Near 20/70
OS Distance 20/20 Near 20/70
Habitual Prescription:
OD, OS: +1.75 OTC Reader; VA near 20/20
Pupils: PERRL, negative APD
EOMs: full, no restrictions OU
Confrontation Fields: full to finger counting OD, OS
Cover Test
Distance: 1 exophoria
Near: 3 exophoria
Slit lamp
Lids/lashes/adnexa:
OD: Unremarkable
OS: Upper lid cannot be voluntarily closed, ectropion
Conjunctiva: clear OD, OS
Cornea:
OD: clear
OS: diffuse 2+ SPK
Anterior chamber: deep and quiet OD, OS
Iris: flat and intact OD, OS
Lens: clear OD, OS
Vitreous: clear OD, OS

IOPs: 16 mmHg OD; 16 mmHg OS via GAT @ 4:10 p.m.
Blood Pressure: 115/79 RAS @ 12:15 p.m.
Pulse 80 bpm, regular
Fundus OD
C/D: 0.30H/ 0.30V
Macula: normal
Posterior pole: unremarkable
Periphery: unremarkable
Fundus OS
C/D: 0.30H/0.30V
Macula: normal
Posterior pole: unremarkable
Periphery: unremarkable

106. What is the MOST LIKELY diagnosis for the patient's chief complaint?
    a. Bell's Palsy
    b. Cranial Nerve 3 Palsy
    c. Cranial Nerve 4 Palsy
    d. Cranial Nerve 5 Palsy
    e. Floppy Eyelid Syndrome
107. What is the MOST LIKELY etiology for this patient's chief complaint?
    a. Compressive tumor
    b. Herpes simplex
    c. Idiopathic
    d. Neural inflammation
    e. Sleep Apnea
    f. Stroke
108. What is the MOST LIKELY location of the neural defect?
    a. Right lower motor neuron lesion
    b. Right upper motor neuron lesion
    c. Left lower motor neuron lesion
    d. Left upper motor neuron lesion
    e. Trigeminal Ganglion
109. What is the MOST APPROPRIATE treatment for this patient's chief complaint?
    a. Emergent MRI
    b. Monitor, this will spontaneously resolve
    c. Perform a sleep test
    d. Prescribe oral Acyclovir
    e. Prescribe oral steroid
110. Which of the following is an EXPECTED finding for this patient (SELECT TWO)?
    a. Drooling
    b. Fixed, dilated left pupil
    c. Left Bell's Reflex intact
    d. Positive Forced Ductions test of left eye
    e. Inability to abduct the left eye.

CASE 23

Demographics
25 year-old African-American female; paralegal
Chief Complaint
Patient complains of photophobia
History of Present Illness
Location: both eyes
Severity: severe
Nature Of Onset: gradual
Duration: this episode started last night
Frequency: this is the third time it has happened in four months
Exacerbations/Remissions: worse when outside during the day
Relationship To Activity Or Function: none
Accompanying Signs/Symptoms: blurry vision in both eyes
Secondary Complaints/Symptoms: none
Patient Ocular History
Unremarkable
Family Ocular History
Mother: unremarkable
Father: unremarkable
Patient Medical History
Unremarkable
Medications Taken By Patient
None
Patient Allergy History
NKDA
Family Medical History
Mother: unremarkable
Father: unremarkable

Review of Systems
Constitutional/General Health: denies
Ear/Nose/Throat: denies
Cardiovascular: denies
Pulmonary: denies
Endocrine: denies
Dermatological: denies
Gastrointestinal: denies
Genitourinary: denies
Musculoskeletal: denies
Neurologic: denies
Psychiatric: denies
Immunologic: denies
Hematologic: denies
Mental Status
Orientation: oriented to time, place, and person.
Mood: appropriate
Affect: appropriate
Clinical Findings
Habitual Rx: none
Entering Acuities:
OD Distance 20/50
OS Distance 20/50
BVA
OD: 20/50
OS: 20/50
Pupils: PERRL, negative APD
EOMs: full, no restrictions OU
Confrontation Fields: full to finger counting OD, OS
Slit lamp
Lids/lashes/adnexa: unremarkable OD, OS
Conjunctiva: perilimbal hyperemia OD, OS
Cornea:
OD: See Image 1
OS: Similar to Image 1
Anterior chamber: 3+ cells OD, OS
Iris: flat and intact OD, OS
Lens: clear OD, OS
Vitreous: clear OD, OS
IOPs: 16 mmHg OD; 16 mmHg OS via GAT @ 10:10 a.m.
Blood Pressure: 115/79 RAS @ 10:15 a.m.
Pulse 75 bpm, regular
Fundus OD: See Image 2
Fundus OS: Similar to Image 2
Chest X-Ray: Noncaseating granulomas on lungs

Image 1

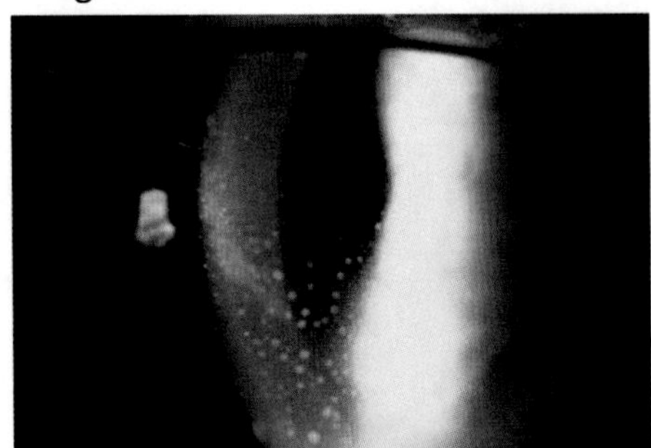

EyeRounds.org University of Iowa

Image 2

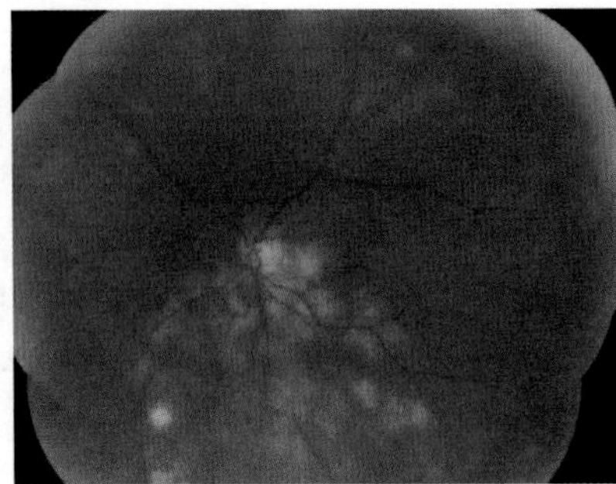

EyeRounds.org University of Iowa

111. What is the MOST LIKELY diagnosis for the patient's systemic disease?
    a. Ankylosing Spondylitis
    b. Sarcoidosis
    c. Syphilis
    d. Tuberculosis
    e. Vogt-Koyanagi-Harada Syndrome
112. Which test would you expect to be abnormal for this patient?
    a. ACE
    b. ANA
    c. PPD
    d. RPR
    e. VDRL
113. Which of the following would be the most appropriate treatment for this patient's anterior segment findings? (SELECT TWO)
    a. Oral Ibuprofen
    b. Oral Prednisone
    c. Topical Cyclopentolate
    d. Topical Ketorolac
    e. Topical Pred Acetate
114. Ocular findings are most likely to be present during which stage of Syphilis?
    a. Primary Syphilis
    b. Secondary Syphilis
    c. Tertiary Syphilis
    d. Quaternary Syphilis
    e. Ocular findings are present during all stages of Syphilis
115. Which of the following tests should you include when following a patient who is taking Plaquenil?
    a. 24-2 Visual Field
    b. Optic Nerve OCT
    c. Ishihara Color Vision
    d. Red Saturation Test
    e. Goldman Applanation Tonometry

CASE 24

Demographics
70 year-old Asian female; Retired
Chief Complaint
Patient is complaining of a red, painful eye
History of Present Illness
Location: OD
Severity: moderate
Nature of Onset: started this morning
Frequency: constant
Exacerbations/Remissions: none
Relationship to Activity or Function: pain is worse in bright light settings
Accompanying Signs/Symptoms: blur OD
Secondary Complaints/Symptoms: none

Patient Ocular History
Cataract Surgery 2 weeks ago
Family Ocular History
Mother: unremarkable
Father: unremarkable
Patient Medical History
Unremarkable
Medications Taken By Patient
None
Patient Allergy History
NKDA
Family Medical History
Mother: unremarkable
Father: unremarkable

Review of Systems
Constitutional/General Health: denies
Ear/Nose/Throat: denies
Cardiovascular: denies
Pulmonary: denies
Endocrine: denies
Dermatological: denies
Gastrointestinal: denies
Genitourinary: denies
Musculoskeletal: denies
Neurologic: denies
Psychiatric: denies
Immunologic: denies
Hematologic: denies
Mental Status
Orientation: oriented to time, place, and person.
Mood: appropriate
Affect: appropriate

Clinical Findings
Habitual Rx: none
BVA
OD: 20/400
OS: 20/20
Pupils: PERRL, negative APD
EOMs: full, no restrictions OU
Confrontation Fields: full to finger counting OD, OS
Slit lamp
OD: See Image 1
OS: Unremarkable
Lens: clear OD, OS
Vitreous:
OD Clear
OS Unable to View
IOPs: 16 mmHg OD; 16 mmHg OS via GAT @ 4:10 p.m.
Blood Pressure: 115/79 RAS @ 4:15 p.m.
Pulse 80 bpm, regular
Fundus OD: Unable to View
Fundus OS
C/D: 0.30H/0.30V
Macula: normal
Posterior pole: unremarkable
Periphery: unremarkable

Image 1

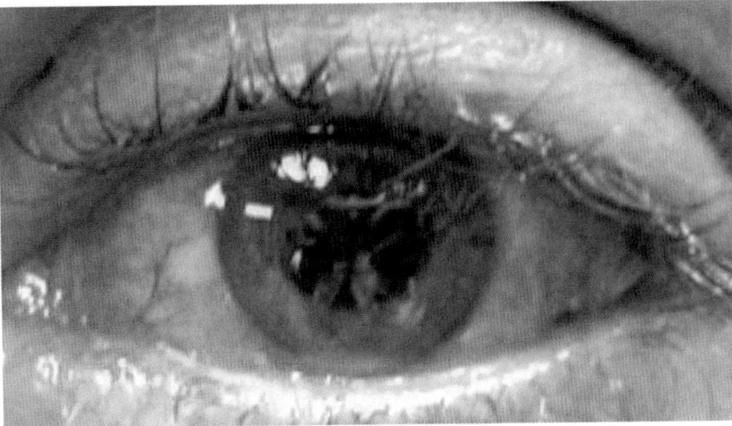

EyeRounds.org University of Iowa

116. What is the MOST LIKELY diagnosis for this patient's chief complaint?
    a. Bacterial Keratitis
    b. Bechet's Disease
    c. Blebitis
    d. Endophthalmitis
    e. Sympathetic Ophthalmia
117. Which of the following is the MOST COMMON cause of this patient's chief complaint?
    a. Corynebacterium diphtheria
    b. Haemophilus influenzae
    c. Moraxella catarrhalis
    d. Neisseria gonorrhoeae
    e. Pseudomonas aeruginosa
    f. Staph aureus
    g. Staph epidermidis
    h. Streptococcus pneumoniae
118. What should be the first step in the management for this patient?
    a. Immediately discontinue all medications
    b. Immediately refer to an ophthalmologist
    c. Monitor IOP hourly
    d. Reassure the patient that she should make a full recovery
    e. STAT testing of ESR and CRP
119. Which of the following should be considered in the treatment for this patient?
    a. Acetylcysteine
    b. Indomethacin
    c. Natamycin
    d. Timolol
    e. Vancomycin
    f. Zirgan
120. IF this patient was only Light Perception OD, which of the following would be indicated?

a. B-Scan
b. Enucleation
c. Laser photocoagulation
d. Pars Plana Vitrectomy
e. Pneumatic retinopexy
f. Trabeculectomy

CASE 25

Demographics
35 year-old Indian male; computer programmer
Chief Complaint
Patient complains of red eyes.
History of Present Illness
Location: both eyes
Severity: moderate
Nature Of Onset: gradual
Duration: started two days ago
Frequency: this is the third time it has happened in the last six months
Exacerbations/Remissions: none
Relationship To Activity Or Function: none
Accompanying Signs/Symptoms: severe light sensitivity
Secondary Complaints/Symptoms: none
Patient Ocular History
Unremarkable
Family Ocular History
Mother: unremarkable
Father: unremarkable
Patient Medical History
Pain on urination
Medications Taken By Patient
None
Patient Allergy History
NKDA
Family Medical History
Mother: unremarkable
Father: unremarkable

Review of Systems
Constitutional/General Health: denies
Ear/Nose/Throat: denies
Cardiovascular: denies
Pulmonary: denies
Endocrine: denies
Dermatological: denies
Gastrointestinal: denies
Genitourinary: Pain on urination
Musculoskeletal: denies
Neurologic: denies
Psychiatric: denies
Immunologic: denies
Hematologic: denies
Mental Status
Orientation: oriented to time, place, and person.
Mood: appropriate
Affect: appropriate
Clinical Findings
BVA
OD: 20/20
OS: 20/20
Pupils: PERRL, negative APD
EOMs: full, no restrictions OU
Confrontation Fields: full to finger counting OD, OS
Slit lamp
Lids/lashes/adnexa: unremarkable OD, OS
Conjunctiva: hyperemia OD, OS
Cornea: keratic precipitates OD, OS
Anterior chamber: 3+ cells OD, OS
Iris: flat and intact OD, OS
Lens: clear OD, OS
Vitreous: clear OD, OS
IOPs: 16 mmHg OD; 16 mmHg OS via GAT @ 4:10 p.m.
Blood Pressure: 115/79 RAS @ 4:15 p.m.
Pulse 85 bpm, regular
Fundus OD
C/D: 0.30H/ 0.30V
Macula: normal
Posterior pole: unremarkable
Periphery: unremarkable
Fundus OS
C/D: 0.30H/0.30V
Macula: normal
Posterior pole: unremarkable
Periphery: unremarkable

Image 1

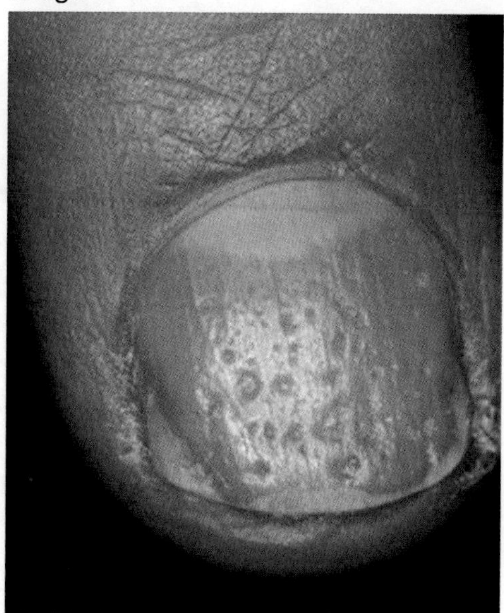

Pinterest 1

121. What is the MOST LIKELY diagnosis for this patient's chief complaint?
    a. Ankylosing Spondylitis
    b. Crohn's Disease
    c. Psoriatic Arthritis
    d. Reiter's Syndrome
    e. Ulcerative Colitis
122. Which of the following tests would you expect to be abnormal for this patient?
    a. HLA-A29
    b. HLA-B12
    c. HLA-B27
    d. HLA-B5
    e. HLA-B7
123. Which of the following is the MOST APPROPRIATE treatment for this patient? (SELECT TWO)
    a. Artificial Tears
    b. Azithromycin
    c. Cyclopentolate
    d. Durezol
    e. Lotemax
124. A DIFFERENT PATIENT presents with the findings as seen in Image 1. Which of the following is MOST LIKELY the diagnosis for this patient?
    a. Ankylosing Spondylitis
    b. Crohn's Disease
    c. Psoriatic Arthritis
    d. Reiter's Syndrome
    e. Ulcerative Colitis

125. Lyme Disease is caused by which of the following?
    a. *Acanthamoeba*
    b. *Actinomyces israelii*
    c. *Borrelia burgdorferi*
    d. *Corynebacterium diphtheria*
    e. *Haemophilus influenzae*
    f. *Moraxella catarrhalis*

CASE 26

Demographics
2 year-old Russian female
Chief Complaint
Parents state that the patient's eyes appear to turn outward.
History of Present Illness
Character/Signs/Symptoms: The patient closes her right eye while in the sun.
Severity: moderate
Nature Of Onset: gradual
Duration: Parents noticed this starting in the last 4-5 weeks
Frequency: three or four times per day
Exacerbations/Remissions: none
Relationship To Activity Or Function: none
Accompanying Signs/Symptoms: none
Secondary Complaints/Symptoms: none

Patient Ocular History
Unremarkable
Family Ocular History
Mother: unremarkable
Father: unremarkable
Patient Medical History
Unremarkable
Medications Taken By Patient
None
Patient Allergy History
NKDA
Family Medical History
Mother: unremarkable
Father: unremarkable

Review of Systems
Constitutional/General Health: denies
Ear/Nose/Throat: denies
Cardiovascular: denies
Pulmonary: denies
Endocrine: denies
Dermatological: denies
Gastrointestinal: denies
Genitourinary: denies
Musculoskeletal: denies
Neurologic: denies
Psychiatric: denies
Immunologic: denies
Hematologic: denies
Mental Status
Orientation: oriented to time, place, and person.
Mood: appropriate
Affect: appropriate

Clinical Findings
Habitual Rx: none
Entering Acuities:
OD Distance 20/30
OS Distance 20/30
Manifest Refraction:
OD: +1.00 DS; VA distance 20/20, VA near 20/20
OS: +1.00 DS; VA distance 20/20, VA near 20/20
BVA
OD: 20/25
OS: 20/25
Pupils: PERRL, negative APD
EOMs: full, no restrictions OU
Confrontation Fields: full to finger counting OD, OS
Cover Test
Distance: 10 exotropia
Near: 10 exotropia
Vergence System
NPC: TTN
Vergences:
Negative fusional convergence (NFC): Far 7/4; Near 12 / 22 / 15
Positive fusional convergence (PFC): Far 9/19/10; Near 13/21/13
Facility: 12 base-out/3 base-in
15 cycles/minute @ 40cm

Stereoacuity (Random dot): 20"
Accommodative System
AC/A: 4/1
Monocular Accommodative Facility: 11 cpm
Slit lamp
Lids/lashes/adnexa: unremarkable OD, OS
Conjunctiva: clear OD, OS
Cornea: clear OD, OS
Anterior chamber: deep and quiet OD, OS
Iris: flat and intact OD, OS
Lens: clear OD, OS
Vitreous: clear OD, OS
IOPs: 16 mmHg OD; 16 mmHg OS via GAT @ 4:10 p.m.
Blood Pressure: 100/60 RAS @ 4:15 p.m.
Pulse 60bpm, regular
Fundus OD
C/D: 0.30H/ 0.30V
Macula: normal
Posterior pole: unremarkable
Periphery: unremarkable
Fundus OS
C/D: 0.30H/0.30V
Macula: normal
Posterior pole: unremarkable
Periphery: unremarkable

Image 1

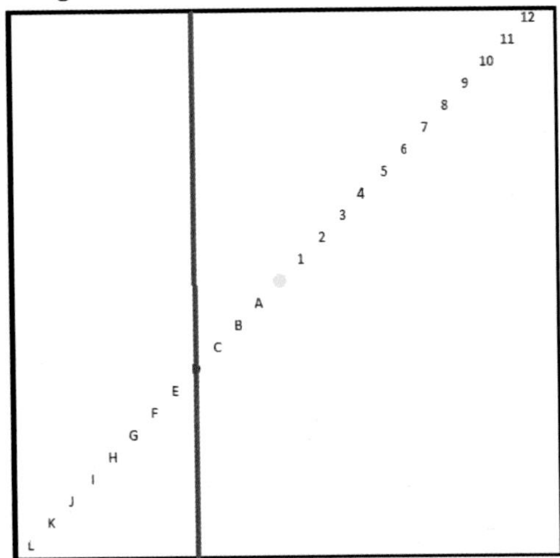

Kimberly Castillo, OD

126. What is the MOST LIKELY diagnosis for this patient's chief complaint?
    a. Basic Exotropia
    b. Convergence Insufficiency Exotropia
    c. Decompensated Exotropia
    d. Divergence Excess Exotropia
    e. Infantile Exotropia
    f. Sensory Exotropia
127. Which of the following is the MOST APPROPRIATE initial prescription for this patient?
    a. Do not prescribe glasses so as to avoid interfering with emmetropization
    b. OD, OS: +0.50 DS to aid with adaptation to prescription
    c. OD, OS: +1.00 DS Add +1.00 for FTW
    d. OD, OS: +1.00 DS for FTW
    e. OD: +1.00 DS, OS +1.00 DS 5BI

128. Five years later this patient decides to undergo vision therapy. Which of the following would be the MOST APPROPRIATE lenses to utilize during therapy exercises?
    a. Plus Lenses
    b. Minus Lenses
    c. Base In Lenses
    d. Base Out Lenses
    e. All of the above
129. A main concern is that this patient will develop amblyopia in the left eye.
    a. True
    b. False
130. You perform Maddox Rod Testing on a DIFFERENT PATIENT as seen in image 1. What can you conclude from this patient's findings?
    a. 4 exophoria
    b. 4 esophoria
    c. 4 exotropia
    d. 4 esotropia
    e. 4 exodeviation
    f. 4 esodeviation

CASE 27

Demographics
45 year-old Caucasian male; farmer
Chief Complaint
Patient is here for an annual eye exam.
History of Present Illness
Character/Signs/Symptoms: Patient is having trouble reading small print on his phone.
Location: both eyes
Severity: moderate
Nature Of Onset: gradual
Duration: slowly getting worse over two years
Frequency: whenever he is looking at his phone
Exacerbations/Remissions: none
Relationship To Activity Or Function: worse in low light settings
Accompanying Signs/Symptoms: headaches when he uses his phone for too long
Secondary Complaints/Symptoms: none

Patient Ocular History
Unremarkable, first eye exam
Patient states that his vision has always been great
Family Ocular History
Mother: unremarkable
Father: unremarkable
Patient Medical History
Unremarkable
Medications Taken By Patient
None
Patient Allergy History
NKDA
Family Medical History
Mother: unremarkable
Father: unremarkable

Review of Systems
Constitutional/General Health: denies
Ear/Nose/Throat: denies
Cardiovascular: denies
Pulmonary: denies
Endocrine: denies
Dermatological: denies
Gastrointestinal: denies
Genitourinary: denies
Musculoskeletal: denies
Neurologic: denies
Psychiatric: denies
Immunologic: denies
Hematologic: denies
Mental Status
Orientation: oriented to time, place, and person.
Mood: appropriate
Affect: appropriate

Clinical Findings
Habitual Rx: none
Entering Acuities:
OD Distance 20/20- Near 20/60
OS Distance 20/200 Near 20/200
Manifest Refraction:
OD: +0.50 DS Add +1.25; VA distance 20/20, VA near 20/20
OS: +0.75 DS Add +1.25; VA distance 20/200, VA near 20/200
Pupils: PERRL, negative APD
EOMs: full, no restrictions OU
Confrontation Fields: full to finger counting OD, OS
Slit lamp
Lids/lashes/adnexa: unremarkable OD, OS
Conjunctiva: clear OD, OS
Cornea: clear OD, OS
Anterior chamber: deep and quiet OD, OS
Iris: flat and intact OD, OS
Lens: clear OD, OS
Vitreous: clear OD, OS
IOPs: 16 mmHg OD; 16 mmHg OS via GAT @ 4:10 p.m.

Blood Pressure: 115/79 RAS @ 4:15 p.m.
Pulse 75 bpm, regular
Fundus OD
C/D: 0.30H/ 0.30V
Macula: normal
Posterior pole: unremarkable
Periphery: unremarkable
Fundus OS
See Image 1

Image 1

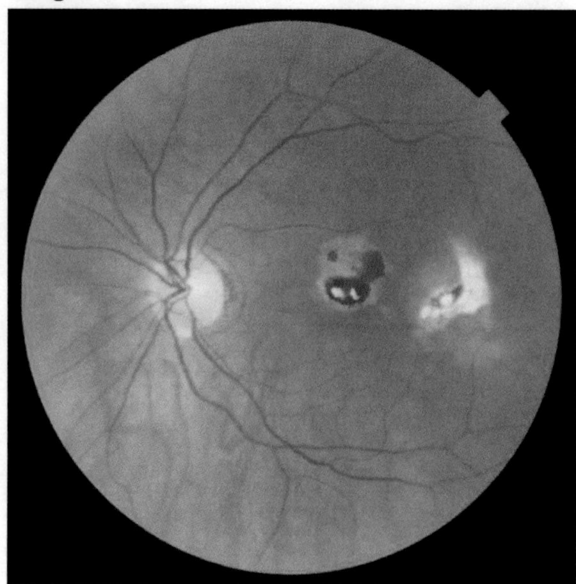

National Vision, Inc.

131. What is the MOST LIKELY diagnosis for the reduced BCVA OS?
    a. Acute Retinal Necrosis
    b. Diffuse Unilateral Subacute Neuroretinitis
    c. Histoplasmosis
    d. Toxocariasis
    e. Toxoplasmosis
132. Which of the following is the MOST LIKELY etiology for this patient's retinal findings OS?
    a. Ancylostoma caninum
    b. Baylisascaris procyonis
    c. Histoplasma capsulatum
    d. Toxocara canis
    e. Toxoplasma gondii
133. This patient's retinal findings OS are MOST COMMONLY associated with which of the following animals?
    a. Armadillos
    b. Bats
    c. Cats
    d. Dogs
    e. Raccoons

134. Which of the following is the MOST APPROPRIATE treatment for this patient's retinal findings OS?
    a. Anti-VEGF injections
    b. Direct laser photocoagulation of the offending organism
    c. Intravitreal steroids
    d. IV antiviral
    e. Pyrimethamine
    f. Topical Natamycin
    g. None of the Above
135. Which of the following complications should you expect for this patient?
    a. Vitritis
    b. Retinal detachment
    c. Strabismus
    d. Uveitis
    e. Pars planitis
    f. Endophthalmitis
    g. None of the Above

CASE 28

Demographics
25 year-old Caucasian female; Bartender
Chief Complaint
"Pink eye"
History of Present Illness
Character/Signs/Symptoms: Eyes feel gritty and teary.
Location: OD
Severity: moderate
Nature Of Onset: gradual
Duration: started yesterday afternoon
Frequency: constant
Exacerbations/Remissions: none
Relationship To Activity Or Function: none
Accompanying Signs/Symptoms: intermittent blurry vision OD
Secondary Complaints/Symptoms: none

Patient Ocular History
Unremarkable
Family Ocular History
Mother: unremarkable
Father: unremarkable
Patient Medical History
Unremarkable
Medications Taken By Patient
None
Patient Allergy History
Vigamox
Family Medical History
Mother: unremarkable
Father: unremarkable

Review of Systems
Constitutional/General Health: Patient is recovering from a recent cold.
Ear/Nose/Throat: denies
Cardiovascular: denies
Pulmonary: denies
Endocrine: denies
Dermatological: denies
Gastrointestinal: denies
Genitourinary: denies
Musculoskeletal: denies
Neurologic: denies
Psychiatric: denies
Immunologic: Palpable preauricular lymph nodes
Hematologic: denies
Mental Status
Orientation: oriented to time, place, and person.
Mood: appropriate
Affect: appropriate

Clinical Findings
BVA
OD: 20/20- distance and near
OS: 20/20 distance and near
Pupils: PERRL, negative APD
EOMs: full, no restrictions OU
Confrontation Fields: full to finger counting OD, OS
Slit lamp
Lids/lashes/adnexa:
OD: See Image 1
OS: unremarkable
Conjunctiva:
OD: See Image 1
OS: clear
Cornea: Clear OD, OS
Anterior chamber: deep and quiet OD, OS
Iris: flat and intact OD, OS
Lens: clear OD, OS
Vitreous: clear OD, OS
IOPs: 16 mmHg OD; 16 mmHg OS via GAT @ 12:05 p.m.
Blood Pressure: 115/79 RAS @ 12:00 p.m.
Pulse 80 bpm, regular
Fundus OD

C/D: 0.30H/ 0.30V
Macula: normal
Posterior pole: unremarkable
Periphery: unremarkable
Fundus OS

C/D: 0.30H/0.30V
Macula: normal
Posterior pole: unremarkable
Periphery: unremarkable

Image 1

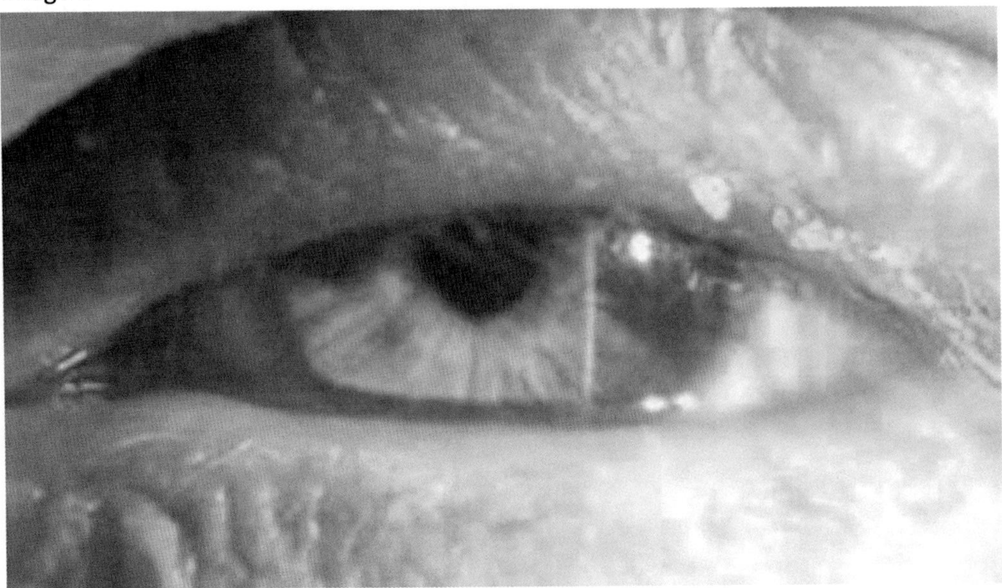

EyeRounds.org University of Iowa

136. Which of the following is the MOST LIKELY diagnosis for this patient's chief complaint?
    a. Adenoviral Conjunctivitis
    b. Bacterial Conjunctivitis
    c. Epidemic Keratoconjunctivitis
    d. Gonococcal Conjunctivitis
    e. Swimming Pool Conjunctivitis
137. Which of the following does NOT need to be included in the education for this patient?
    a. She should avoid touching her eyes
    b. She should clean all towels and bed linens
    c. She should notify her sexual partner(s)
    d. She will be highly contagious for two weeks
    e. This is transmitted via contact
138. Which of the following is the MOST APPROPRIATE treatment for this patient?
    a. Azithromycin OD QID
    b. Ciprofloxacin OD QID
    c. IM Ceftriaxone
    d. Natamycin
    e. Preservative free artificial tears Q2H

139. Which of the following is the MOST APPROPRIATE treatment for Ophthalmia Neonatorum?
    a. Erythromycin ung
    b. Moxifloxacin
    c. Pred Acetate
    d. Silver Nitrate
    e. Vigamox
140. Which of the following bacteria can attack the intact cornea?
    a. Moraxella catarrhalis
    b. Neisseria gonorrhoeae
    c. Staph Aureus
    d. Staph epidermidis
    e. Streptococcus pneumoniae

CASE 29

Demographics
57 year-old African American male; Banker
Chief Complaint
Inability to see
History of Present Illness
Location: both eyes
Severity: severe
Nature of Onset: started this morning
Duration: a few hours
Frequency: constant
Exacerbations/Remissions: none
Relationship To Activity Or Function: none
Accompanying Signs/Symptoms: none
Secondary Complaints/Symptoms: none

Patient Ocular History
Unremarkable
Family Ocular History
Mother: unremarkable
Father: unremarkable
Patient Medical History
Patient a pacemaker implanted yesterday.
Medications Taken By Patient
Azithromycin PO QID
Patient Allergy History
NKDA
Family Medical History
Mother: unremarkable
Father: unremarkable

Review of Systems
Constitutional/General Health: denies
Ear/Nose/Throat: denies
Cardiovascular: heart attack two years ago
Pulmonary: denies
Endocrine: denies
Dermatological: denies
Gastrointestinal: denies
Genitourinary: denies
Musculoskeletal: denies
Neurologic: denies
Psychiatric: denies
Immunologic: denies
Hematologic: denies
Mental Status
Orientation: oriented to time, place, and person.
Mood: appropriate
Affect: appropriate

Clinical Findings
BVA: NLP OD, OS
Pupils: PERRL, negative APD
EOMs: unable OU
Confrontation Fields: unable OD, OS
Slit lamp
Lids/lashes/adnexa: unremarkable OD, OS
Conjunctiva: clear OD, OS
Cornea: clear OD, OS
Anterior chamber: deep and quiet OD, OS
Iris: flat and intact OD, OS
Lens: clear OD, OS
Vitreous: clear OD, OS
IOPs: 16 mmHg OD; 16 mmHg OS via GAT @ 10:10 a.m.
Blood Pressure: 115/79 RAS @ 10:00 a.m.
Pulse 85 bpm, regular
Fundus OD
C/D: 0.30H/ 0.30V
Macula: normal
Posterior pole: unremarkable
Periphery: unremarkable
Fundus OS
C/D: 0.30H/0.30V
Macula: normal
Posterior pole: unremarkable
Periphery: unremarkable

141. What is the MOST LIKELY cause for this patient's Chief Complaint?
    a. Cortical blindness
    b. Malingering
    c. Ocular Migraine
    d. Psychogenic Visual Loss
    e. Vertebrobasilar Insufficiency
142. Which of the following is the most appropriate management for this patient?
    a. Ask the patient to follow up in two weeks.
    b. Educate this patient that recurrent episodes should resolve after thirty minutes.
    c. Educate this patient to avoid triggers.
    d. Reassure this patient that his eyes are healthy and he should make a full recovery.
    e. None of the above.
143. Which part of this patient's brain is most likely involved?
    a. Frontal
    b. Occipital
    c. Parietal
    d. Temporal
    e. None of the above
144. Which of the following is the MOST COMMON type of migraine?
    a. Classic Migraine
    b. Common Migraine
    c. Daily Migraine
    d. Ocular Migraine
    e. Regular Migraine
145. Where would you expect to find the causative lesion for Adie's Tonic Pupil?
    a. Ciliary ganglion
    b. Edinger-Westphal nucleus
    c. Optic Tract
    d. Superior Cervical Ganglion
    e. Trigeminal ganglion

CASE 30

Demographics
43 year-old African American female; High School Principal
Chief Complaint
Patient is here for an annual eye exam.
History of Present Illness
Character/Signs/Symptoms: Patient states her vision has always been perfect but she is now having trouble seeing her phone.
Location: both eyes
Severity: moderate
Nature Of Onset: gradual
Duration: slowly getting worse over two years
Frequency: whenever she is looking at her phone
Exacerbations/Remissions: none
Relationship To Activity Or Function: worse in low light settings
Accompanying Signs/Symptoms: headaches when she uses her phone for too long
Secondary Complaints/Symptoms: none

Patient Ocular History
Unremarkable, this is the patient's first eye exam.
Family Ocular History
Mother: unremarkable
Father: unremarkable
Patient Medical History
Unremarkable
Medications Taken By Patient
None
Patient Allergy History
NKDA
Family Medical History
Mother: unremarkable
Father: unremarkable

Review of Systems
Constitutional/General Health: denies
Ear/Nose/Throat: denies
Cardiovascular: denies
Pulmonary: denies
Endocrine: denies
Dermatological: denies
Gastrointestinal: denies
Genitourinary: denies
Musculoskeletal: denies
Neurologic: denies
Psychiatric: denies
Immunologic: denies
Hematologic: denies
Mental Status
Orientation: oriented to time, place, and person.
Mood: appropriate
Affect: appropriate

Clinical Findings
Habitual Rx: none
Entering Acuities:
OD Distance 20/20- Near 20/30
OS Distance 20/20- Near 20/30
Manifest Refraction:
OD: +0.75 DS Add +1.50; VA distance 20/20, VA near 20/20
OS: +0.75 DS Add +1.50; VA distance 20/20, VA near 20/20
Pupils: PERRL, negative APD
EOMs: full, no restrictions OU
Confrontation Fields: full to finger counting OD, OS
Slit lamp
Lids/lashes/adnexa: unremarkable OD, OS
Conjunctiva: clear OD, OS
Cornea: clear OD, OS
Anterior chamber: deep and quiet OD, OS
Iris: flat and intact OD, OS
Lens: clear OD, OS
Vitreous: clear OD, OS

IOPs: 16 mmHg OD; 16 mmHg OS via GAT @ 4:10 p.m.
Blood Pressure: 115/79 RAS @ 4:15 p.m.
Pulse 65 bpm, regular

Fundus OD
Similar to Image 1
Fundus OS
See Image 1

Image 1

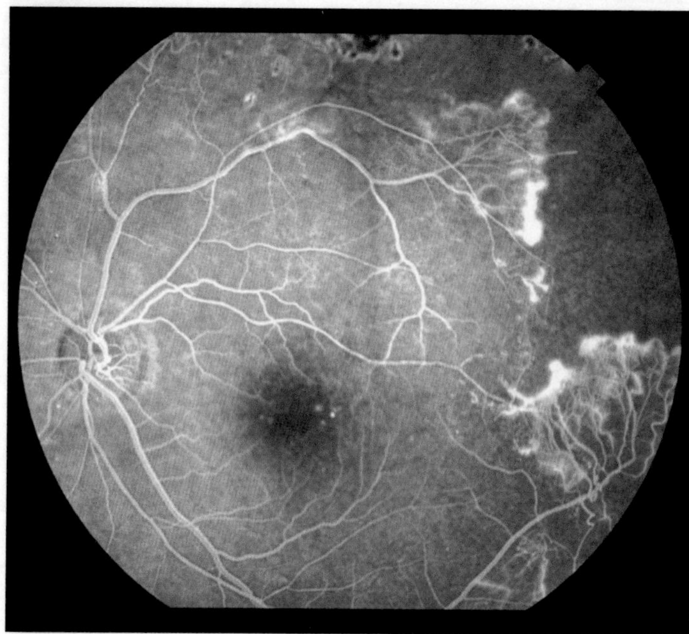

Retina Image Bank 343

146. What is the MOST LIKELY diagnosis for this patient's retinal disease?
    a. Eales Disease
    b. Embolic Retinopathy
    c. Pars Planitis
    d. Sarcoidosis
    e. Sickle Cell Retinopathy
147. Which of the following is the most appropriate stage for this patient's retinal disease?
    a. Stage 1
    b. Stage 2
    c. Stage 3
    d. Stage 4
    e. Stage 5
148. Which of the following should you consider in the treatment/management for this patient's retinal disease?
    a. Anti-VEGF injections
    b. Cryotherapy
    c. Laser Photocoagulation
    d. Refer for a hematology consult
    e. All of the above

149. What is the typical demographic for patients with Coat's Disease?
    a. Boys over 10
    b. Boys under 10
    c. Girls over 10
    d. Girls under 10
    e. Both a and c
    f. Both b and d
150. What is the most common location of the primary tumor in WOMEN who present with Choroidal Metastasis?
    a. Brain
    b. Breast
    c. Colon
    d. Liver
    e. Lung

CASE 31

Demographics
17 year-old Hispanic male; student
Chief Complaint
Patient is here for an annual eye exam.
History of Present Illness
Character/Signs/Symptoms: Patient needs glasses because he didn't pass the vision test at the DMV.
Location: both eyes
Severity: moderate
Nature Of Onset: gradual
Duration: slowly getting worse over two years
Frequency: constant
Exacerbations/Remissions: none
Relationship To Activity Or Function: none
Accompanying Signs/Symptoms: none
Secondary Complaints/Symptoms: none

Patient Ocular History
This is the patient's first eye exam.
Family Ocular History
Mother: unremarkable
Father: unremarkable
Patient Medical History
Unremarkable
Medications Taken By Patient
None
Patient Allergy History
NKDA
Family Medical History
Mother: unremarkable
Father: unremarkable

Review of Systems
Constitutional/General Health: denies
Ear/Nose/Throat: denies
Cardiovascular: denies
Pulmonary: denies
Endocrine: denies
Dermatological: denies
Gastrointestinal: denies
Genitourinary: denies
Musculoskeletal: denies
Neurologic: denies
Psychiatric: denies
Immunologic: denies
Hematologic: denies
Mental Status
Orientation: oriented to time, place, and person.
Mood: appropriate
Affect: appropriate

Clinical Findings
Habitual Rx: none
Entering Acuities:
OD Distance 20/50 Near 20/25
OS Distance 20/200 Near 20/50
Manifest Refraction:
OD: -0.25 -2.50 x052; VA distance 20/20, VA near 20/20
OS: -4.75 -4.50 x135; VA distance 20/70, VA near 20/30
Pupils: PERRL, negative APD
EOMs: full, no restrictions OU
Confrontation Fields: full to finger counting OD, OS
Slit lamp
Lids/lashes/adnexa: unremarkable OD, OS
Conjunctiva: clear OD, OS
Cornea:
OD: Clear
OS: See Image 2
Anterior chamber: deep and quiet OD, OS
Iris: flat and intact OD, OS
Lens: clear OD, OS
Vitreous: clear OD, OS
IOPs: 16 mmHg OD; 16 mmHg OS via GAT @ 4:10 p.m.
Blood Pressure: 117/71 RAS @ 4:15 p.m.

Pulse 63 bpm, regular
Fundus OD
C/D: 0.20H/ 0.20V
Macula: normal
Posterior pole: unremarkable
Periphery: unremarkable

Fundus OS
C/D: 0.20H/0.20V
Macula: normal
Posterior pole: unremarkable
Periphery: unremarkable

Image 1

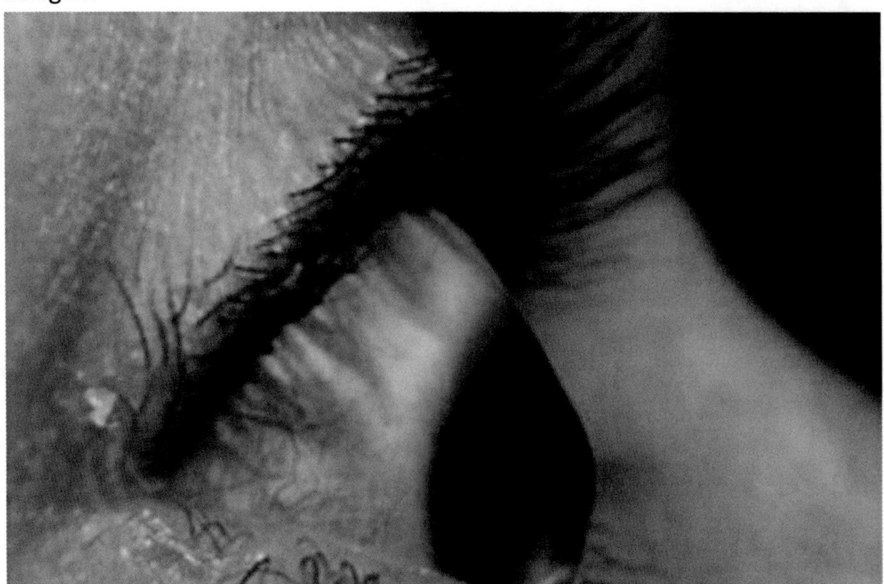

EyeRounds.org University of Iowa

151. What is the MOST LIKELY cause of this patient's reduced BCVA OS?
    a. Astigmatism
    b. Keratoconus
    c. Keratoglobus
    d. Myopia
    e. Pellucid Marginal Degeneration
152. Which of the following is an early sign of this patient's corneal findings?
    a. Corneal Hydrops
    b. Fleischer Ring
    c. Munson's Sign
    d. Stocker's Line
    e. Vogt Striae
153. This patient's corneal findings are associated with which of the following?
    a. Down's Syndrome
    b. Ehlers Danlos Syndrome
    c. Marfan's Syndrome
    d. Osteogenesis Imperfecta
    e. All of the above

154. Which of the following are the MOST LIKELY keratometry findings for this patient's OS?
   a. 39.00 @057, 43.50 @123
   b. 41.00 @155, 45.00 @025
   c. 44.50 @043, 47.50 @133
   d. 51.25 @138, 52.75 @048

155. Which of the following is the MOST APPROPRIATE management for this patient? (SELECT TWO)
   a. Fit with RGP
   b. Fit with soft contact lenses
   c. Prescribe glasses for FTW
   d. Refer for corneal crosslinking
   e. Refer for LASIK

CASE 32

Demographics
55 year-old Caucasian female; Administrator
Chief Complaint
Patient is here for an annual eye exam.
History of Present Illness
Character/Signs/Symptoms: Patient has not noticed any recent changes to her vision.

Patient Ocular History
Oculocutaneous Albinism
Family Ocular History
Mother: unremarkable
Father: unremarkable
Patient Medical History
Albinism
Medications Taken By Patient
None
Patient Allergy History
NKDA
Family Medical History
Mother: unremarkable
Father: unremarkable

Review of Systems
Constitutional/General Health: denies
Ear/Nose/Throat: denies
Cardiovascular: denies
Pulmonary: denies
Endocrine: denies
Dermatological: Oculocutaneous Albinism
Gastrointestinal: denies
Genitourinary: denies
Musculoskeletal: denies
Neurologic: denies
Psychiatric: denies
Immunologic: denies
Hematologic: denies
Mental Status
Orientation: oriented to time, place, and person.
Mood: appropriate
Affect: appropriate
Clinical Findings
Entering Acuities sc:
OD Distance 20/400
OS Distance 20/400
Manifest Refraction:
OD: -7.00 DS; VA distance 20/200
OS: -6.50 DS; VA distance 20/200
Pupils: PERRL, negative APD
EOMs: full, no restrictions OU
Confrontation Fields: full to finger counting OD, OS
Cover Test
Distance: 10 exotropia
Near: 13 exotropia
Nystagmus OU
Stereoacuity: fly
Slit lamp
Lids/lashes/adnexa: unremarkable OD, OS
Conjunctiva: clear OD, OS
Cornea: clear OD, OS
Anterior chamber: deep and quiet OD, OS
Iris: transillumination defects OD, OS
Lens: clear OD, OS
Vitreous: clear OD, OS
IOPs: 16 mmHg OD; 16 mmHg OS via GAT @ 4:10 p.m.
Blood Pressure: 115/79 RAS @ 4:15 p.m.
Pulse 75 bpm, regular
Fundus OD: Hypopigmented
C/D: 0.30H/ 0.30V
Macula: normal
Posterior pole: unremarkable
Periphery: unremarkable
Fundus OS: Hypopigmented
C/D: 0.30H/0.30V
Macula: normal
Posterior pole: unremarkable
Periphery: unremarkable

Image 1

V R S K D R
N H C S O K
S C N O Z V
C N H Z O K
N O D V H R
C D N Z S V
K C H O D K

All About Vision 1

156. True/False: This patient is legally blind.
    a. True
    b. False
157. What would you estimate would be the near add for this patient so that she can read standard print?
    a. +2.50
    b. +4.00
    c. +5.00
    d. +10.00
    e. +20.00
158. At what distance would this patient need to hold her reading materials based on the add you calculated in Question 157?
    a. 40 cm
    b. 25 cm
    c. 20 cm
    d. 10 cm
    e. 5 cm
159. What would you expect would be this patient's Just Noticeable Difference?
    a. 1.00 D
    b. 2.00 D
    c. 3.00 D
    d. 4.00 D
    e. 5.00 D
160. What is the name of the test pictured in Image 1?
    a. Brightness Acuity Test
    b. Feinbloom Chart
    c. Mars Contrast Sensitivity Chart
    d. Pelli-Robson Contrast Sensitivity Chart
    e. Vistech Contrast Sensitivity Chart

SOLO ITEMS

161. Which of the following is the LARGEST purkinje image?
    a. Image I
    b. Image II
    c. Image III
    d. Image IV
    e. Image V
162. During which phase of a clinical trial is a drug's efficacy tested on a small group of sick people?
    a. Phase 1
    b. Phase 2
    c. Phase 3
    d. Phase 4
    e. Phase 5
163. HIPAA applies to which of the following groups?
    a. Health Care Providers
    b. Health Care Plans
    c. Health Care Clearinghouses
    d. A and B only
    e. All of the above
164. Which of the following would be considered a normal APGAR Score?
    a. 0
    b. 3
    c. 6
    d. 9
    e. 12
165. Which of the following materials provides the most UV protection?
    a. CR-39
    b. Crown Glass
    c. Polycarbonate
166. Which of the following filters transmits only one wavelength of light?
    a. Blue Blockers
    b. Interference Filters
    c. Long-Pass Filters
    d. Narrow Band Filters
    e. Neutral Density Filters
167. What is the term for "do no harm?"
    a. Autonomy
    b. Beneficence
    c. Justice
    d. Nonmaleficence
    e. Tort Reform

168. What is the name of the test pictured below?

ProTech Ophthalmics 1

a. Farnsworth D-15
b. Feinbloom Chart
c. HRR Plates
d. Ishihara Plates
e. Nagel Anomaloscope

169. How would you interpret the results from this test?

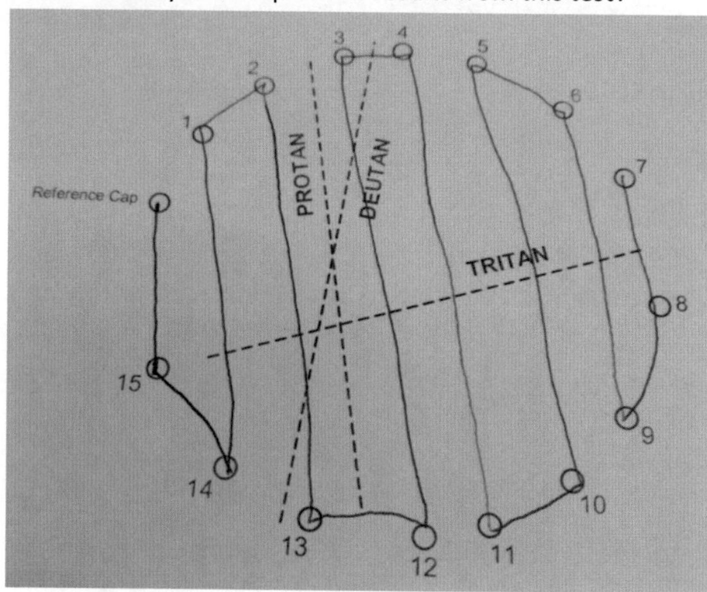

Kimberly Castillo, OD

a. Achromatopsia
b. Deutan
c. Normal
d. Protan
e. Tritan

170. What is the Frame PD of a frame with the following measurements: A 43, B 35, C 40, DBL 15, ED 46?

a. 43
b. 50
c. 55
d. 58
e. 61

171. Which of the following findings would you expect in a patient with CHARGE Syndrome? (SELECT THREE)
    a. Atresia choana
    b. Coloboma
    c. Nystagmus
    d. Retarded growth
    e. Thin upper lip
172. Pantoscopic Tilt on a minus lens will induce astigmatism along which meridian?
    a. Axis 180
    b. Axis 045
    c. Axis 090
    d. Axis 135
173. You are testing a patient using the Nagel Anomaloscope. These are her results: Mixture Field 30, Test Field 17. This is consistent with what type of color deficiency?
    a. Normal
    b. Protanope
    c. Deuteranope
    d. Protanomalous Trichromat
    e. Deuteranomalous Trichromat
174. Which of the following is an example of Incidence?
    a. According to the CDC, at the end of 2015, an estimated 1.1 million persons aged 13 and older were living with HIV infection in the United States.
    b. According to the CDC, in the United States, about 77.9 million adults have high blood pressure.
    c. By the year 2016, 21 million adults in the United States had been diagnosed with diabetes.
    d. In 2018, an estimated 266,120 new cases of invasive breast cancer were diagnosed in women in the United States
    e. Retinitis pigmentosa is estimated to affect 1 in 3,500 people in the United States.
175. A patient picks up his new pair of glasses and his left lens is resting higher than the right lens. Which of the following adjustments could you make? (SELECT TWO)
    a. Bend the left temple arm down.
    b. Bend the left temple arm up.
    c. Bend the right temple arm down.
    d. Bend the right temple arm up.
    e. Increase pantascopic tilt.

Practice Question Answers with Explanations

Case 1 Answers

1. What is the MOST LIKELY diagnosis of the above patient's retinal condition?
    - Correct Answer: e) Malignant hypertensive retinopathy. Malignant hypertension is defined as a blood pressure over 220/120.
2. What is the BEST treatment for the patient's retinal condition?
    - Correct Answer: b) Refer the patient for emergent reduction of high blood pressure. Given this patient's blood pressure findings, he is at risk for stroke or heart attack. Given the life-threatening status of his disease, he needs to have his blood pressure reduced emergently.
3. IF the patient's retinal condition was unilateral, what should you expect?
    - Correct Answer: e) carotid artery obstruction. IF a patient has hypertensive retinopathy in only one eye, then suspect a carotid artery obstruction ipsilateral to the NORMAL eye. The obstructed artery is shielding the ipsilateral eye from the effects of hypertension.
    - Other Answers: Venous Stasis and OIS present with mid-peripheral hemorrhages and are not associated with an elevated blood pressure. A CRVO or CRAO would present unilaterally with significant acute vision loss.
4. This patient is at greatest risk for which of the following?
    - Correct Answer: a) Heart attack. Patients who have a blood pressure greater than 220/120 are at risk of heart attack or stroke, which is why these patients require emergent care.
5. What is the BEST management for the patient's chief complaint?
    - Correct Answer: d) Recheck the refraction after the patient's blood pressure has stabilized. The patient's elevated blood pressure could be impacting the patient's refractive status, and so the refraction found today may not be accurate. Therefore, the refraction should be checked again after the patient's blood pressure has stabilized. Given the patient's chief complaint, age, and refractive findings found today, he will benefit from reading glasses.

Case 2 Answers:

6. Which of the following is another sign you would expect to see with this patient?
    - Correct Answer: a) Exfoliative Material in the Trabecular Meshwork

- Other Answers: Cataracts and a broadened ciliary body band would be seen with Angle Recession Glaucoma. A Krukenberg Spindle is seen with Pigment Dispersion Syndrome/Pigmentary Glaucoma.

7. What is a possible complication for this patient based on the anterior segment findings? (SELECT THREE)
    - Correct Answer: a) Iridodonesis, b) Acute Angle Closure, c) Fluctuating IOP's
    - Other Answers: Rosette Cataracts are associated with Angle Recession Glaucoma. Photophobia is not associated with Exfoliative Glaucoma.
8. What is the MOST LIKELY cause of the patient's increased IOPs?
    - Correct Answer: c) Exfoliative Glaucoma. The classic finding for Exfoliative Glaucoma is a target pattern of exfoliative material on the anterior lens capsule, as is seen in Image 1. This is diagnostic.
    - Other Answers: Primary Open Angle Glaucoma is idiopathic with no known underlying cause. Ocular Hypertension will not present with reduced nerve fiber layer on OCT, large CD ratios, or a reduced visual field. Other findings seen in Pigmentary Glaucoma will include a krukenberg spindle and transillumination defects, which are not seen in this patient. Angle Recession Glaucoma may present with pigment seen on the anterior lens capsule, but not the white exfoliative material seen in Image 1. Angle Recession Glaucoma may also present with an uneven iris insertion, broadened ciliary body band, and a vossius ring.
9. Which of the following is the BEST treatment option for the patient's increased IOPs?
    - Correct Answer: a) Prescribe Timolol BID
    - Other Answers: Latanoprost is contraindicated due to the patient's ocular history of herpes simplex. Cataract surgery, artificial tears, and monitoring the patient will not help reduce the IOP's.
10. Which of the following would be considered a relative contraindication for cataract surgery?
    - Correct Answer: e) All of the above. Diabetes reduces the body's healing process, which can impact recovery from cataract surgery. A history of using Flomax at any time increases the patient's risk of intraoperative floppy iris syndrome. Patients with Fuch's Endothelial Dystrophy have a reduced number of endothelial cells. During surgery the endothelium can get rubbed by the medical equipment, further reducing the endothelial cell count. The lens zonules are weakened with Pseudoexfoliation Syndrome, meaning there is a higher risk of lens dislocation with cataract surgery.

Case 3 answers:

11. Which of the following household items is an acid:
    - Correct answer: a) Vinegar
    - Other answers: Bleach, ammonia, Windex, and drain cleaner are all bases. Remember that bases have a bitter taste while acids have a zingy taste.
12. What is the most appropriate INITIAL treatment option:
    - Correct answer: c) Copious irrigation with a saline solution
    - Other answers: Irrigation with an acid or basic will only further the damage from the

chemical burn. A beta blocker should be used to reduce the IOP only after the pH has been neutralized. The fornices should be swept only after copious irrigation with a saline solution to confirm the pH has been neutralized.

13. Which of the following would be CONTRAINDICATED for this patient?
    - Correct answer: e) Instillation of Pilocarpine. Pilocarpine will cause the blood vessels to constrict, thereby reducing the blood/oxygen flow to the cornea and surrounding structures. It is imperative that maximal oxygen is delivered to these structures to aid in proper healing of the cornea.
    - Other answers: A topical cycloplegic, antibiotic, beta blocker, and artificial tears should all be considered once the pH has been neutralized based on the patient's findings.
14. Which of the following signs indicates a poor prognosis for a chemical burn?
    - Correct answer: c) white cornea. A white cornea has a very poor prognosis because it indicates the blood vessels have been damaged, thereby reducing oxygen flow to the cornea which is imperative for proper healing.
    - Other answers: In contrast to a white cornea, engorged blood vessels indicate that the vessels are not damaged, and so maximum blood flow is arriving to the cornea. Photophobia and an increased IOP are not signs of a poor prognosis. Acid burns are less severe than basic burns.
15. When should you follow up with this patient?
    - Correct answer: a) one day. The patient should be followed daily until the epithelial defect is resolved.

Case 4 Answers

16. What is the MOST LIKELY diagnosis of the patient's chief complaint?
    f) Correct Answer: d) Vernal Conjunctivitis. Vernal Conjunctivitis is most commonly seen in boys under the age of 10 who live in hot climates. Tranta's Dots, superior cobblestone papillae, and a ropy discharge are also signs of Vernal Conjunctivitis.
17. Which of the following is another classic sign you could possibly see with this patient?
    - Correct Answer: b) Shield Ulcer
    - Other Answers: Symblepharon, Keratoconus, and Cataracts are associated with Atopic Conjunctivitis. Uveitis is not associated with Vernal Conjunctivitis.
18. Which of the following should be included in the patient education for the above case?
    - Correct Answer: e) Both A and D. Vernal Conjunctivitis is not contagious and patients should stop having episodes when they reach puberty.
19. What is the BEST treatment for the patient's chief complaint?
    - Correct Answer: d) Pataday QD. Vernal Conjunctivitis is a type of allergic conjunctivitis, and so should be treated with an antihistamine.
    - Other Answers: Vernal Conjunctivitis is not cause by bacteria, and so Cephalosporin and Azithromycin are not indicated. Also, given the patient's Penicillin allergy, Cephalosporin is contraindicated. Artificial tears will not address the etiology.
20. This patient returns a week later stating that your chosen treatment option from question #19 isn't helping. Which of the following options should you now consider?

   a. Correct Answer: c) Topical Lotemax QID. If Pataday is not sufficient in treating the Vernal Conjunctivitis, then consider more aggressive treatment with a topical steroid.
   b. Other Answers: Vernal Conjunctivitis is not cause by bacteria, and so IV antibiotics are not indicated. Durezol is the strongest steroid. It is not necessary to pick a strong steroid because we do not need the steroid to penetrate the cornea. Artificial tears will not address the etiology.

Case 5 Answers

21. With the given information, what is the MOST APPROPRIATE diagnosis for the patient's chief complaint?
    a. Correct Answer: d) Papilledema. Papilledema is defined as bilateral swollen optic nerves in the presence of increased intracranial pressure, all of which is true for this patient.
    b. Other Answers: A pituitary gland tumor would present with a bitemporal hemianopsia, which is not seen with this patient. AAION and optic neuritis are unilateral, which is not the case in this patient. Pseudotumor Cerebri is a diagnosis of exclusion and so we need the results of neuroimaging to rule out an intracranial mass as the culprit.
22. The patient's MRI is found to be unremarkable. What is the MOST LIKELY diagnosis of the patient's chief complaint?
    a. Correct Answer: e) Pseudotumor Cerebri.
    b. Other Answers: A Pituitary Gland Tumor as well as other intracranial masses have been ruled out with the MRI. Papilledema will have an underlying cause, which has not been found in this case, leading to the diagnosis of Pseudotumor Cerebri. AAION and optic neuritis are unilateral, which is not the case in this patient.
23. Which of the following should be considered in the treatment for this patient? (SELECT THREE)
    a. Correct Answers: b) lose weight, d) Discontinue use of birth control pills, e) Diamox 1000mg po QD. Pseudotumor Cerebri is typically found in overweight women of childbearing age (fat fertile females). Therefore, losing weight will help reduce the ICP and also take the patient out of this demographic. Pseudotumor Cerebri is associated with the use of Accutane, Nalidixic Acid, Oral Contraceptives, Tetracyclines, and Vitamin A. Oral Diamox (acetazolamide) should be used to reduce the production of cerebral spinal fluid at the choroidal plexus.
    b. Other Answers: No tumors were identified with MRI and so there are none to remove. Steroids are not indicated for patients with Pseudotumor Cerebri.
24. Which of the following is the definition of INCREASED Cerebrospinal fluid pressure for a patient who is obese?
    a. Correct Answer: e) >250 mmH2O
    b. Other Answers: The definition of increased CSF in patients who are NOT obese is >200 mmH2O.
25. Which of the following would indicate a tumor of the left optic tract?
    a. Correct answer: b) A left optic tract tumor would cause a Right Hemianopsia because the tract is past the optic chiasm.
    b. Other Answers: Answer A would be caused by a RIGHT optic tract tumor. Remember the mnemonic PITS (Parietal Inferior, Temporal, Superior) for Answer options C and D. These

would cause a Quadranopsia and not a Hemianopsia. A Bitemporal Hemianopsia is characteristic of a pituitary gland tumor.

Case 6 Answers

26. Which of the following is the BEST diagnosis for this patient's chief complaint?
    a. Correct Answer: c) Basic Exophoria. Abnormal findings for Basic Exophoria will include a large exophoria at both distance and near which will be within 5 prism diopters of each other. Vergence amplitude and facility will be low at both distance and near. Also both the MEM and NRA will be low. All of these findings are applicable to this case.
    b. Other Answers: This patient has abnormal vergence ranges, and so Accommodative Excess and Ill Sustained Accommodation can be ruled out. Vergence findings will be normal in patients with accommodative conditions. Convergence insufficiency can be ruled out because this patient has a normal near point of convergence. Divergence excess can be ruled out because this patient's distance cover test is within 5 prism diopters of their near cover test.
27. Which of the following BEST supports your diagnosis for the patient's chief complaint?
    a. Correct Answer: a) Cover test findings. An abnormally large exophoria at both distance and near which is within 5 prism diopters of each other is a classic finding unique to Basic Exophoria.
28. Which of the following would be the BEST spectacle prescription for this patient?
    a. Correct Answer: e) Wait to prescribe lenses until after Vision Therapy has been initiated. Basic Exophoria will be exacerbated with plus lenses. Given that hyperopia is corrected with plus lenses, a spectacle prescription will only make the patient's symptoms worse at this time. Wait until the patient can accept plus lenses once he has undergone some vision therapy.
29. What types of lenses should be utilized to train the eyes during vision therapy? (PICK TWO)
    a. Correct Answer: b) Base Out; d) Plus. During vision therapy the patient's visual system is stressed by using the types of lenses which are difficult for the patient. Given that this is a vergence problem, Base Out lenses will be more effective. However, Plus lenses can also be utilized to indirectly stress out the patient's visual system.
30. What type of prism could you consider including in this patient's spectacle prescription?
    a. Correct Answer: a) Base In. Base In prism will direct the light temporally, towards where the eyes deviate. This will make it easier for the patient to maintain a fused image.

Case 7 Answers

31. What is the MOST LIKELY diagnosis of the patient's chief complaint?
    a. Correct Answer: b) Corneal ulcer. A corneal ulcer can be differentiated from an infiltrate because it will have positive NaFl staining.
    b. Other Answers: A corneal infiltrate will not have positive staining with NaFl. Neovascularization will be painless and will not cause photophobia. Tight lens syndrome will present with a red ring around the limbus cause by the lens cutting into the conjunctiva. Contact lens hypersensitivity will present with diffuse infiltrates across the cornea, not one focal infiltrate.
32. What is the MOST LIKELY etiology of the patient's chief complaint?

   a. Correct Answer: a) Immune response to the proteins lodged in the contact lens.
33. Which of the following is the MOST COMMON bacteria to cause corneal ulcers?
   a. Correct Answer: a) *Pseudomonas aeruginosa*
34. What is the BEST initial treatment for the patient's chief complaint? SELECT TWO
   a. Correct Answers: d) AzaSite gt OS Q2H x7days; h) Discontinue contact lens wear. Corneal ulcers must be treated as a corneal infection with a topical antibiotic. The cornea is compromised, and so we need to protect it from opportunistic bacteria. Contact lenses should not be worn because they reduce the cornea's access to oxygen which can slow the healing process.
   b. Other Answers: Lotemax and Durezol are contraindicated at this time because steroids will reduce the patient's immune response and could increase the severity of an infection. Vigamox is contraindicated because the patient is allergic to fluoroquinolones. Pataday will not help the situation because this is not a hypersensitivity reaction. This is not caused by an allergic response to the contact lens solution preservatives, and so changing the solution will not treat the problem with this patient. Patching the eye is contraindicated because it will reduce the cornea's access to oxygen which can slow the healing process.
35. After the patient's chief complaint is fully resolved, what change should be considered in the patient's contact lens fit?
   a. Correct Answer: c) Refit into a contact with a higher DK/t. Greater oxygen permeability will help reduce the change of contact lens complications.
   b. Other Answers: The etiology of this patient's corneal ulcer was not caused by the contact being too loose or tight, and so changing the base curve will not reduce the chance of future corneal ulcers. Given this patient's high prescription and difficulty wearing glasses, she will not be successful with permanently discontinuing the wear of contact lenses.

Case 8 Answers

36. What is the MOST LIKELY cause of this patient's reduced BCVA?
   a. Correct Answer: c) Nuclear Sclerosis. Image 1 is consistent with the typical presentation of a Nuclear Sclerotic cataract.
   b. Other Answers: Given that the BCVA is reduced, this indicates there is a medical issue causing the reduced vision instead of a refractive error. Given that the retinal views are obscured, there is currently no data supporting a diagnosis of Diabetic Retinopathy. Image one is consistent with the presentation of Nuclear Sclerosis and not Snowflake cataracts or Posterior Polar cataracts.
37. What is the MOST LIKELY cause of this patient's secondary complaint?
   a. Correct Answer: Nuclear Sclerosis. Cataracts will cause scatter of light which the patient will perceive as glare resulting in difficulty with night driving.
   b. Other Answers: While uncorrected refractive error can cause difficulty with night driving, the cause is more likely due to cataracts given the patient's anterior segment findings. Dermatochalasis does not cause difficulty with night glare. Headlights on cars have not gotten significantly brighter, this is the patient's own perception and belief that the

problem is external and not with his eyes. The patient does not have posterior polar cataracts.

38. The patient's BCVA is 20/50 OD. See Image 2 for OCT findings. What is the MOST LIKELY cause of the patient's reduced BCVA?
    a. Correct Answer: b) Irvine-Gass syndrome. Cystoid Macular Edema which occurs post cataract surgery is called Irvine-Gass syndrome.
    b. Other Answers: The OCT image is NOT consistent with an Epiretinal Membrane, Pigment Epithelial Detachment, or Retinoschisis. Furthermore, Retinoschisis would cause an absolute visual field defect, which is not present in this case.
39. What would be the MOST APPROPRIATE management for this patient's reduced BCVA?
    a. Correct Answer: a) Acular LS gt QID OD. A NSAID is most appropriate in this case.
    b. Other Answers: Durezol is contraindicated because a steroid will interfere with the healing process post cataract surgery. Membrane peel is indicated for ERM, not for CME or Irvine-Gass syndrome. Pneumatic retinopexy and cryotherapy are appropriate for retinal detachments, not for CME or Irvine-Gass syndrome
40. What is a possible complication if a patient delays cataract surgery for too long?
    a. Correct Answer: a) Phacolytic Glaucoma. A Hypermature cataract can shed lens proteins which can clog the trabecular meshwork subsequently leading to Phacolytic Glaucoma.
    b. Other Answers: Intraoperative Floppy Iris Syndrome is associated with a history of the use of Flomax, not a Hypermature cataract. Lens subluxation is not caused by a Hypermature cataract. Posterior Capsular Opacification is a complication which occurs post cataract surgery.

Case 9 Answers

41. What is the MOST APPROPRIATE diagnosis for the patient's secondary complaint?
    a. Correct Answer: e) Pediculosis. Pediculosis will present with burrowing lice, spots of dried blood (from bites), tiny brown deposits (feces), and white/translucent nits (eggs).
    b. Other Answers: The patient's secondary complaint is ocular itching which is not caused by uncorrected refractive error. Demodicosis presents similarly to Blepharitis, with triangular globs of waste at the base of the patient's eyelashes.
42. What is the MOST LIKELY etiology of the patient's secondary complaint?
    a. Correct Answer: e) *Phthirus pubis*. Pediculosis is caused by an eyelash infection of lice.
43. What should be included in the patient's education regarding his secondary complaint? (SELECT TWO)
    a. Correct Answers: a) His current sexual partner should also be treated; d) Be sure to clean all sheets and towels. Pediculosis is pubic lice which get into the eyelashes, and so is sexually transmitted. Therefore, it is likely that any current sexual partners are also affected. The lice can spread into and live in any sheets and towels, and so it is imperative that the patient either discards or thoroughly cleans all linens in hot water.
    b. Other Answers: Pediculosis initially requires daily follow up. Given Pediculosis is sexually transmitted, it does not occur seasonally. Pediculosis has an excellent prognosis.
44. What is the MOST APPROPRIATE treatment for this patient's secondary complaint? (SELECT TWO)

a. Correct Answers: a) Remove lice with jeweler's forceps; c) Topical erythromycin ointment. Erythromycin ointment should be used TID for 14 days to smother the lice.
b. Other Answers: Lice shampoos are CONTRAINDICATED for ocular use. Artificial tears and Pataday are NOT effective for Pediculosis.

45. What should you consider if a child presents with this eyelid condition?
    a. Correct Answer: e) Child abuse. Given that Pediculosis is sexually transmitted, it is likely that if this is seen in a child then the child is being sexually abused. As optometrists we are mandated reporters, and so we must notify authorities if we suspect a child is being abused.

Case 10 Answers

46. What is the MOST LIKELY diagnosis for the patient's chief complaint?
    a. Correct Answer: c) Diabetic Retinopathy. Diabetic Retinopathy presents with dot and blot hemorrhages and cotton wool spots, as seen in the pictures. It is also associated with increased urination (polyuria) and thirst (polydipsia).
    b. Other Answers: A CRVO would present unilaterally with significant acute vision loss. The patient's blood pressure is normal. Venous stasis and OIS would present with midperipheral hemorrhages, which is not as seen in these pictures. Furthermore, OIS would present with signs of anterior segment neovascularization.
47. What is the highest risk factor for diabetic retinopathy?
    a. Correct Answer: b) Duration which the patient has had diabetes.
48. What is the prognosis for Ocular Ischemic Syndrome?
    a. Correct Answer: d) Fatal in 40% of patients after five years
49. What is the medical term for increased thirst?
    a. Correct Answer: b) Polydipsia
    b. Other Answers: Polyuria is increase urination. Polyphagia is increased hunger. Polymegathism is increased cell size. Pleomorphism describes changes to cell shape.
50. Which of the following BEST describe the blood panels seen in diabetic patients? (SELECT TWO)
    a. Correct Answers: a) A1C greater than 6.0; c) Blood sugar above 100

Case 11 Answers

51. What is the MOST APPROPRIATE diagnosis for this patient's chief complaint?
    a. Correct Answer: c) Compound Myopic Astigmatism
    b. Other Answers: Simple Myopia occurs when patients have spherical prescriptions. Simple Myopic Astigmatism occurs when the patient has a minus prescription in one meridian and no prescription in the other meridian. Mixed astigmatism occurs when the patient is myopic in one meridian and hyperopic in the other meridian.
52. Which of the following is the MOST APPROPRIATE spectacle prescription for this patient?
    a. Correct Answer: e) OD -4.00 -0.75 x009; OS -4.75 -1.00 x171. This patient soaked up a lot of minus during the manifest refraction. Egger's Rule states that the prescription should only change by 0.25D for each line of reduced visual acuity. Meaning, the most change which should be seen when a patient has lost two lines of acuity (20/30) is 0.50D, and the most change which should be seen when the patient has lost three lines of acuity (20/40) is 0.75D.

53. Which is the correct way to write this patient's HABITUAL prescription in Plus (+) Cylinder form?
    a. Correct Answer: a) OD -4.25 +0.75 x099; OS -5.00 +1.00 x081. When transposing from Minus Cylinder to Plus Cylinder, first add the Sphere and Cylinder Powers of the original prescription. This becomes your new Sphere Power. Second change the sign of the Cylinder Power. This is your new Cylinder Power. Add or subtract the axis by 90, be sure not to go over 180. This is your new Axis.
54. Where would you expect to see light converge with no prescription for this patient?
    a. Correct Answer: a) In front of her retina at both axis 009 and 171. This patient is myopic in both meridians. Myopic eyes are "too long" for the patient's secondary focal length, and so light converges within the vitreous in front of the retina. Another way to think about it is myopic eyes are too powerful for their axial length.
55. This patient is viewing the astigmatic dial with no prescription. Which set of lines will she perceive as clearest?
    a. Correct Answer: d) 6:00-12:00. This question is applying the Rule of 30 in reverse. The Rule of 30 states that the axis can be calculated by multiplying the lowest clock hour the patient sees clearest by 30. We know that the patient's axis is around 180 in both eyes. 180/30 = 6. The lowest clock hour the patient will see clearly is 6:00 (12:00 is along the same line but 12 is larger than 6).

Case 12 Answers

56. What is the MOST LIKELY diagnosis for the patient's chief complaint?
    a. Correct Answer: b) Episcleritis
    b. Other Answers: Ocular Rosacea is recurrent in nature, which is not true of this case at this time. Scleritis would present with a deep, boring pain, a blue sclera, will be tender with palpitation, and will NOT blanch with topical phenylephrine. Allergic conjunctivitis will present with itch, papillary conjunctivitis, and will have a diffuse hyperemia rather than sectoral hyperemia. Viral conjunctivitis will present with a watery discharge, follicles, and a recent history of a cold.
57. What is the MOST LIKELY etiology for the patient's chief complaint?
    a. Correct Answer: e) Idiopathic. Episcleritis is most frequently idiopathic.
    b. Other Answers: All of the other answers would cause recurrent episcleritis, which is not true of this case at this time.
58. What is the MOST APPROPRIATE treatment for this patient's chief complaint? SELECT TWO
    a. Correct Answer: e) Topical naphazoline; f) Artificial tears. Naphazoline is a vasoconstrictor, and so will aid in the cosmesis for this patient by reducing the appearance of hyperemia. Artificial tears will help relieve any irritation the patient is experiencing.
    b. Other Answers: Oral medications are not indicated for Episcleritis because it should resolve on its own. Topical Lotemax is only indicated in severe cases.
59. What is now the MOST LIKELY etiology for the patient's chief complaint?
    a. Correct Answer: a) Rosacea. Given the patient's medical history of Acne Rosacea and that this episcleritis is recurrent; the underlying etiology is most likely Rosacea.
    b. Other Answers: Given that this episcleritis is now recurrent and the patient's medical

history, it is likely that there is an underlying etiology (and so not idiopathic). The patient does not have a medical history of RA, Atopy, or Thyroid Disease.

60. Which of the following is now the MOST APPROPRIATE treatment for this patient's chief complaint?
    a. Correct Answer: b) Oral Erythromycin. Recurrent cases of episcleritis can be managed by treating the underlying etiology. Rosacea is treated with oral doxycycline, tetracycline, or erythromycin.
    b. Other Answers: Doxycycline is contraindicated because this patient is allergic to Tetracycline.

Case 13 Answers

61. What is the MOST LIKEY cause of the patient's chief complaint?
    a. Correct Answer: d) Non-Refractive Esotropia. Patients with Non-Refractive Esotropia will have a normal refractive error but a high AC/A ratio. The angle of deviation will be larger at near than at distance.
    b. Other Answers: Congenital esotropia manifests before the age of 6 months. Early onset esotropia manifests between 6 months and 2 years of age. Patients with refractive esotropia will have high hyperopia (greater than +4.75D) with a normal AC/A ratio. Patients with mixed esotropia will have a moderate to high refractive error as well as a high AC/A ratio.
62. Which of the following should be included in your exam for this patient?
    a. Correct Answer: e) Cycloplegic refraction. It is important to prescribe full cycloplegic refraction for patients who have Non-Refractive Esotropia.
    b. Other Answers: Visual information processing including NSUCO and Color Vision testing will not address the patient's chief complaint. Given this patient has an esotropia, Von Graefe Phorias will not be applicable.
63. Prominent epicanthal folds are most likely seen in which of the following patient populations? (SELECT TWO)
    a. Correct Answers: b) Asians, c) Down's Syndrome.
64. Based on the information provided, which of the following would be the MOST APPROPRIATE spectacle prescription for this patient?
    a. Correct Answer: e) +1.00 DS OU Add +2.50 executive bifocal for full time wear. It is important to prescribe full cycloplegic refraction for patients under the age of six who have Accommodative Esotropia. Since this patient still has greater than 8 diopters of esotropia at near with the +1.00, then an add of +2.50 in an executive bifocal is indicated.
65. After writing a spectacle prescription as described in question 64, the patient's chief complaint is still not resolved. Which of the following should be the next treatment considered?
    a. Correct Answer: e) Strabismus surgery. Given this is **Accommodative** Esotropia prisms will not sufficiently resolve the problem.

Case 14 Answers

66. What is the MOST LIKEY cause of the patient's reduced BCVA OU?
    a. Correct Answer: d) Age Related Macular Degeneration.

   b. Other Answers: While this patient has Meibomian Gland Dysfunction and Nuclear Sclerotic Cataracts which could be reducing vision, they are both mild and so most likely not responsible for a reduction of BCVA all the way to 20/70. Familial Dominant Drusen and Stargardt Disease typically manifest before the age of 20, and this patient is in his late 60s.

67. This patient has which of the following risk factors for his retinal findings? (SELECT THREE)
   a. Correct answers: b) Age, c) Sun exposure, e) Caucasian ethnicity. This patient is 68 and so age is one of his risk factors. With a history as a truck driver, he likely experienced a lot of sun exposure during his career. Caucasians are at a higher risk for ARMD due to their light complexions.
   b. Other Answers: While both high cholesterol and a positive family history are also risk factors for ARMD, they are not present for this patient.
68. What should be included in the education for this patient?
   a. Correct Answer: a) Avoid smoking. Smoking has been shown to be a risk factor for ARMD and to increase the progression of the pathology.
   b. Other Answers: Exercise has not been shown to improve ARMD, NSC, or MGD. ARMD has a poor prognosis and is the leading cause of blindness in patients over the age of 50. Treatment is aimed at slowing the progression, there are no known treatments which can improve vision which has been lost. Manifest refraction showed no improvement in BCVA. While ARMD has a familial inheritance, genetic testing is not indicated.
69. Which of the following is the MOST APPROPRIATE treatment for this patient's retinal findings?
   a. Correct Answer: d) AREDS-2 vitamins. The AREDS vitamins are indicated for patients who have moderate ARMD defined as a minimum of 1 large drusen OR extensive intermediate sized drusen OR noncentral geographic atrophy. This patient has extensive intermediate sided drusen, and so the AREDS vitamins are indicated. Patients who smoke should take the AREDS-2 vitamins to avoid the beta carotene found in AREDS-1 (which have been associated with lung cancer in patients who smoke).
   b. Other Answers: This patient has dry ARMD. Focal Laser Photocoagulation and Lucentis Injections are only indicated for wet ARMD.
70. Which of the following would you expect to find for a patient with Best's Disease?
   a. Correct Answer: b) Normal ERG, Abnormal EOG

Case 15 Answers

71. What is the MOST LIKELY cause of the patient's chief complaint?
   a. Correct Answer: e) Trachoma. Given that this patient has been suffering from her "pink eye" for three months, a chronic conjunctivitis should be considered. This will narrow the options down to Inclusion Conjunctivitis or Trachoma. Given that the follicles are located superiorly, the Trachoma is the most appropriate diagnosis.
   b. Other Answers: Viral conjunctivitis will present with a watery discharge and should resolve spontaneously within 2-3 weeks. Bacterial conjunctivitis does not present with tender, palpable preauricular nodes. Allergic Conjunctivitis will present with itch and papillae.
72. Which of the following is true regarding the patient's chief complaint?

   a. Correct Answer: a) it is the most common cause of preventable blindness in the world.
   b. Other Answers: Viral conjunctivitis is most commonly seen in adults. Bacterial conjunctivitis is most commonly seen in children. Vernal or allergic conjunctivitis can be associated with the seasons.

73. Which of the following is a late complication for the patient's chief complaint?
    a. Correct Answer: b) Arlt Lines. Arlt Lines are scars along the superior palpebral conjunctiva due to chronic follicles.
    b. Other Answers: Subepithelial infiltrates may present in early stages of Chlamydial Conjunctivitis or 14 days after the onset of Epidemic Keratoconjunctivitis. Dennie's Lines are seen in Atopic Conjunctivitis.
74. Which of the following is the MOST APPROPRIATE treatment for this patient's chief complaint? (SELECT TWO)
    a. Correct Answers: e) Azithromycin PO, single dose; g) Erythromycin PO QID for two weeks. Given that Chlamydia is a type of bacteria, it needs to be treated with an antibiotic. The patient should start with a single dose of oral Azithromycin followed by two weeks of oral erythromycin, doxycycline, or tetracycline QID. Both Tetracycline and Doxycycline are contraindicated for this patient because she is allergic to Doxycycline.
75. When should you plan on following up with this patient for her chief complaint?
    a. Correct Answer: c) two weeks

Case 16 Answers

76. Which of the following is the MOST LIKELY diagnosis for the patient's chief complaint?
    a. Correct Answer: b) Arteritic Ischemic Optic Neuropathy. Given this patient presents with sudden, unilateral, painless loss of vision with headaches, painful chewing, and a unilateral swollen optic nerve, the most likely diagnosis is AION.
    b. Other Answers: NAION is not typically associated with headaches or jaw claudication. Optic Neuritis would present with pain on eye movement. A swollen optic nerve is not typical of a BRAO or CRAO
77. Which of the following in this patient's case history is a risk factor for his chief complaint?
    a. Correct Answer: c) Optic Nerve Appearance. This patient has a small CD ratio. An optic disc with a small CD ratio is termed a "disc at risk." When the cup is small, there is less real estate for all the nerve fibers and blood vessels to pass. Therefore, when the blood vessels become swollen due to GCA, they are more likely to get blocked.
    b. Other Answers: Hypertension is associated with NAION. Family history, spectacle prescription, and occupation are not risk factors for AAION.
78. Which of the following tests should be ordered for this patient? (SELECT TWO)
    a. Correct Answers: a) ESR; b) CRP. An ESR and CRP should be ordered stat for patients with possible GCA. They will help differentiate AAION from NAION. A temporal biopsy could also be considered. However, they do not always give reliable results due to skip lesions and will also leave the patient with a large scar.
79. Which of the following is the MOST APPROPRIATE INITIAL treatment for this patient?
    a. Correct Answer: a) Emergent IV Steroids. AION is considered an ocular emergency. If left untreated the patient may lose his vision in the other eye within the day. IV steroids

should be initiated even before the results of extra testing are available.

80. Optic Neuritis is MOST COMMONLY associated with which of the following?
    a. Correct Answer: b) Multiple Sclerosis. Optic Neuritis is inflammation of the optic nerve and is frequently the first sign of Multiple Sclerosis (MS). If not yet diagnosed, up to 50% of patients will be diagnosed with MS within 10 years of presentation with Optic Neuritis.

Case 17 Answers

81. Which of the following would be the best RGP design for this patient's right eye?
    a. Correct Answer: e) Cylinder Power Effect Bitoric. Cylinder Power Effect (CPE) Bitoric lenses have a toric back surface for proper fitting on a cornea with a lot of toricity, and a front toric surface to correct for residual astigmatism. They have a combined toric power. They are used to improve fitting comfort on patients who have a lot of corneal astigmatism and also need correction for astigmatism in their contact lenses. They should be used when the patients has >0.75D residual astigmatism and >1.50D of corneal astigmatism
82. Which of the following would be the best power for an RGP in this patient's right eye?
    a. Correct Answer: e) -4.00 -1.25 x090. First you must vertex back the patient's spectacle prescription. -4.25 -3.75 x090 will vertex to -4.00 -3.25 x 090. Then you must account for the corneal astigmatism. In this case this patient has 2.00 diopters of corneal astigmatism, which will correct for 2.00 diopters of this patients astigmatism.
83. See Image 1 for the NaFL pattern for the first trial lens you put on this patient. Which of the following changes could you consider for this lens? (SELECT THREE)
    a. Correct Answers: a) Choose a steeper base curve; c) Increase the diameter; e) Increase the sagittal height. A contact lens that sits low with a lot of peripheral NaFL pooling is characteristic of a loose fit. Therefore, this lens needs to be tightened. Think of the RGP as being like a suction cup. A deep, curvy, large suction cup would stick better (tighter fit) than a shallow, flat, small suction cup (looser fit).
84. This patient returns one year later for her annual eye exam. She is happy with her RGP lenses and has not observed any changes in her vision in the past year. See Image 2 for your slit lamp findings. What is the MOST LIKELY cause of the findings seen in Image 2?
    a. Correct Answer: d) Dimple Veiling. Dimple Veiling occurs when bubbles get trapped under an RGP due to a tight contact lens fit. These bubbles imprint dimples into the cornea which will pool with sodium fluorescein when the RGP is removed. Patients may have no complaints (asymptomatic) or complain of blur, epiphora, and ocular irritation.
    b. Other Answers: **Jelly Bumps** occur when proteins or other deposits lodge themselves into the front of a soft contact lens. This occurs due to contact lens over wear and improper contact lens care. Patients may complain of discomfort with contact lens wear. **Mucin Balls** are found with both soft and hard contact lens wearers. They occur when mechanical rubbing of the contact lens stimulate the goblet cells to produce extra mucin which will form balls that embed themselves in the corneal epithelium. Mucin Balls do not move with blink while the patient is wearing a contact lens. They will become dislodged with blink after the contact lens is removed, leaving behind dimples in the

corneal epithelium in which fluorescein will pool. **Corneal Microcysts** are caused by corneal hypoxia (oxygen deprivation) due to contact lens over wear. Patients may complain of pain if the Microcysts rupture. **Protein Deposits** occur when denatured proteins accumulate on a hard or soft contact lens. This occurs due to contact lens over wear and improper contact lens care. Patients may complain of cloudy uncomfortable contact lenses.

85. Which of the following is the MOST APPROPRIATE management for the patient's finding in Image 2?
    a. Correct Answer: c) The patient needs to be fitted into a flatter RGP. Given that Dimple Veiling is caused by a tight RGP fit, the fit needs to be flattened.
    b. Other Answers: Patients with **Jelly Bumps** need to discard the damaged contact lenses because they cannot be salvaged; removal of the Jelly Bumps will cause dimples in the lens. They should be educated on proper contact lens care and wear time. **Mucin Balls** rarely require treatment. If the Mucin Balls disrupt clarity of vision, then consider fitting the patient into a steeper contact lens. The tighter fit will reduce the mechanical rubbing of the contact lens. Patients can also reduce contact lens wear time and use contact lens rewetting drops. Patients with **Corneal Microcysts** should decrease contact lens wear time and be fit into contact lenses with a higher DK/t, or higher oxygen permeability. Patients need to discard contact lenses which have accumulated **Protein Deposits** because they cannot be salvaged. They should be educated on proper contact lens care and wear time.

Case 18 Answers

86. What is the MOST LIKELY cause of this patient's chief complaint?
    a. Correct Answer: c) Snowflake Cataracts. Snowflake Cataracts may look similar to Rosette Cataracts. They are associated with Diabetes and can have a very rapid onset. They are caused by elevated levels of intraocular glucose and lenticular sorbitol, which causes oxidative stress.
    b. Other Answers: **Cortical Cataracts** are age related and occur when the cortical fibers liquefy. Since the fibers are situated in a radial pattern, the cataracts will look like spokes. Early signs of Cortical Cataracts are vacuoles. Because the spokes occur peripherally, these cataracts are usually most symptomatic at night when the patient is dilated, and the most common complaint will be glare. **Rosette Cataracts** (Traumatic Cataracts) may look similar to Snowflake Cataracts. They are caused by blunt ocular trauma, and can develop within months to years after the trauma occurs. **Subcapsular Cataracts** are plaque-like opacities located either at the anterior or posterior (more common) poles of the lens. They are most easily visualized with retroillumination. These cataracts are often associated with Atopic Dermatitis, steroid use, inflammation, trauma, diabetes, or radiation. Given their central location, these cataracts will cause difficulty with reading. **Sunflower Cataracts** are associated with Wilson's Disease, which is an abnormal accumulation of copper. (Notice the yellow color of the cataract and remember that copper and sunflowers are yellow).

87. What is the MOST LIKELY etiology for this patient's chief complaint?

a. Correct Answer: e) Diabetes. Snowflake Cataracts are associated with Diabetes and can have a very rapid onset. They are caused by elevated levels of intraocular glucose and lenticular sorbitol, which causes oxidative stress
b. Other Answers: Steroids typically cause Posterior Subcapsular Cataracts. Blunt ocular trauma is associated with Rosette Cataracts. Wilson's Disease is associated with Sunflower Cataracts. Sun exposure causes age-related cataracts, and Snowflake Cataracts are not age-related.

88. What is the MOST APPROPRIATE treatment for this patient's chief complaint?
    a. Correct Answer: d) Refer for Cataract Surgery.
    b. Other Answers: This patient's chief complaint is reduced visual acuity. Manifest refraction did not significantly improve the patient's VA, and so an updated spectacle prescription will not resolve the patient's chief complaint. While this patient needs to have be sure to control her diabetes, managing her blood sugar will not resolve the Snowflake Cataract. This patient does not have a Sunflower Cataract, and so there is no evidence of Wilson's Disease. This patient has no history of steroid use and does not have a posterior subcapsular cataract, and so there is no need to educate her to stop using steroids.
89. A DIFFERENT patient with a history of cataract surgery in both eyes comes to your clinic complaining that it appears his cataracts have "come back." See Image 2 for your slit lamp findings. What is the MOST LIKELY cause of this patient's complaint?
    a. Correct Answer: a) Posterior Capsular Opacification. During cataract surgery it is hard to remove every single cell of the natural lens prior to inserting the implant. After the surgery is completed, left over cells on the posterior capsule from the natural lens can begin to grow. The growth of these cells causes a PCO. A PCO can occur between months and years after the cataract surgery. This is a very common complication after cataract surgery (up to 50%).
    b. Other Answers: This patient has had cataract surgery and so cannot have another type of cataract at this time. Pseudoexfoliation Syndrome is usually asymptomatic and will present with a target pattern of exfoliative material on the anterior lens capsule.
90. What is the most appropriate management for this patient's chief complaint?
    a. Correct Answer: a) Refer for YAG Capsulotomy. YAG Capsulotomy (laser treatment) is performed to remove the proliferated lens cells. This procedure only needs to be performed once. The cells do not grow back again after the YAG Capsulotomy has been completed.
    b. Other Answers: Laser Peripheral Iridotomy, Selective Laser Trabeculoplasty, and Latanoprost are all treatments performed to control increased IOP, which is not applicable to this patient. Once a patient has gotten cataract surgery, they cannot get cataracts again and so there is no reason to "redo" cataract surgery.

Case 19 Answers

91. What is the MOST LIKELY cause of this patient's chief complaint?
    a. Correct Answer: b) Acute Angle Closure Glaucoma. Acute Angle Closure Glaucoma will present with a significant IOP increase, a closed angle, and a mid-dilated pupil. Patients

will have corneal edema with bullae because increased IOP interferes with the ability of the endothelium to maintain corneal deturgescence.

b. Other Answers: Glaucomatocyclitic Crisis (POSNER-SCHLOSSMAN SYNDROME) is caused by trabeculitis. Patients present with recurrent attacks of increased IOP (up to 60 mmHg). The trabeculitis will cause a mild anterior chamber reaction of cells/flare. They will have an OPEN angle with NO synechiae. Plateau Iris Configuration is defined by a flat iris which is sharply convex in the periphery due to anteriorly rotated ciliary processes. It is defined as Plateau Iris Syndrome when angle closure with an increased IOP occurs. Plateau Iris Syndrome will initially present the same as Angle Closure Glaucoma. However, after an LPI the IOP will still increase with dilation due to the iris configuration, and this is diagnostic. Aqueous Misdirection Syndrome is the same as Malignant Glaucoma. Malignant Glaucoma occurs when the ciliary body rolls anteriorly causing the aqueous humor to be misdirected posteriorly and pool in Berger's Space. Accumulation of aqueous in the posterior chamber causes the anterior chamber structures to be displaced anteriorly and cause angle closure glaucoma. Patients present with an extremely high IOP with a very shallow anterior chamber.

92. Which of the following spectacle prescriptions would be MOST LIKELY for this patient's OD?
    a. Correct Answer: a) + 6.00 DS. Angle Closure Glaucoma is most commonly found in hyperopes because they have a shorter eyeball. The reduced axial length pushes all of the ocular structures closer together, thus causing the angles to narrow. Given that +6.00 is higher than +1.00, the higher hyperope will have a shorter axial length and so will be more likely to have narrow angles.

93. Which of the following should be considered in the INITIAL treatment for this patient? (SELECT THREE)
    a. Correct Answers: a) Indentation Gonioscopy; d) Topical Brimonidine every 15 minutes; e) IV Acetazolamide. Indentation Gonioscopy can be performed to break the angle closure attack. Topical Brimonidine and oral (or IV) Acetazolamide can be used to reduce the IOP.
    b. Other Answers: Prostaglandins (including Latanoprost) usually take about two weeks to start showing significant reduction of IOP, and so they are not the first line of treatment for an Acute Angle Closure Attack. This patient has asthma, and so Timolol would be contraindicated.

94. Which of the following is the MOST APPROPRIATE treatment once the IOP has been stabilized?
    a. Correct Answer: a) Laser Peripheral Iridotomy (LPI). An LPI will help stabilize the pressure between the anterior and posterior chambers if the angle closes again.
    b. Other Answers: Iridectomy can also be used to prevent future Angle Closure Attacks. However, it is not the first choice because it involves creating a larger hole in the iris than with an LPI. YAG Capsulotomy is used to treat a Posterior Capsular Opacification. Selective Laser Trabeculoplasty and a topical Prostaglandin are treatments for Primary Open Angle Glaucoma.

95. The patient's chief complaint would be MOST LIKELY to occur after which of the following activities?

a. Correct Answer: a) Watching a matinee showing of a movie. Angle closure attacks are known to occur when the patient's pupils are constricting after being dilated. The pupillary border will seal itself off on the anterior surface of the lens. While in a dark movie theatre the patient's pupils would be dilated for a sustained period of time, and then will constrict quickly when the patient steps out into the bright sun.

b. Other Answers: The main concern from Snowboarding is thermal keratopathy due to prolonged exposure to UV-C light without protective eye wear. The main concern related to watching a solar eclipse is Solar Retinopathy, which is basically when the sun burns the retina and causes visual changes. Reading on a computer should cause the eyes to constrict, not dilate.

Case 20 Answers

96. Which diagnosis is the MOST LIKELY cause of this patient's diplopia?
    a. Correct Answer: e) Cranial Nerve 6 Palsy. Patients with a CN6 palsy will present with esotropia with inability to abduct the involved eye.
    b. Other Answers: An esotropia does not present with an ability to abduct the involved eye. Patients with a CN3 palsy will present with an eye which is located down and out with a complete ptosis. Patients with a CN4 Palsy will present with an eye which is located in and up with a possible torsional component.
97. Which of the following should you include in your initial workup for this patient?
    a. Correct Answer: c) Forced Ductions will help determine if the etiology is due to a muscle restriction or a problem with innervation.
    b. Other Answers: Parks 3-Step and Double Maddox Rod test is indicated for a CN4 palsy. Tensilon Test is indicated for Myasthenia Gravis.
98. Which of the following is the MOST COMMON etiology for this patient's diplopia?
    a. Correct Answer: b) Compressive Tumor
99. Which of the following is the MOST APPROPRIATE management for this patient' diplopia?
    a. Correct Answer: d) Refer for an MRI. Given that the most common cause of a CN 6 Palsy is a compressive tumor, an MRI is indicated.
100. If a DIFFERENT PATIENT has Third Nerve palsy and the pupil is NOT involved, what can be concluded?
    a. Correct Answer: a) The etiology is likely due to a microvascular disease.
    b. Other Answers: An aneurysm of the posterior communicating artery will cause a PUPIL INVOLVING CN3 Palsy.

Case 21 Answers

101. What is the spherical equivalent for this patient's right eye based on the MANIFEST REFRACTION?
    a. Correct Answer: b) +0.50 DS. Spherical Equivalency can be calculated with the following equation: Spherical Equivalent = (Cylinder Power / 2) + Sphere Power
102. Which of the following is the MOST APPROPRIATE diagnosis for this patient's chief complaint?
    a. Correct Answer: a) Hyperopia. There is no evidence that this patient has an accommodative or vergence condition.
103. This patient presents with how much LATENT hyperopia in his left eye?

a. Correct Answer: c) +1.50 DS. Latent Hyperopia is the difference between the hyperopia found with the Manifest and Cycloplegic refractions.

104. Which of the following would be the MOST APPROPRIATE prescription for this patient?
    a. Correct Answer: f) OD: +2.25 -0.50 x180 / OS: +2.00 DS for reading only. If a child has latent hyperopia but only complains about difficulty with near vision, then prescribe their full cycloplegic distance refraction for reading only. They do not need correction for distance because they do not have difficulty with distance vision. But, prescribing their cycloplegic distance refraction for near will allow them to use a normal amount of accommodation to achieve clarity of near vision.
105. Which of the following is an example of a Jackson Cross Cylinder?
    a. Correct Answer: d) +1.00 -2.00 x180. A Jackson Cross Cylinder will have a spherical equivalency of zero. Spherical Equivalent = (Cylinder Power / 2) + Sphere Power.

Case 22 Answers

106. What is the MOST LIKELY diagnosis for the patient's chief complaint?
    a. Correct Answer: a) Bell's Palsy will cause flaccid paralysis of one side of the face.
    b. Other Answers: CN 3 and 4 Palsies will cause restriction of EOM movement. CN 5 palsy will cause reduced sensation of the face, not reduced movement. Floppy Eyelid Syndrome is not associated with facial paralysis.
107. What is the MOST LIKELY etiology for this patient's chief complaint?
    a. Correct Answer: c) Idiopathic. There is evidence that Herpes Simplex and Neural inflammation are associated with Bell's Palsy, but it is most commonly idiopathic.
    b. Other Answer: Compressive tumors and Strokes do not cause Bell's Palsy. Sleep Apnea is associated with Floppy Eyelid Syndrome.
108. What is the MOST LIKELY location of the neural defect?
    a. Correct Answer: c) Left lower motor neuron lesion. Bell's Palsy is flaccid paralysis of the lower motor neuron of CN7, affecting the entire ipsilateral side of the face.
109. What is the MOST APPROPRIATE treatment for this patient's chief complaint?
    a. Correct Answer: b) Monitor, this will spontaneously resolve. Bell's Palsy will typically spontaneously improve within 4 months with possible complete resolution within one year or onset.
    b. Other Answers: On oral steroid or oral Acyclovir would be indicated if inflammation or Herpes Simplex were suspected, respectively (which is not true in this case). A sleep test would be indicated if this patient had sleep apnea. An emergent MRI would be indicated if a stroke or brain tumor were suspected, which is not true in this case.
110. Which of the following is an EXPECTED finding for this patient (SELECT TWO)?
    a. Correct Answers: a) drooling; c) Left Bell's Reflex intact. CN7 is responsible for secretions in the mouth. During flaccid paralysis of CN7, the patient may experience drooling. Bell's reflex is controlled by CN3, which is not affected during a Bell's Palsy, and so Bell's reflex should still be intact.
    b. Other Answers: a fixed, dilated pupil would be expected during CN3 palsy due to an aneurysm of the posterior communicating artery. Forced Ductions testing would be positive if the globe could NOT be moved with outside mechanical force, and occurs

when there is muscle entrapment. Neural defects due not cause neural entrapment. An inability to abduct the left eye would be caused by a CN6 lesion, which is not suspected in this case.

Case 23 Answers

111. What is the MOST LIKELY diagnosis for the patient's systemic disease?
    a. Correct Answer: b) Sarcoidosis presents with granulomatous uveitis and NONcaseating granulomas.
    b. Other Answers: Ankylosing Spondylitis presents with NONgranulomatous uveitis, while this case presents with granulomatous uveitis. Syphilis and VKH Syndrome will not present with lung granulomas. Tuberculosis presents with caseating lung granulomas.
112. Which test would you expect to be abnormal for this patient?
    a. Correct Answer: a) ACE. It is important to remember that serum ACE will be elevated in these patients. I remember this by "Sarc-ACE."
    b. Other Answers: An abnormal ANA is not associated with Sarcoidosis. An abnormal PPD is associated with Tuberculosis. RPR and VDRL are associated with Syphilis.
113. Which of the following would be the most appropriate treatment for this patient's anterior segment findings? (SELECT TWO)
    a. Correct Answers: c) Topical Cyclopentolate; e)Topical Pred Acetate. A topical cycloplegic is indicated to treat the uveitis to prevent the formation of peripheral anterior synechiae. A strong steroid is indicated to treat uveitis so that it can penetrate the cornea to reduce inflammation.
    b. Other Answers: Oral medications are usually indicated for systemic or retinal conditions. A topical NSAID (such as Ketorolac) is not indicated for uveitis, a stronger anti-inflammatory is necessary.
114. Ocular findings are most likely to be present during which stage of Syphilis?
    a. Correct Answer: b) Secondary Syphilis.
    b. Other Answers: Primary Syphilis is characterized as a chancre which occurs at the site of infection after a 2-4 week incubation period. Tertiary Syphilis is characterized by cardiovascular and CNS disease. There is no such thing as Quaternary Syphilis.
115. Which of the following tests should you include when following a patient who is taking Plaquenil?
    a. Correct Answer: c) Ishihara Color Vision. A sign of Plaquenil toxicity is color vision defects.
    b. Other Answers: Other tests for Plaquenil toxicity should include a 10-2 Visual Field, Multifocal ERG, Spectral Domain macular OCT. Red Saturation Test is usually performed to evaluate for optic nerve conditions, and we are looking for macular conditions for patients who are taking Plaquenil. IOP is not expected to increase as a result of Plaquenil toxicity.

Case 24 Answers

116. What is the MOST LIKELY diagnosis for this patient's chief complaint?
    a. Correct Answer: d) Endophthalmitis. Endophthalmitis is a very serious infection which typically occurs after intraocular surgery
    b. Other Answers: Bacterial Keratitis can be ruled out because the cornea is not involved in

this case. Bechet's Disease typically presents with a triad of oral ulcers, genital ulcers, and nongranulomatous uveitis. Blebitis occurs when a filtering bleb used to treat glaucoma becomes infected. Sympathetic Ophthalmia is a **bilateral** reaction that occurs after a penetrating ocular injury or intraocular surgery.

117. Which of the following is the MOST COMMON cause of this patient's chief complaint?
    a. Correct Answer: g) *Staph epidermidis*
118. What should be the first step in the management for this patient?
    a. Correct Answer: b) Immediately refer to an ophthalmologist. Endophthalmitis is an ocular emergency which requires immediate management by an ophthalmologist.
119. Which of the following should be considered in the treatment for this patient?
    a. Correct Answer: e) Vancomycin. Endophthalmitis is caused by a bacterial infection. Vancomycin is the only antibiotic on this list.
120. IF this patient was only Light Perception OD, which of the following would be indicated?
    a. Correct Answer: d) Pars Plana Vitrectomy.

Case 25 Answers

121. What is the MOST LIKELY diagnosis for this patient's chief complaint?
    a. Correct Answer: d) Reiter's Syndrome (Reactive Arthritis) has a classic triad of uveitis, urethritis, and polyarthritis (remembered as "can't see, can't pee, can't climb a tree.") If suspected, ask the patient about joint pain and pain on urination. This patient has pain on urination which helps differentiate Reiter's Syndrome from the other causes of nongranulomatous uveitis.
122. Which of the following tests would you expect to be abnormal for this patient?
    a. Correct Answer: c) HLA-B27
    b. Other Answers: HLA-A29 is associated with Birdshot Choroidopathy. HLA-B12 and HLA-B5 are associated with Bechet's Disease. HLA-B7 is associated with Serpiginous Choroidopathy
123. Which of the following is the MOST APPROPRIATE treatment for this patient? (SELECT TWO)
    a. Correct Answers: c) Cyclopentolate; d) Durezol. Uveitis should be treated with a strong topical steroid and cycloplegic. Lotemax is a weak steroid and so would not penetrate the cornea effectively.
124. A DIFFERENT PATIENT presents with the findings as seen in Image 1. Which of the following is MOST LIKELY the diagnosis for this patient?
    a. Correct Answer: c) Psoriatic Arthritis is associated with nail pitting.
125. Lyme Disease is caused by which of the following?
    a. Correct Answer: c) *Borrelia burgdorferi*.

Case 26 Answers

126. What is the MOST LIKELY diagnosis for this patient's chief complaint?
    a. Correct Answer: a) Basic Exotropia occurs in children around the age of 2. It is a type of intermittent exotropia.
    b. Other Answers: Divergence Excess Exotropia typically occurs in older patients and is characterized by a larger angle of deviation at distance than at near. Convergence Insufficiency Exotropia typically occurs in older patients and is characterized by a larger

angle of deviation at near than at distance. Decompensated Exotropia occurs when a patient can no longer compensate for their exotropia with Positive Fusional Vergence (PFV). Consecutive Exotropia occurs after strabismus surgery to correct esotropia. Sensory Exotropia occurs when a congenital organic ocular condition results in decreased vision. Infantile Exotropia manifests before the patient is one year old.

127. Which of the following is the MOST APPROPRIATE initial prescription for this patient?
    a. Correct Answer: d) OD, OS: +1.00 DS for FTW. The first step in aligning an exotropia is to prescribe glasses.
    b. Other Answers: Given that the patient is developing an exotropia, a prescription is indicated despite concerns about emmetropization. The full manifest refraction should be prescribed; children are good at adapting to new prescriptions and we want to be aggressive to prevent the strabismus. There is no evidence of an accommodative disorder or of an increased deviation at near, and so an Add is not required. Prism is only indicated if the deviation is not corrected with lenses.
128. Five years later this patient decides to undergo vision therapy. Which of the following would be the MOST APPROPRIATE lenses to utilize during therapy exercises?
    a. Correct Answer: d) Base Out Lenses. Patients with an exodeviation have difficulty with Base Out prisms. Therefore, their eyes should be "exercised" with Base Out prisms.
    b. Other Answers: Lenses are not the most effective tool in therapy because the issue is not directly associated with the accommodative system.
129. A main concern is that this patient will develop amblyopia in the left eye.
    a. Correct Answer: b) False. Given that the patient's exotropia is intermittent, the left eye is still getting a chance to fixate, and so the patient is not at risk of getting exotropia.
130. You perform Maddox Rod Testing on a DIFFERENT PATIENT as seen in image 1. What can you conclude from this patient's findings?
    a. Correct Answer: e) 4 exodeviation. During Maddox Rod testing, the patient is asked to hold the red lens over their right eye. For horizontal deviations, if the patient states the red line goes through one of the letters on the left side of the card, then the patient is said to have a crossed (or exo) deviation. I remember this by noticing that there is an "x" in exo, which represents a cross.
    b. Other Answers: Maddox Rod testing cannot differentiate a phoria from a tropia. The test will simply give you the magnitude and direction of the deviation.

Case 27 Answers

131. What is the MOST LIKELY diagnosis for the reduced BCVA OS?
    a. Correct Answer: c) Histoplasmosis. Histoplasmosis presents with a classic triad, and two of the three findings need to be present for a diagnosis: 1) Multiple, small, yellow-white, punched-out lesions. 2) Peripapillary atrophy/scarring. 3) Macular choroidal neovascular membrane (CNVM) appearing as a grey-green membrane. This patient definitively presents with 1) yellow-white punched-out lesions and 2) peripapillary atrophy.
    b. Other Answers: Acute Retinal Necrosis presents with peripheral areas of well-demarcated white necrosis which will eventually spread circumferentially around the peripheral retina, sparing the posterior pole until late in the disease course. Toxocariasis will

present with endophthalmitis and leukocoria. Toxoplasmosis will presents with single macular chorioretinal scar (congenital) and possibly headlights in a fog (acquired/reactivated)

132. Which of the following is the MOST LIKELY etiology for this patient's retinal findings OS?
    a. Correct Answer: c) *Histoplasma capsulatum* is the fungus which causes Histoplasmosis.
    b. Other Answers: *Ancylostoma caninum* and *Baylisascaris procyonis* are worms which cause Diffuse Unilateral Subacute Neuroretinitis. *Toxocara canis* is a nematode which causes Toxocariasis. Toxoplasma gondii is a parasite which causes Toxoplasmosis.
133. This patient's retinal findings OS are MOST COMMONLY associated with which of the following animals?
    a. Correct Answer: b) Bats
    b. Other Answers: Armadillos are associated with Leprosy. Cats are associated with Toxoplasmosis. Dogs are associated with Toxocariasis. Raccoons are associated with Diffuse Unilateral Subacute Neuroretinitis.
134. Which of the following is the MOST APPROPRIATE treatment for this patient's retinal findings OS?
    a. Correct Answer: g) None of the Above. Histoplasmosis only requires treatment when there is evidence of inflammation or neovascularization. Neither is present in this case, and so this patient does not require any treatment.
    b. Other Answers: Direct laser photocoagulation is indicated against a nematode which is currently moving through the retina. Histoplasmosis does not have a viral etiology and so an antiviral is not indicated. Pyrimethamine is indicated to treat Toxoplasmosis. Natamycin is an antifungal. While Histoplasmosis has a fungal etiology, antifungals are NOT indicated for treatment (there is no evidence which indicates they are beneficial).
135. Which of the following complications should you expect for this patient?
    a. Correct Answer: g) None of the Above.
    b. Other Answers: Inflammation is not associated with Histoplasmosis, which rules out Vitritis, Uveitis, and Pars planitis. Retinal Detachments and Endophthalmitis are associated with Toxocariasis.

Case 28 Answers

136. Which of the following is the MOST LIKELY diagnosis for this patient's chief complaint?
    a. Correct Answer: a) Adenoviral Conjunctivitis.
    b. Other Answers: Bacterial Conjunctivitis is most commonly seen in children and will present with NEGATIVE lymphadenopathy and mucopurulent discharge. Epidemic Keratoconjunctivitis will present with subepithelial infiltrates 2-3 weeks after onset. Swimming Pool Conjunctivitis (Pharyngoconjunctival fever) presents with fever and pharyngitis (sore throat). Gonococcal Conjunctivitis will have a hyperacute onset of severe mucopurulent discharge with positive lymphadenopathy.
137. Which of the following does NOT need to be included in the education for this patient?
    a. Correct Answer: c) She should notify her sexual partner(s). Adenoviral Conjunctivitis is not sexually transmitted.
138. Which of the following is the MOST APPROPRIATE treatment for this patient?

a. Correct Answer: e) Preservative free artificial tears Q2H. A viral infection will self-resolve within two weeks. Artificial tears can be used for comfort during this time. A mild topical steroid could also be considered to reduce inflammation.
b. Other Answers: This is not a bacterial infection and so an antibiotic is not indicated. Natamycin is an antifungal.

139. Which of the following is the MOST APPROPRIATE treatment for Ophthalmia Neonatorum?
    a. Correct Answer: a) Erythromycin ung is the most modern treatment for Ophthalmia Neonatorum.
    b. Other Answers: Silver Nitrate was historically used to treat Ophthalmia Neonatorum, but now Erythromycin is used.
140. Which of the following bacteria can attack the intact cornea?
    a. Correct Answer: b) *Neisseria gonorrhoeae*. The bacteria which can attack the intact cornea include: *Pseudomonas, Corynebacterium diphtheria, Haemophilus, Listeria, and Neisseria gonorrhea.*

Case 29 Answers

141. What is the MOST LIKELY cause for this patient's Chief Complaint?
    a. Correct Answer: a) Cortical Blindness is sudden, bilateral, complete blindness due to extensive damage to the occipital lobe and may occur within a day of cardiac surgery. The eye exam will be normal aside for bilateral no light perception. The pupillary light reflex will be present because the occipital lobe is not responsible for the pupillary response.
    b. Other Answers: Vertebrobasilar Insufficiency occurs when the Vertebrobasilar arterial blood supply to the brain becomes blocked due to a thrombus, emboli, hypertension, or anything which can cause a hypercoagulable state. An Ocular Migraine is a migraine which presents with an aura without any headache. A patient who is Malingering is a healthy individual who is purposefully pretending to have an ocular condition, usually for financial gain. They will typically be aggressive and combative. A patient with Hysteria genuinely believes they have an ocular condition when they actually do not. They will typically be cooperative and indifferent.
142. Which of the following is the most appropriate management for this patient?
    a. Correct Answer: e) None of the above. The visual loss from Cortical Blindness is usually permanent and has no treatment.
143. Which part of this patient's brain is most likely involved?
    a. Correct Answer: b) Occipital. Cortical Blindness is sudden, bilateral, complete blindness due to extensive damage to the occipital lobe.
144. Which of the following is the MOST COMMON type of migraine?
    a. Correct Answer: b) Common Migraines are Migraines without an Aura.
    b. Other Answers: There is no such thing as Regular or Daily Migraines. Classic Migraines are migraines with an aura. Ocular Migraine occurs when a patient experiences auras without a headache.
145. Where would you expect to find the causative lesion for Adie's Tonic Pupil?
    a. Correct Answer: a) Ciliary ganglion.

b. Other Answers: Argyll Robertson Pupils are caused by damage to the Edinger-Westphal Nucleus. Damage to the optic tract would cause a Contralateral Homonymous Hemianopsia.

Case 30 Answers

146. What is the MOST LIKELY diagnosis for this patient's retinal disease?
    a. Correct Answer: e) Sickle Cell Retinopathy may present with Black Sunbursts, Salmon Patches, Sea Fans, Silver Wire, vitreous detachments, and retinal detachments.
    b. Other Answers: Eales Disease is a diagnosis of exclusion and presents with peripherally located retinal vascular occlusions. Embolic Retinopathy is associated with IV drug use and presents with refractive particles in the retinal vasculature. Sarcoidosis is typically seen with uveitis in addition to Sea Fans. Pars Planitis / Intermediate Uveitis is an inflammation of the vitreous characterized by extensive vitreous cells and fibrovascular exudates.
147. Which of the following is the most appropriate stage for this patient's retinal disease?
    a. Correct Answer: c) Stage 3 Sickle Cell Retinopathy presents with Sea Fans with no associated vitreous or retinal detachment.
148. Which of the following should you consider in the treatment/management for this patient's retinal disease?
    a. Correct Answer: e) All of the above. A Sea Fan is a type of neovascularization. Treatment options for neovascularization include Anti-VEGF injections, cryotherapy, and laser photocoagulation. Patients with Sickle Cell Disease should be referred for a hematology consultation.
149. What is the typical demographic for patients with Coat's Disease?
    a. Correct Answer: b) Boys under 10. The diagnosis is typically made later, between 8 to 16 years old.
150. What is the most common location of the primary tumor in WOMEN who present with Choroidal Metastasis?
    a. Correct Answer: b) Breast.
    b. Other Answers: The most common location of the primary tumor in MEN who present with Choroidal Metastasis is the lung.

Case 31 Answers

151. What is the MOST LIKELY cause of this patient's reduced BCVA OS?
    a. Correct Answer: b) Keratoconus.
    b. Other Answers: Pellucid Marginal Degeneration will present with "kissing doves" on topography. Keratoglobus is thinning of the entire cornea causing it to bulge out entirely; it is not thinning of just the inferior cornea as is seen with Keratoconus. Myopia and astigmatism do not cause a reduced BCVA independently; reduced BCVA is associated with pathology.
152. Which of the following is an early sign of this patient's corneal findings?
    a. Correct Answer: b) Fleischer ring.
    b. Other Answers: Corneal Hydrops, Munson's Sign, and Vogt Striae are all late signs of Keratoconus. Stocker's Line is seen with pterygiums.

153. This patient's corneal findings are associated with which of the following?
    a. Correct Answer: e) All of the Above.
154. Which of the following are the MOST LIKELY keratometry findings for this patient's OS?
    a. Correct Answer: d) 51.25 @138, 52.75 @048. Keratoconus is associated with steep corneal findings. This is the only answer option in which both of the axis are considered steep. Remember that steep is defined as a keratometry findings greater than 45.00D.
155. Which of the following is the MOST APPROPRIATE management for this patient? (SELECT TWO)
    a. Correct Answers: a) Fit with RGP, d) Refer for corneal crosslinking. The tear lens created by an RGP will give this patient maximum clarity of vision. Corneal crosslinking has been shown to either slow or stop the progression of keratoconus in patients under the age of 35.
    b. Other Answers: Soft contacts and glasses will not give the patient maximum clarity of vision. Also, soft contacts could compromise the "good eye." Keratoconus is an absolute contraindication for LASIK. Keratoconus causes progressive thinning and deformation of the cornea. Given that LASIK removes stromal tissue and further thins and weakens the cornea, it would just add fuel to the fire.

CASE 32

156. True/False: This patient is legally blind.
    a. Correct Answer: a) True. Legal blindness is defined as: Patient's best corrected visual acuity is 20/200 or worse in the better seeing eye (in other words, the patient is unable to read the 20/100 line with their better seeing eye). OR Visual field is less than 20 degrees in the better seeing eye.
157. What would you estimate would be the near add for this patient so that she can read standard print?
    a. Correct Answer: d) +10.00. The Kestenbaum Equation allows you to estimate the near add a patient will require to read print at 1M (standard print). It states that the inverse of their distance acuity is the estimated near add. The inverse of 20/200 is 200/20 = 10.
158. At what distance would this patient need to hold her reading materials based on the add you calculated in Question 157?
    a. Correct Answer: d) 10 cm. The equation for determining the distance in centimeters at which a patient needs to hold reading material for clear vision with a given add is Distance = 100 / Add Power. This equation assumes the patient is using no accommodation. 100/10 = 10 cm.
159. What would you expect would be this patient's Just Noticeable Difference?
    a. Correct Answer: b) 2.00 D. A patient's Just Noticeable Difference (JND) can be calculated by dividing the denominator of their best visual acuity by 100. This patient's BCVA is 20/200. Therefore, 200/100 = 2.00 D.
160. What is the name of the test pictured in Image 1?
    a. Correct Answer: d) Pelli-Robson Contrast Sensitivity Chart

SOLO ITEMS

161. Which of the following is the LARGEST purkinje image?
    a. Correct Answer: c) Image III

162. During which phase of a clinical trial is a drug's efficacy tested on a small group of sick people?
    a. Correct Answer: b) Phase 2.
    b. Other Answers: Phase 1 tests the drug's safety on healthy people. Phase 3 tests the drug's efficacy on a large group of sick people and determines adverse reactions. Phase 4 evaluates marketing for the drug. There is no 5th phase.
163. HIPAA applies to which of the following groups?
    a. Correct Answer: e) All of the above.
164. Which of the following would be considered a normal APGAR Score?
    a. Correct Answer: d) 9. An infant is assigned an APGAR Score within 5 minutes after birth, and it will be on a scale from 1-10 with 10 being the healthiest. The score will be based on five criteria which comprise the acronym APGAR: Appearance (skin color), Pulse, Grimace (reflex), Activity, and Respiration. Most babies achieve a score of 7 or above, and this is normal. A score of 4-6 indicates the baby needs help breathing, and a score of 1-3 indicates the baby needs emergent lifesaving intervention.
165. Which of the following materials provides the most UV protection?
    a. Correct Answer: c) Polycarbonate.
166. Which of the following filters transmits only one wavelength of light?
    a. Correct Answer: b) Interference Filters
    b. Other Answers: Blue Blockers are amber colored and prevent short wavelengths of light from transmitting. They can help patients who have complaints about glare sensitivity. Long-Pass Filters transmit only long wavelengths of light. Narrow Band Filters transmit a small range of wavelengths of light. Neutral Density Filters transmit all wavelengths of light. They reduce the amount of light which passes through equally for all wavelengths, and so they do not change color perception. Neutral Density Filters can be used to measure APDs. Neutral Density Filters of increasing intensity are placed over the good eye until the examiner no longer sees the APD.
167. What is the term for "do no harm?"
    a. Correct Answer: d) Nonmaleficence
    b. Other Answers: Autonomy means patients have a right to make their own decisions. Beneficence means helping others. Justice means equal treatment of similar cases and fair distribution of goods and services. Tort Reform caps/limits the fines/damages that may be awarded during lawsuits.
168. What is the name of the test pictured below?
    a. Correct Answer: a) Farnsworth D-15
169. How would you interpret the results from this test?
    a. Correct Answer: d) Protan
170. What is the Frame PD of a frame with the following measurements: A 43, B 35, C 40, DBL 15, ED 46?
    a. Correct Answer: d) 58. Frame PD = A Measurement + DBL
171. Which of the following findings would you expect in a patient with CHARGE Syndrome? (SELECT THREE)
    a. Correct Answers: a) Atresia choana, b) Coloboma, d) Retarded growth. Colobomas are

associated with CHARGE Syndrome which is defined as a collection of findings: Coloboma, Heart conditions, Atresia choana (congenital blockage of the nasal passage), Retarded growth, Genital conditions, and Ear conditions.

b. Other Answers: A Thin upper lip is associated with Fetal Alcohol Syndrome. Nystagmus is not associated with CHARGE Syndrome.

172. Pantoscopic Tilt on a minus lens will induce astigmatism along which meridian?
    a. Correct Answer: a) Axis 180
173. You are testing a patient using the Nagel Anomaloscope. These are her results: Mixture Field 30, Test Field 17. This is consistent with what type of color deficiency?
    a. Correct Answer: e) Deuteranomalous Trichromat
174. Which of the following is an example of Incidence?
    a. Correct Answer: d) In 2018, an estimated 266,120 new cases of invasive breast cancer were diagnosed in women in the United States. Incidence refers to the number of new cases that develop in a given period of time.
175. A patient picks up his new pair of glasses and his left lens is resting higher than the right lens. Which of the following adjustments should you make?
    a. Correct Answers: b) Bend the left temple arm up, c) Bend the right temple arm down.

SOURCES CITED

Cheatham, Kyle M., et al. *KMK Part One: Basic Science Review Guide*. 8th ed., vol. 1, KMK Educational Services, LLC., 2015.

Cheatham, Kyle M., et al. *KMK Part One: Basic Science Review Guide*. 8th ed., vol. 2, KMK Educational Services, LLC., 2015.

Cheatham, Kyle M., and Sarah Dougherty Wood. *KMK Part 2 Diagnosis And Treatment: Board Review Guide*. 5th ed., KMK Educational Services, LLC, 2016.

Gerstenblith, Adam T., et al. *The Wills Eye Manual: Office and Emergency Room Diagnosis and Treatment of Eye Diseases*. 6th ed., Wolters Kluwer, 2012.

Kaiser, Peter K., and Neil J. Friedman. *The Massachusetts Eye And Ear Infirmary Illustrated Manual Of Ophthalmology*. 4th ed., Saunders, Elsevier, 2014.

Kanski, Jack J., and Brad Bowling. *Clinical Ophthalmology: A Systemic Approach*. 7th ed., Butterworth Heinemann Elsevier, 2011.

"National Board of Examiners in Optometry® - NBEO®." *National Board of Examiners in Optometry® - NBEO®*, www.optometry.org/.

Scheimann, Mitchell, and Bruce Wick. *Clinical Management Of Binocular Vision: Heterophoric, Accommodative, And Eye Movement Disorders*. 4th ed., Wolters Kluwer, 2014.

"The Most Trusted Way to Prepare for the NBEO®." *OptoPrep | The Most Trusted Way to Prepare for the NBEO®*, www.optoprep.com/.

IMAGE CREDITS

AAO 1: Steinert, Roger, Ann McColgin, and Sumit Garg. Diffuse Lamellar (interface) Keratitis. Digital image. American Academy of Ophthalmology. N.p., 11 Dec. 2013. Web. 26 Feb. 2018. <https://www.aao.org/munnerlyn-laser-surgery-center/laser-in-situ-keratomileusis-lasik-3>.

AAO 2: Salim, Sarwat. PHACOMORPHIC GLAUCOMA. Digital image. American Academy of Ophthalmology. N.p., Oct. 2016. Web. 27 Feb. 2018. <https://www.aao.org/eyenet/article/lens-induced-glaucoma-diagnosis-management>.

AAO 3: Hung, Crystal, and JoAnn Giaconi. Small, White, Discrete Keratic Precipitates. Digital image. American Academy of Ophthalmology. N.p., 23 Jan. 2015. Web. 27 Feb. 2018. <http://eyewiki.org/testwiki/index.php?title=Glaucomatocyclitic_Crisis_(Posner-Schlossman_Syndrome)>.

AAO 4: Rapoport, Yuna. "Raccoon Eyes" upon Presentation. Digital image. American Academy of Ophthalmology. N.p., 2 May 2015. Web. 27 Feb. 2018. <http://eyewiki.org/testwiki/index.php?title=Neuroblastoma>.

Aibolita 1: Aibolita. Fields of Vision. Digital image. Aibolita. N.p., n.d. Web. 26 Feb. 2018. <http://aibolita.com/nervous-diseases/46788-lesions-of-the-visual-pathways.html>.

Akriti 1033: Cardiff Pediatric Acuity Set of 11 Cards. Digital image. Akriti Oculoplasty Logistics, India. N.p., 2019. Web. 8 Jan. 2019. <https://www.akriti.co.in/index.php?route=product/product&product_id=1033>.

All About Vision 1: Heiting, Gary. The Pelli Robson Contrast Sensitivity Chart. Digital image. All About Vision. N.p., Aug. 2017. Web. 27 Feb. 2018. <http://www.allaboutvision.com/eye-exam/contrast-sensitivity.htm>.

Art of Optics 1: Brightness Acuity Test (BAT). Digital image. Art of Optics. N.p., n.d. Web. 27 Feb. 2018. <https://www.artofoptiks.com/technology/>.

Atlas of Ophthalmology 1812: Ruprecht, Klaus. Tuberous Sclerosis (#4) (Bourneville's Disease). Digital image. Atlas of Ophthalmology. Universitaets Augenklinik, n.d. Web. 26 Feb. 2018. <www.atlasophthalmology.net/photo.jsf?node=1812>.

Atlas of Ophthalmology 2607: Jonathan, Dutton. Squamous Cell Carcinoma of Lid. Digital image. Atlas of Ophthalmology. N.p., n.d. Web. 26 Feb. 2018. <www.atlasophthalmology.net/photo.jsf?node=2607>.

Atlas of Ophthalmology 2645: Jonathan, Dutton. Graves' Ophthalmopathy (Thyroid Eye Disease, Endocrine Orbitopathy), Clinical Signs. Digital image. Atlas of Ophthalmology. N.p., n.d. Web. 26 Feb. 2018. <www.atlasophthalmology.net/photo.jsf?node=2645>.

Atlas of Ophthalmology 2742: Wollensak, Josef. Cogan-Reese Syndrome, Iridocorneal Endothelial Syndrome, ICE, Iris Spots. Digital image. Atlas of Ophthalmology. Univ. Augenklinik, n.d. Web. 26 Feb. 2018. <www.atlasophthalmology.net/photo.jsf?node=2742>.

Atlas of Ophthalmology 2774: Wollensak, Josef. Pediculosis. Digital Image. Atlas of Ophthalmology. Univ. Augenklinik, n.d. Web. 4 Jan. 2019. <www.atlasophthalmology.net/photojsf?node=2774>.

Atlas of Ophthalmology 2832: Wollensak, Josef. Anterior Mosaic Crocodile Mosaic Chagrin (Vogt). Digital image. Atlas of Ophthalmology. Univ. Augenklinik, n.d. Web. 26 Feb. 2018. <www.atlasophthalmology.net/photo.jsf?node=2832>.

Atlas of Ophthalmology 2842: Wollensak, Josef. Capillary Hemangioma of the Lid (Strawberry Nevus). Digital image. Atlas of Ophthalmology. Univ. Augenklinik, n.d. Web. 26 Feb. 2018. <www.atlasophthalmology.net/photo.jsf?node=2842>.

Atlas of Ophthalmology 3274: Benson, William. Avulsion of Optic Nerve. Digital image. Atlas of Ophthalmology. N.p., n.d. Web. 26 Feb. 2018.

<www.atlasophthalmology.net/photo.jsf?node=3274>.

Atlas of Ophthalmology 3411: Meyer, HJ. Orbital Cellulitis. Digital image. Atlas of Ophthalmology. N.p., n.d. Web. 26 Feb. 2018. <www.atlasophthalmology.net/photo.jsf?node=3411>.

Atlas of Ophthalmology 4638: Halabis, J. Lasertrabeculoplasty and Peripheral Anterior Synechiae, Gonioscopy. Digital image. Atlas of Ophthalmology. Durham VAMC, n.d. Web. 26 Feb. 2018. <www.atlasophthalmology.net/photo.jsf?node=4638>.

Atlas of Ophthalmology 4850: Jost, Jonas. Acute Angle-Closure Glaucoma. Digital image. Atlas of Ophthalmology Image. N.p., n.d. Web. 26 Feb. 2018. <www.atlasophthalmology.net/photo.jsf?node=4850>.

Atlas of Ophthalmology 4908: Trachoma, Stage 2a. Digital image. Atlas of Ophthalmology. Web. 4 Jan. 2019. <www.atlasophthalmology.net/photo.jsf?node=4908>.

Atlas of Ophthalmology 5028: Jonathan, Dutton. Capillary Hemangioma. Digital image. Atlas of Ophthalmology. N.p., n.d. Web. 26 Feb. 2018. <www.atlasophthalmology.net/photo.jsf?node=5028>.

Atlas of Ophthalmology 5031: Jonathan, Dutton. Chronic Progressive External Ophthalmoplegia (CPEO). Digital image. Atlas of Ophthalmology. N.p., n.d. Web. 26 Feb. 2018. <www.atlasophthalmology.net/photo.jsf?node=5031>.

Atlas of Ophthalmology 5033: Jonathan, Dutton. Essential Blepharospasm. Digital image. Atlas of Ophthalmology. N.p., n.d. Web. 26 Feb. 2018. <www.atlasophthalmology.net/photo.jsf?node=5033>.

Atlas of Ophthalmology 5132: Denny, John. Third Nerve Palsy. Digital image. Atlas of Ophthalmology. N.p., n.d. Web. 26 Feb. 2018. <https://www.atlasophthalmology.net/photo.jsf?node=5132>.

Atlas of Ophthalmology 5441: Foulks, Gary. Malignant Melanoma of the Iris. Digital image. Atlas of Ophthalmology. N.p., n.d. Web. 26 Feb. 2018. <www.atlasophthalmology.net/photo.jsf?node=5441>.

Atlas of Ophthalmology 5830: Pollock, Stephen. Pupil-involving Third Nerve Palsy. Digital image. Atlas of Ophthalmology. N.p., n.d. Web. 26 Feb. 2018. <www.atlasophthalmology.net/photo.jsf?node=5830>.

Atlas of Ophthalmology 5831: Pollock, Stephen. Tonic Pupil. Digital image. Atlas of Ophthalmology. N.p., n.d. Web. 26 Feb. 2018. <www.atlasophthalmology.net/photo.jsf?node=5831>.

Atlas of Ophthalmology 5843: McCuen, Brooks. Dacryoadenitis, Acute. Digital image. Atlas of Ophthalmology. Duke University Eye Center, n.d. Web. 26 Feb. 2018. <www.atlasophthalmology.net/photo.jsf?node=5843>.

Atlas of Ophthalmology 6201: Ruprecht, Klaus. Canaliculitis. Digital image. Atlas of Ophthalmology. Universitäts Augenklinik, n.d. Web. 26 Feb. 2018. <www.atlasophthalmology.net/photo.jsf?node=6201>.

Atlas of Ophthalmology 7810: Pimenta de Oliveria, Leonardo. Vernal Conjunctivitis, Limbal, Horner-Trantas Dots. Digital Image. Atlas of Ophthalmology. Hospital Santa Luzia, Savador. Web. 4 Jan. 2019. <www.atlasophthalmology.net/photo.jsf?node=7810>.

Atlas of Ophthalmology 8252: Kah, Tan Aik. Corneal Dissecting Bleb (OD). Digital image. Atlas of Ophthalmology. University Sarawak, n.d. Web. 26 Feb. 2018. <www.atlasophthalmology.net/photo.jsf?node=8252>.

Atlas of Ophthalmology 8916: Huchzermeyer, Cord. Ziliolentikulärer Block, Ultraschallbiomikroskopie. Digital image. Atlas of Ophthalmology. Univ. Augenklinik, n.d. Web. 26 Feb. 2018. <www.atlasophthalmology.net/photo.jsf?node=8916>.

Atlas of Ophthalmology 9213: Schumacher, Jaqueline. Effect of Cool Pack Test in Myasthenic Diplopia (Colour Image). Digital image. Atlas of Ophthalmology. N.p., n.d. Web. 26 Feb. 2018. <www.atlasophthalmology.net/photo.jsf?node=9213>.

Atlas of Ophthalmology 9508: Goldblum, David. Macrostriae after LASIK. Digital image. Atlas of Ophthalmology Image. University Hospital Basel, n.d. Web. 26 Feb. 2018. <www.atlasophthalmology.net/photo.jsf?node=9508>.

Bausch + Lomb 1: Dimple Veiling beneath Rigid Lens(82 KB, JPG). Digital image. Bausch + Lomb. Bausch & Lomb Incorporated, 2018. Web. 27 Feb. 2018. <http://www.bausch.com.my/en/ecp/for-your-practice/resource-materials/clinical-photos/epithelium/>.

Bausch + Lomb 2: Tomlinson, Mark. Figure 3 Dimple Veiling. Digital Image. Bausch + Lomb Academy of Vision Care. Web. 1 Jan. 2019. <www.academyofvisioncare.com/files/documents/The%20soft%20approach%20to%20RGPs%20Part%204.pdf>.

Brighton Vision Center 1: Farjo, Ayad. Dimple Veiling. Digital image. Brighton Vision Center. N.p., 2007. Web. 27 Feb. 2018. <http://www.brightonvisioncenter.com/Doctors/Dr_A_Farjo.html>.

Clinica Rementeria 1: Eduardo. CORNEAL DELLEN. Digital image. Clinica Rementeria. N.p., n.d. Web. 26 Feb. 2018. <http://www.clinicarementeria.es/patologias/otras-patologias-de-la-cornea/dellen-corneal>.

Contact Lens Update 1: Bitton, Etty. Everything You Wanted to Know and Were Afraid to Ask about Demodex. Digital image. Contact Lens Update. N.p., 7 Dec. 2015. Web. 27 Feb. 2018. <http://contactlensupdate.com/2015/12/07/everything-you-wanted-to-know-and-were-afraid-to-ask-about-demodex/>.

Cornea Eye Hospital 1: Suman, Santosh. Lens Coloboma. Digital image. Cornea Eye Hospital. N.p., 2018. Web. 27 Feb. 2018. <https://cornea.co.in/eye.php/>.

Donelson R. Manley 1: TIBBETTS, MICHAEL. DEHISCENCE LASIK FLAP. Digital image. Donelson R. Manley. N.p., 16 July 2011. Web. 26 Feb. 2018. <http://donelsonmanley.com/dislodged-lasik-flap-photographed-by-michael-tibbetts-m-d/>.

Ento Key 1: Tuft, Stephen. Acute Phlyctenule at the Limbus. Digital image. Ento Key. N.p., 4 June 2016. Web. 26 Feb. 2018. <https://entokey.com/external-eye-disease-and-the-oculocutaneous-disorders/>.

Etsy 1: RoseleinRarities. BLUE LADIES ARGYLE KNEE-HIGH SOCKS. Digital image. Etsy. N.p., 29 Nov. 2017. Web. 27 Feb. 2018. <www.etsy.com/listing/210125224>.

Eye Care and Cure 1: The Mars Numeral Contrast Sensitivity Test. Digital image. Eye Care and Cure. N.p., n.d. Web. 27 Feb. 2018. <http://www.eyecareandcure.com.sg/mars-number-contrast-sensitivity-test-pi-5011.html?image=0>.

EyeWorld 1: Dalton, Michelle. Retroillumination of Intracorneal Inlay. Digital image. EYEWORLD ASIA-PACIFIC. N.p., n.d. Web. 26 Feb. 2018. <http://aspx.apacrs.org/apacrs-publication/Default2.aspx?id=827>.

Flicker 21939757361: OakleyOriginals. Bee Sting Gone Bad. Digital image. Flicker©. N.p., 3 Oct. 2015. Web. 24 Feb. 2018. <https://www.flickr.com/photos/oakleyoriginals/21939757361/>.

Flicker 2574141467: Jinglejammer. Jack with Erythema Multiforme. Digital image. Flicker©. N.p., 23 Apr. 2008. Web. 24 Feb. 2018. <https://www.flickr.com/photos/jinglejammer/2574141467/>.

Flicker 32271350480: Burton, Matthew. Marginal Keratitis. Digital image. Flicker©. Community Eye Health, 1 Feb. 2017. Web. 24 Feb. 2018. <https://www.flickr.com/photos/communityeyehealth/32271350480/>.

Flicker 32529009371: Dart, John KG. Bacterial Conjunctivitis. Digital image. Flicker©. Community Eye Health, 1 Feb. 2017. Web. 24 Feb. 2018. <https://www.flickr.com/photos/communityeyehealth/32529009371/>.

Flicker 5445430946: Community Eye Health. Esotropia in the Right Eye. Digital image. Flicker©. International Centre for Eye Health, 1 Mar. 2010. Web. 24 Feb. 2018. <https://www.flickr.com/photos/communityeyehealth/5445430946/>.

Flicker 5594570699: Community Eye Health. Bacterial Conjunctivitis. Digital image. Flicker©. International Centre for Eye Health, 1 Mar. 2005. Web. 24 Feb. 2018. <https://www.flickr.com/photos/communityeyehealth/5594570699/>.

Flicker 5686300673: Anderson, Jock. Iridocyclitis. Digital image. Flicker©. Community Eye Health, 1992. Web. 24 Feb. 2018. <https://www.flickr.com/photos/communityeyehealth/5686300673/>.

Flicker 7544734768: National Eye Institute. Visual Acuity Chart. Digital image. Flicker©. National Institutes of Health, 10 July 2012. Web. 24 Feb. 2018. <https://www.flickr.com/photos/nationaleyeinstitute/7544734768/>.

Flicker 8385643520: Heilman, James, MD. Severe Psoriatic Arthritis. Digital image. Flicker©. N.p., 17 Dec. 2009. Web. 24 Feb. 2018. <https://www.flickr.com/photos/myarthritis/8385643520/>.

Flicker 9212534322: Handarmdoc. Rheumatoid Arthritis. Digital image. Flicker©. N.p., 2 Apr. 2008. Web. 24 Feb. 2018. <https://www.flickr.com/photos/handarmdoc/9212534322/>.

iKnowledge 1: Clinical Gate. Pentacam image demonstrating corneal topography and thickness maps of patient with contact-lens-induced corneal warpage. Digital image. iKnowledge. N.p., 3 Oct. 2015. Web. 27 Feb. 2018. <https://clinicalgate.com/cornea/>.

iKnowledge 2: Admin. Globe Subluxation with Equator of Globe and Lacrimal Gland in Front of the Eyelids. Digital image. IKnowledge. N.p., 3 Oct. 2015. Web. 27 Feb. 2018. <https://clinicalgate.com/orbit/>.

Jaypee Journals 1: Mansuri, Mariam, and Purvi Bhagat. Keratic Precipitates. Digital image. Jaypee Journals. N.p., n.d. Web. 27 Feb. 2018. <http://www.jaypeejournals.com/eJournals/ShowText.aspx?ID=3497&Type=FREE&TYP=TOP&IN=_eJournals/images/JPLOGO.gif&IID=276&isPDF=NO>.

Journal of Medical Case Reports 1: Park, Jung Hyun. Posterior subcapsular cataract in the right (a) and left (b) eye which developed 3 days after starting glucose control. Digital image. Journal of Medical Case Reports. N.p., 12 Apr. 2017. Web. 27 Feb. 2018. <https://jmedicalcasereports.biomedcentral.com/articles/10.1186/s13256-017-1268-5>.

Keeler 1: Woolley, Tim. Anterior Chamber Cells and Flare. Digital image. Symphony by Keeler. N.p., n.d. Web. 27 Feb. 2018. <http://www.keeler-symphony.com/making-sense>.

Keeler 2: Acuity Card set for Infants. Digital image. Keeler Ophthalmic Instruments. Web. 7 Jan. 2019. <https://www.keeler.co.uk/acuity-card-set-for-infants-8-cards-5-8-10-12-14-15-17-28.html>.

LASIK Complications 1: Staining at the margin of a LASIK flap. Digital image. LASIK Complications. N.p., n.d. Web. 26 Feb. 2018. <http://www.lasikcomplications.com/flapdislocation.htm>.

Low Vision 253300: Lea Gratings A Preferential Looking Test / 253300. Digital image. Low Vision Resource Center. N.p., 2019. Web. 8 Jan. 2019. <https://www.vision2020lvrc.org.hk/for-an-in-depth-comprehensive-assessment/207-preferentiial-looking-grating-acuity-test-253300.html>.

Mattingly Low Vision 1: Fletcher, Donald. Central California Visual Field Test. Digital image. Mattingly Low Vision. N.p., 2017. Web. 27 Feb. 2018. <http://www.mattinglylowvision.com/content.cfm?n=mprl>.

Medical Observer 1: Chaitow, Jeffrey, and Michael Tran. Juvenile Idiopathic Arthritis. Digital image. Medical Observer. N.p., 3 Mar. 2016. Web. 27 Feb. 2018. <https://www.medicalobserver.com.au/medical-news/rheumatology/a-guide-to-treating-juvenile-idiopathic-arthritis>.

Melanoma Education Foundation 1: Exchemiststeve. Squamous Cell Carcinoma. Digital image. Contact Lens Update. Melanoma Education Foundation, 7 June 2017. Web. 27 Feb. 2018. <http://blog.melanomaeducation.net/squamous-cell-carcinoma/>.

Miriam 1: Miriam. Dorsal Midbrain Syndrom. Digital image. Memorang. N.p., 2017. Web. 27 Feb. 2018. <https://www.memorangapp.com/flashcards/87066/BB+week+3/>.

My Alcon 1: Mucin Balls. Digital image. My Alcon. Academy for Eyecare Excellence and Center for

Contact Lens Research, n.d. Web. 27 Feb. 2018. <https://www.myalcon.com/education/academy-eye-care-excellence/cclm/mucin-balls.shtml>.

My Alcon 2: Deposits – Protein. Digital image. My Alcon. N.p., n.d. Web. 27 Feb. 2018. <https://www.myalcon.com/education/academy-eye-care-excellence/cclm/protein-lens-deposits.shtml>.

My Health 1: Muhanifa, Lily, and Binti Mustafa. Tight Lens Syndrome. Digital image. My Health. N.p., 17 Dec. 2015. Web. 27 Feb. 2018. <http://www.myhealth.gov.my/en/contact-lens-types-mode-of-wearing/>.

NBC 1: Newman, Judith. Blue Viagra Pills. Digital image. NBC News. N.p., 22 Apr. 2011. Web. 2 Mar. 2018. <http://www.nbcnews.com/id/42416956/ns/health-sexual_health/t/how-viagra-can-mess-your-marriage>.

Neupsy Key 1: Moheban, Carol, Matthew Tilem, and Jose Gutrecht. Cluster Headache. Digital image. Neupsy Key. N.p., 4 June 2016. Web. 27 Feb. 2018. <https://neupsykey.com/primary-and-secondary-headache/>.

Neuro-Ophthalmology 1: Brown's syndrome. Digital image. Neuro-Ophthalmology. N.p., n.d. Web. 27 Feb. 2018. <https://sites.google.com/site/neuroophthalmologyfellowship/home/strabismus/browns-syndrome>.

Openi 1: Kashiwagi K, Furuya T, and Kashiwagi F. Biometric Examination of Anterior Ocular Segment. Digital image. Openi. University of Yamanashi, 2008. Web. 27 Feb. 2018. <https://openi.nlm.nih.gov/detailedresult.php?img=PMC2687102_TOOPHTJ-2-1_F1&req=4>.

Openi 2: Bjerrum Tangent Screen. Tangent Screens Are Useful for Testing the Central Visual Field, up to 30°. Digital image. Openi. N.p., 2012. Web. 27 Feb. 2018. <https://openi.nlm.nih.gov/detailedresult.php?img=PMC3588129_jceh_25_79-80_066_f08&req=4>.

Optometry Times 1: Pate, Caroline. Anisocoria in a Patient with Horner's Syndrome OS. Digital image. Optometry Times. N.p., 15 May 2015. Web. 27 Feb. 2018. <http://optometrytimes.modernmedicine.com/optometrytimes/news/proper-procedure-testing-pupils?page=0%2C1>.

Perkins 1: Mayer, Luisa. Visual Acuity Testing, Part 1: History of Preferential Looking and Early Testing. Digital image. Perkins. Web. 7 Jan. 2019. <www.perkinselearning.org/videos/webcast/visual-acuity-testing-part-1-hitory-preferential-looking-and-early-testing>.

Physiopedia 1: Ritchie, Laura. Ankylosing Spondylitis Lumbar Spine. Digital image. Physiopedia. N.p., 24 Aug. 2012. Web. 27 Feb. 2018. <https://www.physio-pedia.com/Ankylosing_Spondylitis>.

Pinterest 1: Wingate, Jane. 7 Things Your Nails Can Tell You. Digital Image. Pinterest. Web. 1 Jan. 2019. <www.pinterest.com/pin/398076054534543564>.

Pinterest 2: Merriam, Meredith. Teller Acuity Cards. Digital image. Pinterest. Web. 7 Jan. 2019. <https://www.pinterest.com/pin/448108231646133710>.

Pollock, Stephen. Optic Nerve Glioma (Pilocytic Astrocytoma) (#2), MRI. Digital image. Atlas of Ophthalmology. N.p., n.d. Web. 26 Feb. 2018. <www.atlasophthalmology.net/photo.jsf?node=6303>.

PRCVI 1: Feinbloom, William. The original distance chart for the partially sighted. Digital image. Provincial Resource Centre for the Visually Impaired. Designs for Vision, Inc., 2011. Web. 27 Feb. 2018. <https://library.prcvi.org/ListDetail?q=&p=4&ps=1&subject_facet=Functional%20vision%20-%20Screening%20tests>.

ProTech Ophthalmics 1: Farnsworth D-15 Dichotomous Color Blindness Test. Digital image. ProTech Ophthalmics. N.p., n.d. Web. 27 Feb. 2018. <http://www.eyedoctorsupply.com/farnsworth-d-

15-dichotomous-color-blindness-test/>.

Psoriasis 1: Finger Nail Pitting. Digital image. Nail Psoriasis Help. N.p., 2014. Web. 27 Feb. 2018. <http://nailpsoriasishelp.blogspot.com/2011/12/nail-psoriasis-pictures.html>.

Recovery.org 1: Marisa, Crane. Fetal Alcohol Syndrome. Digital image. Recovery.org. N.p., 23 May 2016. Web. 27 Feb. 2018. <https://www.recovery.org/topics/fetal-alcohol-syndrome/>.

Retina Image Bank 638: This image was originally published in the Retina Image Bank® website. Ahmadieh, Hamid. Papilledema. Retina Image Bank. 2012; 638. © the American Society of Retina Specialists.

Retina Image Bank 10386: This image was originally published in the Retina Image Bank® website. Jason S. Calhoun. Choroidal Melanoma. Retina Image Bank. 2013; 10386. © the American Society of Retina Specialists.

Retina Image Bank 10818: This image was originally published in the Retina Image Bank® website. Jerald A. Bovino, MD. Phthisis Bulbi. Retina Image Bank. 2013; 10818. © the American Society of Retina Specialists.

Retina Image Bank 11737: This image was originally published in the Retina Image Bank® website. Maria A. Martinez-Castellanos, MD. Angiography of an Intraocular Candidiasis. Retina Image Bank. 2013; Retina Image Bank 11737. © the American Society of Retina Specialists.

Retina Image Bank 12605: This image was originally published in the Retina Image Bank® website. David Callanan, MD. Kaposi's Sarcoma. Retina Image Bank. 2013; 12605. © the American Society of Retina Specialists.

Retina Image Bank 12613: This image was originally published in the Retina Image Bank® website. David Callanan, MD. Allergic Conjunctivitis. Retina Image Bank. 2013; 12613. © the American Society of Retina Specialists.

Retina Image Bank 12755: This image was originally published in the Retina Image Bank® website. David Callanan, MD. Rhabdomyosarcoma R Orbit. Retina Image Bank. 2013; 12755. © the American Society of Retina Specialists.

Retina Image Bank 12845: This image was originally published in the Retina Image Bank® website. David Callanan, MD. Optic Nerve Hypoplasia / Double Ring. Retina Image Bank. 2014; 12845. © the American Society of Retina Specialists.

Retina Image Bank 13398: This image was originally published in the Retina Image Bank® website. Maurice F. Rabb. Optic Neuritis. Retina Image Bank. 2014; 13398. © the American Society of Retina Specialists.

Retina Image Bank 13403: This image was originally published in the Retina Image Bank® website. Maurice F. Rabb. Retinopathy of Prematurity. Retina Image Bank. 2014; 13403. © the American Society of Retina Specialists.

Retina Image Bank 135: This image was originally published in the Retina Image Bank® website. Suber S. Huang, MD, MBA. Primary Ocular Lymphoma. Retina Image Bank. 2012; 135. © the American Society of Retina Specialists.

Retina Image Bank 14240: This image was originally published in the Retina Image Bank® website. Susanna S. Park, MD, PhD. ERM-Post-Op-20100. Retina Image Bank. 2014; 14240. © the American Society of Retina Specialists.

Retina Image Bank 155: This image was originally published in the Retina Image Bank® website. Peter K. Kaiser, MD. Stage 2 Macular Hole. Retina Image Bank. 2012; 155. © the American Society of Retina Specialists.

Retina Image Bank 156: This image was originally published in the Retina Image Bank® website. Peter K. Kaiser, MD. Stage 3 Macular Hole. Retina Image Bank. 2012; 156. © the American Society of Retina Specialists.

Retina Image Bank 15735: This image was originally published in the Retina Image Bank® website. David

Callanan, MD. Methanol Toxicity. Retina Image Bank. 2014; 15735. © the American Society of Retina Specialists.

Retina Image Bank 15753: This image was originally published in the Retina Image Bank® website. David Callanan, MD. Thioridazine Toxicity. Retina Image Bank. 2014; 15753. © the American Society of Retina Specialists.

Retina Image Bank 1643: This image was originally published in the Retina Image Bank® website. Larry Halperin, MD. Sympathetic Ophthalmia after Vitrectomy. Retina Image Bank. 2012; 1643. © the American Society of Retina Specialists.

Retina Image Bank 173: This image was originally published in the Retina Image Bank® website. John T. Thompson, MD. Stage 1 Macular Hole. Retina Image Bank. 2012; 173. © the American Society of Retina Specialists.

Retina Image Bank 1789: This image was originally published in the Retina Image Bank® website Larry Halperin, MD. Sickle Salmon-Patch Hemorrhage. Retina Image Bank. 2012; 1789. © the American Society of Retina Specialists.

Retina Image Bank 1924: This image was originally published in the Retina Image Bank® website. Mallika Goyal, MD. Progressive Outer Retinal Necrosis. Retina Image Bank. 2012; 1924. © the American Society of Retina Specialists.

Retina Image Bank 19561: This image was originally published in the Retina Image Bank® website. David Callanan, MD. Posterior Scleritis (Focal). Retina Image Bank. 2014; 19561. © the American Society of Retina Specialists.

Retina Image Bank 2001: This image was originally published in the Retina Image Bank® website. Norman Byer. Lattice Degeneration. Retina Image Bank. 2012; 2001. © the American Society of Retina Specialists.

Retina Image Bank 2019: This image was originally published in the Retina Image Bank® website. Roy D. Brod, MD. Retinal Angiomas In VHL. Retina Image Bank. 2012; 2910. © the American Society of Retina Specialists.

Retina Image Bank 2161: This image was originally published in the Retina Image Bank® website. Mallika Goyal, MD. Traumatic Optic Neuropathy. Retina Image Bank. 2012; 2161. © the American Society of Retina Specialists.

Retina Image Bank 23305: This image was originally published in the Retina Image Bank® website. H. Michael Lambert, MD. Central Areolar Choroidal Dystrophy. Retina Image Bank. 2015; 23305. © the American Society of Retina Specialists.

Retina Image Bank 24303: This image was originally published in the Retina Image Bank® website. H. Michael Lambert, MD. Lattice Degeneration. Retina Image Bank. 2015; 24303. © the American Society of Retina Specialists.

Retina Image Bank 24325: This image was originally published in the Retina Image Bank® website. H. Michael Lambert, MD. Leber's Congenital Amaurosis. Retina Image Bank. 2015; 24325. © the American Society of Retina Specialists.

Retina Image Bank 24461: This image was originally published in the Retina Image Bank® website. H. Michael Lambert, MD. Venous Stasis Retinopathy. Retina Image Bank. 2015; 24461. © the American Society of Retina Specialists.

Retina Image Bank 24525: This image was originally published in the Retina Image Bank® website. H. Michael Lambert, MD. Wegener's Disease. Retina Image Bank. 2015; 24525. © the American Society of Retina Specialists.

Retina Image Bank 24531: This image was originally published in the Retina Image Bank® website. H. Michael Lambert, MD. Wilson's Disease. Retina Image Bank. 2015; 24531. © the American Society of Retina Specialists.

Retina Image Bank 24974: This image was originally published in the Retina Image Bank® website. Neha

Goel, MS DNB FRCS (Glasg). CME-OCT. Retina Image Bank. 2015; 24974. © the American Society of Retina Specialists.

Retina Image Bank 26040: This image was originally published in the Retina Image Bank® website. David Callanan, MD. Sickle Cell Neovascularization and Vitreous Hemorrhage. Retina Image Bank. 2015; 26040. © the American Society of Retina Specialists.

Retina Image Bank 26174: This image was originally published in the Retina Image Bank® website. Roy Schwartz, MD. Preeclampsia in a 30-Year-Old - Color Fundus Photograph - RE. Retina Image Bank. 2015; 26174. © the American Society of Retina Specialists.

Retina Image Bank 26743: This image was originally published in the Retina Image Bank® website. Asim Mehboob. Valsalva Retinopathy. Retina Image Bank. 2016; 26743. © the American Society of Retina Specialists.

Retina Image Bank 26937: This image was originally published in the Retina Image Bank® website. JEFFERSON R SOUSA. Cysticercosis. Retina Image Bank. 2017; 26937. © the American Society of Retina Specialists.

Retina Image Bank 26972: This image was originally published in the Retina Image Bank® website. Hua Gao, MD, PhD. Cat Scratch. Retina Image Bank. 2017; 26972. © the American Society of Retina Specialists.

Retina Image Bank 27345: This image was originally published in the Retina Image Bank® website. Annal D Meleth, MD, MS. Syphilis CR. Retina Image Bank. 2017; 27345. © the American Society of Retina Specialists.

Retina Image Bank 27627: This image was originally published in the Retina Image Bank® website. Jason Griffith. BB Gun Accident. Retina Image Bank. 2017; 27627. © the American Society of Retina Specialists.

Retina Image Bank 27727: This image was originally published in the Retina Image Bank® website. Olivia Rainey. Endogenous Endophthalmitis With Suspected Systemic Candidiasis. Retina Image Bank. 2018; 27727. © the American Society of Retina Specialists.

Retina Image Bank 28198: This image was originally published in the Retina Image Bank® website. Aaron P. Appiah, MD. Foveoschisis March 2016 OD. Retina Image Bank. 2018; 28198. © the American Society of Retina Specialists.

Retina Image Bank 2856: This image was originally published in the Retina Image Bank® website. Eric A. Postel, MD. Metastatic malignant melanoma. Retina Image Bank. 2012; 2856. © the American Society of Retina Specialists.

Retina Image Bank 3143: This image was originally published in the Retina Image Bank® website. Alex P. Hunyor, MD. Cone dystrophy case 1 LE. Retina Image Bank. 2013; 3143. © the American Society of Retina Specialists.

Retina Image Bank 3343: This image was originally published in the Retina Image Bank® website. Alex P. Hunyor, MD. Ocular ischaemic syndrome colour 1. Retina Image Bank. 2013; 3343. © the American Society of Retina Specialists.

Retina Image Bank 343: This image was originally published in the Retina Image Bank® website. Geoffrey G. Emerson. Sickle Cell Retinopathy with Sea Fans (angiography). Retina Image Bank. 212; 343. © the American Society of Retina Specialists.

Retina Image Bank 3486: This image was originally published in the Retina Image Bank® website. By Thomas M. Aaberg, MD. Tuberous Sclerosis. Retina Image Bank. 2013; 3486. © the American Society of Retina Specialists.

Retina Image Bank 4620: This image was originally published in the Retina Image Bank® website. Thomas M. Aaberg, MD. Racemose Hemangioma. Retina Image Bank. 2013; 4620. © the American Society of Retina Specialists.

Retina Image Bank 5370: This image was originally published in the Retina Image Bank® website. Henry

J. Kaplan, MD. Choroidal Detachment. Retina Image Bank. 2013; 5370. © the American Society of Retina Specialists.

Retina Image Bank 6220: This image was originally published in the Retina Image Bank® website. Henry J. Kaplan, MD. Busacca nodules. Retina Image Bank. 2013; 6220. © the American Society of Retina Specialists.

Retina Image Bank 721: This image was originally published in the Retina Image Bank® website. Michael P. Kelly, FOPS. Sickle Cell Retinopathy. Retina Image Bank. 2012; 721. © the American Society of Retina Specialists.

Retina Image Bank 7220: This image was originally published in the Retina Image Bank® website. Jason S. Calhoun. Central Areolar Choroidal Dystrophy. Retina Image Bank. 2013; 7220. © the American Society of Retina Specialists.

Retina Image Bank 7267: This image was originally published in the Retina Image Bank® website. Jason S. Calhoun. EDI OCT Macular Hole. Retina Image Bank. 2013; 7267. © the American Society of Retina Specialists.

Retina Image Bank 7339: This image was originally published in the Retina Image Bank® website. Jason S. Calhoun. Accordioning Crystalline Lens. Retina Image Bank. 2013; 7339. © the American Society of Retina Specialists.

Retina Image Bank 7828: This image was originally published in the Retina Image Bank® website. Jason S. Calhoun. Corneal Abnormal Blood Vessels. Retina Image Bank. 2013; 7828. © the American Society of Retina Specialists.

Retina Image Bank 801: This image was originally published in the Retina Image Bank® website. Jeffrey G. Gross, MD. Shaken Baby Syndrome. Retina Image Bank. 2012; 801. © the American Society of Retina Specialists.

Retina Image Bank 8039: This image was originally published in the Retina Image Bank® website. H. Michael Lambert, MD. Acne Rosacea Phlyctenular Keratitis. Retina Image Bank. 2013; 8039. © the American Society of Retina Specialists.

Retina Image Bank 8051: This image was originally published in the Retina Image Bank® website. H. Michael Lambert, MD. Acute retinal necrosis. Retina Image Bank. 2014; 8051. © the American Society of Retina Specialists.

Retina Image Bank 8195: This image was originally published in the Retina Image Bank® website. H. Michael Lambert, MD. Angle Closure Glaucoma. Retina Image Bank. 2013; 8195. © the American Society of Retina Specialists.

Scielo 1: Bernardes, Santos Hyun. Olho Esquerdo Com Deslocamento Pupilar Temporal Inferior. Digital image. Scielo. Brazilian Archives of Ophthalmology, 10 Oct. 2005. Web. 27 Feb. 2018. <http://www.scielo.br/scielo.php?script=sci_arttext&pid=S0004-27492005000600024>.

Science Direct 1: Kapoor, Neera, and Kenneth Ciuffreda. An Image of the Developmental Eye Movement (DEM) Test. Digital image. Science Direct. N.p., 1 July 2017. Web. 27 Feb. 2018. <https://www.sciencedirect.com/science/article/pii/S1888429617300407>.

Susan Salvo 1: Salvo, Susan. Massage & Bell's Palsy. Digital image. Susan Salvo's Massage Passport. N.p., 23 Nov. 2016. Web. 27 Feb. 2018. <https://massagepassport.wordpress.com/2016/11/23/bells-palsy-massage-therapy/>.

Topend Sports 1: Wood, Robert. King-Devick Test. Digital image. Topend Sports. N.p., Mar. 2015. Web. 27 Feb. 2018. <http://www.topendsports.com/health/tests/concussion-king-devick.htm>.

University of Calgary 1: Vision Contrast Test System. Digital image. University of Calgary. N.p., n.d. Web. 27 Feb. 2018. <http://www.ucalgary.ca/pip369/mod4/spatial/testingsensitivity>.

VEP 1: Neubert, Sandy. Evoked Potentials – VEP – YouTube. N.p., 16 Jan. 2014. Web. 8 Jan. 2019. <https://www.youtube.com/watch?v=4LCkDwcXMHE>.

Visionary 1: Broken Wheel Eye Chart. Digital image. The Eye Journal. N.p., 13 Julyl 2009. Web. 7 Jan.

2019. <httpsvisionaryeyecare.wordpress.com/2009/07/13/eye-charts-for-childre/>.

Wikipedia 1: Derksen, Bryan. Cup or Faces Paradox. Digital image. Wikipedia. N.p., 2 Mar. 2007. Web. 27 Feb. 2018. <https://en.wikipedia.org/wiki/Figure-ground_(perception)>.

INDEX

A

B

C

D

E

F

G

H

I

J

K

L

M

N

O

P

R

S

T

U

V

W

X

Z

Made in the USA
Middletown, DE
10 September 2024

60795197R00228